Elevating Individual and Societal Success

Life Enabling Enterprise: An Economic System For the Good of Humankind

Elevating Individual and Societal Success

Life Enabling Enterprise: An Economic System for the Good of Humankind

Raphael L. Vitalo, Ph.D. and Christopher J. Bujak, B.S.M.E.

Vital Enterprises: Imprint - Lowrey Press

ISBN: 978-0-9722810-5-8 (Print Edition)

ISBN: 978-0-9722810-6-5 (Electronic Edition - PDF)

Revised Version of: Life Enabling Enterprise: An Alternative Approach to Commerce Volume 1: The Model and Other Critical Knowledge

Cover Designer: Dobromil Nosek

Library of Congress Control Number: 2023901129

To Anne

Always mighty, never a mouse.

All of us teach by the way we live,
Some for better, some for worse.

Some of us teach by intent,
But, without caring or skill, we fail.

You always taught by deed and intent,
Always with caring, never failing.

The basic findings of this book are the following:

1. Commerce is an exchange between people, each giving the other something. What is exchanged can be physical, emotional, or intellectual in form. It encompasses a comprehensive and pervasive set of behaviors that extends across every human life and all arenas of human activity. It is commerce between a man and a woman that creates human life. It is through the commerce between a child and its family that each child is protected, reared, and supported in its development and its family experiences the pride, joy, and excitement of witnessing a human life unfold. It is through our exchanges with others and our physical world that we expand our information and knowledge, develop our skills, hone our proficiencies, and progressively discover who we are as unique individuals. And, yes, it is through commerce that we obtain the material goods and services that we either cannot produce or choose not to produce for ourselves.
2. The traditional economic use of the term that views commerce as the buying and selling of goods is myopic at best. A true understanding of human commerce must incorporate facts descriptive of the full range of its occurrence, including what is exchanged and why.
3. All economic models attempt to describe, predict, explain, and enable the control of commercial activity, as each model defines it, in an effort to ensure its success. Deductive economic models derive their principles from their assumptions about human nature since it is human behavior they explain. Commerce, as a human activity, expresses people's motivations, goals, values, and social orientations. It is a model's assumptions about human nature that determine how it defines the purpose that commerce serves, the behaviors people will engage in to accomplish that purpose, and how they will define success.
4. Capitalism is founded on the assumption that all people everywhere have the same nature (Homo economicus). The core elements of this sameness are that people are materialistically focused, radically individualistic, and always self-serving. They act rationally to maximize their personal profit or received value, both of which are measured monetarily. Essentially, people are egoistic self-maximizers. Capitalism also assumes that, within commercial contexts, no asymmetries of information or power exist between people. Thus, despite their self-maximizing drive, no individual can just take from or otherwise exploit another because no one has power greater than the person whose resource they seek. Hence, all commerce is resolved through negotiated settlements that provide sufficient satisfaction to each party to

warrant agreement. All such transactions are therefore deemed "free and fair."

5. Wealthy people who are materialistically focused and egoistic self-maximizers are served well by Capitalism because, by design, it advantages the already wealthy and serves as a powerful social control mechanism that serves to mask the unrelenting exploitation of the many by the few. As a real-world functional economic system, however, evidence is both overwhelming and indisputable, Capitalism fails. It does not deliver its promised benefits. It is flawed internally as a logical model, produces harmful societal effects, and the assumptions it is built upon do not map to the findings of empirical science.
6. Empirical research demonstrates that not all people match Capitalism's image of humankind. That research reveals that the largest segment of evolved humanity is natively cooperative and other-regarding in their orientation toward others. They value being connected with others and behave in ways that take others into consideration, even at a cost to their material gain and welfare.
7. These cooperative, other-regarding people also strive to emerge as unique individuals. Their striving for individuation is both expressed and advanced through mutually beneficial commerce with others.
8. This portion of humanity has no commercial model to guide their pursuit of commerce in a way that reflects who they are. This book offers such a model.

This chapter explains the purpose of this book and provides a roadmap for understanding its contents.

Chapter 1

Economic Systems

Economic systems have powerful effects on our lives—and not just in material ways. The power of an adopted economic system is exerted directly on our minds, as its understanding of humankind and the values the system endorses constitute a secular ethic that is promulgated directly through teaching in educational institutions and endorsements in public forums. For example, a system may reinforce competition over cooperation, material wealth as a sign of merit, and self-interest over regard for others as a reasonable attitude for living in the world.

An economic system's influence is amplified through the commercial organizations that apply its thinking. Each system defines the purpose a commercial entity pursues, how it organizes its activities and treats those who contribute to its efforts, and how it conducts itself with regard to the public as it acts to realize its purpose. Given our pervasive engagement with commercial enterprises as customers, workers, and members of the public, their conduct exerts unequaled influence in forming the real, not imagined, culture that emerges within a society. That influence on shaping a public's mindset is further enhanced by the portrayal of the conduct of commercial entities back to us by the news and entertainment media, almost always with endorsement. When reproach is expressed, it is usually done with the qualification that the unacceptable conduct was solely an expression of an irresponsible, rogue individual.

And, as if all the power exerted by an adopted economic system in shaping people's social experience were not sufficient to saturate a culture with the system's inherent ethic, each society's government takes actions based on its adopted system's logic, thereby further reinforcing its mindset and principles. In this way, the government itself becomes a promoter of the thinking that underpins the economic system it adopts as it shapes the material reality its citizens must cope with and justifies its actions using its adopted system's rationales.

The False Certainty of a System's Validity

All of the mental impact on us that is exerted by an adopted economic system is largely invisible and goes unchallenged. Most of us imagine that the economic system that envelops us is a given of nature and therefore indisputable. This is especially true of Capitalism, which is often promoted as the only valid economic system in existence. As documented by Häring and Douglas (2012) and Zaitchik (2022) and demonstrated in the Powell Memorandum (Powell, 1971), the proponents of Capitalism have worked diligently to foster this conviction lest voices emerge that threaten its dominance.

But an economic system is not a product of natural law. All economic systems are based on assumptions about humankind, not the laws of nature. Commerce between people is an inherent human activity that spans one's life and every arena in which one operates. How it is manifested expresses people's motives, values, and experience or non-experience of connectedness with others. People who conceive an economic system make assumptions about these features of humankind. It is their assumptions about humankind that determine what their model will define as the purpose of commerce, what it will consider "profit" or gain to be, what measures of progress it will define, and what methods a person will use and not use in pursuing success. And those assumptions model builders adopt may or may not properly reflect the true nature of humankind as judged by existing science.

The premises that underpin Capitalism, for example, are seriously undermined by the empirical findings of human sciences. Its theorems and guidance are based on an assumedly universally applicable definition of human nature. It asserts that all people are materially focused and radically individualistic by nature. They act solely to satisfy their own self-interest without regard for others. Indeed, any regard for others that may appear to be present is simply based on the expectation of achieving greater gains for oneself (Andreoni, 1990).

As you will read in *Chapter 6* of this book, empirical studies have shown that people display two different response dispositions toward others. A portion of humankind acts with self-regard only. Some of these people act egoistically without reserve, as Capitalism posits. That same research also reveals, however, that a second segment of humanity operates on a different basis. They are cooperative and other-regarding by nature. They seek mutually beneficial outcomes when they relate with others, and they regulate their behavior to produce those outcomes. Their mere existence falsifies one of the foundational premises of Capitalism and the derivative theorems and principles that flow from it. But, more pertinent here, it renders all the economic guidance that Capitalism offers irrelevant—if not destructive—for this other-regarding segment of humanity and the societies they constitute. The reason for this is that following Capitalism's guidance requires them to behave in ways that contravene their own native inclinations for cooperation with others in the pursuit of mutual benefit.[1]

The Need for a Different Understanding of and Approach to Commerce

While a number of proposals have been made to adjust Capitalism to

[1] The existence of these two types of people interacting within the same society, as revealed in *Chapter 6*, one resolute "takers" and the other "cooperators," also requires rethinking the underlying causes of society's current state. The reason is that, as *Chapter 6* also reports, repeated studies have demonstrated that, when egoists interact with cooperators, they always seek to exploit them. Consider this finding in the light of the fact, documented in *Chapter 2*, that economic and political power is heavily weighted in the former group.

incorporate concern for others (e.g., B-Corporations, Caux Round Table (CRT) Principles for Responsible Business (2017), Inclusive Capitalism), all fail to recognize that a concern for others is inconsistent with Capitalism's premise about the egoistic nature of humankind. Given that Capitalism is a deductive theory, that premise cannot be "adjusted" because all the dynamics that deliver the benefits Capitalism promises require that it be true. If you modify that premise, the entire model collapses.[2] Only a new approach to commerce based on a different set of premises can adequately provide commercial guidance for people who are natively inclined to cooperate with others and seek mutually benefiting ends in their exchanges with them.

Further, as psychologists and social scientists, we cannot form a correct understanding of the purpose of commerce, the range of human needs commerce must satisfy, and the true nature and role of economic systems *unless* our economic thinking accounts for the makeup and behavior of this second group of humankind. Without such a well-formed understanding of these matters, we will construct systems and shape society in a way that fails to provide all the necessities humankind requires to prosper and grow, and, thus, we will destroy our species.

Finally, we need to appreciate that the mindset embedded in a nation's adopted economic system is expressed both within the nation adopting it and internationally through that nation's relationships worldwide. Indeed, the assumptions about humankind that underpin a nation's choice of an economic system underpin its view of its neighbors and therefore its approach to international relations. If a nation assumes that people are radically individualistic and solely self-serving, acting only to maximize the realization of their self-interest, then that nation will expect international relationships to be contentious by necessity. Given such a view of humankind, it will be anticipated that every other nation will act without regard for the consequences their behavior produces on other nations. A nation with such a worldview must see as its duty the need to preemptively assert itself over other nations so that it does not end up being subject to them. Therefore, hegemony must be the ultimate end goal of such a nation's international relationships. Such a nation might temporarily adapt to a bipolar or multipolar world order whenever hegemony is not possible, but it will always strive to realize hegemony, as that is the solution that best ensures a world order that maximally satisfies its interests in a manner unencumbered by others.

Capitalism's assumptions about humanity are absolutely compatible with the worldview that underpins a hegemonic foreign policy and, more generally, a polar

[2] The deductive nature of Capitalism as a theoretical system and the consequences of that fact are discussed further in *Chapter 2. Why We Need a New Economic Model.* We address the subject in still greater detail in *Chapter 4. How a Model's Foundational Premises Shape Its Contents.*

view of international relationships. No secular economic system recognizing the cooperative and other-regarding qualities of humankind exists. Such a system's perspective on humanity would support a wholly different worldview and solution to international relationships, one that would suggest a harmonious, mutually cooperative approach to meeting each nation's needs. Until now, such thinking has been dismissed as utopian at best. However, science's new understanding of humankind suggests that, for at least a segment of humankind, a harmonious, mutually cooperative approach to nationhood and international relations is both realistic and necessary. Only a new economic system based on assumptions recognizing the existence of this subset of humankind can properly guide such a society and its governance. And only such an economic system can serve the development of a harmonious world since such a world requires a cooperative approach to growth that allows each nation to realize its full potential and humankind as a whole to flourish and prosper.

Overview of This Book

The purpose of this book is to present an empirically valid understanding of who we are as human beings and to provide an economic system derived from this understanding.

This book is organized into three parts. The first part (Chapter 2 and all of Section I) explains why we need a replacement for Capitalism, develops our understanding of commercial models (economic systems) in general, and describes the foundations of the Life Enabling model. The second part (Sections II, III, and IV) presents, in detail, how a Life Enabling commercial enterprise is organized and conducts commerce. The third part (Section V) summarizes the content of this book and presents its implications.

Part One

This book begins by exploring Capitalism itself—its basic tenets, promises, and problems as an economic system. We do this because the proponents of Capitalism present it as the *only* effective economic system. If true, then there really is no need for the rest of this book. Even if not true, we need to understand Capitalism because it dominates our society and all its commercial enterprises. Also, anyone seeking to implement a different approach to commerce must be knowledgeable of how Capitalism works or fails to work. They need to understand the ends Capitalist enterprises seek, how they pursue them, and how they will respond to the presence of an alternative approach to commerce like the Life Enabling approach. Otherwise, implementers of Life Enabling commerce will be unprepared to relate with Capitalist enterprises effectively, and this will ultimately undermine their intent to benefit the people who need their products or services.

Part one next focuses on building people's understanding of economic models in general and the Life Enabling model in specific (Section I). We define the meaning of commerce and introduce a framework for describing the contents of any economic system. We explain the premises that define each model's thinking and show how those premises determine every element of the model's content. We then describe the foundational premises of the Life Enabling approach to commerce, a commercial approach that ensures all organizational decisions and actions protect, nurture, and enrich human life and the ecosystem that supports all life. Next, we test the validity of the model's assumptions against the findings of empirical science. In that process, we uncover facts about who we are as a species, the role commerce plays in the survival and development of humankind, and the range of human needs commerce must serve.

Part Two

The second part of this book (Sections II, III, and IV) provides practical guidance for conducting Life Enabling commerce. In these sections, we elaborate the Strategic, Operations, and Executive Functions guidance that steers the implementation of a Life Enabling enterprise. In each case, we provide examples of how such an enterprise differs in its conduct from one implementing Capitalism.

With regard to its Strategic component, we present the principles that define a Life Enabling enterprise's long-term goal, the specific results it must produce, the marketplace activities it will use to generate those results, and the organizational strategy essential to its success. We explain how it defines profit and how it realizes it. This guidance covers every element within a company's strategic plan and explains the logic that underpins its shaping.

With regard to its Operations component, we provide the knowledge you need to steer the day-to-day activities of every business function within a Life Enabling enterprise. We explain the results operations must produce, the activities that produce those results, and the resources needed to successfully implement those activities. In this guidance, we include how to understand and address the needs and values of customers and stakeholders, how to design outputs and their implementing processes, and how to establish waste-free, optimized processes across all business functions.

Executive Functions keep an organization whole, capable, viable, and accomplishing its purpose. These functions define how organizational decisions are made, the role and power members of the enterprise possess, how the material benefits produced by the enterprise are distributed, and the culture that prevails within it.

Part Three

The third part of this book (Section V) summarizes its content and presents its implications. These include Capitalism's undermining of individual and social well-being and the survival of our species. It also explores the potential for using the Life Enabling model as a guide to forming a nation state.

The Origins of the Life Enabling Model

All sciences assume a rational world in which cause-and-effect relationships are ultimately discernible. Social sciences specifically assume that people's behavior results from the interaction between a person's characteristics—their motives, values, capabilities, and intents—and the contexts within which they behave. The first step in building an economic model therefore is to profile one's assumptions about the nature of people and the context within which commerce occurs.

In building the Life Enabling model, we initially developed the model's thinking about the nature of people and the contexts within which they produce and exchange resources from our observations of human commerce. We deduced the model's assumptions about people and the commercial context from the insights these observations generated as augmented by other resources detailed in *Chapter 5*. We then tested our assumptions and the model's thinking against the findings of empirical research (*Chapter 6*) to ensure that they were valid.

Our observations of human commerce led us to three insights:

1. The traditional economic view of commerce as the buying and selling of goods or services for money with the purpose of satisfying people's material needs is myopic at best.
2. People's natural inclinations toward others are heterogeneous, at least as they are expressed in adults.
3. No economic system can serve both egoists and other-regarding people simultaneously.

A Myopic View of the Nature of Commerce

Our observations revealed that the production and exchange of resources with others is the cardinal element in every individual's experience and an essential factor in every person's survival, growth, health, and ultimate satisfaction in life. Commerce, as circumscribed within the confines of the buying and selling of goods and services, is but a small segment of its occurrence. And its purpose of providing for the material needs of people is a woefully inadequate representation of the essential needs that commerce between people provides.

Indeed, it is the production and exchange of resources between people that creates human life. It is through the exchange of resources with others that we grow, develop our knowledge and skills, and become capable of achieving outcomes that we value. Throughout our living, learning, and working activities, we connect, communicate, and affiliate with others. Our interactions with others and the exchanges they involve are the central means through which we nourish our emotional life, satisfy an essential requirement for physical well-being, and refine our understanding of ourselves as distinct from others, thereby individualizing our personalities. All these acts of commerce and the essential needs they satisfy fall outside the current economic definition of commerce.

The exchange of resources between people therefore represents a comprehensive, pervasive, and essential pattern of behavior that extends across every human life from conception to death and all arenas of human activity. To narrow this wide array of human behavior to a minuscule segment of its occurrence *and* study it in isolation from the whole of its occurrence undermines its understanding. A true science of human commerce must incorporate facts descriptive of the full range of its occurrence and the functions it satisfies.

People Are Not All Self-Serving

Our second insight is that people's natural inclinations toward others differ. One segment of humanity acts in the service of self-interest alone. This conduct is observable across all their interactions with others and well documented in *Chapter 6*. A second segment of people act in other-regarding ways. They prefer to cooperate with others and engage in mutually benefiting exchanges. If they perceive a greater need in someone else, they will sacrifice their own resources to remedy that need, even to the point of putting themselves in harm's way. This conduct is also observable across their interactions with others and well documented in *Chapter 6*. It is this latter group of humans that evolutionary theorists credit with enhancing our species' ability to survive and evolve.

Our investigation of empirical studies refined our understanding of these two categories of people (egoists and other-regarding). The behavior of egoists is nuanced. Some exploit others without reserve to maximize their personal gains (perhaps 10%–20%). They are resolute in their efforts to amass greater and greater gains at the expense of others. Other egoists are less forward leaning. While they remain egoists, they restrain the extent to which they take from others. Their pursuit of personal gain appears to conform to creating an advantaged lifestyle. Their egoistic roots become clear when they feel their advantaged lifestyle is threatened.

Similarly, the behavior of other-regarding people is nuanced. Some are unconditionally altruistic (perhaps 10%–20%). Others are reciprocators. Reciprocators are other-regarding people who end their cooperation when they experience others exploiting them. They will sacrifice for others but only for those they deem worthy of such a commitment. Unconditional altruists do not apply constraints to their expression of cooperation and caring.

No One System Can Serve Both Egoists and Other-Regarding People

Our third insight is that no economic system designed to serve egoists can also serve other-regarding people. The reason is that the end each pursues in commerce and the means they employ are totally different. One excludes concern for others, and the other includes it. As to means, egoists use manipulation, and the latter group uses empowerment. Capitalism serves the former group; no economic model serves the latter. We built the Life Enabling model to serve this unassisted portion of humanity. We included in our thinking the reality that egoists exist. We also included in our thinking the fact that the contexts within which commerce occurs are rife with strong asymmetries in information and power.

Contributions From Other Professionals

With regard to the technical elements of conducting Life Enabling commerce as detailed in Sections II, III, and IV, our main sources of inspiration and thinking have been the teachings of W. Edwards Deming (1950, 1967, 1975, 1982, 1982a, 1988, 2000, 2013) and the implementers of Lean Manufacturing, also referred to as Lean Enterprise (Jones and Womack, 2009; Shimokawa and Fujimoto, 2009; Womack and Jones, 2003; Womack, Jones, and Roos, 1991; among many others).

Deming presented his thinking about commerce in the context of discussing its management. When he spoke about how one should manage a commercial organization, he was in fact addressing how commerce should be conducted. In this way, he discussed issues such as what the purpose of commerce should be, how it should be pursued, and how an enterprise should behave in relation to its customers, its employees, and others.

When fully appreciated, Deming's work provides the most complete thought base for conducting a commercial enterprise with the intent of maximizing the delivery of value to others in ways that benefit all stakeholders inclusively (Vitalo, 2017). It is Deming's thinking that dominates the operational elements of the Life Enabling model and provides the proper perspective for implementing a commercial enterprise. Especially relevant to our purposes, Deming specifically addressed the issue of people's psychology. He understood its significance as the necessary basis for all the guidance he provided about how one conceives, develops, and manages a commercial organization. His operational guidance for conducting commerce is absolutely consistent with his premises. It is Deming who defined the purpose of commerce in terms of enabling the success of every customer in ways that better the lives of everyone. It is he who set the requirement that commerce's purpose must also be achieved in a manner that benefits all stakeholders inclusively. It is he who blueprinted how to satisfy these requirements.

We see no problem with the content of Deming's thinking. The problem we do see is that Deming did not grasp that his understanding of people was inconsistent with the understanding that underpinned the economic model implemented by the very commercial enterprises he hoped his system would improve. Nor did he recognize that the purpose of commerce he defined (benefiting others) and the requirements for conducting that type of commerce were incompatible with Capitalism. Capitalism was seemingly invisible to him. Given its invisibility, he did not address issues that the recognition of its presence provokes. These are issues of ownership, control of decision making, and the sharing of the material surplus that commerce generates, among others. Thus, while his content is whole and valid with respect to its purpose, it is incomplete in its failure to acknowledge that no truly Capitalist enterprise could apply it. We have attempted to close this gap in his perspective.[3]

Lean Manufacturing is a business improvement methodology. James Womack and his colleagues derived the approach from the findings of their study of the Toyota Motor Company and other Japanese companies. They compared the more successful approaches that these companies employed to the approaches used by a wide array of automotive manufacturing companies around the world. The study was implemented in 1985 by the International Motor Vehicle Program located in the Center for Technology, Policy, and Industrial Development at the Massachusetts Institute of Technology. Its goal was to enable automobile manufacturers worldwide to advance the prosperity of their host countries and improve the work life of industry employees by transferring knowledge of the more competitive approaches implemented by Japanese companies such as Toyota. The study lasted five years, had 36 sponsoring governmental and industry organizations, produced 116 scholarly publications, and culminated in the publication of *The Machine That Changed the World* (Womack, Jones, and Roos, 1991). It introduced the term "lean production" to characterize Toyota's manufacturing strategy (i.e., the Toyota Production System or TPS) and contrasted it with "mass production," which was the norm. Absent from that work was the recognition of Deming's contribution to Toyota's success (Nemoto, 2009). Our research indicates that Deming's teaching was, in fact, the foundation of the Toyota Motor Corporation's success during the period of its emergence as an exemplary global automotive manufacturing

[3] Deming did understand that he was asking adopters of his thinking to radically change their personal perspectives. But he viewed their management thinking as vestiges of times past, not as conduct consistent with their goals and values and the economic model they chose to implement. He knew that they needed to undertake a personal transformation in how they understood people and managed a business. But he never grasped that their current perspectives were reflective of the commercial model they embraced. He never sensed that his call for personal transformation was in fact a call for them to embrace a new economic system.

company (circa 1960–1990). Indeed, Dr. Shoichiro Toyoda, the son of the founder of the Toyota Motor Corporation and its chairman from 1992 to 1999, acknowledged this fact. "Everyday I think about what he [Deming] meant to us," said Dr. Toyoda; "Deming is the core of our management" (Burns, 2008). Nonetheless, Deming's role with regard to Lean Enterprise is largely unrecognized, and its incorporation of his teaching is quite limited.

Over the decade and a half following the introduction of Lean Manufacturing, the Lean production model was refined and elaborated into "Lean thinking." Its guidance was applied to a wide variety of commercial enterprises, including both manufacturing and nonmanufacturing businesses. During this period, its authors expanded Lean thinking's guidance by incorporating their understanding of additional elements of Toyota's strategic perspective and operating methods.[4] Despite the model's expansion of perspective, in practice, the main focus of Lean Enterprise has always been on business operations. It is in Section III of this book (*The Operations Component of the Life Enabling Model*) that you will see its major contributions.

The Lean Enterprise thrust has introduced a wide array of enabling tools and methods that support achieving Deming's purpose *when they are used for achieving that end*. With this caveat, Lean thinking has significantly increased the value received by customers, reduced operating costs, and provided employees the opportunity to experience pride in the products they produce and the services they deliver. It has also yielded new learning, improved employee engagement, elevated teamwork, and raised businesses' performance on traditional measures of commercial success.

Lean Enterprise's problems, from our perspective, are twofold. First, there are significant inconsistencies among Lean community members concerning the ultimate aim the Lean approach serves (Vitalo and Bujak, 2022). Second, major gaps exist in Lean's foundational thinking. As to confusion about the aim of Lean Enterprise, that judgment is based on an analysis of the Lean literature and confirmed by a survey of Lean community members conducted by Womack (2010). He found, to his "surprise," that "[m]any of you [Lean community members] identified confusion about the meaning of lean as a barrier to progress in your organization." Based on Vitalo and Bujak's (2022) analysis, about a third of Lean practitioners assert that Lean is all about "efficiency and cost reduction," with the intent of maximizing profitability for the company. Another third defines Lean from a continuous improvement perspective. They see Lean as focusing on the

---

[4] In essence, when new issues arose related to questions about how to conduct Lean Enterprise, Lean authors used Toyota's practices, as known to them, as their "Rosetta stone." See Vitalo and Bujak (2021) for a discussion of the problems associated with this approach.

application of tools (e.g., 6S, Kaizen, TPM) to eliminate all non-productive work (waste) and elevate the utility of workplaces. In this view, its driving force is a striving for perfection. A final third of Lean practitioners see it as a cooperative commercial strategy integrating the contributions of all participants in commerce in an effort to maximize the delivery of value to customers, as judged from the customers' perspective. Vitalo and Bujak (2022) asked,

> Which of these notions or what higher order notion represents the controlling aim of the Lean approach to commerce? Minimization of cost? Maximization of profit? Delivering value to customers? Benefiting all stakeholders inclusively? Which of these ends should constrain the pursuit of the others when trade-offs are required? (Vitalo and Bujak, 2022)

They went on to point out that "[a] set of ideas cohere into a system only when they are organized around a central aim." In essence, if the aim is uncertain, the system can only be unstable.

As regards the second issue, Vitalo and Bujak (2022) described gaps in Lean's foundational knowledge. Foundational knowledge refers to "a set of principles expressed, defined, and applied consistently" that guides the implementation of a particular system. One of the gaps they explored relates to decisions such as how the benefits generated from waste removal should be shared or whether owners should simply retain them exclusively as added profit. Another gap relates to the absence of principles that allow one to understand to what ends Lean tools should be used. Should Lean tools, for example, be used to downsize a business? Womack (2016) clearly said no, but Ohno (1988, p. 53) seemed to say otherwise: "[W]e consider a manpower reduction policy as a means of cost reduction, the most critical condition for a business's success."

An even larger gap concerns Lean's understanding of the nature of people. Lean management literature speaks about how one should treat people and expects that such treatment will yield involvement and striving for perfection. But nowhere does it provide a detailed description of its view of human nature or a definitive statement of the "why" behind its dictates. Its explanations for some of the sacrosanct behaviors it prescribes—such as "Respect for People"—are inconsistent (Vitalo and Bujak, 2019). Some explanations seem predicated on expediency (e.g., it elicits better engagement by people in their work), while others suggest a moral basis for this behavior (e.g., "it's the right thing to do").

What the Life Enabling model has incorporated from Lean Enterprise are its tools. What it has added is a singular statement of what the purpose of commerce is and the foundational knowledge that guides the consistent pursuit of that purpose.

Capitalism is practiced worldwide. The United States espouses Capitalism with fervor. It touts Capitalism as the *only* effective economic system. The country's founding fathers, with few exceptions, were profit-seeking capitalists. They owned land and possessed wealth. They used their land to produce agricultural products and their wealth to speculate in real estate, trade in cotton and slaves, and provide financial services to their new nation for profit. So, given Capitalism's history and significance, one is compelled to ask whether there are reasons why people need a new economic model other than its limited focus on commerce as implemented by a subset of humankind. As you will read in this chapter, there are.

Chapter 2

Shedding Misconceptions About Capitalism

We begin by clarifying what Capitalism is and is not. Capitalism is a theory, a system of ideas that attempts to describe and explain why and how people produce and exchange resources within a society and the cumulative effects these exchanges generate with regard to material wealth. It is used to guide the conduct of individuals and commercial organizations and to formulate governmental actions. Its intellectual pillars are individualism and materialism.[1]

Capitalism has a long history. As a theory of commerce, it was first formalized in the 18th century, but the history of its pronounced emergence in Europe began in the 11th century (Pirenne, 1960). As with all economic systems, its ideas are deduced from a set of assumptions about the nature of humankind (Goodwin, 1991). Its contents are not induced from empirical research. Its theorems do not have the scientific foundations of a natural science such as physics or biology (Vickrey, 1964).

Every commercial model, including Capitalism, asserts that compliance with its dictates is the best way to ensure that the material resources people require to survive and thrive are available to them. In the United States, the public, including the authors, are further conditioned to associate Capitalism with patriotism, democracy, personal freedom, opportunity, and free markets, and perhaps even have it entangled in our religious beliefs. We are conditioned to imagine its alternatives as those "evil" other systems—like Communism or Socialism. But, in fact, Capitalism simply describes one of a number of possible approaches to commerce, including others that share its requirements for private property and freedom of choice.

None of the emotional content we associate with Capitalism resides within the fabric of its theoretical system. It is not, for example, committed to American values or the nation itself. This should be clear given the reality of multinational companies and the global economy. Indeed, the commitment of a Capitalist enterprise to any nation is solely dependent on how well that nation (or locale) enables it to maximize its profits.[2]

[1] The definition of individualism has many variations (Individualism, 2017). Our use of the term refers to an understanding of humankind that places the interests of the individual above the interests of the social group. This meaning reflects the primary dictionary definition (Individualism, 2017a). The term "materialism," as used here, refers to a dominant desire in humans for wealth and material possessions.

[2] That Capitalist enterprises associate preferentially with nations based on how well they enable their maximization of profit is reflected in the fact that nations competing to attract such enterprises universally do so by offering lower taxes and other monetary incentives (Devereux, Lockwood, and Redoano, 2004; Wenner and Zollman, 2017).

Neither is Capitalism committed to freedom per se, except with regard to the rights of commercial property owners to control, as they see fit, the use of their property and the wealth it creates. For example, Capitalism operated effectively in the United States using the regimen of slavery, and indeed trading in slaves was a profitable and acceptable Capitalist enterprise (Beckert, 2014).

Capitalism is also not committed to democracy, as companies implementing this model operate in accordance with oppressive and dictatorial regimes as well as with governments that are more or less democratic.[3] Capitalist enterprises are not even committed to free markets—at least not in their real-world practices, as they use competitive methods that include restricting free market competition (Washington, 2016).[4] And Capitalism certainly is not aligned with Christianity as a religion, as it envisions the maximization of personal profit without regard for others as the sole motive for commerce between people. Its premise is that people always act egoistically and that Capitalist enterprises have no social responsibility. Their only responsibility is to maximize profits for their owners (Friedman, 1970). Such behavior is a far cry from the Christian construct of agape.[5]

Caution: The above statements are *not* an indictment of Capitalism. They are made to clarify that all the emotional overlays stirred by the term are a function of

[3] As just one example, Google, LLC (previously Google, Inc.), is developing a tailored version of its search engine for China that will deny its users access to information that the government does not want them to see. As Gallagher (2018) reports, the tailored search engine "will blacklist websites and search terms about human rights, democracy, religion, and peaceful protest."

[4] Adam Smith (1776) warned the public that it is always the interest of capitalists ("dealers") to narrow the competition (pp. 213—14). A recent practical example of restricting competition (free market operations) is provided by AT&T. It owns DirecTV, a satellite-based television delivery service, and DirecTV Now, an internet delivery system. AT&T recently merged with Time Warner Corporation. Among the Time Warner properties it acquired is HBO, a media channel that has "long been the crown jewel of American television" (Wu, 2018). Despite AT&T promising in a Federal Court hearing prior to the merger that it would "never use Time Warner's media properties as leverage against its rivals" (Wu, 2018), it ceased allowing its major competitors permission to carry the HBO channel. At the time of this writing, Dish TV (satellite) and Sling (internet) (both owned by Dish Network) have been disallowed from broadcasting the channel. They claim that AT&T pulled their right to transmit the HBO channel as a way to force Dish Network "to pay for a guaranteed number of subscribers, regardless of how many of its customers actually do subscribe to HBO" (Blumenthal, 2018). This would mean that Dish Network would need to reimburse AT&T for customers *who did not want to receive the HBO service.* As an interesting side note, Microsoft Incorporated used a similar tactic in the 1980s to squash competition to its MS DOS operating system. It required all computer manufacturers to pay for an MS DOS license *for every machine they made* whether or not it had MS DOS installed. Otherwise, the vendor could not install MS DOS *on any of its machines* (U.S. Department of Justice, 1994).

[5] The authors are aware of Adam Smith's book, *The Theory of Moral Sentiments*, and his discussion of humankind's other-regarding faculty for sympathy, which, in today's terms, might better be labeled empathy. This second of the "*Two faces of Adam Smith*" (Smith, V.L., 1998), however, has no play in his economic model. Capitalism's posited positive dynamic results from the cumulative effects of mutually agreed transactions arrived at freely by equally knowledgeable and powerful parties *who each operate solely with regard to their selfish ends* (Rabin, 1998; Goodwin, Harris, Nelson, Roach, et al., 2017; Hirschman, 1977; Hosseini, 2010; Jensen and Mackling, 1994; Yamagishi, Li, Takagishi, Matsumoto, et al., 2014; Smith, A., 1776).

our indoctrination. Capitalism, as a commercial model, is simply a set of ideas that are deduced from its assumptions about the nature of people and the context within which they exchange resources (Vickrey, 1964). These ideas purport to explain the dynamics of exchange transactions between people and advise how a society can provide for the generation and distribution of the goods and services it needs to sustain itself and maximize its material wealth.

Whether the purpose Capitalism or any other commercial model defines for commerce or its implementing ideas are good, bad, or indifferent is a judgment that must be made from two perspectives. One is scientific; the other relates to the survival of humankind. From a scientific perspective, a deductive theory like Capitalism must be internally consistent, and, *to have practical utility*, it must be derived from empirically valid premises. Internal consistency means that a theory's contents (theorems, principles) logically flow from its assumptions. If they do not, then the theory makes no sense and, from a scientific perspective, deserves no further consideration. As to valid premises, the foundational beliefs upon which a deductive theory rests must be realistic; they must correspond to the empirical findings of science. If they do not, the theory has no practical use. This means that its contents are useless for explaining or guiding real-world economic activity.[6] For example, recall that all economic theories make assumptions about the nature of people, since these theories, by definition, describe and explain human conduct and its consequences. If such a theory assumes that all people act egoistically in the service of their personal self-interests without regard for others and empirical research uncovers that only a minority of people act on that basis, then the contents of the theory that *require* this *universal* premise be true are *necessarily invalid.* All the principles and theorems deduced from that assumption and dependent on its validity have no legitimacy and no explanatory power.

The survival of humankind provides a second and larger perspective for judging an economic theory. If a system of conduct directs people to behave in ways that endanger the survival of the species, then its use is contrary to the interests of humankind at both the individual and the societal level. Thus, if the evolutionary success of a species were benefited by other-regarding cooperativeness and a system of behavior promoted self-regarding, egoistic conduct, then embracing that system would undermine humankind's survival.

The Basic Tenets of Capitalism

The basic unit of commerce in any society is the exchange of resources between two parties (microeconomic level). In Capitalism's view, each party seeks a resource the other possesses. Each is intent on maximizing the value measured monetarily that he or she realizes from every exchange with another. It follows

[6] We address Milton Friedman's (1953) objection to this contention in *Chapter 4*, pages 92–93.

logically, therefore, that each party's ideal outcome is to get *all* the value *without giving anything*. Given other assumptions of Capitalism, however, this cannot happen. The reason is that Capitalism also assumes that commerce takes place between people with equal power; hence, "taking" is not available. Also, each party is equally able to make fully informed rational judgments about what he or she needs and what others are offering. Consequently, neither party can exploit the other. Given this assumed world of zero asymmetries in knowledge, information, decision-making ability, and power, the parties *must* negotiate. Through these negotiations, they arrive at an exchange of resources that is satisfactory to each. Hence, every marketplace transaction ends "fairly" and "justly" by definition.

At the market level,[7] the dynamic of supply, demand, price, and profit reduction operates. Supply is presumed to evoke demand (Say's Law of Markets, 2018). As more producers enter a market seeking profit by providing the commodity buyers require, they compete for that demand. Since the model also assumes that all producers provide *equivalent* offerings, sellers compete on price alone, thereby driving the price down toward actual cost, as each producer seeks to win more sales. Given that buyers choose freely and effectively, they buy the offering with the lowest price. This is so because the functional utility of each alternative offering is equivalent. As price falls, more and more people have their needs satisfied until all demand is met.[8] Also, as profit margins shrink, producers—acting freely and effectively in the pursuit of maximizing their profits—look elsewhere to invest their productive capabilities in order to realize greater material gains. This search results in the opening of new markets that meet previously unserved buyer needs, and the cycle that begins with high profits and ends with price approaching cost repeats itself.

At the societal level (macroeconomic level), this entire supply–demand–price–profit reduction-new market creation dynamic is presumed to ensure that the productive resources of a social unit are always applied where they will generate the greatest gains measured monetarily. Capitalists invest in markets with unmet needs. As profits lessen, they uncover new unmet needs that they apply their resources to fill so that they gain more profit. This means that the productive capacity of a society is always used efficiently. It is always used where it will produce increasing wealth and meet unmet human needs. Thus, Capitalism assures that the exact products society needs to survive will be available to it in the quantities it requires.

[7] We define a market as a physical or virtual setting that allows buyers and sellers of a specific good or service to interact in order to facilitate an exchange.

[8] Capitalism implicitly assumes that people who need a commodity will have the resources required to purchase that commodity. If this assumption were to fail, then society's need for an offering would not be met and the economic model would fall short of its central purpose.

This efficiency in the use of resources and the assured satisfaction of society's needs evolve spontaneously from the choices made by fully informed people who act freely and rationally to maximize their material wealth in marketplaces where no one has an advantage over anyone else. People always choose just what they need and make the correct choices as to value received for value exchanged. Markets self-correct so that the balance between supply and demand equalizes. When demand slackens, producers cut back production. When demand increases, they increase production. New markets emerge as producers seek higher profit-making opportunities by meeting unaddressed needs.

One of Capitalism's major attractions as a theory is its simplicity and automaticity. It is presumed to be rooted in human nature and the found conditions within which people exist. It requires no planning or intervention. Its effects naturally flow from the native inclinations it posits all people to possess and the characteristics it assumes all markets possess. Indeed, intervention in its operations is deemed destructive because such action would disrupt the naturally effective choices and native behaviors of people and the qualities it presumes that markets have. The unfettered exercise of these qualities is necessary for the dynamics of Capitalism to work. In essence, intervention undermines economic success.

What's Wrong With Capitalism?

As far as we can discern, the theory of Capitalism is logically sound in the sense that its conclusions flow from its premises and the constraints it defines with regard to economic factors (e.g., the independence of economic actors and markets). Indeed, computer simulations of economic activity using the model's specifications do produce behaviors that more or less conform to the model's predictions.

Rather, the criticisms made by economists, psychologists, environmentalists, and other professionals address what these authors deem as the model's structural problems and the consequential problems produced by its use. Oddly, we have not uncovered anyone who has identified the most fundamental failing of the theory —the actual root cause of its structural and consequential problems. That failing is the *invalidity of its premises*. As a deductive theory, that invalidity renders the model's knowledge useless from a practical perspective. We will discuss this issue separately at the end of this chapter.

In this section, we highlight Capitalism's structural and consequential problems. Since our purpose is solely to demonstrate a reasonable basis for society needing an alternative economic model, we will only present a small sample of the issues critics have raised.

Capitalism's Structural Problems

A model has a structural problem when a factor that objectively affects the state of the phenomenon the model represents is missing or when a factor it includes does not behave as the model prescribes. One example of a missing structural element in Capitalism is the role of the banks in money creation. That presence increases aggregate demand and undermines economic equilibrium (Keene, 2012, 2017; Tobin, 1963). The theorem of economic equilibrium is an example of a structural element included in Capitalism that does not behave as the theory dictates.

The presence of either missing or invalid structural elements renders a commercial model dysfunctional for use in guiding economic decision making. This is because economic events will be determined by factors the model does not address or wrongly construes. We have selected the misbehaving theorem of economic equilibrium as our exemplary structural problem, since it is fundamental to the model's dynamic operation and its well touted notion that the "market knows best."

The Theorem of Economic Equilibrium

In Capitalism, economic equilibrium is the state where the economic forces of supply and demand are balanced and stable. Equilibrium in an economy as a whole is termed "general equilibrium." When the construct is applied to a single market, it is termed "partial" or "market equilibrium." The term "market" identifies a context where buyers and sellers meet to exchange resources for a particular good or service. Partial (or market) equilibrium occurs when the supply of a market's good or service is equal to its demand. When the market is in equilibrium, there is no tendency for prices to change. That stable price point is referred to as the "market clearing price." At that price, all demand is met, and no supply remains unsold.

How Does It Work?

As stated before, Capitalism assumes that supply evokes demand (Say's Law of Markets, 2018). The balance of supply and demand determines price. When demand exceeds supply, price rises, since sellers seek to maximize their monetary gains and scarcity forces buyers to compete with one another to acquire what they seek. Also, producers increase their production so that they can reap greater profits by satisfying more demand. Conversely, when supply exceeds demand, producers compete for sales by lowering prices. They also reduce production to better match demand.

This cycle of automatic accommodation between supply and demand continues producing ever-narrowing discrepancies until supply and demand are balanced. This adaptive process is envisioned to occur much as a freely swinging pendulum that oscillates in smaller and smaller arcs until it comes to rest.

As this process occurs across all markets, the economy as a whole stabilizes. This process is seen as a natural consequence of human conduct given Capitalism's assumptions about human nature and the characteristics of the marketplace.

Why Is the Theorem of Equilibrium Important?

The theorem of equilibrium explains why government action to regulate markets is unnecessary. It asserts the existence of a self-regulating mechanism that moderates economic cycles and prevents excesses in either supply or demand. Excesses cause inefficiency in the allocation of productive resources. When supply exceeds demand, productive resources are being used to provide unneeded goods and services. When it falls short, people go without their needs being met. Thus, equilibrium is Capitalism's inherent regulator that moderates business cycles, ensuring that periodic recessions[9] either do not occur or cause little harm to all economic agents and to an economy's productive capabilities. Without this regulator, unmoderated cycles could erupt into "economic bubbles" followed by economic depressions. In short, equilibrium is the source of the "wisdom of the market" that regulates economic activity.

What Is the Evidence Against the Theorem?

Critics have raised a number of issues with the theorem of market equilibrium. We will discuss two of them. One addresses whether equilibrium occurs in all markets, as is claimed. The second addresses whether Capitalism—through the mechanism of economic equilibrium—leads to stable, long-term economic performance, and if not, why not.

Studies Invalidate Equilibrium's Expectations in Financial Markets

The theorem of equilibrium does not operate in financial markets. According to the theorem, changes in pricing should occur as information about the expected value of offerings changes. This is so because economic agents are assumed to be rational and effective decision makers who assess the proper value of an offering based on full information. In asset markets,[10] for example, investors are expected to seek with greater demand those offerings that promise better returns and with lessened demand those that do not. Thus, when good news

[9] A decline in general economic activity for two or more consecutive quarters.

[10] Asset markets trade in equities, bonds, currencies, derivatives, and other financial assets. Alternative offerings are valued based on the likely profit they will generate.

about a company's improved profit-generating potential emerges, the equilibrium theorem predicts that we should see increased demand for its stock, and the stock's price should rise. The reverse prediction is expected when bad news about a company's earnings performance appears. Accordingly, dramatic changes in demand and price should only follow some correspondingly dramatic change related to an asset's inherent value.

Reinforcing the strength of this prediction is the realization that, across an entire market, price changes result from the pooled decisions of millions of rational investors. The sum of their collective "wisdom" should absolutely ensure that the market price is an even better match to the true value of the stock than any individual might arrive at on his or her own.[11] Any pricing errors (i.e., swings in the pendulum) should also quickly get dampened as this mass of well-informed, rational, and effective decision makers make their investment decisions. In this way, market forces using available information about an asset's proper value should tend to iron out any problems long before they become large. As Buchanan (2008) states, "An unexpected rise or plunge in values just cannot happen unless there has been some correspondingly good or bad news." This is the scenario that flows from the theorem of market equilibrium. As Farma expresses it: "In an efficient market ... competition will cause the full effects of new information on intrinsic values to be reflected instantaneously in actual prices" (quoted in Singh, 2010).

Given the wealth and continuous flow of information in financial markets, these markets represent the ideal settings for the demonstration of market equilibrium. Contrary to the expectations of the equilibrium theorem, however, a large-scale empirical study of the relationship between stock prices and information relevant to the inherent value of each stock found no evidence to support the theorem's expectation. In fact, the study's findings led its authors to conclude that "Jumps [in prices] seem to occur *for no identifiable reasons* [italics added], and as a consequence spook the market; this perturbation is slow to decay" (Joulin, Lefevre, Grunberg, and Bouchaud, 2008, p. 7).

In their two-year study, Joulin, Lefevre, Grunberg, and Bouchaud (2008) analyzed more than 90,000 news items posted to investors from Reuters and Dow Jones and the movement in the prices of stocks based on the earnings-relevant

[11] This notion of greater accuracy through numbers fits a statistical perspective wherein human behavior is always observed as evidencing variation (or error) and averaging across very many subjects works to minimize its effects on obscuring the truth. Of course, Capitalism is a deductive model. Its premises about human decision making are unconditional. Its conclusions, therefore, are logical necessities. Given that it presumes every individual makes effective decisions using full information, greater numbers of individuals will not add any greater accuracy. Nonetheless, this argument about expecting even greater accuracy when viewing the collective decisions of all market participants exists unchallenged.

positive or negative nature of the news item. They found no relationship between the two data sets. They concluded that "neither idiosyncratic news nor market wide news can explain the frequency and amplitude of price jumps" (2008, p. 1).

Their findings echoed those of an earlier study by Cutler, Poterba, and Summers (1988) about what moves stock prices. Those authors concluded that "large market moves often occur on days without any identifiable major news releases, cast[ing] doubt on the view that stock price movements are fully explicable by news about future cash flows and discount rates." They also noted that the problem of accounting for price changes based on changes in a financial asset's fundamental value is not confined to trading in stocks. Referring to a study by Malkiel (1977) and "several more recent studies," they reported that the problem also occurs in the closed-end mutual funds market.

Equilibrium Does Not Deliver Its Promised Stability

Two historical facts also make it clear that the general equilibrium theorem is flawed with regard to delivering economic stability. The first relates to recessions. The second relates to economic bubbles and busts.

1. Recessions

There have been 47 recessions in the United States from 1790 through 2018. That is an average of one every 4.8 years (List of recessions in the United States, 2018). Of those 47, *only three might be assigned to an action of the U.S. Government.* For example, the recession beginning August 1918 was consequent to the end of World War 1 and the war-level "production, along with an influx of labor from returning troops. This, in turn, caused high unemployment" (ibid.). Another example is the 1807 depression. It was consequent to a government-imposed embargo on trade with the United Kingdom.

The remaining 44 recessions across Capitalism's history in the United States suggest that Capitalism has not produced stable economic development. Indeed, as a result of his extensive research, Piketty (2014) dismissed its contribution to the economic development of the United States. He stated that the massive development of the United States economy over its 200-year-plus life span can be accounted for solely by its dramatic population growth, territorial expansion through expropriation (except for the Louisiana purchase), and the advantages it realized as a result of the harm to the productive infrastructure of other industrial nations consequent to two world wars.

Also, while the average length of U.S. recessions thus far has been 1.6 years, a recession's economic consequences have longer lives than the recession itself. This suggests that the period free of the negative consequences of recessions has been relatively brief. One negative consequence of a recession is unemployment. It tends to peak *after a recession formally ends* and not recover to pre-recession levels for two to fours years. Thus, the effects of a recession may last into the next occurrence of a recession. To this point, Irons (2009) noted that "a substantial body of economic literature shows, the consequences of high unemployment, falling incomes, and reduced economic activity can have lasting consequences" and that these consequences of an economic recession "can lead to 'scarring'—that is, long-lasting damage to individuals' economic situations and the economy more broadly." This scarring is greater for the less wealthy than for the wealthy, as the latter have greater residual resources and reduced reliance on income from wage labor versus from rents.[12]

Interestingly, while the mantra of Capitalism is no government intervention, it appears that the laws and regulations put into effect during the 1930s (e.g., the Glass-Steagall Act of 1932) *actually dampened* the incidence and depth of recessions. As Whaples (1995) noted, "The current [economic] consensus is that the volatility of GNP and unemployment were greater before the Great Depression than they have been since the end of World War II" (1995, p. 51), at least until the recision of the Glass-Steagall Act and other Depression-era volatility-dampening legislation.

2. Bubbles and Busts

Recessions are not the only economic turbulence that speaks against general equilibrium's moderating expectations. Bubbles and busts represent even more dramatic periods of disequilibrium that theoretically should not occur. Investopedia defines an economic bubble as "the rapid escalation of asset prices ... created by a surge in prices unwarranted by the fundamentals of the asset and driven by exuberant market behavior" (Bubble, 2018). Tulip mania in Holland is the first recorded economic bubble in history. It involved escalating contract prices for the then recently introduced and fashionable tulip that reached extraordinarily high levels before prices dramatically collapsed in February 1637 (Tulip mania, 2018).

Bubbles are propelled by continual buying of an asset irrespective of any positive change in the asset's inherent value. Clearly, this behavior is not consistent with the equilibrium theorem or the premises of Capitalism. When no more investors are willing or able to buy at the elevated price, a sell-off occurs, causing the bubble to deflate. Early buyers sell to escape with whatever profits they can realize. Later buyers sell to reduce their losses. As selling

[12] Rents refer to money collected for the use of existing assets—e.g., payments from a tenant, dividends from stocks, and interest on loans extended to borrowers. The income rents generate does not derive from the production of new value.

escalates, prices fall ever more rapidly until the market collapses. Losses become almost universal.

In the United States, we have most recently experienced the "dotcom" bubble in the late 1990s that burst in 2000 and the housing bubble that burst in 2008. Objectively assessed, we are currently in our third bubble—the stock market bubble—as stock prices far exceed their proper values (Bukhari, 2017). Alan Greenspan, a former Federal Reserve chairman, asserted that we actually are in two bubbles—a stock market bubble *and* a bond market bubble (Egan, 2018).

Given the theorem of economic equilibrium, the history of economic bubbles simply should not exist. Why then do they occur? The answer to this question reveals other structural deficiencies in the model of Capitalism.

Based on historical analysis and research findings, the factors that propel bubbles and busts are

(a) moral hazard,

(b) flawed human decision making, and

(c) leveraged investment.

The theory of Capitalism does not recognize any of these factors. Consequently, it cannot predict the emergence of bubbles and busts, nor does it contain any mechanism to prevent them.

a. Moral Hazard

Moral hazard is greed pursued without risk. It occurs when someone can invest money to reap gains while offloading the risk of losses to others (Pritchard, 2018). It is enabled by one party having information that his or her counterparty in a transaction lacks. It is the ideal scenario for people who conform to Capitalism's assumption that human beings are money maximizing, egoistic pursuers of self-interest. It maximizes one's gains while eliminating one's risks. On the other hand, since Capitalism assumes away any market-relevant asymmetries, moral hazard simply cannot exist.

The housing market bubble (2001 to 2007) is a recent example where greed pursued without risk triggered a bubble. Both mortgage brokers and banks exploited this moral hazard opportunity to reap huge gains that they never were required to surrender to any significant degree (Taibbi, 2011, 2014). As Bouchard noted,

> In the case of the sub-prime mortgage market, for instance, brokers were collecting commissions on mortgages that required no deposit and no proof of income. [They collected their fees up front when the loan was

> made.] Since the brokers were not lending their own money, it was for them a risk-free business. Meanwhile, investment banks took on these risky loans and lumped them together into 'collateralised debt obligations' (CDOs). Once the risks were safely blurred [in these bundled loans], the banks were able to sell the CDOs on at a healthy profit [to unsuspecting or misled investors]. (Bouchard, 2008)

As the rewards from these behaviors became realized, the perpetrators accelerated their efforts. Brokers extended loans to people who had less and less capability to pay their debt costs. They created products that deferred interest payments for extended periods of time in order to make the payment doable for the borrower—at least initially. They encouraged "subprime" borrowers to lie on loan applications (so called "liar loans") or left blank the income/asset portion of the loan application, or they altered documents to make it appear as if borrowers were able to afford loans that they really could not (Andrews, 2007; Pritchard, 2018). Banks accepted these ever-riskier products, bundled them with assurances, and passed them on.

These lending practices increased housing demand, as they made it possible for more and more people to buy homes. Housing prices rose as a consequence. Accordingly, the size of mortgages that people required to buy homes increased. This, in turn, raised the fees collected by brokers, since the fees are calculated as a percentage of the mortgage extended. It also raised the revenues earned by the CDO-generating banks. Thus, the bubble grew as this vicious cycle of riskless profit making spiraled upward.

The ingredients required for the housing bubble to be generated by moral hazard include people who selfishly pursue their own money-maximizing ends and asymmetry of information. The party exploiting the moral hazard opportunity must have information that the party being exploited does not. In the above example, brokers and banks knew that the loans were worthless, but investors did not. As well, borrowers were often assured that they were capable of repaying the loans being made to them, but lenders knew they were not.

Capitalism as a model incorporates the first of the moral hazard requirements. It assumes that people are egoistically driven, money-maximizing actors. It does not, however, recognize asymmetry of information. Everyone in a market is presumed to have full access to all relevant information.

b. Flawed Human Decision Making

Empirical studies demonstrate that people's decision making is flawed. They fail to use only value-relevant information in their investment decision making. And they do not correctly assess which among a set of options will maximize their monetary gain (Rabin, 1998). We have already seen that, contrary to the expectations of Capitalism, pricing in asset markets does not fluctuate in accordance with market information about an asset's proper value. In *Chapter 6*, we will discuss a number of the human decision-making flaws psychologists have empirically demonstrated. Most relevant to the issue of booms and busts are two of these flaws. One is people's tendency to overemphasize recent history in predicting the immediate future, and the other is herding or flocking behavior.

Overemphasizing the Recent Past

As Singh (2010) reported, research in psychology has "demonstrated that people tend to make decisions based on whatever information is available at hand, leading to the human tendency to overweight the recent past [which is more readily at hand]. In making judgments about stock prices, the most likely anchor is the recently remembered price." This empirical finding was anticipated by Keynes (1937). He wrote that people "assume that the present is a much more serviceable guide to the future than a candid examination of past experience would show it to have been" (1937, p. 214).

Minsky (1992), expanding on Keynes's observation, noted that a period of steady growth in asset prices leads people to rising expectations about future growth. "Consequently, capitalists develop 'euphoric expectations' about future prospects as the memory of a previous slump recedes" (quoted in Keen, 2012, p. 16). Minsky's conclusion was that "The tendency to transform doing well into a speculative investment boom is the basic instability in a capitalist economy" (quoted in Keen, 2012, p. 16). This is a far cry from Capitalism's moderating and reassuring theorem of economic equilibrium.

Herding and Flocking

Research indicates yet another flawed decision-making factor not incorporated within Capitalism's theory. In its most general form, it is the tendency for investors to align their decisions with those of other investors. The longer this alignment continues and the more uniform the decisions of these actors become, the more reactive and volatile the overall market is to any event that might trigger buying (boom) or selling (bust) behavior. The reason is that anything that triggers a change in decision making by one or more members of these clusters is amplified by its reverberating effects on the actions of the remaining members of the cluster. This coherence of decision makers has been termed "herding" or "flocking behavior." Its emergence generates market fragility and makes markets susceptible to booms and crashes.

This phenomenon may be due to the "information cascade" process described by Bikhchandani, Hirshleifer, and Welch (1992) or to a feedback phenomenon that progressively increases the weight assigned by decision makers to the behavior of other investors (Harras and Sornette, 2008). It might also be due to humankind's use of social learning via imitation and modeling as a success-enhancing strategy. By imitating someone who succeeds at a task, we increase our likelihood of success.

However it occurs, the increasingly uniform behavior it produces enables "small shocks" to "easily shift the behavior of many individuals" (Bikhchandani, Hirshleifer, and Welch, 1992, p. 999). Buchanan reported that the physicist Sornette "reckons that markets reach a state like an avalanche waiting to happen." He quoted Sornette as stating that "Anything can trigger the avalanche once the system is ripe" (Buchanan, 2008). As should be obvious, herding or flocking behavior is inconsistent with the fundamental assumptions of Capitalism.

c. Debt-Fueled Investment

In addition to moral hazard and flawed decision making, *leverage* is a third factor that triggers the emergence of bubbles. Leverage uses borrowed money to invest in assets.[13] Capitalism views debt-financed investment (leverage) as neutral with respect to increasing aggregate demand and therefore having no effect on achieving equilibrium. Borrowers simply put into play money others (savers) have taken out of play. The total amount of money within an economy remains unchanged. It therefore has no additive affect on aggregate demand and no consequence for equilibrium (Krugman, 2012).

Contradicting Capitalism's theory, Thurner, Farmer, and Geanakoplos (2012) found that leveraged investment has a destabilizing, not a neutral effect, on asset markets *even when investors pursue a value-based investment strategy.*[14] The *mere use of leverage* to buy assets magnifies bubbles and busts. The reason is that leverage causes "fat tails" and clustered volatility. "Fat tails" is a statistical term meaning that extreme events become more

---

[13] Leverage involves investing with money borrowed from a bank or broker (lender). The lender requires the investor to maintain an account that contains assets that the lender can claim should the investor default on his or her loan. The amount in the account is a percentage of the total value of the asset being purchased by the investor using the lender's money. This percentage is termed the "margin," and it is set by the lender. Thus, Broker A, for example, might require an investor to keep 10% of the value of the assets he or she is buying using the investor's money in a margin account. Should the price of the purchased asset drop, a lender may make a "margin call." Here, a lender demands that an investor deposit additional money or securities into his or her margin account so that the margin account plus the sale of the now less valuable purchased asset still allows the lender to recover what was loaned should the investor default.

[14] Value-based investment buys assets that have a higher intrinsic value than their current price.

likely to occur than one would normally expect. Volatility refers to periods of extreme price changes, wherein prices suddenly rise or fall. It is the opposite of equilibrium. Clustered volatility means that once volatility erupts, it tends to sustain (Moffatt, 2017).

Thurner, Farmer, and Geanakoplos (2012) built a computer-based simulation of an asset investment market in which virtual hedge funds purchased assets using leverage with margin calls. Their model *did not* include the dynamic of flocking or herding behavior. It simply focused on the pure effects of leverage (borrowing) in a market where multiple investors—here, hedge funds—independently applied the financial strategy of value-based investing—i.e., systematically buying underpriced assets with the expectation of making a profit when the assets realized their true value.

When investors *do not* borrow, the price fluctuation of a purchased asset is approximately normally distributed and uncorrelated across time. Volatility is moderate and unclustered. Prices move randomly up and down. This pattern changes when the hedge funds invest using leverage. When prices of a leveraged asset fall, brokers raise margin requirements to protect their loans. Consequently, investors must come up with more cash to deposit in their margin accounts. This causes more selling of assets, and that makes volatility worse. A vicious cycle is triggered that multiplies losses. Downward paths accelerate, and volatility increases and lasts longer (becomes clustered). Extreme events become more likely (the fat tail scenario) due to accelerating volatility and its clustering.[15]

What Can We Conclude About the Equilibrium Theorem?

Essentially, the evidence reveals that the theorem of market equilibrium does not operate as expected. All markets are not automatically self-correcting, and

[15] Another approach to investing that uses leverage creates even greater market turbulence. It is called *Ponzi investment*. It is a money-making strategy based on the expectation that an asset's market price will rise over time simply due to other investors increasingly buying the asset. Contrary to the value-based investment strategy, buying is not based on the expectation that the purchased asset will generate profit for the investor due to its underrated intrinsic value. Rather, investors do not expect increases in the asset's intrinsic value to pay their borrowing costs. Rather, these investors use *additional borrowing* to cover the debt costs of leveraging as they hold on to their purchased asset. This investment strategy works as long as the asset's price continues to rise—essentially, as long as new buyers come along who will pay more for the asset than its intrinsic value and more than the current holder paid. Under this condition, the asset's market price rises, and new borrowing against the asset's increased market value is enabled to cover debt costs without provoking any margin calls. If the asset's price does not increase sufficiently to finance debt costs, then margins will be increased and assets must be sold to cover them. Ponzi investment magnifies the effects of leveraged buying by adding greater debt loads. Any event—real or imagined—that causes a drop in the demand for the asset triggers margin calls. Ponzi investors are forced to rapidly liquidate their assets to meet these demands. As prices fall due to excess supply, less value is realized, margins cannot be covered, and investors default on their debts, causing creditors to lose their money.

they possess internal dynamics unrecognized by the theorem that are economically destabilizing. The promise of economic stability is not delivered. The dictum of allowing the marketplace to be the arbiter and guide for social, political, and economic decision making therefore is inappropriate.[16]

Further, the investigations into why the theorem fails reveal other errors and omissions in Capitalism. For example, the role of debt and its ability to destabilize financial markets *even when used to pursue value-oriented investment* is contrary to the expectations of Capitalism. The presence of asymmetries in information is incompatible with the assumptions of Capitalism. These asymmetries enable those people who *do* conform to Capitalism's concept of human nature to exercise the money-maximizing advantages of moral hazard. Their actions produce destructive economic consequences that are fully unexpected by Capitalism.

Empirical investigations also reveal Capitalism's incorrect understanding of how people make decisions. They do not, as assumed, always make choices based on rationally assessing the true value of an offering. The quality of their decision making is flawed when judged by Capitalism's standard of rationality (i.e., always selecting the option that maximizes one's monetary gain). And people's economic decision making is clearly affected by social dynamics (e.g., herding or flocking). In each case, the model's assumptions are invalid.

Accordingly, Keen (2017) concluded that Capitalism's structural problems render it incapable of enabling societies to predict, and therefore prevent, the emergence of dramatic economic downturns and their consequent human and societal costs. As Buchanan (2008) noted, the attractive simplicity of the equilibrium theorem stands in stark contrast to the complexities observed in real-world markets:

> Take the recent worldwide credit crisis [2008]. Its main cause, the most sophisticated computer models now suggest, may be a fundamental tendency for markets to evolve, like an uncooled nuclear reactor, towards a dangerously unstable state. Everything from observations of irrationality in traders to the statistics of market fluctuations is telling us something is wrong with received wisdom, and a growing band of researchers has formed the view that we desperately need to develop a new theory of economics. (Buchanan, 2008)

Capitalism's Consequential Problems

Consequentialism evaluates a system of performance based on its effects. The evaluation might compare what a system promises versus what it delivers or what it delivers versus some standard of what is desirable—e.g., its effects on individual and societal well-being.

---

[16] See economist Frank Ackerman's (1999) formal critique of the equilibrium theorem that also concludes its invalidity.

There are many potential effects one might investigate with regard to the practice of Capitalism. Consistent with its premises, the implementers of Capitalism continuously strive to accumulate wealth and egoistically satisfy their self-interests. Growing wealth through large-scale production-based Capitalism requires a supply chain of raw materials and people willing to do the work of production (a labor pool). One set of Capitalism's consequences flows from these needs—specifically, the consequences caused by how Capitalist economies have historically acquired their supply of raw resources and the labor pool needed to enable large-scale manufacturing.

Throughout the history of Capitalism, for example, conquest and colonization have played an important role in securing the raw materials needed by Capitalist economies such as Portugal, Spain, Belgium, Holland, the United Kingdom, France, Germany, and the United States.[17] Indeed, even today, the United States' sponsorship of the overthrow of the elected Venezuelan President Nicolás Maduro has been linked by John Bolton, a National Security Advisor of the United States, to acquiring its enormous oil resources (Durden, 2019).

As to the labor pool needed for large-scale production capitalism, Perelman (1984) noted that, when industrialization was first being introduced, people preferred their self-sufficient lifestyles over working for others. They independently produced or acquired the commodities they needed to survive and thrive. In order to create the labor pool Capitalism required, capitalists[18] in England, for example, used their political power to force people out of their chosen lifestyles to create a labor pool. Instruments of this coercion included imposing taxes they could not pay based on their subsistence lifestyle and enclosing common areas, thereby limiting people's access to food from hunting and grazing land for raising livestock. Given no alternative, people migrated to urban areas and became dependent on wage labor to survive.

The accumulation of wealth through production also requires the continual creation of new markets. Each new market adds a new revenue and profit stream. Since Capitalism neither incorporates nor acknowledges the construct of social

---

[17] Economist Utsa Patnaik's analysis of British economic records estimated that the East India Company and the British Raj siphoned at least $44.6 trillion from India during the period of Britain's colonization (Sreevatsan, 2018).

[18] In this book, the lower-case term "capitalist" refers to a person who uses his or her means for the production of goods and services to egoistically pursue the maximization of personal wealth. Since every functional human being inherently possesses the means of production, the discriminating factor for being a capitalist is one's status as an egoistic self-maximizer. The "wealth" element that is typically associated with the concept of capitalist serves only to amplify the scale of one's capabilities to achieve one's ends. It is the end the person pursues in his or her exchanges with others that defines the person as a capitalist. When we capitalize the "c," we are referring to the economic theory.

responsibility (Friedman, 1970), there is no requirement that these new commodities actually deliver benefit to people. To realize profits, they only require that people want them and buy them. Thus, products that are addictive and harmful to health, such as cigarettes and "junk foods"; pharmaceuticals with initially hidden but known harmful health consequences, such as Celebrex, Vioxx, and OxyContin; chemicals and coatings with known toxic consequences, such as Teflon and asbestos-contaminated talcum powder; and very many other diverse commodities have been conceived, produced, and marketed for profit.

New commodities also require new or additional raw material inputs, all of which are finite and, therefore, exhaustible. The consequences of their exhaustion are not a concern for Capitalism and its implementers. Neither are the pollutants its enterprises generate. These pollutants affect the quality of air, water, and soil and endanger the lives of people and other living beings. Cumulatively, these pollutants can generate environmental changes of global significance like climate change. All of these outcomes are considered "negative externalities." Capitalism, as an economic system, does not recognize negative externalities as a producer's responsibility. When such externalities exist in a free market context, producers take no responsibility for the costs required to remedy their effects or the human harm they produce. Rather, these consequences are passed on to society.

Given the breadth of possible consequences one could investigate and our limited space and intent, we have chosen to focus this section on inequality in the distribution of wealth and income and its consequences. These consequences include the economic and social harm inequality causes and its generation of a self-perpetuating process that causes its harmful effects to spiral upward.

Inequality of Wealth and Income

Economic inequality is the unequal distribution of financial resources among different groups in a society.[19] Economic systems are expected to provide for a society's material well-being (Marshall, 1982), which economists measure monetarily. Achieving broadly based material well-being implies a relatively egalitarian distribution of wealth and income, if not initially, then over time. Indeed, the latter outcome was claimed for Capitalism by the economist Simon Kuznets (1955).

[19] We are using Piketty's (2014) definitions of wealth and income. Wealth is the total of one's assets. An asset is anything tangible or intangible that can be owned and controlled to produce monetary value through sale, rent, or productive use. Examples include non-financial assets such as land, dwellings, commercial inventory, machinery, patents, and financial assets such as bank accounts, mutual funds, stocks, insurance policies, and pension funds, among others. Income is monetary value acquired through either labor (i.e., the expenditure of one's personal time, effort, and expertise) or rents (i.e., money earned from one's existing base of wealth). The former includes wages, salaries, bonuses, and "other remuneration statutorily defined as labor related" (Piketty, 2014, p. 18). The latter includes dividends, interest, profits, capital gains, and other rents.

Three questions are paramount to our interest in inequality. First, does inequality in wealth and income exist? Second, if it does exist, what is Capitalism's role in creating or diminishing it? Third, is inequality a problem society needs to address?

Does It Exist?

Empirical evidence overwhelmingly confirms that inequality in wealth and income does exist. Indeed, it has been with us since the emergence of formalized Capitalism. Additionally, inequality under the regime of Capitalism is increasing. In the United States, for example, income and wealth inequality has persisted and increased since its founding (Lindert and Williamson, 2012).

Wealth

Focusing on wealth inequality, Piketty (2014) reported that, in 1810, the top 10% economic group owned approximately 58% of total wealth in the United States (2014, Figure 10.5, p. 348). In 2010, that ownership had increased to 70% of the total private wealth in the country (Piketty, 2014, Table 7.2, p. 248).

Collins and Hoxlie (2017) found that, in 2017, the "three wealthiest people in the United States ... own[ed] more wealth than the entire bottom half of the American population combined, a total of 160 million people or 63 million households" (2017, p. 2). They also reported that "The median American family ha[d] a net worth of $80,000, excluding the family car. The Forbes 400 [list of the wealthiest people in America] own[ed] more wealth than 33 million of these typical American families" (ibid.).

Wealth inequality is also accelerating. Smith, C. (2017) reported that, from 1986 through 2012, "the [total wealth] share of the top .1% took off, essentially tripling from 8% to over 22%, while the [wealth] share of the bottom [90%] fell precipitously from 36% to 23%." Zucman (2019) added that the accelerating state of inequality "is confirmed by Forbes rankings which show that the share of [U.S.] national wealth owned by the top 0.00025% (roughly 400 richest Americans) has been multiplied by four since the early 1980s .... In sum, a body of independent data sources paint the same picture of sharply rising [wealth] concentration at the top end" (2019, p. 111).

Inequality in wealth ownership is also pronounced in our Capitalist-based global economy. Luhby (2019) reported that "The combined fortunes of the world's 26 richest individuals reached $1.4 trillion last year—the same amount as the total wealth of the 3.8 billion poorest people." He further stated that "The world's billionaires are growing $2.5 billion richer every day, while the poorest half of the global population is seeing its net worth dwindle." Coffey, Revollo, Harvey, Lawson, et al. (2020) reported that "In 2019, the world's billionaires, only 2,153 people, ha[d] more wealth than 4.6 billion people," and "The world's richest 1% ha[d] more than twice as much wealth as 6.9 billion people." The authors provided a graphic image to communicate this inequality. "If everyone were to sit on their wealth piled up in $100 bills, most of humanity would be sitting on the floor. A middle-class person in a rich country would be sitting at the height of a chair. The world's two richest men would be sitting in outer space" (2020, p. 9).

Income

Income inequality in the Untied States was present before its start as a nation. In 1774, people in the top 10% of income earners garnered approximately 32% of all income (Lindert and Williamson, 2012). By 2010, the top 10%'s share was 50% (Piketty, 2014, Table 7.3, p. 249). Using a more recent window of measurement, the economic elite continue to claim an increasingly greater portion of total national income. In the United States between 1980 and 2015, for example, the income of the top .01% increased 322% whereas the increase for the bottom 90% of people was .03% (Gilson and Rios, 2016).

Reinforcing this perspective of increasing income inequality, Chappell (2019) found that "The gap between the richest and the poorest U.S. households is now the largest it's been in the past 50 years." Most recently, the United States Census Bureau found that "U.S. income inequality was 'significantly higher' in 2018 than in 2017 .... The last time a change in the metric was deemed statistically significant was when it grew from 2012–2013" (Chappell, 2019). Echoing Chappell's findings, Saez (2020) reported that, over the past five decades, the top 1% of American earners have nearly doubled their share of national income.

Not only are the economic elite capturing more of the national total income in absolute terms, but they are also capturing a greater portion of its growth. Saez (2020) reported that families in the top 1% of income earnings "captured 45% of total real income growth per family from 2009–2018" (Saez, 2020, p. 1).

As to the global Capitalist economy, Piketty observed that "Since the 1970s, income inequality has increased significantly in the rich countries" (2014, p. 15). Chappello (2020) reported data that confirms Piketty's observation. It involves gauging inequality using the Gini index. The Gini index measures the extent to which the distribution of income among individuals or households within an economy deviates from a perfectly equal distribution. Index values range from zero (absolute equality) to one (absolute inequality). In reporting on the findings of Bourguignon and Morrisson, Chappello (2020) stated that their "work show[ed] a sustained growth in inequality since 1820 when the global Gini coefficient was 0.500." The estimate for 2008 was .705 (Lakner and Milanovic, 2015).

The True Picture of Inequality Is Worse

The various representations of the current state of inequality significantly understate the facts. The reason is that the financial elite have vast stores of offshore, hidden wealth not accounted for by the data reported above (Henry, 2012; International Consortium of Investigative Journalists, 2013; Zucman, 2016). "The mega-rich use complex offshore structures to own mansions, yachts, art masterpieces and other assets, gaining tax advantages and anonymity not available to average people" (International Consortium of Investigative Journalists, 2013). A number of studies reported by Zucman (2019) place the amount of hidden wealth somewhere between $5.6 trillion and $32 trillion. Zucman's own research estimated the amount as $7.6 trillion (Zucman, 2019).

After critically reviewing the methodology of these earlier hidden wealth studies, Henry (2012) devised an expanded methodological approach to estimating offshored money. He concluded that "A significant fraction of global private financial wealth—by our estimates, at least $21 to $32 trillion as of 2010—has been invested virtually tax free through the world's still expanding black hole of more than 80 offshore secrecy jurisdictions" (Henry, 2012, p. 5). Using the average of estimates of the studies referred to above, excluding Henry's, approximately $8 trillion are hidden. This amount is the equivalent of almost half the total gross domestic product of the United States in 2014. Most notably, this wealth is held by less than 1% of the population and is generating income every day of every year, virtually tax free. Again, none of it is incorporated in the inequality data reported above.

What Is Capitalism's Role in Producing Inequality?

Proponents of Capitalism claim that its success will "raise all ships." This claim is embodied in the distributional principle asserted by Kuznets (1955). It holds that, under Capitalism, the balancing forces of growth, competition, and technological progress lead to reduced inequality and produce greater harmony among the classes. Accordingly, the level of inequality should display an *inverted* U shape (termed Kuznets' curve). The curve depicts an initial rise in inequality as Capitalism begins followed by a peak and subsequent decline in inequality as it matures.

Mainstream economists Thomas Piketty and his associates (Anthony Atkinson, Emmanuel Saez, Gabriel Zucman, and others) undertook an exhaustive research project to empirically evaluate Capitalism's effects on the distribution of wealth and income over its 200-plus years of adoption.[20] He and his colleagues collected

[20] Simon Kuznets (1955) did empirically investigate the issue for the period of 1913 through 1948. While his findings formed the basis for Capitalism's position on the fate of inequality, Kuznets was aware of the unusual nature of the time period he studied (two World Wars, the Great Depression) and the highly speculative nature of his interpretation. He stated that it was perhaps "5 percent em-

wealth and income data for a number of developed economies, including France, the United Kingdom, Belgium, and the United States. His findings are documented in his book, *Capital in the Twentieth Century* (Piketty, 2014). Piketty's (2014) analysis concluded that Capitalism *preferentially rewards the already wealthy.* Capitalism does not reduce inequality; it automatically increases it for the already wealthy. Piketty stated that the empirical evidence indicates that "there is no natural, spontaneous process [within Capitalism] to prevent destabilizing, inegalitarian forces from prevailing permanently" (2014, p. 21). Absent some exogenous force (government action, natural disaster, war, etc.), inequality will spiral upward under Capitalism and produce a progressively narrower group of financial elites.

Piketty identified two simple mechanisms within Capitalism that advantage the already wealthy and *accelerate* inequality. Neither of these mechanisms has anything to do with merit. The first is the compounded rate of return on existing wealth which, at the beginning of Capitalism, was unequally shared.[21] The second is inheritance.

Given compound interest on existing wealth, even "an annual rate of return of a few percent, compounded over several decades, automatically results in a very large increase of the initial capital" (Piketty, 2014, pp. 76–77). Existing wealth grows exponentially. People attempting to create a base of wealth from saved income cannot catch up. Piketty stated that inequality accelerates whenever the rate of return on invested capital (r) is greater than the rate of increase in labor income (g). Across Capitalism's history, the rate of return on capital has always been higher than the rate of growth in income. On average, Piketty reported that *r* has been 4–5%, versus an economic growth [income growth] rate (*g*) of just .2% to 1%. More recently, the rate of return on invested capital has been even higher. "[A]round the world, the largest fortunes ... have grown at very high rates in recent decades (on the order of 6–7 percent a year)" (Piketty, 2014, p. 431).

The second mechanism for increasing inequality is inheritance. Wealth passed forward advantages the progeny of the already wealthy. Inherited wealth is received in relatively few people, as documented by the 1998 Federal Reserve Board's survey of consumer finances. It found that 91.9% of all citizens receive *no inheritance.* Only 1.6% receive an inheritance greater than $100,000. In 2016, the wealthiest 1% of the population inherited, on average, just under $5 million in

pirical information and 95 percent speculation, some of it possibly tainted by wishful thinking" (Kuznets, 1955, p. 28).

[21] Piketty reports that in 1810, 80% of the private wealth of France was owned by just 10% of its people (2014, p. 340). In both Britain and Sweden, 10% of the people owned between 80% and 90% of total private wealth, respectively (2014, pp. 344–345).

current dollars (Lewis and Bruenig, 2017). Remember, all this wealth takes advantage of the exponential growth provided by compounding. In addition, as Steverman (2020) pointed out, the estimated $764 billion to be inherited in 2020 will be subject to an average tax of 2.1%. "By contrast, the estimated tax on work and savings is 15.8%, more than seven times higher."

These two mechanisms—compounding and inheritance—ensure that the already wealthy remain apart from all others and that the distance between them and the remainder of society continually grows larger.

Is Inequality Problematic?

Not everyone agrees that inequality is problematic. Some proponents of Capitalism maintain that it is essential to sustaining a vibrant and growing economy.[22] However, the vast majority of scholars find that the relationship between inequality and economic growth is negative. As well, extreme inequality erodes the conditions that support a society's well-being. Finally, the conditions established by extreme inequality enable a human process that self-perpetuates and increases inequality and its harmful effects. It does this by creating broadened opportunities for exploiting moral hazard (Exhibit 1).

Exhibit 1. Interconnected Consequences of Inequality in Wealth and Income

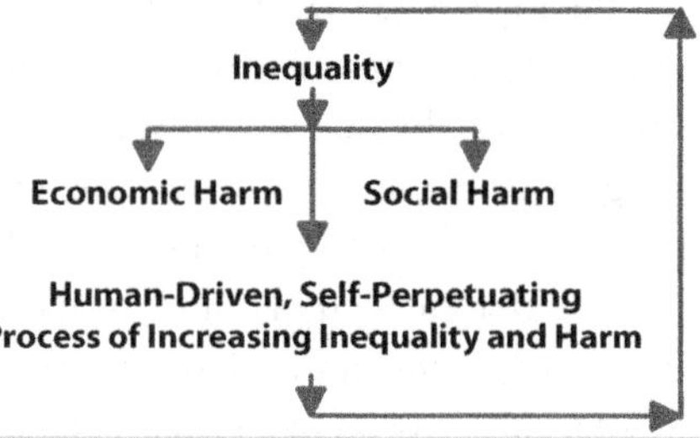

Inequality and Economic Harm

Cingano (2014) found that inequality *hurts* economic growth. Economically developed countries with decreasing income inequality showed higher levels of economic growth than countries where it was rising. He concluded that "The impact of inequality on growth turns out to be sizable" (2014, p. 17) and added,

> Rising inequality is estimated to have knocked more than 10 percentage points off growth in Mexico and New Zealand. In the United States, the United Kingdom, Sweden, Finland and Norway, the growth rate would

[22] See *Appendix A: Is Inequality Problematic: The Naysayers' Perspective* for a more detailed discussion of this topic.

> have been more than one fifth higher had income disparities not widened. On the other hand, greater *equality* helped increase GDP per capita in Spain, France and Ireland prior to the [2008 financial] crisis. (2014, p. 18)

An International Monetary Fund (IMF) study conducted by Dabla-Norris, Kochhar, Ricka, Suphaphiphat, et al. (2015) echoed Cingano's findings. It concluded that inequality negatively affects economic growth and its sustainability:

> We find an inverse relationship between the income share accruing to the rich (top 20 percent) and economic growth. If the income share of the top 20 percent increases by 1 percentage point, GDP growth is actually 0.08 percentage point lower in the following five years, suggesting that the benefits do not trickle down. Instead, a similar increase in the income share of the bottom 20 percent (the poor) is associated with 0.38 percentage point higher growth. (Dabla-Norris, Kochhar, Ricka, Suphaphiphat, et al., 2015, p. 7)

Inequality also retards the upward economic mobility of people within an economy. The concept of upward mobility refers to people's prospects of realizing life earnings greater than their parents'. Corak (2013) reported a finding of a 2011 study done by the Organization for Economic Co-operation and Development (OECD): "'Intergenerational earnings mobility is low in countries with high inequality such as Italy, the United Kingdom, and the United States, and much higher in the Nordic countries, where income is distributed more evenly.'" This finding is dramatically represented in a chart that depicts the relationship between economic mobility and income inequality for 22 developed nations (Corak, 2013, Figure 1, p. 82). The relationship is essentially linear and negative. The higher the inequality, the lower the upward mobility. As reviewed by Krueger (2012), Corak's data revealed that inequality accounts for 76% of the decline in upward mobility in an economy.

The findings of Chetty, Grusky, Hell, Hendren, et al. (2017) further strengthen the negative relationship between inequality and upward mobility. They measured the proportion of U.S. children who earn more than their parents for cohorts of children born at 10-year intervals from 1940 through 1980. Across *all* income groupings, the likelihood of children earning more than their parents decreased significantly from a high of more than 90% for all persons born in 1940 to just 50% for persons born in 1980. Most significantly, for the 1980 cohort, the likelihood of upward mobility for children born into families making up the bottom 80% of income earners *dropped below 20%*. As to the reason for this decline, the authors found that most of the decline in absolute upward mobility was due to the increasingly greater portion of total national income going to the financial elites.

Implications for Capitalism as an Economic System

The economic consequences of the automatic upward spiraling of inequality of wealth and income that Capitalist economies produce undermine economic growth and progressively strangle upward mobility. Rather than "raising all ships," Capitalism preferentially raises the "ships" of the already wealthy and sinks the ships of all others.

Inequality and Social Harm

Upward spiraling inequality in wealth and income also impacts people's opportunities for well-being and personal achievement. This harm rends America's social compact. That rending is evidenced by people's growing disillusionment with the promise of the American Dream; the observation that status, not merit, is the propellant for success; and the consequent breakdown in trust, which is essential for a cohering society.

The "American Dream" is a broad concept with powerful meaning in the United States. For Americans, it means "Being free to say or do what you want," "Being free to accomplish almost anything you want with hard work," and "Being able to succeed regardless of the economic circumstances in which you were born" (Economic Mobility Project, 2009; see Questionnaire and Results, pp. 6 and 7). As Corak noted, "These meanings ... are also likely a reason why Americans have been willing to tolerate a good deal more inequality of outcomes than citizens of many other rich countries (Corak, 2013, p. 79). Bernstein (2013) echoed Corak's judgment. He observed that, in America, "while we do not aspire to equal economic outcomes, we believe strongly in equal opportunity. If inequality were to thwart the opportunities of the 'have-nots,' this would represent a significant violation of a basic American tenet" (Bernstein, 2013, p. 2).

The facts suggest that inequality does thwart the opportunities of the "have-nots." As Piketty (2014) concluded, unequal economic outcomes are *not* the result of people better utilizing the opportunities they experience but from people *differentially experiencing better opportunities.* Capitalism not only skews the accumulation of wealth and income toward the already wealthy, it also produces unequal opportunities for people to realize well-being and fulfill their personal goals.

These differential opportunities are reflected in the more secure and less polluted neighborhoods that the financial elite populate (Badger, 2014; Hoffower, 2018; Katz, 2012; Lucido, 2015), the enrichment opportunities they are able to provide their children (Corak, 2013), their preferential access to elite schools when competing against non-elites *with like abilities* (Giancola and Kalenberg, 2016; Golden, 2003; Gross, 2019; Jerrim, 2013), and their better access to healthcare services (Powell, A., 2016; Willingham, 2019; Woolf, Aron, Dubay, Simon, et al., 2015). They are also reflected in the justice system's preferential treatment of white-collar crime relative to blue-collar crime (Floyd, 2018; Rizzuto and Schoenberg, 2013; Taibbi, 2011, 2014; Washington, 2011) and the reduced tax burdens the financial elite carry due to their offshoring of money, minimal taxation of inheritance, and their preferential capital gains tax rate for income earned on investments as compared to the tax rate assessed on labor-generated income.

The most basic "opportunity advantage" is, of course, longevity. It appears that life expectancy differs by income level, with greater longevity favoring the economic elite. Fletcher (2013) reported that "Even as the nation's life expectancy has marched steadily upward, reaching 78.5 years in 2009, a growing body of research shows that those gains are going mostly to those at the upper end of the income ladder." It also appears that the divergence is growing. Chetty, Stepner, Abraham, Lin, et al. (2016) found that "The gap in life expectancy between the richest 1% and poorest 1% of individuals was 14.6 years ... for men and 10.1 years ... for women" and that the inequality had increased over time: "Between 2001 and 2014, life expectancy increased by 2.34 years for men and 2.91 years for women in the top 5% of the income distribution but by only 0.32 years for men and 0.04 years for women in the bottom 5%." Their study adjusted for differences in race and ethnicity. It included only people who had reached the age of 40 years at the study's beginning. A 2015 National Academy of Science study produced a similar finding. It compared people in the bottom 20% income bracket to those in the top 20% bracket. It found that "the life expectancy gap between the bottom and top income quintiles of women expanded from 3.9 years for the 1930 birth cohort to 13.6 years for the 1960 birth cohort" (Isaacs and Choudhury, 2017).

As to the promise that working hard, acquiring greater skills, and producing more will lead to just rewards—empirical evidence makes that promise ring hollow. Bakija, Cole, and Heim (2012) found that "executives, managers, supervisors, and financial professionals account for about 60 percent of the top 0.1 percent of income earners" (2012, p. 2). Are their exceptional income levels due to their superior performance? Apparently not. Company success accounts for only 1–7% of the exceptional compensation they receive (Cooper, Gulen, and Rau, 2016; Mullaney, 2015; Sigler, 2011). Some 93–99% of the reason CEOs are paid so much *is not due* to their positive effect on company performance. It is *not due* to *merit.* What is it due to? The best evidence supports the judgment that it is due to their control of their own compensation levels.[23]

[23] See *Appendix A* for a fuller explanation of how CEOs control their compensation.

In contrast, consider how, in the absence of personal control of one's compensation level, greater worker productivity has been rewarded. From 1948 to 1973, worker productivity growth tracked closely with wage growth. An Economic Policy Institute analysis using Bureau of Labor Statistics data found that, between those years, productivity grew 95.7% and worker hourly wages grew 90.9%. However, since 1973, despite a 77% improvement in worker productivity, the average hourly wage of workers has grown just 12.4% (Economic Policy Institute, 2018).

What about advancing oneself through higher education? As it turns out, the "earnings premium" higher education yields is not spread evenly across the population of people who invest their money and effort in achieving an education.[24] Bartik and Hershbein (2018) found "that the career *percentage* earnings premium from earning a bachelor's degree, relative to only a high school diploma, is much lower for individuals who grew up in low-income families" (2018, p. 4). In fact, college graduates from low-income families garner only 71% of the average earnings premium realized by bachelor-degreed people versus high school graduates as compared to the 136% realized by graduates from non-low-income families.

Add to this biased outcome the effects of preferential access to elite schools that children of the economically elite experience. While, ironically, attending an elite versus a non-elite school *delivers no added economic value for the already rich* (Dale and Krueger, 2011), it does affect upward mobility for students from the bottom 20% of the income distribution. Chetty, Friedman, Saez, Turner, et al. (2017) found that students from the bottom 20% income bracket who gain access to elite schools achieve higher rates of mobility to the top 1% income group. Thus, when students from the bottom 20% income bracket are denied access to elite schools due to the preferential treatment of financial elites, they suffer economically. In contrast, when a financial elite does not attend an elite school, he or she experiences no economic cost.

This differential benefit from access to elite schools might appear less a matter of concern if access to elite schools was merit based. Jerrim (2013), however, reported that a considerable gap in access to selective colleges and universities existed *even after accounting for differences in academic performance* as measured by grades or standardized tests. "When you take academic achievement into account you can explain some of the difference [in access], but not all of it," said Dr. Jerrim. "[I]n elite private American universities only 48 percent [of the access gap] could be accounted for by differences in academic achievement." One source for the remaining gap is admission based on one's family wealth. Golden (2003)

---

[24] The earnings premium refers to the extra amount of income earned over a lifetime by people with higher-level degrees as compared to those with lower-level degrees.

reported that Duke University admits to relaxing its admission standards "to admit 100 to 125 students annually as a result of family wealth or connections, up from about 20 a decade ago." Duke is not alone in making exceptions for the admission of applicants from wealthy families. Gross (2019) reported on the emergence of "legacy preferences" in applicant selection by top colleges. These preferences go to "students with a family connection to the university," who "are widely seen as a reliable source of alumni donations" (Gross, 2019). Giancola and Kahlenberg (2016) stated that the practice appears to be widespread, as "[o]ver 80 percent of our most selective institutions employ legacy preferences." For example, Harvard's acceptance rate for legacy-preferenced applicants is 33% versus its "overall acceptance rate of under 6%" for all applicants, and Princeton reports a legacy applicant acceptance rate "at roughly four times the rate of applicants overall" (Gross, 2019). The practice is doubly unfair. Firstly, it disregards academic merit and preferentially credits wealth. Second, when students from the bottom 20% income bracket are denied access to elite schools due to the preferential treatment of financial elites, they suffer economically. Meanwhile, when a financial elite does not attend an elite school, he or she experiences no economic cost.

Given the breakdown in the premise of a level playing field and the assumption that merit is what produces success, the American Dream is nullified. This nullification is rending American society and expressing itself in social turbulence. Evidence of turbulence can be found in the escalating lack of trust in American institutions and citizen participation in civil society. Pierson (2015) wrote that "In 1964, Americans agreed, by 64–29%, that government was run for the benefit of all the people. By 2012, the answer had flipped, with voters saying by 79–19% that government was 'run by a few big interests looking after themselves'" (2015, p. 4).

Less dramatic but still consistent with this perspective, Jones (2016) reports that citizens' trust in their political leaders has fallen from 68% in 1974 to just 42% in 2016. The legislative branch has shown the greatest loss in trust, from 65% in 2001 to 35% in 2016. The Judicial branch, the arm that ensures that our constitutional rights are protected, has fallen from 80% in 1999 to 61% in 2016 (Saad, 2016). Worse, only 40% of people believe that judges are not influenced by political parties (Pew Research Center, 2020). As to the nation's fourth estate, Swift (2016) reported that the public's trust in mass media has dropped from 55% in 1999 to just 32% in 2016.

As a summary judgment of people's satisfaction with the direction of their country, just 16% of Americans responded positively to that question in a December 2020 Gallup poll. That satisfaction rate was down from 71% in a February 1999 poll (Gallup, 2020). Worse still, some 55% of Americans reported that they felt helpless to change the political situation in which they found themselves (Staff, 2016).

Implications for Capitalism as an Economic System

The economic theory of Capitalism claims to ensure the material well-being of society. The facts make clear that this claim is false. By its design, it ensures the material well-being of the already wealthy—not the public at large. To our knowledge, Capitalism contains no explicit claims about creating a just or cohering society. It is the people who seek to promote its use who make such claims. To the economic harm created by its biased advantaging of the already rich, however, one must add the just documented social and political harm generated by that use. A society that adopts an economic system that undermines its coherence and confidence in its governance destroys itself.

A Self-Perpetuating Process of Increasing Harm

The economic, social, and political harm caused by Capitalism's generation of upward-spiraling inequality in wealth and income is significant. Yet, in our opinion, it does not represent the worst threat caused by this economic system that concentrates monetary resources into fewer and fewer hands. What is most dangerous is that those resources enable a human-driven process that perpetuates and

Exhibit 2. Human-Driven, Self-Perpetuating Process of Increasing Inequality and Harm

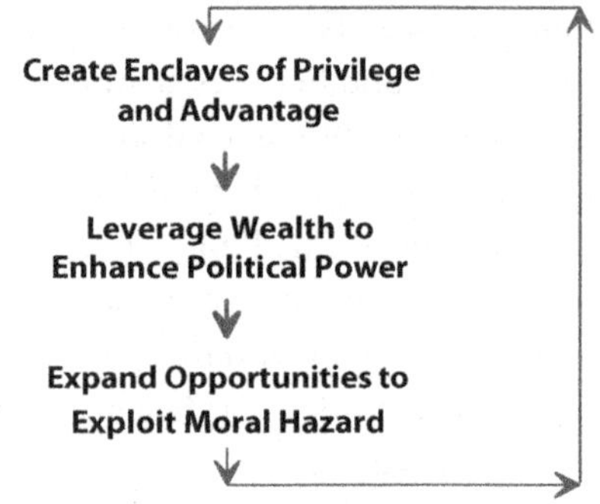

augments the system's mechanical drivers of growing inequality and its harmful societal outcomes (Exhibit 2). Extreme monetary resources enable the financial elite to build enclaves of privilege and advantage. From these enclaves, they seek and acquire political power and—through the exercise of that power—expand their opportunities for the exercise of moral hazard.

Enclaves of Privilege and Advantage

To the extent their means and circumstances permit, all people locate themselves in settings that serve their values. People of wealth have few if any limitations in this regard. They create enclaves that have restricted entry and possess their own security forces. The problems most others experience in their living settings have no presence in these enclaves. There are no potholes, poor garbage collection, polluted water, unreliable transit systems, indifferent schools, and unresponsive vendors of products or services. They are not challenged by issues of pollution, the homeless, limited access to healthcare, people begging for money, or uncertainties about their personal income. They have an inside track for every job for which they compete. By virtue of their means, whatever they want is accessible.

Residents of these enclaves share memberships in private clubs, are chauffeured from place to place, and travel longer distances on their private planes. They have access to the finest healthcare, take rest and recreate as needed, and make use of spas, fitness centers, and personal trainers to support their physical well-being.

They also have networks of contacts that share information and opportunities that enable even greater wealth accumulation. These opportunities include access to investment opportunities with high returns like initial public offerings (IPOs). They also include lucrative positions on boards,[25] access to restricted conferences and forums (e.g., the Bilderberg Conference, Council for Foreign Relations, Trilateral Commission, or World Economic Forum), and other advantaging prospects.

In addition, these enclaves form mini-cultures that pass forward their learning and resources to the next generation. The children of the financial elites attend private schools, have personal tutors, attend summer camps costing $10,000 to $20,000, and have access to whatever resources are required to ensure their success at each stage of their development. When they are ready, they may leverage their parents' networks of contacts to enter well-paid positions of employment or access other wealth-accumulating opportunities. Later, when their parents die, their wealth will be bolstered by their inheritances.

To be clear, the issue with these enclaves *is not what their inhabitants enjoy.* In that regard, they simply represent what all people strive to do—that is, fill their lives with what they value. The issue is what effects these enclaves of privilege have on their inhabitants' experience of connectedness with the remainder of society.

These enclaves become the privileged fiefdoms of what Stewart (2018) labeled a "new American Aristocracy." They have created a society within a society, an

---

[25] Sherman (2018) reported, "The median director pay at the largest U.S. companies was above $250,000 in 2015. This means that half of the directors of major corporations earned more" than this amount. Sherman added that the average board member puts in just "a few hours a week on the job."

enclosed territory that is culturally distinct from the "foreign territory" that surrounds it.

For the residents of these enclaves who are capitalists, their one purpose is to sustain their elite economic status. As true exemplars of Capitalism, they will seek only the further accumulation of the wealth that underpins the lifestyles and privileges they enjoy. Contrary to empirical findings about the role of merit in the accumulation of their wealth, they will imagine that what they possess they earned and that their differentiation from others is simply a reflection of their exceptional giftedness and, perhaps, tenacity of purpose. They will pass their mindsets onto their children, along with their fight to retain and expand their wealth and privilege.

Sharing no common experiences with those who live outside their walls, they have no basis for identifying with them (Murray, 2016). In the course of their living, working, and socializing, they simply do not interact with the typical American—except, perhaps, as people in their employ, whose purpose is to serve their needs and satisfy their wants. As Andrew Yang observed about the members of this aristocracy, their "ties to the greater national fabric will be minimal" (Yang, 2018, p. 100). Consequently, they will have little inclination to address matters that affect the general public but for them are non-existent. Rather, these owners of concentrated wealth and influence distort the politics of the larger society in which they are embedded to preferentially serve their own purposes. And the combined forces of their wealth, exclusivity, and network of relationships with people in decision-making positions empower their success. As Dahl and Lindblom (2000) noted, these enclaves of privilege and advantage "constitute resources that can be used in order to gain influence over other people." The immense, disproportionate wealth they coalesce "foster[s] inequalities in influence, including influence over the government of the state" (Dahl and Lindblom, 2000, pp. xxxi–xxxii).

As to the magnitude of this personal wealth, consider that in 2015 "Just 62 ultra-rich individuals ... ha[d] as much wealth as the bottom half of humanity. Five years ago, it took 388 rich guys to achieve that status" (Peck, 2016). That number continues to fall. It became 43 in 2017 and just 26 in 2018 (Elliott, 2019).

With regard to the wealth of large Capitalist corporations, their revenues rival those of whole nations. Ten companies appeared on a list of "the largest 30 entities in the world. ... All ten of these companies had annual revenue higher than the governments of Switzerland, Norway, and Russia in 2015. Indeed, 69 of the largest 100 corporate and government entities [worldwide] ranked by revenues were corporations" (Zingales, 2017, p. 113).

Political Power

Two centers of exceptional private wealth—the financial elite who are capitalists and Capitalist corporations—are both "in the market for political power" (Hacker and Loewentheil, 2013). They represent overlapping groups, since "six in ten of the richest 0.1 percent of Americans are corporate or financial executives" (ibid.). Zingales (2017) states that the super rich fund political campaigns, seeking to control the government's agenda while, corporations seek to control the outcomes of specific issues relevant to their success.

Private wealth's pursuit of political power is not new. Zingales (2017) pointed out that, throughout Capitalism's history, both financial elites (e.g., the Medici family's rule of Florence and the Della Scalla family's rule of Veronna in Medieval Italy) and corporations (e.g., the British East India Company from the 17th to the 19th century and the *robber barons* in the U.S.'s first Gilded Age) have sought to translate their economic power into political power.[26] Thomas Jefferson observed it occurring during his time. It was one reason why he argued against establishing a separate legislative body of the "aristoi" (the few who are rich and well born) to protect the interests of the wealthy from the actions of the majority of the public. He wrote: "Nor do I believe [such a chamber] necessary to protect the wealthy; because enough of these will find their way into every branch of the legislation, to protect themselves" (Govan, 1950, p. 680). Phillips (2002) documented the influence of wealth on U.S. government decision making from the nation's beginnings to the turn of the 21st century.

Consistent with Jefferson's observation, the most direct way wealthy people and Capitalist businesses obtain political power is by overrepresentation in the roles of government decision makers. Members of both houses of Congress, the presidency, and the Supreme Court are disproportionately members of the financial elite. "Of 534 current members of Congress [in 2014], at least 268 had an average net worth of $1 million or more in 2012 .... The median net worth for the 530 ... lawmakers who were in Congress as of the May [2012] filing deadline was $1,008,767" (Choma, 2014).[27] In 2013, the median net worth of U.S. households was just $63,800—just 6% of the median net worth of their

[26] Zingales (2017) reported a statement by the California railway baron Collis Huntington: "'If you have to pay money [to a politician] to have the right thing done, it is only just and fair to do it. ... If a [politician] has the power to do great evil and won't do right unless he is bribed to do it, I think ... it is a man's duty to go up and bribe'" (2017, p. 116). Zingales further described how corporate political influence was perceived at the end of the 19th century: "In a cartoon by Joseph Keppler that appeared in *Puck* in 1889, the Senate was labeled 'of the Monopolists by the Monopolists and for the Monopolists!'" (ibid.). Today, we hear a similar phrase: "coin operated congress" (Snider, 1994).

[27] The average net worth for the 433 House members for whom 2018 data was available equaled $6.9 million. As of 2018, the average net worth for the 85 senators for whom data was available equaled $11.4 million (OpenSecrets.org, 2020).

"representatives" (Financial Samurai, 2014). With regard to the presidency, Sauter and Suneson (2019) reported that 80% of U.S. Presidents have been millionaires, with 52% having a net worth of more than $10 million in 2019 constant dollars. As for the Supreme Court, all but one of the eight members of the court in 2016 had an estimated net worth greater than $1 million. The annual salary for associate justices was $244,400 at that time (Lamare, 2016).

For corporations and their industry groups, the direct method of influence involves industry or firm representatives rotating between high-level government positions and high-level business positions. This is the "revolving door" phenomenon. One example is Henry Paulson. Paulson worked as an assistant to John Erlichman in the Nixon administration from 1972 to 1973. He joined Goldman Sachs in 1974 and eventually became its chief executive officer. He reentered government as Secretary of the U.S. Treasury under George W. Bush in 2006. "Two years later, Paulson spearheaded advocacy for the federal bailout of the banking industry. Goldman Sachs received $12.9 billion in federal bailout funds; several of the bank's largest competitors received little or no aid and went under" (Clark, 2011). Another example is Robert E. Rubin. Rubin began his finance career at Goldman, Sachs & Company in 1966. He became its vice chairman and co-chief operating officer in 1987 and was named co-senior partner and co-chairman from 1990 to 1992. The Clinton administration appointed Rubin as assistant to the president for economic policy and as director of the newly created National Economic Council (NEC) in 1993 (Council on Foreign Relations, 2019). In January 1995, Rubin was appointed as the Secretary of the Treasury. During his tenure as Treasury Secretary, Citigroup accelerated its "effort to change the Glass–Steagall Act, which severed the economic ties between investment banking and commercial banking" (Zingales 2017, p. 122). In parallel, Citigroup purchased Travelers Insurance, an action that *violated the Glass-Steagall Act, still the law of the land.* In answering why he executed this unlawful merger, Co-Chair of Citigroup Sandy Weill explained that Citigroup had had enough discussions with the U.S. Treasury to believe that its action would not be a problem (Zingales, 2017). Zingales continued:

> The head of the U.S. Treasury then was Richard E. Rubin. Rubin worked very hard to convince his fellow Democrats to change the law [thereby legalizing Citgroup's crime]. His efforts, along with those of other pro-banking advocates (e.g., Alan Greenspan, Lawrence H. Summers, Arthur Levitt, Jr.) succeeded. Rubin left the Treasury in July 1999, the day after the House of Representatives passed its version of the bill .... Three months later, on October 18, 1999, Rubin was hired at Citigroup at a salary of $15 million a year. (Zingales 2017, p. 122)

Another avenue for direct influence by corporations is through representation in presidential cabinets. In Trump's 2017 cabinet, for example, 11 of the heads of the 15 executive departments came from corporations or had been lobbyists for corporations. Former employers included Goldman Sachs, Boeing, and Bank of America, among others. As corporate executives or industry lobbyists, they had represented the interests of companies like Haliburton and Microsoft and industries like gas, oil, big pharma, and agribusiness.

Other methods of direct influence include contributions (Pierson, 2015; Pilkington and Siddiqui, 2019), lobbying (Brill, 2018; Thompson, 2010; Wilson, 2017), deferred offers of jobs to government officials after they leave public office (Zingales, 2017), and promises of other money-generating opportunities (e.g., lucrative speaking engagements, executive board positions, no-show or little-work consulting contracts). Less friendly, but nonetheless effective, are lawsuits against regulatory bodies to prevent the promulgation of regulations should direct efforts fail to prevent unfavorable legislation (Zingales, 2017).

There are also longer-term efforts that focus on inculcation of views in decision makers and the general public. These include the use of mass media to promote specific viewpoints and the wealthy's influence over university programs, hiring, and tenure offers. These efforts produce a false consensus—one manipulated into existence rather than emerging from personal judgment based on objective facts (Herman and Chomsky, 2002). Pierson (2015) wrote that "Powerful actors can gain advantage by inculcating views in others that are to their advantage. ... Those with influence over the media, schools, churches, think tanks, or other key cultural institutions may foster beliefs in others (about what is desirable or possible) that serve the interests of the powerful. Again, what looks like consensus on the surface may reflect underlying inequalities of influence" (Pierson, 2015, p. 7). The Powell Memorandum (Powell, L.F., 1971) provides a wide-ranging, long-term example of a comprehensive indoctrination program using all the methods Pierson identified to establish Capitalism as America's absolute economic system.[28]

Do these efforts translate into greater political power? Most political scientists claim that money "has negligible impact on elections" (Parramore, 2016). Nevertheless, both historical analyses (Ferguson, 1995; Phillips, 2002) and multivariate empirical studies find just the opposite (Jacobs and Page, 2005; Gilens and Page, 2014). When research designs simultaneously evaluate all major voices of influence on policy, "the prior findings [of citizen control] appear to be largely or wholly spurious" (Gilens and Page, 2014, p. 573). In fact, using

[28] *Appendix B: A Detailed Look at the Powell Memorandum* provides a full description of the contents of the Powell memorandum.

multivariate designs, both Jacobs and Paige (2005) and Gilens and Page (2014) showed that the average citizen has no effect on policy decision making when their voice on issues is evaluated in the context of the voices of so-called financial elites and business interest groups. Essentially, "ordinary citizens get what they want from government *only when they happen to agree with elites or interest groups that are really calling the shots* [italics added]" (Gilens and Page, 2014, p. 573). It is the wealthy elite and business interest groups who are the two most powerful influencers of government decision making.

Most relevant to our concerns, the results produced by the two wealth powerhouses can be categorized as preferential to them alone. Those results further enable their accelerated wealth accumulation, enhance their ability to exert political influence, and protect them from the effects of their conduct. They include the huge transfer of wealth from the public to banks by forcing unnecessary borrowing from the banks, reduced enforcement of laws, concentration of market power, giveaways of the people's assets for private wealth accumulation, preferential taxation, and opportunities to exercise moral hazard. *Appendix C* provides detailed examples of each of these achievements.

The cumulative effect of the political influence of the financial elites and Capitalist corporations is "crony capitalism." Wikipedia defines it as being "an economy in which businesses thrive ... as a return on money amassed through a nexus between a business class and the political class" (Crony capitalism, 2019). This knot of wealth and political power results in preferential treatment through "handing out permits, government grants, special tax breaks, or other forms of state intervention over resources where the state exercises ... control over public goods" (ibid.). Crony capitalism turns the collective wealth of a nation's citizens into the private profit of a few. Its effect is to accelerate upward-spiraling economic inequality, with all its destructive consequences.

With greater industry concentration as a result of relaxed anti-trust oversight, citizens pay higher prices and have fewer choices in meeting their needs (Philippon, 2019; Devanny, 2020).[29] Tax breaks for the financial elite and corporations and the Federal Reserve's enforced low interest rates for borrowing are regularly promoted as necessary to stimulate productive investment that will grow industry, create well-paying jobs for the working class, and raise the nation's economic growth. The empirical data says otherwise.

[29] Philippon (2019) estimated that "monopolies cost the median American household about $300 a month." Devanny (2020) reported that just "Twelve corporations control over 400 retail brands. Ninety percent of the legacy media of all kinds, print, television, movies etc. is owned by ten firms. American political economy has never been so centralized and so consolidated."

As to tax breaks, Krueger (2012) documented that "income growth was stronger for lower and middle-income families in the 1990s than it was in the last 40 years overall" (2012, p. 6). At that time, the top level of personal income tax on the wealthy was increased to 39.6% from 35%, and the corporate tax rate was raised to 35% on net income over $10 million. Further, Krueger reported that "Across all businesses, job growth was much weaker" *after the tax reductions* implemented from 2001 through 2007 than in the 1990s. Linden (2011) did a broader analysis. Since the 1950s, the top margin tax rate has ranged from 92% to just 28%. He evaluated the economic growth rates at each of these taxation levels. He found the following:

> Altogether, in years when the top marginal rate was lower than 39.6 percent—the top rate during the 1990s—annual real growth averaged 2.1 percent. In years when the rate was 39.6 percent or higher, real growth averaged 3.8 percent. The pattern is the same regardless of threshold. Take 50 percent, for example. Growth in years when the tax rate was less than 50 percent averaged 2.7 percent. In years with tax rates at or more than 50 percent, growth was 3.7 percent. (Linden, 2011)

Unremarkably, the financial elites use the benefits they receive from lower taxes and the cheaper borrowing enforced by the Federal Reserve to enhance their wealth still further. As Alsin (2017) reported, "American companies have been spending wildly lately, but that cash isn't being used for R&D or innovation. Rather, it's being spent to buy up gobs of company stock." Stock buybacks were illegal until the Securities and Exchange Commission legalized them in 1982. They were considered a form of stock manipulation. By reducing the number of shares outstanding, the same level of income produces a *higher earnings per share* result. This results in higher bonus payouts for CEOs. It also elevates the company's share price by reducing the supply of stock. What it does not do is increase the inherent productive value of the company or provide new economic opportunities to the general public (Almeida, Fos, and Krunkund, 2016; Ayres and Olenick, 2017; Brettell, Gaffen, and Rohde, 2015, 2015a; Lazonick, 2014).

Opportunities for Moral Hazard

The final element in the self-perpetuating process of increasing harm is the elite's use of political power to create opportunities to exploit moral hazard. As explained earlier, moral hazard allows someone to pursue the accumulation of wealth without risk. It is enabled by political influence applied to (1) eliminating laws or regulations that guard against moral hazard, (2) establishing permissive oversight through regulatory capture, (3) creating new laws that limit redress for harm by buyers or third parties negatively affected by commercial acts,[30] and (4) bailing out creditors from losses resulting from poor investments.

Capitalist corporations and financial elites exploit opportunities for exercising moral hazard to accelerate their wealth accumulation. The enhanced wealth they derive increases their ability to influence political decision making to create still more opportunities for moral hazard. Thus, the cycle of exploitation of the non-elites advances with ever greater velocity.

Each cycle begins with a set of enabling parties who argue that laws or regulations restraining some economically hazardous activity are costly and hinder the operation of Capitalism. They argue that such laws are unneeded because markets self-correct. Each cycle ends with some people making huge profits at the expense of the general public and the economy. We will briefly discuss two examples: the savings and loan (S&L) industry debacle of the 1980s and the 2008 banking failure.

S&L Debacle

With the entry of the Reagan administration in 1981, most political, legislative, and regulatory decisions became imbued with the bedrock position of Capitalism. Consistent with this viewpoint, the government reduced the constraints on businesses so they could operate freely, as Capitalism dictates. The savings and loan (S&L) industry debacle of the 1980s began as an opportunity to apply deregulation to save failing banks that specialized in funding home mortgages with savings from depositors (Moysich, 1997). The S&L business problem was real; the promoted solution created the debacle.

Deregulation was the essence of the Garn-St. Germain Depository Institutions Act of 1982 that President Reagan signed into law. The Act allowed banks to make commercial loans, not just homeowner mortgages. It removed restrictions that ensured that loans made had a good likelihood of being repaid; opened up direct investment by S&Ls in speculative real estate development; permitted banks to value the real estate they bought at its *original* price, not the asset's current market value; and allowed S&Ls to create alternative mortgage products (Federal Reserve History, 2019). These alternative products included the "infamous 2/28 adjustable-rate [30-year] mortgages to entice subprime borrowers to initiate loans at low rates [for 2 years], only to find

[30] As an example of blocking redress for harm, Milman (2019) reported on an effort underway to pass legislation that will extend to polluting corporations legal immunity for damages done to the environment by the pollutants they have emitted. The law "would squash [a] raft of climate lawsuits launched by cities and counties across the US seeking compensation for damages." The promoters of this plan are James Baker and George Shultz, both former Secretaries of State, backed by former Federal Reserve chairs Ben Bernanke and Janet Yellen. Their efforts are supported by BP, ExxonMobil, Chevron, ConocoPhillips, Shell Oil Company, and Microsoft Corporation.

that they could not afford the payments when the mortgage quickly reset at a much higher rate" (Federal Reserve History, 2019).

All of these relaxed constraints created opportunities for speculative investment using depositor funds. Worse still, they allowed the risk to be magnified in two ways. First, by allowing S&Ls to value their assets at their *purchased price* rather than their *current market value*, S&Ls appeared to have greater total assets than they could ever realize in the marketplace based on current prices. Second, S&Ls could invest using leverage, thereby magnifying the amount they could buy with their unrealistically valued assets.

States then passed legislation consistent with the new Federal direction. For example, "California, Texas, and Florida passed laws allowing their S&Ls to invest in speculative real estate. In Texas, 40 S&Ls tripled in size" (Amadeo, 2019a).

At the same time, President Reagan *cut* the budgets of the regulatory staff at the Federal Home Loan Bank Board (FHLBB or Bank Board), which had oversight responsibility for the S&L industry. This impaired the FHLBB's ability to monitor lending behavior and investigate bad loans. Thus, with the removal of constraints and the weakening of bank oversight, the opportunity for moral hazard was created.

The consequence was rampant speculation in risky investments, loans that could not be repaid, and what then F.B.I. Director William Sessions reported as "fraud 'pervasive' industrywide" (New York Times Editorial, 1990).

While some 600 persons were convicted of wrongdoing (Holland, 2013), a *New York Times* editorial noted that "most of the perpetrators will escape. For that, the responsible parties are members of Congress who legislated the thrifts' license to splurge and steal, Reagan Administration officials who ignored the storm warnings and hundreds of incompetent and corrupt S&L owners and managers who dallied with their depositors' trust" (New York Times Editorial, 1990).[31] In 1990, then Federal Reserve Chairman Alan Greenspan stated, "the eventual cost of the savings and loan bailout could exceed a half-trillion dollars." Then Treasury Secretary Nicholas Brady admitted

[31] Exposure of the debacle was impeded by the intervention of five U.S. senators who acted to squelch an investigation of one of its major protagonists—Charles H. Keating, Jr., Chairman of the Lincoln Savings and Loan Association. Labeled the *Keating Five* by the press, Senators Alan Cranston, Dennis DeConcini, John Glenn, John McCain, and Donald W. Riegle, Jr. intervened in response to $1.3 million [approximately $3.2 million in 2021 dollars] in contributions by Keating, who called on the senators to help him resist U.S. federal regulators. Senators Cranston, DeConcini, and Riegle were found by the Senate's Ethics investigation to have "substantially and improperly interfered with the FHLBB's investigation," and Senators Glenn and McCain were criticized for having exercised "poor judgment" (Keating five, 2019).

that "taxpayers will bear most of that burden" (New York Times Editorial, 1990).

2008 Banking Failure

The banking failure of 2008 makes the S&L debacle seem trivial. The same cycle described above repeated beginning in the late 1990s. As always, it began with the removal of legal barriers to the exercise of moral hazard and the thwarting of regulatory control. This time, a new economic instrument called *derivatives* was excluded from oversight. The key enabling events were the passage of the Gramm-Leach-Bliley Act in 1999 and the Commodities Futures Modernization Act of 2000.

The first law repealed part of the Glass–Steagall Act of 1933, removing barriers to integrating banks, brokerages, and insurance companies in one institution. This restriction had avoided the amplification of the effects of financial misdeeds on the economy and the creation of the "too big to fail" phenomenon. Glass–Steagall also had prevented banks from using depositor funds for their profit-seeking activities, thereby putting their depositors at risk for their bad investments. As well, under Glass-Steagall, banks were prevented from issuing securities (Rickards, 2012). Thus, for example, banks would not have been able to buy the bad home loans made by mortgage lenders and bundle them up into the mortgage-backed securities (MBSs) that they then sold to unsuspecting investors for a riskless profit.

The second law prevented the Commodities Futures Trade Commission (CFTC) from overseeing the emerging market in derivatives. That action was taken despite CFTC chair Brooksley Born's warning that "derivatives pose a grave danger to our economy."[32] Had derivatives been regulated, the magnification of the impact of risky investing would have been avoided. Through the derivative of credit default swaps (CDSs), for example, banks engaged in risky loans that they backstopped using CDSs as their insurance (hedge) against losses. A CDS used in this way released the asset value of what was lent to be re-leveraged into further investment, then was also backstopped using a different CDS. Worse still, CDS dealers "utilized 'daisy chains' in entering their credit default swap contracts, wherein they hedged [the] protection [they] sold with equivalent protection purchased from another dealer or insurance company, which may do the same" (Mirochnik, 2010, p. 5). If the ultimate seller of the CDS—the party immediately guaranteeing the underlying

[32] Born's position was forcefully reinforced by Warren Buffet, Chairman of Berkshire Hathaway Inc., and Charles T. Munger, Vice Chairman. In the company's 2002 annual report, Buffet stated: "We view [derivatives] as time bombs, both for the parties that deal in them and the economic system" (Berkshire Hathaway Inc., 2002, p. 13).

asset—held many CDSs, then the vulnerability of that party to any financial turbulence would impact the entire daisy chain of insurers.[33] And it did. This elaborate, invisible, and unregulated network of debt reached $67 trillion by 2007, when it collapsed.

The opportunity for moral hazard created by the Gramm-Leach-Bliley Act in 1999 and the Commodities Futures Modernization Act of 2000 ended with the Great Recession and the bailout of the banks whose conduct had precipitated it. As of 2015, the "Special Inspector General for TARP's [the Troubled Asset Relief Program's] summary of the bailout says that the total commitment of government is $16.8 trillion" (Collins, 2015). The bailout continues under the guise of various iterations of Quantitative Easing and other bank liquidity supporting Federal Reserve infusions of money into financial institutions.

As to the exploiters of moral hazard, just one low-level Wall Street executive went to jail (Cohan, 2015). Forty-nine "financial institutions have paid various government entities and private plaintiffs nearly $190 billion in fines and settlements" (ibid.), a paltry amount compared to the sums made by these enterprises. Worse still, it was the shareholders of these institutions who paid, not the bankers who exploited the opportunity for moral hazard and whose compensations soared as a result. Indeed, "just weeks after Jamie Dimon, the CEO of JPMorgan Chase, settled out of court with the Justice Department [for $13 billion], the bank's board of directors gave him a 74 percent raise, bringing his salary to $20 million" (ibid.). The Justice Department had determined that JP Morgan knowingly misrepresented the quality of its securitized mortgage offerings to potential buyers (Cohan, 2017).

Capitalism's Scientific Problem

The significant structural and consequential problems of Capitalism have their origin in the theory's omission of factors that modify economic activity (e.g., the banks' creation of money through lending, the effects of leveraged investment on market stability) and in its unreal foundational premises.

Capitalism's utility is as a theoretical model of an imaginary world. When promoted as a practical model applicable to the real world, it is invalid. All of its premises are false. *Chapter 6* of this book reviews in detail the basis for this judgment.[34] All of Capitalism's premises are stated as universals. Its assumptions

[33] The American International Group (AIG) was an example of such an institution.

[34] See *Chapter 6. What Science Tells Us About Human Nature.* The same research that applies to judging the question that chapter addresses also applies to evaluating Capitalism's premises about the nature of people.

about human nature are posited to apply to all people engaged in commerce, all the time. Its premises about the market context within which commerce occurs are assumed to apply to all markets everywhere. Its premises about human nature eliminate differences in people's purposes, motives, critical resources (self-insight, decision making, information resources), and power. It assumes that all people are rational and effective decision makers who wisely choose exactly what they need from available offerings and only make advantageous exchanges with others. Its assumptions relative to the commercial context deny asymmetries between buyers and sellers in every market. In the world as envisioned in Capitalism, all offerings of a specific product are functionally equivalent. Neither buyer nor seller has power over the other. Every market is functionally equivalent to every other market, and each operates independently. What is produced is needed, since supply drives demand. What is needed can be bought; otherwise, the dynamic that ultimately ensures that a society's materials needs are met would fail. When these premises are baked into a computer simulation of Capitalism, the theory appears to work. It is only in the real world, where its assumptions are not matched by reality, that the model fails.

Empirically, people do not make "rational" decisions as a rule. Their decision making is most often affected by factors unrelated to the value-relevant features of offerings. They do not always choose exactly what they need. In fact, people frequently choose options that they later deem incorrect. Also, asymmetries between buyers and sellers abound (Washington, 2014). These core assumptions of the theory that underpin Capitalism's "wisdom of the market" are fictions.

As to people's nature, some people do fit the materially focused, radically individualistic self-serving premises of Capitalism, but many others do not. There are self-maximizing egoists, and there are people one might label as other-regarding "cooperators." The latter seek mutually beneficial exchanges with others. In the real world, when egoists meet cooperators, they invariably exploit them. This is a logical outcome given the nature of egoists, the presence of asymmetries, and the existence of people who are inclined to be cooperative. Behavioral economists have experimentally demonstrated this phenomenon repeatedly. In these instances, fair and just exchanges do not happen.

The expectation of many offerors in every market and growing competition through entrepreneurship is contradicted empirically by the reduced emergence of new enterprises (LeVine, 2018). Rather, increased market concentration is observed as existing larger enterprises buy up smaller competitors and create barriers to entry (Abdela and Steinbaum, 2018; Devanny, 2020; Grullon, Larkin, and Michaely, 2018). This finding is totally consistent with Adam Smith's warning about the nature of capitalists. Their interest, he stated, is always "to narrow the competition" so as to maximize their profits through the exercise of market power (Smith, A., 1776, pp. 213–214).

The only oddity concerning Capitalism's structural and consequential problems is the failure of scholars and professionals to grasp that the theory with which the very field of economics identifies is invalid as a practical guide to economic decision making. Deductive systems only have practical utility when their contents are logically deduced from their premises *and* those premises are true. This is a simple epistemological fact (Vickrey, 1964). While Capitalism appears to meet the first criterion, it fails on the second. The premises of a deductive system are functionally the same as the supporting columns that hold a building up. Destroy them, and the building collapses. Given Capitalism's invalidity as a practical theory, professionals, at the very least, should expect it to have structural and consequential problems.

So the only puzzle is this: Given the empirical disproof of the premises from which the theorems of Capitalism are deduced, why is there continued promotion of the practical relevance of this theory by mainstream economists and government officials? A deductive system has no "elasticity" with regard to its assumptions. Once a model's assumptions are shown to be empirically invalid, all theorems derived from them lack explanatory utility in the real world. When many premises are disproved, the theory's entire structure of explanations and expectations collapses. One could construct a valid version of Capitalism that would guide the conduct of the people depicted in its premises (materially focused, egoistic self- maximizers). This would entail making its assumptions conform to empirical facts (see *Chapter 17*). Or, one certainly could build an empirically based system. For example, Keen (2017) proposed such an approach to building an effective macroeconomic theory. But, in either case, *you are actually building a new theory*. People who propose ad hoc "fixes" to Capitalism miss this very point. As a deductive model, it is of *whole cloth*. Any modification of premises renders the elements of the theory deduced from those premises null. Any dressing up of its assertion that commerce serves self-interest alone by introducing other-regarding notions of benefiting stakeholder welfare undoes a supporting structure of the model. You certainly can create a new theory based on different assumptions about humankind and the contexts within which commerce occurs. But that new theory is *not* Capitalism.

Given its structural and consequential problems, especially with regard to Capitalism's consistent preferential distribution of rewards to a small minority of society's members, its only conceivable utility is as a *social control mechanism* that serves the most wealthy and politically influential capitalists. Indeed, it is a reasonable observation to make that—for people who egoistically seek to maximize their wealth—the promotion of Capitalism as the "only valid system of commerce" provides an excellent vehicle for their personal success.[35] Understand that, while Capitalism as an economic theory with practical use is invalid, its *utility* for true wealth-maximizing egoists does remain. Real-world asymmetries provide people with wealth superior market and political power. Capitalism's promotion of laissez-faire argues against any action to redress these asymmetries. The biased policies of Capitalist governments toward empowering capitalists—justified as appropriate since they are the providers of benefit for "all" society—further enhances the ability of people with significant wealth to control the political and economic arenas to their singular advantage. Under the cover of Capitalism's mantra of non-interference in the marketplace, they are free to exploit their advantages of power and wealth and advance further their exploitation of the non-egoistic portion of humankind.

Where to From Here?

The remainder of this book explains the Life Enabling commercial model. It is a commercial model that serves people who are natively inclined to cooperate and who seek mutually benefiting ends in their exchanges with others. While the model addresses the existence of egoistic self-maximizers, it has no utility for them. They are by their makeup incapable of implementing it. As we describe the model, we will contrast its approach with that of Capitalism to clarify its distinctiveness.

In the next section of this book (Section I), we present a template that organizes the presentation of any commercial model. We use it in the remainder of the book to detail the contents of the Life Enabling model. The remainder of Section I describes the premises from which the Life Enabling model is deduced and tests their "realisticness" against the findings of science.

---

[35] *Appendix B: A Detailed Look at the Powell Memorandum*, beginning on page 493, describes a long-term, comprehensive indoctrination program targeting the public and political decision makers for the purpose of establishing the value and necessity of upholding Capitalism as the United States' singular economic system. *Appendix C: The Economic Fruits of Political Power*, beginning on page 497, describes a sample of the economic benefits capitalists have reaped from their indoctrination efforts and their achievement of political power.

Section I

The Foundations of Every Commercial Model

This section introduces a framework for describing any commercial model. It explains the framework's structure and rationale and describes, with examples, the content that populates each of its elements. The remainder of Section I describes the assumptions that underpin every commercial model and how that foundational knowledge shapes its contents and guidance. It then presents the Life Enabling commercial model's assumptions and tests whether these assumptions have a valid basis in science.

There are multiple deductive theories explaining the dynamics of commerce and prescribing how commerce should be accomplished (e.g., Capitalism, Islamic economics, command economy, Life Enabling commerce). Each theory derives its contents from a set of premises. Each defines the impetus for the exchange of resources between people and the end that exchange serves. Each guides the conduct of commercial activities, whether undertaken individually or cooperatively with others. These theories are models of commerce. Each model, if implemented at the transactional level, generates a profile of effects at the societal level.

A completely developed commercial model addresses every issue essential to defining and implementing commerce. Its guidance governs formulating the purpose commerce will serve; building the infrastructure needed to achieve that purpose; guiding an enterprise's long-term marketplace activity; managing its day-to-day operations; and maintaining the enterprise as a whole, capable, viable, and achieving commercial entity.

Existing models are incomplete when measured against this list of a complete model's expected contents. To ensure a thorough description of the Life Enabling commercial model, we created a template or framework as a guide. We identified the template's topics by analyzing the guidance one needs to implement a particular approach to commerce *as a producer*. When you populate this schema with the ideas specific to a particular approach, you transform the template into a full description of that commercial model at a microeconomic level.

In this chapter, we explain the makeup of the template using examples to clarify its various elements. In the remainder of this book, we use the template to organize our description of the Life Enabling model.

Chapter 3

The Functions of a Framework

A framework is a structure of topics that denotes the important elements of some object or theory. It provides an intellectual tool that ensures completeness in one's description and documentation of the object or theory it addresses. A properly developed framework does even more:

- It facilitates learning by providing a mental structure a person can use to store and recall what has been taught. Research tells us that students retain their learning of a large array of related ideas better when instruction explicitly uses an organizing framework in communicating it. Absent such a schema, learners retain much less of what is presented (Cooper, 1998).
- It can prompt scientific advancement by showing what is known and unknown about a phenomenon or developed and undeveloped about a theory. Once it is populated with what is known about a phenomenon or developed within theory, any elements left unpopulated denote areas of knowledge that are missing. They represent opportunities for new discovery or development.
- It can facilitate consensus building among people on issues where different persons or groups hold differing understandings of the same phenomenon or theoretical system. Using the same framework, people can populate the framework from their differing perspectives, compare their differences, and resolve their differences rationally.

To support these expanded uses, a framework must contain more than a schema of topics. It must include guidance within each topic that enables the documenter to populate that element with its correct content. It also must contain guidance explaining the relationships between elements. This guidance allows the documenter to check the internal consistency between the various elements of content he or she records. For example, Exhibit 1, next page, presents a simple framework developed by Vitalo (2019) for use in understanding a properly constructed goal statement. It identifies that a goal has six components, tells you what content goes into each component, and provides guidance for testing the goal's internal consistency by describing the interrelationships between its components.

The Framework for a Commercial Model

A deductive commercial model is founded on a set of premises (foundational assumptions) from which its author infers three sets of guidance. Each set of guidance addresses one of the following major components of commercial activity:

- Strategic – Defines the end commerce seeks to realize and the long-term strategy that one implements to achieve success as defined by the model

Exhibit 1. The Components of a Complete Goal Statement

Component	Contents
To	States the result the goal must produce. This content always begins with "To" and names the object to be created or modified and the final state it should be in when the goal is realized. Example: "To produce Widget A," or "To make Product X more customer satisfying," or "To maximize profit from each transaction."
For	States for whom the result is being produced—the beneficiaries of the goal's achievement. Example: "For customers, the business, and all its stakeholders" or "For the owners of the business."
By	Names the method that will be used to accomplish the "To." An example is: "By eliminating unwanted features and adding wanted features." To be correct, the "By" activity must be capable of accomplishing the result specified in the "To" while satisfying the "Conditions" listed below.
So That	Lists the benefits the result should produce for each beneficiary of the goal. Each benefit identifies how a beneficiary of the goal will be better off once the "To" is achieved. Every benefit listed must be immediately producible by accomplishing the "To" and represent a result that advantages the beneficiary. A benefit must be identified for every beneficiary named in the "For" section.
Conditions	States other requirements that the pursuit of the goal must satisfy. These may ▪ limit the resources used (e.g., time, money, people), ▪ state "must do" requirements—e.g., use a specific tool or involve specified people or abide by a certain protocol in pursuing the goal ("must do" constraints), or ▪ list "off-limits" decisions or actions ("must not do" constraints). Once conditions are set, recheck the "To" and "By." The "By" must be able to accomplish the "To" while satisfying every condition. If it fails, modify the "By" or renegotiate the conditions.
Success Criteria	The benchmarks that must be met for the goal to be judged as achieved. These criteria test whether the effort expended ▪ produced the result specified in the "To," ▪ used the method specified in the "By," ▪ delivered the benefits specified in the "So That," and ▪ satisfied the constraints recorded in the "Conditions."

[1] For a tutorial on building a goal statement, go to: http://www.vitalentusa.com/learn/building_a_useful_goal_statement.php

- Operations – Defines the model's guidance for managing each business function's day-to-day operations so that they collectively accomplish the model's Strategic direction
- Executive Functions – Defines how an enterprise maintains itself as a whole and viable business that is accomplishing its purpose

Each component's guidance is organized under three topics: expected results (Results), required activities (Activities), and essential resources (Resources) (Exhibit 2, next page). The Results section describes the outcomes the component should produce. The Activities section describes the approach the model specifies for generating those results. The Resources section identifies the critical-to-success wherewithal needed to implement the component's prescribed activities. These resources enable you to successfully implement the activities that produce the results specified for each component.

The Contents of a Commercial Model

The contents that populate a commercial model do not provide the specific directions for running a particular enterprise. No model directs a person to take Action A on Day N, nor does it specify the *time-specific* solution to any business question. Rather, commercial models provide the thinking that decision makers need to apply to resolve questions and take actions in a manner that complies with the model's dictates.

A Commercial Model and a Business Model Are Not Equivalent

The concept of a "business model" is present in management literature. Business models typically describe different approaches for generating *revenue* in a marketplace. They provide thinking for populating just one cell (Strategic Activities) within the commercial model's framework. They focus on answering questions like: Who will pay for your offering? What will you provide? To whom? And why will they pay for it? (Clarke, 2004). An example of a business model is "bait and hook." Its profit-generating strategy is to offer a product at a low price and gain profit from customers returning to you for some required consumable (e.g., blades for razors, ink cartridge refills for inkjet printers). Rappa (2000) identified nine basic categories of business models and described different alternatives within each category. His focus was on web-based businesses, but his categories apply to non-*e*-businesses as well. While people writing about business models are constantly expanding the "topics" included within their business model frameworks (Lambert, 2010), no business model to date addresses all the elements that constitute a commercial model. Most important, all currently proposed business models assume the same purpose for commerce—namely, to generate revenue

Exhibit 2. The Framework of a Commercial Model and the Knowledge Contained Within Each of Its Components

Foundational Assumptions			
Identifies the model builder's assumptions about the nature of people and the context within which commerce occurs. These are the fundamental premises from which the model builder derives the model's remaining contents.			
Component	**Results**	**Activities**	**Resources**
Strategic	Identifies the end commerce serves and guides one in defining an enterprise's *business intent,* including ▪ its purpose, ▪ its vision, ▪ its core values, ▪ how it defines the meaning of profit, ▪ the stakeholders the enterprise recognizes and its relationship with each, and ▪ the benefits it must produce.	Guides one in defining an enterprise's *commercial strategy*—how it will conduct commerce to produce success. The issues addressed include ▪ how it defines what it will offer to whom, ▪ where it will enter into commerce, ▪ how it will attract, win, and retain customers, and ▪ how it will realize profitability as the model defines it.	Guides one in defining an enterprise's *organizational strategy*, including ▪ what its critical-to-success resources are for long-term success and the essential features each must possess and ▪ how the enterprise should organize itself within (structurally and socially).
Operations	Guides one in defining ▪ what operating results the business should focus on producing and ▪ what key features of day-to-day performance it must realize.	Guides one in defining an organization's general approach to producing the operating results expected by the model and demonstrating the operating characteristics the model requires.	Guides one in defining the critical-to-success resources needed at the Operations level and the essential features each must possess.
Executive Functions	Specifies the results that Executive Functions must realize. These results always include (1) effectiveness, (2) sufficiency, and (3) synergy. Effectiveness means the organization consistently advances towards realizing its purpose. Sufficiency refers to the presence, engagement, and effective contribution of efforts by each person needed to realize the business's aims. Synergy means that those efforts integrate efficiently to accomplish the organization's purposes.	Guides one in the proper implementation of the management activities that accomplish the Executive Functions.	Guides one in defining what critical-to-success resources are required to implement the Executive Functions successfully and the essential features each must possess.

and maximize profit defined monetarily for the producer. Therefore, they all propose ideas, with varying degrees of breadth, that align with and guide the implementation of *just one commercial model*—Capitalism.

Foundational Assumptions

As stated previously, every commercial model's guidance is derived from its assumptions about the nature of people and the context within which commerce occurs. This foundational knowledge controls its explanation of commerce.

Assumptions about people's motives and inclinations toward others, for example, determine the bases on which people will come together to form cooperative commercial endeavors. Consequently, they shape a model's guidance for creating commercial organizations. They also determine the model's guidance for how one engages, involves, and ensures the successful performance of an enterprise's many contributors. The successful execution of these functions requires that one's executive actions conform to the dictates prescribed by the nature of people.

Across human history, two different Western perspectives about the nature of humankind have persisted (Sahlins, 2008).[1] One imagines that people are individualistic by nature and focused solely on gratifying their personal wants and needs. The other imagines that people inherently experience a connection with others and that they instinctively seek to operate in a manner that benefits others as well as themselves. Logically, the notion that people are radically individualistic may seem absurd on its face, given that each human is literally the product of a social interaction, is reared in a social relationship in which he or she actively participates as both a recipient and giver, and almost always lives in a social context from which he or she draws benefit. Yet, radical individualism has been the controlling perspective of American culture and is the perspective upon which Capitalism is founded. It is a matter for empirical research to decide which of these two perspectives on human nature (individualistic or social) is correct or whether some other view is required. That research is examined in *Chapter 6*. For our purposes here, what is important is that you understand that a commercial model's foundational assumptions about the nature of people are one of the two underpinnings for the guidance that model puts forward.

The second root of a commercial model's guidance is its assumptions about the context within which commerce occurs. Human behavior is a function of the makeup of the person and the context within which he or she acts. Features of a

[1] Sahlins's (2008) essay provides an excellent introduction to these views, clarifying their historical roots and highlighting the major exponents of each and their reasoning. Sahlins did take a position on which perspective he supports, but that does not detract from the educational value of his scholarly survey of each position, nor does it impede any reader's option to form his or her own judgment.

commercial context either allow or disallow a person's expression of his or her natural inclinations. For example, imagine a model that assumes people act solely to maximize their personal gain without regard for others. This model also assumes that, in every commercial context, neither the seller nor the buyer has power over the other. Given this structural characteristic of the commercial context, the model deduces that, despite everyone's intent to maximize his or her gain, sellers and buyers must bargain in good faith to conclude transactions that are acceptable to each. Such an inference would be logically correct. The assumption that in every market neither the seller nor the buyer has power over the other effectively blocks each party from exploiting the other or simply taking what he or she wants. Such victimization would be expected given the model's assumptions about the nature of people. The model's assumption about the commercial context, however, negates the expression of this outcome. Consequently, the model's deduction about how commerce unfolds is reasonable. If, however, power asymmetries do exist between sellers and buyers, then whoever has the power over the other would naturally use it to take for themselves all the gains that their power advantage permit. All of the model's derived expectations for how commerce unfolds would not apply.

A model builder may elect to leave the issue of the structural state of the commercial context for empirical investigation and make no assumptions about it. In this case, he or she must specify the structural characteristics that a commercial context *must possess* for people to express their assumed nature and commerce to occur as the model describes.

The Strategic Component of a Commercial Model

The Strategic component of each approach to commerce describes the long-term results a commercial enterprise seeks, the activities it employs to realize them, and the critical resources it needs to achieve success.

Strategic Results

Strategic Results define the end commerce serves and the outcomes it must produce. Its guidance provides the knowledge used to define an enterprise's business intent. A "business intent" states the enterprise's purpose, vision, and core values. It documents its definition of profit, the stakeholders the enterprise recognizes, and its relationship with each of them. A stakeholder is a person, group, or other entity that either affects or is affected by the actions of an enterprise. While each stakeholder has a "stake" in the direction, conduct, and outcomes of a commercial organization's actions, a company only attends to the stakeholders recognized by the commercial model it is applying. Each commercial model offers its own guidance for which stakeholders to recognize and how they should be "attended to."

A statement of business intent is tailored to the business that defines it, since it includes what that business will produce for exchange, with whom, where, and why. Its vision statement—what the company desires to become—is also tailored, as it is usually couched in the language of its owners and the industry to which the business belongs. However, the content of these statements and all other elements of a firm's business intent must be consistent in principle with the dictates of the commercial model the enterprise is applying. For example, two stakeholder-related dictums flow from the foundational premises underpinning the Life Enabling commercial model. One is that businesses must recognize as stakeholders all parties who either are affected by or can affect their conduct, not just those who are direct participants in business transactions. The second is that every business must benefit all its stakeholders inclusively. If your business adheres to the Life Enabling model, your purpose statement must recognize all such stakeholders and identify how it will benefit each.

Also contained in the Results section of the template's Strategic component is the model's definition of profit. Most people assume that profit means money earned in excess of the costs incurred in doing commerce. That monetary definition is dominant in our thinking simply because it is the meaning inherent in Capitalism, today's dominant approach to commerce. Originally, however, *profit meant the advantage or benefit that is gained from doing something.* That is its historical root.[2] One achieves advantage by progressing toward or finally realizing the end that he or she seeks. What advances a person's success depends on the aim he or she pursues and what is required to accomplish it. If your primary end is to amass financial wealth, then profit for you is defined monetarily. If your end is otherwise, then you will measure profit using different metrics that may or may not include monetary gain. For example, you may judge as instances of profit the acquisition of enhanced knowledge, having more capable people working with you, or the improved status of some other resource that achieves your purpose.[3]

Strategic Activities

The Strategic Activities section contains the knowledge that guides an

---

[2] Oxford Living Dictionaries report its root as being, "Middle English (in the sense 'advantage, benefit')." It states its origins as "from Latin profectus 'progress, profit', from proficere 'to advance'" (Profit, 2016).

[3] Some readers may object, asserting that every enterprise must realize monetary gain in order to exist. The issue here is instrumentality. Profit is whatever immediately advances your purpose. If your purpose is to produce products that enable the success of others, for example, then money itself does not advance your purpose. It is inert; it produces nothing. On the other hand, a contributor's elevated proficiency in the skills that generate success-enabling products for customers would directly aid you to better achieve your purpose.

enterprise in realizing its commercial goal. This guidance supports decision makers in defining what the enterprise will provide to whom, where, and how it will pursue marketplace success (commercial strategy). That strategy decides what market(s) the enterprise will enter; how it will attract, win, and retain customers; and how it will achieve profitability as defined by the model. For example, the Life Enabling approach to commerce dictates that a business must compete through the excellence of its offering and the buying-benefiting experience it supports[4] as judged by its customers. It may not use persuasive or coercive techniques to affect the outcome of those judgments. This edict implies that businesses implementing that model should focus their commerce on customers whose purposes, requirements, and expectations they understand and have the expertise to enable or satisfy. It also implies that they only compete in locales where they can effectively service their customers.

In contrast, the premises of the producer-focused, profit-maximizing model (Capitalism), if followed rigorously, would guide one to select markets where monetary gain will be highest. This implies that the critical issues to consider are the degree to which the enterprise can elicit buying behavior from prospective customers and the degree to which a market offers the potential for high profit margins. As to eliciting "buy-behavior," any survey of marketing and consumer psychology literature will quickly reveal that the methods used have little relationship to the excellence of one's offering. Rather, the drivers emphasized by companies seeking to maximize buy-behavior manipulate emotion and people's established conditioning—not the rational processing of features offered versus utility desired. Thus, for example, packaging design, where products are displayed, endorsements, associations established between an offering and the realization of some desired self-image (being glamorous, powerful, "cool," etc.), and other "nudging" techniques are all valued and used to elicit buy-behavior under the Capitalist approach to commerce but would be disallowed under the Life Enabling approach.

Strategic Resources

Strategic Resources are the wherewithal needed to successfully implement the model's Strategic Activities and produce its Strategic Results. They specify both the means needed to achieve long-term success (e.g., people, technology, physical assets) and the features each must possess. This guidance also describes how an enterprise should organize itself both structurally and socially. The structural guidance addresses the issue of *departmentation*—how a business divides itself

[4] A customer's buying-benefiting experience includes all the activities the customer must engage in to access, acquire, prepare to use, and use an offering to accomplish the customer's purpose; maintain it in a useful state between uses; and dispose of it and its byproducts.

into work units and associates these work units so that the business operates most effectively and efficiently. The "social" aspect of organization defines the basic role every organization member is expected to perform, how he or she will be involved in business decision making, and how members will work together to accomplish the purpose of the enterprise. It also details how authority and responsibility are delegated, reporting relationships are defined, human relations are conducted, and resources are allocated. Together, the Strategic resources' guidance expresses the organizational strategy that a commercial enterprise must establish to realize its long-term purpose.

The Operations Component of a Commercial Model

The Operations component provides knowledge that guides decision makers in steering the day-to-day activities of every business function. By following this guidance, decision makers ensure that the daily activities of each business function produce the results that will, in aggregate, achieve the long-term results that the commercial model specifies.

Operations' Results

Operations' Results describes the day-to-day outcomes business activities should produce and the characteristics of their operating performance they must realize. These results are defined logically to ensure that, if realized over time, they will cumulatively deliver the Strategic outcomes the commercial model defines. It is the daily operations of a business that realize its long-term purpose.

From the Life Enabling perspective, for example, Operations must produce outputs that correctly incorporate features customers value and produce them at the pace required by customer demand. At the same time, Operations must satisfy the expectations of all of the business's stakeholders. In addition to these "externally delivered" results, Operations must improve its capabilities for producing value. For example, it must continuously improve work processes so that they have increasing value-added ratios,[5] and it must make every workplace safer and possess greater utility. If these and other related results are realized, then, over time, Operations will produce the model's long-term goal of maximizing every customer's receipt of value while benefiting all stakeholders inclusively.

Operations' Activities

Operations' Activities details the knowledge that guides an organization in producing its prescribed operating results. This guidance applies to every business

[5] The value-added ratio (VAR) is the proportion of a work process's total cycle time that is consumed by activities that materially change its output in a way that satisfies a customer's value. See Bujak and Vitalo (2014) for a detailed discussion of VAR.

function (marketing, production, human resources, etc.) and work process within it. It does not describe how to complete any specific technical task. No approach to commerce tells you how to make shoes, build cars, or construct a credit swap agreement. Rather, it prescribes *how people must approach implementing* the technical work each business function performs. Thus, the guidance the model supplies applies whether you build ships or operate an *e*-marketplace.

For example, if one's business produces instructional products, then an operation called *content development* is one of the technical work processes its people perform. This process gathers or develops and organizes the knowledge that an instructional product teaches. Content development is a methodology belonging to the professional domain of instructional technology. No commercial model provides guidance for how to do "content development." But every commercial model should guide a business in understanding what it should focus on when implementing every one of its work processes, including the content development work process.

The Life Enabling model, for example, directs one to establish flow[6] and pull[7] in all work processes as part of its approach to producing outputs that are waste free.[8] The concepts of flow and pull apply to every work process one can imagine, including content development. Also, the Life Enabling model imposes an overriding constraint on all process improvement actions. Namely, every improvement must enable the better satisfaction of customer values. Thus, efficiency or cost reduction per se is never a sufficient improvement result. Cost reduction only has value when the improvement enhances the value delivered to customers, either in a reduction of the customer's cost or in the improved functionality of the product he or she receives.

In contrast, the producer-focused, profit-maximizing model directs one to improve Operations in ways that maximize profit for owners. Any way profitability can be improved is acceptable, even if the action reduces the value delivered to customers. For example, with regard to food producers, one might maintain the box size of a product and its price per box but reduce the amount of food it contains so that profit is improved (Gelhaus, 2008). The subterfuge of a consistently sized container and price avoids triggering the negative customer reaction that a visible increase in price would cause. Thus, sales are maintained, cost per unit sold

[6] Flow describes a process in which work moves through without interruptions or delays at a pace that matches customer demand.

[7] Pull describes a process in which customer demand triggers the flow of activities that transform input resources into a finished product.

[8] Waste refers to any activity or other expenditure of resources that does not materially change a product or service offering or a customer's buying-benefiting experience in a way that increases the value it delivers.

is reduced, and profit is increased. However, the value delivered to the customer is reduced.

Operations' Resources

Each approach to commerce should also define the critical-to-success resources needed at the Operations level. These resources flow from those defined at the Strategic level but are tailored in their specification to meet Operations' needs. For example, one critical-to-success Strategic Resource for a business adopting the Life Enabling commercial model is having organization members who challenge the current "state of the art." This quality manifests itself in being pioneering—that is, always being interested in bettering whatever activities one performs and the settings in which one works. This general dictum applies across all roles within a business. At the Operations level, this quality is expected to express itself on a daily basis in such activities as increasing the value-added ratio of every work process and the safety and utility of every workplace. Here, the general quality of challenging the current state of the art must be specialized to the particular knowledge, skills, and proficiency levels that enable process and workplace improvements. Improving the value-added ratio of a work process requires mastering the knowledge and skills that implement Kaizen.[9] Similarly, improving the safety and utility of workplaces requires mastering the implementation of 6S.[10] The presence of these proficiencies is an Operations-level requirement for challenging the state of the art. Consequently, organization members possessing these specific attributes represent critical-to-success resources for successfully implementing the Life Enabling model's Operations-level activities.

The Executive Functions Component of a Commercial Model

As defined by Barnard (1968, p. 215),[11] Executive Functions are "the specialized work of *maintaining* the organization in operation." They keep the

[9] The term Kaizen has two referents. Here, it refers to a process improvement method that uses knowledge about waste to detect its presence and a problem-solving strategy to remove it. As a result, it increases a process's value-added ratio. See the *Glossary* for more details about Kaizen's meaning.

[10] 6S is a method that uncovers problems and makes changes to a workplace that maximize the efficiency of the work processes performed within it and improve the safety of workers. Roll (2005) provided a detailed discussion of the method.

[11] Chester I. Barnard (1886–1961) is considered by many scholars to be the premier theorist on the topics of organization and executive functioning. His seminal work, *The Functions of the Executive* (Barnard, 1968), was published in 1938 and is still taught in graduate programs in business and management today. The structure of his thinking has general applicability across all commercial models, but the specific guidance he provided best serves the implementation of Capitalism's approach to commerce. Indeed, Barnard's guidance for the performance executive functions is fully consistent with the premises of Capitalism and is the best representation of how executive functions should be implemented under the theory of Capitalism. Barnard's use of constructs such as common purpose, cooperative activity, authority from below, the moral status and responsibility of the executive, and the executive's need to treat people as "subjects to be satisfied" is credited with introducing a new, more enlightened standard for executive conduct. The problem is that a scrupulous study of Bar-

organization whole, capable, viable, and moving forward towards its goals. There are three Executive Functions (Exhibit 3):

1. Effectiveness,
2. Sufficiency, and
3. Synergy.[12]

Exhibit 3. Executive Functions

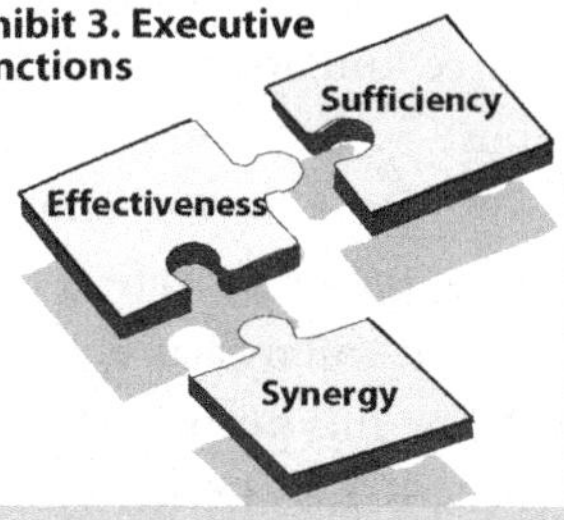

Effectiveness ensures that the enterprise is demonstrably advancing toward fulfilling the aims it has defined. The executive activities that relate to Effectiveness include setting goals, developing plans, solving organizational problems, and improving performance.

Sufficiency ensures the presence, engagement, and successful performance of each person needed to accomplish the business's aim. The importance of Sufficiency flows from the understanding that, without the contribution of cooperative efforts from people, no commerce—and indeed, no human organization—can exist. Executive activities that affect Sufficiency acquire, engage, enable, involve, and ensure the effective performance of the people needed to achieve the organization's purpose. A model's guidance for achieving Sufficiency assists decision makers in determining how an organization should structure its human resource management systems (e.g., recruitment, selection, compensation, training and development, appraisal, recognition and awards, career development, promotion, and separation).

Synergy addresses the integration of the efforts made by all contributors to the business. The knowledge the model provides guides decision makers in how to ensure that the individual efforts of each contributor interact in a manner that efficiently advances the purpose of the organization in a manner consistent with the remaining dictates of the model. Communication and coordination are among the activities critical for realizing Synergy. Both are enabled by the design of the organization (Barnard, 1968).

nard's thinking reveals that his use of these terms does not have the meaning one imagines them to have given today's usage. This is a serious obstacle to understanding Barnard's thinking, especially when approached through writers who summarize it for others. Unlike the case with regard to Mary Parker Follett's writings, when Barnard's constructs are studied in detail and interrelated with one another, *none of his concepts have the "modern, enlightened meaning" people ascribe to them* (Vitalo, 2020). Ironically, however, Barnard's real perspectives, especially about what constitutes "moral" executive action and what are the permissible methods for gaining people's willingness to contribute, are far closer to the reality of modern American Capitalist businesses when their conduct is measured by their actions, not their words.

[12] Barnard (1968) used different language to designate what we term "Sufficiency" and "Synergy." For Sufficiency, he referred to securing essential services and managing people's willingness to cooperate. The purpose of Synergy was addressed in part by his discussion of the function of communication and his concept of coordination and how it is realized.

All Three Functions Are Vital to Achieving a Model's Purpose

Each Executive Function must succeed for a commercial enterprise to sustain and succeed. As Barnard explained, however, the interrelationship among the three functions is complex (Exhibit 4). For example, the definition of purpose—a task within the function of Effectiveness—is a necessary precondition for organizing and constructing an enterprise. This purpose statement defines what the organization will produce for exchange, with whom, where, why, and how it will measure its success. However, given that one or more persons must define this purpose, Sufficiency would appear to have primacy over Effectiveness. But, as Barnard also made clear, without Effectiveness (the progressive achievement of purpose), Sufficiency will wane. For example, if people's contributions are motivated by a promised bonus, lack of success jeopardizes the receipt of that incentive, and the contribution of their cooperative efforts will diminish. If contributors are internally motivated to collectively achieve a personally valued end, failed progress will cause them to reassess whether the current organization is capable of realizing that end. If they conclude it cannot or will not, then they too will move on. Thus, sustaining Sufficiency requires Effectiveness.[13]

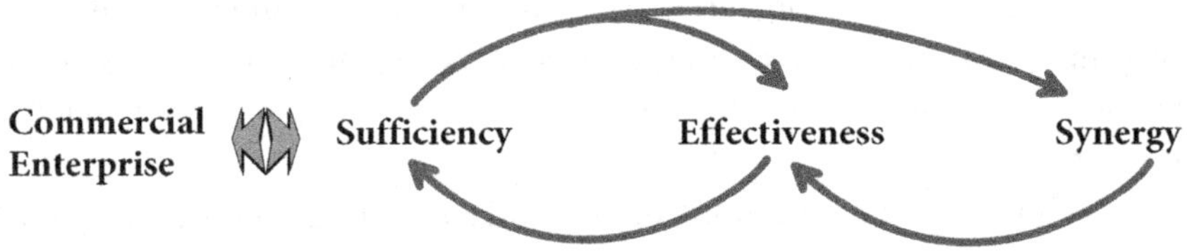

Exhibit 4. The Interrelationships Among the Three Executive Functions

Similarly, without Synergy, there cannot be Effectiveness. Unless the efforts of individual contributors harmonize, goals will not be achieved, and progress will not be made. Finally, without Sufficiency, there cannot be Synergy. You first need people present, engaged, and performing effectively before you can harmonize their individual work efforts.

In essence, an organization remains whole, capable, viable, and achieving when it has the people it needs to accomplish its purpose engaged fully, performing effectively, and working together in a manner that collectively advances its success. Absent *any* of these elements, an organization dissipates, and its prospects of success evaporate.

---

[13] As Barnard stated, the "willingness [of individuals to contribute their resources to an organization] requires the belief that the purpose can be carried out, a faith that diminishes to the vanishing point as it appears that it is not in fact in process of being attained" (Barnard, 1968, p. 87).

Who Is an Executive?

Do not assume that "Executive Functions" means activities performed by people in specially designated executive or managerial roles. It is a person's activities that decide whether he or she is implementing an Executive Function—not the person's role title, compensation type (salary versus hourly), or bargaining unit status. As Barnard (1968, p. 216) clarified, anyone who completes a task with the *maintenance of the organization* as its intent is functionally an "executive" irrespective of the person's formal role title.

While Executive Functions are required in every systematically implemented endeavor, Barnard explained that their performance *does not necessitate* the definition of special roles termed "supervisors," "managers," or "executives." The creation of such roles is simply a choice that decision makers make when they design their enterprise. That choice flows logically from the approach to commerce the decision makers adopt. For example, within a Life Enabling enterprise, every member performs Executive Functions. Within a producer-focused, profit-maximizing company, authority to perform Executive Functions is assigned to a special class of people termed "management."

The Results Executive Functions Must Produce

At the most general level, all commercial models have a common perspective as to what results Executive Functions must produce.

Effectiveness

Ultimately, Effectiveness means that an enterprise is realizing the outcomes specified in the model's Strategic and Operations components. At the Strategic level, this means that the business is accomplishing its long-term purpose, delivering the benefits it has promised to its stakeholders, and abiding by the constraints the model places on its conduct. These constraints are expressed in the model's core values and the requirement that its marketplace behaviors comply with the dictates of the model's guidance. At the Operations level, Effectiveness requires that the business's daily activities produce the Operations-level results dictated by the commercial model. Short of final success, Effectiveness means that the business is advancing toward realizing all of the above outcomes.

Sufficiency

Sufficiency succeeds when the people the business needs to accomplish its purpose are present, engaged, and succeeding in their roles. The guidance for defining these criteria and for how to satisfy each feature varies by commercial model.

Presence of the People Needed to Implement an Enterprise

All commercial models recognize that an organization requires the presence of the people needed to implement it. Where models differ is in the methods they allow for use in satisfying that necessity. One model may propose offering objective inducements as the preferred method for eliciting people's willingness to contribute but also permit the use of persuasion, even coercive persuasion, as an alternative. As Barnard explained, "An organization can secure the efforts necessary to its existence ... either by the objective inducements it provides or by changing minds. ... We shall call the process of offering [objective inducements] 'the method of incentives'; and the method of changing subjective attitudes 'the method of persuasion'" (Barnard, 1968, p. 141). Barnard explicitly stated that the use of coercion is one method of persuasion that has been an effective means by which executives have "elicit[ed] the willingness of people to contribute their cooperative efforts to an organization" (Barnard, 1968, p. 149).[14]

In contrast, the Life Enabling commercial model rejects the use of inducements and persuasion. It advances an approach that elicits people's contribution of their cooperative efforts by supporting their rational decision making about what choice best serves their purposes. Thus, a Life Enabling enterprise equips potential contributors with the factual information they need to make evidence-based decisions as to the match between their personal capabilities, interests, values, and goals and the purpose the business is pursuing, the role it asks the person to fulfill, and the contribution it needs from its contributors. For a Life Enabling enterprise to succeed, the contribution provided by each of its members must be based on a factual alignment between the makeup of the individual as a person and the corporation's purpose, values, and conduct.

Engagement

Engagement means that contributors are aligned with the organization's purpose, energized, focused, and striving to accomplish its work—including investing discretionary effort to that end. Discretionary effort expresses itself in the form of extra time, brain power, and energy invested (Vazirani, 2007). What constitutes "alignment with the organization's purpose" varies in

---

[14] So that you properly understand Barnard's meaning with regard to "coercive conditions," here is what he stated: "(*a*) Coercion is used both to exclude and to secure the contribution of individuals to an organization. Exclusion is often intended to be exclusion permanently and nothing more. ... But forced exclusion is also employed as a means of persuasion *by example*, to create fear among those not directly affected, so that they will be disposed to render to an organization certain contributions. ... The grades of exclusion are numerous, beginning with homicide, outlawing, ostracism, corporal punishment, incarceration, withholding of specific benefits, discharge, etc." (Barnard, 1968, p. 149).

meaning based on the commercial model being applied. From Barnard's perspective, it means adherence to the organization's perspective on issues and "submission to its requirements" (Barnard, 1968, p. 259). From the Life Enabling model's perspective, it means understanding and sharing the organization's purpose and using that understanding and all available information to make decisions and take actions that advance it. It also means challenging any organizational position that is inconsistent with its stated purpose and values.

Success

Success as a contributor has two facets that are applicable in all commercial models. First, it means satisfying an organization's expectations that are common to all its contributors. Second, it means satisfying its expectations that are specific to the technical role(s) a contributor performs. As regards the former, the expectations common to all contributors are dictated by the contents of an organization's adopted commercial model. As to the latter, expectations related to one's technical role depend on the technologies the person employs and the particular activities he or she must accomplish.

Given the Life Enabling model's understanding of human nature, success has a third meaning. It means enabling a person's striving for individuation.[15] A person's striving for individuation seeks to develop his or her singular personality and to acquire the capabilities needed to realize the individual's potential. For a contributor to advance in this striving, the enterprise must support its members in refining their understanding of their individual likes and dislikes, their talents and enjoyments, what they most value, and what roles would best serve the fulfillment of their unique potential. How this is accomplished in a Life Enabling enterprise is discussed in *Chapter 14.*

Synergy

Synergy succeeds when the contributions of effort by the people implementing a commercial organization integrate to collectively advance the business's success. While Synergy is required in all cooperative endeavors, what constitutes Synergy and how it is realized vary based on the commercial model being applied. For example, consider a commercial model that emphasizes centralized control, wherein direction comes from the top echelon and suborganizations are solely responsible for the execution of their individual mandates. In this case, Synergy may be realized by executives effectively transmitting downward prescriptions for action (Barnard, 1968, p. 184) and employees (1) performing their assigned tasks, (2) passing specified information between them at designated points in time, and (3) scheduling in advance their use of common

[15] The topic of individuation is discussed in *Chapter 5. The Life Enabling Model's Premises.*

resources. If all contributors satisfy these requirements, then Synergy is said to be present. The work of the various contributors to the organization is coordinated by following the directions dictated from above. Following those directions ensures that the efforts of the individual contributors integrate to produce the organization's purpose.

A different commercial model, one that emphasizes the decentralized and diffuse pursuit of the organization's purpose; will achieve Synergy differently. Here, the coherence of contributions from various people is maintained by the aligned decision making and actions of people who have internalized a common understanding of their collective purpose and roles. This internalized understanding guides their individual thinking, acting, and relating. Role performance may be adjusted by each individual, in real time, to accommodate changing circumstances. This occurs, for example, when a contributor stops a production process because he or she detects a problem in its execution and focuses on solving the problem.

In such a dynamic network of actors, communication must be fluid. Its content must be determined by the shared work being done at each point in time, an understanding of each other's roles and needs, and the shaping of timely communications that satisfy those needs. Adjustment in one performer's behavior must be broadcast rapidly to all other affected performers, who then adjust their performance so that coherence is retained and the common purpose advanced. This latter perspective on Synergy is consistent with the Life Enabling commercial model.

The Activities That Produce the Executive Functions' Expected Results

In general, all commercial models have a common list of *tasks* that implement Executive Functions (Exhibit 5, next page). Where they differ is in who performs those tasks and the mindset that controls their execution. Related to mindset, for example, the producer-focused, profit-maximizing commercial model views employees as necessary for success, but they also represent a cost. Since employees are a cost, they reduce profit. Also, the model assumes that employees, as all people, seek to maximize their gains from employment. This means that they strive to realize the greatest reward for the least effort expended (profit maximization). Hence, there is an inherent antagonism between the goal of the producer and the goal of his or her employees. This affects how Sufficiency is implemented. The people implementing Sufficiency accept that the owner's interest is primary. Consequently, their approach to ensuring Sufficiency seeks to advance management's ends by maximizing the monetary value delivered by employees while minimizing the cost of extracting that value from them. Ideally, the goal would be to find ways to eliminate the cost of employees while retaining their profit-generating contributions.

Exhibit 5. The Tasks That Implement Each Executive Function

Tasks Accomplishing the Function of *Effectiveness*

- Define the organization's business intent.
- Configure the organization structurally and socially.
- Develop the business's yearly goals and plan.
- Monitor performance.
- Detect barriers hindering progress and opportunities for accelerating progress.
- Eliminate barriers to progress and realize accelerating opportunities.
- Assess performance and extract learning.
- Refine and enhance the organization's definition of its business intent.
- Recycle the tasks accomplishing Effectiveness.

Tasks Accomplishing the Function of *Sufficiency*

- Identify the enterprise's needs for contributors.
- Plan to meet contributor needs using internal and external sourcing.
- Recruit, select, and onboard the people the enterprise needs.
- Align contributors' performance to the organization's purposes.
- Ensure that all contributors are engaged in the performance of their roles.
- Ensure that contributors succeed in their roles.
- Sustain engagement by every contributor.
- Ensure every contributor's adherence to the organization's purpose.

Tasks Accomplishing the Function of *Synergy*

- Implement an effective communication system.
- Ensure the coordination of contributions between and among contributors.

In a Life Enabling enterprise, members own the enterprise. There is no inherent conflict between owners and workers.[16] Every owner/contributor has the same valued end—maximizing the delivery of value to customers in ways that better the lives of everyone. The satisfaction realized when this goal is achieved is not reduced when shared. Sufficiency, therefore, is based on the understanding that enabling the success of the individual enables the success of the organization as a whole.

[16] The form of business assumed by a Life Enabling enterprise is discussed in *Chapter 14.*

The Resources Required to Accomplish Executive Functions

The resources critical to the successful implementation of Executive Functions always include people and information. People are currently the only performers of the entire suite of Executive Functions; hence, they are necessary. Information is the required input people use to manage the state of the organization and its contributors. In any cooperative enterprise, a third critical-to-success Executive Functions' resource is a communications infrastructure. This resource supports the implementation of executive actions across the organization. The presence of other resources critical to success and the qualities each resource must possess vary based on the nature of the commercial model. The priority assigned each resource also varies.

As to variations in the qualities resources must possess, the required qualities of people performing Executive Functions, for example, change based on the model's approach to the issue of control and the methods it permits for achieving Effectiveness, Sufficiency, and its version of Synergy. If a model's guidance aligns with Barnard's view of how executives must function, which Capitalism does, it will require an individual singularly committed to the organization's purpose and proficient in manipulating other people's conduct through inducements and persuasion and through the manipulation of the informal organizations to which they belong. It is through these means that executives ensure workers contribute their efforts and adhere to the organization's purpose and dictates. Such executives plan, direct, and control the work of the organization's contributors. They must be sensitive to the state of each contributor and adjust organizational conditions *or their perception* to ensure that the individual's contribution of cooperative efforts sustains. The effective executive must also be knowledgeable of the nature of the "informal organizations" that spring up within any cooperative enterprise. These associations of people operate to transfer information. They also affect attitudes and influence behavior. Every executive must understand his or her need to control the content of the communications that pass through them so that adherence to corporate purpose and positions is not undermined.

If, on the other hand, a commercial approach aligns with the Life Enabling model's perspective on executive behavior, it would require an individual committed to providing ever-improved products and services that enhance people's lives. They also would be committed to elevating the success of every contributor to that effort. This individual would see the path to that end as involving all contributors in a team effort to understand customer needs and values and discover ways to better satisfy them. He or she would deem nurturing and developing every contributor's natural inclination to learn, achieve, and produce value as critical to success, since those qualities enable and energize continuous improvement. Such a person would "be a colleague, counseling and leading ... people on a day-to-day basis, learning from them and with them" (Deming, 1982a, p. 117). He or she would seek to unleash creative thought and empower people to challenge current corporate thinking so that they could uncover better approaches to delivering greater value to customers.

An Economic System and a Commercial Model Are One

An economic system is a theory that attempts to describe, predict, explain, and enable the control of commerce in an effort to ensure its success. Such theories guide the conduct of entrepreneurs and advise how a society can provide for the generation and distribution of the necessities of human life. Mainstream economic theory focuses on satisfying just one of the necessities for human life, the generation and distribution of material goods. The Life Enabling model addresses all the human necessities that commerce between people must satisfy. Economic models may be empirically developed or deduced from a set of assumptions about the nature of people and the context within which they exchange resources (Vickrey, 1964). Both Capitalism and the Life Enabling model are examples of deductive commercial models.

We view an economic system and a commercial model as being the same. Commerce is the umbrella activity under which people produce and exchange resources, meet their human needs, and develop themselves as productive agents. Why and how that happens and what results such activities produce are the substance of economic theory—certainly at the individual agent level. A commercial model addresses these same issues. It is simply a different label for the same entity. We prefer it because it better identifies with the activity that is being studied and carries less baggage. "Economics" is popularly understood to be about money and tunnels people's thinking into a restrictive subset of commercial activity with a singular purpose.

The dictums of an economic system address three levels of commerce. These are the microeconomic, macroeconomic, and political economy levels. Commercial activity at the individual agent level (producer/seller-buyer) is referred to as the "microeconomic" level. Across an economy, the aggregated effects of these commercial transactions are presumed to describe an economic system's behavior at the macroeconomic level. The study of a particular commercial model's micro- and macroeconomic effects enables one to devise guidance for how a society—through its governing bodies—should act if it should choose to enable the success of that model. This level of thinking is the level of "political economy."[17]

[17] Political economy is the study of the role of public policy in influencing the economic and social welfare of a political unit. Its purpose is to devise ways by which governmental action or non-action

The commercial model template we have described in this chapter guides the description of commerce at the individual commercial agent or microeconomic level. Nonetheless, by aggregating the effects of the conduct of individuals following the model's guidance or by using some other suitable method, one can derive its macroeconomic effects for a society.[18] Thus, while the template presented in this chapter focuses on the microeconomic level of economic activity, it can support the development of a model's macroeconomic implications. Also, since the template includes knowledge that describes the requirements for the successful implementation of the approach to commerce it documents, it also supplies the knowledge needed to guide decision making at the political economy level.

Finally, the guidance a commercial model provides addresses the conduct of both parties to commerce. However, the template displayed in Exhibit 2 on page 63 has language aimed at producers. The reason is that this book's primary function is to explain the Life Enabling commercial model to producers and enable them to use it. Nonetheless, the framework can be populated using language pertinent to buyers whenever that purpose becomes relevant.

The Utility of Documenting Approaches to Commerce

Documenting a commercial model offers many benefits (Exhibit 6, next page). First, the documented model—assuming that it is well formed—explains the aim served by the commerce it describes and the requirements that must be satisfied in order to use its approach successfully.[19] Given a set of documented commercial models, an entrepreneur can select from them the one whose purpose is consistent with his or her goals and values and whose requirements for implementation he or she is willing and able to meet.

Once the selection is made, the individual may use the model to recruit, educate, and align partners in the commercial endeavor, thereby expanding his or her resource base for pursuing it. Together, these leaders can use the model to plan, build, and implement their enterprise. They can apply the model's guidance to

can enable the economic growth and success of a society.

[18] Keen (2017) contended that a macroeconomic model cannot be generated by aggregation from a microeconomic model. He argued from two directions. The first is specific to Capitalism. He stated that a valid macroeconomic model cannot be derived from Capitalism's microeconomic model due essentially to its false premises—false, that is, when compared to empirical facts. His second direction is based on the complexity of economic activities at the macroeconomic level. His position was that a macroeconomic model needs to be constructed based on variables that *emerge* and *express their effects at that level.* His second argument addressed how "emergent systems" generate dynamics in aggregate that are not observable when analyzed in their desegregated state. If he is correct, then a different path is required to generate the Life Enabling model's macroeconomic behavior.

[19] Here, the term "well formed" means having all the elements of knowledge needed to guide a person in performing commerce as defined by the model. It also presumes that the knowledge contained in the model is internally consistent and logically deduced from the model's assumptions.

check whether the business they have built is consistent with the enterprise they desired to create and whether it is generating the benefits the model dictates. Should their efforts go awry, they can use the model's documentation to detect where their decision making or actions strayed from the model and use that diagnosis to correct their efforts.

Exhibit 6. The Activities a Documented Commercial Model Enables

- Define the purpose an organization will pursue.
- Select an approach to commerce that matches your purpose.
- Recruit, educate, and align prospective partners.
- Plan the enterprise.
- Build the enterprise.
- Implement the enterprise.
- Ensure the enterprise operates as designed.
- Validate the model's assumptions.
- Research the actual versus expected consequences the model's guidance produces.
- Improve the model's guidance.

Apart from entrepreneurs, academics can use the model's contents to think through the consequences of pursuing commerce in the particular way it defines. Researchers can create simulations that allow them to study empirically the long-term, real-world effects of the model on a particular business, the economy, and the society within which it operates. Also, researchers can design experiments to test the model's assumptions about people and the commercial context. For example, behavioral economists have conducted experiments to test whether people are inclined to maximize gain for themselves alone in situations where they can control the distribution of an amount of money between them and others with whom they have no personal connection. In these experiments, each subject is paired with an unknown other they never meet. The subject is given money and told that he or she can choose to keep all the money, share some of it, or give it all to the other party. The choice has no consequences for the decider beyond determining how much money he or she keeps. Based on people's assumed singular drive to maximize self-gain, one would expect people to keep all the money for themselves. Should such empirical research prove that a model's assumptions are in error—e.g., all people are not driven to maximize their personal gain from every money-related interaction with others—then the model itself or the components therein that derive from the falsified assumption are invalidated.[20]

[20] In *Chapter 6*, we discuss further these experiments and their outcomes and the larger issue of the "realisticness" (Goodwin, 1991) of a model's assumptions.

On the other hand, if the model's assumptions are supported by empirical research, its guidance can be elaborated by more detailed research so that the guidance better achieves the model's purpose. But such enhancements cannot alter the essence of the original guidance, since that is controlled logically by the model's assumptions.

All of these uses, especially those related to validating and improving the model's guidance, have special importance to practitioners of the Life Enabling commercial model. The reason is that one of its central tenets is *to use learning to improve everything an enterprise does and all the resources with which it does those things*. This includes the Life Enabling commercial model itself.

This chapter explains the wide and deep effects on an economic model's contents that its assumptions about human nature and the commercial context have. With this knowledge, you will recognize why the study of a model's foundations is essential to understanding the model itself. Also, it will become clear why you cannot "tinker" with a model's assumptions without undoing the integrity of the model as a whole. Finally, you will see why a model's assumptions must be empirically valid for its guidance to be useful.

Chapter 4 also clarifies what features of human nature and the commercial context are most relevant to building a commercial model. It closes by discussing why the study of a model's foundations is also important from a personal and social perspective.

Chapter 4

Appreciating the Relevance of a Model's Assumptions About Human Nature

The formative effects of a model builder's assumptions about human nature become clear after a simple reflection on the nature of commerce. Commerce is an exchange between people where each gives the other something. It is both a personal *and* a social event. At a personal level, each individual decides whether to engage in commerce and to what end. Each person chooses what he or she will exchange, with whom, and under what circumstances. At the social level, people must connect with potential partners in commerce, engage them in considering an exchange of resources, and involve them in making that exchange. Prior to that moment, people must shape their offering or its presentation so that it at least appears to satisfy the needs/wants of the person with whom they are seeking to make an exchange.

Further, think about the nexus of social activities that creates and maintains a cooperative enterprise such as a modern business. Included in this "nexus of social activities" are the interactions that occur within and between every group that contributes to the ultimate exchange between a business and its customer. As just a few examples, consider the commerce that occurs between a commercial organization and (a) its employees concerning their employment, (b) its suppliers concerning ordering and receiving its needed inputs, (c) its governmental regulators concerning compliance with regulations and license to operate, and (d) any other entity from which the business needs something. Even if one intends to use pure power to expropriate needed resources from others (physical force or psychological threat or some other form of coercive persuasion), these methods are also ways of relating, and their successful application requires an understanding of people.

Thus, every significant facet of commerce is both an expression of our nature as people *and* a behavior calculated based on our understanding of what people's nature is. Any guidance for conducting commerce therefore must be founded on one's assumptions about that nature. Exhibit 1, next page, lists Capitalism's assumptions about the nature of people. In *Chapter 5*, we will present the Life Enabling model's assumptions about human nature.

The Contents Shaped by the Model Builder's Assumptions About People

In the previous chapter, we explained the elements within the framework for describing any economic model. As we described these elements, we clarified through examples how a model builder's premises about people affect his or her model's content and guidance. Those examples should have made clear that people's assumed motivations, goals, values, and social orientation, for example, determine the purpose commerce will serve and how they will define profit. They

Exhibit 1. Capitalism's Assumptions About the Nature of People[1]

1. Humankind is atomistic. The individual is the fundamental unit of the species, and the interests of the individual are paramount.
2. People possess a universal nature that is expressed in Capitalism's remaining assumptions about people.
3. Material well-being and its furtherance are the individual's highest values.
4. People are egoistic. They act solely to satisfy their needs or wants. They have no other-regarding inclinations.
5. People engage with others to obtain the means for self-satisfaction.
6. People continue to act and interact because the satisfaction of self-interest is never satiated.
7. People pursue the maximum level of personal gain measured monetarily from every interaction with others.
8. When taking as the means to satisfying one's self-interest is blocked, people relate with others on a *quid pro quo* basis. Exchanges are made as long as the benefit received is judged to be greater than the resources expended to acquire that benefit.
9. People have free choice. They exercise it every time they act or choose not to act.
10. People are effective decision makers. They make rational decisions calculated to maximize their advantage by choosing options based on their value-relevant features only.

[1] Derived from the following sources: Bardsley (2008); Barnard (1968); Goodwin, Harris, Nelson, Roach, et al. (2017); Hirschman (1977); Hosseini (2010); Jensen (1994); Jensen and Mackling (1994); Mill, (1844); Smith, A. (1776); and Yamagishi, Li, Takagishi, and Kiyonari (2014).

will also expand or constrict a model's view of the stakeholders to commerce and the type of relationship a producer will seek to establish with each. If people are assumed to be radically individualistic and to egoistically seek wealth maximization, for example, their commercial approach will recognize no social responsibility. Producers will solely pursue their own ends. Commerce will be dominated by the *caveat emptor* principle. Unless constrained by the model builder's assumption about the commercial context, their marketplace conduct will use whatever methods maximize their profit, defined monetarily, without any concern for how those methods affect buyers or society as a whole.

All these content elements (e.g., the purpose of commerce, the meaning of profit, who are recognized stakeholders, how profit is realized) populate the Strategic component of an economic model. All are defined by one's understanding of human nature. In turn, the model's Strategic guidance cascades down to shape its Operations guidance. Operations exist solely as the instrumentality for realizing an enterprise's strategic purposes.

The model builder's understanding of people also shapes his or her guidance for the performance of Executive Functions. Every task executives perform ultimately involves working with or through people. One's understanding of people, therefore, drives a model's approach to Executive Functions and shapes how each executive makes decisions.

Exhibit 2, next page, graphically summarizes the various paths through which a model's assumptions about people affect its contents. The two first-order effects of the model's assumptions are on its Strategic and Executive Functions guidance. Its effects on the contents of its Strategic guidance flow down to shape its Operations guidance (second-order effect).

Throughout the remainder of this book, we will be contrasting how the different understandings of people's nature maintained by the Life Enabling model and Capitalism result in different solutions for accomplishing commerce.

How a Model's Assumptions About the Commercial Context Shape Its Contents

A commercial context includes all situational factors of a structural, rather than transient, nature that affect the actions of people who seek to exchange resources. Structural factors are embedded and enduring. Transient factors are features of the context that come up from time to time. They are temporary in nature, such as storms, natural disasters, etc.

A commercial context includes the marketplace itself and its surrounding political, social, economic, and physical environment. A structural factor of the marketplace might be the availability of information to buyers about offerings and offerors or the number and independence of sellers offering the same product or service. A structural factor of the political environment might be the right to private ownership of property, freedom of choice for sellers and buyers, or the degree to which government decisions preferentially advantage sellers over buyers or vice versa. A social structural factor might be the presence of people in a society who are willing and able to contribute their efforts to undertaking cooperative commercial ventures. An economic structural factor might be the availability of

Exhibit 2. How a Model's Understanding of People Shapes Its Content

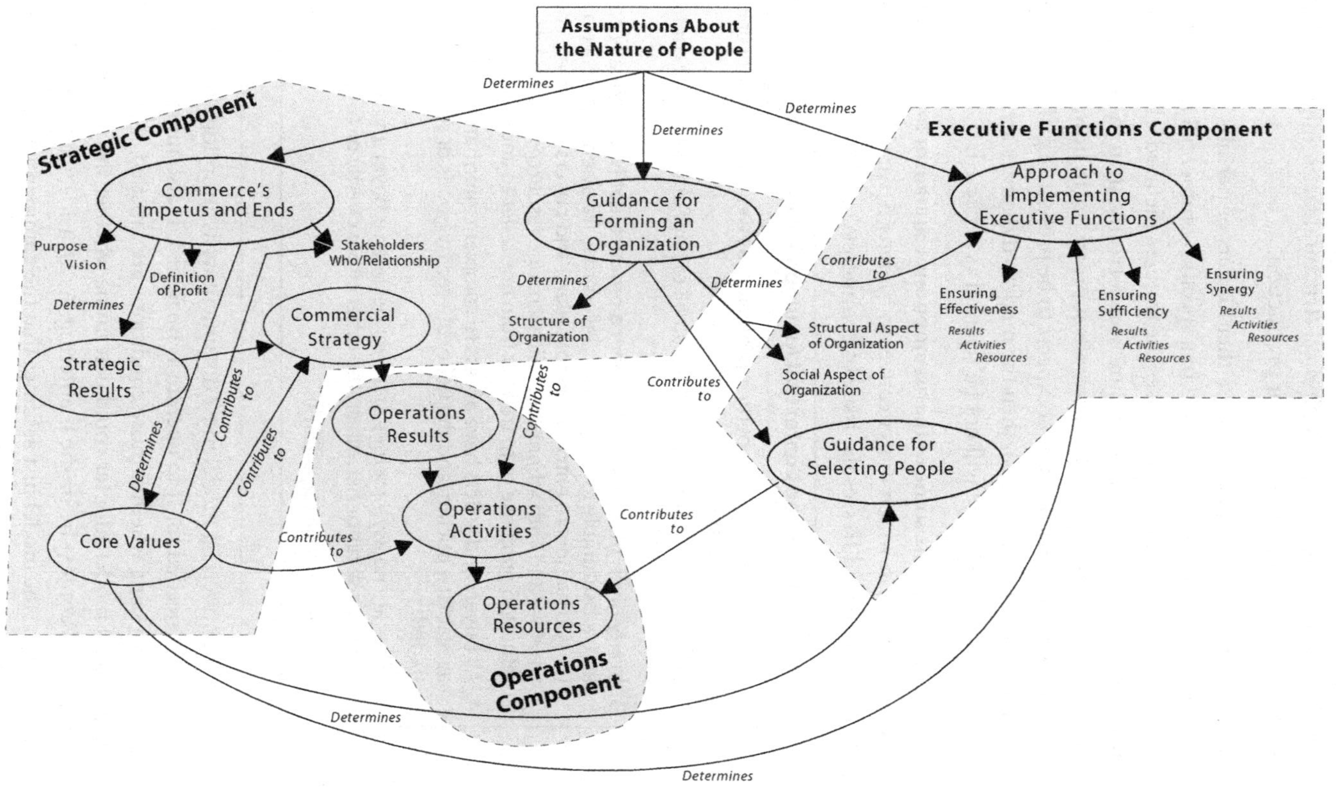

surplus resources for trade.[1] A physical structural factor might be climate or the availability of resources needed for production.

The state of a commercial context either hinders or permits people's expression of their native inclinations as defined in a specific commercial model. If the real-world commercial context possesses the features the model builder assumes are necessary for his or her model to function correctly, then the model should operate as described and generate the results it promises. If, however, a commercial context lacks features the model expects to be present (e.g., free choice, multiple offerers competing for sales), then the model's dynamics are altered, and the end that it claims to facilitate will not be realized as expected.

Exhibit 3 presents some of the assumptions Capitalism makes about the commercial context in which it is effective. In *Chapter 5*, we will describe how the Life Enabling model addresses the issue of commercial context.

Exhibit 3. Some of the Contextual Assumptions the Capitalist Model Makes[1]

1. The right to private property is protected, as well as the control of its use and the benefits obtained from that use.
2. Sellers are too numerous and too small to have any degree of control over prices.
3. In any given market, all sellers offer a product that is functionally equivalent and substitutable for each other. Sellers may freely enter or leave a market (i.e., no barriers to entry or exit for sellers) and buyers may freely choose whether and with whom they will exchange resources (i.e., no barriers to refusal to purchase or to transfer from one seller to another).
4. All buyers and sellers have access to complete information regarding availability, pricing, and the utility offered by goods or services being traded.
5. There are no asymmetries in power between a buyer and a seller. Neither can impose his or her will on the other either overtly or covertly.

[1] Adapted in part from Hayes (2019).

Every commercial model must document its assumptions about the commercial context needed for it to operate as imagined. It also must incorporate guidance for assessing whether those conditions are satisfied. Without such guidance, no potential model adopter could determine whether the model will work in the commercial context he or she is entering. As an aside, Capitalism lacks such guidance. Rather, the model just assumes that the commercial context possesses the

[1] Surplus resources are resources not needed for one's self-subsistence and therefore are available for exchange with others. Self-interest-driven models of commerce require the presence of surplus resources; otherwise, according to such models, nothing would be offered to another.

features it requires and provides no guidance for ensuring that presence.[2]

Every model should also clarify what action a person implementing that model should take to correct actual market deficiencies. For example, if a model requires that people be free to pursue their commercial intents unfettered by regulation because it presumes that they already possess the capabilities to make informed, rational choices that best advance their individual self-interests—then it should declare this requirement and guide one in determining whether a marketplace is regulated. If it is regulated, it should guide its adopters in how to correct that deficiency. A model adopter, using this guidance, would judge whether the marketplace he or she was entering was regulated and, using the model's guidance, act to remedy this deficiency, perhaps by advocating the position that governments pursue a *laissez-faire* approach toward commerce.

For the same reason, the model just referenced should also include guidance for ensuring that information relevant to customer buying decisions is available to them so that they can effectively satisfy their self-interests. For example, faced with a marketplace in which buyers are denied information about the presence of genetically modified organisms (GMOs) in food products, an issue that is apparently important to buyers (Prupis, 2016; Swanson, 2013), the model should guide its adopters as to what action to take to correct this deficiency.

Do Economists Agree With Our Perspective on the Significance of a Model's Fundamental Assumptions?

The answer is both "Yes" and "No." The field of economics has been in the midst of a significant, albeit slow and incomplete, transition. From its inception as a formal discipline, Western economics has maintained a fixed identification with just one model of commerce—Capitalism.[3] That identity includes the implicit acceptance of the premises from which the Capitalist model is deduced. The identification of economics with Capitalism is so complete that, when economists make recommendations, they do not even name the model they are applying. It is as though their utterances issue from fundamental economic truths, not from a

[2] Economists have identified deviations from Capitalism's marketplace assumptions (e.g., presence of asymmetric information, deviations from rational decision making). What is missing is a rigorous investigation, both logically and empirically, of the impact of these deviations on the Capitalist model as a whole. Of special importance, no one has cataloged and attempted to analyze the impact of the *interactive effects of the multiple deviations* that have been uncovered. These include flawed decision making, information asymmetries, and power asymmetries, as in the abridged rights of consumers to seek redress for harm experienced.

[3] We are incorporating under this label all the variations of Capitalism (e.g., classical, neoclassical, and neoliberal Capitalism), as well as those schools of thought within Capitalism that vary in their understanding of specific issues (e.g., Austrian versus Keynesian perspectives on the need for governmental action to ensure efficiency at the macroeconomic level).

specific theoretical perspective. These economists are referred to as "mainstream economists" (see Mainstream economics, 2015). The transition taking place within economics is toward an open, empirically based investigation of the assumptions underpinning the Capitalist model and the exploration of alternative approaches to commerce (Goodwin, 2014; Hossein-Zadeh, 2014; Hosseini, 2003; Keen, 2016; Pluralism in economics, 2014). Whether it will succeed is uncertain (Goodwin, 2014).

On the "Yes" Side

On the "Yes" side, empirically oriented economists accept that a model's assumptions about both the nature of people and the commercial context have fundamental importance to a model's utility. Goodwin stated, "Economics ... is almost entirely concerned with the way human beings behave. Understandings, descriptions and predictions of human behavior are based upon beliefs about human nature" (Goodwin, 1991, p. 228).

Behavioral economists have implicitly acknowledged the importance of a model's fundamental assumptions about people by empirically studying them for the past 60-plus years. Their work has produced a wealth of research investigating how people behave in situations where self-interest and other human qualities that are presumed to exist by Capitalism should exhibit themselves (Hosseini, 2003). Just a few examples of this body of research include Beugelsdijk, de Groot, and van Schaik (2004); Diekmann (2004); Kahneman, Knetsch, and Thaler (1986, 1986a); Kahneman and Tversky (1979); Rabin (1998); and Sippel (1997).

Other esteemed economists also support this position. For example, William Vickrey, a Nobel Laureate economist, stated, "Economic theory proper ... is nothing more than a system of logical relations between certain sets of assumptions and the conclusions derived from them. The propositions of economic theory are derived by logical reasoning from these basic assumptions" (Vickrey, 1964, p. 5).

There are also articles by Jensen (1994) and Jensen and Meckling (1994) that discuss the nature of man. Both Jensen and Meckling are mainstream economists. Their articles recognized the economic relevance of Capitalism's understanding of human nature for the utility of its guidance.

With the exceptions of Jensen and Meckling, when mainstream economists do incorporate some "human" quality into their thinking, it is most commonly a surface feature. It is not a detailed depiction of the nature of people, including their motives, ends, and the principles that regulate their conduct. Nonetheless, such inclusions do reveal the importance of assumptions about people for economic theory.

Consider, for example, the Capitalist model's transaction cost principle. It explains when management chooses to internalize a business function (e.g., human resource management, legal, information technology).[4] According to this principle, firms internalize a business function whenever that choice minimizes the cost of acquiring the service it provides. This principle provides a clear—if unrecognized—example of the significance of a model builder's assumptions about people for the economic guidance he or she generates.

The transaction cost principle implicitly assumes that people operate purely on the basis of rational assessments of cost and benefits from the perspective of the firm they represent. Embedded in its thinking are two premises. One is that people are rational decision makers. The second is that, as employees, people act to maximize profits *for their employers*. While these two assertions do not constitute a fully formed perspective on human nature, they are nonetheless helpful. By investigating them, we can see how a model's assumptions affect the validity of its contents and why testing a model's assumptions is important. For example, knowing the two assumptions that underpin the transaction cost principle allows us to ask and answer questions such as the following: What evidence do we have that people make rational decisions based on factual information? If this behavior does occur, how prevalent is it, and under what circumstances does it occur? What factors enable or deter such conduct? Is this characteristic universal to all people or just a subset? And in whose interest do people behave? Their own or others?

In fact, the empirical evidence is that executives—the employees who are the "internalization of functions decision makers"—are poor users of factual information. They make decisions largely using unreasoned intuition and the untested opinions of others (Keen, 1981; Mintzberg, 1990; Pfeffer and Sutton, 2006).[5] And what of the second assumption, that executives operate to maximize profits for their employers? First, this assumption makes no sense within the context of Capitalism, wherein all people operate based on *self-interest* and the maximization of *personal* gain.[6] At a minimum, one would have to add an additional constraint

---

[4] A transaction cost is a cost incurred in making an economic exchange. External transaction cost relates to exchanges between a company and an outside vendor. Internal transaction cost relates to exchanges between two parts of the same company. When a company contracts with a vendor to supply it human resource management services, for example, the cost incurred is external. When a company receives those same services from its human resource department, the cost incurred is internal.

[5] It is not just executives who are irrational decision makers. Rabin's (1998) summary of findings about decision making presented an even more powerful challenge to the assumption of rational decision making by people in general.

[6] Jensen might disagree with this characterization. He seems to equate "self-interest" with any act whose intent is to advance a purpose held by the actor (Jensen, 1994). Thus, making one's employer richer would qualify as acting on self-interest if that were one's purpose. Charity too may be seen as an act of self-interest when the person's purpose is to be charitable—i.e., to benefit another at one's own expense. A critical analysis of this understanding of "self-interest" quickly uncovers that the term

to the transaction cost principle—namely, that maximizing the firm's profits through the application of the transaction cost rule *must also maximize the executive's personal profit* (self-interest). There is considerable empirical evidence that supports the addition of this constraint. As we will discuss more fully in *Chapter 9*, research indicates that executives make choices for their firms that maximize their personal gains *even when those choices detract from the firm's best interest* (Abrahamson and Park, 1994; Amihud and Lev, 1981; Eisenhardt, 1989). Thus, the universally stated transaction cost principle is invalid *as presented* because its assumptions about people are contradicted by empirical facts.

On the "No" Side

On the "No" side is the fact that the thinking offered by Goodwin and Vickrey and the consistent research findings of behavioral economists are largely ignored by mainstream economists, who teach and consult based on the precepts of the Capitalist model. Mainstream economics has been unaffected by the mounting evidence that the fundamental premises of Capitalism are contradicted by repeated empirical studies stretching across six decades (Goodwin, 2014; Rabin, 1998). For example, while Jensen and Meckling's (1994) paper stated that a growing body of social science research supports their preferred model of human nature (the "Resourceful, Evaluative, Maximizing Model"), the research they cited—based on our scrutiny of each of their papers' references—did not include the findings of any behavioral economics studies.

The most notable naysayer as to the importance of a model's assumptions is the famed mainstream economist and Noble laureate Milton Friedman. In his paper on the methodology of positive economics (Friedman, 1953), he appeared to contend that a model's assumptions might be unreal, yet its specific hypotheses could remain useful in predicting the behavior of a phenomenon. The correspondence between a hypothesis and observed facts trumps theory.

Friedman's paper suffers from a number of problems. Mäki (1986), for example, documented serious inconsistencies in its content. One inconsistency not identified by Mäki is Friedman's declaration later in the article of the importance of knowledge in understanding observed facts. Friedman stated, "A theory is the way we perceive 'facts,' and we cannot perceive 'facts' without a theory" (Friedman, 1953, p. 21 in the electronic document listed in the references). As Vickrey (1964) pointed out, a theory's contents are derived from its assumptions. As Friedman acknowledged, it is these derived contents that we use to explain why a

---

is devoid of useful meaning. "Self-interest" becomes synonymous with "having acted toward any end." For example, if I choose to destroy myself, that obviously served my self-interest as it fulfilled my purpose. A concept that encompasses any and all behavior has no utility.

predicted behavior occurs and under what conditions it will and will not occur. How a model's assumptions can be unreal while the knowledge derived from them is valid and useful in interpreting data defies reason. As we stated previously, a model's assumptions represent the support columns in a deductive model. Dismissing their significance while asserting the integrity of the structure built on them is tantamount to removing a building's supporting columns and expecting the building to stay standing.

Another problem with Friedman's assertion that predictions are sufficient to demonstrate the utility of hypotheses is that the field of statistics contradicts him. Statistics holds that the mere presence of a correspondence between a prediction and an observed result does not *in itself* validate the explanation assumed to underpin the prediction. A correspondence between a predicted event and its observation may occur for reasons unrelated to the hypothesis (knowledge) that generated the prediction. A model, for example, might hypothesize that variable A will predict an object's status on variable B. Perhaps the theory asserts that a person's IQ (A) will determine (predict) his or her level of real-world job success (B). This relationship may be confirmed empirically using some form of correlational analysis. That finding, however, does not mean that A is the cause of B, nor that the observed concurrence of A and B has any necessary utility. Correlations between independent variables (such as A) and dependent variables (like B) may be due to other variables that *are not included in the hypothesis* and therefore not measured (e.g., physical fitness, motivation to succeed, family wealth, social connections). When such "confounding variables" are measured and their effects are experimentally controlled, the previously observed statistically significant relationship between A and B disappears. *Appendix C* provides an actual example of how a found bivariate relationship between median voter preferences and political decision making was misleading by failing to consider other variables of influence. In that example, the hypothesis being tested was that governments act according to the will of their citizens. Early research consistently confirmed this hypothesis until researchers simultaneously investigated the effects of other influencers of government action (i.e., the financial elite, business corporations). When that was done, the initially discovered predictive relationship between median voter opinions and political decision making disappeared.

The Features of Human Nature Most Relevant to Forming a Commercial Model

Seven features of human nature have special significance for formulating an approach to commerce:

1. whether human nature is fixed and universal,

2. whether people are fundamentally individualistic, social, or have some other orientation,
3. whether people have free choice and, if so, what that means,
4. whether people are effective choice makers and, if so, what that means,
5. what propels human behavior,
6. what requirements does human nature impose on working cooperatively with others, and
7. what determines the outcome of human performance.

The contents of a commercial model differ based on its builder's implicit or explicit position on each feature. Given a particular perspective, he or she may need to address some issues that another model builder with a different perspective would not.

1. Whether Human Nature Is Fixed and Universal

If humankind is assumed to universally express an underlying and fixed set of qualities, then one model can be asserted to fit everyone, everywhere. Consequently, just one model for conducting commerce is necessary. By definition, all people and, therefore, all parties to commerce would possess the same ultimate intent and operate according to the set of values required to realize that intent. They may, of course, vary as to their success in accomplishing their purpose based on their "giftedness" or life circumstances, for example, but their fundamental purpose and conduct would be the same.

A universal model of commerce may, over time, have variants reflecting the particular insights and ideas of its different contributors or as a result of changes in the historical context within which the model is being applied. But all versions will share a common core of controlling premises and pursue the same commercial end. Capitalism is an example of a universal model for conducting commerce. It assumes that people everywhere have the same fixed nature. (It also posits that its assumptions about the commercial context apply to all markets.)

If, on the other hand, human nature is seen to possess a common core of features that are modifiable in fundamental ways by interactions with others, by personal choice, or as a result of life experiences, then no "one size fits all" model is possible. A model builder holding this latter view must choose to address all the variations of commercial purposes people pursue based on their different makeup or select a specific subset of people sharing a common makeup and commercial purpose. The Life Enabling commercial model is of this latter type. It addresses how to conduct commerce to realize a specific commercial purpose that people of a specific makeup pursue.

A selective commercial model, such as the Life Enabling model, must make clear for which subset of people it is relevant and what particular personal qualities are essential to its proper implementation. Otherwise, no one would know for whom it was intended. It also must explain with which alternative commercial models it is compatible and under what conditions. And it must identify the models of commerce with which it is incompatible and what remedy, if any, a person implementing the model might employ in such circumstances. For example, the Life Enabling approach to commerce must explain whether a business implementing its model can successfully operate and sustain its existence in a marketplace dominated by Capitalist enterprises. It also must address whether its commercial strategy requires special guidance for addressing such a context and, if so, provide that guidance.[7]

2. Whether People Are Fundamentally Individualistic, Social, or Have Some Other Orientation

People's orientation toward themselves and others defines the perspective from which they will evaluate all choices they face. Will they include concern for others in their decision making? If so, in what way? Will they be instinctively cooperative or competitive in their relationships? What conduct toward others will they deem acceptable?

Assumptions about this feature of human nature shape what the model builder deduces about the origins of commerce, the bases for establishing cooperative endeavors, and the nature of the relationships people develop during commerce. If the model builder assumes that people are atomistic beings—as Capitalism does—they will apply a "self only" perspective to the choices they encounter. Thinking about others will only occur in the service of satisfying oneself. Absent any inherent connection or affinity with others, commerce will only occur when an individual needs something another possesses. People's focus in each transaction will be on satisfying their personal need alone. Their choice making will not concern itself with the effects their decisions have on others. Their contribution of

[7] As an aside, it is interesting to consider the effect a diverse view of adult human nature would have on the field of economics. Assuming that viewpoint, people would have different bases for engaging in commerce. Some of them might have other-regarding purposes, not just self-regarding ones. The relevance of money and the meaning of "profit" would differ among them. Economics would become a domain embracing multiple commercial models. Each model would reflect a different understanding of human nature. The exchange of resources between people would emerge for different reasons and pursue different ends. Economists would experimentally study the assumptions of each model and how the dynamics of commerce were affected when agents operating from different perspectives make exchanges. Or they could empirically investigate real-world marketplaces and progressively build from their observations the knowledge needed to inductively construct a comprehensive commercial model.

cooperative efforts to any multi-person enterprise will need to be induced by either incentives or persuasion.

On the other hand, if a model assumes that people are fundamentally social in nature, its explanation for commerce changes. The builder of such a model may have observed that people's social nature begins before birth with the exchange of resources between mother and child in the womb. It continues after birth with the child offering others the exhilarating experience of new life and them providing the child the nurturing, protection, and guidance needed for his or her development. Based on these and similar observations, the model builder might assert that people are inherently social. Their instinct is to relate with others in mutually satisfying ways. If this is the assumptive base for the model, then commerce is as natural an act for each person as breathing. One might deduce from this thinking that, based on the affinity felt between people and one's history of mutually beneficial interactions, the end that commerce serves would naturally be to generate mutual benefit and not maximum self-benefit.

Alternatively, a model builder's observations of human life might suggest that people's orientation toward themselves and others has *two* aspects—one social (as described above) and one personal. The personal aspect is expressed in their striving for effectiveness in action and individuation of identity. From conception onward, people grow physically. From birth forward, they show excitement about learning and seek to acquire new skills. A first instance of such observations might be the child's efforts to crawl, stand, walk, and then run. Or to touch, hold, manipulate, and use objects in his or her world. And with each instance of mastery, the child beams. Children also demonstrate personal preferences from their earliest age—preferring to be fed from one side or another or liking one food and rejecting another. Such observations might lead the model builder to assume that the striving for efficacy and the expression of one's individuality are also fundamental features of human beings. He or she might assert that the striving for growth and mastery is further revealed by people's life-long effort to expand their competencies and broaden their life experiences so that they maximize their effectiveness in accomplishing the ends they value.

That model builder might further observe that the striving for individuation reveals itself through the child's progressive discovery of his or her likes and dislikes, speech preferences, and interests and indifferences. Through these developments, a personality specific to each individual progressively emerges. With it comes a sharpened understanding of what values the person holds dear and what ends best serve him or her. This sharpened understanding facilitates better decision making about what choices a person should elect.

These insights about the personal aspect of human nature would complement the model builder's recognition of the social aspect of human nature. Thus, such a model builder—acknowledging both aspects of human existence—might conclude that people are fundamentally both social and individual by nature. People naturally seek both mutually benefiting relationships with others and personal growth and individuation.

3. and 4. Whether People Have Free Choice and Make Effective Choices

Free choice refers to a person's ability or discretion to elect an option. Effective choice making is a person's ability to elect that option from a set of options that best serves his or her purpose.[8]

Capitalism incorporates the assumptions that people have free choice and make effective choices. These assumptions underpin important Capitalist theorems. For example, the market dynamic of supply, demand, pricing, profit, and their aggregated effects on the efficient allocation of productive resources depends on people making free and effective decisions. Supply is presumed to evoke demand. As more producers enter a market, they compete for that demand. Since the model assumes that all producers provide equivalent offerings, they compete on price, thereby driving the price down toward actual cost. Given that people seek to maximize their self- interest *and choose freely and effectively*, they choose to buy the offering with the lowest price. As profit margins decrease, producers—also acting freely and effectively in the service of their self-interest—look elsewhere to invest their productive capabilities, since they always seek greater profit. This opens new markets that have not yet been saturated.

This entire dynamic is presumed to ensure that the collective resources of a social unit are always applied where they will generate the greatest gains for everyone. The operation of this dynamic, however, clearly depends on buyers and sellers being free and able to make the choice that best advantages their individual self-interests. Should a seller be able to preempt the "free and effective choice" of the buyer and force the purchase of an offering at whatever price the seller demanded, then the supply–demand–price–profit dynamic would not operate. Similarly, should buyers be able to exert influence on sellers so that sellers were prevented from shifting resources to a more profitable activity, the dynamic would also be undermined. As well, if the buyer or seller lacks the personal or contextual resources to make effective decisions from his or her point of view, the dynamic

[8] Effectiveness of decision making is the underlying meaning of the more common mainstream economic phrase "rational choice."

again fails.[9] Thus, the benefits promised by Capitalism require that personal choice be both free *and* effective.

Similarly, the Life Enabling model requires that sellers and buyers make free and effective choices. One of the model's dynamics is continuous improvement. It drives growth in personal and organizational capabilities and in the utility of the products and services people produce and receive. One vehicle for continuous improvement is learning from one's prior performance. This activity analyzes a prior performance, understands its sources of success, and identifies what factors retarded even greater success. It extracts learning and uses it to improve one's next performance. A critical input to this activity for producers is valid information about their products' utility. Customers supply that information by their free and effective choice making. As a Life Enabling entrepreneur, if people do not buy my product because they are coerced to buy another or because they do not make effective choices, then their choice making fails to tell me anything useful about what I have produced. Only free and effective decision making by customers can feed my learning and help me grow in productive capability.

Two differences distinguish Capitalism's and the Life Enabling model's incorporation of the constructs of free and effective choosing. One is how each model defines the meaning of these terms. The second is that Capitalism assumes the presence of free and effective choosing, while the Life Enabling model does not.

Differing Meanings

The mere use of the same words (e.g., "free choice") by different speakers does not guarantee they have the same meaning. The best way to uncover the meaning of any term is by having its user state the criteria for determining its presence in a given context. For example, Barnard's (1968) criterion for labeling a choice as freely made was simply the fact that the person made the choice. His perspective was founded on the understanding that the mechanism of action (the expression of having made a choice) is *always under the control of the individual* who performs that act. Thus, if I act, then I must have exercised my free will, since no one but me can initiate my acting. Using Barnard's operational definition, one would conclude that the outcomes of commercial transactions are *always freely made and therefore are "fair and just"*—the underlying thought being: "I would not accept an alternative unless I preferred it." The status of a person's choice as "free" is not evaluated based either on the conditions under which it was made (e.g., coercion, withheld information, disinformation).

[9] Examples of lacking resources include when sellers lack the ability to correctly evaluate cost through the absence of needed information, thereby undermining their effective choice in setting the price of their offerings. Similarly, if buyers lacked the information needed to correctly evaluate the features of alternative offerings, their choices would not reliably be effective. Either circumstance would undermine the dynamic driving the efficient allocation of resources.

Indeed, given his conception of free choice, the conditions under which it was made are irrelevant. The fact that the act of choosing occurred is sufficient to demonstrate that it was freely undertaken.[10]

As you will see in *Chapter 5*, the Life Enabling model's definition of free and effective choice is dramatically different from Capitalism's. For example, for a choice to be free, it must be unencumbered by artificial impediments, including coercion.

There are other features that need to be addressed in clarifying a model's meaning of the constructs of free and effective choosing. For example, are these constructs Boolean (all or none) or Bayesian (permitting degrees of presence from none to absolute)? In Capitalism, each construct is presumed to be fully present so that its degree of presence has no theoretical relevance. In the Life Enabling model, each construct is Bayesian. Finally, if either free or effective choosing is a Bayesian construct, to what degree must each be present for the model to operate and produce the results it promises?

5. What Propels Human Behavior

What drives human behavior, especially with regard to the exchange of resources with others? The answer to this question is the basis for a model builder's deductions about important features of commerce. These deductions explain the initial impetus for human commerce, the purpose that shapes the content of each exchange, and why commerce repeatedly occurs across time.

Thomas Hobbes, for example, one of the contributing thinkers to Capitalism's perspective of human nature (Hirschman, 1977), considered the satisfaction of one's passions to be what impels human action. These passions include fear, avarice, lust, and the drive for dominance. Commerce with others occurs in the service of satisfying one's security or satiating one of these appetites. Passions are only temporarily satiated; hence, passion-driven commerce reoccurs continuously. The Life Enabling model sees the impetus for commerce as a person's natural expression of his or her human sociality and as a path for personal emergence. Both these sources of action are spontaneous and continuing.

---

[10] Barnard's (1968) view of free choice is complex. On the one hand, he stated that it is a *necessary* requirement for social order. He reasoned that accountability required that a person's choice be freely made. And without accountability, large-scale commerce is not possible. On the other, he supported the bending of people's choices to a commercial organization's purposes. This was revealed when he wrote about how people's contribution of cooperative efforts may be realized by offering inducements or by means of persuasion—including coercive persuasion. His view of free choice as the act of selecting an alternative allowed him to bridge these apparently conflicting positions. It nullified the significance of the conditions under which a person acted—e.g., the threat of death. This perspective seems especially clear in Barnard's discussion of slavery (pp. 149–150). He deemed, for example, that a slave freely made his or her choice to become a slave by not choosing to be killed.

6. What Requirements Does Human Nature Impose on Working Cooperatively With Others

As Barnard noted (1968), whether or not one assumes that people are fundamentally atomistic by nature, it is readily observable that they do operate collectively. For whatever reason and in whatever forum, they do work with each other to accomplish specific tasks. From the earliest times, people have hunted together in groups and engaged in commercial trade.[11] Given these observable facts, what are the requirements people impose for contributing their efforts to accomplishing a task with others? The model builder's assumptions about this facet of human nature are vital to deducing how a collective commercial endeavor, like a corporation, can be formed and sustained. In exploring the phenomenon of cooperation, Barnard asked, "What are the limitations of cooperation?" and "What are the causes of instability in cooperative systems?" (Barnard, 1968, p. 23). The model builder's perspective on these issues determines his or her guidance for implementing Executive Functions. It is these functions that create and maintain the organization as a whole and functioning entity.

Also, recognize that every commercial transaction is, itself, an instance of cooperative action. Two or more people must come together, form an agreement, and conclude a transfer of resources. A model builder's thinking about the conditions under which people act cooperatively is relevant, therefore, to every commercial transaction. It provides the knowledge from which one can deduce some of the requirements that buyers and sellers must satisfy for them to engage together in commerce.

7. What Determines the Outcome of Human Performance

All commercial models implicitly assume that the individual agents of commerce correctly execute their roles. It is their correct execution of their roles that cumulatively creates the benefits the model promises. Can a model just assume that people will perform their roles in commerce correctly? The answer is no. As real-life experiences reveal, people's performance as buyers or sellers varies as to effectiveness. Some people are skillful, while others are woefully deficient. Given that a model has no utility unless people perform their commercial roles as expected, must not each model clarify its understanding of what factors produce correct performance? Certainly, such understanding would be an important input

---

[11] Examples of human cooperation through commerce extend back to early Western history. Two examples of such commerce are the Salt Road and the Amber Road. Over the Salt Road, salt was shipped from Northern Europe to Liguria, Italy, for trade. This commerce extends back to at least the second century B.C. Over the Amber Road, amber was shipped from the shores of the North and Baltic Seas down through Russia and Eastern Europe to the Mediterranean Sea. Its history extends even further back to at least the 16th century B.C. (de Navarro, 1925).

for political economy decision making. One obvious approach to bolstering economic success would be to raise people's capabilities to execute commerce effectively.

One perspective on what factors affect the outcome of human performance is that differential success is simply a function of one's inherent giftedness augmented by disciplined effort. If so, then the outcomes of commercial activities flow naturally from the giftedness and willpower of its implementers.[12] Success itself will reflect clearly and positively on an individual's personal merits. There will be winners and losers, and the losers will eventually fall by the wayside. This appears to be the perspective underlying capitalist thinking.

If, on the other hand, success is a function of both personal and nonpersonal factors, those non-personal factors need to be known. Only then can we act to ensure that the people implementing a particular commercial model will produce the outcomes the model predicts. This is the perspective of the Life Enabling model.

The Determinants of Human Performance and Executive Guidance

A model builder's assumptions about why some people succeed and others fail inform his or her guidance for implementing the Executive Functions of Effectiveness and Sufficiency, apart from its relevance for political economy decision making.

One task within the Executive Function of Effectiveness is to uncover sources of nonperformance in commercial operations and correct them. Unless this is done, commerce will fail, and the benefits it is expected to provide will not be realized. If the model builder assumes that successful personal performance is a function of biological givens and motivation, then his or her guidance for remedying nonperformance would be to detect which of these two elements was lacking. If the issue was giftedness, then the executive would simply replace the person with another who is "more gifted." If the deficient performance reflected a lack of will, then the executive might choose to prod greater investment of effort on the person's part. Such a model need not address issues related to developing the knowledge and skills of contributors so that they can accomplish their work more effectively. It also need not provide guidance for uncovering and eliminating situational factors that might hinder or undermine a person's success. Indeed, an executive might simply choose to replace the failing person

[12] One expression of the construct that success is a function of giftedness and will is the notion that, among all peoples, there is always a *natural aristocracy*. As John Adams wrote to Thomas Jefferson, "Few men will deny that there is a natural aristocracy of virtues and talents in every nation and in every part, in every city and village. Inequalities are a part of the natural history of man" (Peek, 2003).

with someone who shows promise of greater "merit" (giftedness plus will) and save the resource expenditure required to "motivate" better performance.

On the other hand, if the model builder assumes that people's effectiveness is a function of both personal and nonpersonal factors, any of which may be alterable, then the builder's guidance would need to address how to detect which factor is impeding the contributor's success. Consider, for example, Contributor C who performs Job J. This work occurs at a particular work site (W). C uses a prescribed process that generates an output to satisfy a certain specification. The process requires specific inputs that are transformed using machines, tools, and the decisions and actions of Contributor C. Recognize that, in almost all commercial organizations, most of these factors are not under C's control (e.g., the output specification; the process used; and the input resources, tools, and machines used). Any of these elements can undermine C's success. If in fact one or more of these factors were defective in some way, then replacing C as your simple solution to improving effectiveness or pressing him or her to "do better" would be ineffective in correcting the organization's effectiveness problem.

As to the Executive Function of Sufficiency, its purpose is to ensure the presence of people who are capable, engaged, and accomplishing the work of the organization. Accomplishing these ends requires knowledge of what determines people's success in contributing their efforts to a cooperative venture. For example, one task of Sufficiency is to select people to fill jobs. In a modern business, tasks within roles change to adapt to new requirements. Should an executive replace people who were hired to do a discontinued task with people who can do the new task? Or should he or she develop current workers so that they can do the new task, and if so, how? If giftedness decides competence, then replacement is the only option. If competency results from learning, then retraining becomes an option.

Thus, the model builder's assumptions as to what factors determine the outcome of human performance are critical to forming his or her guidance for the functions of both Effectiveness and Sufficiency. It is this knowledge that executives use to decide how best to correct performance failures and enable and ensure the success of the business's contributors and, through them, the business as a whole.

Implications for Political Economy

At the level of political economy, governments seek ways to advance commercial success. If success is simply the expression of "natural merit," then one might argue that—to advance commerce—the people who have succeeded in commerce deserve a favored place in society and a greater role in economic decision making. Following this thought, a government might set aside a special deliberating body populated by such people. That group might be charged with advising and consenting about policy formation and appointments to important government positions that affect the economy. The voices of these "meritorious people" might rightly have a say greater than the general public. And economic policy itself might rightly focus preferentially on advancing the interests of these people, since they are the ones most likely to advance commerce and thereby benefit everyone.

Governmental action to facilitate commerce would differ if success were a function of people's knowledge, skills, and proficiencies and the performance-enabling aspects of the settings within which they live, learn, and work. It might, for example, follow the advice of Campbell (1969) and use the findings of social science research to focus governmental efforts on advancing people's productive capabilities and improving the success-enabling features of the contexts within which they live, learn, and work.

Thus, a commercial model builder's assumptions about the origins of people's successful performance have significant impact at both the microeconomic and the political economy levels.

The Features of the Commercial Context Most Relevant to Building a Commercial Model

Every commercial model has requirements with regard to the structural characteristics of the context within which commerce occurs. Requirements express what features a context must possess for commerce to thrive given the nature of the people engaged in it. A commercial model may or may not make assumptions about the *actual* state of the commercial context.

A model's requirements about the commercial context depend on the model builder's view of human nature. Those human qualities that the model builder views as advancing commerce require features of the commercial context that enable their expression (e.g., freedom to decide whether to engage in commerce or not). Those qualities the model builder views as potentially retarding commerce require features of the commercial context that block their expression.

Exhibit 3, page 88, provides examples of the structural characteristics of the commercial context that Capitalism requires *and* assumes to be present. These marketplace features ensure that commercial transactions result from people freely expressing those aspects of their innate nature that propel commerce through negotiated agreements while retarding the expression of those aspects that would undermine such commerce. They describe a competitive marketplace where neither buyer nor seller has power over the other and both are able to act freely in the pursuit of their own self-interest. In *Chapter 5*, we will describe the Life Enabling model's commercial context requirements. That model makes no assumptions about the actual state of the commercial context.

The Personal and Social Relevance of a Model's Premises

It should be clear from what you have read that the significance of a model's assumptions about people and the commercial context shapes its contents. In addition to this theory-shaping significance, a model's premises also have a personal and social significance.

Personal Significance

Each of us is affected by the economic thinking that guides our government's decision making. As citizens, we have a right and a responsibility to have input on that decision making. How do we non-economists formulate a position we can share?

Government decision making is driven by the economic model it adopts. One way for us to form a position about its proposed decisions is to learn about and evaluate the assumptions about the nature of people and the commercial context that underpin the government's economic model. While few of us are trained in economic theory, every adult has a wealth of experience in living as a person and observing others doing likewise. Everyone is involved in a wide variety of human relationships in which we exchange resources with others in a number of contexts, including home, school, community, marketplace, and work. We each possess a cache of experiential facts with which to test out a theory's assumptions about people and the commercial contexts in which people act. Our personal evaluation of a model's assumptions about people and the commercial context allows each of us to form an opinion about the relevance and likely usefulness of that model's guidance for civic decision making.

Certainly, a more scientific approach that verifies those "experiential facts" and ensures their breadth and depth is preferred for civic decision making. But how different in quality would an experiential evaluation be from blindly accepting what the "pundits" of economics, with their potential conflicts of interest (Häring and Douglas, 2012), express as certitudes for us to adopt? Furthermore, if someone desired to move beyond "personal opinion"—as we would heartily recommend—that person could formulate his or her own experientially based hypotheses for testing. He or she could use the existing body of psychological and behavioral economics research to evaluate those hypotheses and form a more rigorous appraisal.

Apart from judging, either experientially or experimentally, the validity of a model's assumptions, our knowledge of those assumptions allows us to test the logic of governmental assertions. For example, take the issue of lowering business taxes. Governments that embrace Capitalism authoritatively assert that lowering business taxes will spur business executives to invest in expanding their companies' productive capabilities. That would mean more jobs for citizens. If we know the assumptions about people that the government's adopted economic model makes, we could evaluate that prediction. Should the government's model assume that people egoistically pursue the maximization of their personal wealth, as Capitalism does, we would recognize that the government's assertion makes no sense in light of how businesses currently reward their executives. When corporate executives are given more monetary resources, they use those resources to obtain the greatest personal gain possible at the least risk. That is the choice that best maximizes their accumulation of greater wealth. For a chief executive officer who is incentivized by bonuses based on the business's stock price, stock buybacks provide the best path for maximizing personal gain, not business expansion. Expansion of production has risks, but buybacks are a sure win when it comes to personal gain (see *Appendix A* for a discussion of the research related to this issue).

Social Significance

When a government adopts an economic model, it also adopts that model's view of humankind, since that viewpoint is the foundation of the model. Governments promote the model they adopt through laws, regulations, and laudatory speech. These actions can shape people's behavior in conformance with the model's thinking. This shaping effect can be enhanced when acceptance of a model is also identified with loyalty to one's nation.[13] Should not the members of each society assess their government's adopted model's assumptions about human nature so they can see the kind of person the model supports? What if citizens looked at the underlying portrait of people painted by an adopted model's assumptions and found that portrait problematic from a societal perspective, even if that portrait did apply to a *subset* of individuals? Might they not rightfully reject that economic model if that subset of people the model favors possess qualities of character inimical to social well-being that ultimately threaten to destroy society itself?

---

[13] Former U.S. Supreme Court Justice Stewart Powell, for example, identified Capitalism as "the American system," essentially making it unpatriotic to consider any alternative. *Appendix B* explains in detail Powell's message and its purpose.

There is plenty of science to support the legitimacy of the concern about the direct and indirect effects of conduct prescribed by people in authority and reinforced by one's social context. This body of work demonstrates the behavior-shaping effects of social learning and modeling (Bandura, 1997; Bushman and Anderson, 2001; Deci, Koestner, and Ryan, 1999; Miller and Dollard, 1941), people's inclination to conform to authority's dictates (Asch, 1955; Berns, Chappelow, Zink, Pagnoni, et al., 2005; Burger, 2009; Haney, Banks, and Zimbardo, 1973; Hofling, Brotzman, Dalrymple, Graves, et al., 1966; Milgram, 1963; Rosenthal, 1994; Rosenthal and Rubin, 1978), the effects of priming (Dijksterhuis and Knippenberg, 1998) and nudging (Lerner and Arias, 2017; Meehan, Rosenberg, and Duke, 2018) on human behavior, and the effects of propaganda, indoctrination, and coercive persuasion (Bernays, 1928; Fehr, Kamm, and Jäger, 2014; Hunter, 1983).

Also recognize that we, as living organisms, adapt our makeup to enable us to perform the behaviors we adopt. If, for example, I lift progressively heavier weights regularly, my body will build the musculature needed to support that activity up to the limit of its capability. Human behavior itself can reverberate backwards to change who we are. Those changes may distort some or many aspects of a person in ways that progressively mirror culturally prescribed conduct.

This mechanism of adaptation has special significance from a sociological point of view. The imposition of an economic model with its underlying memes could—over time—alter a society's makeup by modifying the personal orientations of its members, including their goals, values, and manner of relating.[14] This concern is more than speculative. Indeed, behavioral economics research has repeatedly found that, after training in mainstream economics (Capitalism), students become more aggressive, less cooperative, and more pessimistic about the prospects of cooperation. They also are more prone to cheating than students who have not undertaken any economics subjects (Bauman and Rose, 2011; Etzioni, 2015; Frank, Gilovich, and Regan, 1993, 1996; Goodwin, 2014; Marwell and Ames, 1981). These effects are most pronounced when studies focused on behavior as opposed to the verbal statements of subjects. Also, research to date supports the conclusion that instruction in economics itself accounts for at least part of this less cooperative behavior (Etzioni, 2015). Finally, note that the characteristics that develop as a result of taking these economics courses persist (Goodwin, 2014). Thus, the importance of every citizen understanding and assessing the social desirability of a particular economic model's view of humankind has real and consequential significance.

---

[14] This issue will be explored further in *Chapters 6* and *17*.

As stated in Chapter 1, we initially developed the model's foundational assumptions about people and the commercial context from our observations of human commerce. The model's view of human nature was augmented with the thinking of W. Edwards Deming. It also aligns with and draws from the humanistic school of psychology (Abraham Maslow, Gordon Allport, Carl Rogers, etc.) and those elements of the human relations approach to management expressed by Mary Parker Follett. Finally, the model draws from the findings of social science research.

The chapter begins with a brief digression that reviews Deming's thinking about the significance of knowledge and the four areas of knowledge he deemed profoundly important for commerce. The Life Enabling model incorporates all four knowledge sets. One of the four sets—knowledge about the psychology of people—is specifically relevant to the Life Enabling model's view of humankind.

Chapter 5

Deming's View About the Importance of Knowledge

A basic tenet of Deming's thinking was that knowledge is the necessary foundation for all action that attempts to control any aspect of our experience. This is especially true with regard to complex phenomena, such as managing a commercial organization. "Knowledge is built on theory" (Deming, 2000, p. 102). Theory is a system of ideas we use to recognize a phenomenon when it occurs and explain its behavior. It is that explanation that allows us to predict and control a phenomenon's behavior.

Deming stated that the path to uncovering what knowledge one should apply to a given situation required stepping back from immediate events and viewing them from the "outside." Deming's phrase, "a view from the outside" (2000, p. 92), means understanding a phenomenon by placing it in its larger context and using an appropriate set of knowledge to reveal its dynamics. For example, an organization is an instance of a *system*. By stepping outside the immediacy of our experience of a specific organization, we can view it through the lens of our knowledge of systems to describe, predict, explain, and manage its operation. Similarly, in working with people, we need to apply the set of knowledge that elucidates human nature so that we can properly understand people's motives, values, and actions. With this understanding, we can relate to them appropriately.

"Profound Knowledge"

Deming identified four sets of knowledge that are critical to managing commerce: (1) a theory of organization, (2) the concept of variation and its significance, (3) a theory of knowledge, and (4) the "basic principles that reveal the nature of people and the source of their striving" (Deming, 2000, p. 92). These four sets of knowledge constituted his system of "profound knowledge" (ibid.). He termed these sets of knowledge "profound" based on his judgment that, once internalized, this knowledge would have transformational effects on one's thinking and acting. Deming wrote:

> The individual, transformed, will perceive new meaning to his life, to events, to numbers, to interactions between people.
>
> Once the individual understands the system of profound knowledge, he will apply its principles in every kind of relationship with other people. He will have a basis for judgment of his own decisions and for transformation of the organizations that he belongs to. (Deming, 2000, pp. 92–93)[1]

---

[1] See *Deming Revisited: The Real Quality Model* (Vitalo, 2017) for a complete analysis of Deming's thinking, including the full content of his system of profound knowledge.

A Theory of Organization

Deming viewed the commercial organization as a system. A system is a set of components that operate together to accomplish a purpose. The essential feature of a system is that it succeeds only through the integrated activities of its constituent elements. As such, it must be managed from a holistic perspective. Each of its elements must be understood in terms of its specific role and its interdependent relationship with all other elements. Given this understanding, no management action affecting a single person or organizational unit may be treated in isolation.

The Concept of Variation and Its Significance

Variation is the observed differences in the measured value of some feature of a process or its output across instances of its occurrence. No two observations of the same process or behavior yield exactly the same results when measured with sufficient sensitivity. Recognizing the pervasive presence of variation in naturally occurring and humanly devised processes—from individual performance through system performance—means having to conceive an entirely different approach to describing, analyzing, interpreting, and improving that performance. One can only evaluate an observed result in the context of the pattern of prior results. A snapshot of performance may seem to yield an anomalous finding at first glance, but when placed within the pattern of all prior results, it may be a commonly occurring result. And when assessed statistically, it will have no special significance.

A Theory of Knowledge

Knowledge labels or describes a class or category of objects and their characteristics, operation, and relationships. Understanding the difference between knowledge and information causes one to reformulate his or her basis for decision making and action. Information tells about a person, place, thing, or activity at a given point in time. What happened in the past cannot simply be used to predict what will occur in the future, given the ubiquitous presence of variation and the absence of understanding of what conditions produced the prior observation. Similarly, one cannot simply adopt and apply the choices made by others or use one's "gut feeling" or personal intuition to make decisions. Such decision making is arbitrary at best. Deming referred to action in the absence of knowledge as "tampering." He used his "Funnel Experiment" exercise to demonstrate its futility as a means of making improvements (Deming, 1982a, 327–332).

"Management is about prediction," Deming asserted (2000, p. 101). Experience data, whether registered phenomenally or represented numerically, is information. In its given state, it is not useful for prediction. Its utility arises when it is interpreted by theory, whose explanation for its occurrence is established as valid by research. Experience data only becomes useful when such knowledge is applied to it. It is this explanatory knowledge that reveals the conditions that produced the facts we observed. To the degree that these conditions continue to prevail, we can use statistical solutions developed from past observations to predict future events.[2]

The Nature of People and the Source of Their Striving

Finally, knowledge about the nature of people "helps us to understand people, interaction between people and circumstances, interaction between customer and supplier, interaction between teacher and pupil, interaction between manager and his people and any system of management" (Deming, 2000, pp. 107–108). It is this knowledge that guides how one engages people in cooperative commercial endeavors, enables their effective performance, supports their engagement in any endeavor, and ensures synergy across their collective efforts.

Our Focus

Each of Deming's areas of profound knowledge has a place in the Life Enabling model. For example, *Chapter 9. The Resources Critical to Strategic Success* provides a detailed discussion of the meaning and importance of seeing the organization as a system. A complete discussion of the nature and significance of variation appears in *Chapter 10*. Our immediate focus here is on the makeup of the people whose commerce the Life Enabling model expresses.

The Life Enabling Model's Assumptions About People

There are nine assumptions about people that underpin the Life Enabling model. It views these assumptions as describing the dominant features of evolved humankind. However, the model does not assume that all people express these qualities throughout their lives. It only assumes that a subset of people retain or recover them. It is commerce conducted by such people that the model explains and guides. The model posits the following assumptions about people:

1. People possess features that are common to all but are expressed differently in each person.
2. Human nature is both social and personal in character.
3. Cooperation and sharing are people's default behaviors, but, for most people, the continuance of these behaviors is conditional.
4. People possess an "inherent inclination to learn" and a striving for mastery (Deming, 2000, p. 108).

---

[2] See *Appendix D* for an additional discussion of the differences between knowledge and information.

5. Success through learning builds self-esteem, an accurate and positive sense of self-efficacy, and fuels continued striving for excellence.
6. People's inherent qualities may be enabled, thwarted, or altered by their life experiences and the history of their personal choices.
7. Freedom of choice is an inherent potential in people, but its development and maintenance has requirements.
8. Effective decision making requires self-knowledge, the mastery of specific skills, and the discipline to apply them.
9. The outcome of human performance is a function of the person, the process he or she uses, and the context within which the person performs.

Assumption 1: Sameness and Differentness

This first assumption expresses an important paradox about people. It asserts that the whole of humanity shares universal qualities (sameness) and, at the same time, is also characterized by diversity (differentness). Thus, while our foundational nature is the same, people express their shared nature in progressively distinctive ways as they discover and act on their personal preferences, strengths, and interests and adapt to their specific circumstances. This process of individuation (discussed further below) does not alter our basic nature; it simply makes its expression increasingly unique in each person. Thus, diversity emerges as each person develops his or her own personality with its nuanced mix of values, interests, expectations, concerns, competencies, goals, and sense of self.

Effective action by you in relation to any one person therefore requires you to understand *the uniqueness of the individual.* You must do this to personalize your application of the knowledge that applies to all people based on the unique personality of the specific person to whom you are relating. For example, while people are born with an inherent striving to learn and be effective in their pursuits, not everyone has the same talents, finds pleasure in the same activities, seeks to learn the same things, or desires to apply their learning to achieve the same goals.

Assumption 2: Human Nature Is Both Social and Personal in Character

The Life Enabling model maintains that people are *both* social and personal in their orientation. Being connected with others is necessary to each person's full development and satisfaction. Additionally, striving for individuation, the emergence of one's singular personality, is also basic to our nature and necessary to our ultimate fulfillment. These two orientations complement each other and are the primary sources of human motivation.

Humankind's social orientation is reflected in people's inclination to associate in groups and form cooperative societies[3] and in their other-regarding nature. It expresses itself in people's inclination to live communally and cooperate with others; their altruism toward others, even strangers; and their demonstration of positive and negative reciprocity.

Humankind's personal orientation is expressed in people's striving for *individuation*. Individuation is distinct from individualism. In contrast to individualism, it neither implies nor asserts the precedence of the individual's interests over the interests of the social group. Rather, the Life Enabling model asserts that both interests—connectedness with others and individuation—operate interdependently. Each is necessary for the other to thrive. Without the social element, the individual cannot realize his or her fullest capabilities, as the social dimension is the source of their nurturance. It provides the stimulation that promotes the individual's physical, emotional, and intellectual development. It equips the individual with skills essential for survival and learning. It supplies the connection to others that enriches personal experiences, elevates well-being, and provides a sense of completion. On the other hand, without the emergence of the individual, a social unit cannot grow either in membership or in the discovery of new ways to benefit each other and live within the world in a manner that fully develops the human species. The actualized individual, whether working alone or interactively with others, is the fundamental source of innovation.

Assumption 3: Cooperation and Sharing Are People's Default Behaviors, but, for Most People, the Continuance of These Behaviors Is Conditional

Assuming that one's basic inclinations are intact (see Assumption 6, below), people's default behavior is to cooperate and share. They will work with others to achieve a commonly valued end and share resources with them. They will act at a cost to themselves to improve the welfare of others, even strangers. However, for most people, this inclination is not unconditional.[4] People are inclined to cooperate and share as a default but also to reciprocate both positively and negatively once one or more interactions have occurred. They reciprocate positively even at a cost to themselves when they experience being helped by another who is now in need. They reciprocate negatively even at a cost to themselves when they experience a person being selfish, manipulative, or disrespectful. They cease cooperation with such people and act correctively toward them. In essence, both altruism and

[3] "Sociality" is a formal label for this inclination in the jargon of sociobiology and evolutionary theory.

[4] There is empirical research that finds a small segment of people will act cooperatively and even altruistically *unconditionally*. This research is discussed in *Chapter 6*.

reciprocity are fundamental features of human relating. Altruism is displayed in the absence of past or the expectation of future interactions. Reciprocity comes into play when there is a history of past interaction, either with or without an expectation of future interactions.

One implication of Assumption 3 is that people who relate positively with us intensify and sustain our cooperative inclinations toward them. Expressions of respect, empathy, honesty, and fairness satisfy this requirement. Essentially, these interpersonal qualities are necessary conditions for positive human relationships. In the context of such relationships, people spontaneously cooperate and sustain their cooperation, assuming that their basic inclinations are intact. Absent these conditions, people tend to respond non-cooperatively or defensively. Thus, the model posits that most people follow their natural inclination to cooperate with others until the behavior of the other fails to display one or more of the necessary conditions for constructive relating.

The implications of Assumption 3 for organizational development are clear. If one seeks to establish a cooperative endeavor—such as a commercial organization—relationships among contributors must exhibit the interpersonal qualities identified above. Similarly, if one seeks to develop repeated commerce with another party (buyer–seller relationship), their transactional relationship must exhibit these qualities. Manipulative, competitive, or deceptive acts undermine cooperation and teamwork. Here, competitiveness means individuals pitted against one another, each attempting to maximize his or her personal gain.

Assumption 3 further implies that people must be proficient in the interpersonal skills that enable the expression of these decisive social qualities (respect, empathy, honesty, and fairness). Only the effective expression of these qualities will maximize cooperation in collective endeavors and ensure free-flowing communication among all participants.

Assumption 4: People Inherently Strive to Learn and Achieve Mastery

This assumption asserts that people strive for mastery through learning. This process is internally driven and naturally flowing. It expresses itself from birth through adulthood—assuming it is not thwarted. As stated before, a first instance of such observations is the child's efforts to crawl, stand, walk, and then run—or to touch, hold, manipulate, and use objects in his or her world. In adulthood, it is expressed by people who continually strive to refine and extend their knowledge and skills and expand their proficiency in using them.

Deming stated, "One is born with intrinsic motivation, self-esteem, dignity, co-operation, curiosity, [and] joy in learning" (Deming, 2000, p. 122). People seek to develop new competencies and become more effective in realizing the ends they pursue. This intrinsic striving for mastery in activities that are personally meaningful sustains unless negatively affected by other forces.

Assumption 5: Success Through Learning Builds Self-Esteem, an Accurate and Positive Sense of Self-Efficacy, and Fuels Continued Striving

This assumption states that achievement through one's own instrumentality is a positive and powerful force in human development. Success feeds self-esteem and the experience of accurate and positive self-efficacy (Bandura, 1982, 1997). Self-efficacy refers to a person's belief in his or her ability to complete tasks and attain goals. It is a personal judgment of "how well one can execute courses of action required to deal with prospective situations" (Bandura, 1982, p. 122). That judgment may be accurate or inaccurate and positive or negative. When accurate and positive, one's sense of self-efficacy enhances personal success. It excites people to take on new tasks. It sustains their efforts when encountering difficulties. When one's sense of self-efficacy is inaccurate and positive, it undermines success by leading a person to overestimate his or her capabilities. That overestimation results in failure, as people take on tasks they are incapable of fulfilling. When it is negative, it retards future learning because it renders one hesitant to undertake new activities.

Success in mastering a task or controlling an environment is the most effective way to raise accurate, positive self-efficacy (Bandura, 1982). To have a resilient sense of positive self-efficacy, a person needs repeated experiences in overcoming obstacles through effort, perseverance, and learning.

In a work context, Deming referred to these experiences of mastery and success as instances of "pride of workmanship." He asserted that everyone has the *right* to experience these moments of growth and satisfaction (Deming, 1982a, p. 77). He meant that no one should be constrained by the decisions or actions of others from realizing success to the full degree to which he or she is capable.

Assumption 6: People's Inherent Qualities May Be Enabled, Thwarted, or Altered

This assumption reflects the understanding that human beings are malleable and that life's experiences may be "for better or for worse." Who people become may stray far from the native qualities with which they were born. As Deming stated, while the native features that people are born with (intrinsic motivation, self-esteem, dignity, cooperation, curiosity, joy in learning) "are high at the beginning of life" (Deming, 2000, p. 122), life experiences may enhance or retard their development. Indeed, they may even be "gradually crushed by the forces of destruction" (Deming, 2000, p. 122).

Retarding and destructive experiences can begin at the earliest times in one's life. Deming observed that one's "[f]amily environment may shatter at an early age dignity [and] self-esteem, and thereby shatter also intrinsic motivation" (Deming, 2000, p. 108). It may also aggressively destroy or fail to nurture one's natural affinity for others. In contrast, Deming stated,

> The loving mother, the kind teacher, the patient coach, can through praise, respect, and support for improvement, reinforce the child's dignity and self-esteem. Children feel good about themselves when they learn how to master a new activity. ... They develop self-esteem and confidence. They develop [positive] self-efficacy. Their work is meaningful, and they will make improvements in what they do. (Deming, 2000, p. 111)

Besides the home environment, Deming singled out two other environments that can have powerful enabling or destructive effects on the expression of people's native qualities. These are school and the workplace. With regard to school, he repeatedly discussed what he termed the "gold star" schedule. This refers to a behavior-shaping process that replaces children's intrinsic motivation to learn and achieve with extrinsic motivation. He saw this activity as beginning from an early age and being continued throughout later life, especially in the workplace. It begins innocently enough by apparently recognizing a child's achievements with a reward. And then, as Carkhuff (1975) described in his short story, *Gold Star Schedule*, the rewards are used to alter the child's behavior to address tasks and display interest in activities the teacher deems important but the child does not. Soon, the child defers his or her preferences to the teacher's and progressively becomes the teacher's image of who he or she should be.

This process not only undermines the emergence of the child's personality but also undoes the child's intrinsic motivation to learn and achieve. "When children are given rewards such as toys and money for doing well in school, music, and sports, they learn to expect rewards for good performance. As they become adults, their desire for tangible rewards begins to govern action. They are now extrinsically motivated" (Deming, 2000, pp. 110–111). Deming stated that "[n]o one, child or grown-up, can enjoy learning if he must constantly be concerned about grading and gold stars for his performance" (2000, pp. 109–110). He stated that "competition for [a] gold star, high grade, high rating on the job" causes the child or adult to surrender to external pressure. It generates humiliation, fear, and self-defensiveness when he or she fails to satisfy others' expectations. "They lead anyone to play to win, not for fun. They crush out joy in learning, joy in the job, [and] innovation. Extrinsic motivation (complete resignation to external pressures) gradually replaces intrinsic motivation, self-esteem, [and] dignity" (2000, p. 122).

As regards the work environment, Deming added that "[s]ome practices of management ... complete the destruction" (Deming, 2000, p. 108). He referred to these practices as "diseases" in *Out of Crisis* (Deming, 1982a) and "forces of destruction" in *The New Economics* (Deming, 2000). He included in such practices setting *numerical* goals for people *without* knowing whether the process they are required to use is capable of achieving them and without providing any guidance on how they might realize those goals.[5] Other destructive practices he identified include

- indifference to worker feedback about obstacles to success that, if acted on, would enable the worker to succeed and the business to benefit;
- the use of fear to maintain adherence to management dictates;
- inconsistency in corporate direction; and
- ignorance of the processes and technologies that produce the company's offerings, thereby rendering management unable to provide guidance when needed.

Deming saw these forces of destruction as undermining the human spirit and therefore as inherently corrupt and uniquely evil. He had special contempt for those in executive roles who announced new business initiatives that promised to leverage employee ideas to improve business operations, only to later betray that promise. These initiatives excite employees, as they uncover ways to better business performance and remove barriers to their experience of pride of workmanship. In the end, however, management blocks action on these improvements by refusing to make any change that threatens their privileged position. He characterized such initiatives as "smoke screens" and labeled them "devastatingly cruel devices" (Deming, 1982a, p. 85). In contrast, he asserted, "We must replace these forces [of destruction] with management that will restore the power of the individual" (Deming, 2000, p. 122). "Good management helps to nurture and preserve [the] innate attributes of people" (Deming, 2000, p. 108).

The civic arena is still another setting that can have powerful enabling or destructive effects on the expression of people's native qualities. Consider a society

[5] Deming was not against *goals* per se. He wrote, "An individual will of course have his goals. A man may set his heart on a college education. He may resolve to study harder to pass a course or an examination. I resolve to finish this chapter before morning: I give myself a deadline. Goals are necessary for you and for me, but numerical goals set for other people, without provision of a road map to reach them, have effects opposite to the effects sought. They generate frustration and resentment. The message they communicate to everyone is that the management is dumping their responsibilities on to the work force. Why advertise the helplessness of management?" (1982, pp. 38–40).

where governing officials are manipulative and duplicitous and take actions that are contrary to the people's will and harmful to their well-being. Those political actors violate the social compact that unites people and their government. When the people caught in such a society have no power to correct the insults and abuses imposed by their governing representatives, the civic arena becomes an agent of personal destruction. It provides a steady regimen of frustration and conditioned impotence, as all its institutions are controlled by a small segment of people whose actions are self-serving.

How people react to such a circumstance varies. Frequently, their responses have ill effects. Many withdraw from civic involvement to block further undermining. Some react violently. Some displace their frustration onto targets they feel they can act against effectively, even when such action will not eliminate the source of their misery. In their different ways, people strive to survive as the spirit of life within them is under incessant attack. Consider the effects of these conditions of frustration on the American public, as described earlier in the section *Inequality and Social Harm* (pages 38–42). As cited there, only 16% of the public reported being satisfied with the direction of the country, while 55% of Americans reported that they felt helpless to change the political situation in which they found themselves (page 41).

The effects of demoralizing and destructive home, school, work, and civic settings continue unless interdicted by constructive personal action. Such action may require the assistance of others.

Assumption 7: Freedom of Choice Is an Inherent Potential in People, but Its Development and Maintenance Has Requirements

Free choice is present whenever a person selects an object, defines a goal, or chooses a course of action that expresses his or her preferences *unaffected by artificial impediments*. Such impediments to free choice may be internal or external. The model designates as "artificial" any impediment that is not a limit defined by one's inherent capabilities. Examples of artificial impediments include

- limited awareness of options due to restricted life experiences;
- the imposition of preferences by another person, group, or organization; or
- the reflexive avoidance of options due to passively acquired conditioned inhibitions.[6]

Thus, if one's restrictive life experiences were undone, the limitation would disappear, and the person's choice would change. Similarly, the person's choice

[6] A conditioned inhibition is a learned internal state that prevents a person from making some response they would otherwise make. The inhibition results from punishment training or withholding of positive reinforcement.

would change if the coercive actions of others intent on controlling the individual's choice were nullified or one's passively acquired conditioned inhibitions were removed.

Understanding Freedom of Choice

The following statements clarify the Life Enabling model's understanding of free choice:

1. From the beginning of life, freedom of choice is constrained by one's personal and contextual limitations. These limitations include the child's restricted mobility, the constrained physical and social contexts within which he or she exists, and the child's limited understanding of the objects in his or her world and the consequences that flow from interacting with them.
2. Freedom of choice expands as a result of physical maturation and the exercise of curiosity, striving to learn, and the progressive mastery of new skills. These skills expand the child's ability to accomplish a wider variety of tasks. This progressive development adds degrees of freedom by widening the possible ends and actions a child can entertain. This development of the child's freedom must be nurtured by the adults responsible for the child until the process becomes self-sustaining.
3. The personal process of expanding freedom is continuous as long as the native features of human nature persist and thrive within an individual and no exogenous forces impede their expression. Progressively, the contexts within which the maturing person lives, learns, works, and engages in social and civic activities widen. With this widening, the person acquires more information and knowledge about others and his or her surrounding world. With increasing knowledge and information, more options and alternatives are revealed. As people act upon their world, they develop increased instrumental and social skills and self-understanding. With success in learning and achievement, factually based positive self-efficacy grows and, with it, one's readiness to undertake new endeavors, explore new settings, entertain new courses of action, and realize new successes. As a consequence of this growth, one's freedom of choice further increases. It is enhanced still further by the person's continued development of physical and emotional fitness, improved well-being and self-understanding, and the additional knowledge and skills he or she develops that permit the person to transform a given set of inputs into a desired result.
4. Conversely, freedom of choice can be compromised by physical, emotional, intellectual, or experiential deprivations. These deprivations may be the direct consequences of the determined actions of others or byproducts of

happenstance. Their methods of effect are through the depletion of energy and physical capabilities, the engendering of confusion about oneself, the undermining of one's positive self-efficacy, and the limiting of available opportunities for exploring one's world and learning new skills. It can also be undermined by withheld information or misinformation, inculcation of beliefs that erode self-worth or rule out avenues for exploration and discovery that otherwise would be pursued, and trained avoidance behaviors (actively implanted conditioned inhibitions) that automatically close off options for thought or behavior. Essentially, any action or event that restricts what a person might entertain doing or the means he or she might use to do it reduces an individual's freedom of choice. The loss of freedom may be compounded by a person's progressive submission to the debilitating effects of deprivation until he or she has functionally surrendered to the dictates of internal and external circumstances.

Special Relationship Between Freedom of Choice and Individuation

Freedom of choice is a requirement for the process of individuation to succeed. Reciprocally, the process of individuation is the essential vehicle for expanding a person's freedom of choice. Individuation requires that people be able to explore their world based on their personal interests and curiosity. These interactions provide the feedback needed to learn about oneself—one's likes and dislikes. This enables a person to distinguish real from apparent interests and separate the values and goals that are vital to him or her from those that are not. With each venture forward, we expand our knowledge and master new instrumental skills or strengthen existing ones. New potential goals enter our awareness. More options for action are conceived. More of these options become possible for us to accomplish. With each expansion, a broader array of opportunities unfolds that invites the person to engage in further discovery, learning, and achievement. We become less restricted in what we can conceive, undertake, and succeed at. In this way, the process of individuation expands one's freedom of choice.

Assumption 8: Effective Decision Making Requires Self-Knowledge, the Mastery of Specific Skills, and the Discipline to Apply Them

The model defines effective decision making by the process the person uses to make a decision and by the outcome that decision produces.

As to the process, effective decision making uses either information- or knowledge-based methods that are goal driven and evidence based (*Appendix E*). Information-based methods analyze and interpret facts to make a decision. They maximize the options a person considers and operationalize the values that the "best choice" must satisfy. They systematically evaluate each option with respect to its likely success in achieving the person's goal and satisfying the decision maker's values. Knowledge-based methods apply a set of knowledge to logically deduce from relevant facts which choice to elect or how to correct a problem. Both information- and knowledge-based methods permit documentation of how a decision was made, allow participation and review by others, and support the use of outcome information to extract learning that can improve a person's future decision making. Given the probabilistic nature of all assessments due to the absence of complete information and knowledge, the use of information- or knowledge-based methods does not guarantee success. It just maximizes the likelihood that a person will realize success.

As to the outcome, effective decisions should elect that alternative that best enables a person to achieve his or her goal in ways that satisfy his or her values. The outcome of all decisions of significance must be objectively assessed by comparing what results each decision produced versus what was desired. Also, each such decision must be analyzed to uncover what enabled or hindered the success that was realized. Each decision maker must use the learning derived from these assessments to progressively advance and ultimately realize his or her proficiency in effective decision making.

Both internal and external factors influence the effectiveness of decision making. The fundamental internal factors are one's accuracy in understanding his or her purpose, mastery of the knowledge and skills needed to implement information- and knowledge-based decision-making methods, and demonstrated discipline in applying these methods correctly. To the degree these elements are lacking, the effectiveness of decision making is compromised.

With regard to information-based methods, a person needs proficiency in completing the following tasks:

- operationalizing a decision goal and the values that a best approach to accomplishing that goal must satisfy,
- expanding one's options for realizing a goal,
- separating valid and relevant from invalid or irrelevant information,
- assessing the effectiveness of options for goal achievement, and
- selecting that option which offers the best chance of achieving success in a manner that best satisfies one's goal and all of one's values.

With regard to knowledge-based decision-making methods, one must be able to distinguish knowledge from information and be able to uncover, verify, and apply knowledge to infer the best choice in a given situation.

Decision makers also need proficiency in learning from their prior performance when choosing the best course of action to realize their purpose. This learning eliminates prior errors, elevates proficiency, and improves future decision making.

The fundamental external factors that influence the effectiveness of decision making are the legal right to choose, the availability of and access to all valid information and knowledge relevant to making one's choice, and the material resources needed to process that content or develop it if it is absent.

Assumption 9: The Factors Determining the Outcome of Human Performance Are the Person, the Process, and the Setting

The Life Enabling model adopts Gilbert's (1996) definition of human performance as including both what the performer does (*behavior*) and what he or she produces (*results*). Analyzing either alone yields no useful learning, and it is learning that propels continuous improvement. Without a measured result, behavior has no known utility. Without assessing the process used, one cannot say whether the result produced was a product of the behavior performed or simply chance. One also cannot judge whether the behavior satisfied one's requirements for acceptable conduct.

The model organizes the specific factors that shape the outcome of human performance into three categories—the Person, the Work Process he or she used, and the Work Setting within which the work was done. Examples of specific factors in the Person category include the performer's knowledge and skills, distractedness, and task-relevant physical fitness. As to Work Processes, examples of specific factors include the absence of documentation and the inherent adequacy/inadequacy of the process based on its design. As to Work Setting, examples include the adequacy/inadequacy of inputs, effectiveness of machines, adequacy/inadequacy of coordination from other interfacing operations, and the presence/absence of supervisory support and know-how, among others.

A more detailed development of the model's view of the factors determining the outcome of human performance is provided later in this chapter.

The Model's Position on the Features of Humankind Deemed Most Relevant to Commerce

In *Chapter 4*, we introduced a minimal set of elemental features of humankind most relevant to understanding commerce between people. A model's position on each feature is either explicitly stated in its assumptions or deducible from them. Here, we explain the Life Enabling model's position on each feature.

Whether Human Nature Is Fixed and Universal

The Life Enabling model maintains that people initially express a common set of features and native dispositions that have evolved over time. Their initial expression assumes that no preemptive biological deficiencies are present (Exhibit 1). Assumption 6 of the model (pages 114–117), however, makes clear that these features are not fixed in their expression. Each commercial agent's life experiences and personal choices may enable, hinder, block, or replace these native dispositions with other inclinations and patterns of behavior. Given the variation and multiplicity of human decisions and interpersonal experiences across a lifetime and the malleability of people, a universal commercial model is implausible. Motives and purposes will vary. Assertions to the contrary are unreasonable based on available empirical evidence. As you will read in *Chapter* 6, that empirical evidence, thus far, is overwhelmingly against the view that the motive and purpose that drive human commerce are fixed and universal.

Exhibit 1. Human Nature as Fixed and Universal

- People initially express a common set of evolved features and native dispositions.
- People's disposition not fixed but subject to modification by others and self.
- A universal commercial model is implausible given the number and uncertainty of life experiences.
- Every commercial model must describe for whom it applies and how interaction with people operating under different models will affect its implementation.

Given the implausibility of a universal commercial model, every commercial model must describe the people for whom it has utility. This is the set of people who correspond to the model's assumptions about human nature. Thus, the Life Enabling model profiles those people for whom it applies. This group is composed of those individuals whose native inclinations, as described in the model's assumptions, remain intact or have been recovered. The model guides a person in conducting commerce in a manner consistent with these qualities and in a world where people operate from different motivational bases and with different inclinations toward others and therefore apply different approaches to commerce.

People's Native Orientation and What Propels Human Behavior

Evolved humankind is both social and personal in its orientation (Exhibit 2, next page). People are propelled from within by their desire for connectedness with others in mutually benefiting relationships and their striving to grow, learn, master new capabilities, and individuate themselves. Commerce serves both these strivings. It expresses our human sociality and provides a path for our personal emergence. The exchange of mutually benefiting resources creates closeness and satisfies our desires to be helpful to others. In parallel, the stimulation and benefit received from interacting with others and from one's productive efforts and achievements advances our personal development.

The model's understanding of people's native orientation also has significance for developing and maintaining viable and effective cooperative endeavors. The organizational context of such endeavors must enable their contributors to satisfy both their social and personal inclinations. Contributors must have opportunities to work together helpfully and to advance their individuation through the application of their talents. Their common enterprise must provide them opportunities to experience pride of workmanship and to explore and master new roles and responsibilities.

Exhibit 2. Native Orientation and Drive

- People are both social and personal in their orientation.
- People are propelled by their desire for connectedness with others in mutually benefiting relationships and their striving to grow, learn, master new capabilities, and individuate themselves.
- Commerce is a vehicle for the expression of human sociality and personal emergence.
- The internal organization and operations of cooperative enterprises must enable the expression of human sociality and provide a path for every contributor's personal emergence.

Whether Humans Have Free Choice and, if so, What That Means

The Life Enabling model's premise is that people have the potential for free choice. It identifies freedom of choice as essential to the expression of human nature and to the realization of both individual and social well-being. It also identifies free choice as a requirement for commerce.

The model views free choice as existing on a continuum. At its highest level, a person is able to make choices uncorrupted by artificial limitations, including the lack of awareness of alternatives due to limited life experiences or the influence of others who seek to shape the person's choice to satisfy *their* preferences. At the lowest level, the person's choice is fully a function of artificial internal or external limitations.

How the Model Incorporates This Understanding

A producer can only succeed in Life Enabling commerce if all parties to commerce have free choice. Every potential producer must assess the state of people's freedom of choice in every market he or she contemplates entering. If a producer chooses to engage in commerce in a market where people's freedom of choice is compromised, he or she must assume responsibility for advancing their freedom of choice. Otherwise, the producer's efforts to implement Life Enabling commerce cannot succeed.

How does a Life Enabling enterprise act to realize this producer responsibility? First, as its standard approach, the enterprise ensures that all its contributors have the opportunity to expand their work experiences, improve their understanding of themselves, build their sense of positive self-efficacy through experiencing pride of workmanship, and continue their growth in knowledge, skills, proficiencies, and achievements (Exhibit 3).

With regard to prospective customers, the enterprise—first and foremost—ensures that it produces offerings that deliver maximum value. By "value" we mean something that enables its recipients to achieve the purpose they seek to accomplish in a way that satisfies their values and provides a better life for everyone. By enabling a customer's instrumental success, each customer's positive self-efficacy grows, and, with that growth, their freedom of choice increases.

Exhibit 3. Barriers and Life Enabling Enterprise Solutions to Advancing Free Choice

Definition: Free choice is present whenever a person selects an object, defines a goal, or chooses a course of action that expresses the person's preferences, *unaffected by artificial impediments.*[1]

Barriers	Solutions
Barriers include any state of physical, emotional, intellectual, or experiential deprivation that is a direct consequence of the determined actions of others or a byproduct of happenstance, not inheritance. For example ▪ restricted life experiences due to lack of opportunities, ▪ lack of accurate, positive self-efficacy, ▪ passively acquired conditioned inhibitions, ▪ coercive persuasion by others, ▪ restricted range of acquired skills and knowledge due to lack of learning opportunities, and ▪ restrictions that limit offerings available in a market, customer transfer between vendors, or one's right to redress for harm experienced.	**Standard** ▪ Within the organization, the enterprise enables its contributors to deepen their understanding of themselves, enhance their sense of positive self-efficacy, and continue their growth in knowledge, skills, and achievements. ▪ With customers, it expands the alternatives customers can elect and produces offerings that advance their personal success in a way that satisfies their preferences, thereby building their experience of positive self-efficacy. **Tailored** ▪ The enterprise uncovers the barriers that hinder the free choice of its customers and stakeholders, and it acts to remove them both directly and in concert with other concerned parties.

[1] An artificial impediment is any impediment that is not a limit defined by one's inherent capabilities.

A Life Enabling enterprise also implements tailored solutions to advance people's freedom of choice. It does this by identifying the specific barriers preventing its greater expression in its customers and stakeholders. It uses this information to guide its problem solving to find ways for it to elevate each party's free choice. These solutions, for example, may involve offering training in better understanding oneself or expanding decision options, or it may undertake actions that increase the decision-relevant information available to all parties. The enterprise uses its Marketing function to execute such tailored solutions. Marketing ensures that the public has all the information people need or deem relevant to their decision making. It assists people in understanding their real needs. It educates them about alternate solutions for meeting their needs. It also supports people in objectively evaluating alternative ways to meet their needs from their points of view and in choosing that offering which best serves their needs. This is done without regard for the effects of those choices on the enterprise itself.

At a market level, the enterprise advocates for creating marketplaces free of barriers that restrict choice and limit a person's opportunities to reward or punish those producers who fail to deliver the benefits they promised.

Ultimately, a Life Enabling enterprise uses its research and development capabilities to discover ways that enable its customers *not to need its offering in the future*. Not requiring an external resource to enable one's success frees up the time and effort a person expends in acquiring and using that resource. These personal and material resources become available for use in pursuing other purposes. In this way, eliminating a person's need for one's offering expands that individual's degrees of freedom.

What Determines the Effectiveness of Decision Making

As stated earlier, effective decision making uses either information- or knowledge-based methods that are goal driven and evidence based and produce outcomes that enable the decision maker's success in ways that satisfy his or her values. Becoming an effective decision maker also requires learning from one's past performance and using that learning to advance one's decision-making proficiency.

The model maintains that effective decision making can be compromised by both internal and external factors. Unless these factors are eliminated, people's choices will neither efficiently advance their purposes nor provide others with valid information about what best serves people's needs.

How the Life Enabling Model Incorporates This Understanding

As with free choice, the model recognizes the producer as responsible for ensuring the presence of effective choice making among its partners in commerce (Exhibit 4). This includes its customers, enterprise contributors, and all its stakeholders. The reasoning is the same. A Life Enabling enterprise cannot accomplish its purpose unless people are making effective decisions. Given the producer's intent and the absence of effective decision making in any of his or her partners in commerce, the producer must either act to remedy that deficiency or choose not to do Life Enabling commerce.

Exhibit 4. Barriers and Solutions to Advancing Effective Choice-Making

Definition: Effective decision making uses information- or knowledge-based methods that employ all relevant information and yield outcomes that advance one's purposes.

Barriers	Solutions
▪ Lack of self-understanding ▪ Lack of information- or knowledge-based decision-making skills ▪ Lack of skills in vetting choice-relevant information ▪ Lack of material resources to develop or process missing information or knowledge ▪ Lack of discipline in applying the correct process to decision making ▪ Lack of skill in learning from prior performance	**Standard** ▪ Within the organization, it models effective decision making by ensuring that all business decision making uses information- or knowledge-based methods and trains its contributors in decision-making skills, provides them access to the resources they need to make effective decisions, and supports members in improving their decision-making proficiency. ▪ With prospective customers and stakeholders, it encourages their learning and use of information- or knowledge-based methods and improving their proficiency in using these methods by learning from their prior efforts. ▪ With the communities in which it participates, it supports civic efforts to neutralize the actions that manipulate people's choice making. **Tailored** ▪ It uncovers the barriers that hinder its customers' and stakeholders' effective choice making and acts to remove them both directly and in concert with other concerned parties.

Every Life Enabling enterprise therefore must assess the degree to which its prospective members, customers, and all stakeholders are capable of making effective choices. Where deficiencies exist, such an enterprise acts to remedy them. It advances effective decision making among its contributors by training them in decision-making skills and ensuring that they have access to the knowledge and information they need. It also advances it by ensuring that all its business decision making uses either information- or knowledge-based procedures. Finally, it supports contributors in evaluating their completed decisions and in using the learning they derive to improve their effectiveness.

The enterprise elevates the effective decision making of its prospective customers and stakeholders by offering them training that develops in them the knowledge, skills, and proficiency levels required to make effective choices. It also supports them in obtaining access to the knowledge and information they require to make effective choices. To elevate effective decision making by the citizens of the communities in which the enterprise operates, the enterprise supports civic efforts to neutralize attempts to manipulate people's choice making and eliminate restrictions on citizens' access to the knowledge and information they need to make their choices. It also works with them to expose propaganda and disinformation campaigns and any other attempts to distort citizen choice making to reflect the preferences of others rather than serve their own goals and values.[7] It does not, however, endorse censorship. Its focus is on empowering people by providing them the competencies they require to evaluate the information available to them and to expand their access to such information. It does not seek to control them. Finally, it provides community training programs in effective decision making as part of its efforts to recruit new members. This effort is described further in *Chapter 15.*

The Life Enabling enterprise also develops tailored approaches to advancing effective decision making by its customers and stakeholders. It uncovers the barriers that hinder their effective choice making and acts to remove them, both directly and in concert with other concerned parties.

People's Requirements for Working Cooperatively

The Life Enabling model acknowledges that cooperation has natural ground rules. Relations with customers, suppliers, delivery chain members, and other parties to commerce must abide by these ground rules. This understanding also

[7] An recent example of citizen-targeted disinformation relates to choosing to use carbon-based fuels. Beginning in the 1980s, Exxon funded a propaganda campaign to sow doubt in the public's minds about climate-change projections. This action contradicted its own internal research completed in the 1970s, which confirmed the correctness of those projections. Exxon, in fact, used that data to plan how they would profit from climate change as the change progressed. Yet Exxon withheld their findings and actions from the public. Instead, it fostered doubt about climate-change concerns. Full disclosure would reasonably have affected the public's use of their products and governmental subsidization of the fossil fuel industry, plus government support for various industry-related foreign policy matters. See the five-part series, *Exxon: The Road Not Taken*, reported using internal Exxon documents (Banerjee and Song, 2015; Banerjee, Song, and Hasemyer, 2015; Banerjee, Song, and Hasemyer, 2015a; Cushman, Jr., 2015; Hasemyer and Cushman, Jr., 2015). Please note, however, that a Life Enabling enterprise's efforts to neutralize citizen-targeted disinformation *would never align* itself with current efforts at censorship that are being promulgated by mainstream media, some social media outlets, and members of the U.S. Congress. First, the inconsistent behavior of these entities suggests strongly that they are involved in a propaganda endeavor and not a genuine effort to eliminate disinformation (Greenwald, 2021, 2021a, 2021b). Second, they seek to remove access to information *they deem* harmful. A Life Enabling enterprise's approach never denies people access to information. Rather, it equips people to evaluate information objectively for themselves based on their frames of reference, thereby enabling them to make their own judgments and choices rather than have them made for them.

applies to developing and sustaining an effective organization.

Constructive and satisfying human relationships require mutual respect, empathy, honesty, and fairness. Such relationships alone intensify and sustain people's cooperative inclinations and satisfy their desire for affinity. All relationships within the commercial organization itself and between it and all its partners in commerce must embody these necessary interpersonal qualities.

Exhibit 5. Factors Determining the Outcome of Human Performance

Person
- Competencies
- Capacity
- Motivation
  - Effort applied
  - Sustainment
- Self-efficacy
  - Accuracy
  - Positive/Negative
- Distraction

Work Process
- Effectiveness
- Documentation
  - Complete
  - Correct
  - Understandable for average performer
  - Inclusive of "think" and "do" steps
  - Contains metrics and a method for gauging progress and results
  - Available to performer

Work Setting
- Resources
- Coordination
- Expectations/Feedback
- Incentives

Factors Determining the Outcome of Human Performance: A More Detailed Look

As stated earlier, the Life Enabling model adopts Gilbert's (1996) definition of human performance as including both one's behavior and the results one produces. The model also builds on Gilbert's list of the factors that generate the outcome of human performance. Using Deming's observations of failed outcomes in a work context, we expanded Gilbert's factors and organized them into three groups: the Person, the Work Process implemented, and the Work Setting within which work was done.

Below, we describe in detail each group and the factors of performance within it. Exhibit 5 summarizes this description. For an example of how this construction of the factors that determine the outcome of human performance is applied to uncovering the reasons an observed outcome occurred, see Vitalo (2022).[8]

Person – This group of factors relates to the makeup of the person who performs the process used to produce a specified outcome. Factors within this group include the performer's competence, capacity, motivation, self-efficacy, and freedom from distraction. Competence refers to the person's possession of the knowledge and skills needed to perform the process correctly at the level of proficiency required for success. It also includes one's demonstration of those "other personal characteristics" needed for success. These are sometimes referred to as *traits*. One example is "cooperativeness," especially if the task being done requires multiple people coordinating their efforts. Capacity refers to the

[8] The article is available at https://www.vitalentusa.com/learn/cause_analysis_failure.php.

person's capability to handle the physical, emotional-interpersonal, and intellectual demands of the work. Physically, does the person possess the strength, endurance, flexibility, or other physical fitness qualities needed to do the work? With regard to the emotional-interpersonal sphere, is the person able to sustain the number and complexity of relationships required to coordinate the work as expected? Intellectually, can he or she manage the multitasking or concurrent processing demands of the process being implemented? Motivation refers to both the level of effort a person applies to a given task and the sustainment of that effort until his or her work is completed. Self-efficacy refers to the accuracy and valence of the performer's judgment about his or her abilities. Freedom from distraction means absence of any factor that interferes with one's ability to apply themselves to a task (e.g., worry about a sick loved one).

Work Process – This group of factors refers to characteristics of the process used to produce an outcome. The method used, by its design, may not be effective. That is, even if one implemented it exactly as prescribed, the process used might not be able to produce the result the performer is expected to produce. If the process *is* effective, it may or may not be documented. Without documentation, what does a performer use to ensure he or she is doing the process correctly? Even if a method is documented, that documentation may not be complete, correct, current, understandable by the average performer, or available to him or her. It should contain both "do" and "think" steps. "Do" steps tell you what action to take. "Think" steps tell you how you can check to see if you are doing that action correctly and how to avoid doing it incorrectly. The documentation also should contain metrics and guidance for gauging progress and results. Absent such metrics and guidance, the performer is left guessing about how he or she is progressing and whether he or she got the desired results.

Work Setting – This third group of factors relates to the context within which a performer completes his or her work. Four types of work setting issues affect the outcome of human performance. These are (1) resources, (2) coordination, (3) expectations/feedback, and (4) incentives.

Resource issues include the workspace, machines and tools, raw materials, supervision and other performance-support aids, and all other wherewithal a person needs to accomplish a task as prescribed. The adequacy of these resources affects a worker's success in implementing a process. Moreover, the availability and effectiveness of coaching from an expert or other performance support resources may affect the outcome of a person's performance.

Coordination addresses the impact on success that others have whose work affects the success of the performer. Coordination issues include the adequacy of execution by others of interrelated tasks (timeliness, correctness, consistency) and the alignment of perspectives of the people who direct (not support) task performance. If multiple decision makers direct a worker in conflicting ways, no performer can succeed.

Expectations/Feedback issues address the adequacy of information about what a performer is expected to do and produce and how he or she is doing in satisfying those expectations. Expectations/Feedback issues include the completeness of assignment information provided to the performer (e.g., task, objective, product, process, schedule, performance criteria that the worker must satisfy) and the adequacy of the achievement information provided (e.g., feedback on both approach and results, correctness of feedback, timeliness of feedback).

Incentives issues affect one's motivation to do work. Items in this category address the following questions: Do the incentives offered have motivational value from the performer's perspective?[9] Does the setting consistently recognize and reward good performance as promised? Is poor performance pointed out, and are consequences forthcoming if it is not corrected? Are poor performers sometimes rewarded? Are rewards and consequences aligned with the organization's established performance expectations?

Whether an individual undertakes commerce alone or cooperatively, that person's execution and outcome will be an interactive consequence of the adequacy of the three groups of factors described above.

The Commercial Context Required by the Life Enabling Model

The Life Enabling model makes no assumptions about the current state of the commercial context. Its status is purely an empirical question that each enterprise must assess. The model does have requirements that the commercial context must satisfy for its dynamics to operate correctly. These requirements are as follows:

1. People have the right of ownership to whatever resources they acquire or generate.
2. People have the political freedom to choose whether or not to enter into commerce.
3. Prospective buyers have a correct understanding of their real needs.
4. Prospective buyers use information- or knowledge-based decision-making methods to select the best offering available to them based on their value-relevant features.

---

[9] For example, extrinsically motivated people will find inducements of pay, awards, and other positive or negative consequences motivating, but intrinsically motivated people will not. They find factual information about their progress and results energizing. Material rewards are meaningful only when they are under the performer's control. That is, the reward is directly generated by their own performance. In contrast, they respond negatively to motivators that are controlled externally (Cerasoli, Nicklin, and Ford, 2014; Deci, Koestner, and Ryan, 1999).

5. Prospective buyers have access to complete and valid information about each offering.
6. Prospective buyers assess the value delivered by their choices and use that assessment to elevate their own decision-making effectiveness.
7. Prospective buyers must be able to make choices based on their personal preferences unaffected by artificial impediments.
8. Prospective buyers must be effective decision makers.
9. Third-party adjudications of disputes use evidence-based, unbiased, information- or knowledge-based methods and be easily accessible.
10. The marketplace is free of artificial barriers to competition,[10] as evidenced by:
    - the absence of coordination among producers;[11]
    - the absence of conditions created by law, regulation, or the exercise of economic power that preferentially benefit one or a subset of producers, hinder market entry by new producers, or hinder the transfer by customers from one producer to another;
    - the absence of conditions created by law, regulation, or the exercise of economic power that restrict the actions of producers in ways that compromise any of the other necessary features of the commercial context; and
    - the presence of the unrestricted right of buyers to seek redress for harm resulting from a producer's offering, the buying–benefiting experience a producer provides, or for failure to follow-through on any commitment the producer makes to the buyer.

Why Are These Conditions Necessary?

The Life Enabling model views the function of commerce as serving people's growth and emergence both individually and collectively. For commerce to

---

[10] An artificial barrier to competition is one constructed to prevent individuals qualified by their capabilities from undertaking commerce within a market or to prohibit an action that might result in the dilution of control by the producers who currently service that market. It may be expressed through protectionist tariffs, the use of influence to deny another entrepreneur access to credit he or she would otherwise qualify for, legislation that provides special advantages to one or more current producers (e.g., extending patent rights on pharmaceuticals, thereby impeding the introduction of cheaper, generic versions of the drugs), or any of a very wide range of activities.

[11] Coordination among producers refers to an action by a group of firms that is intended to improve their profits by aligning their reactions to each other's business decisions. One example might be producers in an industry agreeing to uniformly raise prices, not based on each firm's own capabilities or circumstances but in response to a price rise announced by one producer. Coordination among producers may include tacit or expressed collusion, which may or may not be lawful. It always disadvantages the buyer by limiting competition among sellers and raising prices.

realize this function, people must be free to choose whether or not to engage in it. They need to be able to own the resources they acquire or create. Ownership allows people to use, shape, and otherwise process their resources as best they can so that they express the intent and capabilities of the producer. Thus, people can decide what resource(s) they will work with, who they will serve, what they will offer, and all the myriad other decisions commerce entails. People can select for themselves those avenues of activity that seem to best advance their personal emergence while providing benefit to others. With the feedback they receive from the people they serve, they can hone their capabilities and sharpen their definition of what they seek to produce and provide to others. With the feedback they obtain from their decisions and actions, they can advance their emergence as unique individuals.

Similarly, buyers' freedom of choice requires that every market be served by multiple producers, each attempting to address the buyers' needs. To make valid selections, buyers must understand their real needs. They must use information- or knowledge-based methods to select the best offering available to them based on their value-relevant features. This requires that they have access to all the information relevant to their decision making. It also requires that they be free from pressures and other hindrances that compromise effective decision making.

Once the product or service is acquired, buyers must assess the value delivered by their choices and use the learning from that assessment to elevate their decision-making proficiency. They also must seek redress for any harm they experience from producers, as that is valuable feedback that producers need to improve their performance. For this to occur, third-party adjudication of claims of harm must be evidence based, unbiased, and use information- or knowledge-based methods.

For markets to support Life Enabling commerce, they must satisfy certain additional requirements. Specifically, they must be free of artificial barriers to competition. This includes the absence of coordination among producers and any elements that preferentially benefit one or a subset of producers, hinder market entry by new producers, or hinder the transfer by customers from one producer to another. Each marketplace must be free of any conditions that restrict the actions of producers in ways that compromise any of the model's required features of the commercial context.

When these commercial context requirements are not satisfied, neither buyers nor sellers can fully learn and thereby advance their personal emergence and provide the social benefit their commerce seeks to deliver.

Since the Life Enabling model does not assume that any commercial context satisfies the conditions necessary for its use, it incorporates guidance for assessing the presence of these conditions. This assessment provides potential producers the information they need to decide whether to enter that market using the Life Enabling approach to commerce (see *Chapter 8*). If one chooses to enter a marketplace lacking one or more of the required conditions, he or she assumes responsibility for correcting those deficiencies, since, without correction, that person's effort to implement Life Enabling commerce will fail. The model also includes guidance on accomplishing these corrective efforts.

To What Degree Must These Conditions Be Met?

Initially, a marketplace's compliance with the model's commercial context requirements must be sufficient to allow a Life Enabling entrepreneur to establish his or her enterprise's presence in that marketplace. If an enterprise can sustain its operation, it can work progressively to expand the marketplace's satisfaction of the model's full requirements. However, as a Life Enabling entrepreneur, you can only expand a market's freedom from within if you can initially compete through excellence with sufficient success to sustain your commerce. Ultimately, the marketplace must fully comply with the model's commercial context requirements for your enterprise to thrive and fully deliver its benefits.

The "Realisticness" of the Life Enabling Model's Assumptions

Goodwin (1991) introduced the requirement that the "realisticness" of an economic model's assumptions needs to be established. The term "realisticness" refers to whether the assumptions made by a given theory map to the empirically established facts of the state they describe. If they do not, that failure would falsify the model's assumptions and the theory derived from them.

At this point, you have learned the assumptions underlying the Life Enabling Model. *Chapter 6* explores the scientific basis for judging whether the model's assumptions map to the findings of science. It provides you the resource you need to make an evidence-based judgment about the model's assumptions. The remaining sections of this book explain how commerce conducted by people who possess the qualities defined in the model's assumptions unfolds and provides practical guidance for implementing the Life Enabling approach to commerce.

If mainstream news media shapes your view of humankind, you will find it difficult to imagine that there is any mapping between the facts of human nature and the assumptions made by the Life Enabling model. Yearly, for example, the news is full of reports about killings at schools in the United States which, in 2025, totaled 233. International news regularly reports on the dire straits of victims of armed conflicts being fought around the globe. In the economic arena, there are regular reports of the U.S. imposing punitive tariffs and sanctions against other countries that fail to comply with its will and threatening the annexation of countries it deems important to its purposes. And, beginning in 2023, before our very eyes, our nation joined with Israel to pursue the genocide of an entire people, the Palestinians, and the destruction of Middle East nations and their peoples in order to realize their aims of hegemony over their collective resources. In times like these, science, as a method for discerning and balancing facts, becomes critical to testing our impressions. In this chapter, we will review the science concerning human nature. Its findings stand in stark contrast to the impression of humanity conveyed by the actions of leaders of nations controlled by capitalists.

Chapter 6

Science Determines a Model's Realisticness

The Life Enabling model has a much lower bar to hurdle to establish the realisticness of its assumptions than, for example, Capitalism. Unlike Capitalism, the model does *not* claim that its assumptions about human nature apply to the current state of *all* people. While the model posits that, at the beginning of life, people share a common set of features and native dispositions that have evolved over time, it makes clear that these features are not fixed in their expression. Thus, if the model's posited features of human nature map to even a subset of adults, then its assumptions and the principles of commerce derived from them should be judged as realistic with regard to that subset of humanity. As you will see, the empirical evidence suggests that the model's assumptions about human nature are evidenced by far more than a small subset of people.

An exhaustive exploration of scientific findings relevant to judging the realisticness of the Life Enabling model's assumptions would take one into many different fields of science. These sciences include anthropology, archaeology, biology, psychology, sociology, sociobiology, management science, organizational effectiveness, and behavioral economics, among others. Such an undertaking is outside the scope of this book. It would require a volume of its own. Nevertheless, we can address, to a sufficient extent, the issue of the model's realisticness. Additionally, we invite empirical scientists to systematically evaluate the Life Enabling model's assumptions and report their findings. We firmly accept that the model has no practical utility if its assumptions are invalid. If one or another assumption is invalid, the model must be made consistent with that fact by eliminating the contents derived from the invalidated assumptions or be dismissed as a useful commercial model.

The Essence of the Model's Assumptions About the Nature of People

The model assumes that people possess features that are common to all but are developed differently in each person (sameness and differentness). While our foundational nature is the same, people develop their shared nature in progressively distinctive ways as they discover and act on their personal preferences, strengths, and interests and adapt to their specific circumstances. This process of individuation does not alter one's fundamental nature; it simply allows it to flower in different ways.

The model further asserts that humankind is both social and personal by nature (Exhibit 1, next page). These two qualities are the primary sources of human motivation.

Humankind's social orientation expresses itself in people's other-regarding nature and their desire to be connected with others in mutually benefiting relationships. These relationships are essential to each person's growth and development and his or her realization of well-being and fulfillment. People's relationships with others exhibit cooperation, sharing, altruism, and caring. They extend beyond kin to people unrelated to us by blood or marriage. These qualities of relating, despite being initial defaults in one's conduct toward others, become conditional for most of us when we experience others who are exploitive or harmful to us.

Exhibit 1. Salient Features of the Life Enabling Model's Assumptions About People

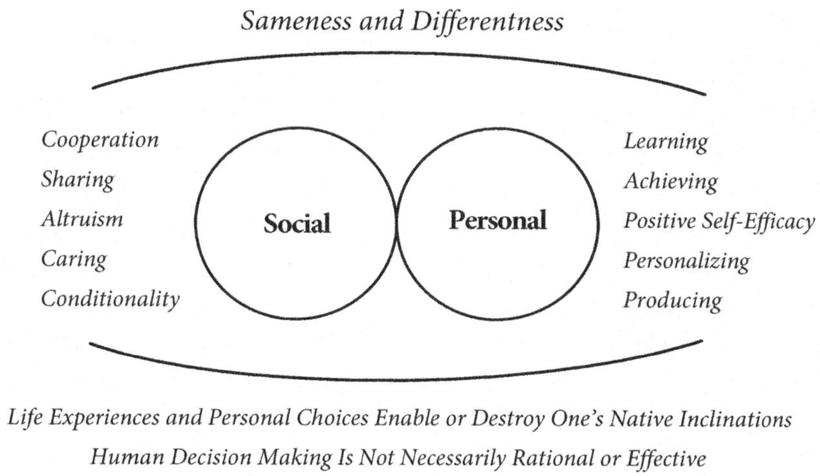

People's personal orientation is expressed in their progressive individuation and striving for personal emergence. This process is enabled by our inherent striving to learn, master new skills, and produce results. Our learning clarifies for us our personal likes and dislikes, our talents and enjoyments, and what we most value. As this process of living and learning unfolds, our unique personalities emerge. We sharpen our unique profiles of interest, values, concerns, goals, and preferences. As we act on what we learn, we delineate ever more clearly who we are as persons and progressively solidify our character and identity. Our achievements of mastery strengthen our sense of positive self-efficacy. The products we create and share with others become expressions of our unique identity and offerings that form the substance of our life-enabling commerce with others.

As this last sentence suggests, the two core drives within us are complementary and mutually enabling. They are not antagonistic. Each is necessary for the other to thrive. Without social connectedness, an individual cannot realize his or her fullest capabilities, as the social dimension is the source of our nurturance and learning. It also provides the stimulation that promotes the individual's physical, emotional, and intellectual development. It enriches our personal experiences and provides us a sense of completion. On the other hand, without the emerging individual, a social unit cannot grow either in membership or in the discovery of new ways to benefit each other and live within the world in a manner that fully develops the human species while enriching the ecosystem that sustains it.

Our dual social and personal strivings, however, are not immutable. Life experiences and our personal choices may enable, hinder, block, or replace our foundational nature with other patterns of motives and inclinations.

The model views free choice (free will) as a potential feature people can develop. Its emergence, however, is not a given. The model defines free choice as the election of an object, goal, or course of action that expresses the person's preferences *unaffected by artificial impediments.*

The model also views effective choice making as a potential feature people can develop. Its emergence is also not a given. It defines effective decision making by the process the person uses to make a decision and by the outcome that decision produces. Effective decision making uses either information- or knowledge-based methods that are goal driven and evidence based. As to the outcome, effective decisions elect alternatives that enable the decision maker's success in ways that satisfy his or her values.

Assessing the Assumption of Sameness and Differentness

The first assumption of the model—sameness and differentness—is axiomatic. It is the fundamental assumption of every science that generalizations can be made about the objects it investigates, including human beings. All the generalizations science makes about a class of objects (e.g., humankind) apply universally to class members (e.g., requirements for oxygen, nutrition, excretion of waste products, etc.). Hence, all science implicitly accepts the assumption of "sameness."

No generalizations about physical objects, however, are without qualification or variations in expression. For example, every aspect of a human being—anatomy, physiology, personality, individual behavior, and social relating—displays variation in its expression when its structure and function are measured across humans. That distribution has both a central tendency that represents our commonality and variation in its expression, which represents our differentness one from another.

There also is empirical support for the Life Enabling model's expectation that human nature is *not* fixed across adult humankind. Ironically, the support comes from research into Capitalism's assumption about the universally selfish nature of people. That premise asserts that people act solely to maximize the satisfaction of their individual self-interests. A great number of studies using game theory scenarios have investigated the validity of this premise. The overwhelming finding is that *some people do act* from the basis Capitalism specifies, but as many and usually slightly more people act from a basis that considers the welfare of the other party, not just oneself. The research related to this issue is discussed in detail later in this chapter. Suffice it to say that, at this point, the firmly established research finding is emphatically that people are motivationally and behaviorally heterogeneous.

Assessing the Assumption That Humans Are Social Beings

The Life Enabling model's assumption about the social nature of people fundamentally differentiates it from Capitalism. In Capitalism, with its emphasis on radical individualism, the impetus for and end of commerce are exclusive of concern for others. Independent, equally knowledgeable and powerful actors contend to maximally satisfy their respective self-interests. Their interactions are resolved through negotiation that yields exchanges that each finds acceptable but not ideal. While the summative effect of these exchanges is expected to produce societal benefits, each actor behaves selfishly. In contrast, the Life Enabling model assumes that people's inherently social nature leads them to act with regard for others, not just themselves. Hence, the model's assumption about the social nature of people is pivotal to its realisticness. For that reason, we will address this assumption in some detail, even though the construct is undisputed across many sciences, including anthropology, archaeology, biology, psychology, and sociology. The evidence we will review concerning the social nature of people is drawn from basic observations about human conduct and the discoveries of life sciences.

Human Behavior Demonstrates That Humans Are Social Beings

To appreciate the realisticness of human sociality, one only needs to review some observational facts. Such facts are, after all, the basis for all science.

Observable Facts That Support People's Social Nature

- Humans almost always live in groups, and when they leave a group, they almost always develop a new group or associate with other existing groups.

- Human communities encompass mostly unrelated others. People work in organizations, associate with others in formal and informal organizations, and purposefully seek out personal companionship. Almost all of these relationships are with unrelated others.
- Humans reproduce sexually, not asexually. They procreate by pairing.[1] Each person, therefore, is the product of a human relationship.
- Human offspring are atricial at birth. They are immature and helpless. They are incapable of caring for themselves and require a long developmental period before they are able to survive on their own. Each person's life is initially secured only through the caring of others.
- The human child's long developmental period requires that adults divert their energies from ensuring their personal survival to invest them in protecting, nurturing, instructing, and guiding their child's development. This transfer of benefit from self to another diminishes the survival chances of the adult.
- Human generations overlap and cooperate in the caring of their young.
- Human relationships are not solely task based. They have an *affective* component which, when positive, creates a strong sense of connection and, at the highest level, intimacy. This connectedness is amply demonstrated when a relationship is interrupted by a death. That loss results in the survivor's expressions of pain, grief, and mourning. People also experience loss when they merely separate locationally from someone with whom they have affiliative bonds.
- Human survival and development are enhanced through social learning. People acquire fitness-improving tools and skills through modeling and instruction. These resources enable them to solve survival-threatening problems more quickly and with less risk of harm than by self-implemented trial-and-error learning.

While observations are not proof, the behaviors they record require that any assertions about the nature of people must be capable of explaining them. As you will see, the suggestion that human sociality is an epiphenomenon cloaking people's basic egoistic drive to survive and satisfy their individual self-interests is not supported by the empirical findings of science.

---

[1] Even artificial insemination requires the contribution of two parties. And while single parenthood has risen in developed nations, the incidence worldwide in 2017 was 17% (The Spaced-Out Scientist, 2017). And, even in these circumstances, parenting occurs and the parent's extended family often assists in child rearing.

Evolutionary Science Accepts That Humans Are Social Beings

The phenomenon of human sociality is fully accepted within evolutionary biology. The judgment is that the human species is a "social animal" (Sociality, 2020) with the eminent sociobiologist E. O. Wilson arguing that it possesses the highest level of sociality, eusociality (Wilson and Hölldobler, 2005). The only issue that remains hotly debated within the context of evolutionary theory is how our social nature evolved. This is because evolutionary theory *assumes* that the original state of all living beings was solitary, with each individual organism operating independently, each propelled by the egoistic drive to survive. Indeed, most people associate evolutionary theory with the concept of the *survival of the fittest,* wherein individual organisms compete for survival against each other and against other fitness challenges (e.g., limited food supply). The genetic material of the individual who survives longest and, presumably, propagates the most (Darwinian fitness) passes forward to subsequent generations those features that enabled its superior survival. The individual's greater procreation through its longer survival cascades forward. The feature that enabled its better survival becomes progressively more prevalent in the species, assuming that its superior survival advantage sustains.

This image of evolutionary theory has been greatly complicated over the past century, as it has embraced the observed fact that a large number of species along the evolutionary ladder evidence other-regarding qualities. As Melis and Semmann (2010) stated, "Even very simple organisms such as viruses, bacteria and social amoebas [dictyostelid] cooperate with each other. Solitary amoebas for example form a multicellular differentiated 'slug' when they are starving, which is able to pass through soil barriers that [a] solitary amoeba cannot cross" (p. 2,663). Rutherford and Bassler (2012) described how bacteria coordinate among themselves to modulate gene expression in order to shape their behavior in a way that maximizes their virulence while conserving their energy resources.

Over the last 60 years, three main hypotheses have been proposed to explain how sociality could have evolved given the notion of each organism as a selfish actor. These are kin selection (Hamilton, 1964, 1964a), reciprocal altruism (Trivers, 1971), and group selection (Goodnight and Stevens, 1997; Wade, 1977).[2]

Both kin selection theory and Trivers' extension of it have problems. Kin selection theory has encountered a number of challenges (Alonzo, 1998; Milius, 1998; Nowak, Tarnita, and Wilson, 2010; Wilson and Hölldobler, 2005). For one, its projection of greater numbers of progeny for individuals who are altruistic toward

---

[2] A fourth theory, multilevel selection, incorporates both individual and group selection, with individual fitness operating as the focus of selection within a group and group fitness operating between groups.

their kin is based on a since-superseded understanding of how traits are passed forward between generations.[3] Trivers' reciprocal altruism hypothesis assumes that humans' other-regarding behavior emerged because it produces a reciprocal and benefiting response from other humans at a later time. The hypothesis found early confirmation in simulations and small network experiments. However, it failed when the networks of actors grew even by small numbers (Boyd and Richerson, 1988). Also, it cannot explain the phenomenon of people expressing altruistic behavior toward others they *neither know nor will have any further relationship with* (Fehr, Fishbacher, and Gächter, 2002).[4]

From our point of view, how sociality emerged in the human species or whether it has always been present has no importance. From a naive perspective, one would imagine it emerged from whatever point the human species began paired reproduction and cooperative child rearing. If pair-bonded reproduction and cooperative child rearing have always been a feature of humankind, then so has sociality. The fact that it is present and that it is a recognized feature of the human species is what is important. This acceptance supports the Life Enabling model's assumption about the social nature of people.

The Benefits of Human Sociality

From the perspective of evolutionary theory, new traits remain *only when they provide a fitness advantage*. That means that the new trait enhances survival and propagation. The exploration of the role of sociality in human evolution has uncovered important ways it contributes to the human species' evolutionary fitness. These contributions address its role in brain development, human evolvability, and science. Understanding these benefits strengthens one's appreciation of the fitness-enhancing power of sociality in humans.

[3] Hamilton's model assumes a "one trait, one gene" relationship and transmission according to pure Mendelian laws. The notion of one trait, one gene is false (Bethell, 2001; Greenwood, 2018). Almost every expressed trait is the result of multiple genes in interaction with each other and with epigenetic factors. Even something as simple as eye color is now believed to be the result of the interaction between 61 discrete genomic regions (Simcoe, Valdes, Liu, Furlotte, et al., 2021). Also, contrary to Mendel's fixed probability of gene transmission from parent to child, the probability of transmission of specific genes from parent to child is uncertain. Genes are spread across the genome. The likelihood that a gene will be selected during meiosis depends on its location within the genome. Genes—even those that operate together to express a single trait—therefore have different likelihoods of being selected to pass forward, making it uncertain whether the entire set of genes needed to produce a trait's expression will be selected. The dynamic of differential selection based on location is just one of many factors affecting gene selection and the calculation of the probability of trait transmission and expression from parent to progeny. All of the transmission-affecting dynamics operate independent of the utility of a given phylogenetic trait. Adding to the complexity of projecting transmission rates, traits sometimes emerge in an offspring that are very different from those possessed by either parent and *not as a result of mutation*. Some of the dynamics affecting what genetic material passes are epigenetic inheritance, gene transposition, intragenomic conflict, and recombination, among others.

[4] As research reviewed later in this chapter will make clear, every other effort to explain other-regarding behavior as fundamentally motivated by self-regarding interests has also failed.

Brain Development

Dunbar (1998) demonstrated that the significant development of the neocortex in humans versus other primates is best explained by the species' advanced social development. The neocortex is the area of the mammalian brain involved in higher-order mental processes (e.g., analysis, planning, inferencing, and social relations). These capabilities contribute greatly to increasing the fitness of humankind.

The neocortex is the newest part of the cerebral cortex to evolve. In humans, 90% of the cerebral cortex and 76% of the entire brain is neocortex. The problem with this development from an evolutionary perspective is the heavy cost to the organism's fitness that such brain development imposes. As Dunbar (1998) noted, "The adult human brain weighs about 2% of body weight but consumes about 20% of total energy intake" (1998, p. 178). Given the heavy cost of maintaining a large brain, "it is intrinsically unlikely that large brains will evolve merely because they can. Large brains will evolve only when the selection factor in their favor [i.e., fitness advantage] is sufficient to overcome the steep cost gradient" such development incurs (Dunbar, 1998, p. 179).

Dunbar stepped through the four answers to this question that scientists have proposed. These are the epiphenomenal, developmental, ecological, and social solutions. The first (epiphenomenal) asserts that brain size increase is a simple expression of body size increase. Its emergence has no other reason. The second (developmental) suggests that brain size growth in any species is a function of the energy richness of that species' diet. A richer diet makes the growth in brain size a "no cost" situation. These two hypotheses are easily discounted. The first fails to satisfy the rule of natural selection—nothing that has a fitness cost sustains unless it has a net fitness-enhancing value. The second is not supported by studies of dietary richness across taxa (groups of animals classified as a unit) and brain development. There is no relationship between the richness of a species' diet and its brain size.

The third hypothesis (ecological) asserts that species that forage or must survive by processing a larger, more complex ecological area are advantaged by added brain growth, and that advantage (improved food gathering ability) is the offsetting benefit of its cost. The fourth hypothesis (social) is that the increase in the sociality of a species results in more complex social contexts that present greater information-processing demands as the number of relationships increases. A species that lives singularly has but one relationship to process—i.e., with oneself. As the number of social relationships increases, the complexity of managing social contacts grows exponentially. According to this hypothesis, the enhanced individual and group fitness benefits of sociality offset the cost of the added brain development required to process all these social connections.

Dunbar tested the power of each of the two viable hypotheses (ecological and social) in predicting neocortical brain size among various anthropoid primates. He used several measures of the ecological hypothesis (e.g., ranging area—the space moved across and used for survival purposes) and of the social hypothesis (e.g., social group size). "Neocortex size, however measured, does not correlate with any index of the ecological hypothesis, but does correlate with social group size" (p. 181). Moreover, Dunbar reported that the findings have been confirmed by the research of Barton and Purvis. Further, he reported that this "relationship has now been shown to hold for at least four other mammalian orders: bats, carnivores and insectivores, and odontocete cetaceans" (1998, p. 183).

Dunbar and Schultz (2017) updated Dunbar's original explanation of the relationship between brain size and neocortical development. In doing so, they corrected some misunderstandings of Dunbar's prior work and stepped once more through the multiple alternative explanations that have been proposed. First, they clarified that the proper understanding of the social brain hypothesis is that brain development was selectively preferred because it enabled the creation of "functional, cohesive, bonded social groups as a means of solving an ecological problem" (2017, p. 5). The proper understanding of this event is as "an explicitly two-step process: an ecological problem is solved socially (i.e. as a cooperative process) and a big brain is needed to allow the requisite level of sociality to do this" (2017, p. 5). In other words, the fitness advantage of cooperative processing becomes the selective pressure for brain development. Second, the enhanced fitness benefits of cooperation apply to the individual, not just to the group. Thus, the emergence of increased neocortical capabilities is not viewed as an instance of group selection. The individual's fitness is also advantaged by the capabilities that a larger neocortex provides. Third, the relationship between brain development and sociality is not simply about group size. Dunbar and Schultz (2017) stated, "the quantitative relationship between brain size and group size does not apply outside the anthropoid primates" (p. 6). Also, they clarified that group size is simply one "emergent property of the animals' abilities to maintain and coordinate social relationships" (p. 6). In all other mammals and birds, the key relationship is between brain size development and the presence in the species of pair-bonded versus polygynous sexual mating relationships. The facilitation of pair bonding by increased brain size provides "a unitary explanation for brain evolution across all mammals and birds" (ibid.).

After making these clarifications, the authors evaluated again each alternative explanation for brain size development in terms of its ability to explain six observations: (1) that primates have larger brains than other animals, (2) that there is quantitative variation in primate brain size, (3) that brain size correlates with group size in primates, (4) that primate sociality is complex (bonded), (5) that pair-bonded non-primates have large brains, and (6) that some primates are more technically innovative. Based on empirical findings, only the Social Brain Hypothesis provides an explanation for all six.

The Fitness Benefits of Neocortex Development

The area of the brain whose development sociality appears to have promoted enables people to manipulate information, not simply to remember it. Thus, humans demonstrate the capability for interpretation of emotional cues, tailored exchange of information within dyads (triads, quadriads, etc.), definition of roles, coordination of complex activities with others, the development of complex language systems, and the interpretation of metaphor, among other higher-order cognitive behaviors. These added intellectual capabilities have additional utility in enabling humans to survive and prosper by cognitively generating adaptations to environmental pressures (tools, knowledge, skills) both individually and collaboratively. These capabilities provide a whole new facet for enhancing the fitness of the species and its members. This suggests the possibility that *the advanced development of sociality has generated both direct and indirect fitness benefits*. The direct benefit is the advantage collective performance has over individual performance in solving complex problems like survival in a changing world. The indirect benefits are mediated by the development of the neocortex. Its enhanced development enabled the emergence of cognitively generated fitness enhancements (tools, knowledge) and new methods for propagating forward fitness-improvement capabilities (training). Training enables one generation to pass forward survival-enhancing solutions to the next. Each member and the species as a whole benefit from these learned fitness-improving capabilities. This forward propagation of learned fitness-enhancing improvements through cultural transmission elevates the human species' evolvability.

Evolvability

Evolvability is the capacity of a genome to generate adaptive solutions to selective pressures.[5] This biological capability enhances a species' survivability and represents, as a phenotypic feature, a selective trait from an evolutionary

[5] Selective pressures refer to factors that challenge an organism's survival—e.g., reduced food supply, climate change, population density, emergence of a new predator, or other life-challenging problems.

perspective. The higher-order mental capabilities provided by neocortical development add a new, non-biological way to elevate human evolvability. These mental capabilities generate fitness-benefiting knowledge, skills, and tools and other cultural memes with survival-enhancing value that people can pass forward to subsequent generations.

These cognitively generated, fitness-enhancing solutions are passed forward in two ways. The first method is through teaching/learning from generation to generation. Each group's future members' ability to survive and thrive is enhanced by acquiring previously developed solutions through modeling and instruction. Learning from others augments one's innate skill set (instincts) and accelerates an individual's survival proficiency more than trial-and-error learning (van Schaik and Burkart, 2011). The social nature of the human species creates a context that enables this teaching/learning. Parents and other adults within a social network instruct through modeling behaviors and through behavioral shaping (differential reinforcement). This conclusion is supported by the work of Bandura (1977), van Schaik (2006), and van Schaik and Burkhart (2011).

The second method for passing forward learned solutions is through natural selection itself. Survival-enhancing solutions that are culturally passed forward over a sufficient period of time can have *indirect* genetic effects. The explanatory mechanism is termed the Baldwin effect. It was introduced by James Mark Baldwin, a psychologist, in 1896. The principle states that an advantageous behavior, once it has appeared in a population, will *indirectly* reshape the genes of the species which has adopted it by generating a selective pressure for retaining mutant traits that facilitate its learning and use, assuming its utility sustains (Baldwin effect, 2018). Thus, for example, imagine that a tool was devised that was critical to survival and is passed down from generation to generation with sustaining survival value. Imagine further that the tool worked best for people who happened to have added thumb-index finger dexterity. The survival-enhancing value of that tool's use would become a selective pressure advantaging those who, by mutation, emerged with better thumb-index finger dexterity. In this way, culture itself becomes an *indirect* avenue for human evolution. In this way also, sociality's fitness-benefiting advantages (cognition and sharing) further elevate human evolvability and benefit both individuals and the group inclusively.

Science as an Advanced Expression of Human Sociality

Still another advantage of human sociality is the emergence of science itself. The recent commercialization of scientific endeavors under the model of Capitalism (Nelson, 2003; Shibayama, 2014) has blurred a basic fact—namely, science originally was a collegial endeavor to advance human knowledge, not a competitive endeavor seeking privatized economic gains. Historically, science as the systematic development of knowledge has been a cooperative endeavor of people sharing a common set of methods and rules for concluding what constitutes new knowledge. It was dominated by the Mertonian norms of universalism, communalism, disinterestedness, and skepticism (Mertonian norms, 2020).

Universalism refers to ensuring the validity of new findings. It is realized by the common use of the scientific method and the sharing of all data underpinning new discoveries. Thus, every reported finding can be assessed against the method used to generate it and confirmed through replication. *Communalism* refers to the open sharing of intellectual knowledge, the promotion of collaboration, and the rejection of secrecy. *Disinterestedness* refers to all parties in the scientific endeavor acting solely for the benefit of the common scientific enterprise, rather than for personal gain. *Skepticism* asserts that all claims of discovery should be exposed to critical scrutiny before being accepted.

In concert with these Mertonian norms, the benefits of new discoveries were publicized and used broadly within society. In essence, one might assert that the emergence of science as a cooperative knowledge-building effort represents another fitness-enhancing gain derived from the advanced sociality of humankind.

Is Human Sociality Real or Just Masked Self-Serving Behavior?

As mentioned earlier, the phenomenon of human sociality was initially in conflict with classical evolutionary thinking. One of the first approaches to explaining other-regarding behavior, such as altruism, was essentially to reinterpret it as self-serving. For example, the warning calls issued by a member of a species that alert others to danger appear to benefit others while endangering the caller. The caller's vocalizations signal its location to the approaching predator. As reported by Alonzo (1998),

> Charnov and Krebs (1975) suggested that this act may in fact favor the 'caller,' who would benefit from the confusion caused, thus increasing its chance of flight. Trivers (1971) attributed an advantage to the 'caller' because, by preventing the successful hunting of the predator, the former [the caller] would lower the frequency of the predator returning. (Alonzo, 1998, p. 1).

If these speculations were true, then one might infer that the other-regarding feature of human sociality was actually a self-serving behavior and simply a different expression of humankind's radical individualism. Milius (1998), however, described an exhaustive field study of ground squirrels by Paul W. Sherman of Cornell University to test whether sticking one's neck out to the benefit of other ground squirrels was self-serving. Sherman found that the calling did not advantage the caller. Milius reported: "He [Sherman] found no mobbing, ventriloquism, or pandemonium. No predators were startled or confused by the squeals and whistles." Even more pointedly, Sherman found that "[a]nimals who gave the alarm whistle raised their odds of being killed" (pp. 1–2). This, joined with the findings of behavioral research on humans that we will discuss below, demonstrates that at least some other-regarding behavior is about benefiting the "other" and not oneself.

Human Physiology Indicates That Humans Are Social Beings

The reality of humankind's social nature is further supported by our biological makeup, the effects of isolation on species members, and our methods of learning.

Biological Makeup and Sociality

Two examples of our biological makeup that appear designed to support sociality are mirror neurons and oxytocin. Both features of human physiology enable social relating and learning. Again, according to evolutionary theory, they would only have emerged and sustained if they offered some fitness advantage.

Mirror Neurons

Mirror neurons are neurons that fire "both when an animal acts and when the animal observes the same action performed by another" (Mirror neuron, 2018). These neurons enable one to internally experience the behavior of others as though the observer were performing it. Iacoboni (2009) stated, "Neural mirroring solves the 'problem of other minds' (how we can access and understand the minds of others) and makes intersubjectivity possible, thus facilitating social behavior" (2009, p. 653). Mirror neurons activate in an observer the same circuitry that is active in the person being observed. This creates a phenomenal state in the observer that mirrors the phenomenal state of the person being observed. In essence, it allows one person to share another person's inner experience.

Mirror neurons have been directly observed and studied in monkeys. In humans, a meta-analysis of magnetic resonance imaging (MRI) research has shown that "there are brain areas in humans that exhibit overlapping activation for observed and executed actions" (Molenberghs, Cunnington, and Mattingley, 2009, p. 976).

"The effect of mirror neurons on empathy has been shown in different studies" (Wudneh, Acharya, Ashraf, Krishnan, et al., 2016, p. 3). For example, research has found that the "same neural circuits that fire when a person is happy are also activated when we see someone is feeling happy" (2016, p. 3). Similar empathic findings have been found for witnessing pain. This phenomenon also supports *anticipating* another person's experience. The mirror neurons of observers who viewed people not currently in pain "also fired when noticing people who [the observer knew] would be painfully stimulated" (2016, p. 3).

The phenomenon of learning through observation is referred to as "social learning" (Bandura, 1977). Social learning is another function enabled by mirror neurons and another fitness-enhancing benefit of sociality. This ability to anticipate a future state based on observing another's experience enhances survival. It enables an individual to learn to avoid doing a harmful behavior without directly performing it.

Oxytocin

Oxytocin is a peptide hormone. It is a short chain of amino acid monomers that serve as signaling molecules that target distant organs to regulate physiology and behavior. Behaviorally, oxytocin has been found to trigger social bonding and empathy. Its presence is part of our evolved biological makeup. It suggests that people have an inborn orientation to connect and relate with each other in caring ways. Its effect on behavior, however, is not unconditional. Oxytocin's effect appears to be associated with the relational context in which it is expressed (Clark, Boothby, Clark-Polner, and Reis, 2015). "People who have reason to trust others seem to react to the administration of exogenous oxytocin with increased prosociality. But if the relational context is one of distrust, oxytocin's effect is reversed" (p. 341). That reversal may be expressed as unresponsiveness, mistrust, or hostile behavior depending on the circumstances that prevail between the parties.

We can draw two inferences from the oxytocin research. One is that we seem to have evolved a biological mechanism that supports us in connecting and sharing in positive ways with others. The second is that the expression of this inclination is modulated by our perception of who that other is and whether he or she is trustworthy and caring in return. Our affective response is positive if we experience the other as being positive and negative if otherwise. One might reasonably surmise from this fact that, in a relationship with another who seeks to gain advantage over us, we will react negatively. This should inform one's conceptualization of commerce, since it is an exchange between people. If that exchange is with another who is perceived to operate from a basis of egoistic self-interest, the transaction and its follow-ups should be negative. This surmise is supported by the research into the phenomenon of positive and negative reciprocity, which we will discuss later. It is also supported by the research of Dincer and Uslaner (2010), who found a positive relationship between trust and economic growth. Other research findings confirm this relationship (Beugelsdijk, de Groot, and van Schaik, 2004; Cardenas and Carpenter, 2008; Zak and Knack, 2001). The type of trust that facilitates growth is "'generalized trust' defined as trust between strangers" (Dincer and Uslaner, 2010, p. 59). Dincer and Uslaner concluded: "high trust regions [in the U.S.] achieve faster economic growth" (2010, p. 67).

Social Isolation and Immunological Resilience

The effect of social relating on people's biological well-being and development further reinforces the critical importance of sociality for humankind. Research has shown that social isolation predicts mortality and the incidence of disease in both the general population and individuals with established illnesses. For example, Kreibig, Whooley, and Gross (2014) found that socially isolated coronary heart disease patients "had a 50% greater risk of death than did nonisolated patients" (p. 659). This finding was made after adjustments for demographic and disease-relevant confounding variables.

In his editorial comment concerning the repeated findings that social isolation kills, House (2001) stated that the "deleterious effects on health of social isolation, first recognized in epidemiologic research of the late 1970s and 1980s[,] [has been] replicated and extended for more than a decade since then" (p. 273). From House's perspective, the real issue for science now is to uncover "how and why social isolation is risky for health—or conversely—how and why social ties and relationships are protective of health" (House, 2001, p. 273).

Karelina, Norman, Zhang, Morris, et al. (2009) used a mouse analog to study this question. Mice, living either isolated or in pairs, were subjected to an experimentally induced stroke. The study's results confirmed the deleterious effects of isolation. Mice living in the isolated condition experienced a significant decrease in their post-stroke survival rate. They also experienced greater tissue damage from the stroke and increased edema. The research's findings suggested that socially isolated mice evidenced an "altered neuroinflammatory response; specifically, central interleukin-6 (IL-6) signaling" (p. 5,895).

Liu and Wang (2005), also using a mouse analog, studied the survival rates of mice infected with liver cancer under two conditions—reared individually or in a group. They found that the survival time for the group-reared mice was significantly longer than that in the individually reared control group.

Using a pig analog, Tuchscherer, Kanitza, Puppea, Tuchschererb, et al. (2004) assessed the impact of postnatal social isolation on the hormonal and immune responses of pigs to an acute endotoxin challenge. Their results indicated that pigs that experienced repeated social isolation showed long-term effects on their bodies' ability to control inflammation at the periphery and in the brain following an immune challenge.

Human studies have found similar results. Pressman, Cohen, Miller, Barkin, et al. (2005) studied the antibody response to influenza immunization in healthy college freshmen. They related that response to the subjects' reported experience of loneliness. They found that

> [e]levated levels of loneliness throughout the semester and small social networks were independently associated with poorer antibody response to 1 component of the vaccine. Those students with both high levels of loneliness and a small social network had the lowest antibody response. Loneliness was also associated with greater psychological stress and negative affect, less positive affect, poorer sleep efficiency and quality, and elevations in circulating levels of cortisol. (Pressman, Cohen, Miller, Barkin, et al., 2005, p. 297).

Cole, Hawkley, Arevalo, and Cacioppo (2011) investigated gene expression as a possible mechanism for the impact of psychological states like loneliness on physiological well-being. Their study involved 93 chronically lonely people. Its purpose was to identify the specific immune cell types whose biological expression was affected by subjective social isolation. Previous studies had shown that alterations in the expression of these cells appear to place socially stressed individuals at increased risk for chronic inflammation-related illnesses. This study sought to clarify how and why social environments regulate immune function. Using genetic analysis, they found that "antigen-presenting cells appear to have evolved a transcriptional sensitivity to socioenvironmental conditions" (p. 3,080). The expression of these antigen-presenting cells was significantly different in people reporting chronic loneliness as compared to the normative expression recorded in the GEO GSE1133 Human Gene Atlas reference study.

How Does the Reality of Human Sociality Affect Commerce?

The social aspect of human nature is an accepted evolutionary fact that has advantaged both the species and its individual members. It has rendered the species fitter in a Darwinian sense and enabled the cooperative processing of life challenges. It has elevated each individual's ability to cognitively solve problems in living and accelerated the transfer of survival-enhancing tools and solutions between members of the same generation and from generation to generation.

Humankind's biology displays features that both enable sociality and benefit from it with respect to growth, development, health, and well-being. The nature of these social relationships appears to be overwhelmingly affiliative, not combative or competitive. Sussman, Garber, and Cheverud (2005) reviewed 81 observational studies of primate relating and found "the rates of agonistic behaviors are extremely low," being only 10% of the social activity observed. Also, it appears that the quality of our relationship with another interacts with our biology to provoke a negative response when we experience another as behaving negatively toward us.

Commerce is an instance of human sociality. Given the significance of sociality for humankind, *every theory of commerce must incorporate a correct understanding of what research has revealed about human sociality.* On its face, a model built on the premise of individualism (not individuality) appears to deny the findings of science regarding human sociality and threatens to undermine the benefits sociality has delivered to both individuals and our species. It does this by enforcing a perspective and proposing courses of action that pit one person against another. It promotes acting on the basis of one's self-interest alone. In denying the reality of human sociality, it promotes asociality, thereby advancing a manner of living that annihilates the fitness benefits human sociality delivers to each of us personally and collectively.

In contrast, a commercial model built on premises that recognize human sociality is aligned with the findings of life sciences. Such a commercial model will guide the development of commercial organizations in a way that enables connectedness among its members, fosters learning from others, and promotes the transfer of knowledge and tools across the organization. It will extend this understanding to its relations with its customers and all its stakeholders. It conceives commerce as an instance of cooperative processing wherein people work together to realize a common benefit that advances their collective and individual well-being.

Assessing Whether Cooperation and Sharing Are Default Behaviors but Their Continuance Is Conditional

Given that people are social beings, what is the behavioral evidence concerning their inclination to cooperate and share? As it turns out, the research investigating the presence of cooperation and sharing in humans is broad, deep, and consistent in its findings. It supports the following conclusions as descriptive of a substantial portion of humankind:

- People will cooperate with others—including strangers—even when noncooperation offers greater personal reward.

- People self-initiate reductions in benefits to themselves to provide benefits for another.
- People shape the benefit they provide another person even more favorably toward the other if the giver is aware of the other's added need.
- People will enforce fairness and equity in their relationships with others, even at a cost to themselves, if they have the opportunity to do so.
- People will act to protect themselves from others who attempt to exploit their cooperative and sharing natures by suspending those behaviors in situations where they lack the opportunity to correct the other's exploitive or harmful behavior.

Cooperation

We define cooperation as people working together to accomplish a purpose that benefits all contributors. Cooperation is an expression of human sociality. In this section, we review evidence of human cooperation from behavioral economists and psychologists. Ironically, much of that evidence derives from experimental studies designed to test the validity of Capitalism's assumptions about the atomistic and egoistic nature of people, where each person competes against all others to realize the maximum personal gain. As Dawes and Thaler stated:

> Much [mainstream] economic analysis—and virtually all game theory—starts with the assumption that people are both rational and selfish. For example, predictions that players will defect [betray their partner] in the prisoner's dilemma game and free ride [not contribute] in public goods environments are based on both assumptions. People are assumed to be clever enough to figure out that defection or free riding[6] is the dominant [most self-benefiting] strategy, and are assumed to care nothing for outcomes to other players. (Dawes and Thaler, 1988, p. 187)

While the research shows that some people do conform to these expectations, it also shows that just as many and, most often, more people act cooperatively to the mutual benefit of all parties. We will briefly review the findings from numerous studies exploring cooperation. Most of these studies use two different experimental paradigms—the prisoner's dilemma (PD) game and the public goods (PGs) game. Exhibit 2, next page, explains each of these games.

Prisoner's Dilemma (PD) Game Findings

The PD game pairs two people who make a choice that either benefits themselves alone or both parties together. Neither party knows the other nor

---

[6] Free riding refers to a person who elects to enjoy a benefit accruing from the collective efforts of others while contributing nothing to those efforts.

Exhibit 2. The Basic Prisoner's Dilemma and Public Goods Paradigms

Prisoner's Dilemma (PD)

In the PD game, two people are virtually "paired" as criminals who partnered in committing a crime. In the basic version of this game, neither subject has any direct knowledge of the other except that he or she exists and is being offered the same options. Each party is *separately* confronted with a set of choices and their consequences. The choices either benefit themselves alone or them and their "partners" together. Each party is offered two options: (a) betray the other by testifying that the other party committed the crime or (b) cooperate with the other by remaining silent. Once each player makes his or her choice, the game ends (termed the "one-off" version of the game). The following consequences of the possible choices participants make are made known to each participant *prior* to his or her decision:

- If both parties remain silent, then each gets one year in prison.
- If Party A and Party B each betray the other, then each of them serves two years in prison.
- If A betrays B *but* B remains silent, then A will be set free and B will serve three years, or vice versa.

People operating from the motive of self-interest should choose betrayal (termed "defection"). This choice promises the highest payoff while minimizing one's potential loss. People operating from the motive of cooperation should choose silence (termed "cooperation") (Prisoner's dilemma, 2018).

Public Goods (PGs)

The PGs game tests whether people will act cooperatively with others or selfishly with harm to others. The simplest scenario involves four to 10 subjects, each of whom has no knowledge of the others or what each decides. Each subject is given an endowment, say $10. Each participant may contribute any amount of the $10 or nothing to a common pot. Each person's contribution to the pot is deducted from his or her personal holdings. The total amount contributed by all players to the pot is *multiplied* by a factor preset by the experimenter and known to the subjects. The pot is then shared equally among all players *irrespective* of whether or how much each contributed. From a cooperative, common good perspective, each player would contribute the maximum amount possible, as that would generate the greatest common pot to share. From a pure self-interest perspective, the "dominant strategy" (i.e., most self-aggrandizing strategy) is to contribute nothing to the pot. This is called *free riding*. Under that condition, you always keep $10 as a minimum payout. And if others donate, you get a 1/nth portion of their contributions multiplied by the preset multiplier. Essentially, you risk nothing and, if others make any contribution at all, you end up with the greatest *individual* gain.

For example, assume five players: A, B, C, D, and E. Each has $10 and the multiplier is 4. Players A through D contribute $10; Player E $0. The pot is $40 x 4 = $160 shared five ways = $32 each. The net benefit to players A through D is $22 ($32 received - $10 contributed). The net benefit to Player E is $42. ($32 received + $10 not contributed). If E had contributed his/her $10, he or she would only net $30 (total pot = $50 x 4 = $200/5 = $40 to each player; net gain $40 - $10 contributed = $30 net gain).

interacts with him or her. Both are cast in the role of criminals who acted together. The game paradigm was introduced in 1950 by Merrill M. Flood and soon after given its current name by Albert W. Tucker (Khadjavi and Lange, 2013). It has been used as a research paradigm and reported on by countless articles and books. Across some 70 years of research, the findings have remained quite consistent. As regards single-game experiments (one-off version), people tend to choose cooperation over defection (betrayal) despite the fact that betrayal promises the greater personal benefit. For example, van Vugt, Roberts, and Hardy (2009) reported that between 40% and 60% of subjects participating in a one-off PD game with an anonymous partner chose the non-egoistic, cooperative course of action. In a "one-off PD" game, there is no subsequent interaction between the anonymous participants and therefore no chance for the decision maker to be punished should he or she choose to defect. Molina, Giménez-Nadal, Cuesta, Gracia-Lazaro, et al. (2013) found, in their study of 1,229 subjects, that the percentage of subjects choosing cooperation in an initial PD game (equivalent to a one-off version) was 50%. Strikingly, Khadjavi and Lange (2013) reported that 56% of *actual prisoners* tested in the one-off PD game cooperated with rather than betrayed their anonymous partner.[7] Clearly, the findings of one-off prisoner dilemma games support the assumption that many, if not most, people are inclined to cooperate with others.

Public Goods (PGs) Game

The PGs game involves a group of people, each of whom is given an amount of money (endowment). Group members have the option to contribute any or all of their endowment to a common pot. That pot is then multiplied by a given factor and then shared equally with all members, whether or not they contributed. Each person's contribution to the pot is deducted from his or her personal holdings.

[7] Equally striking, Khadjavi and Lange (2013) found a cooperative response rate of only 36% for *economics students*. Herein lies a cautionary tale about sampling bias. Prior research has shown that persons trained in economics are a skewed population that demonstrate less sharing and cooperation, on average, than non-economics students and even less than the general population (Bauman and Rose, 2011; Etzioni, 2015; Frank, Gilovich, and Regan, 1993, 1996; Goodwin, 2014; Lazear, Malmendier, and Weber, 2012; Marwell and Ames, 1981). Indeed, Marwell and Ames found that, while non-economics students tended to contribute some 40% to 60% of their endowment in public goods games, the average contribution fell to just 20% when economics students were the subjects. Lazear, Malmendier, and Weber (2012) compared the giving of 53 Business/Economics (B/E) majors and 114 non-Business/Economics (nB/E) majors in a basic dictator game experiment. On average, B/E students shared ~31% less of their received money than nB/E students. Hence, experimental studies of cooperation and sharing using economics students as subjects result in observing lower levels of each behavior than would be observed if non-economics students were the subjects. Unfortunately, in almost all the research we have reviewed, neither behavioral economists nor psychologists attempted to control for this confounding variable, thereby making their measurements of cooperation and sharing *negatively biased*. Note that the performance of economics students does not reflect a superior understanding of the game. As you will read, research has shown that cooperative/sharing behavior is not a function of ignorance of the game.

As Exhibit 2 explains, the pure self-interest strategy is to contribute nothing to the pot. Assuming egoistic self-interest as people's basic motive, 100% of the participants in the basic public goods (PGs) game would contribute zero dollars. Contrary to that expectation, however, most subjects choose to contribute. These subjects typically begin by investing about half of their endowments. Andreoni (1995) found, for example, that players who chose to contribute put into the common pot an average of 56% of their endowment. *Only 20% of the players contributed nothing (free riders).* That is, 80% behaved cooperatively for the common good, and 20% acted from pure self-interest to maximize their personal gains. In a separate study by the same author, the average percentage of *free riders* over 10 iterations of a PGs experiment was 20.5% in a situation where the participants in each iteration changed.

As to the percentage of endowment contributed, Marwell and Ames (1981) reported that, over many iterations of PGs experiments, *non-economics* subjects (see Footnote 7, page 155) consistently contribute between 40% and 60% of their stake to the public good. Dawes and Thaler stated that the findings of Marwell and Ames held true "for subjects playing the game for the first time, or after a previous experience" (Dawes and Thaler, 1988, p. 189). They also stated that the finding held true for subjects playing in small groups (4) and large groups (80) and "for subjects playing for a range of monetary stakes."

Dawes and Thaler (1988) described a study by James Andreoni in which he attempted to discern whether cooperation was a product of intent or error. Did subjects who violated egoistic self-interest by cooperating do so simply because they did not understand the game? To test this ignorance hypothesis, Andreoni used a series of iterative one-off PGs. Iterative PGs games involve multiple rounds of decision making about whether to contribute to the public good. These rounds may involve the same or different participants. A payout is made after each round. Andreoni repeated a set of 10 one-off PGs experiments multiple times, thereby giving subjects an opportunity to learn how to play. Subjects were told they would play a series of one-off PGs games. When the 10 iterations were completed, the subjects were told they would play again for another 10 rounds with the same set of players. Dawes and Thaler reported that, upon restarting each set of 10 games, Andreoni found contributions went back up to virtually the same contribution rate observed on the initial trial in the first game (e.g., 44 percent on trial one of the second set of games vs. 48 percent on trial one in the first set). "Such results seem to rule out any explanation of cooperation based on subjects' misunderstanding the task" (Dawes and Thaler, 1988, p. 190).

Researchers, however, have consistently noted that both subject contributions and the number of people contributing fall over the course of repeated games *involving the same people*. In the Andreoni study just described, Dawes and Thaler also reported that he replicated the decaying contribution rate found by previous investigators. In a later study, Andreoni (1995) found that contribution dropped from 56% to 26% on average, and the percentage of subjects not contributing rose from 20% to 45% (Andreoni, 1995, p. 896). Some have speculated that the fall-off reflects the phenomenon of learning, where subjects gradually understand how to play the game in a manner consistent with their drive to maximize their personal gains. The learning explanation for the decline in contributions across repeated cycles *with the same players* appears untenable given the results Andreoni found in his learning experiment. In its place, Andreoni (1995) suggested another interpretation. He proposed that people do, in fact, have an inclination to cooperate. He termed this a taste for "kindness." He hypothesized "that the decline in cooperation often observed in the multiple trials of public-goods experiments [with the same players] ... may be due to frustrated attempts at kindness" (p. 892). That is, people's initial cooperation was met by exploitation by some players. Andreoni's speculation received empirical support from the research of Fehr and Gächter (2000) and Fehr, Fischbacher, and Gächter (2002). In fact, their work showed that, when people who cooperate encountered people who free ride (egoistic self-maximizers), each affected the other's behavior. The direction of the effect depended on the circumstances. When cooperators find themselves being exploited by free riders, they reduce their cooperation if they cannot otherwise control being exploited. When cooperators are experimentally given ways of affecting the free riders' behavior, they use those methods. As a result, the free riders actually become cooperators in the context of the experiment. We will explore this phenomenon further below in the section on *Conditionality*.

Sharing/Caring

Sharing refers to instances where someone voluntarily gives up a portion of his or her resources or the opportunity to gain resources to benefit another. We use the term "caring" to refer to instances where a person adjusts what he or she chooses to share so that it better serves the needs of another. The Life Enabling model asserts that people have an inherent inclination to relate to others in helpful ways. It maintains that they are inclined to show concern for the welfare of others and that this inclination is expressed, in part, by their willingness to invest their own resources in helping others. Sharing and caring are expressions of these posited native human inclinations.

As to people's inclination to share, Indiana University's Lilly Family School of Philanthropy reported that the share of households contributing to charity was 49.6% in 2018 (CBS News, 2021). However, there can be many reasons for giving, some of which may be termed self-serving. Here, again, experimental studies help clarify whether people's sharing is truly other-regarding (prosocial) or just masked self-regarding behavior (proself). Studies can also clarify to what extent prosocial versus proself sharing occurs. For the sake of brevity, we will discuss the findings of just two experimental thrusts that have investigated sharing and caring. The first has focused on "behavioral distributive justice." The second has investigated the phenomenon of altruism. These two investigative tracks do, however, overlap, especially when researchers add novel conditions to their experimental designs.

Behavioral Distributive Justice

Behavioral distributive justice experiments investigate people's thoughts and behavior regarding how a found or given resource should be shared among others *not including themselves*. The decision-making person is acting as a disinterested third party. This research has uncovered facts related to the following four questions relevant to the sharing/caring aspect of human nature:

1. Are people inclined to distribute a found resource among involved others or assign it to one party?
2. If yes, on what basis do they make this decision?
3. Do people factor need into their distribution judgments?
4. Does people's inclination to share, if present, change when the resource is their own?

In response to the first question, Rabin (1998) reported that people predominantly split a found resource between the parties identified as possible recipients. To the second question, he reported that, in the absence of other information about the potential recipients, people apply the *equality principle* in sharing a resource. They split the resource evenly. To the third question, Rabin reported that the principle of distribution changes when information is provided that enlightens the disinterested party about the potential recipients' differential needs. When such information is introduced, Rabin (1998) stated that "[m]any people feel goods should be allocated according to a *'maximin' criterion* which equalizes welfare improvements between the two people" (1998, p. 18). The *maximin principle* divides a given bundle of goods in such a way that, after the division, the welfare of the person having the greater need (initially least advantaged individual) is as close as possible or equal to the person having the lesser need (initially more advantaged individual).[8] The use of this principle implies a concern by the decision maker for the well-being of each party (*caring*).

Yaari and Bar-Hillel (1984) conducted a complex series of experiments that revealed people's preference for the maximin principle. Their experiments sought to ferret out what allocation principles applied under different circumstances where a resource was to be distributed by a disinterested party. In the *differences-in-needs* component of their study, the researchers presented subjects with the question of how to distribute a shipment of grapefruits and avocados between two persons, Jones and Smith. Each needed the Vitamin F the fruits supplied, but each party differed in his ability to extract Vitamin F from the respective fruits (1984, p. 8). The study offered the subjects five different alternative distributions. Eighty-two (82%) of the subjects chose to split the fruits between the parties in a way that best equalized the ability of each party to derive the benefit each needed to realize his or her well-being. This choice demonstrated caring by showing people's regard for the differential needs of each party and for ensuring their respective welfare. The authors modified this scenario two additional times, and each time the maximin principle prevailed, reinforcing the notion of caring.

But what will people do in situations where the resource to be shared *is theirs*? This is the fourth question posed above. Here, sharing causes a personal loss.

Andreoni and Miller (2002) investigated this question, along with what principle people used to distribute a resource under the condition of ownership of that resource. In their study, each subject received an amount of money and could choose to give an anonymous other any portion of it or nothing. If they gave nothing, they kept it all. Rabin (1998), reporting from Andreoni and Miller's prepublication manuscript (1996), stated that the authors found "[o]ver half the subjects behaved in a way significantly inconsistent with pure self-interest" (1998, p. 19). That is, they shared their own resource, thereby incurring a loss to themselves. In the published version of the paper, Andreoni and Miller (2002) stated, "We found that subjects exhibit a significant degree of ... altruistic behavior. ... Only a quarter of subjects are selfish money maximizers" (2002, p. 737).

Andreoni and Miller also sought to uncover what principle people used to divide their owned resource—e.g., an equal split between the parties. They created different experimental conditions that modified what an anonymous

---

[8] Definitions of the maximin principle vary. The one presented here is based on the studies we reviewed, wherein the principle people chose to apply was in allocating a needed resource *so that the division equated, to the highest degree possible, the final state of welfare among recipients.*

recipient received if a subject chose to share money with him or her. For example, in one condition, if the subject of the experiment (the decider) chose to give $1 of his or her allocation to an anonymous other (the recipient), that recipient would get $3. The experimenters were trying to see if people distributed based on benefit received (the $3) or simply based on what the decider possessed (e.g., an even split wherein the decider is endowed with $10 and gives $5 away). Rabin (1998) reported that two-thirds of the deciders who shared their endowment with their anonymous other *adjusted* the amount they shared to equalize the benefit the decider and the recipient realized (the maximin allocation rule). Thus, if the decider was given $10 and the anonymous other got $1 for every dollar given, the decider would give the recipient $5. If the anonymous other got $3 for every dollar the decider gave, then the decider would give $2.50 and keep $7.50. In this latter example, $2.50 given is $7.50 received by the recipient—$2.50 ×3 = $7.50. Both approaches equalize the realized benefit to each party. However, the second example required that the decider take into account the multiplier and adjust his or her giving based on *its effect on the other*, not simply on what the decider possessed. Thus, sharing in this instance showed attention to the end state of the other person, and the action taken sought to produce *mutual and equal benefits.*

The research studies reviewed above are just a few examples of the phenomenon of sharing/caring in human behavior explored in the context of resource distribution. The summative finding of this wealth of research is that people are inclined to share a resource in a way that attempts to equalize the benefit each party receives and that this behavior does not change even when the resource is theirs and sharing means a loss to them of some part of it.

Altruism

In the behavioral economics literature, the term "altruism" has multiple meanings. Here, we define it as an intentionally taken action that benefits another at a cost to oneself and from which no secondary benefit is derived. The "cost" may involve a reduction in one's material wealth or placing one's own well-being at risk. The action is observed in situations where the "other" appears to have been treated unfairly or where his or her welfare appears to be in jeopardy. This definition is similar to that of Fehr (2005). Altruism, thus defined, definitively expresses caring.[9]

[9] Altruism is not kindness, although at least one author, Bardsley (2008), seems to use the terms interchangeably. "Kindness" refers to an act that expresses sympathy, affection, or consideration for another's feelings. Kindness does not require the loss of personal resources or the assumption of risk to one's well-being. Neither is altruism the spontaneous giving of one's possessions to others irrespective of their needs. Nor is it the expending of one's resources to help others who need no help. Altruists do not jump into pools to save people who are swimming just fine.

Our definition of altruism corresponds to its common use. It differs from the concept of *biological altruism* in that biological altruism does not incorporate conscious intent. It also differs from *reciprocal altruism* (Trivers, 1971) in that there is neither a preceding receipt of benefit from the person for whom the altruistic act is done nor the potential for future reward or punishment. It differs from *impure altruism* (Andreoni, 1990) in that the actor is not motivated by the receipt of any secondary gain, such as the expectation of a positive internal feeling (i.e., a "warm glow" for doing a good deed) or relief from a negative internal feeling (e.g., guilt). Finally, it also differs from "altruism" as understood by some authors (e.g., Cox, Sadiraj, and Sadiraj, 2002; Bardsley, 2008) who include within its meaning giving to others even when there is no apparent welfare issue (e.g., injustice, danger) the other is experiencing.[10]

As reported by Okasha (2013), "Altruistic behaviour is common throughout the animal kingdom, particularly in species with complex social structures," and is fully recognized by evolutionary scientists. Okasha, of course, was referring to biological altruism. One example we discussed earlier is the signaling behavior of ground squirrels.

As to altruism in human behavior, as we define it, one source of evidence is the Carnegie Hero Fund Commission. It was endowed by Andrew Carnegie in 1904 to recognize any citizen in the United States or Canada who "voluntarily risks his or her own life, knowingly, to an extraordinary degree while saving or attempting to save the life of another person" (Carnegie Hero Fund Commission, 2018). The award *excludes* people acting in the context of their work roles that require them to perform such acts. The number of awardees as of December 19, 2017, was 9,991 (Carnegie Hero Fund Commission, 2018). Becker and Eagerly (2004) reported that the "[t]ypical acts that merit Carnegie Hero Medals include saving people from fires, drowning, attacks by animals, assaults by criminals, electrocution, and suffocation." The inherent risk of such acts is attested to by the fact that, "since 1994, 20% [of the awards] were posthumous" (2004, p. 167). This mortality rate is actually an underestimate of the harm to well-being that the altruistic actors incurred. It does not include people injured either temporarily or permanently as a result of their altruistic deeds.

Another source of evidence involves incidences where people risk their lives or well-being to save an animal. Chen (2016) reported one such event that involved saving both a human and an animal. A woman was trapped in her car with her dog. The car was swept away and sinking in raging flood waters.

---

[10] For example, Bardsley (2008) expected "altruistic" people in the dictator role to give their anonymous others part of their endowments, even though both dictators and their anonymous others were each given the *same amount of money initially* and *the dictator was aware of this fact.*

Terrified, she cried out, "Oh my God, I'm drowning!" After rescuers failed to save the woman from an emergency boat, the car slipped deeper into the flood water. From the shore, "a man jumped into dangerous floodwaters to save [her] from drowning in Baton Rouge, Louisiana." After being pulled from the submerged vehicle, the terrified woman came topside *and immediately attempted to dive back down to save her dog*. The man who saved her stopped her. Then, he dove twice for the dog, saving him on the second try.

A second example involving an animal alone was reported by Betts (2018). The youngest daughter in a family living in Hope, Maine, witnessed an attack of her pet dog by a rabid raccoon. She cried out for assistance. Then, unarmed and unprotected, she tried to kick the rabid animal free from her dog. The raccoon "had the dog by its face" (2018, p. A10). She succeeded in kicking the animal free. It was at that point that her father, who had just arrived at the scene, killed it. Hope residents are familiar with raccoons appearing at the end of winter during daytime. These are almost always rabid, as the raccoon is a nocturnal animal and generally avoids dogs. The daughter and father were both treated with rabies shots.

The Experimental Study of Altruism

The experimental study of altruism is limited by scientific ethics, as true tests would expose subjects and other participants to potential harm. The most frequently used experimental paradigm for studying human altruism by economists is the one-off dictator game (DG). While the subjects in such studies are not exposed to physical harm, their elected actions can produce loss of money to them. Money is the metric of value in mainstream economics, and its loss is their surrogate for harm.[11]

Obviously, this paradigm is an extraordinarily weak example of risking one's well-being to benefit another as compared to real-life altruism. The salient features of real-world altruistic acts and the economic decision making in one-off DGs are, on their face, totally different. The economically based DG paradigm seems more a venue for exploring people's inclination to share money versus seeking to maximize their possession of it. The paradigm itself introduces a potential response bias.[12] By its design—the use of money as the

[11] Capitalism posits that people always act to maximize their accumulation of wealth (Classical Capitalism) or their received value (Neoclassical Capitalism). Both are measured monetarily. Indeed, the use of money as the measure of commercial behavior is assumed to free economics from psychology (Marshall, 1982).

[12] Response bias refers to experimental subject behavior that is triggered by the conditions of an experiment rather than the underlying factor being studied. Subject behavior may be influenced by the nature of the experimental setting, the experiment's design, the experimenter's behavior, the instruction set used, and, here, with regard to the DG paradigm, the use of money as the metric of value.

metric of value—the experiment might activate people's notions of correct economic behavior as defined by the promulgated principles of Capitalism, America's economic system. Nonetheless, the DG paradigm does provide findings of some value for judging the realisticness of the Life Enabling model's assumptions about human nature.

The One-Off Dictator Game (DG)

The one-off DG involves strangers who never interact in any way. The experimental subject is the "dictator." The dictator is only told that there is a second party involved in the experiment, but, again, they never meet or interact. The dictator is given a sum of money. In the basic game, the other party is given nothing. As the recipient of the money, the dictator is free to share his or her money with that unknown other person, keep it all, or give it all to the other person. There are absolutely *no* consequences for the dictator should he or she keep all the money except being richer. Thus, the dictator may act with impunity.

If people behave according to Capitalism's assumptions about human nature, they will always keep *all* the money. If people have a tendency toward altruism—*as operationalized by economists in this paradigm*—they will choose to share some of what they receive.

Dictator Game (DG) Findings

Camerer (2003) recorded that "[i]n the first dictator game experiment, Kahneman, Knetsch, and Thaler (1986) gave subjects a [fixed] choice between dictating an even split of $20 with another student, or an uneven (keep $18 and give $2) split favoring themselves" (2003, p. 56). A full 75% of the subjects in that first experiment chose an even split. This fixed-choice scenario has been replaced in almost all experiments with the option to provide or keep any amount from all to none.

A great many subsequent DG studies using the revised distribution option have been performed since then. Across 22 studies completed before the year 2000 using the one-off basic DG paradigm, only 38% of subjects, on average, elected not to allot any of their received endowment to their anonymous partner (Camerer, 2003).[13] In contrast, 62% gave a portion of their endowment to their anonymous other. This general result was essentially confirmed in more recent studies by many other researchers. List (2006), for

[13] This calculation used the data reported in Tables 2.4 of Camerer's (2003, pp. 56–57) book, excluding seven data points. We omitted one study because it reported a frequency of giving nothing to the other party that is nearly twice the level of any other study reviewed by Camerer or ourselves. Another study was omitted because it offered no zero-giving option. Five studies were omitted because the partnered people were apparently not both anonymous to each other.

example, found that 71% of subjects in a baseline dictator condition gave a positive amount to their unknown other. Approximately 42% of them gave 40% or more of their allotment. More recently, Engel's (2011) analysis of 616 DG experiments with varying design features found that, on average, 74% of all the dictators studied gave a positive amount to their "others," and 29% of those dictators gave 50% or more of their endowments.

The findings from DG experiments vary based on modifications in the game's design, the instruction set used, and the options offered to the subjects (Engel, 2011; Lazear, Malmendier, and Weber, 2012). Studies have varied

- the subjects' exposure to the experimenter,
- their awareness of who the other party is,
- whether the other party also receives an endowment,
- the amount of discrepancy between the dictator's and the other's endowments,
- the features of the other party (e.g., charity versus an anonymous person, the neediness of the other),
- whether the dictator's money is earned versus unearned, and
- whether the amount given to the other is multiplied or just the face value offered.

Two variables *not* acknowledged by experimenters and therefore not controlled relate to whether subjects in the experiment were economics students and whether subjects perceived that they were participating in an economics experiment.

As we explained earlier (see Footnote 7, page 155), economics students represent a negatively biased response group compared to non-economics students and even more so compared to the general public. Experimenters need to control for this confounding variable, and, thus far, only a few of the DG studies we have reviewed have done so. The bottom line is that the findings of studies using economics students are not generalizable to the general population of people.

The use of money and the identification of the study itself with economics provide two potentially reinforcing biasing factors, as they may well activate in subjects notions about what their *expected conduct* should be, as defined by Capitalism. Capitalism is our nationally embraced economic model. It is not unreasonable that subjects would perceive their expected behavior to conform to its notions of economic behavior and act as "priming" agents for that behavior. Both features may also create "demand characteristics" of the experiment. This construct (the demand characteristic) was introduced by Martin Orne (McCambridge, Witton, and Elbourne, 2014). It refers to biased responses by participants due to their "being aware of what the researcher is trying to investigate" or by what the experimenter anticipates finding and what this implies for how participants are expected to behave (McCambridge, Witton, and Elbourne, 2014). As Draper (2016) pointed out:

> After all, even conversations have strong demand characteristics (being relevant, being polite, etc.) which strongly modify what we say; and given also that in most human experiments, the participants are either paid or are volunteers, it must be expected that they try hard to do what they perceive is wanted. So interpreting any such experiment as somehow showing what the participants themselves want or prefer is obviously problematic. (Draper, 2016).

The construct of demand characteristics overlaps with the subject-biasing effect that results from experimenter expectations, as identified by Rosenthal (Rosenthal and Rubin, 1978; Rosenthal, 1994).

Nonetheless, *despite all the tested variations* in the game and the absence of controls for subjects' exposure to economics training and other possible negatively biasing variables, *a sizable percentage of people consistently choose to equitably share their given resources with others.* Engel (2011) found that in only six out of 616 studies did dictators not give money to their others. As Engel concluded, "It by now is undisputed that human populations are systematically more benevolent than *homo oeconomicus* [sic]" (2011, p. 5).[14]

Trying to Explain Away Cooperation, Sharing, and Caring and Failing

Faced with the experimental finding that people demonstrate cooperation, sharing, and caring rather than Capitalism's expected egoistic money-maximizing behavior, mainstream economists have looked for ways to explain how these unexpected behaviors might really be *disguised self-interest.*

One reasonable possibility for not observing egoistic money-maximizing behavior is that subjects did not understand the consequences of the options they were presented.[15] We discussed this "ignorance" hypothesis earlier (pages 156–

[14] "Homo economicus" (not "*homo oeconomicus*") is the commonly used term to refer to Capitalism's assumptions that people are consistently rational and operate solely to maximize their self-interest. See also Caporael, Dawes, Orbell, and Van de Kragt (1989) for additional experimental evidence that undermines the construct of Homo economicus. For cross-cultural evidence undermining the validity of the construct, see Cardenas and Carpenter (2008) and Henrich, Boyd, Bowles, Camerer, et al. (2005).

[15] Of course, this explanation would still violate the assumptions of Capitalism. It posits that people have full information and *always* make rational and effective choices that maximally benefit their

157) and will not deal with it again here. Another is that a different dynamic may be at play—not an inclination to cooperate, for example, but a strategic use of cooperative behavior *in order to reap even bigger future gains* (termed "reciprocal cooperation"). A third is to simply dismiss the other-regarding nature of cooperation and sharing as a "faux" phenomenon. Cooperation and sharing behavior are not about the other party's well-being but simply actions that gratify oneself. With specific reference to altruistic behavior, a fourth tack is to suggest that observed altruism in DGs is an artifact of how the game context is constructed. None of these arguments withstand empirical scrutiny.

Future Benefits and Reciprocal Cooperation

The potential for reaping more significant future benefits renders cooperation a strategic way to maximize one's self-interest. The rationale is that egoists learn that appearing cooperative yields superior self-benefits *in the long run*. The phrase *reciprocal cooperation* captures this thinking: "I cooperate now because I have come to expect future, added benefits to myself for doing so." This construction is based on the understanding that many social interactions take place repeatedly and that one's reputation as being selfish might harm his or her future possibilities for repeated commerce with others and, therefore, additional gains from them.

Initial exploration of this argument seemed promising. Indeed, game theorists showed that "when the chances for repeated interactions are sufficiently high, rational egoists ... can establish an equilibrium [stable strategy] with full cooperation despite the existence of short-run cheating incentives" (Fehr, Fishbacher, and Gächter, 2002, pp. 1–2). Further study by these researchers revealed, however, that this conclusion required significant refinement. *First*, the movement from exploiting others to cooperating with others requires that the exploited players know that they have been exploited *and* can punish the players who exploit them.[16] Only when these two conditions are satisfied do proself egoists simulate cooperative behavior. *Second*, further research demonstrated that cooperativeness by selfish people breaks down as the number of parties involved in a network of relations increases. Boyd and Richerson (1988) found that "the conditions that allow the evolution of reciprocal cooperation become extremely restrictive as group size increases" (1988, p. 337). For "quite small groups," cooperation based on reciprocity can evolve. Larger networks of relationships reduce the frequency of specific dyadic encounters and make full knowledge of other people's behavior more difficult to acquire and counter. Finally, even in the restrictive case of a small network of repeatedly interacting

[16] Examples of punishments include suspending cooperation or penalizing a partner by deducting money from the total amount of money the partner holds (when the game permits such action).

people who are aware of and punish each other's exploitive behavior, the concept of reciprocal cooperation does not explain why some people always cooperate in a one-off prisoner's dilemma game. *In one-off PD games, there are no repeated encounters and no potential for future benefit.* Therefore, there is no basis on which cooperation is the strategy that best serves one's egoistic money-maximizing purpose. The same observation holds true for the last trial in a repeated-trials PD game. In this version of the PD paradigm, people repeatedly interact with the same party and know what option that person chose on the previous trial. Thus, each person is exposed to being punished on the next round if they act selfishly in the previous round. *But, in the last round of the experiment, there is no possibility for punishment because there is no next round.* Hence, there is no basis for reciprocal cooperation. Yet, people do cooperate.

Thus, after reviewing the experimental evidence on the issue of reciprocal altruism, Dawes and Thaler (1988) concluded, "Once again, however, the data rule out ... [the reciprocal cooperation] explanation. Cooperation never falls to zero, even in one-trial games or in the last period of multi-trial games when it can never be selfishly rational to cooperate" (p. 191).

Social Preference

It has been hypothesized that other-regarding behavior might be a *self-regarding response* to one's preference for certain internal states. Andreoni (1990) had raised the issue that feelings of "social pressure, guilt, sympathy, or simply a desire for a 'warm glow' may play important roles in the decisions of agents" to contribute their resources to others (1990, p. 464). He termed this type of cooperation "impure altruism." It is a faux altruism in that it is *self-regarding* behavior and not other-regarding behavior, as altruism is defined. It is driven by the desire to obtain personal relief from some negative inner experience (e.g., guilt or shame) or to acquire some positive inner experience (e.g., the "warm glow" resulting from having done something viewed as good). The behavior simply represents the social preference of the person when the value of acquiring the internal state is greater than the loss of monetary gain.[17]

Impure altruism was introduced, in part, to explain why public giving to community-benefiting efforts sustains when Capitalism's model predicts that it should decline. According to Capitalism, government grants and subsidies should *crowd out* the public goods participation from citizens. Seeing that money was already being provided, people would experience reduced utility in

[17] Be aware that if this construct were valid, it would still invalidate Capitalism's posited nature of people. In that model, humans are fundamentally singleton beings. The construct of shame or guilt, or the notion of a warm glow from doing "good," implies a social consciousness, as none of these experiences have meaning outside of a social existence.

added giving, and their contribution would decline. Yet, empirical evidence falsifies this expectation (Andreoni, 1990). "Field studies of charitable giving, however, find that the amount of crowding out is actually quite small, with estimates ranging from 5 to 28 percent. There are several possible explanations for the inconsistency" (Bolton and Katok, 1998, p. 317). Andreoni proposed that this inner drive for relief from a negative feeling or for acquiring positive satisfaction sustains giving when rationality, as defined by Capitalism, would predict decreased giving.

In scrutinizing Andreoni's proposed explanation, several issues emerge that appear to weaken its utility. First, contributions decline when participants detect they are being exploited in repeated Public Goods (PGs) games. This presumably *should not occur if contributing were a self-regarding* behavior. A self-regarding behavior should, by definition, be unaffected by the behavior of others. That would make it an other-regarding behavior. Also, research has shown that public goods giving is inversely related to people's income level, at least in economies with high-income inequality (Côté, House, and Willer, 2015). If giving were due to people's desire to experience the "warm glow" of decency, why would individuals with less income be more inclined to give than those with higher incomes? Would not the relationship be reversed, as more wealth would provide a greater opportunity to acquire one's pleasurable "warm glow" experiences?

Empirical studies also challenge Andreoni's analysis. Bolton and Katok (1998) reported an experimental study using the DG that attempted to contrast the effects of pure and impure altruism. Here, subjects were given an amount of money they could choose to share or not share with another anonymous player. The game was played once. Then, it was repeated, but with a different other player. In one version, the subject received $15 in tokens and was told that the other player had received $5 (Condition A). In the second version, the player was given $18 in tokens and had been told that the other player was given $2 (Condition B). The hypothesis was that, given pure altruism and the implicit unfairness of the allocations, the amount of money contributed to the other would be less in Condition A than in Condition B, since the inequity was less. Impure altruism, which is self-regarding, would be unaffected. The data supported the construct of pure altruism. Subjects who shared their received tokens in Condition B offered more on average to the other player than subjects in Condition A. Interestingly, the modal donations in each condition "corresponded to the simple fairness norm of splitting the money 50/50 ($10 each for donor and recipient)" (1998, p. 325), a finding consistent with other DG studies.

Also undermining the impure altruism argument is the extensive research showing that human decisions are guided by the person's interpretations of the other party's condition, intent, and conduct. This "attribution-based decision making" (Rabin, 1998) is manifestly other-regarding—not self-regarding. Again, in impure altruism, the warm glow comes from *my* action judged against my personal criteria. It is unaffected by who the other is or what condition he or she is experiencing. We will discuss attribution-based decision making further in the section below, titled *Conditionality.*

Taking—Not Just Giving

The dilemma for mainstream economic researchers was put nicely by Cox, Sadiraj, and Sadiraj:

> Economics traditionally focused on the model of self-regarding (or "economic man") preferences in which agents are assumed to be exclusively concerned with their own material payoffs. ... But there is now a large body of experimental literature that has produced replicable patterns of inconsistencies with the self-regarding preferences model's predictions in contexts involving salient fairness considerations or opportunities for cooperation. (Cox, Sadiraj, and Sadiraj, 2006, p. 1)

A final response to this failure to validate the universal presence of self-regarding behavior has been to doubt the validity of the discrepant research. One tactic has been to label the "aberrant data" of altruism as an "artifact" due to the choice set presented to subjects. If one allows subjects to "take" and not just give money, altruism will disappear. As Bardsley (2008) asserted, "Experimental dictator games have been used to explore unselfish behaviour. Evidence is presented here, however, that subjects' generosity can be reversed by allowing them to take a partner's money" (2008, p. 122). This strongly stated conclusion, however, is not supported by Bardsley's study or by other experiments. What the research has revealed is that extending the subject's response set to include "taking" does change the distribution of dictator responses, *but it does not eliminate giving.* While giving declines in frequency, giving *sustains* even when subjects are *punished for not taking* (Korenok, Millner, and Razzolini, 2014).

The research also reveals that the "taking" behavior is a complex phenomenon whose determinants are not at all clear. It is, in fact, riddled with contradictions. Bardsley's assertion would have us think that taking was a consistently expressed preference whenever it was offered. However, there is considerable variation in the frequency and extent of taking behavior as exhibited by research subjects within and across experiments. That variation suggests that there are a number of unknown variables affecting its expression, not all of which may be germane to the phenomenon per se (e.g., experimenter bias, biased sampling of subjects, demand characteristics of the study context).

This variation is observed in Bardsley's (2008) study itself. That study encompassed three separate experiments. The observed occurrence of taking behavior ranged from 77% of the time in his Experiment 1 to just 39% of the time in his Experiment 2. *The opportunity to give or take was the same in both these experiments.* Variation in the preference for taking is also exhibited in other research. In List's multiple-experiment study (2007), for example, taking varied from 21% to 60% between experiments. List suggested that the reason was that the difference in taking between his Experiment 2 (21%) and his Experiment 3 (60%) was an artifact of the taking options given subjects. Experiment 3 allowed subjects to take as much or as little as they wanted, but Experiment 2 had them choose among fixed amounts of taking. However, List's Experiment 4 replicated the range of taking offered in Experiment 3, yet produced only 28% taking. Thus, his own data contradicted his explanation of the variability within his findings.

Still more evidence of the variability in "taking" behavior is provided by Korenok, Millner, and Razzolini (2014). One of the conditions (labeled "Decision 3") in their study was comparable to the high taking condition (77%) in Bardsley's (2008) study and the high taking condition (60%) in List's (2007) study. Rather than the high taking percentage these earlier authors found, Korenok, Millner, and Razzolini found that 46% of subjects *gave* money and just 40% took money. Similar findings were obtained by Cappelen, Nielsen, Sorensen, Tungodden, et al. (2012). They measured taking and giving under two conditions. In each condition where taking was possible, just 42% and 44% took.

Apart from the issue of variability in taking behavior, a second sign of the complexity associated with interpreting what "taking" behavior means is revealed by the contradictions uncovered in various other studies. One such contradiction is that taking does not necessarily reduce the final payout that the "other" receives. Korenok, Millner, and Razzolini (2014) found that, as the opportunity to take increased, payouts to recipients actually *increased.* It is almost like the "givers" in a subject sample recoil and increase their giving whenever an experiment allows taking. This interpretation, of course, is speculative and would need targeted research to verify. But whatever this finding means, it clearly does not support the simple assumption that people act purely to maximize their wealth.

Also indicating the complexity of the taking phenomenon is the finding that people are *averse* to participating in a DG experiment that has a "taking" option. Korenok, Millner, and Razzolini (2014) created a scenario where people could choose to participate in either a give-only DG or a give/take DG game. An astounding 86% of the 121 subjects chose the give-only DG game. Next, the researchers tested how committed subjects were to that option. Subjects who picked the give-only game were later asked repeatedly to make the same decision (give-only DG vs. give/take DG) in nine different situations. In each subsequent situation, sticking to the give-only option cost them more and more money. The longer they held to their "give only" preference, the more money they lost. Thirty-one percent of the subjects *never switched from the give-only to the take DG* game in spite of losing money. The authors concluded that the aversion to taking is prevalent and strong.

Given the available research, what can firmly be said about expanding the choice set to include taking in a DG is that it does appear to change the distribution of giving behavior in DGs but not the form of distribution. The data from non-taking, basic DGs has *consistently* displayed a bimodal distribution that has generally been unrecognized, as researchers typically report univariate statistics in describing these data. In the non-taking DG, there is usually one mode of responders that give nothing and a second mode of responders who give an amount somewhere between 50% and 100% of their endowment. This has always suggested that people have two distinct response sets—one selfish and one giving. The "taking" version of DG clarifies this dual response set by extending the range of possible subject responses from not giving anything to taking all (absolute selfishness). But we can still see the two distinct response sets—one on the left side of the distribution (taking) and one on the right side (giving). Giving remains a demonstrated response even in the context of being able to take with impunity.

Conditionality

Conditionality refers to modifying a behavior based on circumstances. We discussed earlier the differential effects of oxytocin expression on people's experience of affective connectivity with others (pages 149–150). The hormone can either trigger bonding and empathy in contexts where the subject in whom it is being expressed trusts the other person or it can provoke hostility and guardedness in situations where the person distrusts the other.

A large number of behavioral studies reinforce the presence of conditionality in our everyday social relating. People's decision making with regard to others considers issues related to the other person's perceived fairness, intentions, prior behavior, and welfare needs (e.g., Forsythe, Horowitz, Savin, and Sefton, 1994; Kagel, Kim, and Moser, 1996; Kahneman, Knetsch, and Thaler, 1986, 1986a; Rabin,

1998). This phenomenon was referred to by Rabin (1998) as *attribution-guided judgments*. Conditionality is also reflected in the separate but related phenomenon termed *reciprocity* (Coyle-Shapiro and Kessler, 2002; Diekmann, 2004; Falk and Fischbacher, 2000, 2001; Fehr, Fishbacher, and Gächter, 2002; Henrich, Boyd, Bowles, Camerer, et al., 2001).

With regard to the behavior of cooperation, absent any specific information about another person, many people's default response is to cooperate and be helpful. Given information about another person, those inclinations are most often modified by how we perceive that person. These findings are consistent with the Life Enabling model's assumptions about people. Moreover, conditionality has important implications for society in general and sustainable commerce in particular. We will review a few of the most relevant studies in this area to provide a sense of what has been empirically demonstrated and what these findings imply.

Attribution-Based Judgment and Cooperation

One example of attribution-guided decision making is revealed in DG experiments. Based on the premises of Capitalism, one would expect the recipients of a dictator's monetary gift to accept any amount offered, since rejection of an offer results in the recipient receiving nothing. However, people *do reject* offers they perceive as being unfair or demeaning, even though that rejection leaves them with no money and *has no effect whatsoever on the dictator*.

> A robust result ... is that proposals that give the [recipient] positive shares below 20 percent of the available sum [to share] are rejected with a very high probability. This shows that [recipients] do not behave in a self-interest maximizing manner. In general, the motive indicated for the rejection of positive yet 'low' offers is that subjects view them as unfair, (Fehr, Fischbacher, and Gächter, 2002, p. 11).

The threshold for rejecting varies across studies. It is typically about 20% of the total amount given to the dictator and sometimes as high as 30%. The threshold for acceptance is higher when the recipients are presented with the percentage of the total endowment being offered to them by the dictator as compared to when recipients are presented with the numerical amount (e.g., a 29% share rather than $20 of a total of $70). One might infer from this that the percentage makes clearer the "fairness level" of the offer. The phenomenon of rejecting offers deemed unfair has been observed cross-culturally and even when high amounts of money are at stake (Cameron, 1999; Henrich, Boyd, Bowles, Camerer, et al., 2001; Roth, Prasnikar, Okuno-Fujiwara, and Zamir, 1991).

Our perception of the conduct of others also affects the giving side of people's decision making. Goranson and Berkowitz (1966) performed an experiment that demonstrated people's conditional quality of cooperativeness and the importance of people's inferences about whether another's positive behavior toward us was voluntary. In their experiment, confederates of the experimenter posed as fellow subjects within the pool of real subjects. These confederates were designated to help real subjects fill out some worksheets that were part of the experiment. "One third of the [real] subjects were told that the confederate had voluntarily offered to help; one third were told that the experimenter had instructed the confederate to help; and one third were told that the confederate might be willing to help but, *unknown to the real subject*, the confederate was instructed to refuse help" (Rabin 1998, p. 22).

Afterward, subjects were given an opportunity to assist the confederate who had either previously assisted them or refused to do so. "Subjects provided significantly more help to their [assigned confederate] when [the confederate's helping was] voluntary than when it was involuntary" (Rabin, 1998, p. 22). As Goranson and Berkowitz (1966) reported, subjects worked harder in an effort to help the person who had helped them voluntarily than when the help they received was the decision of the experimenter. Subjects who had been refused prior help from their assigned confederate were least willing to help them.

Reciprocity

Falk and Fischbacher (2001) defined reciprocity as people's inclination to "reward kind actions and punish unkind ones" (2001, p. 1). The construct assumes that the person is acting in relation to a prior experience with another person or an anticipated future experience. The response people make varies based on the person's assessment of the kindness or unkindness of an action, "not only by its consequences but also by the intention underlying this action" (2001, p. 1). Rabin (1998) stated, "Reciprocity motives manifest themselves not only in people's refusal to cooperate with others who are being uncooperative, but also in their willingness to sacrifice [suffer a loss] to hurt others who are being unfair" (1998, p. 22).[18]

Negative reciprocity is observed in a wide variety of cultures, and people will incur a rather high monetary loss to punish someone perceived to be unfair. The ultimatum game (UG) has been used to explore this phenomenon. A UG is a version of the dictator game. In it, the "dictator" is labeled the "proposer." The proposer suggests a split of his or her received funds to an unknown other, and the recipient may accept or reject what is proposed. If the recipient rejects the proposed offer, neither party gets anything. By now there are literally

---

[18] The word "hurt" is incorrect. Subjects never physically harm anyone. The word "punish" fits the factual nature of action studied in reciprocity experiments.

hundreds of studies of one-shot UGs in which a proposed offer to share an amount of money is rejected based on its perceived unfairness. As just stated, a rejection in the context of a UG results in *neither party getting anything.*

Rejections of positive offers have been observed in Israel, Japan, many European countries, Russia, Indonesia, the United States, and 15 other societies worldwide. For comparisons across countries, see Roth, Prasnikar, Okuno-Fujiwara, and Zamir (1991) and Henrich, Boyd, Bowles, Camerer, et al. (2006). In the study by Cameron (1999), the phenomenon was observed even when the amount to be divided by the Indonesian subjects represented three months' income for them.

Attribution-Based Decision Making and Reciprocity

As with the expression of cooperation, attribution-based decision making affects the expression of reciprocity. Two actions, both having the same negative or positive outcome, will be treated differently by the person affected depending on how that person views the actor's motive and control. Rabin (1998) stated that "if you think somebody has been generous to you solely to get a bigger favor from you in the future, then you do not view his generosity to be as pure as if he had expected no reciprocity from you" (p. 23). With regard to control, Rabin (1998), in reporting a study by Blount (1995), stated that people imposed the least standard for acceptance of money offered in a UG when they thought the split was *decided randomly* as compared to when they thought the split was *the choice of the proposer.* Rabin concluded that people were "less keen to reject offers which were not the result of volition by the person who would be hurt by the rejections" (1998, p. 23).

What Happens When Proself and Prosocial People Interact?

Clearly, the research reviewed above supports the conclusion that *some* people do indeed behave in a manner consistent with Capitalism's premises and act egoistically to maximize their personal gain. But the research also shows that many others do not. They behave in a manner consistent with the assumptions of the Life Enabling model. They are sensitive to the needs of others and adjust their behavior based on how it will affect others. What happens in a society that is constituted of both types of people? How do they interrelate? How does that interaction affect the civic milieu and alter the normative behavior observed in a society?

One of the truly significant social insights provided by reciprocity research is supplied by studies that analyze what happens when persons acting egoistically interact with people who act cooperatively. Fehr and Gächter (2000) conducted a complex set of experiments using a version of the PGs game to isolate how people's behavior changes over time when they have the opportunity to be generous but are in a mixed group of egoistically self-maximizing parties and cooperators. They assessed people's behavior when they have full information and when they do not. They also assessed situations in which people were able to punish others who exploited them and in which they were not.

The experimental context for these investigations was a set of multiple-trial PGs games. The researchers used a two-factor experimental design (Exhibit 4). One factor was the ability of subjects to punish exploitive behavior (punishment option–absent or present). The second factor manipulated whether players in the PGs games were new in each trial or the same (group membership–random or constant). Multiple sets of four subjects played 10 PGs games within each of these four conditions. In all conditions, people were informed about the behavior of the other participants at the end of each of the 10 games.

Exhibit 4. Fehr and Gächter (2000) Study Design

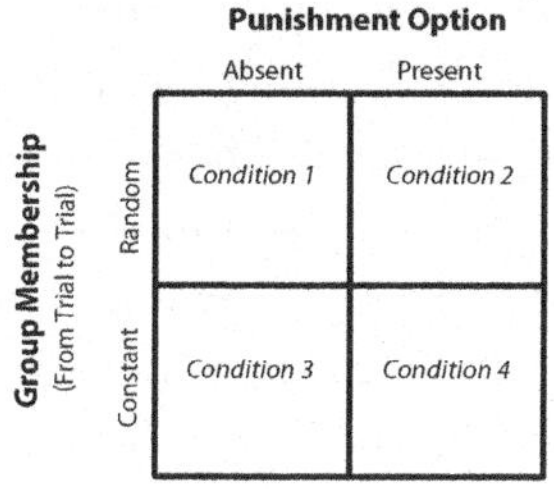

1. Condition 1 (new players each game, informed, no punishment possible). Each of the 10 games played was populated by *a new set of players*. None of the players knew what the other players were contributing to the common pot *when* each made his/her personal choice. However, at the end of each game, they were informed about the contributions of the other group members. Because the participants in each game changed, there was no possible way to act on the information about what others had contributed in the just completed game, since they were not in the current game.
2. Condition 2 (new players each game, informed, punishment possible). Each game played is populated by *a new set of players*. Again, at the time each person decided his/her contribution, no one knew what the other participants were contributing. In this setup, however, there was an opportunity to punish. At the end of each game, subjects were told each other player's investment decision. Subjects were allowed to assign punishment points to each of the other group members if they so chose. Each subject could assign up to 10 punishment points to each of the other group members. There was a cost, however, for exacting punishment. For each punishment point a person assigned another player, he or she lost three tokens.[19] Assigning no

[19] In such games, each token has a monetary value. At the end of the experiment, subjects receive the monetary value of the tokens they retain. The authors did not report the monetary value assigned to each token in this study.

punishment points costs the punisher nothing.
For each received punishment point, the monetary income of the punished subject was reduced by 10%. A reduction of 10% implies, on average, an income reduction of between two and three tokens. While people knew that Player A, for example, made X contribution, they did not know who Player A was, nor was the person designated Player A in one game the same as the person designated Player A in the next game. Hence, no player could establish a personalized reputation.

3. Condition 3 (same players each game, informed, no punishment possible). Each game was populated by *the same set of players*. At the time each person decided his/her contribution, no one knew what the other players chose to contribute to the common pot. However, at the end of each game, each player was informed about the contribution made by each other group member. That information informed each player's decision making about how to act in the new game, which had in it all the same players. There was *no* opportunity to punish a person's behavior at the end of each round.
4. Condition 4 (same players each game, informed, punishment possible). The same conditions prevailed as in Condition 3, *except* there was an opportunity to punish at the end of each round. The method for punishing and its consequences were identical to those described in Condition 2 above.

Findings

- In all conditions, some people initially acted in a proself manner (egoistic self-maximizer) as premised by Capitalism, and some people acted in a prosocial manner (cooperator) contrary to the premises of Capitalism.
- In Condition 3, the average contribution to the common pot deteriorated across trials to less than a fourth of its early high point. In essence, the proself free riders did not give, and the prosocial givers who *could punish* that selfish behavior increasingly held back on contributing. With the prosocial cooperators ceasing to give, the group as a whole became less generous. From a social perspective, the figurative "good guys" (prosocials) acted the same as the figurative "bad guys" (proselfs). The common *behavior* drifted toward the egoistic self-maximizing behavioral norm. The expression of "societal concern" deteriorated. This, however, *does not mean that the inclination of prosocial people had changed.* It simply reflects that they

Exhibit 5. Average Investment Over Time in Public Goods Games With Stable Groups (All Subjects)

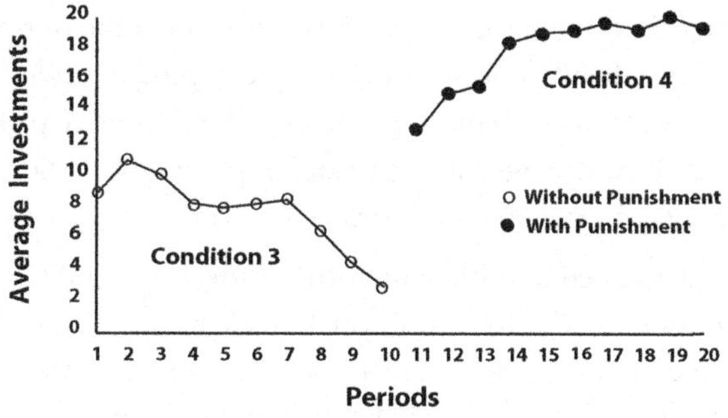

Condition 3 - Same people in each game; information provided at end of each game; no opportunity to punish.

Condition 4 - Same people in each game; information provided at end of each game; opportunity to punish.

Exhibit 6. Average Investment Over Time in Public Goods Games With Random Groups (All Subjects)

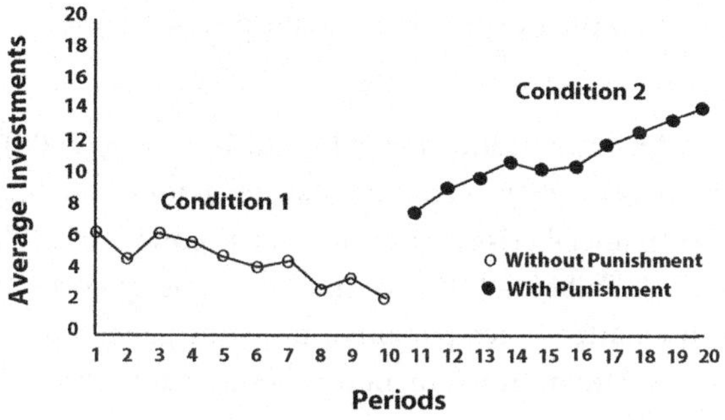

Condition 1 - New players in each game; information provided at end of each game; no opportunity to punish.

Condition 2 - New players in each game; information provided at end of each game; opportunity to punish.

had ceased to display their previously revealed inclination when forced to interact with people who operated exploitively. Exhibit 5, next page, shows the plots of the giving behavior for Condition 3.

- In Condition 4, the average contribution to the common pot improved to a third higher than the initial level. In essence, given the option for selfish people to act selfishly *and* prosocial people *to punish exploitive behavior*, the group as a whole became more generous. The figurative proself "bad guys" acted the same as the figurative prosocial "good guys." "Societal concern" improved, *at least in terms of outward behavior.*
- Condition 1 showed a trend similar to Condition 3, and Condition 2 showed a trend similar to Condition 4, in each case, to a lesser degree. Thus, when people interacted with new people in a series of games where they experienced their prior partners behaving exploitively, their own cooperative behavior deteriorated toward the selfish norm *under the condition that they could not punish the previously experienced exploitive behavior* (Condition 1; Exhibit 6, previous page). Also, the behavior of players in Condition 2 mirrored that observed in Condition 4 but to a lesser degree. The collective behavior of participants improved in terms of generosity when members were informed about the exploitive behavior of other members and *could punish* the specific persons who had been exploitive. Even with that capability, however, the observed collective behavior in Condition 2 was never as high as in Condition 4. This finding suggests that prosocial people experiencing exploitive behavior from different people across different encounters over time may restrict their expression of their prosocial orientation.

The Social and Commercial Implications of Conditionality

Consider the societal implications of Fehr and Gächter's (2000) finding about conditionality for a society where the selfish behavior of the financiers who caused the 2008 financial crisis, for example, has gone unpunished (Phillips, 2009; Rakoff, 2014; Taibbi, 2011). Consider the consequences for civic participation where, no matter which person or party the general public votes in, once in office, those individuals implement policies unwanted by the general public but desired by the very small segment of people who were the politicians' major funding sources (Ferguson, 1995; Ferguson, Jorgensen, and Chen, 2016; Gilens and Page, 2014; Parramore, 2016).

The empirical data suggests that, given those circumstances, the prosocial people will restrain their native inclination to participate and limit their contribution of effort in civic endeavors. It also suggests that the egoists will continue to exploit the prosocial members of society as long as they face no consequences for their actions. These research studies provide a new context for appreciating the civic consequences of, for example, the Obama-Holder principle of "too big to jail" (Berman, 2013; Holder, 1999; Sirotta, 2014) and the many other practical ways in which wealth has leveraged the political apparatus to advantage the wealthy over others (*Appendix C*).

Also consider the commercial implications of Fehr and Gächter's (2000) findings. In a sense, commerce itself is no different than a public goods game. When one party seeks to exploit its wealth-induced advantage in political power and judicial protection, the other party must guard against that exploitation. Commerce becomes a fraught experience. Its growth is diminished. Every market becomes a place of exploitation dominated by the greater wealth and power of producers. Each becomes just another place where "the strong do what they [will] and the weak suffer what they must" (Thucydides, 1951, p. 331). The wariness produced in people by being exploited without the option to act against the exploiter grinds down their native inclination to cooperate, share, and act fairly. And with that diminution, commerce atrophies. Now, also consider the consequences for civility in a society where such a state exists.

Evidence for the Personal Aspect of Human Nature–The Striving for Individuation

The Life Enabling model assumes that people have two basic drives, the second of which is individuation. Is the striving for individuation an accepted construct? As far as our research can discover, it appears to be an uncontested construct in psychology, marketing, and the popular media—at least within Western cultures.

Developmental psychology recognizes striving for independence and self-identity as a stage in early human development (Erikson, 1988). Adolescents labor to create a personal identity distinct from their parents. From childhood forward, people demonstrate a propensity for personalizing their existence with all the choices they make as regards their appearance, interests, associations, living and work settings, etc.

Marketers also appear to recognize people's striving for individuation. Certainly, the concept of "tailoring" as a marketing strategy implies that people individualize their identity. Tailoring is claimed to deliver added benefits to producers who vary their products and marketing messages so that they respond to the unique preferences and values of different segments of their target customers (Oaks, 2015; Smith, D. 2011).

Popular communications media readily incorporate the concept of tailoring in the design of their media products. Each offering targets a specific segment of people differentiated by demographics and personal preferences. Media executives shape each product's content, presentation, format, and appearance to appeal to the unique characteristics of their chosen target audience.

Based on these facts, one might reasonably conclude that the striving for individuation does map to empirically observed human behavior. However, the construct of a human striving for individuation has subtle implications that, from a scientific perspective, require empirical evidence to support. For example, it implies consciousness of oneself as distinct from others and a person's understanding that his or her mental perspective may differ from that of others. Is there any empirical basis for the conscious awareness of self, one's recognition of having an identity different from others, and people's awareness of the motives and purposes of others?

We have already reviewed one avenue of empirical support—the phenomenon of attribution-guided decision making. People do infer the mental states of others, and those inferences shape their choices of action. This implies both people's awareness of mental states and their recognition that the mental states of people vary. Some clever experimentation into these issues provides additional empirical support for the validity of the subtleties underlying the construct of individuation. This experimentation investigates the "theory of the mind" (ToM), which refers to people's ability to "attribute mental states—beliefs, intents, desires, pretending, knowledge, etc.—to oneself, and to others, and to understand that others may have beliefs, desires, intentions, and perspectives that are different from one's own" (Theory of mind, 2018).

A basic scenario used in ToM research involves a child, a mother, an experimenter, and the shell game. The child and mother witness the experimenter revealing what is under each of three shells. One has a pea under it, perhaps the center shell. The mother leaves the room and, out of her sight but in the presence of the child, the experimenter moves the location of the pea to another shell. The mother returns and the experimenter asks the child which shell the child thinks his/her mother will pick when asked where the pea is. After getting this answer, the experiment then asks the child where the pea is. Before age four, most children answer that the mother will pick where the experimenter *moved* the pea, suggesting that the child does not distinguish between his or her awareness and that of the absent mother. Beginning around four years of age, the majority of children will correctly anticipate which shell the mother will select and then correctly state where the pea *actually* is. When debriefed, children explain that their mothers' wrong understanding is due to their not being present when the experimenter changed the pea's location.

There are many variations of this scenario and more complex questions that ToM experiments address. But this simple scenario demonstrates the early development in humans of the distinction between what is in one's own mind and what is in another's (Baron-Cohen, Leslie, and Frith, 1985; Wimmer and Perner, 1983). It empirically reveals both the presence of self-awareness and the awareness of other perspectives distinct from one's own.

Thus, in addition to the manifest acceptance of the concept of individuation in Western cultures by psychology and marketing, there is experimental evidence that demonstrates that the underlying mental mechanisms necessary for a person's pursuit of individuation—awareness of self and differentiation of self from others—do exist.

Evidence That Human Decision Making Is Not Necessarily Effective

Both Capitalism and the Life Enabling model require that people make effective choices. Such choices best advantage their purposes. Economic research uses the term "rational decision making" to characterize what we refer to as "effective decision making." The word "rational" is somewhat misleading in that it suggests a systematic mental process, but, almost always, the economic research tests people's decision making by its result, not its process.[21]

Mainstream economic research defines a rational decision as the election of an alternative that results in someone maximizing his or her monetary gains (expected value) or receipt of value (expected utility). The choice that satisfies either criterion is determined by its statistical likelihood of yielding the outcome each prescribes. Thus, if I am offered two bets, A and B, and B has the higher likelihood of yielding the best monetary payoff, Capitalism assumes that I will always choose B (superior expected value). Or, if I am offered two treatments for my disease and one has the greater likelihood of succeeding, I will always pick that alternative (superior expected utility). Some decision-making research has also evaluated the rationality of people's decisions by assessing *post facto* whether the choice people made actually did satisfy them as they expected. If people always choose the utility-maximizing option, then they will always answer "Yes" when asked whether the choice they elected satisfied them.

[21] From the perspective of neoclassical Capitalism, rational choice does have a process requirement. Samuelson and Zeckhauser (1988) stated that a "fundamental property of the rational choice model, under certainty or uncertainty, is that only preference-relevant features of the alternatives influence the individual's decision" (1988, p. 8). The inclusion of this criterion of including only preference-relevant features in decision making only appears in studies of rational decision making when it is the specific focus of study. Otherwise, the rationality of a choice is solely decided by the outcome it produces.

Capitalism assumes that people are always rational (effective) decision makers. The Life Enabling model maintains that people can develop and apply this capability, but not all people do. The results of empirical studies support the Life Enabling model's premises.

The issue of rational decision making has been studied from the early 1970s. As summarized by Rabin (1998), people's decision making and judgment are typically not rational. They do not always elect the option that offers the best monetary payout or the one that is most likely to provide them the benefit they seek. Also, people's election of an option is subject to a number of factors other than which choice offers the greatest utility. Moreover, the assumptions that people know what desire or need they seek to satisfy, correctly assess what alternative delivers that outcome, and make judgments purely on the basis of the preference-related features have all been falsified. Here are some examples of the relevant findings:

- People falsely imagined differences between equivalent options. They wrongly differentiate between two equally valued options simply because they are described using different language that actually has the same meaning. For instance, given the choice to accept a single treatment option presented two different ways—either as having a 50% likelihood of success or as having a 50% likelihood of failure—significantly more people pick the former alternative, *even though the alternatives being offered are the same.*
- People demonstrate a "status quo bias." People "prefer the status quo to changes that involve [potential] losses of some goods, even when these losses are offset by gains" (Rabin, 1998, p. 14). Valuing "standing pat" when another choice offers a gain is not rational decision making from the perspective of mainstream economics. Status quo bias is evident when people prefer things to stay the same by doing nothing or by sticking with a decision made previously, even when a change will objectively deliver greater value.[22]
- People misjudge the value that a choice will deliver when that choice's value is measured by the satisfaction it actually provides. Kahneman (1997) differentiated two ways of viewing utility (i.e., value satisfaction). You can measure it at the point of decision making, which he terms "decision utility." Or you can measure it at the point of experiencing the option one selects (hedonic utility). From the perspective of Capitalism, "the utility of an

[22] A related phenomenon is "risk aversion." Risk aversion expresses itself when people elect an option that they *experience* as more predictable but offers a lower payoff than another option, *even when the superior payoff of the other option is adjusted for the likelihood of receiving it.* The "rational choice" would be the opposite.

outcome" is determined at the point of choice based on each option's value-relevant characteristics (Kahneman, 1997, p. 21). However, unless that elected option delivers the hedonic satisfaction the decision maker expects, it does not maximize a person's utility. According to Rabin (1998), the collective research on this question indicates that people mistake the actual value (i.e., hedonic satisfaction) delivered by the options they elect. Thus, when you evaluate the post-selection effects of an elected option, it frequently falls short of delivering the satisfaction the person expected at the time he or she chose it. In essence, people frequently do not make value-maximizing choices.

- People use reference points in making their decisions. These reference points subjectively modify their objective assessment of alternatives. People show "greater sensitivity to how a current situation differs from some reference level than to [the] absolute characteristics of the situation" (Rabin, 1998, p. 13). For example, when a person is poor, $50 is a large sum. Yet, after becoming rich, obtaining $50 no longer provides the same hedonic satisfaction the person previously experienced. Reference-level decision making violates Capitalism's rational decision-making standard because $50 is still $50—hence, the option should deliver the same value satisfaction.
- Another source of failed rationality is that people modify their choice making based on the perceived characteristics of the offerer or other issues unrelated to the preference-related features of the offering. For example, Meyers-Levy, Zhu, and Jiang (2010) found that bodily sensations prompted by the texture of flooring can modify a buyer's assessment of a product he or she is evaluating. In retailing, it is widely known that people will more frequently buy a product if its in-store placement is near the checkout or at eye level.

These are but a few of the empirically documented phenomena that demonstrate that rational decision making is not a given. Two others such phenomena are: people's propensity to pursue immediate gratification that results in long-term loss (e.g., overeating) and their making errors of application. Errors of application appear in the form of missed information or wrongly remembered prior satisfactions, incorrectly applied judgment principles, and the failure to apply one's assessment expertise based on overconfidence in one's intuitive judgment. Rabin (1998) stated, "An error of application is most convincingly demonstrated when a person, spontaneously or with minimal prompting, clutches his head and exclaims: 'How could I have missed that?'" (1998, p. 31).

Conclusions About the Realisticness of the Life Enabling Model's Assumptions

Based on the research reviewed in this chapter, there should be little doubt that the premises of the Life Enabling model concerning the native inclinations of people pass the test of realisticness.

The premises of the Life Enabling model stand consistent with the inclinations of very many adults. Its assumptions about people's sameness and differentness are consistent with the premises of empirical science. The facts of evolutionary theory, anthropology, biology, medicine, and psychology support the proposition that sociality is a fundamental quality of human nature and that connectedness with others is essential to our individual survival, growth, learning, and well-being. Indeed, sociality is a critical component of humankind's evolutionary fitness.

While behavioral science has clearly shown that there is a segment of people who do operate egoistically to maximize their personal gains, that same research also supports that cooperation and sharing are default behaviors for as many and often more adults. Additionally, the evidence makes clear that people's cooperation and sharing depend on their experience of the others with whom they are interacting and the conditions that prevail as they relate with them. Thus, most cooperative-oriented people will cease their cooperation if they perceive themselves as being treated unfairly. They will act to punish egoists who exploit them if they have that option. If not, they will discontinue their cooperation. Egoists, on the other hand, will continue to exploit others as long as they experience no negative consequences for their actions. If they do experience such consequences, they restrain their exploitive behavior and behave cooperatively.

The findings of research also support the assertion that people develop and pursue their own individuation. They possess an awareness of self and recognize others as distinct beings, each with his or her own perspective. Within the context of our sociality, we continuously differentiate who we each are and reveal in finer detail our unique personalities.

Finally, the preponderance of evidence makes clear that no one can reasonably assume that people universally make rational or effective decisions. Such an assumption is patently false. Any theory that requires people to make effective decisions must also require that entrepreneurs verify that people do so. If people do not make effective choices, as the model requires, that deficiency must be corrected for the theory to have practical utility.

How Commerce Consistent With the Life Enabling Model's Premises Is Implemented

Given that the premises of the Life Enabling model pass the test of realisticness, how is commerce conducted according to this model? Sections II, III, and IV of this book answer this question. They provide practical guidance for implementing a commercial enterprise in a manner consistent with the makeup of the people who satisfy the Life Enabling model's premises.

The Framework of a Commercial Model and the Knowledge Contained Within Each of Its Components

Component	Results	Activities	Resources
Strategic	Identifies the end commerce serves and guides one in defining an enterprise's *business intent,* including ▪ its purpose, ▪ its vision, ▪ its core values, ▪ how it defines the meaning of profit, ▪ the stakeholders the enterprise recognizes and its relationship with each, and ▪ the benefits it must produce.	Guides one in defining an enterprise's *commercial strategy*—how it will conduct commerce to produce success. The issues addressed include ▪ how it defines what it will offer to whom, ▪ where it will enter into commerce, ▪ how it will attract, win, and retain customers, and ▪ how it will realize profitability as the model defines it.	Guides one in defining an enterprise's *organizational strategy*, including ▪ what its critical-to-success resources are for long-term success and the essential features each must possess and ▪ how the enterprise should organize itself within (structurally and socially).

Section II

The Strategic Component of the Life Enabling Model

This section provides the knowledge you need to define the long-term goal your enterprise must realize and specify the Strategic results it must produce, the marketplace activities it will use to generate them, and the organizational strategy essential to its success.

This chapter describes the long-term results a Life Enabling enterprise produces. It defines the purpose commerce serves, the core values its conduct abides by, and the outcomes it produces. In doing so, it clarifies how the enterprise defines profit, what stakeholders the enterprise recognizes, and how the enterprise relates with each of them.

Use the guidance in this chapter to define your Life Enabling enterprise's business intent, its principles of conduct, and its strategic-level key performance measures.

Chapter 7

Preview of the Model's Guidance

Exhibit 1, beginning on the next page, previews the Life Enabling model's Strategic Results guidance. It clarifies the scope of issues this chapter discusses and provides a brief summary of the model's guidance with respect to each.

The Purpose Commerce Serves

The purpose of commerce at the enterprise level is to maximally deliver value to customers while benefiting all stakeholders inclusively. A "value" is some feature of an object, activity, or setting that enables its recipients to achieve the purpose they seek to accomplish in a way that satisfies their preferences and provides a better life for everyone. Within Life Enabling commerce, value received is judged both objectively and subjectively. Objective assessment uses measurements of the effects of the enterprise's offering on the achievement and well-being of customers and stakeholders. Subjective assessment measures the benefit received as experienced by each recipient.

The Logic of the Model's Commercial Purpose

The purpose the model defines for commerce is a straightforward deduction from its understanding of human nature and the role commerce serves in fulfilling the human drives of sociality and personal emergence. If the model's purpose is accomplished, then individuals connect with others in mutually benefiting relationships. Each enables the success of the other, grows in productive capabilities, and advances the emergence of his or her unique personality. Society prospers, and our ecosystem is unharmed.[1] Both individually and collectively, people raise their proficiency as learners, achievers, and contributors. They expand their ability to engage in future commerce. The repetition of these outcomes initiates and sustains a virtuous cycle of life-enhancing benefits delivered, growth realized, and expanded opportunities for commerce produced.

Elevating Productive Capabilities

The model's approach to commerce elevates people's ability to produce value in both personal and instrumental ways. The agent of both these effects is *success.*

On the personal level, both the producer's and the customer's increased success strengthens their respective experiences of positive self-efficacy. Positive self-efficacy enhances their readiness to take on new initiatives, set challenging goals, and achieve greater future success.[2]

[1] As will be discussed later in this chapter, the model recognizes the ecosystem that sustains all life as a stakeholder in commerce.

[2] See Bandura (1982, 1997) for a comprehensive discussion of the construct of self-efficacy and its ef-

Exhibit 1. Summary of the Life Enabling Model's Strategic Results Guidance

Purpose of Commerce	To maximally deliver value to customers while benefiting all stakeholders to commerce inclusively. A "value" is some feature of an object, activity, or setting that enables its recipients to achieve the purpose they seek to accomplish in a way that satisfies their preferences and provides a better life for everyone. **Requirements** ▪ The utility delivered must be real. ▪ Both the offering and its provision must be life enhancing to its recipients and, at a minimum, do no harm to the ecosystem that supports them. ▪ The information used to judge success must be evidence based.
Motive Force for Commerce	Commerce is the natural expression of people's social and personal nature. It is a vehicle for connecting with others in mutually benefiting ways and for the emergence of one's unique personality.
Definition of Profit	Profit is registered whenever an enterprise produces a result that elevates its capability to engage in Life Enabling commerce. This occurs when an enterprise grows in ways that immediately increase its ability to produce and deliver value to its customers and all stakeholders. It also occurs when, by its agency, the commercial context better satisfies the context requirements for Life Enabling commerce so that it may thrive and fully deliver its benefits.
Producer's Responsibility	▪ The producer or seller, as the initiator of commerce, is responsible for ensuring that all parties to commerce are capable of fulfilling their responsibilities. If deficiencies exist, it is the producer or seller's responsibility to remedy them (e.g., make valid market information available and accessible; ensure parties possess the knowledge, skills, and proficiencies needed to correctly identify their needs and evaluate the benefits each receives; etc.). ▪ The model maintains that responsibility is ubiquitous and indivisible among all parties to commerce. Therefore, the producer's special responsibility does not mitigate, for example, each other party's responsibility to be fully informed, make free and effective choices, and fulfill the terms of each exchange.
Customer	The customer is the user of the product or service offering. Enabling that individual's success in a way that betters *Continued ...*

fects. Bandura (1997) also provides a review of the multi-decade empirical support for these assertions.

Exhibit 1. Summary of the Life Enabling Model's Strategic Results Guidance (continued)

Customer (continued)	everyone's life is the *raison d'être* of Life Enabling commerce. All decisions and actions taken by the enterprise must first accomplish this commitment to customers and then satisfy the expectations of all stakeholders.
Stakeholders to Be Benefited	▪ The model recognizes as a stakeholder any individual, group, or entity that either is affected by or may affect the success of commerce. It includes our life-sustaining ecosystem as one of commerce's stakeholders. ▪ Stakeholders always present in Life Enabling commerce are contributors/owners, suppliers, the communities within which the enterprise operates, the government bodies that represent those communities, and the ecosystem that supports their lives. Others are included when present (e.g., creditors). ▪ By "community" we mean all the localities within which the enterprise operates. This includes the communities in which it has facilities; those through which its products pass on their way to customers; those that are affected by the by-products of its activities; those where its products are received, used, and disposed of; and those from whom it recruits its contributors and to whom it sells its offerings.

Core Values That Must Be Abided By	**Individual conduct**
	▪ Be accountable.
	▪ Act with integrity.
	▪ Be honest in all dealings.
	▪ Hold the validity of information sacrosanct.
	▪ Strive for perfection in all personal and professional endeavors.
	▪ Be pioneering.
	Social conduct
	▪ Respect others.
	▪ Act fairly in all interactions with others.
	▪ Show understanding for the perspectives of others.
	▪ Find inclusive solutions to realize opportunities or solve problems that affect others.
	▪ Be a good citizen by
	  ▪ honoring the language and spirit of the law,
	  ▪ promoting the strengthening of communities,
	  ▪ contributing to the enrichment of society, and
	  ▪ doing no harm to our collective ecosystem.
	Continued ...

Exhibit 1. Summary of the Life Enabling Model's Strategic Results Guidance (continued)

Core Values That Must Be Abided By (continued)	**Executive activities**
	▪ Structure the organization functionally, not politically.
	▪ Use a team approach to working with others.
	▪ Promote, facilitate, and leverage learning throughout the enterprise and across all stakeholders.
	▪ Document all commerce-guiding knowledge.
	▪ Ensure the success of all contributors.
	▪ Understand the aims, performance settings, and perspectives of customers and all stakeholders.
	▪ Ensure the meaningful involvement of all stakeholders.
	▪ Ensure full and open communication with all parties to commerce.
	▪ Use decision-making and problem-solving methods that enable participation and public discourse.
	▪ Think long term, anticipate change, and offer solutions that continue to work for the people you are serving as their circumstances evolve.
	▪ Foster free markets by
	  ▪ removing artificial barriers to competition;
	  ▪ advancing the availability and accessibility of valid information about offerings;
	  ▪ enabling citizens to make free, informed, and effective choices that best meet their needs;
	  ▪ eliminating the effects of coercive pressures that corrupt rational decision making; and
	  ▪ ensuring that every market you operate in satisfies the model's 10 commercial context requirements.

Expected Outcomes of Commerce	▪ Customers grow in success and their capability to produce value by (1) receiving an offering that measurably advances their success in ways that provide a better life for everyone and (2) experiencing a buying–benefiting experience that is increasingly value adding and non-resource consuming. ▪ Organization members are fully engaged in the enterprise, enhance their capabilities to produce value, and find fulfillment of their social and personal work-related goals. ▪ Suppliers/delivery agents achieve greater success in realizing their commercial goals through their collaboration with the Life Enabling enterprise and their application of the Life Enabling model to their commercial endeavors. *Continued ...*

Exhibit 1. Summary of the Life Enabling Model's Strategic Results Guidance (continued)

Expected Outcomes of Commerce (continued)	▪ Communities that the Life Enabling enterprise touches have more wealth, more choice, smarter and more capable citizens, and increased career opportunities as a result of its business operations. ▪ Government agencies that work with the Life Enabling enterprise have greater success in accomplishing the citizen mandates each serves. ▪ The human ecosystem is either unharmed or enhanced by the enterprise's commercial activities. ▪ The markets within which the enterprise does commerce either satisfy the 10 requirements of a commercial context as defined by the model or are advanced toward satisfying those requirements. ▪ The enterprise has a record of conduct consistent with the Life Enabling model's core values and all other conditions of performance as specified by the model. ▪ The enterprise grows in its capability to produce value for others and in its reputation as one that reliably enables its customers' success, provides its stakeholders the benefits they seek, and conducts itself in a life-enhancing manner.

On the instrumental side, prior commerce will have provided each party increased resources for use in launching new or expanded commercial efforts. Those resources might be new learning (knowledge and skills); higher levels of proficiency in skills needed for success; or new technologies, equipment, tools, or other value-producing resources that can be applied to productive ends.

With these elevated personal and instrumental capabilities, people grow in their ability to create value (productive capabilities) and exchange that value with others (new commerce).

Increased Proficiency as Learners

The second way the model's approach to commerce promotes increased commerce is by raising people's learning proficiency. In Life Enabling commerce, learning is the engine of success. It drives continuous improvement and, with it, the delivery of increasing value. A Life Enabling enterprise by design elevates the learning proficiency of its members. It teaches its members the competencies they need to more rapidly acquire knowledge from others. It also instructs them in applying systematic problem-solving methods that uncover and eliminate barriers to producing maximum value. It trains its members in how to analyze their own prior performance and extract principles they can use to improve their future performance. It supports their use of learning skills by encouraging them to explore, discover, and experiment with new ideas. It facilitates people's daily efforts to uncover and eliminate barriers to organizational success, explore better ways to accomplish the organization's operations, and think in new ways to envision how it can better accomplish its purpose.

The enterprise's learning focus and its pioneering contributors enable it to respond quickly when existing commercial activities cease to be viable or new forms of commerce emerge or are required. Indeed, its members become the originators of such transitions and the creators of new commerce.

But beyond the organization itself, a member's elevated proficiency in learning is theirs to own and use in improving their lives. Its use in their living, learning, and relating in social and civic contexts opens them up to new ideas, suggests new goals, and reveals new opportunities for them to explore. It enables people to efficiently acquire or create new methods for realizing newly uncovered opportunities and for developing the expertise they need to act on them successfully. Collectively, this personal growth elevates society's ability to conceive new ways to prosper. People's elevated ability to learn therefore yields improvements in their ability to produce value in both their personal living and their social and civic roles. This further expands people's opportunities for commerce and commerce's sustainability.

The Motive Force for Commerce

Capitalism and the Life Enabling model define the motive force for commerce in dramatically different ways. In the dominant model, the producer solely seeks to maximize his or her profit from every transaction. Profit is defined monetarily. The driving force for continued commerce is the never-satiated desire to accumulate more wealth. The perspective guiding the individual is one of absolute self-interest.

For the Life Enabling approach, commerce is the natural expression of people's social and personal nature. People are propelled from within by their desire to connect with others in mutually benefiting relationships and their striving to grow, learn, master new capabilities, and individuate themselves. Commerce serves both these ends, and its continued pursuit is self-sustaining. Each instance of enterprise is an avenue for connecting with others in mutually benefiting ways. Each effort to produce value is an opportunity for personal emergence. Each provides an avenue for pursuing one's interests, applying one's talents, expressing and enhancing one's productive capabilities, and refining one's self-understanding.

The Life Enabling Model's Definition of Profit

Given the purpose of Life Enabling commerce pursues, a Life Enabling enterprise registers profit whenever its capability to engage in commerce is elevated as an immediate result of its commercial activities. This occurs when the enterprise grows in ways that increase its ability to produce and deliver value to its customers and all its stakeholders. Thus, an increase in the enterprise's documented knowledge that guides better performance on the metrics that calibrate its success is profit. Growth in the personal productivity of its contributors is profit. Similarly, acquiring material resources that, by their design, produce added value for customers is also an instance of profit (e.g., a machine that produces an output that better satisfies customer values). Profit is also realized when the enterprise's efforts transform the commercial context within which it operates in a way that better satisfies the model's context requirements (e.g., more consumers are able to make effective choices or are freer to transfer from one to another producer). All of these examples directly advance a producer's capability to implement the Life Enabling approach to commerce. The model does not, however, consider money to be profit. Money is merely a medium of exchange. It is passive by nature. It possesses no inherent meaning or agency. In itself, it is unproductive.

Requirements for Declaring the Model's Purpose Achieved

A Life Enabling enterprise must satisfy three requirements in order to declare its aim realized. First, value delivered must be real. Second, the utility provided must be life enhancing to its recipients and, at a minimum, do no harm to the ecosystem that supports them. Third, the information used to judge success must be evidence based.

Value Delivered Must Be Real

Commerce only succeeds when the utility it provides is real. Utility is real when its effects measurably advance a purpose of its recipient. If the utility received is apparent but not real, then it has not benefited its recipient in the way he or she sought. The illusion of benefit a recipient may experience only diminishes the recipient. It drains the recipient's resources and does not enable the person to achieve his or her purpose. As a result, the recipient grows less capable of future commerce. Thus, if a person seeking nourishment acquires a food product that is capable of stimulating a temporary feeling of satiation in him or her but is not actually nourishing, that instance of commerce fails its purpose. Since that person expended resources but failed to realize the purpose he or she pursued, his or her ability to produce value is diminished, not enhanced. Opportunities for future commerce by and with that person are reduced.

Utility Provided Must Be Life Enhancing

Given the enterprise's intent to provide a better life for everyone, its offering, resourcing, and operations may not harm people or the ecosystem that supports their lives. The utility provided, therefore, must also enable people to realize an end that enhances their ability to live, learn, work, or relate. Any offering or its provision that, to whatever extent, diminishes the well-being of its recipients or any other affected party is invalid by definition. It diminishes commerce, which is an expression of life. As Deming stated, the aim of commerce "must always relate to a better life for everyone" (Deming, 2000, p. 52). If an offering fails in accomplishing this purpose, its recipients and all other affected parties will not grow in their capability to be productive, and their potential to engage in future commerce will be lessened.

Utility also requires that neither the offering itself nor its manner of provision may diminish or corrupt the ecosystem that supports all life. No facet of commerce may compromise our ecosystem's provision of life-essential resources such as clean air, food, water, or any other component of the ecological environment that enables our continuance.

Information About Performance Must Be Evidence Based

Each party to commerce must judge performance using valid information that is rigorously evaluated. From the business's perspective, faulty information or its evaluation prevents knowing to what extent the enterprise has realized its commercial purpose. This undermines its ability to improve what it offers and its capability to produce even greater value. Faulty information or its evaluation by customers undermines their effective decision making, and it jeopardizes their well-being and success.

The evidence-based evaluation of benefit requires that each party systematically assesses the quantity and quality of utility he or she receives using objectively acquired empirical information. Subjective data are only sufficient when evaluating a party's *experience* of a transaction or its outcome. The enterprise also must assess its impact on the ecosystem using objectively acquired empirical information.

The Responsibilities of the Producer and the Other Parties to Commerce

The model views the producer, the party offering a resource to enable another person's success, as responsible for ensuring that all parties to commerce are capable of fulfilling their commercial responsibilities.[3] Thus, it is up to Life Enabling

[3] We use the word "producer" to identify the initiator of commerce. In some commerce, this party will not have made what he or she offers and would be more correctly referred to as a "seller."

enterprises to advance people's capability to act freely, make effective choices, and perform effectively. Likewise, the producer is responsible for ensuring that the commercial context satisfies the model's requirements. This special responsibility *does not* negate any other party's responsibility for ensuring the same outcomes. Thus, for example, customers remain responsible for ensuring their ability to understand their needs, evaluate their options, and make correct judgments about what best satisfies their requirements. Similarly, citizens, through their governmental representatives, remain responsible for ensuring that markets are competitive and otherwise satisfy the requirements detailed in the Life Enabling model. In the model's perspective, responsibility is ubiquitous and indivisible. It cannot be put off to another nor reduced by any other party's actions to assume it.

Why then does the producer have a special responsibility if all other participants retain theirs? As explained earlier, the reason is twofold. One, it is the producer's free choice to enter any market. Two, it is the producer's desire to succeed in commerce using the Life Enabling model. Each of these choices is elective. If you elect both, you can only accomplish your intent if all parties to commerce are capable of fulfilling their responsibilities and the market context satisfies the model's requirements. The model, therefore, incorporates this producer responsibility not from a moral sense but because it is a practical requirement for realizing the producer's desire to succeed in commerce using the Life Enabling approach.

Implications of the Producer's Special Responsibility for Its Marketplace Conduct

There are a number of practical implications that flow from the producer's special responsibility. One example is that a food processing company implementing the Life Enabling commercial model would never lobby for laws or regulations that block the public's right to know what ingredients its products contain and whether those ingredients have been genetically modified. Instead, the company would argue against such a restriction of information. Similarly, a bank or other commercial lender would always ensure that the documents governing the borrower's rights and obligations were written in a language and style that its borrowers could understand. Also, if such an enterprise detected that its prospective customers lacked the knowledge, skills, or proficiencies required to make informed and reasonable judgments about its offerings, that producer would undertake education efforts to correct the deficit. This is what the Toyota Motor Company did when it started business in 1938. At that time, the Japanese public were largely unfamiliar with cars, how they worked, what they could do, and how one selected a car that would serve his or her needs. Toyota's head of marketing and sales, Shotaro Kamiya, initiated a door-to-door program through which his staff educated prospective consumers about automobiles and how to select a car that would meet their needs (Toyota Traditions, 2007). In the process, Toyota learned about their prospective customers' wants, needs, and preferences.[4]

The Customer

Following Deming (1982a), we define the customer as the *user* of a producer's product or service. He or she is the person whose purpose the offering must enable. Enabling that individual's success in a way that betters everyone's life is the *raison d'être* of Life Enabling commerce.

In sales to businesses, there may be others involved in the acquisition, installation, maintenance, support, etc. of one's product or service offering. We treat these people as stakeholders. As such, their needs, expectations, and concerns must be understood and addressed. They too must be benefited by the enterprise. But the enterprise's first and foremost concern is the utility of the output for the customer (user). Unless that is secured, all else is meaningless.

One implication of the primary status of the customer is that if, at a given point in time, an enterprise is only capable of generating an incomplete solution to its mandate to enable its customers' success and satisfy the expectations of all its stakeholders, that solution, *at the very least*, must meet its customers' effectiveness needs.[5] That is, the offering must enable customers to successfully achieve their

[4] Contrast this customer-educating approach with that implemented by Capitalist commercial mortgage lenders targeting low-income first-time home buyers. These borrowers lacked prior experience in obtaining mortgages but had a great desire to own a home. According to Brian Montgomery, the Federal Housing Administration commissioner under President George W. Bush, mortgage lenders lured these low-income borrowers away from traditional, cheaper, and less risky FHA mortgages to what he termed the "fool's gold" of subprime loans (Becker, Stolberg, and Labaton, 2008). They offered them complicated products that contained hidden risks and made them attractive with low initial teaser rates. The offerors frequently obscured the much higher rates the borrower would have to pay after a year or two. Many of the loans came with big fees that were hidden in the overall interest rate. And many had prepayment penalties that effectively blocked people from getting cheaper loans for two years or longer. The products themselves were considered "exotic and often inscrutable" by banking regulators (Andrews, 2007). Edward M. Gramlich, the Chair of the Federal Reserve's Committee on Consumer and Community Affairs from 1997 to 2005, concluded that the industry was selling its most risky loan products to the least sophisticated borrowers because "the least sophisticated borrowers are probably duped into taking these products" (Andrews, 2007). Risk to the mortgage lenders was minimal. Each transaction brought fees that were paid on signing. Reselling the mortgages immediately to investment banks ended their lending risk completely. Banks profited by turning these poor loans into securities they sold to unsuspecting investors. This also eliminated the banks' risk from loan defaults. The conduct of these mortgage lenders and banks has been a subject of disapprobation, but as implementers of the Capitalist commercial model, *they were absolutely correct.* They maximized their profits while minimizing their risk. The negative economic effects produced for the general citizenry as a result of their conduct were inconsequential to the lenders, as they were not exposed to them. Their profits were in hand, preventing the possibility of loss. The positive benefits of running up the price of homes was also captured in subsequent mortgages that required higher loan values and therefore resulted in higher fees. In all its facets, this appears to have been a very effective realization of the egoistic self-maximizing purpose commerce serves as defined by Capitalism.

[5] "Effectiveness needs" are requirements that enable the customer's successful performance. To fully service a customer, you must also satisfy all their remaining needs and preferences.

purposes. No action to satisfy the expectations of stakeholders may detract from this responsibility.

The commitment of all customers to learning and improving their understanding of their purpose, values, capabilities, needs, and approach is essential to the ultimate success of Life Enabling enterprise. Errors in understanding or unwillingness to discover and adopt improved methods for accomplishing one's purpose creates waste. Waste squanders resources, and that diminishes both the value a producer can deliver and customers receive. Therefore, the extent to which customers commit to learning and improving their understanding and approach represents a constraint on the performance of a Life Enabling enterprise. Engaging customers in learning that improves their capabilities and methods for realizing their purposes is therefore a producer responsibility that is essential to successful Life Enabling commerce.

Stakeholders Recognized by the Model

A Life Enabling enterprise recognizes as stakeholders all individuals, groups, and other entities that affect or are affected by its efforts to serve customers. Each provides an element of the support an enterprise needs to succeed in commerce, either by the contribution of a resource or by acceptance of or adaptation to an effect commerce has on the party. Therefore, each has a "stake" in the direction, conduct, and outcomes of commerce. From the perspective of the enterprise, the greater the support such parties provide, the more likely its commercial efforts are to succeed. The following individuals and groups are viewed as stakeholders in commerce:

- contributors/owners,[6]
- suppliers/delivery agents,
- the communities within which commerce takes place,
- the governmental bodies that represent those communities, and
- the ecosystem that supports all human and natural life.

The list of stakeholders expands to include all other contributing parties, such as creditors, should they be present.

About Stakeholders

Each stakeholder contributes an element of assistance that enables successful commerce.

---

[6] As you will read in *Chapter 14*, a Life Enabling enterprise is a member-owned business. See *Choosing the Right Form of Business*, pages 422–424, for more details.

Organizational members/owners contribute the energy, expertise, and ideas that guide, implement, and improve the enterprise and accomplish its purpose. Their personal commitment to learn, improve their own performance, and support each other's growth in productive capability enriches the enterprise's ability to produce value. They may also contribute material resources to support the enterprise.

Suppliers provide the resource inputs needed to generate the enterprise's offering. Delivery agents assist the enterprise in transferring its offering to its customers for their use. Supplier resources must meet certain specifications to allow the enterprise to produce its offering with maximum value and minimum waste. The performance of delivery agents must also satisfy the enterprise's goals in servicing its customers. How both parties fulfill the enterprise's needs and expectations affects the level of value it can deliver. Waste in a supplier or delivery agent's operations shows up as unproductive cost in the producer's operations. Thus, the commitment of suppliers and delivery agents to learning and improving their production of value is yet another contribution they make to the Life Enabling enterprise.

The community provides the infrastructure the enterprise relies on to conduct its business. It also nurtures, protects, rears, educates, and supports the people who directly contribute to the enterprise or who may in the future contribute to it. And it is the source of the enterprise's customers. Understand that by "community" we mean all those localities within which the enterprise operates. This includes the communities in which it has facilities; those from which its inputs are obtained; those through which its products pass on their way to customers; those that are affected by the byproducts of its activities; those where its products are received, used, and disposed of; and those from whom it recruits its contributors and to whom it sells its offerings.

Governments support their communities' efforts to sustain and thrive. Their role is to address issues critical to accomplishing community goals that are greater than any one individual, family, or neighborhood within the community can realize. When effective, they enable their communities to survive and thrive, and, as a consequence, those communities become better able to support commerce.

The ecosystem provides the matrix that sustains all life. It includes all the living and non-living components that, functioning interdependently, are essential for life to exist. Its *least* contribution to enterprise is the raw materials which producers use to generate their products and implement their services.

Together, stakeholders are the sources of the wherewithal needed for an enterprise's success. Without them, no commercial enterprise can realize its purpose. With them growing and thriving, there is an ever-expanding opportunity for commerce. It is this reality that underpins the model's recognition of the importance of all stakeholders and its commitment to ensure that all stakeholders benefit inclusively from its efforts.

Appreciating the Implications of the Model's View of Stakeholders

One way to internalize the implications of the Life Enabling model's view of stakeholders is to contrast its treatment of externalities with the way Capitalism treats externalities. An externality is a cost or benefit incurred by a party who did not agree to the action causing the cost or benefit. A cost is called a negative externality. A benefit is called a positive externality.

Air pollution of eastern states in the United States caused by coal-burning power-generating companies operating in the western states is an example of a *negative externality*. The citizens of the affected eastern states, though not parties to the commercial activities that generate the pollution, must bear the costs associated with receiving that pollution. There are both direct and indirect costs. They include, for example, lost earnings due to pollution-stimulated illnesses, increased medical costs, lost revenue due to fall-off in business from vacation visitors, and increased taxes to pay for remediation efforts to recover the use of streams and waterways or prevent the blighting of needed forest acreage.

With regard to *positive externalities*, consider the owner of an apple orchard located adjacent to a bee yard. The beekeeper's bees will pollinate the nearby apple orchard during the normal course of their daily activity and not as a contracted service. The apple orchard's owner benefits from the pollination, as it enables his or her trees to bear the fruit that the orchard sells. The benefits the orchard owner receives are unsolicited and not remunerated. This is an instance of a positive externality.

Recall that a Capitalist business has no social responsibility. Its singular responsibility is to maximize profits for its owners (Friedman, 1970). To this end, a Capitalist business eliminates negative externalities by offloading their cost onto others outside the business (e.g., citizens of eastern states). It internalizes positive externalities by capturing their value without remunerating the source of that value. Both actions maximize its profits. Thus, for example, a power company implementing Capitalism will not attend to pollution abatement unless forced to, since it involves a cost. Also, it will invest money in political action to prevent being required to do pollution abatement as long as that investment nets a return.[7]

In contrast, a Life Enabling enterprise addresses negative externalities by *eliminating them in fact,* not simply from its balance sheet. It would recognize the distant communities affected by its activities as stakeholders and voluntarily implement pollution abatement actions. Simultaneously, it would seek ways to generate power in a way that did not involve the need for abatement. A Life Enabling enterprise does not advantage itself at the cost of its stakeholders. It sees itself in commerce *with them* and thus sees their well-being as a value to be protected.

With regard to positive externalities, consider the pharmaceutical companies. They receive government grants to do research into developing compounds that will treat various diseases. In return, the business provides the government its research findings. A positive externality to that research-for-pay commerce is the occasional identification of a compound that can actually treat a disease and provide benefits to people. Presumably, that externality belongs, at least in part, to the people whose government paid for the research that uncovered the useful compound. A Capitalist pharmaceutical company, however, would seek to capture that positive externality for itself. Thus, it might spend money to influence lawmakers to create regulations or pass laws prohibiting the government from owning any useful compounds uncovered by the research it performed on behalf of the public. The law might also force the sponsoring government agency to pass ownership rights of such compounds from the public to the company whose work it subsidized (Zaitchik, 2018). Under these circumstances, the pharmaceutical company can sell the drug back to the public who paid for its discovery at whatever profit it defines.[8]

In contrast, a Life Enabling pharmaceutical company would recognize the public's ownership of the compound, in whole or part, and seek a partnership with their government that puts the company's production and distribution expertise in the service of the public's interest in exchange for sharing the benefits such commerce would generate. From the model's perspective, advantage is pursued by

[7] See Footnote 27, page 50, for an example of an effort by Capitalist enterprises to escape the consequences of the negative externality of pollution.

[8] Gilead Sciences, Inc. offers a recent example of a Capitalist pharmaceutical company making the most of citizen risk-taking. It developed the drug Remdesivir "with at least $79 million in U.S. government funding" supplied by the citizens of the United States (Fang and Lerner, 2020). While research (Hill, Wang, Levi, Heath, and Fortunak, 2020) indicates that the minimum cost for production of this drug is 93 cents per dose, or $4.65 per a 5-day course of treatment, Gilead announced that it will charge U.S. citizens with health insurance $624 per dose, or $3,120 for a course of treatment (Macleod, 2020a).

sharing in, not usurping, the benefits positive externalities yield. Shared benefits generate more opportunities for commerce through the positive relationships they engender and the shared well-being they create. And to reiterate once more, the model's guidance flows logically from its empirically supported premises about people and their intent to maximize the well-being of individuals and humankind as a whole. They do not derive from some moral philosophy or set of religious beliefs.

The Concept of Core Values

Core values are the principles of conduct that people implementing an enterprise abide by as they pursue their commercial purpose. In general, values derive from training or indoctrination, personal beliefs or convictions, or learning extracted from one's experience of actions taken and their consequences. *Concerning commercial models, however, core values are derived logically from the purpose commerce serves and verified against the relevant findings of the social sciences.* They specify principles of conduct necessary to the successful use of a specific economic model.

The core values of an approach to commerce have no "moral" underpinning. They are not founded in personal convictions about right or wrong or in the beliefs of a religion or a theory of ethical behavior. Despite what the label "values" connotes, they have no inherent claim to "goodness," "correctness," or "worth." The core values of a commercial enterprise are simply principles of conduct that must regulate its commercial activities so that its actions realize the purpose of commerce defined in the commercial model it adopts. They are grounded in the logic of the model and the findings of social science.

Also, they are not aspirational in nature but mandatory. The practices that flow from a model's core values are required for the realization of its commercial purpose. Finally, almost always, the core values of Capitalist companies are not the "public speech" versions of the core values that these companies publish on their web sites or in their promotional materials. By our analyses, these public speech expressions of "core values" are constructed for persuasive purposes only. They reflect neither the real conduct of the companies communicating them nor the conduct required by the commercial model they embrace. As U.S. District Court Judge Sidney S. Stein concluded, they are "mere commercial puffery" (Neumann, 2013).[9]

---

[9] We use an inductive method to derive the actual core values that drive a business's observed commercial behavior. We analyze the organization's documented decisions and actions and infer whose ends those behaviors factually benefit ("cui bono") and what benefits each provides. We compare these ends to the company's publicly stated purpose, vision, and values. Wherever a discrepancy exists, we apply the empiricist's rule that *behavior trumps speech* or imagined intents. See *Appendix F:*

Different Commercial Models Require Different Values

If one commercial model defines its intent communally (e.g., to generate benefits for customers and all stakeholders inclusively) and another defines it egoistically (e.g., maximize the producer's profit from each transaction), the core values or principles of conduct that guide commerce in each of these models must differ.

A communal intent requires a collaborative effort among all participants. Based on social science findings—highlights of which were reviewed in *Chapter 6*—such collaboration requires relationships typified by trust, respect for each other's expectations and concerns, fairness, and the open and honest sharing of information. The absence of these qualities undermines people's ability to define a common purpose and work together to realize it. Once a common purpose is defined, its collaborative pursuit requires sharing power among the participants in determining how that purpose is realized (Mary Parker Follett's "power with" model; Follett, 1995). The form of working together such an enterprise uses is that of a team (Follett, 1995a).

In contrast, a commercial model whose end is maximizing producer profit must operate using different principles of conduct. This end is *exclusive* in nature. It specifies that the initiator of commerce seeks all the benefits possible from a commercial transaction, since "all" defines the maximum. Given this end, open and honest sharing of information, for example, may undermine one's success. For instance, if I am a pharmaceutical company seeking to promote a new drug, I may not want to share the results of studies that show adverse effects. Rather, I might withhold the results of these studies, claiming they lacked rigor, while I submit studies of equal credibility that produced less problematic results. In fact, Capitalist pharmaceutical companies employ such practices (AboutLawsuits, 2009; Cooper, 2014).[10]

Given a commercial model where the pursued outcome is exclusive in nature, a required value for success is control or "power over" the other parties to commerce (Follett, 1995). When one party in a commercial transaction has control of the information flow, control over what alternatives the other party has for consideration, and control of any other factor that may limit them from dictating the terms of a commercial transaction—that party can construct a transaction that most advantages him or her.[11] Maximizing personal gain is the

Testing Speech Against Corporate Conduct in the *The Lean Champion's Resource Guide* (Vitalo, Bujak, Vitalo, Bierley, et al., 2023) for a detailed explanation of this method.

[10] Indeed, such practices led the former editor of the prestigious *New England Journal of Medicine*, Marcia Angell, M.D., to conclude: "It is simply no longer possible to believe much of the clinical research that is published, or to rely on the judgment of trusted physicians or authoritative medical guidelines. I take no pleasure in this conclusion, which I reached slowly and reluctantly over my two decades as editor of *The New England Journal of Medicine*" (Gyles, 2015; Kendrick, 2020).

[11] Warren Buffet's statement about how he picks the companies in which he invests affirms this point.

purpose defined by Capitalism. Hence, establishing control over all parties to commerce is a core value for fully implementing that model. Without control, people must negotiate and, in the end, settle for less than all. If this sounds like an extreme and asocial view of Capitalism, recall that Nobel laureate Milton Friedman argued that the corporation in a Capitalist system has *no social responsibility*. Its sole purpose is "to use its resources and engage in activities designed to increase its profits" (Friedman, 1970).[12]

Also, recognize that applying the principle of control within a commercial context reaps great monetary benefits with relatively few consequences. As mentioned previously, Microsoft Corporation coerced computer manufacturers to pay for a copy of its operating system, MS-DOS, for every computer they *made* whether or not they loaded a copy of MS-DOS on the computer (per-processor licensing agreements; U.S. Department of Justice, 1994).[13] This produced enormous profits both directly from the revenues it generated and indirectly by pressuring computer manufacturers to cease selling computers with operating systems other than MS-DOS (e.g., CP/M, DOS Plus). Dominance of the operating system market opened up other advantages that Microsoft leveraged to sell its application suites. For example, it was able to tailor the coding of its office applications (e.g., MS Word, Excel) to take advantage of proprietary elements in the DOS operating system that allowed those applications to perform better than competitor applications. Without control of the operating environment, this advantage and the windfall in profits it produced would not have occurred. The benefits derived from this early activity extend even to today. Monetarily, they range in the tens of billions of dollars.[14] For these benefits, Microsoft paid no fine. It admitted no wrongdoing. It simply agreed to end its "monopolistic practices."

He stated, "The extraordinary business does not require good management. ... The single most important decision in evaluating a business is pricing power" (Frye and Campbell, 2011). *Pricing power* is a euphemism for a company's ability to set prices independent of market conditions. It is interesting that neither Buffet nor any reporter or commentator on his remarks recognized that he was endorsing "unfree markets" as the best profit-generating investment bet in our supposedly "free market economy."

[12] Friedman did add that, while Capitalist businesses have no social responsibility, they should operate "within the rules of the game" and engage "in open and free competition without deception or fraud" (Friedman, 1970). Given his assertion that Capitalist enterprises have no social responsibility, it is clear that his caveat is *not an element* of the Capitalist economic system. Otherwise, his call for socially responsible behavior (operating "within the rules of the game") would contradict his argument that a Capitalist enterprise has no social responsibility.

[13] According to the Department of Justice's judgment, Microsoft engaged in monopolistic practices, and Microsoft accepted that judgment. It stated, in part, "Microsoft ... agreed to end its illegal monopolistic practices after the Department of Justice charged that the company used unfair contracts that choked off competition and preserved its monopoly position" (U.S. Department of Justice, 1994). "Per processor licenses" were one of the anticompetitive practices listed in the finding.

[14] In 2007 alone, Microsoft's Office Suite accounted for 41% of its profits—$13.4 billion in 2020 dollars (Dilger, 2007).

If you are imagining that the "marketplace" will correct for deceit, it is true that exploitation, *when recognized*, provokes disengagement or retaliation. Hence, another principle of conduct or core value one applies when implementing Capitalism is to *always maintain the appearance of being trustworthy.* Manipulative actions should be kept hidden. This end is embedded in notions such as "maintain credible deniability" and expressed in actions such as the use of "cutouts" like law firms, spurious "grassroots" organizations, subsidized "think tanks," or sponsored news stories to ensure that no blowback from exploitive behavior adheres to the party doing the exploiting.[15] If these methods fail, then companies use crisis management techniques to salvage their "image" or "brand," including, if necessary, renaming themselves (Harness, 2009).

On a day-to-day basis, however, rationalization may be a sufficient device to obscure intent. For example, one might explain the complexity of credit card agreements and the use of very small font sizes for printing them under the subterfuge that they result from the requirements of law and regulation or the desire to save money and keep costs down. Proactively, one might use propaganda to make a self-advantageous action appear proper and socially necessary. For example, Capitalist businesses pursue advantage over their customers by encouraging legislators to limit a customer's right to redress for harm done via lawsuits. To make that action appear nonexploitive, they invest in propaganda efforts to persuade the public that tort reform is required because many lawsuits pursue trivial claims for personal advantage. The actions of these "venal individuals," they assert, harm the public by clogging the courts and running up the cost of business. Since neither of these claims appears to withstand scientific scrutiny, they qualify as likely subterfuges that permit the reduction of consumer rights through "tort reform" while not appearing as a citizen-exploitive behavior by the producers driving that effort.[16]

The point here is that it is the purpose a commercial model pursues that generates the core values or principles of conduct that enterprises adopting the model must implement. With the producer-focused, profit-maximizing model, the singular goal is to maximize one's financial benefit from every transaction. Capitalism, as a

---

[15] The New York Times obtained access to a secretly recorded presentation by Richard Berman, the founder and chief executive of the Washington-based Berman & Company consulting firm. In that presentation, he refers to the use of cutouts as he reassures the Capitalist corporations in his audience that they can hide their roles in funding their propaganda efforts. Berman stated, "People always ask me one question all the time: 'How do I know that I won't be found out as a supporter of what you're doing?' ... We run all of this stuff through nonprofit organizations that are insulated from having to disclose donors. There is total anonymity. People don't know who supports us" (Lipton, 2014).

[16] With regard to the tort reform propaganda, see Baker (2005), Bialik (2007), Chimerine and Eisenbrey (2005), Democracy Now! (2011), Klein (2006), Lane (2006), Liebeck v. McDonald's Restaurants (2011), and Sutter (2006).

commercial model, contains no restraints on the means one uses as long as the use of those means does not undermine the utility of the profit-generating advantage obtained by their users. The principle of behavior that flows from that purpose is to establish control over every other party to commerce so that one can unilaterally dictate the terms of a transaction. Under this condition, one can reliably maximize personal gain. The corollary principle that also must guide behavior is to ensure that one's control and the means used to accomplish it are not revealed or, if revealed, do not produce a negative consequence for the producer.[17]

While people may find the factual principles of conduct of one or another model more appealing or consistent with their moral ideas or their thinking about what values best serve a society, *no set of core values derived from any commercial model has an inherently higher claim to "moral rectitude."* They simply specify the conduct that is consistent with the model's purpose and content and that enables its successful implementation. The judgment of moral rectitude stands outside science. However, it seems quite appropriate for people seeking to live together within a society to assess the principles of conduct each commercial model requires and endorse only those models whose principles enable the development and sustaining of a healthy and vibrant human society.

The Core Values of the Life Enabling Commercial Model

We defined the core values of the Life Enabling model by identifying the performance factors critical for realizing its strategic purpose. We listed each of the salient features of its Strategic component (e.g., maximize the delivery of value to customers, use learning to improve products and processes, involve all contributors in decision making and problem solving) and organized the features into like groupings (affinity analysis).[18] We then labeled each grouping according to the common theme the features expressed. We uncovered four critical performance factors:

1. success through enabling others,
2. collaboration,

---

[17] Barnard's guidance for executive functioning fully supports the judgment that control is a core value for executives of enterprises implementing the dominant commercial model. He considered it critical to both forming and maintaining the organization. With regard to forming the organization, he stated: "*Organization results from the modification of the action of the individual through control of or influence upon one of these categories* [purposes, desires, impulses of the moment, and alternatives]. Deliberate conscious and specialized control of them is the essence of the executive functions" (Barnard, 1968, p. 17). As to maintaining the organization, see his discussion of personnel and how one forms the executive organization (1968, pp. 221–227). Note especially his guidance on how to populate the membership of the informal organization with individuals who will be receptive to and compliant with executive direction. These are simply a few examples of Barnard's thinking about the importance of control in forming and maintaining an organization.

[18] This analysis included contents you will read about in *Chapters 8* and *9*.

3. continuous improvement, and
4. competition through excellence.

We then introduced the findings of the social sciences to determine the principles of conduct one must evidence to enable the success of others, use collaboration to accomplish a common purpose, continuously improve one's performance, and compete successfully through excellence.[19] The principles of conduct required to implement these four critical performances form the model's core values. Our findings are recorded below.

Success Through Enabling Others

The Life Enabling enterprise aims to advance the success of customers and all stakeholders inclusively. This is a "helper's" purpose. To succeed as a helper, you must communicate respect for the person you seek to help, accept personal responsibility for all your decisions and actions (accountability), adhere steadfastly to the purpose of helping (integrity), and be truthful and act fairly in all dealings (honesty); otherwise, you will not be perceived as genuine or be trusted. Without trust as the basis of a relationship, helping will not occur (Carkhuff, 1969, 1971, 1983a; Carkhuff and Anthony, 1979; Carkhuff and Berenson, 1967; Zak, 2017; Zak and Knack, 2001). Clearly, *caveat emptor* has no place in this approach to commerce, as it rules out the quality of relationship between producer, customers, and stakeholders that is needed for Life Enabling commerce (Exhibit 2).

Exhibit 2. Conduct Essential to "Success Through Enabling Others"

- Respect others.
- Be accountable.
- Act with integrity.
- Be honest in all dealings.
- Act fairly in all interactions.
- Understand the aims, performance setting, and perspectives of customers and all stakeholders.
- Offer solutions that work for the person you are serving within the circumstances he or she faces.
- Think long term, anticipate change.
- Strive for perfection in all personal and professional endeavors.

Additionally, to help another, you must act in ways that respond effectively to their needs and preferences. This means that a Life Enabling business must understand what each party to commerce seeks to accomplish, the context in which each party operates, and each party's values and concerns with respect to

[19] Some of the relevant social science research includes Bandura (1994, 1997); Carkhuff (1969, 1983); Carkhuff and Berenson (1967); Cerasoli, Nicklin, and Ford (2014); Coyle-Shapiro and Kessler (2002); Deci, Koestner, and Ryan (1999); Gibbs (1980); Goulder (1960); Harter, Schmidt, Agrawal, and Plowman (2013); Harter, Schmidt, and Killham (2003); Herzberg, (1987); Spreitzer (1995, 2007); Truax and Carkhuff (1967); Vitalo, Byron, Bierley, and Holmberg (2008); and Zak (2017); Zak and Knack (2001), among others. Also relevant is the research discussed in *Chapter 6*.

accomplishing his or her aims. Otherwise, you will not offer solutions that fit the purpose and setting and satisfy the needs and concerns of your customer and each stakeholder.

You also must look ahead to anticipate how changing circumstances will impact your customers' and stakeholders' needs and wants. If you fail to look ahead, you will be unprepared to meet each party's new needs. Additionally, given that success on the first try is not a common occurrence in human performance, you must demonstrate a sustained striving for perfection in all your commercial activities. This striving, when evidenced by your deeds, demonstrates to others the genuineness of your commitment to acting in their service. It also promises that each helping effort you make, while perhaps imperfect, will be followed by a still more effective effort.

Collaboration

Your commercial success requires a high level of cooperation among all people who participate in it. Absent such an aligned and collaborative effort, your enterprise will incur waste that will limit its ability to deliver value to its customers. Only a team approach provides the highest degree of aligned collaboration, and only that level of collaboration supports cooperative enterprise that is waste free. A team is two or more people who pursue a common purpose together. Teaming removes the need for centralized control of each party's performance, as is required in a group approach to cooperative endeavors.[20] Teamwork is realized through the inherent alignment of purpose among members and their common assumption of responsibility for ensuring that their behavior is consistent with the team's purpose and values and integrated with the efforts of each other contributor.

To operate as a team, people must respect one another, show understanding for one another's perspective and abilities, find common ground, define a common goal, agree on the results the goal should produce, and work together to accomplish it. They must share information and ideas freely and completely and support one another's success. Their guideline for decision making must be to elect options that best advance the common purpose they are pursuing while satisfying the values necessary for realizing their purpose. Working as a team, people rise above their individual perspectives to envision alternatives that leverage their different views into superior, integrative solutions.

A team approach to enterprise also requires that team members have access to all the information relevant to their efforts and possess the skills needed to

[20] How people must work together in a Life Enabling enterprise is discussed in detail in *Chapter 9*, especially pages 274–278.

participate and lead in their teamwork. See chapters *Task 4 Lead Teams* and *Task 5 Participate in Teams* in *The Lean Champion Resource Guide* (Vitalo, Bujak, Vitalo, Bierley, et al., 2023) for other behaviors that enable successful teamwork.

Successful teamwork requires conduct that demonstrates the values summarized in Exhibit 2, since team members act as helpers to one another as well as contributors to a common effort. Effective teaming also requires additional principles of conduct (Exhibit 3). These include ensuring the meaningful involvement of all stakeholders in the team's work. Teams must communicate fully and consistently with their stakeholders as they strive to accomplish their mandates, and they must incorporate their stakeholders' perspectives in all their deliberations.

Exhibit 3. Conduct Essential to "Collaboration"

- Use a team approach to working with others.
  - Show understanding for each team member's perspective and abilities.
  - Find common ground and define a common goal.
  - Agree on the results the goal should produce.
  - Work together to accomplish the team goal.
  - Share information and ideas freely and completely.
  - Support each team member's success.
  - Find integrative solutions to issues that leverage each person's unique perspective to maximally advance achieving the team's goal.
- Ensure the meaningful involvement of all stakeholders.
- Ensure full and open communication with all parties to commerce.
- Use decision-making and problem-solving methods that enable participation and public discourse.
- Be a good citizen by:
  - honoring the language and spirit of the law,
  - promoting the strengthening of communities,
  - contributing to the enrichment of society, and
  - doing no harm to our collective ecosystem.

As to decision making and problem solving, biological approaches ("gut feelings," intuition, "tacit knowledge") are private, personal approaches that lack transparency.[21] They result in a proposed choice or solution whose rationale cannot be represented, shared, and discussed. Their conclusions can only be stated along with the proposing party's conviction about them. This limits the participation of others to either accepting or rejecting a proposed conclusion. Consequently, they are inappropriate for decision making within a collaborative effort. Only information- and knowledge-based methods support collaborative decision making and problem solving.

[21] See *Appendix E: Three Categories of Methods for Decision Making/Problem Solving* for a brief explanation of the different types of decision-making and problem-solving methods.

Concerning the enterprise's collaboration with communities, one of its stakeholders, the essential core value may be best expressed as good citizenship. It encompasses honoring the language and spirit of the law, promoting the strengthening of communities, and contributing to the enrichment of society. It also includes ensuring that no actions are taken that endanger the health or safety of the community or degrade the quality of its ecosystem.

Continuous Improvement

Continuous improvement is the Life Enabling model's primary means for advancing commercial success. Exhibit 4 summarizes the principles of conduct required to achieve continuous improvement.

Exhibit 4. Conduct Essential to "Continuous Improvement"

- Promote, facilitate, and leverage learning throughout the enterprise and across all stakeholders.
- Document all commerce-guiding knowledge.
- Measure performance.
- Be pioneering.
- Hold the validity of information sacrosanct.
- Structure the organization functionally, not politically.

Learning is the engine of continuous improvement. It is promoted by encouraging and supporting every contributor every day and in imagining ways to improve existing practices. The knowledge generated from learning must be made explicit and documented so that it can be shared across the enterprise. This sharing maximizes the advantage realized from it. Within a Life Enabling enterprise, learning is promoted and disseminated by a variety of means. One key method is through the creation and dissemination of standardized work documents that record the current best practice for implementing each business process. These documents are updated as new or improved methods are devised. Another is by providing training and coaching to support contributors in applying standardized work guidance.

Learning, in turn, requires the measurement of performance and the dissemination of this information. People implementing a Life Enabling enterprise use this performance information to guide their problem solving. It clarifies where opportunities for improvement exist and whether the ideas developed to realize those opportunities have utility. Without performance information, no one can empirically decide the validity of a proposed improvement.

The role of continuous improvement within the Life Enabling commercial model reinforces the previously documented principles of conduct and suggests additional ones. To the personal values of honesty, integrity, and striving for perfection in both personal and professional life is added the quality of being pioneering. People who are pioneering exhibit openness to new information and ideas and a willingness to venture into imagining and trying new solutions. They hold sacrosanct the responsibility to ensure that the information they develop and use is evidence based and valid. Invalid or inaccurate information frustrates the pursuit of new ideas, as it undermines learning. Those who use opinions instead of evidence-based information sabotage their own growth and the growth of others.

Pioneering people also appreciate the importance of promoting and facilitating learning by all others involved with them. The stimulation produced by associates who are themselves pioneers accelerates one's own discovery of new opportunities and extends the horizons of growth for everyone. Together, pioneering people turn the Life Enabling enterprise into a de facto applied research center that continuously uncovers better ideas for what to offer and better ways to implement commerce.

The importance of continuous improvement and learning extends to an overlooked area of executive action—the structuring of the enterprise. The business must be structured to enable the development and sharing of learning and not just the effective and efficient performance of work. Departmentation must be functional, not political.[22] Functional departmentation breaks the work of the enterprise into the major business activities that accomplish its purpose (e.g., production or service fulfillment, product development, sales, marketing, human capital management, information technology). Each of these business functions relies on a unique set of expertise. Each has a unique workflow that accomplishes its purpose by progressively transforming the inputs it receives into the outputs it contributes to the business. This end-to-end flow of work is called a *value stream*.[23] A Life Enabling business is organized into these value streams, and within each value steam, it is decomposed into work units that accomplish the work processes that implement the value stream. The organization and juxtaposition of work units serves to maintain clarity about the substance of the work being accomplished and the linkages between elements of work. It also serves to maximize direct communication between contributors and minimize handoffs. All of these features allow contributors to focus on the work they must accomplish and, together, probe ways to improve it. It allows them to pursue improvements in association with others who affect and are affected by their work. It also speeds the transfer of new learning and the realization of benefits from it.[24]

---

[22] Politics drive departmentation when, for example, organizations are divided in ways that protect one or another manager's turf or status or reward or punish individuals based on their perceived support or lack of support for the person deciding departmentation.

[23] The construct of the value stream was first introduced by W. Edwards Deming in 1952 to Japanese industrialists (Deming, 1982a). It became commonly known through the work of Womack, Jones, and Roos (1991) and Womack and Jones (2003).

[24] *Chapter 9. The Resources Critical to Strategic Success* discusses further the organizational structuring of a Life Enabling enterprise.

Compete Through Excellence

A Life Enabling enterprise competes for customers based on the excellence of its offering and the buying–benefiting experience it provides. This excellence is judged by its customers' experience and, objectively, by the measured success that its offerings enable for them.

Competing through excellence requires every other principle of conduct already discussed. There is an additional requirement, however, that is most often not recognized (Exhibit 5). Specifically, markets must be free. Barriers to competition must be removed so that all parties that are capable of producing an alternative offering can do so. This ensures that a Life Enabling enterprise can enter and compete in every marketplace. Also, valid information about offerings must be available and accessible to customers. People must make free, informed, and effective choices that best meet their needs. Coercive pressures that corrupt free and effective decision making must be eliminated. In essence, a Life Enabling enterprise must ensure that every market it operates in satisfies its model's 10 commercial context requirements (pages 130–131) in order for it to compete based on excellence.

Exhibit 5. Additional Behaviors Essential to "Compete Through Excellence"

Foster free markets by
- removing artificial barriers to competition;
- advancing the availability and accessibility of valid information about offerings;
- enabling citizens to make free, informed, and effective choices that best meet their needs;
- eliminating the effects of coercive pressures that corrupt rational decision making; and
- ensuring that every market you operate in satisfies the model's 10 commercial context requirements.

In general, the failure to satisfy these 10 requirements creates markets where the seller has power over the buyer. The buyer either lacks options due to limited offerings; is limited as to redress from harm by law, regulation, court decision,[25]

[25] One example of a court decision limiting customer redress from harm involves Standard & Poor's financial asset rating service. Standard & Poor's (S&P's) Financial Services ratings service, now named S&P Global Ratings, analyzes and rates stocks, bonds, and commodities based on their creditworthiness. It has long declared that its letter-grade ratings are *independent and objective*, part of a bid to allay concerns over its business model (S&P is paid by the issuers of the securities they rate). The Justice Department filed civil fraud charges against S&P's on February 4, 2013 in U.S. District Court in Los Angeles. Based on its conduct leading up to the 2008 financial crisis (Taibbi, 2013), the Department charged "that the rating firm committed fraud when it allegedly misrepresented its ratings as independent and objective" (Neumann, 2013). In its defense, the company indirectly made clear that "honesty" was *not* one of this Capitalist company's core values. "In its formal defense ... S&P pointed to two earlier court decisions where judges ruled that such statements by [a business] were puffery and therefore can't form the basis for a fraud claim" (ibid.). Indeed, in one of the cases cited by S&P, U.S. District Court Judge Sidney S. Stein concluded that such claims "were mere commercial puffery" and could not be used to support a fraud claim. The Court's judgment denied the misled customers

or contract; or lacks the competencies or informational resources needed to make valid, evidence-based choices.

Any factor that compromises a buyer's effective decision making also undermines a market's capability to support competition through excellence and, therefore, must be addressed. This includes factors extrinsic to the market itself. For example, people may be buried by debt or limited by poverty. In these instances, a buyer may be forced to defer selecting any product despite his or her need or to select an offering that is inferior as regards its overall utility but is affordable.

Whichever commercial context requirement for free markets is violated, its distortion of choice is detectable by virtue of the fact that the person elects an option that he or she *would not otherwise* elect based on the value it delivers. Any distortion in the customer's free and effective decision making necessarily undermines an organization's ability to compete through excellence. Life Enabling enterprises absolutely depend on undistorted feedback from customers to guide their assessments of their performance and their continuous improvement efforts.

Given the necessity of free markets for the Life Enabling enterprise, the model mandates that every Life Enabling enterprise must ensure the presence and continuation of free markets wherever they exist and work to make free any market that is not.

Summary of the Life Enabling Model's Core Values

Our analysis generated a large number of principles of conduct. To facilitate retention, we factored our list of into three groups (Exhibit 6, beginning on the next page):

- *Values related to conduct as an individual* – these principles apply to the conduct of every member of the enterprise operating on his or her own.
- *Values related to social conduct* – these principles apply to the conduct of every member of the enterprise as he or she interacts with others.
- *Values related to executive activities* – these principles apply to the conduct of every member of the enterprise as he or she works to ensure the commercial organization's continuance and success and the presence and continued effective contribution of cooperative efforts by all its contributors.

The Strategic Outcomes Commerce Must Produce

The model's guidance ensures that all commercial transactions protect, nurture, and enrich human and natural life. It creates a context within which all parties to commerce can fulfill their dual drives of sociality and personal emergence.

---

any redress for the harm caused them by the company's deception.

Exhibit 6. The Core Values That Guide the Life Enabling Approach to Commerce

Individual conduct

- Be accountable.
- Measure performance.
- Act with integrity.
- Be honest in all dealings.
- Hold the validity of information sacrosanct.
- Strive for perfection in all personal and professional endeavors.
- Be pioneering.

Social conduct

- Respect others.
- Act fairly in all interactions .
- Show understanding for the perspectives of others.
- Find inclusive solutions for realizing opportunities or solving problems.
- Be a good citizen by
  - honoring the language and spirit of the law,
  - promoting the strengthening of communities,
  - contributing to the enrichment of society, and
  - doing no harm to our collective ecosystem.

Executive activities

- Structure the organization functionally, not politically.
- Use a team approach to working with others.
- Promote, facilitate, and leverage learning throughout the enterprise and across all stakeholders.
- Document all commerce-guiding knowledge.
- Understand the aims, performance settings, and perspectives of customers and all stakeholders.
- Offer solutions that work for the person you are serving within the circumstances he or she faces.
- Ensure the meaningful involvement of all stakeholders.
- Ensure full and open communication with all parties to commerce.
- Use decision-making and problem-solving methods that enable participation and public discourse.
- Think long term, anticipate change, and offer solutions that continue to work for the people you are serving as their circumstances evolve.

Continued ...

Exhibit 6. The Core Values That Guide the Life Enabling Approach to Commerce (continued)

- Foster free markets by
  - removing artificial barriers to competition;
  - advancing the availability and accessibility of valid information about offerings;
  - enabling citizens to make free, informed, and rational choices that best meet their needs;
  - eliminating the effects of coercive pressures that corrupt rational decision making; and
  - ensuring that every market you operate in satisfies the model's 10 commercial context requirements.

The model's Strategic outcomes express this intent. The Strategic outcomes expected from commercial activities are the observable and measurable results that accomplish the enterprise's long-term purpose. Each outcome forms the anchor for a success criterion against which the enterprise judges its performance.

Anchors for Measuring Strategic Success

- Customers grow in success and their capability to produce value by (1) receiving an offering that measurably advances their success in ways that provide a better life for everyone and (2) experiencing a buying–benefiting experience that is increasingly value adding and non-resource consuming.
- Organization members are fully engaged in the enterprise, enhance their capabilities to produce value, and find fulfillment of their social and personal work-related goals.
- Suppliers/delivery agents achieve greater success in realizing their commercial goals through their collaboration with the Life Enabling enterprise and their application of the Life Enabling model to their commercial endeavors.
- Communities that the Life Enabling enterprise touches have more wealth, more choice, smarter and more capable citizens, and increased career opportunities as a result of its business operations.
- Government agencies that work with the Life Enabling enterprise have greater success in accomplishing the citizen mandates each serves.
- The human ecosystem is either unharmed or enhanced by the enterprise's commercial activities.

- The markets within which the enterprise does commerce either satisfy the 10 requirements of a commercial context as defined by the model or are advancing toward satisfying those requirements.
- The enterprise has a record of conduct consistent with the Life Enabling model's core values and all other conditions of performance as specified by the model.
- The enterprise grows in its capability to produce value for others and in its reputation as a business that reliably enables its customers' success, provides its stakeholders the benefits they seek, and conducts itself in a life-enhancing manner.

Making Anchors Measurable

To measure an enterprise's strategic success, you must decompose each of the above-listed outcome anchors and construct a success criterion for each item's component elements. A success criterion is a statement that specifies what is to be achieved (anchor for measurement), how the status of the anchor will be gauged (method of measurement), and the result that defines success (target). Using a success criterion to measure your performance enables you to verify whether you are properly implementing the Life Enabling model and whether your efforts are succeeding. Detailed guidance on forming success criteria and establishing an enterprise-wide measurement system is provided in chapter *Task 9 – Measure Results* of the *The Lean Champion Resource Guide* (Vitalo, Bujak, Vitalo, Bierley, et al., 2023).

This chapter describes the activities that produce strategic success. It provides the model's guidance for defining a business's commercial strategy. A commercial strategy specifies what an enterprise will offer to whom; where it will enter into commerce; how it will attract, win, and retain customers; and how it will realize profit. A successfully implemented commercial strategy produces the Strategic Results that the model defines.

Chapter 8

Preview of the Model's Guidance

Exhibit 1, beginning on the next page, previews the Life Enabling model's Strategic Activities guidance. Use it to appreciate the scope of the issues this chapter discusses and the model's guidance with respect to each.

The Model's Strategic Activities

The Life Enabling model specifies six guidelines that regulate the contents of an enterprise's commercial strategy:

1. Focus on customers you are maximally able to help.
2. Create and sustain a cooperative system capable of Life Enabling commerce.
3. Win and retain customers by delivering offerings that have exceptional value.
4. Win and retain customers by providing an exceptional buying–benefiting experience.
5. Free markets to enable the success of Life Enabling commerce.
6. Strive for perfection at the Strategic level.

1. Focus on Customers You Are Maximally Able to Help

Your impetus for initiating commerce is the desire to enable people's success. Those people whom you will be maximally able to benefit will have one or more qualities you respect and a purpose you value and possess the expertise to support. They must also live in a geographic area where your enterprise can reasonably expect to serve them either directly or through intermediaries.

Focusing on serving someone you respect who is pursuing a purpose you value is necessary for several reasons. First, respect for another is an essential requirement for working collaboratively with that person, and commerce is a collaborative endeavor between producer and customer. Second, that respect is also a basis for the concern and caring you express in your effort to understand your prospective customers' needs and wants and advance their success. Third, valuing the purpose a person is pursuing energizes further your investment of effort in finding ways to advance its achievement. Enabling an activity you value for a person you respect, therefore, provides the strongest motivational basis for any commercial endeavor. Internally rooted motivation such as this is most likely to sustain your commercial efforts during times of difficulty (Barnard, 1968).

Exhibit 1. Summary of the Life Enabling Approach to Commerce's Strategic Activities

Commercial Strategy Guidelines	1. **Focus on customers you are maximally able to help.** Select as your target customers people who have one or more qualities you respect and whose purpose you value. Make sure that the customer purpose you select to support is one you are competent to enable. Focus your commerce in geographical areas where you can reliably produce a value-adding offering, deliver it to your customers, and support them in benefiting from it. Ensure that the marketplace you enter is sufficiently free of constraints to allow you to compete through excellence. Otherwise, you will not have a chance to succeed. 2. **Create and sustain a cooperative system capable of Life Enabling commerce.** Select members based on their ability to deliver value to your efforts to serve your customers. Engage, enable, and support all members of your business's cooperative system in understanding and applying the Life Enabling model. Establish between the business and all its cooperative system members the communications infrastructure needed to work together to eliminate waste and maximize every customer's receipt of benefit. 3. **Win and retain customers by delivering offerings that have exceptional value.** Deliver offerings that maximize their user's success while satisfying all other values the user maintains. Ensure that your offering provides a better life for everyone. Educate prospective customers about the utility your offering provides. Support them in making evidence-based decisions about which alternative offering best satisfies their needs and preferences. 4. **Win and retain customers by providing an exceptional buying–benefiting experience.** Make your buying–benefiting experience least burdensome to customers. To the extent possible, build in features that customers derive value from as they access, acquire, prepare to use, and use your offering to accomplish their purpose; maintain it in a useful state between uses; and dispose of it and its byproducts. Educate prospective customers about the utility your buying–benefiting experience provides. Support them in incorporating this information into their evidence-based decisions about which producer best satisfies their needs and preferences. 5. **Free markets to enable the success of Life Enabling commerce.** Expand the possibility to compete through *Continued ...*

Exhibit 1. Summary of the Life Enabling Approach to Commerce's Strategic Activities (continued)

Commercial Strategy Guidelines (continued)	excellence within every marketplace you enter by providing customers superior value as judged from their perspectives. Understand the dynamics of each marketplace. Assess the degree to which each marketplace satisfies the model's commercial context requirements. Improve deficient markets by introducing competition as a substitute for concentration and coordination, expanding the availability and accessibility of information about offerings and offerors, eliminating producer-preferential laws or regulations, and elevating consumer capabilities to make free and effective purchasing decisions. **6. Strive for perfection at the strategic level.** Continuously improve the implementation of each of the six Strategic Activities. Elevate both the methods and the means by which each activity is performed. Improve each activity's outcomes and the results the entire cycle produces. Use learning to ▪ sharpen your focus on those customers you are maximally able to help and improve your understanding of what to provide them and where to serve them; ▪ refine and deepen your understanding of all members of your cooperative system and find better ways to engage, enable, and elevate each member's receipt of value from their participation in your cooperative system; ▪ improve your ability to conceive and deliver an offering that delivers superior value and to continually enhance its satisfaction of all your customers' values; ▪ improve your ability to create and provide a buying–benefiting experience that is less burdensome and adds value for your customers; ▪ more effectively free markets to enable the success of Life Enabling commerce; and ▪ refine and extend your generation and leveraging of learning and its use in further improving your performance of Strategic Activities. The enterprise must also undertake research and development efforts that generate innovations and prepare the business to continuously improve its delivery of value to its customers.
How Profit Is Realized	Profit is any outcome that immediately enhances the enterprise's capability to engage in future life-enabling commerce. *Continued ...*

Exhibit 1. Summary of the Life Enabling Approach to Commerce's Strategic Activities (continued)

How Profit Is Realized (continued)	The following are examples of profit that a Life Enabling enterprise produces: ▪ knowledge guiding how to better produce greater value, waste free; ▪ enterprise members who are elevated in their capability to produce value and do so; ▪ stakeholders benefited in ways they value and that advance their success; ▪ a cooperative system better able to sustain the creation and delivery of greater value; ▪ workplaces and work processes that are waste free and more capable of producing the highest-valued outputs every time; ▪ supply and delivery chain members who are elevated in their capabilities to produce value and do so; and ▪ marketplaces that better satisfy the 10 conditions that define them as truly free and competitive. Monetary surplus (traditionally defined as profit) is not considered profit. This surplus may be transformed into resources that can themselves advance the production of value for customers and stakeholders, but money itself is inert and produces nothing.

Your need for expertise in all the areas related to addressing the needs of the people you seek to help is self-evident. Without such expertise, you will not be able to conceive and produce a success-enabling offering and support your customers in its use.

Finally, it also self-evident that you must focus your commerce in a region where you can reliably produce your value-adding offering, deliver it to your customers, and support them in benefiting from it. Otherwise, your enterprise will fail.

The first step in defining a focus for your commerce begins with a personal reflection. There are three areas to explore. One is to discover what expertise we possess that we most value. The second is to uncover the people who interest us most and whom we most desire to help. The third is to discover what purposes people pursue that we most admire. In one of these three areas we will discover our natural anchor for commerce. Some of us are wrapped around an area of expertise we possess. We see great value in it and experience enjoyment in developing and applying it and would like to put it in the service of others. Others of us are focused on people and usually some subset of people with whom we experience a positive emotional connection. We value their lives and seek to enrich them. Still others of us experience the pursuit of a purpose as especially meaningful and regard it highly. Begin your effort to focus your enterprise with whichever of these three concerns represents your strongest interest.

If your strongest interest is an area of expertise, explore what purposes it can enable and who might undertake those pursuits. If your anchor is a group of people with whom you have a positive emotional connection, explore their life circumstances and understand their interests, concerns, and aspirations. Learn about the challenges they face in their living, learning, working, and relating contexts. Appreciate their goals and values and identify how you might enable their better achievement of some end they seek to realize. If your anchor is a purpose people undertake that you especially value, discover who pursues this purpose, what ends they seek to realize, in what contexts they pursue it, and what challenges they encounter in accomplishing it. From whichever of these entry points you begin in focusing your enterprise, you must end up having identified whom you seek to help, the purpose you will enable them to succeed at, and the expertise you will apply to accomplish that end. You must find value in both the person and purpose you identify and either possess or develop the expertise needed to enable your target customer's success.

Build on your focus for commerce by exploring and understanding the answers to the remaining questions you must address to form an enterprise: What offering might you provide? How would it benefit your target customer? What process would produce that offering? What resource inputs would you need to produce it? How would you deliver and support its successful use? Create a map of the end-to-end stream of activities that would fulfill the following needs: acquire and supply the input resources your production process requires; produce and deliver your intended offering; and support your target customers' receipt, use, and extraction of benefit from it.

Next, resolve in which of the geographies where your target customers reside you can successfully implement this enterprise. Judge in which of these regions you can reliably access the inputs you will need to produce your offering. Determine in which you can construct, equip, and reliably implement a production system that can provide your customers what they need, where they need it, in the quantity they require, and at a price they can afford. Assess also in which locales you can create and sustain a delivery and support solution that will satisfy your customers' needs. Prioritize those locales in terms of how well each satisfies these requirements.

Continue your evaluation by assessing each candidate marketplace's openness to competition based on excellence. Identify which are sufficiently free to allow competition through excellence. To this end, research the social, political, economic, and technological factors that affect competitiveness in each market region. Answer the critical question: To what extent does each market satisfy the 10 commercial context requirements (pages 130–131) that define a free and competitive marketplace? Use the results of this analysis to identify what barriers to entry and competition exist and to what degree they limit competition based on the value of one's offering. Also evaluate how amenable these barriers are to elimination. As part of this assessment, evaluate the factors that affect customer choice, such as the accuracy with which prospective customers understand their real needs, their ability to make evidence-based choices among available offerings, and the presence of any factors that may pressure them to elect a choice on a basis other than merit.

With regard to a marketplace's satisfaction of the model's requirements, remember that you only need a degree of compliance sufficient to allow you to establish your presence in that marketplace. If you can win an initial customer base as a result of the quality of your offering and the buying–benefiting experience you provide, you can work progressively to expand the marketplace's satisfaction of the model's 10 requirements.

Finally, for your selected geographies, identify what is currently provided to your target customers and how it is provided. Consider both the offering itself and its associated buying–benefiting experience. Assess whether the offering and buying–benefiting experience you would provide would exceed to any degree what is already available to your target customer. You need to advance the current value delivered to customers in that market to succeed.

2. Create and Sustain a Cooperative System Capable of Life Enabling Commerce

The concept of a cooperative system was introduced in 1938 by Barnard. It refers to a commercial organization's need for support from all the outside entities necessary to its commerce. It recognizes that the commercial success of a business is possible only if its internal efforts are augmented by the cooperative efforts of outside entities, such as supplying businesses, communities, governmental bodies, and others who provide resources essential to conducting commerce (Exhibit 2, next page).

Both Barnard (1968) and Deming (1982a, 2000) viewed the commercial organization as a system both within itself and as the central element within a larger system that extends beyond itself. Both scholars viewed commercial success as requiring the aligned, interdependent efforts of both the organization proper and those outside entities. Barnard's focus for that cooperation was the achievement of the commercial organization's self-defined purpose. Deming's focus was on benefiting customers and all stakeholders inclusively and bettering the lives of everyone.

Exhibit 2. The Members of the Business's Cooperative System as Defined by the Life Enabling Model

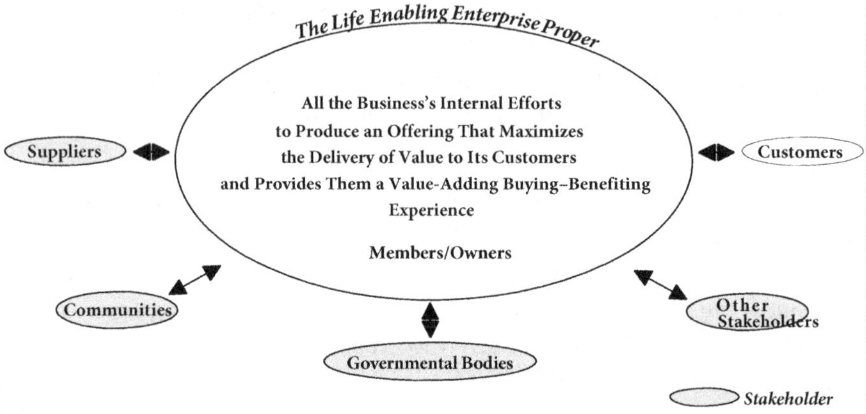

Barnard referred to this larger system as a "system of cooperation." Within this "cooperative system," the organization proper is only one element. It is, however, the cooperative system's central element, since it is the enterprise's makeup and the commerce it conducts that define the system's remaining members. The members of this cooperative system provide the business the resources it needs to produce value and deliver and support its use (e.g., technical support for its operations, licenses, the use of the community's transportation and communications infrastructure). Each business acquires these resources through exchange transactions. Barnard asserted that the organization could not function without its cooperative system.[1] He stressed that success of an enterprise depends on all the elements of this larger system operating together.

The aim and means of cooperation espoused by Barnard are not the same as those described in either Deming's work or the Life Enabling commercial model. Nonetheless, all agree that successful commerce requires that the organization

[1] Barnard (1968) used the phrase "cooperative system" in two ways in his book, *The Functions of the Executive.* In the early part of the book, he used the term interchangeably with the word "organization." In this sense, it simply refers to the business itself. Beginning on page 65, the term refers to what we describe above. For an analysis of Barnard's thinking, see Vitalo (2020).

elicit and sustain the contribution of cooperative efforts from all members of its cooperative system.

Who Is Included in a Business's Cooperative System?

The Life Enabling model views customers and all stakeholders as "parties to commerce" and therefore members of a business's cooperative system. While this view is consistent with Barnard's perspective, the term "parties to commerce" as used in Capitalism is a less inclusive group. It only includes people or groups who are *direct participants* in a commercial transaction. As mentioned earlier, our concept of stakeholders includes all parties *who either can affect or are affected by* commerce, including those who are not direct participants in that commerce.

Deming too held a similarly inclusive view about the breadth of membership in a business's cooperative system. His most expansive notion, however, incorporates elements not included in the Life Enabling perspective. For example, he suggested that the industry within which a company exists be included and that a type of enlightened cooperation replace the "adversarial competition" between companies in the same industry. The Life Enabling model agrees with the jettisoning of adversarial competition. While it views the pursuit of perfection as value-adding, competitiveness is seen as waste because it focuses the enterprise on its competitors rather than its customers. On the other hand, at this time, the Life Enabling model does not incorporate the notion that competitors are part of the enterprise's cooperative system.

What Are a Business's Responsibilities as Related to Its Cooperative System?

Consistent with the Life Enabling model's position on the special responsibility of the producer (pages 197–198), it holds the producer responsible for establishing social cohesion and effectiveness within and across its business's cooperative system. Initially, cooperation may be based on the practical alignments between the different purposes parties pursue. Ultimately, cohesion must be centered on a common commitment by all participants to applying the Life Enabling approach to commerce. Recall that you will not be able to maximize the value you deliver to your customers unless all your collaborators in commerce join in that effort. Waste within a collaborator's activities eventually produces waste within your producer activities. If a company supplying resources critical to your business does not invest in improving the products or services it provides, for example, it limits how effectively and efficiently you can advance in elevating the value you deliver to your customers. Similarly, on the customer side, if your customers fail to understand the pace of their need for an offering you provide and consequently make large, unexpected swings in their demand for it, those demand swings will strain your production system and cause inefficiencies in your operations. Hence, the degree to which all collaborators are aligned and engaged in pursuing perfection in the conduct of their affairs is one of the critical factors that determines the extent to which your Life Enabling enterprise can ultimately succeed.

Given the critical role of the cooperative system in realizing the model's purpose, the producer must perform the following tasks:

1. Assess whether an effective cooperative system can be established.
2. Select cooperative system members who can support a Life Enabling enterprise.
3. Develop the capabilities of all members to fulfill their responsibilities and make an informed decision about adopting the Life Enabling model for their own enterprises.
4. Collaborate with them in a common effort to realize the cooperative system's goal.

Assess

This assessment is part of your work in evaluating the geographies in which you can successfully implement your enterprise. An acceptable marketplace must offer potential cooperative system members who can support you in reliably delivering value to your target customers. After you define who you will serve, what you will provide, and how you will produce, deliver, and support that offering, you must determine in which geographical regions you can successfully undertake such commerce. As part of your evaluation of each market region, you must assess the potential membership of your enterprise's cooperative system. The region in which you will do commerce circumscribes its membership. Supply and delivery agents, for example, can only be companies that are able to support your business's activities in the localities you will serve. The communities your commerce will impact exist in these selected geographies, and any government regulators that affect your commerce will come from those communities.

Initially, when judging whether an effective cooperative system can be constructed within a geographical region, cohesion among the system's members may be based on the practical alignment between the different purposes parties pursue and each party's satisfaction of five criteria:

1. ability to produce value (competence),
2. responsibleness as regards fulfilling the commitments each makes,

3. adaptability to changing circumstances,
4. openness as regards communications around issues relevant to the relationship between members, and
5. absence of any behaviors that violate one of the Life Enabling model's core values (e.g., exploiting labor's weakened bargaining state, acting deceptively toward others).

To the degree that you can assemble a cooperative system with members meeting these minimal requirements, you can successfully initiate a Life Enabling enterprise.

Select

You will only be able to select some members of your enterprise's cooperative system. For example, you choose your supply and delivery chain agents, but you do not have a choice with regard to other members. These include government regulators who are chosen by the governments they work for and the members of the communities that will be affected by or could affect the operation of your enterprise.

The model's guidance for selecting supply and delivery agents follows that offered by Deming (1982a). He advised that a business complete two assessments of a potential supplier/delvery agent.[2] The first assessment evaluates the input or service a potential supplier/delivery agent proposes to provide you, and the second assesses each candidate's effectiveness as a business. You must base each assessment on objective data (testing and measurement), not impressions.

Your assessment of the candidate's offering evaluates the utility it provides you in two ways. First, you must judge its offering in terms of how well it enables your enterprise to deliver value to your customers. Second, you must judge each potential business partner in terms of the buying–benefiting experience it provides you, its customer.

In addition, you must assess the degree to which each supplier/delivery agent's conduct as an enterprise aligns with the Life Enabling approach to commerce. To this end, you need to research each candidate's Strategic, Operations, and Executive Functions conduct. Using this research, you evaluate the inclusiveness of the business's intent to provide benefit and its reputation for fulfilling the commitments it makes. You also assess its adaptability to changing circumstances, its openness as regards communication about issues

[2] Deming did not discuss "delivery" agents per se. But his guidance readily generalizes from suppliers to delivery agents. The only difference between them is at which end of the value stream each provides assistance.

relevant to the relationship between it and its customers, and the absence of any behaviors that violate one of the Life Enabling model's core values.

Once your assessments are complete, you select those supply/delivery agents with whom there is practical alignment with regard to purpose and who satisfy the five criteria listed above.

Develop

It is your task as the producer to develop your business's cooperative system so that it fully enables your enterprise's success. To this end, you must engage, enable, and support each cooperative system member in deciding whether to apply the Life Enabling model within its own business. As part of this effort, your enterprise should exchange on-site visits with its cooperative system members so each party better understands how the other operates. You should also share education and training programs with members and, if they desire it, provide them on-site coaching on their efforts to optimize their operations. Cooperative system members also should be invited to participate in improvement efforts conducted by your enterprise on your own operations. Such experiences will augment their learning and provide observational information to support their decision making.

Through these efforts, you support each member in understanding the Life Enabling model. You provide them an opportunity to experience its utility and master the skills needed to implement it. *However*, the choice to adopt the model must be freely made by each cooperative system member based on their evidence-based understanding of what adoption of the model means and its congruence with their enterprise's purposes and values. Adoption also requires that the makeup of the owners of a cooperative system member aligns with the native dispositions essential to a Life Enabling entrepreneur.

Collaborate

As partners in the cooperative system, the members work together to discover ever more effective ways to enhance the value each member contributes to the others and to the common goal of maximizing the delivery of value to the customers your Life Enabling enterprise serves.

A fully functional cooperative system operates as a team. Teamwork requires that you establish a communications infrastructure that supports your business and its cooperative system members in working together. This infrastructure enables members to share information about current activities, needs, and any problems they are encountering. It also enables them to work together to solve those problems and share the learning each generates from their research and improvement efforts. In all respects, the teamwork among system members evidences all the qualities that describe how members of the Life Enabling organization itself relate to and enable one another's success.

3. Win and Retain Customers by Delivering Offerings That Have Exceptional Value

A Life Enabling enterprise's absolute imperative is to provide an offering that enables its users' success. Only a useful offering benefits a customer. This guideline extends that imperative. It states that your approach to attracting and winning customers is based on the *superior* effectiveness of your offering over alternative offerings in enabling your customers' success.

Beyond the superior effectiveness of its offering, your enterprise wins and retains customers by maximally satisfying all *other* customer values pertaining to your offering. Customers maintain an array of values as regards offerings and their buying–benefiting experiences. In Noriaki Kano's terms, these values are of three types: "Must Be," "Satisfier," and "Delighter" (Walden, 1993). "Must Be" values are features of an offering or the customer's buying–benefiting experience that, when absent, lead to rejection of the offering. If present, your offering qualifies for consideration. If absent, it is rejected. "Satisfier" values relate to features that create greater satisfaction the more they are present and less satisfaction the more they are missing. "Delighter" values relate to features that are not expected by the customer; hence, their absence goes unnoticed and has no significance. But when these features are present, they delight the customer.

To deliver exceptional value to your customers, you must develop a correct understanding of their needs, wants, and preferences. You base this understanding on an analysis of their purpose, capabilities, and values; the context within which they operate; and the wherewithal they require to succeed. From this information, you conceive an offering and derive the features it must possess to support your customers' success (*effectiveness* features). After your offering's effectiveness is assured, you focus on enhancing its value by adding features that satisfy all your customers' other "must have" values and as many of your customers' "satisfier values" as feasible. Lastly, to the extent possible, you add features that would delight your customers. The constraints you will experience in accomplishing these ends are

1. your current state of expertise and resourcing,
2. the state of the technology you are applying,
3. the need to constrain cost to a level that customers can afford,
4. your need to benefit stakeholders inclusively, and

5. your commitment to abide by the model's core values.

Once you have conceived your offering, you must shape your production or service fulfillment process so that it reliably produces it waste free. You also must design a supply chain and a delivery/support system. The latter conveys your offering to your customers and ensures its correct operation and delivery of benefit.

Once you launch the production of your product or service, your marketing efforts must educate prospective customers about the value your offering provides. They must support prospective customers in using this information in their decision making about which market alternative best satisfies their needs and preferences.

Your continued success also requires that you engage in activities that evaluate your offering's value-satisfying status and conceive and implement ways to elevate that status. In addition, you must invest in research that has two points of focus. One focus is to uncover emerging developments that may modify your customer's needs or wants. The second focus is to discover ways to satisfy your customer's needs that require less expenditure of resources by them.

The first focus of research seeks to anticipate changes in a customer's needs and preferences and develop responses to these new requirements in advance of their emergence. This research activity uncovers factors that may alter how the customer pursues his or her objective or require the customer to adapt to changes in the circumstances within which he or she operates. You must conceive ways to make your offering responsive to these expected changes. If a business does not anticipate its customers' future needs, it will not be able to provide a value-adding solution to them when they need it.

The second focus of research discovers new solutions to the customer's needs that require less resource expenditure by the customer. These solutions may involve the introduction of new technologies, the use of new materials, or applying totally different methods to resourcing, producing, and delivering your offering. Ultimately, this research seeks to discover how your customers might accomplish their purpose *without* any need for your offering. Only this solution delivers maximum utility to your customers.

4. Win and Retain Customers by Providing an Exceptional Buying–Benefiting Experience

Begin by recognizing all the elements that make up the customer's buying–benefiting experience. This experience includes all the activities the customer must engage in to access, acquire, prepare to use, and use an offering to accomplish the customer's purpose; maintain it in a useful state between uses; and dispose of it and its byproducts. You need to understand how each affects your customer. Use this knowledge to uncover what elements of the buying–benefiting experience are resource-demanding. Find ways to reduce and, ultimately, eliminate these customer resource expenditures.

Also find ways to add value to your customers' buying–benefiting experience. Begin with understanding your customers' needs, wants, capabilities, and preferences as regards this experience. Uncover what features must be present to meet your customers' "must have" values. Discover what features, if present, would elevate your customers' satisfaction with their buying–benefiting experience. Uncover and add any features that would delight your customers.

Once implemented, you must continue to develop ways to reduce your buying–benefiting experience's resource burden and elevate the satisfaction and delight it delivers. Some of the solutions may feed back into redesigning your offering or how it is delivered so that its acquisition, use, and disposal are less burdensome.

Educate prospective customers about the utility your buying–benefiting experience provides. Support them in using this information in their decision making about which producer best satisfies their needs and preferences.

Finally, you also must look forward to anticipate any changes that might affect the type of buying–benefiting experience your customer will require in the future and prepare to satisfy those expectations once they emerge. Ultimately, when you eliminate your customers' need for your offering, you will free them completely from having to engage in any buying–benefiting experience.

5. Free Markets to Enable the Success of Life Enabling Commerce

To succeed as a Life Enabling enterprise, you must ensure that—over time—the markets you serve fully satisfy the model's 10 commercial context requirements (pages 130–131). As stated previously, your first step in moving any market toward fully enabling competition through excellence is to provide your customers a superior value-adding offering and buying–benefiting experience. That action alone expands customer options within any marketplace.

Next, you must ensure that all people in your target market who require your offering can access, acquire, and derive benefit from it. You must identify and remove all barriers that hinder access to your offering, its acquisition, and its successful use.

You may achieve the removal of barriers to access and successful use of your offering in several ways. One way is to ensure that your offering has an affordable price and work continuously to reduce that price. These actions are relevant if money is the exchange resource required to obtain your offering. If money remains a barrier, you may be able to partially finance a customer's purchase and receive payment over time. You also may advance ways to elevate the income earnings of the people you seek to serve. For example, you may support efforts to improve labor's bargaining power or to uncover and eliminate employer actions that limit people's job options and earnings.[3]

If awareness of your offering is the issue, you need to seek ways to better inform prospective customers about your product or service. If prospective customers lack free choice or the knowledge or skills needed to make effective choices, you will implement programs to eliminate these barriers. By freeing your prospective customers and heightening their ability to make effective choices, you also enable your own improved value production. Such prospective customers provide more accurate information about their needs and better feedback on your current offering and their buying–benefiting experience. This improved information accelerates your learning, which yields improved growth in your productive capability.

In parallel with these steps, you need to undertake progressively expansive efforts to advance each market's satisfaction of the model's commercial context requirements. Use your understanding of the dynamics of your marketplace and its failings to focus these efforts. You seek to introduce competition as a substitute for concentration and coordination, expand the availability and accessibility of information about offerings and offerors, eliminate producer preferential laws and regulations, improve each customer's understanding of his or her real needs, and elevate your customers' capabilities to make fully informed, evidence-based purchase decisions free of coercive pressure.

If the barriers constraining competition through excellence are due to the political control possessed by one group of people who use that control to aggrandize themselves at the expense of others, then you need to act in the political arena. In eliminating such barriers, your enterprise should align itself with community organizations that have a similar intent, such as consumer rights organizations and other public accountability initiatives.

---

[3] An example of Capitalist employers acting to limit employee job options (freedom of choice) and earnings was reported in 2014. "In early 2005, ... Apple's Steve Jobs sealed a secret and illegal pact with Google's Eric Schmidt to artificially push their workers' wages lower by agreeing not to recruit each other's employees, sharing wage scale information, and punishing violators" (Ames, 2014). The participants in this agreement expanded to include Intel, Adobe, Intuit, and Pixar (Knoczal, 2014). With this collusion among employers, employee wages were effectively suppressed and their options for alternative employment restricted.

6. Strive for Perfection at the Strategic Level

The concept of striving for perfection derives from Deming's teaching to the Japanese leaders of industry in 1950 at his first Hakone lecture. He initially represented this striving as a spiraling cycle of learning and improvement that must continue forever (Deming, 1950). Later in his career, he expressed it in the fifth of his 14 Management Points: "Improve constantly and forever the system of production and service" (Deming, 1982a, p. 49).

The goal of this striving is to realize what Deming termed a "zero loss function." This means that all of the enterprise's resources are successfully transformed into an offering and customer buying–benefiting experience that maximally advances the customer's success and betters the lives of everyone. Nothing is wasted. No instance of performance is off the mark. The Life Enabling model adds the requirement that your enterprise achieve this end without producing any negative externalities and at a continuously lower cost to your customer. These last two elements are reasonably implied but not explicit in Deming's original construct.

The general principle of striving for perfection applies across the enterprise and permeates through all levels of its activity (Strategic, Operations, and Executive Functions). All contributors to a Life Enabling enterprise pursue this end on both a daily and a yearly basis. The daily activity of continuous improvement is owned and practiced everywhere by everyone. Each person detects opportunities for improvement, shares them with all affected parties, and works with those parties to generate and implement an improvement action. The yearly cycle is expressed in a businesswide Policy Planning and Deployment process that involves all contributors in building next year's business and continuous improvement plans (see *Chapter 13*).

Striving for perfection *at the Strategic level* uses learning to continuously improve each of the six Strategic Activities (Exhibit 3, next page). It elevates both the methods and the means by which each activity is performed. It improves each activity's outcomes and the results the entire cycle produces. It uses learning to

- sharpen the enterprise's focus on those customers it is maximally able to help and improve its understanding of what to provide them and where to serve them;
- refine and deepen the enterprise's understanding of all members of your cooperative system and discover better ways to engage, enable, and elevate each member's receipt of value from their participation in the enterprise's cooperative system and their ability to contribute to its success;

- improve the enterprise's ability to conceive and deliver an offering that delivers superior value and to continually enhance its satisfaction of all your customers' values;
- improve the enterprise's ability to create a buying–benefiting experience that is less burdensome and adds more value for its customers;
- more effectively free markets to enable the success of Life Enabling commerce; and
- refine and extend the enterprise's generation and leveraging of learning and its use in further improving your performance of Strategic Activities.

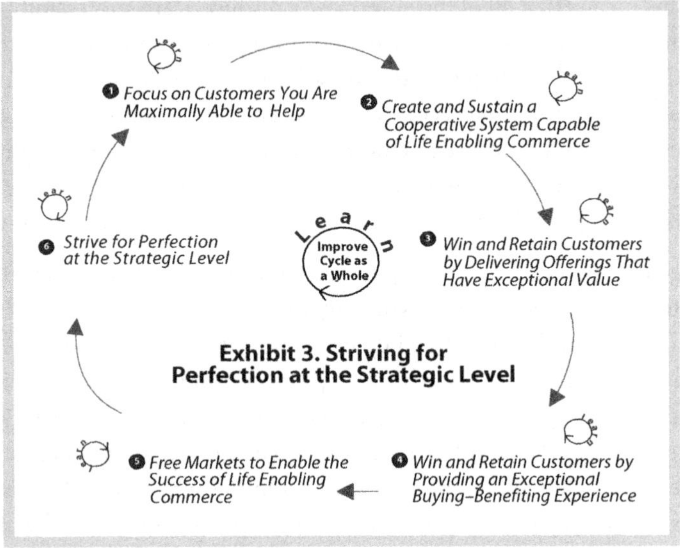

Exhibit 3. Striving for Perfection at the Strategic Level

In its pursuit of perfection at the Strategic level, the enterprise also undertakes research and development (R&D) efforts that generate innovations and prepare the enterprise for the future. These R&D investments focus on

- improving the design of current products and services;
- innovating new offerings, better methods, and the use of improved materials;
- developing improved design, development, production, and service fulfillment methods and infrastructure;
- developing improved methods and means for supporting every contributor's successful performance;
- uncovering new skill requirements and improving the training and support of all contributors; and
- discovering ways to eliminate your customers' need for your offering while enabling them to accomplish the purpose they seek to realize.

How Profit Is Realized

Recall that an enterprise registers profit whenever its capability to engage in Life Enabling commerce is elevated as a result of its commercial activities. It generates profit both directly and indirectly. Profit is realized directly from the subset of the enterprise's outputs that immediately raise its internal capability to produce value or render its commercial context more enabling of Life Enabling commerce. One way your enterprise indirectly generates profit is by elevating the success of its customers.

In addition to profit, your enterprise will produce a monetary surplus. This surplus is not "profit" because money itself has no inherent productive utility. In the words of Henry Ford (1922), "Money cannot make anything and money cannot manage anything." It is only when you transform money into new means for producing value for customers and all stakeholders that your enterprise profits.

Exhibit 4 lists the outputs produced by a Life Enabling enterprise. It identifies which of those outputs generate profit directly.

Exhibit 4. Outputs and Their Status as Direct or Indirect Profit

Output	Direct?
Offerings that measurably advance their users' success and better their lives	No
Buying–benefiting experiences that are increasingly value-adding and non-resource-consuming	No
Stakeholders benefited in ways they value and that advance their success	Yes
Knowledge guiding how to better produce greater value, waste free	Yes
Enterprise members who are elevated in their capability to produce value and do so	Yes
A cooperative system better able to sustain the creation and delivery of greater value	Yes
Workplaces and work processes that are waste free and more capable of producing the highest-valued outputs every time (zero loss function)	Yes
Supply and delivery chain members who are elevated in their capabilities to produce value and do so	Yes
A record of conduct consistent with the model's core values and all other conditions of performance	No
Marketplaces that better satisfy the 10 conditions that define them as truly free and competitive	Yes
Human ecosystem is unharmed or improved	No

This chapter explains a Life Enabling enterprise's organizational strategy. That strategy assembles the wherewithal needed to successfully implement the Strategic component of Life Enabling commerce. It identifies the enterprise's critical-to-success resources and describes the essential features each resource must possess. It includes guidance on how the enterprise must organize itself, both structurally and socially, and the culture that prevails within it.

Chapter 9

Preview of the Model's Guidance

Exhibit 1, beginning on the next page, summarizes the Life Enabling model's organizational strategy guidance. Use it to preview the scope of issues this chapter discusses and the model's guidance with respect to each.

A Life Enabling Enterprise's Organizational Strategy

Exhibit 1. The Elements of an Organizational Strategy

Three elements make up a commercial model's organizational strategy (Exhibit 1). The first element identifies what the model dictates as its critical-to-success resources. Without these resources, no organization can implement the model successfully. Hence, establishing and sustaining these resources is an organization's first priority. The second element prescribes the rules that govern the organization's design. The design of the organization determines the flow of work, the formal connections between people, and the speed of communication. The third element describes the culture that is present in a Life Enabling enterprise. Culture encompasses how people work together and the nature of their relationships with one another, their organization as a whole, and others outside their group.

Critical-to-Success Resources – An Overview

The critical-to-success resources an enterprise requires depend on the commercial model it is implementing. If your approach to marketplace success uses *control* as a key strategy, for example, then financial resources have a critical importance. Money buys influence and enables a company to employ techniques that can establish and sustain control over a market. A business with a sufficient financial cushion, for example, can undercut the price of its competitors and drive them from the marketplace despite incurring losses.

In contrast, consider a model that pursues market success based on the utility of its offering to customers, its continuous improvement of that offering, and the waste-free alignment and integration of contributor efforts across the organization. Its critical-to-success resources will be different. The Life Enabling approach to commerce is such a commercial model. Its real-time demands for understanding, creativity, problem solving, self-management, and collaboration among its

Exhibit 1. Summary of the Life Enabling Model's Organizational Strategy

<table>
<tr><td>Critical-to-Success Resources</td><td>
There are five critical-to-success strategic resources:
1. people,
2. knowledge,
3. information,
4. a communications infrastructure, and
5. a functional measurement and feedback system.
People
The model's primary critical-to-success resource is people who are cooperative and other-regarding by nature and possess the desire to enable the success of others and to pursue their own emergence. They must also possess the following qualities of character:
▪ aligns with a purpose based on intrinsic motivation,
▪ teams with others,
▪ is self-starting and sustaining,
▪ esteems competence as well as results, and
▪ challenges the current "state of the art."
The specific competencies people must possess are listed in Exhibit 3 on page 250 and described on pages 249–251.
Knowledge
▪ Knowledge documenting the Life Enabling commercial model
▪ Knowledge explaining what customer values are and how they are uncovered, verified, and used within a Life Enabling enterprise
▪ Knowledge explaining what stakeholder values are and how they are uncovered, verified, and used within a Life Enabling enterprise
▪ Guides, manuals, and other resources that support the mastery and use of business methods (e.g., Policy Planning and Deployment process, Kaizen, Total Productive Maintenance)
▪ Guides, manuals, and other performance-support resources that guide the use, maintenance, and repair of facilities, equipment, tools, and materials
▪ Documented learning developed from improvement efforts
▪ An extended value stream map for each business function
▪ A standardized work document for every work process
Continued...
</td></tr>
</table>

Exhibit 1. Summary of the Life Enabling Model's Organizational Strategy (continued)

Critical-to-Success Resources (continued)	**Information** ▪ The enterprise's business intent, including its purpose, vision, and core values; how it defines the meaning of profit; the stakeholders the enterprise recognizes; and its relationship with each. It also specifies the outcomes the business must produce to claim success. ▪ Descriptive information about the enterprise's current customers or customer segments including their purposes, the setting within which they operate, how they judge success, and their capabilities in pursuing their purposes. ▪ Current customer values information (identity of values, type, importance [when applicable], the critical-to-quality metrics associated with each value, and the degree to which each is satisfied). ▪ The identity of the enterprise's current stakeholders and a description of their connections to the enterprise and their awareness of, concerns about, and expectations for the enterprise. ▪ Current stakeholder values information (identity of values, type, importance [when applicable], the critical-to-quality metrics associated with each value, and the degree to which each is satisfied). ▪ The current state of performance at the business level, the business function level, the value stream component level, the work process level, the work unit level, and the performer level. ▪ The current year's continuous improvement plan and the status of its achievement ▪ The current year's business plan and the status of its achievement. **Communications infrastructure** The underlying facilities, services, and other resources needed to share knowledge and information and allow people to connect, communicate, and collaborate with one another. It provides ▪ immediate access to the information and knowledge that is needed to support individual performance within each work setting (e.g., work status information, work standards, job aids) and *Continued...*

Exhibit 1. Summary of the Life Enabling Model's Organizational Strategy (continued)

Critical-to-Success Resources (continued)	▪ the means by which people can connect, communicate, and collaborate with one another across distances in real time. It allows people to contact one another, share information and ideas conversationally, store and retrieve facts and learning, and otherwise work together to accomplish business goals, improve business operations, and leverage the products of their improvement efforts. **Functional Measurement and Feedback System** The Functional Measurement and Feedback System supplies the information that guides decision making in realizing personal and organizational effectiveness. A measurement system is functional when its contents are accessible by every contributor and it ▪ is complete, ▪ contains sound measures, ▪ has integrity, and ▪ is fully documented.
Organization Structure	The enterprise's organization structure must enable ▪ the waste-free implementation of value-adding work; ▪ the affirmative adding of value to the producer's offering and the customer's buying–benefiting experience; ▪ the connection of people to the outcomes they produce; ▪ each contributor's ability to control the work for which he or she is responsible; ▪ the implementation of a functional business measurement system that clarifies the status of model-relevant performance at the business level, business function level, and value stream component level and at the work process, work unit, and performer level; ▪ the rapid communication of knowledge and information among contributors; ▪ the proximity of contributors who are working together to implement a particular process and produce a needed output; and ▪ the efficient implementation of the enterprise's yearly Policy Planning and Deployment process. Departmentation is done by decomposing the business into its functions, value streams, work processes, operations, and *Continued ...*

Exhibit 1. Summary of the Life Enabling Model's Organizational Strategy (continued)

Organization Structure (continued)	tasks. Work cells are formed to maximize communication, minimize handoffs and other sources of waste, and ensure line of sight to outputs produced. Once completed, each work unit's mandate (purpose, conditions of performance, accountabilities, provided inputs, approach, and expected outputs) is documented. Authority, responsibility, and reporting relationships are distributed or assigned in a manner that ensures ▪ authority flows with task responsibility; ▪ responsibility includes both the performance of the technical work of each contributor's position and the common organizational role every contributor performs; and ▪ reporting relationships define the customary path for communication, but information sharing is omnidirectional.
Organization Culture	**Basis for Individual Contribution** ▪ Intrinsic – This means that every contributor's purpose and values naturally align with the purpose and values of the Life Enabling model. They experience commerce as an opportunity to apply their capabilities to benefit another while advancing their own emergence as an individual. They also find satisfaction in the activities of continuous improvement, working with others in a team format, and the technical work they will perform. **The Role Each Contributor Must Perform** Each person who contributes to a Life Enabling Enterprise's functions fulfills the following role responsibilities: 1. Master the Life Enabling model and the company's approach to implementing it. 2. Add value as defined by customers in a manner that benefits all stakeholders. 3. Measure one's impact on value delivered to customers and other stakeholders. 4. Improve personal and collective performance continuously. 5. Share personal learning with others and enable their improved success. 6. Team with others to accomplish the common purpose. Teaming must extend across one's work unit, one's business function, and the business as a whole, as well as all members of each business function's extended value stream and the company's cooperative system. *Continued ...*

Exhibit 1. Summary of the Life Enabling Model's Organizational Strategy (continued)

Organization Culture (continued)	**How People Must Work Together** People work together as a team to accomplish their work unit, work process, value stream component, business function, and corporate goals. Each individual is accountable for his or her personal performance *and* for ensuring the success of the team as a whole. Personal success requires that the team as a whole succeed. **How People Within the Organization Relate With One Another** The people who implement a Life Enabling Enterprise create relationships with one another that are ▪ formed around accomplishing the organization's purpose, ▪ permeated by accountability but focused on learning in the service of improving the value delivered to customers and stakeholders inclusively, ▪ governed by the principles of the Life Enabling commercial model, ▪ devoid of principal-agent conflicts (Jensen and Meckling, 1976), ▪ typified by a striving for perfection that drives toward realizing the organization's goal while enabling the success and fulfillment of each member, and ▪ based on the fundamentals of decency, respect, empathy, fairness, and valuing each other member. The culture they create ▪ thrives on valid information, as it is critical to learning and performance improvement; ▪ holds ensuring the validity of information sacrosanct; ▪ leverages diverse perspectives into integrative solutions that elevate the value of everyone's thinking; ▪ uses only information- and knowledge-based methods to make decisions and solve problems; ▪ enables and supports the growth and achievement of each member in the service of their common purpose; ▪ challenges every member to reach the limit of his or her own personal capabilities; and ▪ celebrates each member's growth and achievements. In summary, the people who power a Life Enabling enterprise operate together as a community of professionals dedicated to a common purpose and a common code of conduct that extends not just outward to the others they encounter in the marketplace but inward to one another as well.

contributors determine its five critical-to-success resources. These are people, information, knowledge, a communications infrastructure, and a measurement and feedback system.

People Are the Primary Resource

The model's primary critical-to-success resource is people whose native inclinations align with those described in *Chapter 5*. They are cooperative and other-regarding by nature and possess the desire to enable the success of others while pursuing their own emergence. These people must also possess the qualities of character and specific competencies needed to implement Life Enabling commerce. Only these people can transform the model's thinking into practice (Exhibit 2). Only they will genuinely pursue the model's purpose and conduct

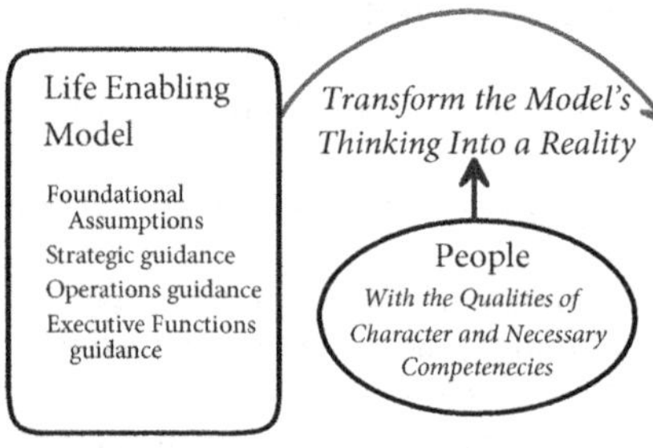

Exhibit 2. People Create a Life Enabling Enterprise

themselves in a manner consistent with its core values. Only they will continuously uncover and remove barriers to performance, recognize and realize opportunities to enhance performance, extract learning from their experiences, share their learning with other contributors, and apply that learning to improve themselves and everything they do.[1] They will self-manage their behavior and create and maintain the networks of collaboration needed to ensure collective success. Ultimately, their collective efforts will make processes waste-free and capable of delivering maximum value to customers while benefiting all stakeholders inclusively and improving the lives of everyone.

[1] Computer-based artificial intelligence systems have been developed that can detect and solve problems in specific domains. Some have been developed that can learn and improve their problem-solving performance within a domain. While many of these systems function better than most or all humans in specific domains (e.g., chess playing, nautical chart making, medical diagnosis), none to date match the broad flexibility and agility that skilled and motivated people can demonstrate as problem solvers and learning producers across domains. Some types of neural networks do perform unscripted learning (e.g., speech recognition), but, to our knowledge, none have demonstrated proficiency at accomplishing complex endeavors such as conducting real-world market-based commerce. This does not mean such development may not happen, just that it has not yet happened.

The Qualities of Character and Competencies People Must Possess

Two categories of features distinguish people who both retain or reinstate the native inclinations described in *Chapter 5* and are capable of implementing Life Enabling commerce. The first describes qualities of character. These qualities are termed "other personal characteristics" by professionals in the field of human resource management. The term refers to traits or broad dispositions that consistently evidence themselves in a person's behavior. Such qualities are not inherited—rather, they are the reflection of one's pattern of decisions and actions. Their presence is a product of one's personal choices and deeds. The second category identifies the specific competencies a person must possess to successfully implement the common role every contributor to a Life Enabling enterprise performs. These competencies are learnable and teachable.

These qualities of character and competencies are qualifications people must possess to build and sustain a Life Enabling enterprise. Knowledge of these qualifications informs your enterprise's recruitment and selection methods. It also is the basis for constructing your enterprise's onboarding process that orients new members and the design and development of the training curricula it uses to develop contributors with the proficiency levels they require to succeed.[2]

Qualities of Character

The following five personal characteristics are required of every contributor to a Life Enabling enterprise:

1. aligns with a purpose based on intrinsic motivation,
2. teams with others,
3. esteems competence as well as results,
4. is self-starting and sustaining, and
5. challenges the current "state of the art."

1. Aligns with a purpose based on intrinsic motivation

This means that people base their commitment to any organization on the substantive alignment between the organization's purpose, values, conduct, and needs and their personal goals, values, interests, and capabilities. The person's investment of effort is *not* controlled by external inducements. Rather, the satisfaction the person realizes derives from the nature of the work he or she performs, the investment of effort in an endeavor he or she values, and the achievement of the purpose being pursued. This common, intrinsically based alignment of contributors to the organization facilitates coherent

[2] These topics are addressed in detail in *Chapter 14. The Executive Function of Sufficiency.*

performance across people and their unified advancement of the business's success.

2. Teams with others

This means the individual is comfortable with the idea that his or her personal success depends on the success of the team as a whole and finds the added tasks that teaming requires satisfying. Some people do not. They favor singleton performance. They focus laser-like on their tasks and responsibilities, and they find satisfaction in accomplishing them through the application of their own capabilities. Teaming introduces a large social aspect to work that some people find detracts from their real enjoyment, which is the technical aspect of work.

Since a Life Enabling enterprise uses a team approach to accomplishing its purpose, every member must be comfortable with the idea that success depends on *the integrative achievement of multiple contributors.* The person must find satisfying the tasks of knowing who their fellow teammates are, understanding their capabilities and requirements, and connecting with them regularly. They must find value in working with their teammates to find solutions to problems that work across the organization and its cooperative system.

Also, as a team member, one must uphold the dual responsibility of acting as a leader and a member. As a leader, each contributor evaluates the implications of what the team is doing for its effects on the larger corporate purpose that the team's work is enabling. Each ensures that the team's current direction aligns with that purpose. If not, he or she acts to correct any deviations. Also, as a leader, each contributor also strives to envision better ways to formulate and realize the team's goal. As a member, each contributor manages his or her own performance, supports each other teammate's performance, and shares information and learning with others across the enterprise and its extended value streams.

3. Esteems competence as well as results

This means that the person demonstrates a persistent inclination to succeed by mastering the skills needed to produce success. A person with this trait is not satisfied with a positive result happening. Rather, such a person seeks to ensure that he or she has the observable and measurable knowledge, skills, and levels of proficiency needed to *produce that result consistently.* Being competent is valued as much as producing a measurable result. Such people strive to make themselves reliable achievers and to always operate from a base of explicit knowledge. They are exemplars for building mastery. Their example supports others in developing their own mastery. The expression of this trait by every contributor continuously elevates each person's consistency in performance and that of their teammates and the business as a whole.

4. Is self-starting and sustaining

This means the people who power Life Enabling commerce are active and initiating in the performance of their work. They are energized from within and consistently apply themselves with intensity. Their energy is fueled by the challenges they encounter, the results they produce with others, the learning they create, and their attention to maintaining their physical fitness. Their morale flows from these sources, their valid experience of positive self-efficacy, and their personal sense of the importance of what they are pursuing.

5. Challenges the current "state of the art"

This means that the individual is pioneering. He or she consistently pushes to expand the envelope of personal and collective achievement. This quality extends beyond a readiness to take on each day's new problems or challenges. It manifests itself in always being interested in what *could be* and willing to invest effort in imagining and experimenting with ways to make it real. Such people do not require carrots and sticks to "bust bureaucracy" or "challenge the current paradigm." People who must be moved or "incented" to expand the envelope of current achievement are not pioneering. They are *reactive.* Once the carrot and stick are removed or cease to be sufficiently potent, they revert back to their inert state. This is the fatal flaw in the "burning bridge" notion for energizing efforts to adopt a transformational change. Once the bridge ceases to burn, the investment of effort evaporates. People whose investment is externally controlled continue to need that external force in order for their actions to sustain or for their readiness to change to repeat itself. Implementing the Life Enabling model requires people who are paradigm breakers *intrinsically.* Only such people demonstrate no "rubber band" qualities, stretching when circumstances pressure them to try new ideas, then rebounding to their "comfort zone" once the pressure is removed.

Specific Competencies

Competency requirements refer to the set of knowledge, skills, and proficiency levels a person needs to enable the success of a Life Enabling enterprise. There are two sets of competencies contributors require. One set refers to the competencies a contributor needs to successfully perform his or her specific technical role within the enterprise. The second set of competencies are those a person needs to successfully fulfill the common role every Life Enabling enterprise contributor must carry out. The content of that role is described later in this chapter (pages 273–274). We term this second competency set "core competencies" because they are needed by all workers. Exhibit 3 lists these core competencies. Together, these competencies, when mastered with sufficient proficiency, enable each performer to

- self-manage his or her efforts, including aligning those efforts with the organization's purpose;
- collaborate with others;
- continuously improve his or her own performance and the effectiveness of the organization's offerings, work processes, and workplaces;
- improve the performance of others; and
- fulfill the role of a leader and a member within teams.

Exhibit 3. The Core Competencies Every Contributor to a Life Enabling Enterprise Requires

Knowledge	Skills
▪ Being able to explain the Life Enabling approach to commerce, including its Strategic, Operations, and Executive Functions components and the concepts and principles critical to its implementation (e.g., value, waste, flow, pull, etc.) ▪ Being able to define what customer values are and explain how they are uncovered, verified, and used within a Life Enabling enterprise ▪ Being able to define what stakeholder values are and explain how they are uncovered, verified, and used within a Life Enabling enterprise	▪ Action planning ▪ Goal setting ▪ Information- and knowledge-based decision making ▪ Information- and knowledge-based problem solving ▪ Learning from performance ▪ Measurement ▪ Teaching and coaching others ▪ Value detection ▪ Waste detection ▪ Working with others as a team

Core Knowledge Requirements

Every contributor must possess knowledge of the Life Enabling approach to commerce and an understanding of customer and stakeholder values. Knowledge of the model's approach to commerce is required because it guides decision making and action and ensures the alignment of individual performances. An understanding of customer and stakeholder values is essential because it enables contributors to gather, assess, and interpret the business's current information about these values. This interpretation informs every decision made in a Life Enabling enterprise, as it is the mandate of all contributors to satisfy customer values while benefiting all stakeholders inclusively.

Core Skills

Goal setting, action planning, measurement, and learning from performance are required to manage one's own performance and implement information-based problem solving. Value detection is required in order to decide what enhances the business's offerings and operations. Waste detection is required in order to detect opportunities for waste removal by uncovering non-value-adding work or product features. The methods of information- and knowledge-based problem solving and decision making are needed to stabilize work processes, eliminate waste, add value, and improve personal and collective performance. The working with others skills of clarifying and confirming, constructive criticism, and hitchhiking (Byron and Bierley, 2003), along with other skills essential to leading and participating in teams, enable the collaborative approach to enterprise dictated by the model. Teaching and coaching skills allow each contributor to share their knowledge with others and support the success of other contributors.

Exhibit 4, beginning on the next page, provides added information about each skill.

Proficiency Levels Required

Proficiency refers to the degree to which a person has mastered a skill and its correct application. The level of proficiency required for each core skill by a contributor to a specific enterprise is determined by the conditions of performance that exist within that enterprise. The more diverse, complex, and novel the work required by the enterprise is and the narrower its tolerances for error are, the greater the proficiency levels required in each of its contributors.

Knowledge and Information Are Essential Resources

People who are aligned, teamed, capable, energized, and pioneering need both knowledge and information to implement the Life Enabling model's commercial strategy. Both knowledge and information must be explicit and documented in order to be useful in a cooperative effort.

Knowledge

Knowledge allows us to label, organize, explain, predict, and control the contents of our world. It also enables us to accomplish tasks in a consistent manner.

Exhibit 4. An Elaboration of Each Core Skill

Skill	Description
Action planning	Organizes and documents how to accomplish a goal. It contains a statement of the goal to be accomplished and defines the steps to be taken to realize that goal, the resources needed to implement the plan, a list of anticipated barriers to success and possible solutions, and the action people will take should they not be able to execute the plan.
Goal setting	Defines what is to be achieved in observable, measurable terms. It specifies the result to be produced, who it is to benefit, and the name of the method to be used to produce the result. It records the benefits to be produced and what constraints on resources, decision making, or action must be abided by. Finally, it specifies the benchmark that must be met for the goal to be judged as achieved (see Exhibit 1, page 61).
Information- and knowledge-based decision making	Methods for making decisions either by collecting and analyzing information (e.g., criterion-based decision making) or by applying knowledge to infer the best or correct choice (e.g., decision table).
Information- and knowledge-based problem solving	Methods that solve problems either by collecting and analyzing information (e.g., A3 problem solving) or by applying knowledge to infer the proper solution (e.g., fault tree analysis).
Learning from performance	The systematic analysis of a task's outcome that generates learning one uses to improve his or her next performance of the task. The skill uncovers what enabled the success that was realized and what limited it from being even greater. It then extracts learning from this analysis and produces guidance for making improvements (Vitalo and Vitalo, 2020).
Measurement	A group of skills that enables one to calibrate the status of something on a designated attribute.
Teaching and coaching others	A group of skills that enable people to transfer expertise from themselves to another individual and support the improvement of another's mastery of that expertise.
Value detection	The ability to detect features of an output or activity that add value to an offering received by the customer or to his or her buying–benefiting experience. *Continued ...*

Exhibit 4. An Elaboration of Each Core Skill (continued)

Skill	Description
Waste detection	The ability to detect features of an output or activity that do not add value to an offering received by the customer or to his or her buying–benefiting experience.
Working with others as a team	A group of skills that enable one to effectively lead and participate in teams and be a helper to others. Includes basic communication skills (clarifying, confirming, constructive criticism, and hitchhiking), helping skills, skill in forming useful communications, and skill in detecting when communication has been successful.

To appreciate its utility, consider the label "house." It refers to a category of structures that serve as dwellings for one or more persons. That chunk of knowledge (label plus definition) allows you to identify whether any building you encounter is a house. Our knowledge of the structure of an apple allows us to predict that, when we slice an apple in half, we will find at its center a hard core with seeds. When a piece of equipment breaks down, we use the knowledge contained in its troubleshooting manual to discover why. That knowledge guides us in observing the equipment's status, interpreting what that status means, and understanding what the cause of the problem is. That same manual may also guide us in fixing the problem. If its instructions are complete, it will support us in managing our performance of the repair. The instructions will tell us what tools and materials we need, educate us on the sequence of steps we must execute, and provide tips to ensure each step is done correctly. When we finish, the instructions will guide us in checking whether we did the task correctly. In this way, knowledge allows us to control our own performance and ensure our success.

A uniquely important feature of knowledge is that it applies across instances of time, place, and person. When people do the same work in different but equivalent locations, the same written instructions support them in being consistent in their distributed execution of that work. When multiple people must operate together on a task, documented instructions enable them to coordinate their efforts by clarifying what each person will do and how their activities must flow together. Finally, knowledge, when taught to new hires, enables them to more rapidly master the work they must accomplish and progress from novice to master in their roles.

Examples of knowledge are everywhere in a Life Enabling enterprise. Here are a few:

- the directions for implementing a particular problem-solving strategy (e.g., A3),[3]
- an exploded diagram of a device with its parts labeled and pointers identifying where it resides in the device,
- a repair manual that guides one in diagnosing and correcting the operation of a piece of equipment,
- standardized work documents that broadcast current best practices for implementing each work process, and
- the work flow diagram posted in a workplace to guide contributors in the performance of a work process.

All the above listed items are examples of knowledge. Below is a list of the knowledge resources critical to the successful performance of the Life Enabling model's commercial strategy:

- knowledge documenting the Life Enabling commercial model;
- knowledge explaining what customer values are and how they are uncovered, verified, and used within a Life Enabling enterprise;
- knowledge explaining what stakeholder values are and how they are uncovered, verified, and used within a Life Enabling enterprise;
- guides, manuals, and other resources that support the mastery and use of business methods (e.g., Policy Planning and Deployment process, Kaizen, Total Productive Maintenance);[4]
- guides, manuals, and other performance support resources that guide the use, maintenance, and repair of facilities and equipment, tools, and materials;
- documented learning developed from improvement efforts;
- an extended value stream map for each business function; and
- a standardized work document for every work process.

---

[3] A3 is a version of information-based problem solving that (1) identifies the problem, (2) describes the context within which it occurs, (3) measures its impact, (4) specifies a goal for improvement, (5) uncovers root causes using the 5 Whys method, (6) generates and implements solutions, (7) measures the improvements made, (8) reports the results of the effort, and (9) follows up to ensure that the improvements are sustained. First used by the Toyota Motor Company, it is one of many tools in the Lean Manufacturing toolbox.

[4] The tools listed in parentheses are adopted from Lean Manufacturing. The Life Enabling model uses all Lean tools with the caveat that their use abides by the dictates of the Life Enabling commercial model.

Information

Information describes what we or others have experienced or imagine we will experience. It tells the status of persons, places, things, or activities at a point in time (e.g., "Today, at lunch, John was shaking his fist. Mike was sweating."). When it describes past experiences, it records history. When it presents what we imagine will happen, it tells our premonitions about the future. When it reports the results of an experiment, it documents the study's results, observations, or measurements and their analysis and interpretation. "In our experiment, Method A produced the course materials in 23 hours. Method B produced the materials in 61 hours." It can also describe the *apparent* connections between two or more persons, places, things, or activities (e.g., "When Mac studied more than 15 hours a week, his grades were B or higher").

Information, however, cannot *guide* our decisions or actions. The reason is that it only describes the state of something at *a particular time and place*. It does not explain why it occurred, tell us whether the same observation would be made at another time or place, or whether another observer would report it the same way.

While information cannot guide decision making or action, it is an important resource for accomplishing both purposes. It can point us to the knowledge we should use to guide our decisions and actions. For example, the model number on a piece of equipment tells us which repair manual to use in servicing it. When we repair that equipment, we need information about the status of its various gauges. The manual's guidance uses that information to diagnose the problem and decide what action we should take.

Below is a list of the specific information resources critical to the successful performance of the Life Enabling model's commercial strategy:

- The business intent of the Life Enabling enterprise, including its purpose, vision, and core values; how it defines the meaning of profit; the stakeholders the enterprise recognizes; and the state of its relationship with each. It also specifies the outcomes the business must produce to claim success.
- Descriptive information about the enterprise's current customers or customer segments, including their purposes, the setting within which they operate, how they judge success, and their capabilities in pursuing their purposes.
- Current customer values information (identity of each value and its type and importance [when applicable], the critical-to-quality metrics associated with each value, and the degree to which each is satisfied).

- The identity of the enterprise's current stakeholders and a description of their connections to the enterprise and their awareness of, concerns about, and expectations for the enterprise.
- Current stakeholder values information (identity of values, type, importance [when applicable], the critical-to-quality metrics associated with each value, and the degree to which each is satisfied).
- The current state of the business's performance at the business level, the business function level, the value stream component level, the work process level, the work unit level, and the performer level.
- The current year's business improvement plan and the status of its achievement (an output of the Policy Planning and Deployment process; see *Chapter 13*).
- The current year's business plan and the status of its achievement (an output of the Policy Planning and Deployment process; see *Chapter 13*).

Communications Infrastructure

The communications infrastructure is also a necessary resource. It is made up of the facilities, services, and other elements needed to share knowledge and information and allow people to connect, communicate, and collaborate with one another. This sharing and collaboration must extend across each business function's extended value stream, the enterprise as a whole, and the enterprise's cooperative system.

Within a Life Enabling enterprise, this communications infrastructure conveys the representation of information and knowledge in all required media. The point-of-use for information or knowledge determines where it is displayed. The importance of the information or knowledge for supporting the immediate performance of contributors in a particular setting determines its prominence. The information displayed may report, for example, the status of current performance for the individual or work unit or the work process being implemented. The knowledge displayed might be a work process map of the process being implemented in a work area or job aids that support the correct execution of tasks.

In addition to the content that is displayed, the communications infrastructure must provide access to stored content important to success but only needed from time to time. It also must enable people who are not proximate to each other to work together on a task. To accomplish this end, people must be able to connect with each other across distances in real time, interactively share information and ideas, store and retrieve facts and learning, and otherwise cooperatively accomplish business goals and improve business operations.

Through its support, the communications infrastructure plays a critical role in sustaining alignment among contributors and enabling their personal efforts to coherently advance the achievement of the Life Enabling enterprise's purpose.

The choice of media used to store and distribute content (paper-based, computer-based, etc.) across the infrastructure is made based on its utility alone. Issues of technological sophistication have no inherent significance. Within the Life Enabling enterprise, there is no confusion between *information technology* (IT) as a surrogate term for computer-based systems and *communications infrastructure*. The former may be an element in the latter, but its role, as with any artifact, is in the service of enabling contributors to add value to the customer's efforts and experience. Therefore, the preferred medium is the one that best serves the goals of communication with the least human burden and cost. That may or may not be the IT option.

Functional Measurement and Feedback System

A Functional Measurement and Feedback System (FM&FS) supplies the information needed to guide decision making in realizing personal and organizational effectiveness. A measurement system is deemed functional when it is complete, contains sound measures, has integrity, and is fully documented.

A *complete* measurement system includes measures that report the status of the business's results, activities, and resources at the Strategic, Operations, and Executive Functions levels. It also must report the status of performance at the business level, the business function level, the value stream component level, the work process level, the work unit level, and the performer level.

A measurement system has *sound* metrics when the information the metrics report is reliable, valid, and interpretable. Reliability means that each of its measurement operations consistently reports the same value for a given state every time it is correctly executed. Validity means that a metric does, in fact, report the status of the specific feature it claims to report about. Interpretability means that what a metric reports can be understood in a way that guides decision making and action.

A measurement system has *integrity* when both what it measures and how it executes its measurements align with the dictates of the business's commercial model. Thus, its results-focused measures make clear how well the business is realizing its commercial model's expected outcomes. Its activities-focused metrics clarify whether its manner of performance in realizing the model's desired ends is consistent with the model's dictates. Its resource-focused metrics clarify whether the business has and is appropriately using the resources critical to the successful implementation of its business model. Also, its methods of measurement must comply with the dictates of the model.

A functional measurement system also must be fully *documented.* Only a documented system is publicly knowable and therefore can be assessed and improved by any contributor to the enterprise. Without such documentation, no metric within the business measurement system will be reliable or valid.

In addition to satisfying the requirements for being complete, having sound measures, possessing integrity, and being documented—a functional system also requires that its contents be accessible by every contributor.

A more detailed description of the measurement system required by the Life Enabling enterprise appears in the section titled *Functional Measurement and Feedback System* in *Chapter 13*.

Organizational Design

Organizations larger than a single work unit or implementing processes more complex than a single activity must divide their work into subsets of operations with progressively more specific focuses. This division of the work is called *departmentation.*[5] Its output is represented by the various "boxes" that appear on a company's organization chart. Each box identifies a distinct work group. Each lower tier represents a more limited level of activity.

Beyond structuring its work, an organization's designer must distribute authority and responsibility for accomplishing the organization's goals across its work units. The designer also must define the reporting relationships among work units. His or her purpose is to clarify accountability for segments of the company's performance and to define the default communication path members should use. This task draws the solid or dotted lines that connect the boxes in an organization chart. An organization's designer completes the definition of the social aspect of an organization by clarifying the basic role organization members are expected to perform, their involvement in business decision making, and how they will work together to accomplish the purpose of the enterprise.

How an organization executes departmentation and the definition of the social aspect of an organization depends on the commercial model its designer is implementing. Each model has its own specific requirements. If, for example, your model emphasizes control over information, authority, and contributor actions, then a top-down structure that retains authority at the top makes sense. On the other hand, if your commercial model requires all members of the enterprise to continuously improve its performance through pervasive waste removal and

---

[5] Departmentation can be done using approaches other than work decomposition, but work decomposition is the most relevant method for our purposes.

innovation and that effort requires the ability of members to share ideas and solutions rapidly, then a top-down, control-oriented structure fails. Thus, depending on its characteristics, an organization's structure can either impede or facilitate a commercial model's operation.

How a Life Enabling Enterprise Must Be Structured

Enomoto (1995) told us that, from as early as 1950, the writing of Barnard, among others, shaped Japanese management's thinking about the structural aspects of organizations. Enomoto stated: "So great, in fact, was Barnard's influence on our management thinking that the phenomenon came to be called 'the Barnard Revolution'" (Enomoto, 1995, p. 241). While Barnard's guidance appears absent from the management guidelines offered by Lean Manufacturing, we understood it to be critical to enabling the continuous improvement efforts inherent in that approach. Therefore, we incorporated this thinking into the Life Enabling model.[6]

Following Barnard's the thinking, Japanese managers recognized that an organization's structure establishes its formal lines of communication; the paths for cascading goals, plans, and performance expectations; and, typically, the path for budget development. In other words, an organization's structure establishes the grid across which executive and operating information and work flows. *Unless it is designed to enable those functions, it will undermine their performance.* To enable the effective performance of this work in a Life Enabling enterprise, its organization's structure must be defined in a way that supports the following ends:

- the waste-free implementation of value-adding work and the affirmative adding of value to the enterprise's offering and the buying–benefiting experience it provides the customer,
- the connection of contributors to the outcomes they produce,
- each contributor's ability to control the work for which he or she is responsible,
- the implementation of a functional business measurement system that clarifies the status of its resources, activities, and results at the business level, the business function level, the value stream component level, the work process level, the work unit level, and the performer level,
- the rapid communication of knowledge and information among contributors,
- the proximity of contributors who are working together to implement a particular process and produce a needed output, and
- the efficient implementation of the enterprise's yearly Policy Planning and Deployment process.

[6] Enomoto also named Mary Parker Follett as another formative influence on Japanese thinking about organization. Her work is also incorporated into our model, especially with regard to the social aspect of organizations.

The Model's Approach to Departmentation

Following Barnard, the Life Enabling model's approach to departmentation decomposes the technical work that must be done to realize the organization's aim. This analysis correlates "the efforts of individuals in such a way ... that purpose may be accomplished" (Barnard, 1968, p. 136). Barnard's ideas about departmentation are largely addressed in his chapter The *Bases and Kinds of Specialization* (Barnard, 1968, pp. 127–138).[7] His process for departmentation begins with analyzing how one accomplishes the purpose of the organization.

"Purpose" for Barnard is defined concretely by the product or service output a commercial organization produces for its customers. One example he offers in *The Functions of an Executive* is "to make shoes." "A manufacturing organization," he wrote, "is said to exist to make, say, shoes; this is its 'purpose'" (Barnard, 1968, p. 92). As he stated it, departmentation's first step is "the recognition of what means may be effectively employed cooperatively, that is, what specialization of activity will work" to accomplish the organization's purpose (Barnard, 1968, p. 134). He saw this analysis as focusing on the processes, operations, and tasks that must be performed to produce the organization's intended offering. Consequently, decomposition of the organization begins with the production value stream (Exhibit 5, next page). This is the set of technical operations that produce the business's final output.

The departmentation process may use either the method of process decomposition (as depicted in Exhibit 5) or a mix of object and process decomposition. Both methods begin with a precise definition of what the function being decomposed must produce. Process decomposition starts with mapping the overall flow of activity that transforms a function's initial inputs into its final product or service output. It progressively breaks down each major component of that workflow into processes, operations, and tasks. It is essentially equivalent to a work breakdown analysis that repeats itself until the desired level of detail (granularity) is achieved.

Object decomposition begins with the function's final output. It breaks up the final output into its component parts. It temporarily sets aside those components sourced externally as either initial inputs or in-process inputs. Then, it sequences the production and assembly of the remaining components to identify the main work flow. Once all components are identified and arranged in their order of production, it applies process decomposition to uncover the activities that produce each component.[8]

[7] "Specialization" is the word Barnard used for what is referred to here as *departmentation*.

[8] Demand Flow Technology® (DFT), developed by John R. Costanza and popular in the 1990s, used an object decomposition approach to construct a work process that was balanced and free of wait states.

Irrespective of the method used (process or object decomposition), at each level of decomposition, the value stream components are aligned by order of performance. The lower-level activities are depicted below the higher-level activity they accomplish. Barnard referred to this analysis as the "discovery or invention of the

Exhibit 5. Departmentation of the Production or Service Fulfillment Value Stream

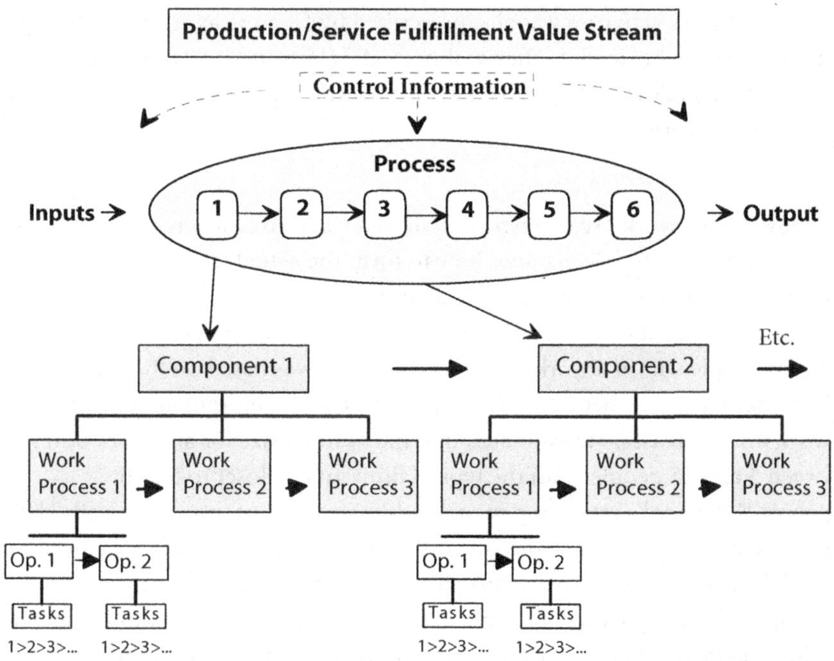

correct order of cooperative acts" (Barnard, 1968, p. 133). When finished, one has identified all the processes, operations, and tasks that must be completed to produce the output a business function provides and their order of occurrence.

All Value Streams Within the Business Are Decomposed

A modern commercial organization is composed of many functions that work together to produce the offering it provides its customers. These functions are of two types. The first type delivers value directly to the business's customer (e.g., the Production or Service Fulfillment function). The second type delivers value indirectly by enabling the success of the function(s) that serve the customer directly. These are called *enabling functions.* Enabling functions include, for example, Product Development, Order-to-Delivery,[9] and Human Resource

[9] The order-to-delivery function receives customer orders, triggers and tracks their fulfillment and de-

Management. Exhibit 6, next page, depicts the relationship between these two types of functions.

The Life Enabling model extends Barnard's thinking with regard to structuring the organization. Once the decomposition of the production value stream is completed, a Life Enabling enterprise applies the same process to each remaining business function (e.g., Product Development, Purchasing) whose outputs support the operation of the production value stream. This operationalizing of each function's activities was also prescribed by Deming as an essential step in transforming a business to the Quality model (Deming 1982a, p. 87). A technical work breakdown is done for every function's value stream in order to structure the enterprise.

Forming Work Units

Following the work breakdown analysis of a value stream, a reasoning process is implemented that determines how to form the actual work units within it. In performing this step, Barnard identified the primary concern as satisfying the needs for communication. For Barnard, this implied a restriction on the number of people within a work unit. His reasoning was based on the exponential increase in the number of interrelationships that occur as membership of a work unit increases. He estimated that the optimal size for any work unit is between 5 and 15 people, with the typical limit much closer to 5 or 6 people.[10] Barnard's reasoning process addresses other concerns as well. These include the nature of the work, the order of its performance, and the need that work be done in a specific location due to the sharing of a common resource.[11] Other factors are applied in forming work units within a Life Enabling enterprise. These include the intent to minimize handoffs; eliminate sources of waste, especially travel/transport; and ensure that contributors have a line of sight to the outputs they produce. Handoffs can increase interruptions,

---

livery, bills customers for completed orders, and receives and records their payments.

[10] Barnard pointed out, for example, that a work unit of just eight people has 28 potential one-to-one relationships (8! / (2! x (8-2)!)). When the number of relationships to be maintained exceeds people's ability to maintain them, the work effectiveness and social organization of the unit deteriorates (see Barnard, 1968, p. 108–109).

[11] One issue Barnard considered in forming work units is *not included* in the Life Enabling model. This is the issue of "associational specialization." It refers to Barnard's requirement that the definition of work units "create social conditions which are attractive to such persons ... as an inducement to participation in [the] organization" (Barnard, 1968, p. 134). For Barnard, this means ensuring that there will be people within each work unit who are comfortable with each other's race, religion, skin color, social status, or education. With regard to departmentation, Barnard sees associational specialization's unique relevance as its ability to benefit communication and the fact that it populates the informal organization with people who are likely to support adherence to the organization's direction (Barnard, 1968, p. 134). While Barnard's concerns about obliging people's prejudices and manipulating people's adherence to corporate policies are relevant within a control-oriented commercial model, neither is relevant within the Life Enabling approach to commerce.

motion, setup, and wait—all forms of waste. Line of sight to output maintains the connection of contributors to the end result they are participating in producing. This enhances their sense of ownership for it, the flow of feedback to them about the result they have produced, and their experience of pride of workmanship.

Exhibit 6. Top-Level Structure of a Life Enabling Enterprise

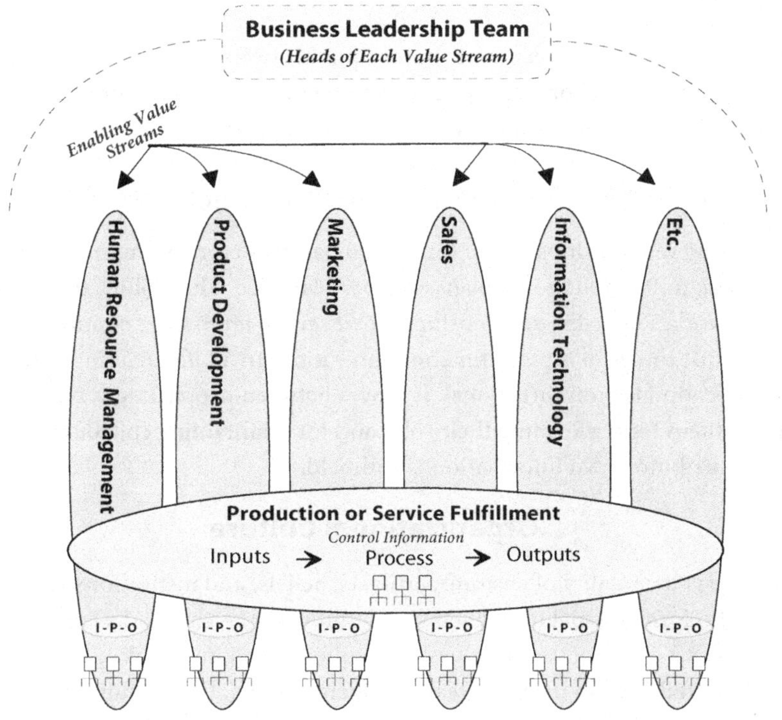

The reasoning that defines work units interrelates with all these issues. The process for defining work groups generates and refines the definition of work units until a fully satisfying solution is uncovered. Based on what Barnard stated elsewhere in his book, when the departmentation process is completed, the finishing step is to document each work unit's mandate or purpose statement. He identified five elements that a work unit's purpose statement should include—"(*a*) the place where work is done; (*b*) the time at which work is done; (*c*) the persons with whom work is done; (*d*) the things upon which work is done (inputs); and (*e*) the method or process by which work is done" (Barnard, 1968, pp. 128–129). To this list we add what is produced, to whom it is provided, and what requirements that output must satisfy.

The Model's Approach to Distributing Authority, Responsibility, and Defining Reporting Relationships

In a Life Enabling enterprise, authority flows with responsibility. Every contributor has the right to make those decisions required to accomplish his or her role's responsibilities. Since the enterprise is implemented using a team approach, the execution of this authority must address the impact of decisions on every other team member locally and across the enterprise and on the enterprise as a whole.

As to responsibility, every contributor upholds two sets of responsibilities. The first is common to all contributors and defined in the role each contributor must perform. This is discussed later in this chapter on pages 273–274. The second is specific to the technical tasks each contributor must accomplish. This set of responsibilities is defined in his or her position description.

Reporting relationships define the formal pathways for communication between work units about goals, plans, and performance. They follow the decomposition of work. Reporting relationships, however, *do not restrict* communication. They are just the default paths for communication. In a Life Enabling enterprise, communication is omnidirectional. It moves between people freely, based on its utility to them for performing their roles and for maintaining collaboration between contributors. No information is withheld.

Organizational Culture

Culture is the totality of customs, artifacts, beliefs, and institutions created by people who form a social unit. Each social unit is aligned around a common goal and upholds a common set of values. The culture of a Life Enabling enterprise, for example, is reflected in its use of team problem solving, the ubiquitous presence of information displays in work areas, broad participation by contributors in the enterprise's idea generation and process improvement events, the use of standardized work documents, and the implementation of an all-hands, organization-wide yearly planning activity. As a social unit, it is aligned around the goal of helping others succeed and the set of core values that guide that effort.

There are two features of culture that have special significance. One is distinctive of a commercial enterprise's culture, and the other is common to all cultures. They are, however, interrelated.

Unlike the culture emerging in other social units, a commercial organization's culture is not evolutionary. It does not gradually emerge, only taking its final form after a certain period of development. It is present from the organization's beginning as the predictable milieu produced by the people who implement a specific commercial model. This is because the people who control a commercial organization select its commercial model to represent their purposes and values. That model defines how the enterprise must be formed and operated to realize its owner's intent. It specifies the people who must populate it, how they will work together, and the artifacts they must select or create and use to support their efforts. If the model is properly implemented, the organization's culture expresses itself from the enterprise's very beginning. Any observed variation between the cultures of organizations correctly implementing the same commercial model are only within the margins tolerated by the specific model that the people in authority have chosen to implement.

The second feature, common to all cultures, is that, despite the above statements, the culture that prevails in any organization is determined by the makeup of the people that implement that organization. The model itself is a logical entity. It is an artifact of the mind. It prescribes but does not think or act. Only people think, act, and relate. It is the people who implement an organization that determine its culture. While a commercial model may specify how its agents *should relate* to each other, how agents *do relate* is wholly determined by the character and capabilities of the people it selects as agents.

The fact that the nature of the people who implement an organization determines its culture does not negate a commercial model's contributions to that culture. On the contrary, it clarifies how its effect is realized: through the model's specification of the character and makeup of the people it designates as needed to implement it. If owners who find a particular commercial model expressive of their personal makeup follow its guidance, the behavior of an organization's selected leaders will reflect the required character and capabilities defined by the model they were chosen to implement. It is only in this indirect way that each commercial model determines the relationships that emerge between contributors and the organization's culture as a whole.

Thus, a firm implementing commerce based on self-interest that is directed toward maximizing its owner's gain from each commercial transaction will populate itself with people whose values align with this intent, *at least in its executive roles.* Such people will establish and maintain relationships within the firm that reflect this value set, establish the artifacts that support it, and evidence in their behavior the methods that best serve these ends (e.g., maintaining control, using any means available to maximize personal gain as long as the appearance of "clean hands" can be maintained). Exhibit 8, beginning on the next page, expands the implications of this insight.

Exhibit 8. Some Implications of the Fact That People Decide Culture

The understanding that the makeup of people, not the dictates of policy, decides an organization's culture has a number of implications. One is that "culture change" in an organization requires personal transformations on the part of the company's leaders and contributors, since the culture that must be changed is an expression of who they have been. Put simply, if the culture must change, then they must change first. Personal transformation cannot be imposed from without. By definition, it must be assented to from within the individual. No "edict from above" will alter people's character. A second implication is that, assuming the current culture matches the requirements of the business's commercial model, a company must change its commercial model if it intends to change its culture. Otherwise, it will change its people in ways that would make them no longer appropriate to implement the organization's approach to commerce. A third implication is that culture change within an organization implementing the dominant commercial model is implausible. In such organizations, control is maintained at the top. This means that the people who must decide to change the organization's culture—and implicitly, its commercial model—are precisely the ones most advantaged by the company's current approach to commerce and its associated culture.[1]

Two examples may clarify the consequences of these implications. The first relates to the adoption of *employee involvement*, and the second relates to the status of *employee engagement*.

Employee Involvement

Employee involvement refers to the role that nonmanagement employees have in business decision making and action. At the lowest level of involvement, management tells employees what is expected of them, and employees contribute by fulfilling those expectations. At the highest level of involvement, employees participate fully in setting the direction of the business, deciding its approach for realizing that direction, and ensuring that it is accomplished. The essence of the concept, as applied to businesses, reaches at least as far back as the 1920s to the writings of Mary Parker Follett (Follett, 1995). It is most recently identified with the work of Edward E. Lawler. Empirical research indicates that high-involvement workplaces generate employee engagement, improved job satisfaction, reduced turnover, and improved financial results. Either directly or indirectly, these effects mean improved net monetary performance for Capitalist businesses.[2] Business gurus have, for decades,

Continued ...

[1] This third insight has specific relevance for the current efforts of capitalists who seek to redefine Capitalism to be inclusive or to reset our world economic system to be fairer and more just.

[2] It is unclear to what extent the contribution of employee involvement to improved financial performance is direct or is mediated by its influence on other factors, such as job satisfaction, morale, turnover, and retention. It does appear clear, however, that the potency of its effects are moderated by a number of factors, such as employee readiness to be involved and the meaningfulness of the involvement solicited by management. Nonetheless, its positive effects on business metrics is well documented (Beaty, 1996; Benson and Lawler, 2015; Benson, Kimmel, and Lawler, 2013; Combs, Liu, Hall, and Ketchen, 2006; Cottini, Kato, and Nielsen, 2009; Guerrero and Barraud-Didier, 2004; Harter, Schmidt, and Killham, 2003;

Exhibit 8. Some Implications of the Fact That People Decide Culture (continued)

advised such companies to redefine their organization's relationship with its employees to one typified by higher employee involvement (e.g., Deming, Drucker, Peters, Pfeffer, Lawler). Despite the fact that many companies claim they involve their employees in business decision making, the factual results of investigations indicate that businesses do not devolve decision-making authority downward and share power with frontline workers. While upwards of 70% of the businesses surveyed report that they use an "involving management approach," 73% indicate that they almost never or never use self-managing teams, and 74% indicate that they almost never or never involve nonmanagement employees in policy and strategy issues (Lawler, Mohrman, and Ledford, 1995). More recent research by Lawler, Mohrman, and Benson (2001) found the percentages on these factors indicating limited involvement to be much higher, perhaps as high as 94%.[3]

Why would the people responsible for leading a Capitalist enterprise not introduce high levels of employee involvement and reap the greater profits it appears to generate? That makes no business sense!

The fact is that the adoption of employee involvement is inconsistent with the makeup of the people who lead producer-focused, profit-driven companies. Here is why. To implement high levels of employee involvement, one must disperse authority broadly to people outside executive and managerial roles. These people must receive business information that usually is kept within those ranks, thereby reducing the asymmetrical information relationship that advantages managers and is one source of their power and control (e.g., in wage negotiations). If the involvement of nonmanagement employees is expanded to include a significant role in making business improvements, their contribution to successful change making would stimulate their expectations for greater participation in the business benefits they generate. Their status and stake in the enterprise would grow. All of these consequences would dissipate the basis for differential status and rewards that are expected and realized by executives and managers. These developments would lessen the power of executives to control their own destinies.

Leaders of Capitalist companies are themselves capitalists in their personal commerce. As Agency Theory (Jensen and Meckling, 1976) and research (Abrahamson and Park, 1994; Amihud and Lev, 1981; Eisenhardt, 1989) make clear, they operate out of self-interest and seek to maximize the rewards they realize from their *quid pro quo* agreements with the organization. Their special status is based on their differential responsibility and control over corporate actions. Their ability to maximize the benefits they receive depends on their control of business decision making (see *Appendix A*). Both their special status and their control would be diluted by broad and significant involvement of all

Continued ...

[2] Jones and Kato, 2005; Kuyea and Sulaimonb, 2011; Lawler, 1999; Lawler, Mohrman, and Benson, 2001; Lawler, Mohrman, and Ledford, 1995; Meckstroth, 1991; Spreitzer, 1995, 2007).

[3] The 2001 study used a slightly different measurement scale. This difference makes an exact statement of the percentage impossible.

Exhibit 8. Some Implications of the Fact That People Decide Culture (continued)

employees. Hence, implementing employee involvement is antagonistic to their best interests.[4]

Employee Engagement

A similar analysis can be made with regard to elevating employee engagement. The work of Harter, Schmidt, and Killham (2003); Khan (2007); Schweyer (2009); Wellins, Bernthal, and Phelps (2005); and others supports the efficacy of employee engagement in improving business performance. Yet, despite a broad push by organizational consultants (e.g., the Gallup Organization, BlessingWhite, Development Dimensions International [DDI], the HayGroup) for companies to adopt programs for improving engagement, there has been no significant advancement in the degree to which companies engage their employees. Engagement scores for employees of traditional companies hover in the 20% to 33% range (Gallup, 2017; Gallup Management Journal, 2002; BlessingWhite, Inc., 2008; Towers Perrins, 2008). We suggest that the reason for this failure to elevate employee engagement is that the factors that elevate engagement include higher levels of employee involvement and thus also dilute management power and compromise their control of decisions that affect their self-interest.

The takeaway lesson from understanding who or what determines culture is that, once you have identified the commercial model that expresses who you are, choosing your people correctly is the only way to ensure that the model and its required culture will exist. A second lesson is that if you have correctly chosen the model that fits your makeup and the people to implement it and you seek to change the existing culture, you must first change yourself, then select a new commercial model expressive of your new makeup and acquire contributors that satisfy the people requirements of your new model.

4. As an extension of this thinking, realize that if capitalists lead the redefinition of the political and economic regime that will lead societies in the future (e.g., the Great Reset), you can be sure that such systems will not reset the power asymmetries that currently exist between them and the remainder of society.

Based on this understanding of how a culture is created, an organization's culture is a *dependent variable*—i.e., a result of other factors. Namely, it is the product of people whose makeup and conduct match the requirements of the commercial model they have been chosen to implement. In the end, however, culture becomes both a dependent and an independent variable. While initially it is *a product of prior and current members' behavior, it becomes an influencer of future behavior.* Once established, its customs and contents enable and reinforce the behaviors of the people who created it. In this way, a culture makes its own contribution to supporting its continuance.

Describing the Life Enabling Organization's Culture

The culture of a commercial organization can be described by documenting how it resolves the following four issues:

1. Why do people contribute their cooperative efforts to the enterprise?
2. What is the role of each contributor in accomplishing the enterprise's success?
3. How must people work together in order to successfully implement the enterprise's commercial strategy?
4. How must the organization relate with its contributors if it is to attract, hire, develop, and retain the people it needs?

The answers to these questions clarify important aspects of an organization's culture. For example, the reason why a person contributes his or her cooperative efforts affects the basis for social cohesion within the culture. It shapes the individual member's relationship with each other and with the organization as a whole. It can create a culture dominated by individualistic agendas wherein people compete against each other for material rewards or a culture of cooperation and mutual support as people seek to realize a common end. The answers also further clarify the type of people you need to bring on board to implement your approach to commerce. This information has critical significance for shaping the human resource management systems that will serve your organization.

1. The Basis for Contributing Cooperative Efforts

There is no organization unless there are people who invest their talents and efforts in doing its work. Why do people make that investment, and of what significance is that reason? The reason a person joins an organization has implications for that person's connection to the work he or she assumes and how the person will behave as a contributor across time.

Barnard (1968) considered the question of why people contribute their efforts to an organization from an organization-building perspective. He identified two types of reasons. The first is based on the "natural alignment" between one's purpose and values and the purpose and values of the organization. In this instance, the basis for an individual's investment of effort in a collective endeavor is *intrinsic*. The second is *induced*—that is, it is elicited based on the organization offering incentives and/or applying persuasion. Essentially, the person's commitment to work is made as a *quid pro quo*. The person contributes only to realize some promised reward or benefits. Together, these two types of reasons (intrinsic and induced) encompass all the reasons people take jobs or become contributors. Each type has different implications for an organization.

Intrinsic Motivation

Barnard's writing about natural alliances as a basis for contributing one's efforts to an organization is oddly inconsistent. As to frequency of their occurrence, for example, he termed personal commitments based on a "natural alignment" an "aberration." Indeed, in *The Functions of the Executive*, he stated that the occurrence of common purpose between a person and an organization is "never the case" in modern businesses and also claimed that it "rarely even appears to be the case" (1968, p. 88). Yet, he later contradicted himself by writing that it occurs "very frequently," that "a considerable number of family organizations are of this origin," and that "out of many thousands of cases one will last for a considerable period" (Barnard, 1968, p. 102). Further, he identified the natural alliance between people who have the same purpose as one of the four ways organizations are created. He termed these organizations *spontaneous organizations* (Barnard, 1968, p. 102).

Barnard identified two organizational advantages of intrinsic motivation as the basis for individual contribution. First, it supplies a more stable commitment and contribution of effort, especially during times of uncertainty. Second, he asserted that an intrinsically driven commitment generates a greater intensity of effort. As Barnard wrote, intensity of cooperative effort relates to the "intensity of attachment to the 'cause'" (Barnard, 1968, p. 84). The more internally rooted one's commitment of effort is, the greater the person's "attachment to the 'cause.'"

There is a third benefit that Barnard did not identify but is implied by his remaining ideas. The omission is striking, given that Barnard spent a chapter discussing the problematic side of this issue.[12] When a commitment to an organization emanates from the alignment between one's purpose and values and the purpose and values of the organization, its maintenance requires *no* special expenditure of organizational resources. The organization need only focus on remaining true to its purpose and accomplishing its goals. Essentially, a person's intrinsically based commitment is self-managing, assuming there is no change in the individual's or the organization's purpose and values. Of course, people and organizations do change, but radical transformations in purpose and values are not frequent occurrences.

Induced Motivation

Despite the advantages of intrinsic motivation, Barnard stated that the use of induced motivation is the *only proper basis* for acquiring people's investment in accomplishing a commercial organization's purpose. "*Organization results from*

[12] *Chapter IX The Economy of Incentives* (Barnard, 1968, pp. 140–160).

the modification of the action of the individual through control of or influence upon one of these categories [the individual's purposes, desires, impulses of the moment, and alternatives]. Deliberate conscious and specialized control of them is the essence of the executive functions" (Barnard, 1968, p. 17, italics in original).

Barnard identified the use of objective incentives (e.g., money, status) and "persuasion" as the two means for accomplishing this task of control (Barnard, 1968, p. 141). His concept of persuasion is important to explain, as he included methods one might not assume to be present in a commercial enterprise. All methods of persuasion have the purpose of changing people's minds. Barnard stated, "Persuasion in the broad sense in which I am here using the word includes: (a) the creation of coercive conditions; (b) the rationalization of opportunity; (c) the inculcation of motives" (Barnard, 1968, p. 149).

The terms "coercive conditions" and "coercion" are meant literally. If you are wondering what "benefit" creating coercive conditions offers the person being coerced, it is in not having the threatened negative act implemented—e.g., the threat to eliminate your job is not executed. Rationalization is another means of persuasion. It communicates reasons why it is in the person's best interest "to perform services or conform to requirements of specific organizations" (Barnard, 1968, p. 150). These reasons *need not be fact-based,* just intellectually persuasive. The inculcation of motives uses "propaganda" (Barnard, 1968, p. 152) to instill in the person the desire to "join up" with the organization. It is a strategy that manipulates emotions.

Barnard did not identify what advantages the method of induced commitment provides. He simply stated it is the only approach that fits a correct understanding of an organization and how its executive functions must be performed. One might infer, based on his broader thinking, that its advantage is that it protects the executive's ability to control the organization as he or she sees fit. In that sense, it is the only appropriate means for an organization implementing a control-oriented commercial model such as Capitalism.

For example, one control-benefiting advantage of induced over intrinsic motivation is that the definition of purpose is wholly a matter of the owner's discretion. An owner is free to define or redefine the organization's purpose and values without concern for its effects on contributors as long as the factors inducing their contribution remain unchanged. Another control-benefiting advantage of induced motivation is that it allows an executive greater flexibility in determining how resources are applied. If an executive seeks to shift resources from sustaining employee cooperation, he or she is free to move from offering objective incentives to persuasion, even coercive persuasion. A common example of this is when management tells its employees that unless they take a pay cut, they may lose their jobs entirely. Here, the threat of loss of all income is the means for changing people's minds, retaining their contribution of effort, and lowering their cost to the business.

Barnard did identify a significant downside to induced motivation, although he did not label it as such. The *quid pro quo* basis for eliciting a person's contribution of efforts is sensitive to changing material circumstances. Any event that makes uncertain whether the promised "reward" will be received disturbs the person's investment of effort. For example, if the inducement to work were the expectation of future wealth due to the accrual of stock and the company's stock price falls, the person's confidence in receiving his or her reward would lessen and, theoretically, so would his or her investment of effort in work. Also, when incentives are used, the emergence of an alternative employer offering a higher level of one's promised incentive might well entice the contributor to change his or her commitment. Thus, if the job market improves, people who have been "persuaded" to work for low pay in unpleasant circumstances due to the lack of alternatives would likely leave those jobs.[13]

Agency Theory (Jensen and Meckling, 1976) offers another perspective on the downside of commitment based on external inducements, one that recognizes both the owner (principal) and the employee (agent) as capable actors. A *quid pro quo* basis for contributing one's talents and efforts implies that both the individual and the organization are operating out of self-interest. As Agency Theory clarifies, given two parties (a principal and his or her agent), each of whom is operating out of self-interest, what benefits one may not benefit the other. An action that would most advantage the organization may clash with an alternative action that would most enhance the individual's personal interest (Jensen and Meckling, 1976). The logical resolution of such conflicts is for the individual, given the motive of self-interest, to ensure benefit for him- or herself.

This reasoning is consistent with the findings of empirical research. Abrahamson and Park (1994), for example, found that corporate officers intentionally conceal negative organizational outcomes from shareholders and that this behavior is followed by their subsequent selling of stock in their companies before the negative information becomes public. Amihud and Lev (1981) found support for personal gain as a driver in management decisions to engage in

---

[13] A perpetually weakened job market obviates this danger. Indeed, a "heightened sense of job insecurity" was lauded by Alan Greenspan, former Federal Reserve Chairman, in his testimony to the U.S. Congress, as a major factor in suppressing wages and enhancing business profits during the 1990s (Pollin, 2002).

conglomerate mergers despite the uncertain benefits such mergers offer shareholders. And Eisenhardt's (1989) review of the literature on executive behavior found that whenever the interests of shareholders and top executives diverged—as, for example, on issues of "takeover attempts, debt versus equity financing, acquisitions, and divestitures, and for the mitigation of agency problems"—self-interest drove executive action unless checked by owner controls. In every such instance, Agency Theory's predictions were supported.

Both Barnard's theorizing and the formulations of Agency Theory converge on the judgment that collective efforts, populated by induced contributors, require oversight of their members, accountability systems to ensure they conduct themselves in the best interest of the business, and other costly "overhead" type activities to manage employees' adherence to corporate purposes.[14]

The Life Enabling Enterprise's Required Basis for Contributing Cooperative Efforts

People's contributions of effort to a Life Enabling enterprise must be based on intrinsic motivation. This means that every contributor's purpose and values naturally align with the purpose and values of the Life Enabling model. Thus, they experience commerce as an opportunity to apply their capabilities to benefiting another while advancing their own emergence as an individual. It also means that they find satisfaction in the activities of continuous improvement, working with others in a team format, and the technical work they will perform. They naturally embrace the model's core values and the specific business intent of the company they contribute to. Thus, both contributor and organization pursue a common goal in a common way and derive satisfaction from their efforts and outcomes. The achievement of one party's ends substantively realizes the other party's ends.

In a Life Enabling enterprise, the problems that Agency Theory clarifies do not exist. Nor does the enterprise need to assume the overhead required to manage the inducement of people's willingness to contribute. From the perspective of a Life Enabling enterprise, all such activity is waste, and its approach to commerce requires that all waste be eliminated from its offerings, operations, and work settings. This is why intrinsically motivated contributors are essential for realizing the goals of the Life Enabling model.

2. The Role Each Contributor Must Perform

An analysis of the contributions required from every member of a Life Enabling enterprise reveals the common role each contributor must perform to realize the

[14] See Barnard's (1968) statements on pp. 6, 44, 57, 156, 200–201, 244–245 of *The Functions of the Executive* to appreciate the challenge management faces in maintaining the continuance of induced cooperative efforts.

enterprise's commercial goals. When these requirements are translated into a generic job description, six responsibilities emerge:

1. Master the Life Enabling model and the company's approach to implementing it.
2. Add value as defined by customers in a manner that benefits all stakeholders and betters the lives of everyone.
3. Measure one's impact on value delivered to customers and all stakeholders.
4. Improve personal and collective performance continuously.
5. Share personal learning with others and enable their improved success.
6. Team with others to accomplish the common purpose. Teaming must extend across one's work unit, value stream component, business function, and the business as a whole. Also, it must extend across all members of each business function's extended value stream and the company's cooperative system.

Essentially, each person implementing a Life Enabling enterprise operates as a self-managing contributor/owner/executive who maintains the enterprise as capable and succeeding in its purpose. Every contributor ensures his or her understanding of the Life Enabling model and how the business is accomplishing it. Each strives for perfection as he or she works to maximize the delivery of value to customers while benefiting all stakeholders inclusively and bettering the lives of everyone. Each contributor thinks and acts in a manner that aligns with the organization's purpose and seamlessly integrates with the efforts of others. And everyone focuses on enabling his or her teammates to do likewise. In doing so, all contributors strive to implement current best practices flawlessly while devising and sharing improved practices for the future.

3. How People Must Work Together in a Life Enabling Enterprise

Multiple people can work together in two ways: as a group or as a team. In each instance, the work unit has a goal, and each member has a responsibility for achieving that goal. However, the person's relationship to the goal and his or her responsibility for achieving it vary based on whether they are operating as a group or a team.

Group Approach

In the group approach, each member's responsibility is to complete an assignment. Each individual is accountable for his or her assignment only. An individual succeeds or fails solely based on how well he or she accomplishes that assignment. The "group," meaning the members *as a whole*, has no responsibility in itself. It is solely a collection of people performing individual assignments.

Groups always require leaders. The leader is responsible for performing the executive functions needed to maintain the group. He or she must set the group's goal; plan its achievement; make assignments; communicate needed information about direction, performance, and the coordination of resources and activities; and ensure that each individual performs his or her assigned responsibilities. Whether the leader is directive or participative in his or her approach, the performance of the executive functions remains the leader's *singular* responsibility. If each member of the group fulfills his or her assignment and the group's goal is not realized, it is the group leader alone who fails.

The group approach does best when the nature of the work to be done satisfies the following criteria:

- The work required to accomplish the group's goal is well understood and explicitly documented.
- The interdependencies among the elements of work accomplished by different members are known and predictable.

In addition, the group approach works best if people's connection to the group is through their specific assignments, as opposed to directly identifying with the group's overall goal. If the latter were true, people might have a tendency to second-guess the group's direction or otherwise be distracted from executing their specific mandates.

Under these conditions, the centralized management and discrete implementation of portions of a work unit's mandate can be effective in accomplishing technical work. People work together by simply focusing on their individual assignments and doing them well. Any requirements for communication between them is planned into their assignments or conveyed to them by the group leader. Group members do not require an overall understanding of the group's goal or what other members are doing. They just need to know what it is they must do. Thus, a group can accommodate circumstances where contributors are less than fully proficient in managing their own performance or the interfaces between their performance and the performance of other group members. This is because the group leader ensures that each individual's performance meets expectations and that the various individual performances coordinate with one another to realize the overall goal.

Team Approach

In the team approach, the team *as a whole* is responsible for accomplishing the unit's goal. Each individual member has a dual responsibility. One is to accomplish the specialty assignments he or she undertakes. The other is to ensure the success of the team as a whole. Thus, in a team, each individual is accountable for his or her personal assignment *and* for the collective achievement of the team's goal. Success in one's personal assignment is not sufficient. A team member succeeds only when the team succeeds. This dual responsibility requires members to adjust their performances (what, how, when, etc.) to ensure that the team collectively advances to its common goal. For example, given emerging circumstances, one team member may need to assist another in the completion of his or her assignment in addition to fulfilling the member's specialty assignment.

The team's cohesion results from its members' personal commitment to achieving their commonly valued goal *together*. Since the responsibility for overall team success is distributed to all members, a team does not require a dedicated leader. It may, however, designate a member or rotate members to chair team meetings and answer external inquiries about the team. It is each team member's responsibility, while working with his or her teammates, to perform the Executive Functions needed to maintain the team's integrity. This is done through virtual or physical meetings. The team sets its goal, plans the achievement of that goal, and decides assignments. It ensures the communication of information about its direction and performance to all parties and coordinates its resource use and activities with them. Decisions are made by consensus. While the planning of and accountability for Executive Function tasks is done collectively, the tasks are executed individually by each team member. Each member ensures that all members are engaged, energized, enabled, supported, and successful in accomplishing their team responsibilities. Each member ensures that the team is moving forward toward achieving its goal. Essentially, the effecting of each executive responsibility—communication, engagement, learning, teaching, and supporting team member success—is accomplished by *each team member* for him- or herself and in support of each fellow teammate.

Teamwork requires that each member commit to achieving a commonly valued goal together. Team members must be proficient in managing their own performances, understanding the roles and needs of other team members, managing the interfaces between their performances and the performances of teammates, and ensuring that all efforts align. Further, effective teamwork requires that team members are capable of assuming multiple roles and enabling the success of other teammates.

A Life Enabling Enterprise Requires a Team Approach

If one's approach to commerce (a) requires maximum engagement from its contributors, (b) involves the fluid adjustment of cooperatively implemented processes, and (c) seeks to eliminate overhead, then the team approach is the superior choice for working together. Teams use distributed performance, aligned based on a common understanding of purpose, to effect the real-time coordination of efforts. This approach eliminates management overhead. Also, it enables real-time integration of efforts among contributors, allowing them to continuously regulate their behavior to better respond to changing circumstances. Clearly, these characteristics fit the Life Enabling model's commercial strategy and, as you will see in Section III, its approach to operations.

Scaling Up a Team Approach

To support a team approach across a large business, you structure the enterprise in the manner described in the Life Enabling model (pages 258–264). A leadership team leads each business function, and a business-level leadership team umbrellas all of them (Exhibit 7). The current chair of each business

Exhibit 7. Tiered Interlocking Leadership Teams

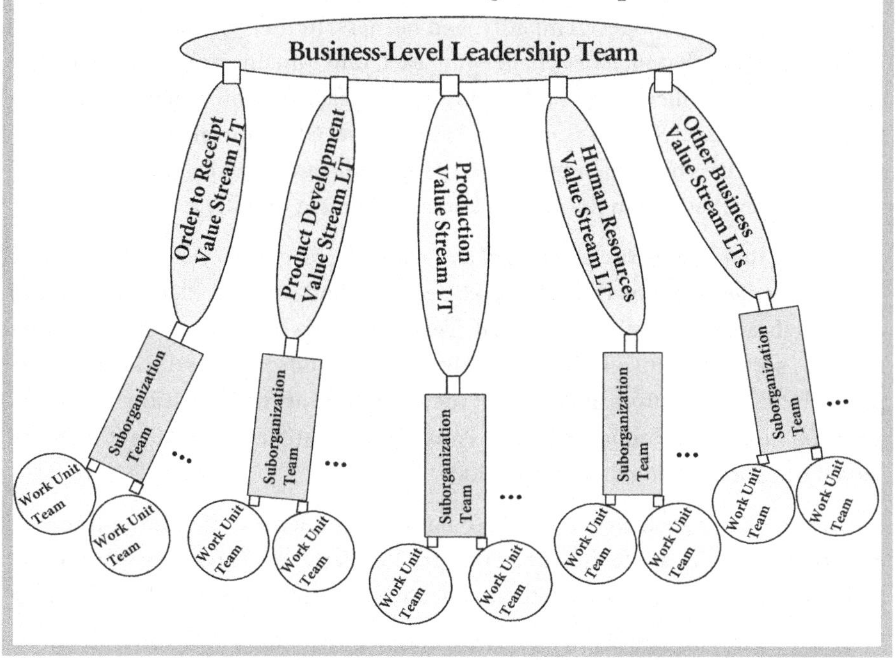

function's leadership team sits on the business-level leadership team. Each business function leadership team is composed of the representatives of the top-level process components within the function's value stream. Each of these components has its own "leadership" team that mirrors in membership the one above it. This cascaded team formation with its vertically interlocking membership is continued until each work unit is reached. Team membership in every higher-level team is rotated based on who on the next lower-level team is currently acting as its head. This structure of tiered, interlocking teams allows one to apply a team approach to a complex organization.

4. How the Life Enabling Organization Must Relate with Its Contributors

First, it should be clear by now that an organization is an artifact of the mind. It does not think, act, or relate.[15] People think, act, and relate. Therefore, a correct formulation of this question would be: how do the members of a Life Enabling enterprise relate with one another?

Given the character, values, and capabilities of the people who elect Life Enabling commerce and their alignment with the purpose of helping others succeed in ways that better the lives of everyone, their behavior expresses the principles of the Life Enabling commerce. Each member conducts him- or herself consistently with the core values of a Life Enabling enterprise. Consequently, their interrelationships are typified by respect, empathy, and fairness. In this regard, each is a helper to the other, and that includes challenging each other member to be all he or she can be. Every member enjoys and celebrates their factual achievements as well as those of their peers. Success is unitary. When achieved by any member, it advances the success of all members. Also, people who are growing and achieving simply find excitement in the growth and achievement of others.

Because their enterprise is pursued as a team, they rigorously use information- and knowledge-based methods to make decisions and solve problems. Both types of methods are systematic and explicit. Team members understand that only these methods support teamwork because only these methods permit reasoned participation by all contributors. Both sets of methods contrast with decision making based on one's "gut feeling," personal conviction, or unreasoned imitation of observed behavior (Pfeffer and Sutton, 2006).[16]

Every member is natively inclined to faithfully implement the common role each contributor to a Life Enabling enterprise undertakes. Thus, they work together to continuously improve their collective commercial success by enhancing

[15] Barnard did reify the organization. He viewed it as a living thing. "Systems of cooperation which we call organizations I regard as social creatures, 'alive', just as I regard an individual human being" (Barnard, 1968, p. 79). Today, the notion of an organization as a "person" is a legal one. It serves to protect owners/managers from liability while allowing them greater freedom to apply their organization's resources to whatever ends they choose.

[16] See *Appendix D* to understand our distinction between information and knowledge. See *Appendix E* for a brief introduction to information- and knowledge-based methods. For detailed descriptions of these methods, see chapters *Task 6 Solve Problems* and *Task 7 Make Decisions* in *The Lean Champion Resource Guide* (Vitalo, Bujak, Vitalo, Bierley, et al., 2023).

the features of their organization's offering and the buying–benefiting experience it provides. They improve the enterprise by removing waste from all its offerings and operations and by adding value to each of them.

They appreciate the importance of valid and timely information to supporting their striving for perfection. Consequently, everyone works to gather, disseminate, and systematically use such information to enable his or her learning. And since false facts are useless, all contributors uphold the principle that the validity of information is sacrosanct.

No one places opinion higher than fact in making judgments. No one claims more than is objectively verifiable. This does not mean that people may not have "hunches" or "intuitions" about one or another issue. It just means that their hunches trigger their research to determine the validity of those hunches, thereby rendering them useful for collective decision making and action. No one expects or extends to others special privileges based on role, rank, or professional status. Indeed, everyone in a Life Enabling enterprise is a professional in the true sense of the term. Each is a person who has mastered a body of knowledge and places it in the service of others—namely, the firm's customers, its stakeholders, and their fellow teammates.

The human resource functions such people conceive and implement serve the purpose of ensuring that the individuals needed to implement a Life Enabling enterprise are available when needed and that each person possesses the qualities and competencies required to perform within a Life Enabling enterprise. Concretely, this means that selection and hiring decisions rely on behavioral measures that place evidence of one's ability to do what is needed first and not one's résumé, submitted recommendations, score on a generic test of intelligence, or any other paper or social network credential. Thus, a doctoral degree from a prestigious university is not a substitute for being able to clarify and confirm what another is saying, correctly apply information- and knowledge-based methods, or effectively represent and share one's knowledge and information with others.[17]

Development opportunities are open to all whose needs match the learning each opportunity offers. Such development programs are accountable for producing behaviorally demonstrated gains in their participants' knowledge, skills, and/or proficiency levels. These gains in capabilities must also translate into elevated personal and business success as a result of their application in the workplace.

---

[17] *Chapter 14* addresses in detail the human resource functions as implemented within a Life Enabling enterprise.

Advancement in responsibilities is solely based on factual performance, as is the sharing in the monetary surplus the organization generates. From the business-level leadership team to every individual work station, what one measurably contributes to success determines one's remuneration. Any other approach undermines the logic and values of a Life Enabling enterprise.

The people who power a Life Enabling enterprise therefore create a work setting permeated by accountability *but not focused on it*. Its focus is on learning in the service of benefiting its customers and stakeholders and bettering the lives of everyone. Thus, every member fiercely holds to the need for objective information about his or her capabilities and performance. Valid information is seen as the critical resource for personal and professional development and the realization of their common goals.

Summing It Up

So, how does one summarize the relationships produced by people who power a Life Enabling Enterprise with one another? We really cannot find a simple phrase to encapsulate it. Yes, the contributors that constitute the enterprise function as a true team. Yes, as a team, they are singularly focused on accomplishing their common goal. Yes, they work studiously to realize that goal. Yes, they exhibit the fundamentals of decency, respect, empathy, and support for one another's success. Yes, they challenge one another to reach the limit of their individual capabilities. Yes, they seek ways to leverage diverse perspectives into integrative solutions that elevate the value of everyone's thinking and doing. Yes, they support and celebrate one another's growth and achievement. Yes, they require verifiable facts and eschew opinions as the bases for their judgments. Yes, they maintain with absolute rigor the principles that define the Life Enabling commercial model. No, they do not see themselves as ends but as means for realizing the common end they value. Yes, they do grow and change and may very well move on to other endeavors as their learning about themselves sharpens their understanding of themselves and their purposes. No, they never violate the basic understanding that functional people are the *sine qua non* for Life Enabling commerce. So, in the end, they always act to enable and support the growth and achievement of one another in the service of their common purpose.

The struggle one has in providing a simple summary of their relationship is due to the fact that it has so many facets, all of which are significant. Perhaps the best we can do is to say that the people who power a Life Enabling enterprise operate together as a community of professionals dedicated to a common purpose and a common code of conduct that extends not just outward to the others they encounter in the marketplace but inward to one another as well. *That purpose is to enable the success of others and better the lives of everyone. Their code is defined by the requirements for accomplishing their helping intent.*

The Framework of a Commercial Model and the Knowledge Contained Within Each of Its Components

Component	Results	Activities	Resources
Operations	Guides one in defining ▪ what operating results the business should focus on producing and ▪ what key features of day-to-day performance it must realize.	Guides one in defining an organization's general approach to producing the results expected by the model and demonstrating the operating characteristics the model requires.	Guides one in defining the critical-to-success resources needed at the operating level and the essential features each must possess.

Section III

The Operations Component of the Life Enabling Model

This section provides the knowledge you need to steer the day-to-day activities of every business function. It explains the results Operations must produce, the activities that produce those results, and the resources needed to successfully implement those activities.

Operations executes the business's day-to-day activities that, over time, cumulatively deliver a model's long-term results and realize the purpose it defines for commerce. These activities conceive, design, develop, resource, produce, market, sell, distribute, and support an enterprise's product or service offering. They also construct and implement the buying–benefiting experience associated with each offering. A commercial model builder deduces the results Operations must produce from the strategic purpose and outcomes these results must realize.

We begin this chapter by briefly reviewing the structure of a Life Enabling enterprise. This review will refresh your understanding of the different types of business functions within it. While there is a core set of operating results expected from every business function, the model defines additional results that vary by a function's type.

Chapter 10

Preview of the Model's Guidance

Exhibit 1, next page, overviews the operating results a Life Enabling enterprise must produce. It clarifies the scope of issues this chapter discusses and provides a brief summary of the model's guidance with respect to each.

The Structure of a Life Enabling Enterprise

Recall that the Life Enabling enterprise is organized by business functions. Each business function uses a unique set of expertise to generate an output that contributes to a business's success. The central business function is Production or Service Fulfillment, since it generates the business's final output and it is that output that enables customers' success. The remaining functions support its operation.

Each value stream is defined by decomposing the workflow that transforms the function's initial inputs into its final output. The value stream depicts the major operations that complete this transformation (Exhibit 2).

Exhibit 2. Structure of a Life Enabling Enterprise

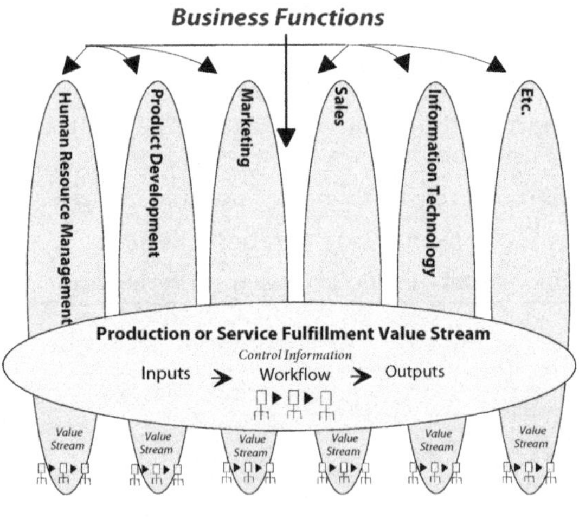

Also recall that each value stream has both a supply and a delivery chain (Exhibit 3, page 288). Each is made up of organizations external to the business. The supply chain is made up of organizations that produce and deliver the business's inputs. The delivery chain is made up of the organizations that deliver its outputs to its customers and support customers in extracting benefit from them. Together, a business function's value stream, joined with its supply and delivery chains, constitute its *extended value stream.*

Exhibit 1. Preview of the Results Operations Must Produce

Results Expected From All Business Functions

- New knowledge that guides better performance in adding value and eliminating waste
- Value stream contributors who are elevated in their capability to produce value
- Workplaces that are improved in their utility and safety
- Work processes that are increasingly waste-free and optimized, as evidenced by their
  - stable operation (zero special cause variation),
  - increasing value-added ratios (VAR),
  - decreasing defect rates,
  - improving cycle-to-takt time and throughput-to-demand ratios,
  - decreasing need for inventory,
  - decreasing generation of scrap,
  - decreasing common cause variation,
  - decreasing cost-to-customers for operations implemented and outputs produced, and
  - an increasing convergence between the work process's typical output and the output that maximally enables customer success, satisfies customer values, and benefits all stakeholders.
- Supply and delivery chain members that are elevated in their capability to produce value
- Stakeholders whose expectations, as related to day-to-day operations, are satisfied and whose ability to produce value in their own operations is elevated
- Conduct that is consistent with the Life Enabling model's core values

Results Expected From Business Functions That Deliver Benefit Directly to Customers

- Outputs or service outcomes that fully advance each customer's achievement of his or her purpose in a way that satisfies their preferences, benefits all stakeholders, and provides a better life for everyone
- A buying–benefiting experience that is increasingly value-adding and non-resource-consuming

Results Expected From Enabling Business Functions

- Outputs or service outcomes for other business functions that enable them to maximize the delivery of value to the enterprise's customers in ways that benefit all stakeholders and provide a better life for everyone
- A receiving function's acquiring–benefiting experience that is increasingly value-adding and non-resource-consuming

Exhibit 3. A Value Stream and Its Extended Value Stream

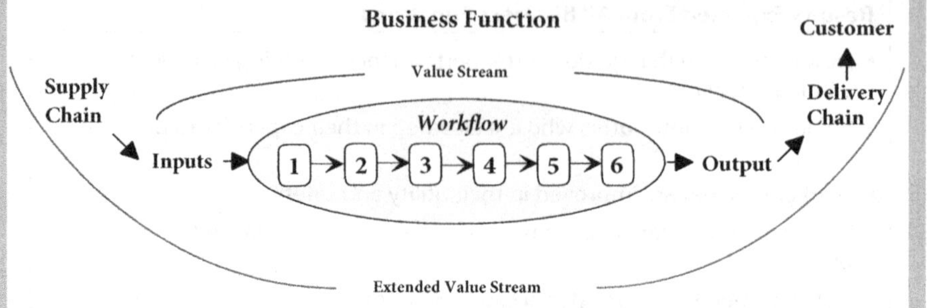

Types of Business Functions

Also recall that there are two types of functions within a modern business. *Both types are responsible for delivering value to the business's customer.* The first type delivers value *directly* to the business's customer (e.g., the Production or Service Fulfillment function). The second type delivers value *indirectly* by enabling the success of those functions that serve the customer directly. These are called *enabling* functions. Exhibit 4 provides examples of the respective contributions of a few of the enabling business functions commonly present in modern businesses.

Exhibit 4. Examples of Enabling Functions and What Each Contributes

Enabling Function	Generic Statement of Contribution
Facilities Maintenance	Work settings whose waste-free and safe implementation of work is maintained, thereby enabling the people performing within them to maximize the delivery of value to customers.
Human Resource Management	People—when needed, where needed, in the number required—who: (a) satisfy the requirements for performing the role common to all members within a business, (b) possess the technical expertise needed to perform their specific roles, and (c) perform at the level required for success.
Information Technology	Computer-based systems that retain, process, and distribute the knowledge and information needed to support contributors in delivering value to customers. These systems operate with the speed, ready access, ease of use, reliability, currency, and interoperability needed to enable successful performance.

The Results Expected From All Business Functions

The results expected from *every* business function within a Life Enabling enterprise express the model's perspective that Operations must leverage learning to improve its performance continuously and work with firm adherence to the model's dictates. Learning drives the progressive elimination of waste and the affirmative adding of value to all business activities, work settings, and outputs. Together, these improvements maximize the delivery of value to customers. Consequently, the following results are expected from *every* business function within a Life Enabling enterprise:

- new knowledge that guides better performance in adding value and eliminating waste;
- value stream contributors who are elevated in their capability to produce value;
- workplaces that are improved in their utility and safety;
- work processes that are increasingly waste-free and optimized, as evidenced by their
  - stable operation (zero special cause variation),[1]
  - increasing value-added ratios (VAR),[2]
  - decreasing defect rates,
  - improving cycle-to-takt time and throughput-to-demand ratios,[3]
  - decreasing need for inventory,
  - decreasing generation of scrap,
  - decreasing common cause variation,[4]

---

[1] Special cause variation is anomalous performance due to some event or action that causes a process to *not* be implemented as designed. The reason for problematic behavior is detectable and correctable through the application of problem-solving methods.

[2] The value-added ratio (VAR) is the proportion of the time it takes to complete a cycle of a process that is consumed by work that adds value—i.e., materially changes an offering in a manner the customer values. The judgment of whether an improved VAR advances the Life Enabling enterprise's purpose requires consideration of how it was realized, not just that it occurred. See Bujak and Vitalo (2014) for a discussion of this issue.

[3] Following Rother and Shook (2003), we define cycle time as the rate at which a unit of output exits a work process. For example, if a process completes an output every 11 minutes, its cycle time is 11 minutes (or 1 output/11 minutes). See Vitalo (2014) for a discussion of other definitions of cycle time. Takt time is the rate at which a unit of output *must exit* a work process to satisfy customer demand. Consistent with Lean thinking, the Life Enabling commercial model expects cycle and takt time to coincide so that throughput and demand are in balance and customers have what they need when they need it.

[4] Common cause variation is due to the design of the process and its incomplete control of all the variables that affect its performance. It is present even if the process is performed perfectly every time.

- decreasing cost to customers for operations implemented and outputs produced, and
- an increasing convergence between the work process's typical output and the output that maximally enables customer success, satisfies customer values, and benefits all stakeholders.

- supply and delivery chain members that are elevated in their capability to produce value;
- stakeholders whose expectations, as related to day-to-day operations, are satisfied and whose ability to produce value in their own operations is elevated;[5] and
- conduct that is consistent with the Life Enabling model's core values.

The Results Expected From Business Functions That Deliver Benefit Directly to Customers

A function delivers value to the business's customers *directly* in one of two ways. It may produce the offering that enables the customer's success, or it may implement the customer's buying–benefiting experience. If it produces the business's offering, that function is judged by how effectively its offering enables its user's success in a way that satisfies all the user's preferences, benefits all stakeholders, and provides a better life for everyone.[6] An offering is maximally value-adding when all these criteria are satisfied. If the function implements the customer's buying–benefiting experience, then the experience it provides must be maximally value-adding as determined from the customer's perspective and must progressively become less resource-consuming for the customer. The following statements express these outcomes:

- outputs or service outcomes that fully advance each customer's achievement of his or her purpose in a way that satisfies their preferences, benefits all stakeholders, and provides a better life for everyone and
- a buying–benefiting experience that is increasingly value-adding and non-resource-consuming.

The Results Expected From Enabling Business Functions

Before companies internalized enabling business functions, they purchased the resources these functions provide from other freestanding enterprises. For

[5] An example of satisfying expectations would be the timely reporting of accidents and incidents in conformance with the Occupational Safety and Health Administration requirements.

[6] The minimum requirement for satisfying "provides a better life for everyone" is that the output harms no one. By definition, this requires the output to enable the success of its user and create no problems for any stakeholder.

example, if a business's facility needed repairs, it would contract with an appropriate craftsperson to accomplish that work. Today, a medium to large business would likely have its facilities maintenance department complete the work internally. Since the 1800s, modern businesses have progressively internalized these enabling activities, making each a *captive* enterprise that operates solely for the business within which it exists (Johnson and Kaplan, 1991).[7] These enabling functions serve the Production or Service Fulfillment function as well as other internal business functions. Facilities maintenance is a good example. It serves all business functions.

No matter which business function it serves, an enabling function's responsibility remains the same—to advance the delivery of value to the *business's customers in ways that benefit all stakeholders and provide a better life for everyone.* It is the achievement of this end that determines its effectiveness. To measure its flow-through impact, every enabling function's primary success criterion is whether what it delivers enables its recipient to maximize the delivery of its value-delivering output. Its purpose is never simply to meet the expressed expectations of the function that immediately receives its offering.

The reasoning for this flow-through expectation is straightforward. Each enabling function is presumed to possess the specialized expertise needed to shape its value-adding offering. Information Technology (IT) personnel, for example, are experts in the fields required to deliver computing support to all business functions. In this sense, IT is an "internal producer," and, as such, it assumes responsibility for ensuring that the offering it delivers to its receiving function has utility, as defined by its ability to enable that receiving function to accomplish its purpose.

Thus, while being responsive to its receiving function's *expressed* needs, expectations, and preferences, it must shape its offering by also *looking past* that function's expressed request. To do this, it must understand the needs and values of the customer and the other utility requirements that the receiving function's value stream must satisfy. It uses this understanding of the receiving function's mandate to evaluate the specifications given to it by the receiving function. By applying its specialty area expertise, it confirms that the output the receiving function is requesting will actually enable its value stream to succeed. *In the Life Enabling model, no producer—even an "internal producer"—accepts and creates an output to a specification that will fail to meet its recipient's real needs.* If they did so, they would fail as a teammate, and the organization as a whole would fail in its

[7] Over the past 30 years, there has been a movement to outscource certain support or enabling functions, including, for example, human resource management. Nonetheless, the historical movement of modern businesses as having internalized enabling functions remains valid and is still relevant for almost all commercial organizations.

Exhibit 5. Two Examples of How Enabling Business Functions Anchor Their Thinking in the Business's Customers

As an example, consider Company A. It provides several variations of its basic customer offering (Models 1, 2, and 3). Each variation addresses the special circumstances that a different subset of its customers face.

Company A's Marketing function, given its analysis of the company's marketplace, understands that customer values vary across these three subsets of customers, each of which is termed a "customer segment." It recognizes that the people producing Models 1, 2, and 3 need to be aware of how these values vary from segment to segment so that they can produce each model in a way that satisfies its targeted customer segment. If the Production function failed to ask for the differentiation of customer values by customer segment, Marketing would alert the people in Production to their need for this information. It would do this so that the value-adding and waste removal efforts that Production implemented to better satisfy one customer segment were not generalized across all the models. It would take the initiative in educating Production about its need for the differentiated values information, and, with the function's concurrence, Marketing would collect and provide values information for each segment.

As a second example, Company A's Information Technology function (IT) provides for the storage, distribution, access, and retrieval of customer values information for both the Marketing and the Production value streams. It too must look to the end customer to appreciate what these recipient value streams require from IT. In studying customer values information, IT discovers that rapid response to changing needs was especially important to its business's customers. With this insight, IT would recognize that the computing infrastructure it provides needs a means for updating its stored information that is exceptionally speedy. IT would also deduce that the infrastructure needs to incorporate an alerting function. That function would make members of the Marketing and Production value streams swiftly aware of any new or changed customer values information. It would enable them to respond quickly to address these changes and thereby sustain a high level of customer satisfaction.

Naturally, the reasoning done by Marketing and IT with regard to shaping their respective offerings is not accomplished unilaterally. Given that this is a Life Enabling enterprise, the uncovering of a recipient function's real needs and the thinking through of the best response—while initiated by each enabling function as part of its responsibilities—would be accomplished collegially with the recipient function each is serving.

purpose. Exhibit 5 provides an example of how an enabling business function might accomplish this responsibility.

Based on the logic just described, every enabling business function must produce the following results:

- outputs or service outcomes for other business functions that enable them to maximize the delivery of value to the enterprise's customers in ways that benefit all stakeholders and provide a better life for everyone and

- a receiving function's acquiring–benefiting experience that is increasingly value-adding and non-resource-consuming.[8]

Illustrative Metrics for Evaluating Operations' Results

Exhibit 6 lists some possible metrics for measuring whether Operations is producing the results expected from it. The success criteria presented in Exhibit 6 are for illustrative purposes. As discussed previously, a metric must be expressed as a complete *success criterion* to be useful. The examples in Exhibit 6 are not complete statements of success criteria. For example, the measures stated in the exhibit do not include a description of the method by which status on each anchor is gauged.

Exhibit 6. Illustrative Success Criteria for Gauging Operations' Results[1]

Anchor	Measure	Target
Business-Level Results		
Value-Added Offering - Customers	▪ Average percentage of values satisfied by the business's offering, as judged by customers responding to the yearly customer satisfaction survey[1]	▪ 92%
Value-Added Buying–Benefiting Experience	▪ Average percentage of values satisfied by the customers' buying–benefiting experience, as judged by customers responding to the yearly customer satisfaction survey	▪ 92%
Human Resource Management Results		
Quality of New Hires	▪ Percentage of new hires passing proficiency tests in each of the core skills required to contribute to a Life Enabling enterprise (see Exhibit 3 for list, page 250)	▪ 100%
Work Processes Improvement		
	▪ Mean percentage across business functions of work processes improved in their value-added ratios	▪ 100%
	▪ Mean percentage across business functions of work processes operating at takt time (quarterly)	▪ 90%
	▪ Mean percentage across business functions of non-optimized[2] work processes improved in throughput-to-demand ratio	▪ 85%
	▪ Mean percentage across business functions of work processes with zero scrap ratios	▪ 85%

Continued ...

[1] All metrics are measured yearly unless otherwise stated. Targets reflect improvement goals.
[2] Non-optimized means not having already reached the highest level of performance.

[8] The "acquiring–benefiting" experience is a recipient function's equivalent to a customer's buying–benefiting experience.

Exhibit 6. Illustrative Success Criteria for Gauging Operations' Results (continued)

Anchor	Measure	Target
Workplace Improvement		
	▪ Mean percentage across business functions of non-optimized work areas improved in utility (e.g., reduced waste, increased worker safety)	▪ 100%
	▪ Mean frequency across business functions of lost or restricted workdays due to work-related injury or illness per 100 employees (assumes 200,000 hours worked)	▪ ≤4
Supply/Delivery Chain Members		
	▪ Percentage of all business function supply and delivery chain members reporting greater success with regard to the effectiveness of their operations as a result of assistance received	▪ 80%
Stakeholders' Satisfaction With Operations		
	▪ Percentage of business functions for which all stakeholders report that their expectations as related to day-to-day operations are satisfied (quarterly)	▪ 100%
Knowledge Development		
	▪ Percentage of business functions producing 10 or more validated, improved methods for adding value and eliminating waste (each improvement must be empirically verified, documented, and disseminated across the enterprise)	▪ 100%

This portion of each measure is omitted for space reasons. Detailed guidance on forming success criteria and establishing an enterprise-wide measurement system is provided in chapter *Task 9 – Measure Results* of the *The Lean Champion Resource Guide* (Vitalo, Bujak, Vitalo, Bierley, et al., 2023).

The Life Enabling Model's Image of Operating Perfection

Exhibit 7, next page, graphically represents the state of Operations that the Life Enabling model strives to create. This image captures the model's notion of striving for perfection. It integrates Deming's concept of a "zero loss function" with the role of waste removal, which, we think, is a special contribution of Lean thinking (Womack and Jones, 2003). It also incorporates the learning and growth of members of the organization and the development of new knowledge. It represents explicitly Operations' responsibility for satisfying stakeholder expectations and elevating the performance of its supply and delivery chain members. It adds to these continuously decreasing the cost to customers for the enterprise's product or service without reducing the value it delivers. A lower cost is a universal customer value that increasingly satisfies a customer the more it is realized. With each decrease in cost, utility delivered is increased, assuming that the satisfaction of all other values remains constant.[9]

Exhibit 7. Life Enabling Model's Image of Operating Perfection

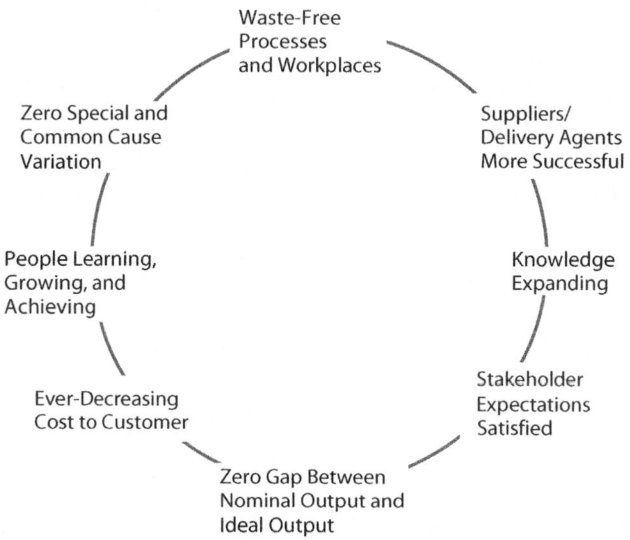

Exhibit 7 depicts striving for operating perfection. Its realization is only achieved when the cost to the customer for accomplishing his or her purpose is zero. This is achieved by eliminating your customers' need for your offering. This outcome realizes operational perfection. It is accomplished when you develop an alternative solution that enables your customers to accomplish their purpose without your assistance or a substitute for it. This is the ultimate end of all helping—freeing the person from his or her need for assistance. It enables customers to apply their recovered resources to pursue new ends and realize new achievements. It also creates for the enterprise an opportunity to enter new areas of commerce. In essence, it establishes a new mechanism for *creative destruction.* As we are using the term, creative destruction means the ending of a commercial market by actively rendering unnecessary the product or service need it was satisfying.

---

[9] A decrease in cost to the customer that results from a subsidy from the producer or a third party is not counted as contributing to this targeted result.

Until that endpoint is reached, only incremental improvement in realizing operating perfection is achievable. In the interim, Operations' people and knowledge outcomes and decreasing cost to the customer should be continuously achievable. Also achievable with increasing success are all the remaining expected results Operations must produce: waste elimination, reduction in common and special cause variation, satisfaction of stakeholder expectations, development of ever more effective extended value streams, and production of typical outputs that more closely match the ideal output.

This chapter explains how a Life Enabling enterprise produces Operations' expected results.

Chapter 11

Preview of the Model's Operations Guidance

The model's guidance for managing the business's day-to-day operations reintegrates the contributions of W. Edwards Deming with those of Lean Manufacturing (Womack and Jones, 2003). This reintegration rationalizes the use of Lean tools to achieve overall operational perfection. It also corrects the glaring omission of Deming's contributions in the original presentation of Lean Manufacturing (Womack, Jones, and Roos, 1991). Masao Nemoto, a senior managing director at Toyota in the 1960s, noted this omission in *The Birth of Lean* (Nemoto, 2009, pp. 175–176).

From Deming, we include Total Quality Control's emphasis on using research to understand your customers' needs, wants, and concerns. You use this understanding to build quality into products and service offerings. We also reincorporate the concept of variation (special and common cause) and its elimination. We especially emphasize the importance of stabilizing processes before attempting to improve them.

From Lean Manufacturing, we incorporate all Lean tools. Lean tools are a set of concepts and methods that facilitate the discovery of waste and its elimination. They can also support adding value to a business's offering. People familiar with the Lean literature will find this content most familiar to them. For people unfamiliar with Lean literature, we provide a brief description of each tool we identify either in the text or in this book's *Glossary*.

What will be unfamiliar to people who have studied Lean thinking is how we have fitted together the use of the various tools to form a coherent system of application. The usual presentation of Lean tools offers no defined sequence for their use. In fact, many Lean community members refer to Lean tools collectively as items in a "tool box." A tool is selected based on the type of improvement one intends to make. But when you reintegrate Deming's work with Lean thinking, you discover that there is a rational framework that guides the use of Lean tools. This framework is the logic that defines the content and sequence of activities that produce Operations' expected results. By following its guidance, you ensure that value is built into your offerings and your customers' buying–benefiting experience and that all your processes are stable and optimized.

Exhibit 1, beginning on the next page, overviews the model's guidance for how Operations produces its expected results. Use it to preview the contents of this chapter.

Exhibit 1. The Activities That Produce Operations' Expected Results

1. Understand what customers need and value.

Understand your customers' needs and values so that you can conceive an offering and buying–benefiting solution that enables their success and satisfies all their remaining values. Research to uncover the goal your customers seek to accomplish, the nature and resourcing of the settings within which they pursue this goal, and how your customers define "success." Know what your customers' personal capabilities and limitations are with regard to accomplishing their goal. Understand why there is a gap between what they seek to accomplish and what they are able to accomplish given no offering. Use this information to conceive an offering that enables their success.

Go beyond utility to build into your offering features that maximally satisfy your customers' other values. Connect with your target customers and learn about their values directly from them using one-on-one interviews, focus groups, and surveys. "Walk in your customers' shoes" to better appreciate what they do, how they do it, and what helps or hinders their success. Learn about your customers' values from information your business currently collects and from industry research. Gather values information in sufficient detail to define metrics that you can use to design your product or service offering and evaluate whether what you produce satisfies your customers' expectations.

Ensure that each value fulfills three conditions: (1) it satisfies a customer preference while not detracting from the effectiveness of what is provided, (2) it is recognized by customers as beneficial to them, and (3) it does no harm to the customer or anyone else.

Do additional research to learn what buying–benefiting experience will best serve your customers. Learn what barriers hinder their ability to access and acquire your offering, maintain it in a usable state, use it successfully, and dispose of it or its byproducts when done. Use this knowledge to conceive a buying–benefiting experience that is least burdensome to your customer, makes your offering available to the greatest number of people, and maximizes their likelihood of successfully using it.

2. Understand stakeholder expectations and concerns.

Recognize the right of stakeholders to be involved in the operation of your enterprise as a whole and each of the business functions that they affect or are affected by. Relate with them from a basis of respect. Work to benefit their efforts in ways that maximizes the benefit you deliver your customers and advances all life.

Constructively involve stakeholders at the corporate level and the business function level. At the corporate level, constructively involve every party with a stake in the enterprise's strategic direction and approach. At the business function level, constructively work with the subset of all stakeholders who relate to the work of that function.

Understand each stakeholder's interests, expectations, and concerns. Disseminate this stakeholder information to every contributor whose work relates to each stakeholder. Support contributors in incorporating this understanding into their decision making and actions. Work cooperatively with stakeholders to satisfy each of their expectations and address each of their concerns.

Establish a contact person in each business function to monitor and manage each stakeholder relationship. Maintain regular contact with each stakeholder. Obtain each stakeholder's assessment of how well your function is addressing his or her expectations and concerns. Make sure this information is disseminated to every relevant contributor. Support contributors in continuously improving their responsiveness to each stakeholder's perspective.

Continued ...

Exhibit 1. The Activities That Produce Operations' Expected Results

3. Manage from a systems perspective.

Know what a system is and why this knowledge is important to managing an organization. Learn the four principles that guide managing from a systems perspective. Recognize that a commercial organization is an open, dynamic system. Know that a system succeeds only when all its components work together cooperatively. Understand that, in a dynamic system, success requires *the interactive responsiveness of all its constituent elements*. Know that membership in an open system includes all its internal contributors and those entities outside it that affect or are affected by its operation. Understand that complex, dynamic systems must be managed by the application of knowledge, not conditioning, intuition, or imitation. Finally, know how the qualities of an open, dynamic system determine what a Life Enabling enterprise's most critical-to-success resources are.

Recognize that managing from a systems perspective must occur at every level within a commercial organization. These levels extend from the corporate cooperative system level through each business function's extended value stream to the work process level and, ultimately, to the work unit and individual workstation levels. Detail the membership and interconnections of every system. Map, analyze, and improve each system in a way that incorporates referencing the whole system and all its interconnections. Never fail to apply the rule that the improvement of any element within the enterprise *must* also improve the performance of the whole enterprise.

4. Design outputs and implementing processes that maximize the benefit delivered to customers and all stakeholders inclusively.

Build quality into your offering and its buying–benefiting experience by using your understanding of your customers' needs and values. Have a cross-functional product team conceive and design an offering that enables your customers' success. Add to it features that your customers value. Ensure that the design also satisfies stakeholders' expectations and addresses their concerns. Test your design using prototypes and with a sample of your customers to ensure its utility and desirability. Evaluate its capabilities against customer needs and values and stakeholder expectations and concerns.

Conceive and design processes for input sourcing, production, delivery, and customer support. Make sure the processes can reliably source, produce, deliver, and support your customer's successful use of your offering at a cost the customer can afford and at a pace that meets their demand. Conceive, design, resource, and test the buying–benefiting experience you will implement. Once processes with the required features and capabilities are established, identify and eliminate all vulnerability points in them. For those that cannot be eliminated, build in methods and devices to detect breakdowns. Pilot test your processes to ensure their effectiveness.

Finalize each process design by specifying its requirements for implementation (people, training, infrastructure, workplace layout) and producing its standardized work documentation. Plan the rollout of the new offering and its buying–benefiting experience.

5. Establish waste-free, optimized processes across all extended value streams.

Recognize that a waste-free, optimized process is one that is stable, is free of common cause variation, and produces an output that exactly matches what the customer needs and values every time at the least cost to the customer. Optimize

Continued ...

Exhibit 1. The Activities That Produce Operations' Expected Results

5. Establish waste-free, optimized processes across all extended value streams (continued).

each function's extended value stream by making every operation in its value stream stable, establishing "flow" and then "pull" across each value stream and subprocess, eliminating all waste, and continuously reducing common cause variation and its output's cost to the customer. Broadcast the value stream improvements you make to all members of its extended value stream.

Make processes stable by (a) establishing standardized work; (b) effectively selecting, training, and supporting process implementers; (c) using tools such as Total Productive Management, 6S, and Supply Chain Management to manage process resources; and (d) detecting and eliminating all instances of special cause variation.

Establish flow in each process to ensure that work moves through it continuously as a single piece and at a pace that matches customer demand (takt).

Establish pull to ensure that all work is triggered by customer demand.

Optimize the performance of every value stream and its subordinate work processes by eliminating all remaining waste in every business setting and operation, driving out common cause variation, and continuously reducing the cost of your offering to your customers while not compromising the value delivered.

Finally, optimize process performance across the extended value stream. Engage all members of your extended value stream in learning and employing the Life Enabling approach to commerce. Support them in stabilizing their processes and establishing flow. Incorporate their operations into the Life Enabling enterprise's pull system. Assist them in optimizing their work processes and realizing ever-greater success in accomplishing their business goals.

With regard to each business function's stakeholders, educate them on your use of the Life Enabling model. Help them understand its purpose and approach. Share with them how it benefits their interests, addresses their concerns, and fulfills their expectations. Always involve stakeholders by gathering their input on any issue that affects them. Share with them how you will use their input and obtain their feedback on your thinking. Work with them to uncover the best solution that will advance your enterprise's purpose and meet their needs. Remember always that their positive involvement in your work is essential to your ultimate success.

6. Strive for perfection at the Operations level.

Continuously develop and apply learning to improve the implementation of each of the six tasks that make up Operations' cycle of performance (Exhibit 5, page 350):

- Elevate the speed and effectiveness with which customer values and stakeholder expectations and concerns are recognized and understood.
- Refine and extend people's understanding of what managing from a systems perspective means and how to better apply that understanding.
- Improve how products and processes are designed and vetted so that they deliver greater value to customers from their first implementation.
- Elevate the enterprise's methods and means for establishing waste-free, optimized processes across all extended value streams.
- Refine and extend people's understanding of how to generate and leverage learning and use that knowledge to improve how Operations strives for perfection.

Six Activities Produce Operations' Expected Results

The following six tasks produce Operations' expected results:

1. Understand what customers need and value.
2. Understand stakeholders' expectations and concerns.
3. Manage from a systems perspective.
4. Design outputs and implementing processes that maximize the benefit delivered to customers and all stakeholders inclusively.
5. Establish waste-free, optimized processes across all extended value streams.
6. Strive for perfection at the Operations level.

Once initiated, each of these six tasks is performed continuously. The *cycle of the six activities* as a whole, however, is renewed whenever changes in customer values, stakeholder expectations, market conditions, or business solutions require adjustments in the business's offerings or the buying–benefiting experience it provides. By implementing these six tasks, you

- ensure that all decision making is anchored in an understanding of customer needs and values and how well those are currently being served;
- address stakeholder expectations and concerns in your execution of day-to-day operations;
- avoid optimizing any work unit, work process, or value stream's performance at the expense of the enterprise's overall effectiveness;
- stabilize and continuously improve all offerings and processes;
- make all processes flow continuously with each cycle controlled by customer demand;
- render the business waste-free and fully value-adding, with both judgments made objectively and from the customer's perspective; and
- reliably produce offerings and a buying–benefiting experience that maximize the delivery of value to customers and benefit all stakeholders inclusively.

1. Understand What Customers Need and Value

Your purpose in understanding your target customers' needs and values is twofold. First, you must conceive an offering and buying–benefiting solution that enables your customers' success. Then, you must strive to maximize the degree to which both satisfy all your customers' remaining values.

Ensuring Your Offering's Utility

Your first responsibility is to provide your target customer the means he or she needs to successfully accomplish the customer purpose you have chosen to support. Unless your offering has utility, you have no basis for commerce. To have utility, your offering must close the gap between what your customer is able to achieve without it and what he or she desires to achieve. This gap closing must be done in a way that betters the lives of everyone or, at a minimum, causes no harm.

Your first step in conceiving such an offering is to fully understand the purpose your customer seeks to accomplish. Use the goal statement template discussed on page 61 and the guide provided by Vitalo (2019) to support your discovery and documentation of your customer's purpose.

Learn how successful your target customer is in accomplishing his or her goal. Use the success criteria you document in the customer's goal statement as your standard for judging success. Elicit your customer's perspective on how well these criteria are currently satisfied. Gather any objective information available to confirm your customer's perception. If none is available, develop it. Resolve in dialog with your customer any discrepancies that you uncover.

Next, understand the reasons for your target customer's shortfall in success. Use the framework provided by the *Factors Determining the Outcome of Human Performance: A More Detailed Look*, pages 128–130, and the guidance provided in Vitalo (2022) to assist you in this task. Begin with the method your target customer currently uses to accomplish his or her goal. Uncover what customers find helpful and problematic about their current approach. What are its strengths and shortcomings? Determine what latitude your target customers have with regard to altering the method they use.

Follow up this discovery by learning about the settings within which the customer seeks to accomplish his or her purpose. How are these settings organized and resourced as regards supporting what your customer seeks to do? What about them enables or hinders the customer's success? Determine what latitude your target customers have with regard to altering the settings within which they pursue their goal.

Finally, discover what your customers' personal capabilities and limitations are with regard to accomplishing their goal given the success criteria they define. How well does the profile of their personal capabilities satisfy the requirements for successfully using their current method for accomplishing their goal within the setting in which they operate? Use this information to uncover what personal factors are enabling your customers' current success and hindering them from even greater success.

By analyzing this information, you can uncover the resource your customers need to realize their goal and the features that resource must possess. You will also have the information you need to ensure that your target customer is able to employ your offering within the settings in which he or she operates. With this information, conceive an offering that enables your customers to close the gap between what they seek to realize and what they are currently able to realize.

Ensuring the Utility of the Buying–Benefiting Experience You Provide

Do additional research to learn what buying–benefiting experience will maximally benefit your target customers. Learn about their current buying–benefiting experience, should one exist. Discover their likes and dislikes concerning it. Understand what barriers may hinder their ability to learn about your offering, understand the value it delivers, access and acquire it, maintain it in a usable state, use it successfully, and dispose of it or its byproducts when done. Use this understanding to conceive a buying–benefiting experience that is least burdensome to your customer, makes your offering available to the greatest number of people, and maximizes their likelihood of successfully using it.

Maximizing Your Delivery of Value

After you have understood the requirements for enabling your target customers' success, learn what other values your offering and its buying–benefiting experience should satisfy. Customer values are characteristics of an offering or a buying–benefiting experience that, when present, satisfy customer preferences. Every customer value relates to one or more features of the business's offering or its associated buying–benefiting experience. A feature of an offering is a specific characteristics of some aspect of its content, shape, appearance, or performance (form, fit, finish, or functionality). A feature of the buying–benefiting experience is a characteristic of one or more of the activities required to access, acquire, prepare to use, and use an offering; extract benefit from it; maintain it in a useful state between uses; or dispose of it or its byproducts.

Every valued feature you incorporate in your offering must meet three conditions. Each feature must

1. satisfy a customer preference while not detracting from the functional effectiveness of what you provide,
2. be recognized by customers as beneficial to them, and
3. do no harm, either directly or indirectly, to the customer or anyone else.

When the features of an offering and its associated buying–benefiting experience satisfy these conditions, then

- each customer's successful performance is fully enabled,

- all customer expectations are fulfilled,
- customers experience your business as delivering exceptional value, and
- they judge that commerce with your enterprise is preferable.

Methods for Learning About Customer Values

There are four general approaches to learning about your target customers' values:

1. Reach out to your target customers and learn about their values directly from them. Use one-on-one interviews, focus groups, and surveys (e.g., paper-based or web-based surveys). Repeat these activities on a regular basis. Use them to uncover new values and verify the values that you have deduced from indirect sources (see 2, 3, and 4 below). Surveys are especially useful in connecting with a broad representation of your target customers. They can be structured to confirm values, clarify what type each value is, gauge its relative importance to your customer, and measure how well your business is currently satisfying it.[1]
2. "Walk in your customers' shoes" to deepen your grasp of your customers' spoken values and to uncover unspoken ones. "Unspoken values" are characteristics of an offering or elements of a buying–benefiting experience that customers do not spontaneously identify as values but acknowledge as such when they are pointed out. One way to "walk in your customers' shoes" is by observing your customers' buying–benefiting experience. Another is by studying simulations of that experience. The simulations can be as simple as a person role-playing the customer as he or she acquires and uses the offering in a setting that replicates the customer's actual setting. It can be as sophisticated as a mathematically driven computer simulation of use and setting. In either case, you analyze the facts obtained from your observations or simulations to uncover what factors advance or impede your customers' success or their experience of satisfaction. Then, you test the validity of your inferences by sharing back what you learned with your customers and obtaining their confirmation or corrections.
3. Mine the customer information your business already collects and the information posted by customers on the Internet. The information typical businesses collect includes customer-initiated complaints and praise. Also available to you are the observations and insights of sales and marketing teams, distributors and retailers, and the technical representatives who visit

[1] Chapter *Task 3 Understanding Customer Values* in *The Lean Champion Resource Guide* (Vitalo, Bujak, Vitalo, Bierley, et al., 2023) provides detailed guidance for conducting customer values surveys.

customer sites. Still another resource is the information posted by customers on web sites, including their reviews of the business's offering and their comments about their experience in doing business with your company. Also pay attention to their comments about offerings that are alternatives to yours. Use all these sources to expand and deepen your understanding of your customers' needs and preferences.

4. Study the findings of your industry's research into what features of a particular offering customers value, the value each feature satisfies, and its importance to prospective customers. Also, monitor the emergence of new materials and technologies and how customers perceive these new developments.

Guiding Principles for Understanding Customer Values

Apply three principles as you attempt to understand value from your customer's perspective:

1. The more detailed the information you gather about each value, the more useful the information is.
2. A target customer's stated needs and real needs must align.
3. Values information must be current, made measurable, disseminated, and used in all decision making.

As to the first principle, the more detailed the information about each value you capture is, the more precisely you can shape your business's offerings and its buying–benefiting experience to satisfy each value. For example, with regard to a car's engine noise, it is more useful to know what decibel level of noise is acceptable to customers than to simply know that customers value noise suppression.

The second principle advises that you must always make certain that you distinguish between your customers' stated and real needs. In any sector where you, as a producer, have deeper technical knowledge of your offering and its capabilities than your customer—as, for example, in medicine or engineering—a customer may ask for features he or she does not actually need and leave out others that are essential to his or her success. When you uncover discrepancies between what customers say they need and what factual information indicates they need, you must explore that discrepancy with your customers. Your first task is to discover whether you correctly understand what your customer is trying to accomplish and the context within which he or she is operating. An error in your understanding of either might change the status of a value from "apparently needed" to "actually needed." If your understanding of your customer's needs is correct and the discrepancy remains, then you must educate your customers so that they comprehend their real needs. Also educate customers about how they will benefit from eliminating apparent needs and meeting only their real needs. Only in this way can your enterprise be an honest partner with them in commerce.

The third principle is that knowing what customers value is only useful when it is (a) maintained as current, (b) put into a useful form, (c) disseminated to all contributors, and (d) used in making every business decision. To make values useful, each customer value must be transformed into a critical-to-quality (CTQ) metric. A CTQ metric is an observable and measurable standard used to gauge the presence of a customer value. It translates a need or value of the user into a measurable characteristic of your offering (Deming, 1982a, p. 169). The concept of CTQs was first introduced by Shewhart in 1931 (Shewhart, 1980, p. 54). You build each metric by linking each customer value to a feature of your offering or its buying–benefiting experience. Then you define a scale that calibrates its level of presence and provide a method for gauging the status of the relevant feature on the scale. You use the scale to specify how a feature is to be executed and the method of measurement to judge how well you succeeded in satisfying the value.[2]

How You Use Your Understanding of Customer Values

There are six basic ways you use your understanding of customer values:

1. Design value-delivering offerings and buying–benefiting experiences.
2. Drive quality into every level of business performance.
3. Guide waste removal actions.
4. Inform your business's marketing efforts.
5. Assess your business's performance at every level of its activity.
6. Guide your business's yearly planning process.

Design Value-Delivering Offerings and Buying–Benefiting Experiences

Use your customer values information to ensure that the design of your offerings and your customer's buying–benefiting experience maximally benefit your customers. Your first step is to break out the components and features of your proposed offering. Chapter *Task 3 Understanding Customer Values* in *The Lean Champion Resource Guide* (Vitalo, Bujak, Vitalo, Bierley, et al., 2023) provides detailed guidance on accomplishing this task.

Your next task is to link your customers' values information (value, type, importance, desired state, status of satisfaction) to each feature. Once you have completed this linkage, several important facts become clear. First, you recognize what values link with each feature of your offering. Second, you uncover

[2] CTQs and the previously discussed "success criteria" are essentially equivalent.

which features of your current offering serve no values. Third, you also immediately see how well each feature, as currently designed, satisfies the values associated with it. Fourth, you detect what features desired by your customers are missing by noting the customer values that have no feature linkage.

This information stimulates your thinking about how to improve your current or proposed offering. Immediately, any feature not linked to a customer value represents waste and is a target for removal. Any missing but valued feature should be considered for addition. Any feature not adequately satisfying customer values should be targeted for improvement.

You use this same process of analysis, linkage, and discovery to improve your offering's current buying–benefiting experience.

Drive Quality Into Every Level of Business Performance

Use CTQ metrics to educate contributors about what customers value and how their work delivers value to customers. This education drives the understanding of quality into every level of performance. It enables each contributor to experience personal responsibility and satisfaction for benefiting customers. Also, it enables contributors to verify the quality of their outputs prior to passing them forward. This allows them to experience pride of workmanship, an experience important to every individual.

Guide Waste Removal Actions

Eliminating certain types of waste—e.g., hazards, interruptions, inventory, motion, rework, search, setup, travel/transport, and wait—always improves an operation's value-added ratio. Customer values information is not needed to detect these types of waste because there is no circumstance under which their presence adds value. However, to detect other categories of waste correctly, you must know your customers' values.

For example, consider the type of waste termed "inspection." Checking for errors at the end of a value stream is considered waste because it adds cost but does not itself add a new increment of value to an offering. Yet, some customers have exact requirements for product purity and need a post-production inspection certificate from the manufacturer as proof of purity. This documentation of the product's purity may be required by government regulation or to meet a demand of their customers. Without it, they would not be able to sell their products. For them, inspection is a "must have" value.

Consider also the type of waste termed "unnecessary processing." Most times, unnecessary processing can be detected by simply applying logic. Clearly, one can detect that entering information into a database that is not legally required, is never accessed, and has no identifiable relevance to business decision making is unnecessary processing. Sometimes, however, unnecessary processing is not easy to detect without specific knowledge of your customers' thinking. For example, a manufacturer we worked with changed over to a specially designed packaging and packing system to better secure its products for shipment. The company assumed that its customers valued this new approach's extra protection, since damaged units would cause the customer lost production time while the customer waited for replacements. When the business finally consulted its customers, however, the company discovered that its new system did not solve any problem the *customer experienced.* Its presence did not connect to any value the customer held. Worse, the new system created problems for the customer. The packaging caused difficulty for the customer's receiving team, who had to extract the units from it and discard the packing materials. Both added cost that the customer bore. Hence, the specially designed packaging system proved to be unnecessary processing for the producer when viewed from the perspective of customer values. It detracted from the customer's buying–benefiting experience.

Inform Your Business's Marketing Efforts

Marketing within a Life Enabling enterprise has an educational function, not a motivational function. It does not seek to change people's attitudes or "nudge" them to make buy decisions. Rather, it informs customers about the effectiveness of the business's offering in supporting their success and satisfying their values. It seeks to enable prospective customers to make evidence-based choices that best meet their needs.

Marketing cannot accomplish its task without customer values information. This information clarifies the features of your offering and its buying–benefiting experience that prospective customers need information about so that they can make evidence-based choices. With it, Marketing can build tools that support people's decision making. For example, it could use its understanding of customer values to create a decision checklist that customers could use to compare alternative offerings.

If Marketing understood that customers needed training in making evidence-based buying decisions, it also could build a simple, online training offering to meet this need and incorporate the checklist and information search as "application steps" in that training program. With such an approach, Marketing would leverage its understanding of customer values to create a value-adding educational offering for customers that accomplished its marketing purpose, elevated customer competencies, and advanced the enterprise in accomplishing its commercial purpose.

Assess Your Business's Performance at Every Level of Its Activity

Use customer values information to assess at the Strategic level how well your business is maximizing its delivery of value. For example, you can compute the percentage of customer values your offering and its buying–benefiting experience currently fully satisfy. Or you can compare the average percentage of customer values your enterprise is satisfying fully during its current year against the level it satisfied during its prior year.

With regard to Operations, you can use the ongoing measurements of performance against CTQs to gauge how well customer-valued features are being executed at every workstation on a daily basis.[3]

At the Executive Functions level, you can use the results of the two assessments just mentioned to determine how well the executive purpose of Effectiveness is being realized. If the satisfaction of customer values in both Strategic and Operations results show success, then the executive purpose of Effectiveness is, to that degree, being achieved.

Guide Your Business's Yearly Planning Process

Use your customer values information to formulate and prioritize improvement goals during your yearly businesswide Policy Planning and Deployment process. Begin with the results of your assessment of business performance.[4] Identify where the business is succeeding and what is enabling that success. Set goals for leveraging those identified strengths elsewhere in the business. Identify where the business is falling short and what is hindering greater success. Determine ways to eliminate those barriers to success. Set goals for implementing those remedies. Use your customer values information to prioritize your goals. The greater a goal's impact on improving the satisfaction of customer values, the higher its priority.

2. Understand Stakeholder Expectations and Concerns

Stakeholder awareness and involvement is widely recognized by business consultants as a crucial ingredient for success in endeavors that affect stakeholders either directly or indirectly (Alexander, Miesing, and Parsons, 2004). Certainly, in the absence of sufficient power over others, even producer-focused, profit-maximizing enterprises will work to identify and win over every party that can

[3] See examples for measuring effectiveness at the Operations level in Exhibit 6, pages 293–294.

[4] This assessment is part of the business's yearly Renewal process. See *Chapter 13* for a discussion of this process.

thwart their purposes. While the "public speech" of such a company may suggest otherwise, the purpose of each of these relationships will be to persuade stakeholders to support the ends and actions that serve the business's goals. The more successful a Capitalist enterprise is in this endeavor, the fewer barriers for realizing its egoistic aims it will encounter (Barnard, 1968).

The person undertaking Life Enabling commerce acts from a different appreciation of stakeholders. If you are a person whose qualities match those required for implementing Life Enabling commerce, you will understand that stakeholders are people who have genuine grounds for being aware of and involved in how you conduct your enterprise. You will recognize their right to be involved in anything that affects them or their areas of responsibility. You will want to understand their interests, expectations, and concerns so that you can incorporate them into your thinking, deciding, and acting. Your relationship with each of them will be based on respect. Your intent will be to benefit their efforts in ways that advance all life.

Life Enabling entrepreneurs proceed at two levels to constructively involve stakeholders—the corporate level and the business function level. At the corporate level, involvement focuses on the business's long-term goal and its methods to accomplish it. At the business function level, it focuses on satisfying each stakeholder's expectations with regard to each function's day-to-day operations.

In both cases, your first action is to understand who your stakeholders are and what your stakeholders' interests, expectations, and concerns are as related to your business. You will incorporate this understanding into your decision making and use it as the basis for working cooperatively with them.

Identifying Your Business Function's Stakeholders

Each business function's leadership team is responsible for identifying who its function's stakeholders are. One approach to accomplishing this involves generating a draft list of stakeholders using a work team of function members and then finalizing the list by drawing on the knowledge of every function member.

Your business function's work team should have representatives from each of its major value stream components. Each component's representatives should generate an initial list of stakeholders by analyzing the work processes their component implements and identifying every entity outside the business that their work affects or may be affected by. They should use the list of members of the business cooperative system as a starting point. For each identified stakeholder, the representatives record with which business activities the stakeholder is connected. If a named stakeholder is a large organization, they record the specific suborganization that connects to the identified function activity. They also record the title of the person representing the stakeholder with whom the component interacts. For example, if one of your stakeholders is the Department of Labor, identify the subgroup within Labor you interact with (e.g., Occupational Safety and Health Administration, OSHA) and the role of the person with whom you relate (e.g., OSHA inspector). As another example, within the Department of Commerce, it might be the United States Patent and Trademark Office, and your contact person might be a patent examiner for electrical engineering devices. With communities, consider whether your element affects neighborhoods or the community at large. If it is a neighborhood, identify it by its location or name. If it is the community at large, identify the community and any organizations within that community that focus on an issue related to your business activity.

Next, send the draft stakeholder list with its associated information to all the members of the business function for their confirmation, correction, or addition of stakeholders and their associated information. Use a survey approach. Last, integrate the findings from the survey with your initial list. Document a final list of your business function's stakeholders, including the information associated with each. It is the task of each function's leadership team to update this document whenever a change in operations is made and repeat the survey on a semi-annual basis.[5]

Understanding Each Stakeholder's Perspective

Each function's leadership team is also responsible for maintaining an up-to-date understanding of each stakeholder's perspective. It uses research and face-to-face communication by function members to clarify and confirm its understanding.

Know Each Stakeholder's Interests

You need to identify what each stakeholder's interests are in your function and why they are important to the stakeholder. Begin by doing research to educate yourself about what their interests might be. For government regulators, their interests are defined in the mandate that established their organizations. That mandate is documented in the law that authorized their creation. Similarly, the interest of any corporate entity will be expressed in their charters of incorporation and their current mission and functions statements. Community interests will need to be uncovered by meeting with community members. Begin with real grassroots advocacy groups associated with whatever issues relate to the element of your business function your stakeholder analysis connected to the

[5] Chapter *Task 2 Involve Stakeholders* in *The Lean Champion Resource Guide* (Vitalo, Bujak, Vitalo, Bierley, et al., 2023) provides detailed guidance on working with stakeholders.

community.[6] Proceed to engage the community directly through focus groups, town meetings, or surveys. Use these vehicles to confirm what the public's interest is and gather other needed information. Such opportunities allow you to educate the public about your enterprise as well as be educated by them about their perspectives on issues important to them and related to your business function.

Know Their Expectations

Learn what each stakeholder's expectations are with regard to your business function's conduct. For regulatory bodies, these will include compliance with specific laws and regulations and fulfillment of reporting requirements. Be certain to learn the identity and contents of the laws or regulations that apply. Document any reporting requirements, including what information must be conveyed, how, when, and to whom. In addition, uncover any personalized reporting requirements your specific liaison person expects you to meet.

Learn also what criteria each stakeholder will use to judge whether you have satisfied their expectations. You need this information to evaluate for yourself how well you are satisfying your stakeholder's expectations. This information is necessary for you to manage each stakeholder relationship.

Know Their Concerns

Learn what, if anything, troubles the stakeholder about your business function's operation. Understand what the stakeholder's concerns are, why the stakeholder has them, and what harm the stakeholder sees occurring if you do not address each concern. Do not challenge any concern that stakeholders express. Focus on understanding their concerns and appreciating their significance from the stakeholder's perspective. Be certain that the stakeholder recognizes that you do in fact comprehend and respect their concerns. Only when you have evidence that you have satisfied these relationship requirements should you engage in discussions about differences in perspectives. Even then, be certain to first establish a common, acceptable method for resolving such differences. Begin by establishing a common goal that captures what both the stakeholder and you acknowledge as important to ensure. Use evidence-based methods to evaluate the validity of each party's perspective, beginning with your perspective. Be sure the methods are agreeable to the stakeholder and validly address the stakeholder's concerns. Provide stakeholders the opportunity

---

[6] Profit-maximizing corporations and their lobbying associations have taken to using covertly sponsored "grassroots organizations" as vehicles for advocating positions favorable to their self-interest. The practice is called *astroturfing* (Grandia, 2011). You will need to examine carefully any grassroots advocacy group you identify to ensure that it is in fact rooted in the public's interest and not the self-interest of one or another profit-seeking entity.

to verify for themselves any facts that are introduced and add any facts they deem relevant. Only with a common goal and set of decision values and an agreed-upon, evidence-based approach to evaluating facts can you agreeably resolve differences with one another.

Always Confirm Your Understanding

With every contact, be certain to clarify and confirm your understanding of each stakeholder's communications to you. Never assume that the other party experiences you as understanding what they shared and why they shared it. Put your understanding into words and elicit their judgment as to whether you have correctly expressed their thinking and feeling. Also, verify their acknowledgment of your correct understanding of their perspective by observing their openness in sharing additional information with you and their willingness to use ideas you share. Hesitancy in sharing is usually a sign that you have incorrectly understood the other person's perspective or failed to communicate respect for them. When you have verified your understanding of your stakeholder's position, discuss ways in which you hope to integrate the stakeholder's perspective in the conduct of your function and seek their feedback as to whether they see those actions as responsive to their interests, expectations, and concerns.

Monitor and Manage Your Delivery of Benefit to Each Stakeholder

Maintain an open channel for ongoing communication with each stakeholder. Establish a liaison role in your function to work with each stakeholder. Rotate this role assignment periodically among all the contributors who do work that relates to each stakeholder. This maximizes learning by contributors about the stakeholder and exposes the stakeholder to all the people who implement the work that concerns them.

The business function's liaison with each stakeholder is responsible for maintaining regular contact with the stakeholder, updating and disseminating changes in the stakeholder's perspective, and verifying how satisfied the stakeholder is with the function's responsiveness to his or her interests, expectations, and concerns. This person must record what they learn and share it with all contributors whose work affects the specific stakeholder. In this way, every relevant contributor will understand the current status of the function's relationship with the stakeholders he or she affects. This enables contributors to review their own decisions and actions with regard to how responsive they have been to the stakeholder's perspective. Each contributor can then extract learning from their prior performance and adjust their behaviors accordingly. It also positions each contributor to generate ways the function can improve in fulfilling its commitment to benefit customers and all stakeholders inclusively.

3. Manage From a Systems Perspective

Managing from a systems perspective is a mindset, a way of looking at things that determines how you evaluate and respond to situations. It is based on the recognition that a commercial enterprise is a holistic entity, not a collection of independent components. It ensures that any local action to improve performance will not result in a decrement in performance by the enterprise as a whole. Contributors to a Life Enabling enterprise incorporate this systems perspective at every level of performance. These levels of use extend from the business level through each function's extended value stream level to the work process level and, ultimately, the work unit and individual performer levels.

Both Barnard (1968) and Deming (1982, 2000) recognized an organization as being a system and the importance of managing it from that perspective. However, the origin of the concept of a system extends far back into human history. Deming (2000, p. 65), for example, reproduced a quotation from the epistles of Saint Paul (1 Corinthians 12:14–21; circa 56 AD) that uses the analogy of the body as a system that must be understood as a whole. The 20th century root for *general systems theory* is assigned to Karl Ludwig von Bertalanffy. Its development has many contributors. One especially notable contributor was Jay Wright Forrester, the founder of the field of Systems Dynamics. In addition, other authors have promoted the use and importance of systems thinking in business settings. Two of these contributors are Robert R. Carkhuff (1983, 1986, 1988) and Peter Michael Senge (1990).

What Is a System?

A system is a set of components that operate together to accomplish a purpose. The essential feature of a system is that it succeeds only through the integrated activities of its constituent elements. The time reported by a mechanical clock, for example, is produced by the coordinated operation of all its gears, levers, and springs. No single component or subset of components alone can produce the correct time.

Every system serves a defined function and is made up of components and the processes that accomplish its purpose. Systems do vary in how they operate to accomplish their functions. Systems may be fixed or dynamic in their operation and open or closed with regard to their external contexts.

Fixed Versus Dynamic Systems

Within fixed systems, internal operations are preset and do not vary their behavior. Each component is designed to execute in exactly the same way every time the system is activated. The action of each gear, lever, and spring in a mechanical watch never varies—assuming the watch retains its designed state and its materials retain their integrity.

The components within dynamic systems vary their behavior in response to changes in the system's internal state. Thus, the temperature control system within the human body seeks to maintain a body temperature between 97.6°F and 99.6°F for an adult. This function is its contribution to the body's survival. How its components operate to achieve this function varies continuously. Depending on conditions within the body, the system may use sweating to reduce heat, vasoconstriction to retain heat, or shivering to increase heat production, or it may stimulate the production of hormones to accomplish its regulating function. It may alternate or combine these actions and sensitively regulate each action as it processes the current state of the body. While the system's function does not change, its performance is dynamic.

Open Versus Closed Systems

Systems also vary by whether or not they interact with their environments. Closed systems do not. A mechanical watch, as it operates, does not take in any information from its setting or produce any effect on its setting. Closed systems are insular. Open systems interact with the contexts within which they operate. A tree, for example, is an open system. Its components interact with its physical environment (soil, climate, etc.). A tree uses the information it receives from its environment to regulate its behavior (e.g., leaves may open to receive sunlight or fold to reduce transpiration).

Managing an Organization From a Systems Perspective

A commercial organization clearly satisfies the definition of a system. Its various business functions operate together to accomplish a common purpose. Without the integrative efforts of all its components, a business cannot accomplish its purpose.

It is also clear that a commercial organization is an open, dynamic system. It operates within a marketplace within which it exchanges information and resources with other entities (customers, suppliers, regulators, etc.). It adjusts its behavior in part based on the information it receives. Hence it is an open system. It is also a dynamic system, since its internal operations vary their behavior based on their interactions with one another. Each business component processes the information it receives from other internal components as it regulates its operations. An increase in production will cause downstream functions like shipping to modify their operations so that they can handle the greater output from production. Information that an employee is absent from a particular workstation may cause other employees to adjust their schedules and roles to cover that person's absence so that operations can be maintained.[7]

Four principles are most relevant to the purpose of managing a commercial organization from a systems perspective:

1. Only a system operating as a whole can accomplish its function.
2. The membership of open systems includes both their internal components and the external entities with which they interact.
3. Dynamic systems succeed based on how well their components respond to the current state of all other components with which they interact.
4. Complex systems—especially social systems—require contributors to act based on knowledge, not reflex or intuition.

Principle 1: A System Operates as a Whole or Not at All

By definition, it is the collective action of all components of the system working together that produces its success. This simple piece of knowledge is the foundation for managing from a systems perspective. "For our purposes we say that a system is something which must be treated as a whole because each part is related to every other part included in it in a significant way" (Barnard, 1968, p. 77).

Within a business context, this means that any action that alters the performance of one element of the business must account for its impact on the performance of all other elements of the business's system. No issue or action can be considered in isolation from the whole. As Deming stated, "An important part of management is to recognize and manage the interdependence between components" (2000, p. 64). The alteration of any component or subset of components that occurs in isolation from other system members will most likely detract from and not enhance the organization's overall performance.[8]

---

[7] While a commercial organization is a dynamic system, it does contain within it fixed systems. Many machines and most tools are examples of fixed systems. The organization needs these fixed systems to operate exactly the same way every time. The success of a fixed system depends on the adequacy of its design and fabrication, the continued fitness of its components, and whether its use requirements are followed.

[8] Deming (2000) offered a number of simple examples of the consequences of optimizing a function or work unit in isolation from the whole business. See *The New Economics*, especially his comments about the "Destruction of a System" (pp. 65–72) and on competition versus cooperation (pp. 82–87).

To satisfy Principle 1, every member of a complex commercial organization must understand that the enterprise is one whole system made up of many layers of interlocking subsystems (Exhibit 2, next page). The cooperative system represents the highest-level system view. Within the organization, its set of business functions forms its internal top-level system. They operate together to accomplish the organization's purpose. Each function is itself a major subsystem. It has, at its center, a value stream made up of components that represent its internal membership. Each function also has an *extended value stream* that includes the supply and delivery chain agents that complement its performance. The extended value stream provides a complete view of a business function's system.

Within each function's value stream, there are multiple operating components. This set of major components represents another level of subsystems. Each is organized around its central workflow. That workflow is made up of the operations that the component uses to produce its contribution. Each operation involves the performance of a series of tasks. Each task in this workflow is implemented by a workstation. These workstations may be viewed as perhaps the most detailed level subsystem within a commercial organization's layers of systems.

At each level within the organization, contributors must manage their performance from a systems perspective. Each of their decisions and actions must be evaluated based on its potential impact on all members of their immediate system and all other systems with which their system interconnects.

Principle 2: Open Systems Have Both Internal and External Members

Each open system has both internal and external members, and their interaction determines the system's performance. Unless you identify both sets of members, you will not be able to apply Principle 1. Internal members are work units within the boundary of your own business function. External members are entities with whom your internal members interact but are outside your business function. Some of these external members may be work units that reside in other business functions but not outside the enterprise. Others may be outside your enterprise (i.e., stakeholders). As with Principle 1, the application of Principle 2 needs to be propagated downward through all subsystems.

Principle 3: The Components of Dynamic Systems Must Act Responsively to One Another's Current State

A dynamic system requires each element within it to correctly read the state of each other element with which it interacts. It must infer from that information how best to adapt its behavior so that it enables the success of all the elements

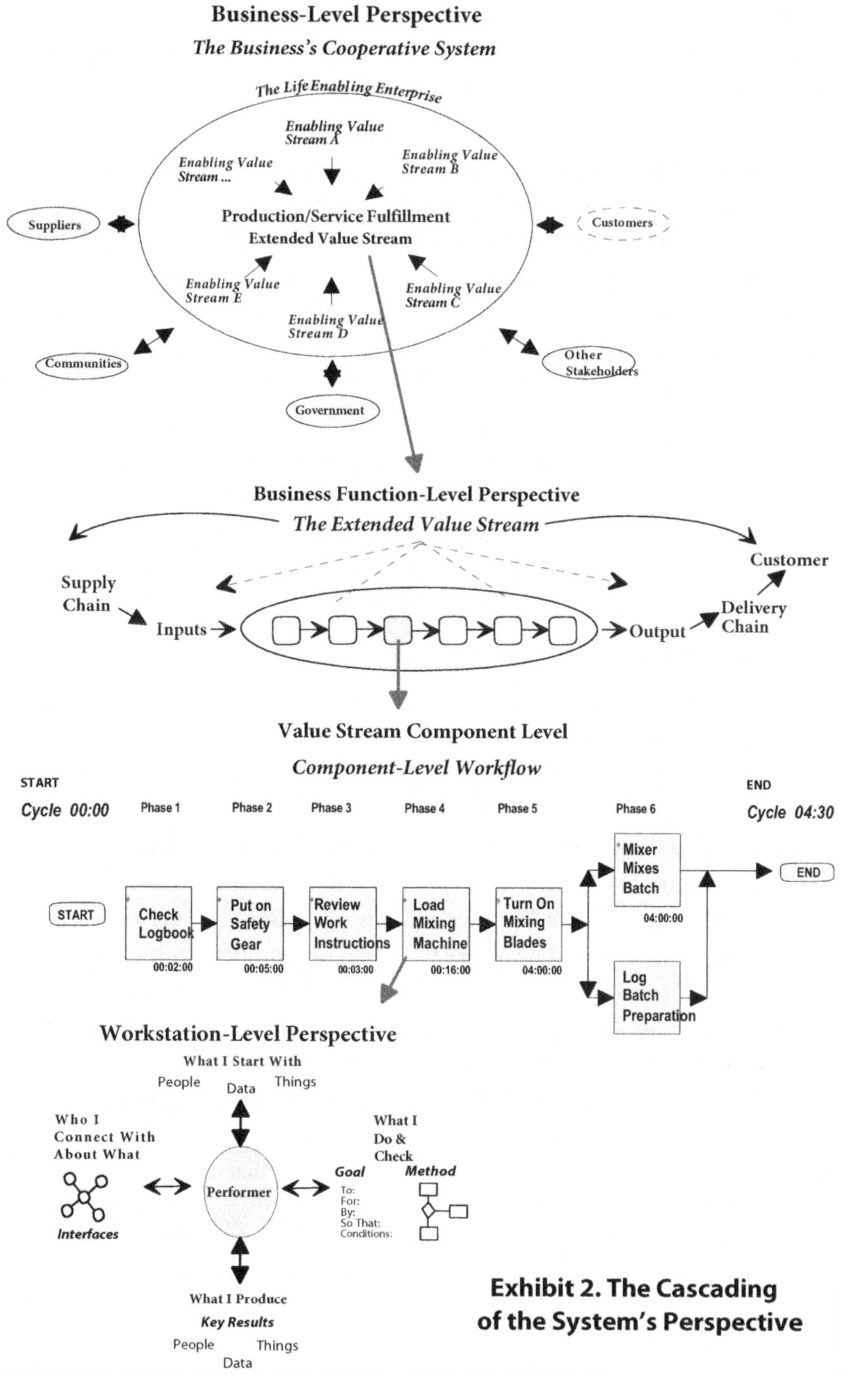

Exhibit 2. The Cascading of the System's Perspective

it affects. If it misreads the state of another element or fails to optimally adapt its behavior to that state, then the system's performance will be compromised. The degree of compromise depends on the failing component's scope of effect, the magnitude of its error, and the system's tolerance for error.

This principle of responsive action has importance for understanding what resources are critical to the success of a Life Enabling organization. As a dynamic, open human system, its members must be able to relate with one another, get and give relevant information correctly, process that information into effective adaptations to their own performance, and—over time—generate improved ways of performing. Only people with the ability to think, relate, learn, and act can currently satisfy those requirements with the level of scope and flexibility needed. Such people, therefore, are the *sine qua non* resource of Life Enabling enterprise.

Also, two other resources that are critical to success become clear. One is the information such people need so that they can correctly process the facts of their current situation. The other critical resource is a communications system that allows them to exchange information and interact with one another in real time.

Principle 4: Managing Complex Systems Requires Knowledge

Complex systems are those composed of many elements. Open, dynamic systems with many elements are the most complex systems. This describes a human organization. Every member is receiving, interpreting, acting on, and creating new information that he or she passes on to others. Jay W. Forrester stated that social systems are far more complex than the technological systems faced by engineers. He asserted that such complex systems cannot be managed intuitively. Even with the "simpler systems of chemical refineries and space flight, an engineer would never try to design by simply thinking and depending on intuition" (Forrester, 2010, p. 1). In this light, he ridiculed what *he* termed systems thinking. "By 'systems thinking' I mean the very popular process of talking about systems, agreeing that systems are important, and believing that intuition will lead to effective decisions" (ibid.) in managing them.

> In designing an engineering system, say a chemical plant, engineers realize that the dynamic behavior is complicated and that the design can not successfully be based only on rules of thumb and experience. ... On the other hand, although political, economic, and managerial systems are far more complex than engineering systems, only intuition and debate have ordinarily been used in building social systems. (Forrester, 1991, p. 6)

Given the complexity of social systems, knowledge and systematic experimentation must drive the design and management of complex dynamic human systems such as commercial organizations.[9]

Managing From a Systems Perspective in Multilevel Organizations

There are three requirements for cascading a systems perspective throughout a multilevel organization. First, people must understand the necessity of managing from a systems perspective. Second, they must be aware of the system they are a member of and all the other systems with which it is connected. Third, they must have an approach to system improvement that incorporates a systems perspective. You satisfy the first requirement by educating each contributor about the concept of managing from a systems perspective. To satisfy the second requirement, you need a method for enabling each contributor to become aware of his or her local system and its interconnections with all other systems within the organization. You also need a process for maintaining and disseminating that information. To satisfy the third requirement, you need to adopt and instruct all contributors in mapping, analyzing, and making improvements from a systems perspective.

Becoming Aware of One's Connections

In a complex, multi-tiered organization, how do people stay abreast of everyone who immediately affects their work or is affected by it? These people constitute each contributor's local system. While this may seem a daunting task, remember two facts. *First*, at the level of each contributor, identification of the linkages between one's work and others who either affect or are affected by it is straightforward. Basically

- anything you receive comes from someone, and *that* someone represents one member of your "local system";
- anything you hand off goes to someone, and *that* person represents another member of your local system;
- anything that you require (e.g., license, permit, someone's approval) or use (information, tools, equipment, machines, facilities) but do not supply or maintain is supplied or maintained by people somewhere, and each of these people is another member of your local system; and

[9] Deming used the "funnel" experiment (Deming, 1982, pp. 327–337) to teach his students the effects of using intuition to manage a system whose components and dynamics were unknown. In the experiment, students drop a marble through a funnel onto a target marked on the surface on which the funnel sits. The funnel is centered over the target's bullseye. When the marble comes to rest, its position is marked and plotted. Successive trials display a pattern of "errors"—final positions that are not at the center of the target. Students are allowed to try and correct these errors by making whatever adjustments they deem appropriate. Each "correction" produces new results that are also plotted. Invariably, intuitively "corrected" performance displays a wider pattern of error than the original performance.

- any person with whom you share a resource is another member of your local system.

Once uncovered, this set of linkages describes the members of your local system. Its membership does not change dramatically unless the basic nature of your work or the organization changes. For each person you identify as a member of your local system, record their job title, work unit, and business function.

Second, with regard to revealing the membership of ever-more distant system segments, every contributor who populates one's local system also does the same linkage-recognizing exercise (Exhibit 3). When the results of these individual efforts are integrated, a holistic network view of the connections between local systems that span the enterprise is easily constructed without any unusual burden of discovery falling on any one person's shoulders. Every contributor can see the connections that exist between his or her performance and others who directly affect or are affected by it, the connections of those individuals to others, and so forth.

This graphic view of the network of interconnectedness among contributors and local systems renders concrete the abstract notion of a systems perspective. The reverberated effects that one's decisions can have on every other component across the organization and its cooperative system become perfectly clear. This network of connections also remains relatively constant. It is easily represented and distributed using social network analysis software (e.g., Cuttlefish or similar applications), modern computing technology, and a hypertext presentation approach.[10] It becomes a key resource for supporting people in managing from a systems perspective and teaming.

Exhibit 3. Mapping the Network of Relationships Across an Organization

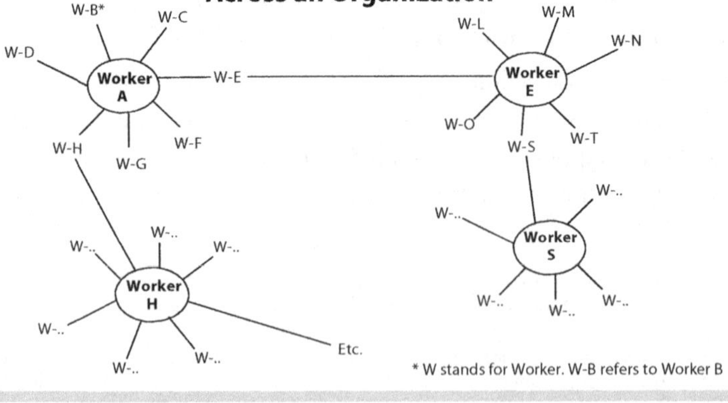

* W stands for Worker. W-B refers to Worker B

[10] See Moody, McFarland, and Bender-de Moll (2005) for a discussion of dynamic network visualization.

A Method for System Improvements That References the Whole

Managing from a systems perspective requires making improvements in a way that incorporates referencing the whole. Both Rother and Shook (2003) and Jones and Womack (2009) have introduced methodologies that can be adapted to accomplish this task. Each involves mapping, analyzing, and improving the way work is done while considering the system within which it is done. Jones and Womack's approach focused on the extended value stream and is the closest to incorporating a full view of all system members. Its typical use would be at a business function level, with the business function's leadership team using its process to manage its function's extended value stream and improve its performance as a whole.

Mapping is done as a team. Team members include representatives from the various components that make up the business function's extended value stream. Mapping documents the flow of work from suppliers to the recipients of the function's outputs. It also documents the information that controls this workflow. That information triggers its startup, controls its rate of flow, and otherwise regulates its operation.

Mapping produces a graphic representation of the function-level system that the function's leadership team manages and seeks to continuously improve. During mapping, the team also collects and records information that describes the present state of the performance of all mapped workflow components (e.g., cycle time, throughput, error rates).

We adapt Jones and Womack's approach to the Life Enabling enterprise perspective by including in our system view not only the supply and delivery chain members but also all other involved parties. Attach to the map three items: a statement listing the key values and current state of satisfaction of the function's customers, a list of function's stakeholders, and a list of all the other enterprise systems with which the mapped extended value stream interfaces. Reference this attached information to check whether any issue you are addressing with regard to improving the mapped extended value stream either impacts or may be impacted by the functions' customers, stakeholders, or interfacing enterprise systems.

Once the business function's system is represented, the team works to analyze the system's strengths and weaknesses in delivering value to the recipients of its outputs and the enterprise's customers. Members work together to uncover opportunities to ensure that the function's throughput matches demand. They identify and eliminate all forms of waste in its current design. They also look to affirmatively add value to the system's operations and outputs. Each potential improvement is examined with regard to its impact on the function's system as a whole, the recipient of the function's output, the enterprise's end customers and all its other stakeholders, and each of the other systems with which the function interfaces. Proposed improvements are reshaped to ensure inclusive benefit to all affected parties and the enterprise as a whole. At a minimum, the accomplishment of each selected improvement must improve the value-adding contribution that the business function makes to its recipient's success in a way that also elevates the enterprise's delivery of value as a whole.

Vetted improvement ideas are then prioritized, scheduled, and executed. When changes are made to the function's system, its map is updated. Information about each improvement made (what, why, where, when, how, participants, results) and the revised map are shared with all members and affected parties. This process of mapping, analysis, improvement, and updating is recycled periodically (not less than yearly).

Generalizing the Use of the Systems Approach to Improvement

The process of mapping, analyzing, improving, and updating is applied at every level of performance within the Life Enabling enterprise. Thus, at the corporate level, the enterprise's leadership team uses this strategy to enhance the performance of its entire cooperative system. As just described, each business function's leadership team does likewise for its extended value stream. Each major value stream component uses mapping, analyzing, and improving to manage and improve its operation. And so forth. At each subsystem level, improvement opportunities are uncovered, vetted as to their effects on all stakeholders and systems with which the subsystem interacts, prioritized, and accomplished.

This mapping, analysis, improvement, and updating approach is also applied at the work unit and performer levels. Throughout, contributors prevent actions that optimize one element within the enterprise while hindering another. They do so by maintaining a holistic perspective from the business level through to the performer level and by incorporating into decision making the potential effects of their choices as they reverberate across the enterprise. In this way, they ensure that each of their local actions elevates the performance of the business as a whole.

4. Design Outputs and Implementing Processes That Maximize the Benefit Delivered to Customers and All Stakeholders Inclusively

Your first use for your understanding of customer and stakeholder values is to *build value into* your product and service offerings. This practice follows Deming's teachings to the Japanese leaders of industry in the 1950s (Deming, 1982a, p. 175). To do this, you develop cross-functional "product teams" for each of your proposed offerings.[11] Team members first conceive and design each offering so that it enables its user's success. They add in other value-satisfying features so that each offering maximally fulfills customer preferences. They also incorporate features in their design that satisfy the expectations and concerns of all stakeholders. The team then conceives the processes that will reliably supply resource inputs and produce, deliver, and support each offering.

Each product team is made up of people in research, design, sales, and production and any other function (e.g., IT) whose activities affect the input sourcing, production, delivery, or support of the product or service (Deming, 1982a). In this way, all the expertise relevant to ensuring that customers receive, use, and benefit from an offering contributes to its development. In completing its work, the team employs concepts, principles, and activities from various engineering tools—e.g., value engineering, quality function deployment (QFD), design failure mode and effects analysis (DFMEA), design for excellence (DfX), and Production Preparation Process (3P). In each case, however, they ensure that the application of these tools is consistent with the Life Enabling model's core values and its intent to benefit customers and all stakeholders inclusively.

The advantages of using the systematic approach to designing products and processes described below are twofold. First, its use yields offerings that are most likely to enable customers to realize their purpose. Second, its use ensures the enterprise can deliver and support its offering when and where customers require them, at the volume they need, and at a cost they find acceptable.

General Flow of Work

The general flow for creating a product/service offering and its associated processes begins with your understanding customers' needs and values and formulating a concept of an offering that will satisfy them. It proceeds through developing a general design and continues with the drafting of a detailed design. All design solutions are evaluated from the perspective of enabling your target customer's success and satisfying his or her preferences. Both the general and the detailed designs are also evaluated from a sourcing, production, delivery, support, and cost to customer perspective and the perspectives of stakeholder expectations and concerns.

Once a going-forward detailed design is concluded, the process-focused product team members complete the design of the processes. These product team

[11] For the sake of simplicity, we will focus this discussion on products. Its generalization to services should be straightforward.

members execute roles in logistics, production or service fulfillment, and product support, among others. They design the processes that supply the offering's resource inputs and produce, deliver, and support its use.

Product development continues with the production of one or more prototypes. Each prototype is evaluated for conformity to design specifications and tested with a sample of target customers. Using the learning from this testing, the product's design and associated processes are improved, finalized, and documented. The product team then plans the rollout of the offering—that is, the introduction and reintegration of a new product or service into its target market (Exhibit 4, next page).

Initiating Product and Process Designs

To create a product or service concept, the product team reviews the customer's purpose and how he or she defines success. The team also reviews the customer's capabilities for being successful in the setting(s) within which the customer operates. The team then evaluates what key resource the customer needs to be successful. This judgment may confirm, correct, or enhance prior notions of what the offering should be or current industry solutions. Next, the team conceives a business offering that would supply that resource. The team's initial focus is on ensuring that the offering incorporates features that will satisfy the customer's effectiveness requirements. This ensures that the offering will satisfy the minimal requirement for enabling its user's success.

With an acceptable product concept completed, the team creates a general design of the offering. In this design, it adds features that will satisfy as many other customer values as feasible within the product's cost constraint. This cost constraint is set by estimating what price the target customer would find reasonable for the offering.

Every iteration of the general design must provide the same or improved levels of effectiveness while adding preference-satisfying features. Through discussion, the product team concludes the offering's general design. It then verifies the general design's compatibility with stakeholder expectations and concerns. Once a satisfactory general design is developed, the team produces a mock-up of the offering. This mock-up provides an observable representation of the offering.[12] For physical and intellectual products, it represents the product's form, fit, and finish but not its functioning.[13]

[12] The equivalent of a mock-up for a service offering would be a storyboard or a workflow map.

[13] Intellectual products include procedural documents, training courseware, research reports, marketing materials, etc. Mock-ups would express the final product's topic list, organization, delivery medium, format and style, and other specifications that define its form, fit, and finish but would not contain its final intellectual content.

Exhibit 4. Building Value Into an Offering

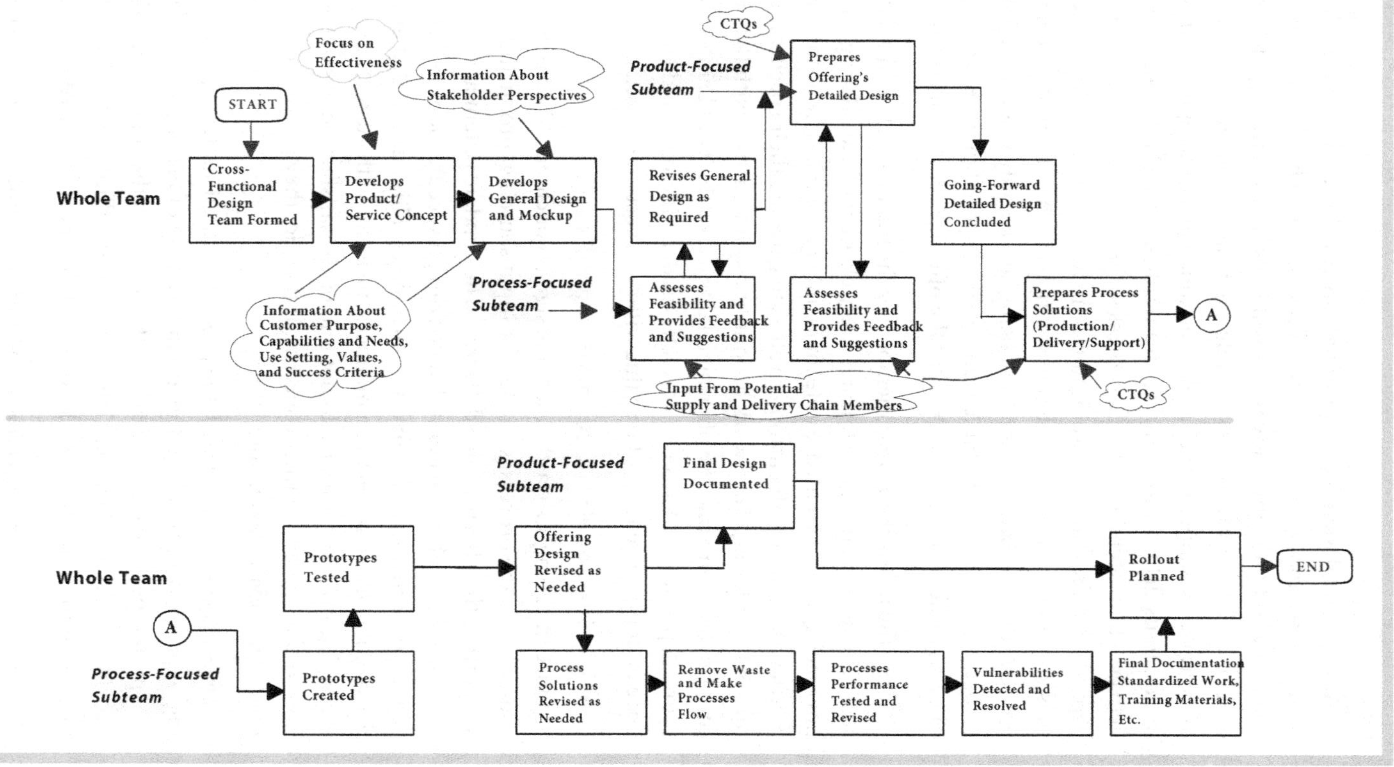

As a general design is being formed, process-focused members discuss potential materials, technologies, and production solutions. They make suggestions, raise concerns, and offer alternatives that will improve the offering's feasibility. Once a general design is formed, they complete a detailed evaluation of the design's feasibility as regards input sourcing, production, delivery, support, and cost to the customer. In its deliberations, this subteam solicits input from potential supply and delivery chain members. As the process subteam's assessment unfolds, its members educate the team as a whole about their subteam's findings. They clarify issues and provide alternative design solutions to the full product team that would improve the offering's likelihood of being successfully resourced, produced, delivered, correctly used, maintained, and easily disposed of once no longer needed. They also offer solutions that reduce the offering's cost while retaining its value.

Next, the product-focused members of the full product team draft a detailed design. The detailed design delineates every element of the offering and specifies how each is to be executed. Subteam members use the critical-to-quality (CTQ) metrics associated with customer values to generate their specification of each feature of the offering. They work in continuous interaction with the process-focused subteam to ensure that the offering retains its feasibility of being successfully resourced, produced, delivered, correctly used, maintained, and easily disposed of once no longer needed and remains within its cost constraint.

Completing the Product and Process Designs

Once the going-forward detailed design is concluded, the process-focused subteam designs the processes needed for input sourcing, producing, delivering, and supporting the offering once delivered. They update potential supply and delivery chain members about relevant detailed design specifications and reconfirm its feasibility for sourcing and delivery to customers. This ensures that any supply and delivery needs can be met in a manner consistent with customer values. They also verify that process solutions do not impair the satisfaction of stakeholder expectations or the remedy of their concerns. If they do, they adjust their process designs to accommodate stakeholder issues.

Once processes are defined, the process-focused subteam prototypes the offering. A prototype provides a functioning version of the offering.[14] The production of a prototype provides feedback on the processes the subteam has developed. It provides direct information about materials handling, assembly, and other facts important to understanding the production process required to manufacture the

[14] The equivalent for a service offering is a pilot test of the service. For intellectual products such as procedural manuals, the team produces a draft of a selected procedure in accordance with the product's detailed design. This sample output allows people to evaluate the offering's form, fit, finish, and functionality.

offering. Once the prototypes are completed, the team as a whole tests them. Initial testing is done against the product's design and anticipated cost. It verifies that the prototype offering's features satisfy the CTQ metrics specified in its detailed design. If problems of fidelity are detected, their causes are identified, and processes are modified to eliminate them. If problems of cost are detected, alternative approaches to satisfying the product's specifications are discussed, and trade-offs are made to ensure that customers can afford the final offering.

Once the prototype's fidelity and cost acceptability are verified, testing with a sample of prospective customers verifies the offering's utility and desirability from the customers' perspective. A final check is made to ensure that the offering and its associated process satisfy stakeholder expectations and harm no one. Finally, the team as a whole concludes a final detailed design incorporating all the learning derived from testing. The process-focused team members revise their process solutions as needed.

Tools Used/Issues Addressed

The process-focused team members apply the concepts and principles of the various tools mentioned above (DfX, DFMEA, etc.) in completing their designs. These tools ensure that their solutions are technically feasible and can be produced reliably, at the least cost, while satisfying customer values. They also address issues related to environmental concerns, producibility, safety, timely delivery of the offering, maintainability of the product, and support of the offering post-delivery. Finally, they evaluate and address the ultimate disposal of the offering.

Eliminating Waste From Initial Process Designs

In designing the product's implementing processes, the process subteam members use a "Paper Kaizen" to uncover and eliminate waste in its initial designs. Paper Kaizen is a team process improvement activity that does not require a process to exist and be observed in operation. The team maps each proposed work process. Using this map, it conducts a virtual walkthrough of the process to detect instances of waste. It revises the work process to eliminate the waste it uncovers and documents the improved work process. Changes in any one process must account for their propagated effects on the performance of all related processes. Each improvement must elevate the whole and not just the single process where waste was detected.

Organizing Workstations and Ensuring Flow

The improved processes are organized into work units. Work units group machines, people, and equipment into teamed units. Each unit accomplishes a portion of a work process. In designing work units, process team members seek to balance the cycle times between units to ensure a continuous *flow* of work through the process. The rate of flow must yield the throughput required to meet estimated customer demand. This even flow of work through the new product's value stream reduces the need for work-in-process (WIP) and final inventory. The pace of the process ensures that customers will have the products they seek when they need them.

This effort to establish workload balance, an even pace, and a continuous flow of work also seeks to eliminate *mura* and *muri*. Mura means unevenness, irregularity, or inconsistency. An example would be a work process that has workload demands that vary greatly over time. Muri means overburden, unreasonableness, or absurdity. It refers to any form of stress due to excess demands on workers, the overburdening of equipment, or the accumulation of WIP inventory.

As the team proceeds in its work, it continuously updates each process's design document with any changes it devises. The team documents both how each process is organized into work units and the workplace layouts needed to support the continuous flow of work.

Next, the team tests these improved process designs. Every process must be capable of producing its needed contribution reliably and effectively with the yield research suggests is required and at a cost acceptable to the customer. Each design is tested in a pilot application or through simulations. Each test measures the process's performance and determines whether it satisfies the organization's needs. This evaluation includes estimations of the process's typical output, cycle time, throughput, yield, and capability indices (Cp and Cpk).[15] These tests determine whether the process can satisfy the current estimate of customer demand and requirements. If a process fails, its design is revised and the pilot is recycled.

Eliminating Vulnerabilities in Process Designs

Once a process design satisfies the established performance criteria, the team proceeds to detect and eliminate any points in the process where breakdowns might occur. Breakdowns make a process unstable in its performance. Each

[15] Cp calculates whether the width of variation in a desired feature of an output matches the width of the tolerances for acceptability of the feature by a customer. For example, assume that a customer value is satisfied if the valued feature's measurement falls between unit 21 and unit 30, inclusively, on some measure. That is a 10-unit range of acceptable variation. If the production process's band of variation in producing that feature is no more than 10 units in width, then its Cp is acceptable. Cpk verifies that a process's band of variation *always includes an acceptable output value.* A process may possess an acceptable band of variation, but if the typical output it produces is not centered within that band, then some of its outputs will fail to satisfy customer expectations. Such a process would fail this second quality test. Cpk, therefore, measures a process's reliability of producing an output acceptable to a customer every time. A process may have a band of variation that is acceptable (Cp) but not be reliable in producing outputs that satisfy customers (Cpk).

detected vulnerability is addressed. The team either modifies the process to eliminate the vulnerability or adds a poka-yoke device (Robinson, 1997) that will prevent the breakdown from occurring.[16] If the process is modified, then its performance on criteria must be re-checked.

For those vulnerabilities that are not preventable, the team builds detection capabilities into the process. Detection of a breakdown leads to the stoppage of the process. This stoppage minimizes the negative impact of the breakdown. Once the process is stopped, a fix is made. As Harada (2010) reports, building in these detection capabilities is part of the planning of the process from long before a process launches.

Error detection capabilities may be automated or manual. The placement of an automated detection system in a machine is termed *autonomation* ("Jidoka" in Japanese). The word means "automation with a human touch." The human touch added to the machine is vigilance and judgment. Essentially, the automated component detects instances of out-of-bounds performance, signals its occurrence, and stops the machine's operation and the process to which it is contributing.[17]

Manual detection solutions depend on workers to detect operating problems. A signaling device is placed in the work area where the vulnerable process is performed. When detection occurs, the worker signals that a breakdown has occurred, and that signal stops the process. One type of signaling device is the "andon cord." It is triggered by pulling a cord mounted in the work area. When activated, it signals that a process has gone awry and stops the process. Manual detection by workers is consistent with a broad understanding of the Japanese concept of Jikoda. That understanding views every contributor as responsible for detecting when a process they implement goes awry. In the words of Akio Toyoda, the president of the Toyota Motor Company,

> For much of Toyota's history, we have ensured the quality and reliability of our vehicles by placing a device called an andon cord on every production line—and empowering any team member to halt production if there's an assembly problem. Only when the problem is resolved does the line begin to move again. (Toyoda, A. 2010)[18]

---

[16] Poka-yoke is a Japanese term that means "mistake-proofing." A poka-yoke device is either a physical or mental aid that ensures that a task is done correctly. A jig is an example of a physical poka-yoke device. A conceptual template or framework that guides a person in describing a commercial model is an example of a mental poka-yoke device.

[17] "Out-of-bounds" performance refers to values on metrics that fall either above the acceptable upper limit or below the acceptable lower limit established statistically for the process being monitored.

[18] In a distributed service fulfillment context, the andon cord might be an instant message (IM) sent to all process implementers signaling that they should halt their work and convene as a team to resolve the uncovered issue.

Final Documentation and Rollout Plan

The process subteam's final focus is on documenting each proven process's requirements. These requirements are the resources that must be present for the process to operate as designed. This documentation records

- the number of people needed to implement the process and the skills and proficiency levels they require;
- the manuals, guides, and other training products required to prepare process implementers;
- the input resources the process needs and the features those inputs must possess; and
- the infrastructure (space, equipment, tools, etc.) required to support people in implementing the process.

Once this is complete, the team finalizes the process's standardized work documentation (discussed below). This documentation fully describes how the process should be set up and executed.

Finally, the whole product team plans the rollout of the offering. This rollout plan must resolve the selection of the location(s) where the offering will be implemented. It must setup the offering's supply and delivery chains and decide how people will be readied to implement the processes that market, sell, produce, deliver, and support the offering once delivered. It must plan how the infrastructure (e.g., space, utilities, equipment, computer systems) needed to support process implementation will be established and workspaces will be configured in accordance with each process's design specification. It prepares a formal rollout plan that designates roles, responsibilities, and specifies a timeline for performance.

5. Establish Waste-Free, Optimized Processes Across All Extended Value Streams

A waste-free, optimized process is one that is stable, is free of common cause variation, and produces an output that exactly matches what the customer needs and values at the least cost to the customer. The design phase provides a "best but not final" solution to realize these ends. The Life Enabling model prescribes five actions that realize the aim of establishing waste-free, optimized processes across all extended value streams:

A. Make processes stable.

B. Establish flow in all value streams.

C. Establish pull in all value streams.

D. Optimize the performance of all value streams and subprocesses.

E. Broadcast the use of the Life Enabling model across all extended value streams.

A. Make Processes Stable

A process is stable when it is executed *as designed* every time. A stable process consistently performs within the bounds of its capability. To understand stability, you first need to understand the concept of variation and its significance to business management.

Variation

Variation is the observed differences in the measured values of some feature of a process or its output across instances of its occurrence. For example, given a sufficiently precise measurement instrument, successively produced #2 steel screws almost never have precisely the same thread or exactly the same dimensions.[19] The differences may be exceedingly small and of no consequence as to the screw's utility to a user, but variation will be present.

All commercial processes exhibit variation. They are examples of what is termed "random processes." They are "random" in the sense that we have incomplete control of all the variables that affect how the process behaves. Control is incomplete because we do not know all the variables that influence the process's performance; hence, we cannot control them. This type of variation is called "common cause variation."

The good news about random processes is that they do produce a *consistent pattern* of results *when implemented as designed.* This pattern can be calculated and represented as a distribution of values. The salient features of this pattern (central tendency, amount of variation, upper and lower limit values) can be described quantitatively. This pattern can also be used to predict future performance (e.g., 95% of the time, screws will fall within .0001 inches of the target width). With this information, we can judge whether a process will meet our customer's needs and preferences. We can set goals, make plans, and manage our resources.

But variation can have a second reason for occurring. That reason is due to the process not being *performed as designed.* That type of variation is termed *special cause variation.* It occurs when some event or action makes a process deviate from the way it is supposed to be implemented. In a sense, it is the result of

[19] This assertion assumes the same measurement instrument is applied every time. Theoretically, as the measurement instrument's precision improves, the likelihood of the same value being produced repeatedly approaches zero.

"stuff that happens." It may be an out-of-specification input that slips through inspection. It could be a machine that unexpectedly goes out of alignment, a power surge or voltage drop that disrupts the operation of sensors, or inattention on the part of a performer due to being distracted by fatigue or personal issues.

The presence of special cause variation destabilizes a process. Its cause, however, can be detected because it is an observable happening that is *always a deviation* from the usual and proper way the process is supposed to be performed. It can, therefore, be discovered and corrected through the application of problem-solving methods. Also, its reoccurrence can be minimized by the introduction of preventive actions.

Special Cause Variation Blocks Planning and Improvement

If a process is not stable, its pattern of performance becomes unpredictable. Consequently, you cannot rely on the pattern of performance the process displayed during testing or across its history of correct operation to predict what it will produce. This means that you cannot perform the essential management tasks of setting goals, making plans, and managing resources. You cannot be certain that customers will receive what they need, when they need it, and in the quantity they require. Moreover, unstable processes cannot be improved. If a process is not performed consistently, whatever you change about it today may not be done tomorrow. The first challenge in optimizing a work process, therefore, is to make each process stable (Deming, 1982a).

Requirements for Stabilizing a Process

You must satisfy the following four conditions to ensure that a process is stable:

- First, you must document the process. Without a written guide that accurately documents how the process is to be implemented, there is no process per se. There is only whatever is being done, by whoever is doing it, at whatever time it is happening. The likelihood of any of these being consistent across time, place, and performers is essentially zero.
- Second, you must install the process correctly. This means that all the resources required for the correct implementation of the process (people, machines, input materials, workplace layout, etc.) are put in place and meet specifications. If this condition is not met, then whatever is occurring cannot be the process as designed.
- Third, people and machines must execute the process correctly. If people or machines deviate from the documented method of execution, the process is not being executed as designed. It cannot be stable. Rather, it is again

relegated to an unknown process performed in uncertain ways. For it to be executed consistently, every person must perform his or her role in the manner specified in the process's design. Every machine must operate in a manner consistent with its design specifications.

- Fourth, you must detect and eliminate instances of special cause variation. Their causes must be understood, and action must be taken to prevent their reoccurrence. This application of information- or knowledge-based problem solving, triggered by instances of special cause variation, progressively frees a system from the "stuff that happens."

Satisfying these conditions involves (1) establishing standardized work; (2) selecting, training, and supporting process implementers in mastering their roles; (3) implementing proper management of the process's resources and work setting; and (4) detecting and eliminating instances of special cause variation.

1. Establish Standardized Work

Standardized work refers to the development, maintenance, and use of a written description of each process's goal and output; how the process should be set up, implemented, and checked; and what its expected performance is. The document records the current "best practice" version of the process. It supports the stable operation of the process by recording the information required to install, operate, and improve it. It is used as the basis for teaching, coaching, managing, and optimizing a process. The documentation should include the following contents:

- Document identification – This content records information used to organize, store, retrieve, and control access to and revision of a standardized work document. This information includes the name of the work process, the value stream to which it contributes, and the work unit responsible for implementing it. It lists the roles that implement the process (department and job title) and records the alphanumerical identifier assigned to the standardized work document, its revision number, and its issue date. It also lists the machines, specialized tools, informational resources (documents, forms, and data files), and software applications used in the process with the identifying number of each process step in which each resource is employed.
- Work procedure – This content provides an overview of the process and a detailed description of the workflow that implements it. The overview records what triggers the startup of the process. It documents the process's goal, the resource inputs needed to complete it, the output it produces, and the other processes with which it interfaces as it executes. The detailed description section contains a flow diagram of the work process. It also

includes a narrative description of the process steps listing each action performed in its sequence of occurrence. For each action, it registers its sequence number, who does it, where, and the names of all documents, forms, data files, or other informational items used in doing the action. It records the materials, tools, and machines used. It also records each action's average cycle time and the percentage of cycle time implemented by machines and consumed by materials drying, setup, or curing.

- Workplace layout – This content visually depicts the space within which the process should be implemented and the correct layout of the equipment, tools, materials, storage, and inventory that must exist within that work area.
- Current profile of performance – This content records the process's average cycle time and current value-added ratio, throughput, inventory requirements, non-conformity (defect) rate, scrap rate, and rate of recordable incidents.

The initial version of this standardized work documentation is produced by the design team using data from its testing cycles. Maintenance of documentation is completed by process implementers and by process improvement teams whenever an improvement is made in the process. The development, maintenance, and modification of a standardized work document is itself guided by a standardized work document.

2. Select, Train, and Support Contributors

You must properly select and train the people who will perform the process and correctly organize the work setting in which they will work.

Before any process can move from a proven design to correct implementation, you must choose people who possess the knowledge, skills, and proficiency levels required to learn and perform the roles specified in the process's design. If training is required, that training must effectively transfer to contributors the proficiencies they need to perform successfully. It also must support the transfer of learning from the classroom to the actual work setting. The goals of training must be to ensure that every contributor understands his or her role, can accomplish it successfully, and does so in the actual work context. You must verify the successful achievement of these goals before contributors begin carrying out their roles. Complete this verification by measuring the degree to which contributors acquire and successfully use the knowledge and skills they are taught. Make the use assessment in a simulated work context or the actual work context while the process is offline.

Further, you must support the transfer of learning from training to the job by ensuring that the work setting is laid out and equipped correctly. Also ensure that each contributor's supervisor is knowledgeable and skilled in the process the contributor is performing *and* in coaching performance. Supervisors need both task and coaching expertise to aid contributors. Their goal in coaching is to support each contributor in accomplishing his or her role to at least the level of proficiency that enables the process to perform at its level of capability. Further, supervisors must ensure that the performance of each contributor is stable. This means that each contributor consistently exhibits the proficiency he or she has mastered.

Within the Life Enabling model, this entire effort of ensuring contributor success is accomplished collegially. Instructor, contributor, and supervisor each assume full responsibility and work together to ensure that the contributor succeeds and experiences pride in his or her accomplishments and that the process itself is performed as designed.

3. Implement the Proper Management of Resources and Work Settings

The proper management of resources and work settings realizes the following three goals:

1. Tools and equipment function to specifications.
2. Each work setting is maintained in accordance with the requirements specified in the process's standardized work document.
3. Input materials are available as required.

Life Enabling enterprises use Lean Manufacturing programs, such as Total Productive Maintenance (TPM), 6S, and supply chain management, to accomplish these three goals and proactively prevent process anomalies (special cause variability).

TPM. TPM is a set of activities focused on ensuring that every machine is always able to perform its required tasks as expected. The multiple activities that constitute the TPM system act to prevent breakdowns. Hence, they contribute to making processes stable.

TPM's activities include

- autonomous maintenance,
- predictive maintenance, and
- equipment improvement.

Autonomous maintenance means that operators regularly inspect the status of their equipment; perform routine maintenance to ensure its readiness for operation; and provide feedback about its design, performance, and wear patterns.

Predictive maintenance uses experience data about the wear patterns of machines and their components to set up tailored schedules to address wear issues *before* they create breakdowns or defective outputs. It is preventive maintenance tailored to the unique operating characteristics of a particular machine.

Equipment improvement turns ideas from operators and from the problem solving of breakdowns into better designs for future equipment. This latter activity also relates to process optimization (see below), and TPM has this second application as well.

6S. 6S is often included within the TPM program but is also applied as a free-standing method in manufacturing and non-manufacturing businesses. It extends the "5S" method by adding *Safety* as the sixth concern.

The six "Ss" stand for each of the following responsibilities:

- Sort – Distinguish between what is needed and not needed in a work setting and remove the latter.
- Straighten – Neatly arrange and identify needed materials for ease of access.
- Shine – Clean up the workplace and look for ways to keep it clean.
- Standardize – Make the 6S work practices consistent and formalize people's roles in implementing them.
- Sustain – Maintain and improve 6S policies.
- Safety – Eliminate hazards.

Like TPM, 6S has two different uses. The first is to ensure that the work setting is continuously maintained in a manner specified in each process's standardized work document. This use helps stabilize processes by eliminating performance anomalies due to an improperly organized workplace (e.g., a missing resource, materials not stored in their proper place). It requires that each process's standardized work document include a workplace layout that clarifies the location of each element used within the process.

Its second use is to improve the original design of a work setting so that it better supports the efficient, reliable, and safe performance of a process. It does this by uncovering and eliminating selected forms of waste (e.g., motion, inventory, search, travel/transport, hazard) that were previously undetected or for which a solution could not then be discovered. It also eliminates interruptions and harm due to safety incidents by uncovering and removing hazards. With these improvements, it contributes to optimizing a process.[20]

Supply Chain Management. Supply chain management oversees all activities involved in sourcing and procurement, conversion, and logistics management activities.[21] It includes coordination and collaboration with supply chain partners (suppliers, intermediaries, third-party service providers) to ensure the timely and uninterrupted flow of input resources to the business so that its processes operate as designed. The logistical elements of supply chain management coordinate the production, movement, and storage of needed goods and materials. The information-sharing aspect allows the various supply chain partners to coordinate their long-term plans and to control the day-to-day flow of goods and materials up and down the supply chain (Handfield, 2011). Effective supply chain management ensures the uninterrupted presence of the resources needed to sustain process performance. It thereby prevents process anomalies due to a failure in the supply of needed materials to the process.

4. Detect and Eliminate Instances of Special Cause Variation

Despite everyone's best efforts, anomalies in the execution of a process will occur. This is why vigilance and a proper response to a detected anomaly are essential to stabilizing the performance of every process once it is operational.

As described earlier, either or both automated or manual detection methods are built into each process's design. These methods are embedded in machines and equipment (autonomation) or rely on the vigilance and skill of contributors. In the latter case, contributors signal the detection of a process anomaly and stop the process. Every stoppage triggers a problem-solving activity. Workers come together and use a team problem-solving approach to investigate and identify the cause of the breakdown, conceive a solution, and identify ways to prevent its reoccurrence. If the problem-solving process is likely to be lengthy, they put in place an immediate fix or work-around, and the problem solving is done offline.

To prevent the repetition of an observed anomaly, problem-solving teams use methods such as poka-yoke. This method was previously applied during process design to negate process vulnerabilities. Here, it is applied to prevent the future occurrence of an observed anomaly that was not anticipated. Poka-yoke, or "mistake-proofing," involves conceiving, designing, and installing a

[20] For guidance on how to use 6S to optimize a process, see Roll (2005).

[21] Definition adopted from the Council of Supply Chain Management Professionals (CSCMP).

method or a device that prevents an error in performance.[22]

Poka-yoke's use to eliminate special cause variation is triggered when the investigation of a performance anomaly uncovers human error as its cause. Problem solvers conceive and install a poka-yoke method or device that prevents such errors in the future. In this use, the inherent capabilities of the process are unchanged. The device simply ensures that the process will not be subject to an anomaly that detracts from the expression of its capabilities.

B. Establish Flow in All Value Streams

Flow describes a value stream through which work moves continuously as a single piece and at a pace that matches customer demand (takt).[23] It establishes a consistent rhythm for the process's operation and balances workloads across it. It ensures that only what is needed is produced without straining the capabilities of people or infrastructure. It also eliminates wait states, one example of waste (*muda*).

When work processes flow, there is no build-up of work-in-progress (WIP) inventory (mura), since each output moves continuously through the value stream. In its ideal state, there also is no need for final product inventory, as the rate of output matches the customer's demand for that output. People and machines are spared the strain of sudden surges in activity (muri) because work is balanced across the system and its demands are matched to their capabilities.

All of the improvements that flow introduces eliminate physical and financial waste and harm to contributors. For example, flow eliminates excess inventory, improves finances by shortening the cash-to-cash cycle (Bierley, 2008), and prevents work from overburdening people and causing fatigue-provoked injuries. Flow also ensures that customers have what they need in the quantity they require when they require it.

Following Womack and Jones (2003), the Life Enabling model dictates that a process must satisfy three conditions before it can be made to flow. Contributors

---

[22] Many people credit Shigeo Shingo (Robinson, 1997) as poka-yoke's originator. However, the use of such devices extends at least as far back as Frederick Taylor's famous efforts to optimize the performance of the Midvale Steel Works in the 1870s (Kanigel, 1997). His work, The *Principles of Scientific Management*, was translated into Japanese and published in Japan in 1913. This book was systematically studied, and Taylor's ideas were incorporated into management training in Japan from that date forward. Kanigel reported that "[s]oon, [Japanese] students, industrialists, and educators were making the pilgrimage to Boxly [Taylor's home] ... returning to Japan with the received gospel" (Kanigel, 1997, p. 491).

[23] In misguided applications of Lean thinking, flow has a different meaning. Yes, a product or service output moves through the business with no delays, but the pace of production is not dictated by customer demand (takt). Rather, it fits a schedule devised from other bases—e.g., the most cost-efficient rate at which to run one's machinery. In fact, in our experience, businesses implementing "flow" do not even compute takt time.

to a value stream must

1. view the value-adding activities that produce a function's final output as a single process;
2. recognize the importance of moving outputs as single units of production, not in batches; and
3. understand the pace of their customers' demand.

Flow is first introduced into a process when a value stream and its subordinate work processes are initially designed. But, once operational, it requires review and fine-tuning because circumstances change—for example, customer demand may increase or decrease or value stream improvements may modify a process's original design.

A Single Process

Contributors need to view the value-adding activities that produce a function's final output as a single process not segmented by specialty areas into different silos. For example, in a typical company producing custom-designed gas-producing plants for industry, the customer request through product receipt value stream is segmented into multiple independently implemented disciplines. The company's sales group performs the front-end discussions with customers. These discussions specify the plant to be delivered to the customer and decide the contract that will control its execution. The engineering design group controls the plant's physical design. The technology group controls the development of new technologies that engineering will include in the plant. The project management department manages the execution of the contract to specification, timeline, and budget. The construction group controls the building of the plant. The plant operations group controls the commissioning and transfer of the plant to the customer. Yet, it is only all these activities working together that can deliver to a customer what he or she needs, on time, and at the cost specified in the original contract. A balkanized approach to implementing a single production value stream creates discontinuities in thinking, promising, and execution that make the fulfillment process unstable. This instability leads to increased cost and failed timelines, and it frustrates both workers and customers. Flow requires breaking down the artificial barriers between discipline-based components of a single value stream. It requires considering a business function's production system as one value-adding stream of work.[24]

[24] A similar example can be constructed for the value stream depicting hospital-provided x-rays on an outpatient basis. An external physician orders the x-ray, client reception is controlled by the hospital's administrative services, client registration by its accounting services, provision of the x-ray and its interpretation by the hospital's radiology department, and delivery of the results by the referring physician. Typically, each party in this process has its own protocol and focuses on its own role.

The Superiority of Single Units Over Batches

People implementing each value stream must recognize the value of moving outputs as single units of production, not in batches. Batch processing works on multiple units as a group. The first unit in the group that is finished waits until the final unit in the group is done before it can move forward. Womack and Jones (2003) made the point that people's mindset, at least in businesses that deal with tangible goods, seems bent on seeing batch processing as more efficient than one-piece processing. These authors provided examples that clarify how reducing batch sizes and accomplishing the transformation of inputs to outputs for a single piece almost always maximizes efficiency and minimizes work-in-progress inventory. This occurs because you are not holding up the first piece of output in a batch until the last piece is finished.

Knowing Takt Time

The business as a whole must understand the pace of its customers' demand. This pace is called *takt time*. It specifies the rate at which an output must exit a business to satisfy customer demand. You use this information to synchronize all work processes within the production or service fulfillment value stream so that it produces outputs at a rate that ensures their availability when customers request them.[25]

While work can be balanced within a value stream without the use of takt times, the matching of output rate to customer demand is the only way to limit excess production (mura) and the pressure to increase production (muri).

Creating Flow

Once the prerequisite conditions for flow are satisfied, each business function within a Life Enabling enterprise establishes flow by involving a cross-functional team in analyzing the current state of flow in each workstream, beginning at the value stream level. It also involves members of the function's extended value stream, since changes in the pace or content of a function's value stream may require supply- or delivery-side adjustments. As with all activities, achieving flow requires maintaining a systems perspective.

The process used at each level from the value stream down through to workstations is similar. The first task contributors perform ensures that the workstream's sequence of major activities represents the critical path through the process. The critical path is the series of steps that must be executed *in sequence* in order for a process to finish. All other tasks in a process can be done *in*

[25] Members implementing enabling value streams must also understand the rate at which their outputs are required by each of the business functions they serve. Otherwise, they will fail to support the business function they are serving in maintaining its performance to takt.

parallel to this sequence. That is, they can be implemented while tasks on the critical path are being executed and completed before any task on the critical path needs their outputs.

The time consumed by all the tasks on the critical path determines the *minimum time* needed for an output to pass through the workstream. Once the critical path is revealed, the non-critical path activities become feeder processes that operate in parallel to the critical path.

Next, contributors identify and eliminate unnecessary operations within the workstream. They then seek to balance the time it takes to pass through each workstream operation by re-grouping work, if possible, into sets that minimize handoffs and can be accomplished with a timing that matches takt. Finally, they document the revised workstream.

Once work is regrouped, balanced, and documented, the flow team revises, as needed, the locations of work and the workplace layouts to minimize waste and ensure safe operation.

At the workstation level, the teams right-size machines, ensuring that the capability of each machine meets *but does not exceed* the needs of each workstation and that each machine's performance supports the process's performance to takt. Where one machine produces multiple outputs, teams quicken the changeover from producing one component on a machine to producing a different component on the same machine. Quickening the changeover activity eliminates waste (setup), reduces cycle time, and allows you to reduce batch sizes.

As a final step in establishing flow, each business function cross-trains its personnel to ensure that people can switch between roles if needed. This prevents the interruption of flow if one or another contributor is absent.

Throughout this effort to establish flow, contributors use waste-removal events like 6S and Kaizen to support its establishment. Their efforts eliminate waste that detracts from the process's delivery of maximum value to customers.

As a last point, recognize two facts. First, absolute flow is an ideal state you strive to realize but may never achieve. There may be practical barriers due, for example, to the current state of the technologies you employ that prevent flow's full realization. Nonetheless, you pursue it. You challenge every barrier to flow's accomplishment that you encounter with the intent of ultimately removing it. Second, recognize that every change in the design of a process requires that the process's standardized work documentation be updated and that the modified process be made stable.

C. Establish Pull in All Value Streams

Pull means that customer demand activates the value stream's operation. In a pull system, action is triggered from the value stream's endpoint back to its beginning. A customer order (or shipped product), for example, cascades a signal backwards through the production value stream. This signal triggers production and replenishment activities from the last workstation to its preceding workstation.[26] As each workstation produces its output, it signals the need for a new input from its supplying workstation(s). This "finish, pass forward, signal backward, and be replenished" sequence is the cycle of a pull system.

Pull contrasts with the typical "push" approach to production and replenishment in non-service industries.[27] With the push approach, activity is *driven* by targets and schedules that are based on factors such as machine sizing, changeover times, and supply availability. The intent is to operate the production system with maximum efficiency from an accounting perspective. At best, the factors that drive a push approach only partially relate to customer demand.

Once flow is established, pull is implemented by creating a system of signals (termed kanbans) that start at the fulfillment end of the value stream and trigger the startup of earlier operations (in-process or production kanban). The kanban system is extended to supplier operations (materials or transport kanban). A combined production and materials kanban system is termed an integrated kanban system. Together, this system carries the signal of customer demand back through the value stream and out to its suppliers.

By establishing pull, a business further reduces its inventory needs and improves its cash-to-cash cycle. It lowers its costs and can therefore lower the cost of its offering to its customers. A waste-free pull system, however, is not achievable without having first established flow. Only then can a process operate continuously at a pace dictated by customer demand (Womack and Jones, 2003).

D. Optimize the Performance of All Value Streams and Subprocesses

Optimizing the performance of every value stream and its subordinate work processes involves three activities. First, you eliminate all remaining traditionally

[26] Replenishment refers to restocking a workstation with the unit of work in progress produced by its preceding workstation and any other materials it uses to complete the production of its contribution to the value stream.

[27] In service industries, pull is always present. No one can initiate a service operation until a customer requests it. An automotive repair shop cannot initiate an oil change for your car until you deliver your car to it and request the service. Neither can a healthcare provider respond to a person's illness until the person presents him- or herself and requests care. The challenge in the service sector is to be available to serve when service is needed. This is the challenge of making the service flow. On the other hand, the supply processes associated with service delivery (restocking materials, for example) will generally not be pulled, and those areas should be targeted for implementing pull.

defined waste in every business setting and operation.[28] Second, you drive out common cause variation. And, third, you continuously reduce the cost to the customer for the product or service you provide while not compromising the value delivered.

Waste Elimination

Waste is eliminated by each contributor's performance of daily kaizen and through special improvement events. In daily kaizen, each contributor detects instances of waste. This occurs continuously at every workstation in every workplace. The contributor records each instance on a display set up in the work area for this purpose. On a daily or weekly basis, contributors in that work area meet to discuss what team members have found. They select items to remedy and problem solve how to eliminate them.

Waste is also eliminated by periodically recycling special Kaizen events (Vitalo, Butz, and Vitalo, 2003) on each process. These are multi-day, teamed workplace and work process improvement activities. The Kaizen team includes representatives from all affected parties. The team assesses the current state of the workplace and work process, identifies opportunities for improvement, devises ways to make those improvements, verifies that improvements will have no negative impact on interconnecting processes, implements the changes, and measures their effects. After the event, the team reports to contributors and stakeholders what was learned, what improvements were made, and what results were produced. Each event leaves behind a set of measures with which to monitor the sustained use of the improvement and the benefits it generates. The measures and findings are openly displayed in the workplace. They allow people to experience pride in their improvement efforts, and should implementation or benefits fall off, they trigger a round of problem solving to remedy the fall-off.

Reduction in Common Cause Variation

To reduce common cause variation, you need to uncover the hidden variables that affect a process's baseline performance. You use research to accomplish this end. Ideas for research come from different sources. They arise from suggestion systems that contributors use to advance their thinking about ways to improve the business. They emerge from studying relevant professional literature or from attending presentations at professional conferences in the different areas of expertise a process uses. They also come from team members as a result of their participation in improvement events meant to eliminate waste. Finally,

---

[28] The traditional list of waste types includes hazards, interruptions, inventory, motion, rework, search, setup, travel/transport, and wait (Vitalo, Butz, and Vitalo, 2003).

they come from laboratory-based scientific investigation that generates ideas about possible sources of variation.

As your research uncovers new possible sources of baseline variation, you test your hypotheses and, if they prove valid, explore ways to control them. This may involve experimentation with new materials, methods, or equipment. When solutions are uncovered, the revised process is treated as a new design. It is subjected to the same set of activities previously described for developing, finalizing, and fielding new processes.

As you eliminate common cause variation, you improve the precision of a process's typical output. You increase the useful yield from that process. This eliminates waste.

Lowering Cost to Customers

Both waste removal and, usually, the elimination of common cause variation reduce the cost of your offering to your customers. It is possible, however, that a process that produces the ideal output *every time, waste-free* can still be improved from a cost perspective. For example, an innovation in a product's design, materials, or production methods may further reduce cost without affecting any other value delivered. New technologies may provide the opportunity to produce an offering of equal customer value less expensively or replace an offering with a totally different solution that is equally beneficial to the customer but less expensive. Since cost to the customer is a universal "Satisfier" value, every reduction in cost that does not reduce other valued features of an offering adds an increment in customer satisfaction. Hence, when all other aspects of operational perfection are realized, research into ways to further reduce cost should still be pursued.

The ultimate way to reduce cost to customers, as mentioned previously, is to eliminate the customer's need for your offering. This solution optimizes the enterprise as a whole as it fulfills the ultimate purpose of its commerce.

E. Broadcast the Use of the Model Across All Extended Value Streams

Each business function helps its supply and delivery agents understand and use the Life Enabling model to better their own success. It also works with its other stakeholders to realize the same end. This effort with supply and delivery chain members builds on their already demonstrated alignment with your enterprise's purpose and approach. It was their alignment with your purpose and their business capabilities that was the basis for their selection to be members of the function's extended value stream.

All business functions should employ a variety of methods to support their supply and delivery chain members' use of the model. They should exchange on-site visits to improve understanding of one another's operations. They should share education and training programs, allowing their partners to participate in their in-house training programs. They should provide on-site coaching of each partner's efforts to optimize their Operations. Each business function also should encourage partners to participate in the improvement efforts it conducts on its own operations.

Through these multiple methods, each business function supports its supply and delivery agents in making their processes stable, establishing flow and pull in their value streams, and optimizing all their operations. The introduction of flow within these members' processes ensures that they deliver to their customers—including your enterprise—what is needed, when it is needed, and in the quantity each requires.

With the introduction of pull within every external member's processes, the Life Enabling enterprise is able to transform its internal kanban system into an integrated kanban system that extends from itself out to its extended value stream members. With this improvement, just-in-time performance[29] becomes better realized. As each external member's own value stream is elevated, the Life Enabling enterprise's current Operations are further improved.

With regard to other function-specific stakeholders, your purpose should be to educate them on your use of the Life Enabling model. Begin by using your understanding of each stakeholder's expectations and concerns to guide you in educating each stakeholder about how your enterprise is addressing their interests, meeting their expectations, and handling their concerns. Always involve each stakeholder by gathering their input on any issue you intend to address that affects them. Share with them how you will use that input and obtain their feedback. Work with them to uncover the best solution that will advance your enterprise and meet their needs. Remember always that their positive involvement in your work is essential to your success.

As stakeholders express their interest in your enterprise, help them understand its purpose and approach. Share with them its effects on the people who implement it and who receive its value-adding outputs. Show them its operating efficiencies and how it fulfills its purpose and satisfies its model's core values. Help

---

[29] Just-in-time performance means that the quantity of on-site inputs matches your immediate need, there is no build-up of work in progress, and the volume you produce exactly matches customer demand. No resources wait around to be processed. No performers wait for materials they need to do their work.

them see how their use of its approach could further their success in accomplishing their purposes. Finally, support them in learning how to apply the Life Enabling model in their endeavors *should they be interested in doing so.*

6. Strive for Perfection at the Operations Level

Learning continuously improves the implementation of each of the six tasks that make up Operations' cycle of performance (Exhibit 5, next page). It elevates both the methods and the means by which each activity is performed, each task's outcomes, and the results the entire cycle produces.

- It increases the speed and effectiveness with which customer values and stakeholder expectations and concerns are recognized and understood.
- It deepens and extends people's understanding of what managing from a systems perspective means and how to better apply that understanding.
- It improves how products and processes are designed and vetted so that they deliver greater value to customers from their first implementation.
- It elevates the enterprise's methods and means for establishing waste-free, optimized processes across all extended value streams.
- It refines and extends people's understanding of how to generate and leverage learning and use that knowledge to improve how Operations strives for perfection.

Understanding Customers

By applying new learning, you create faster and more accurate ways to gauge your customers' experience of your offering and the buying–benefiting experience you provide and their changing needs and wants. Faster gauging of your customers' experience enables you to respond more rapidly to changes in customer experience and better anticipate and respond to new customers needs. More accurate registering of your customers' values enables you to translate those values into more precise critical-to-quality metrics (CTQs). New learning also enables you to improve how you apply CTQs to the production of your offering and the shaping of the customers' buying–benefiting. Finally, new learning improves how your enterprise disseminates customer values information to its contributors so they use the most up-to-date information in their decision making and action.

Understanding Stakeholders

New learning enables you to improve the speed and accuracy of your understanding of your stakeholders' interests, expectations, and concerns. It accelerates your ability to gauge their experience of how responsive you are being to their perspectives. It improves your effectiveness in engaging and involving your stakeholders in working together to ensure that your function satisfies their expectations and addresses their concerns. Finally, it increases your ability to discover better ways to benefit your stakeholders while maximizing the delivery of value to your customers.

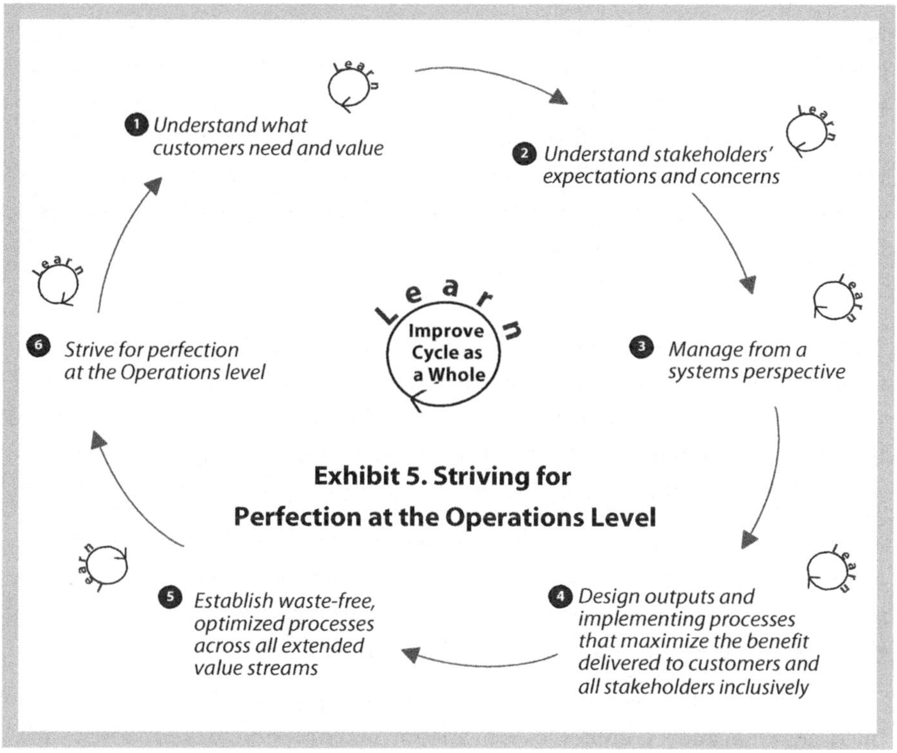

Exhibit 5. Striving for Perfection at the Operations Level

Managing Systems

Contributors improve their understanding and implementation of managing from a systems perspective in several ways. They explore the concept of managing from a systems perspective to develop new insights into its meaning and derive new principles and methods to guide its implementation. They develop through personal learning and research ways to improve their teamwork across each system. An element of that personal learning derives from analyzing feedback from other system members on how well each contributor currently recognizes and supports each other contributor's work.

Contributors also improve their understanding of how different roles and activities interact within and across business functions. The new insights they develop expand their awareness of their system's members and how each is affected by their own decisions and actions. Finally, they use their learning to improve their personal decision making with regard to performing their own roles.

Designing Products and Processes

With regard to designing products, contributors explore and develop new ways to better conceive initial solutions to customer needs. They use learning to improve how they incorporate customer-valued features and satisfy the values customers seek. They also use learning to improve how they advance conceptual solutions through to detailed designs, prototypes, and testing into maximally value-adding offerings. Similarly, with regard to designing processes, they explore and develop new ways to make the cycle of development more efficient and render its outcome more certain of success.

Eliminating Waste and Optimizing Processes

With regard to improving waste removal from all operations, contributors develop and share insights into the nature of waste and how it might better be detected. They improve their waste removal techniques. These improvements speed the implementation of waste removal activities, broaden their application, and render them more effective.

Contributors also improve the effectiveness of the suggestion systems they use to collect, analyze, and follow through on the improvement ideas they share. And they discover ways to more effectively transfer learning across the organization so that processes everywhere are more quickly optimized.

Contributors also sharpen their skills in designing and implementing studies on the factors that affect common cause variation and how best to control that variation. They use learning from the implementation of previous pilot programs to better construct and execute future pilots of improved methods and processes.

Finally, contributors uncover ways to improve how they engage and involve the external members of their extended value streams and all other stakeholders. With improved engagement and involvement, they better extend waste removal and optimization efforts across each function's extended value stream. These efforts enhance their members' ability to apply Life Enabling thinking in their own Operations. As they do so, they better support your Life Enabling enterprise while realizing their own company goals.

Striving for Perfection

Improving how one strives for perfection means that the methods used for learning itself are subject to analysis. This analysis uncovers ways to improve how people extract, test, and deploy new learning. This investigation also focuses on how to better enable people to generate, share, and leverage learning within and across Operations and throughout every business function's extended value streams. The insights and solutions people generate are used to improve all of Operations' striving for perfection.

This chapter describes the resources critical to producing Operations' results. It also clarifies the essential features that each resource must possess. This knowledge guides you in selecting the people needed to implement Operations' guidance and building the infrastructure required for them to successfully accomplish Operations' activities and generate its expected results.

Chapter 12

Preview of the Model's Guidance

Exhibit 1, beginning on the next page, overviews Operations' critical-to-success resources. Use it to preview the contents that this chapter discusses.

Operations' Critical-to-Success Resources

Resources critical to Operations' success are those essential to accomplishing the six activities (page 302) that ensure it produces its expected results. An analysis of these tasks reveals the following:

- All six tasks are largely intellectual and social as opposed to physical in nature.
- All tasks are implemented using a team approach.
- All the tasks require ongoing communication between members, since the tasks are done as a team.
- All the tasks require developing or gathering knowledge and information and storing, retrieving, and sharing it across the enterprise.

It becomes clear from this analysis that the critical-to-success resources for Operations mirror those required to accomplish the model's Strategic component. They are people, the knowledge and information they develop and use in accomplishing their work, and the infrastructure essential to enabling ongoing communication between them and their sharing of the knowledge and information they develop and use.

People

The qualities people need to successfully implement a Life Enabling enterprise's Operations component are subsets of those defined at the Strategic level. The Strategic-level qualities required to implement the Life Enabling model are detailed in *Chapter 9*, pages 247–251. An analysis of the activities people must perform at the Operations level within a Life Enabling enterprise adds additional requirements.

Knowledge Mastery

- Flow and pull – This knowledge enables a person to define each state and explain each state's purpose and benefits and the concepts, principles, and methods associated with establishing flow and pull in a work process.
- Information and its value – This knowledge enables a person to define what information is, describe the uses to which it is applied within a Life Enabling enterprise, and explain how information is developed, tested, documented, refined, and extended.

Exhibit 1. The Resources Needed to Accomplish Operations Activities Successfully

<table>
<tr><td>Resources</td><td>People
To the qualities of character and specific competencies detailed in Chapter 9, add the following list of knowledge and skills.
Mastery of the following knowledge:
▪ flow and pull,
▪ information and its value,
▪ knowledge and its value,
▪ systems and how they are improved, and
▪ variation, including its types and how to eliminate it.
Proficiency in the skills of:
▪ affirmatively adding value,
▪ analyzing variation and testing hypotheses,
▪ designing and conducting experiments,
▪ distinguishing knowledge from information,
▪ establishing flow and pull,
▪ gathering and representing knowledge,
▪ helping,
▪ identifying members of one's local system,
▪ improving systems,
▪ information processing, and
▪ root cause analysis.
Knowledge
All items listed in the Strategic component of the Life Enabling model (pages 255–256), plus job descriptions and team charters. A job description defines a role's purpose, responsibilities, authorities, resources, reporting relationship, coordination, performance expectations, and competency requirements. It provides the knowledge an incumbent uses to prepare to successfully accomplish his or her expected contribution to the business. It educates the person about what his or her role is, how it needs to be performed, what it must produce, and the competencies required for effectiveness.
Information
All items listed in the Strategic component of the Life Enabling model (pages 255–256). In addition, every performer must have the information that connects current customer and stakeholder values information to the features of the business's offering and its buying–benefiting experience
Continued ...</td></tr>
</table>

Exhibit 1. The Resources Needed to Accomplish Operations Activities Successfully (continued)

Resources (continued)	**Information (cont'd)** that they address. Team charter information performs a role analogous to a job description but for a single team. It documents each team's goal, its responsibilities, and how it will accomplish both. It sets the team's direction and accountability. It aids efficient team operation by resolving up front basic decisions about the team's responsibilities and methods. It serves as an effective tool for orienting new members— as well as non-members—about the team. **Communications Infrastructure** As described in the Strategic component of the Life Enabling model (pages 256–257). In addition, it needs to seamlessly interface with three systems essential for realizing Operations' success. These are the Knowledge Management and Sharing System (KMSS), the Businesswide Suggestion System (BwSS), and the Functional Measurement and Feedback System (FM&FS). KMSS ensures that contributors can share the knowledge they uncover, develop, or create to improve their performance and the performance of the enterprise as a whole. It is also the repository for all other knowledge documents, including the standardized work documents for every process. The BwSS collects and processes ideas for improvement from contributors that apply to the organization as a whole or to processes other than the ones that the idea's contributor is involved in implementing. The FM&FS supplies the information needed to assess the current status and progress of all performers and business activities and guide contributors in realizing success at every level of performance. It must satisfy the requirements specified in the model's Strategic component (pages 257–258), as amplified in *Chapter 13*.

- Knowledge and its value – This knowledge enables a person to define what knowledge is, explain how it differs from information, describe the uses to which knowledge is applied within a Life Enabling enterprise, and explain how it is developed, tested, refined, and extended.
- Systems and how they are improved – This knowledge equips a person to explain what a system is and the types of systems that exist. It enables people to understand what it means to say that a commercial organization is an open, dynamic system. It clarifies why social systems, like a commercial organization, are the most complex of all systems to understand and manage. It makes clear why complex systems must be managed from a

basis of knowledge. Finally, it provides a person with the principles that guide managing from a systems perspective. People who master this knowledge can correctly define the scope and membership of every system at every level within an organization. They can explain the role of each component in a system, why conflicts between components must be avoided, and how system performance is improved.

- Variation, including its types and how to eliminate it – This knowledge enables a person to appreciate the challenge a business faces in representing the performance of people and processes over time. It explains the need for the use of statistics to describe performance and predict what a process will produce, with what degree of likelihood, how fast, and at what cost. It equips the person with an understanding of the types of variation that performance may evidence (special and common cause), how to discriminate which is being observed, and what response is effective to eliminate each. It makes clear the importance of acquiring competence in the statistics of variation (see below).

Skill Proficiencies

- Affirmatively adding value – These skills include the use of quality function deployment (QFD),[1] building values frameworks, and defining critical-to-quality metrics, among others. They enable a person to apply his or her understanding of customer values to add features to an offering and to the customer's buying–benefiting experience that maximize the benefit delivered to customers and their satisfaction.
- Analyzing variation and testing hypotheses – These competencies are required to detect, measure, and represent variation and interpret its type. They permit a person to compare an observed status to an expected result and detect whether the observed difference is significant. They also enable us to design experiments to test possible sources of common cause variation and ways to eliminate it. These skills are required for stabilizing work processes and researching ways to optimize their performance. They are also used when collecting and analyzing customer and stakeholder values and measuring and evaluating current performance at every level in the enterprise.

---

[1] QFD is a criterion-based approach to selecting what to improve in an output or process. It uses an evaluation matrix to assess proposed or existing features of an offering or work process against customer values and other decision criteria. The criteria you use when implementing this method must be consistent with the dictates of the Life Enabling model. Many, if not most, examples of the application of QFD do not satisfy this requirement.

- Designing and conducting experiments – These skills enable a person to uncover the factors that affect the performance of people and systems, test ways to control their behavior so that they better enable successful performance, and develop new knowledge that enables the elimination of common cause variation.
- Distinguishing knowledge from information – This skill allows a person to accurately label information and knowledge when presented with examples of each. It ensures that one's ability to verbally describe the difference between these resources translates into behaviorally correct discriminations between examples of these different resources.
- Establishing flow and pull—This set of skills enables a person to define the critical path for a workflow, streamline its operations, eliminate all waste within it, balance workloads across the workflow, estimate takt time, establish a pace of operation that matches takt, enable a process to transform inputs to outputs as single units, and have the process be triggered by customer demand.
- Gathering and representing knowledge – Knowledge-gathering skills enable a person to rapidly and accurately learn from another individual the concepts, principles, and methods that individual has mastered. Knowledge representation skills enable one to record ideas for transfer and application by others in a manner that facilitates their learning and successful use. Life Enabling enterprises advance their success by their members learning and applying the knowledge each develops. The efficient and effective acquisition and documentation of knowledge are critical to the success of this strategy. Performers need to understand how to gather and record both procedural and decision knowledge.[2] Procedural knowledge guides one in accomplishing an instrumental task. A work process map is an example of documented procedural knowledge. Decision knowledge guides one in determining what action to take in a given situation. A decision tree is an example of documented decision knowledge.
- Helping – Helping skills enable a person to assist others in exploring, understanding, and resolving problems that hinder their personal success. They include responding, personalizing, and initiating skills (Carkhuff, 1977). Responding goes beyond clarifying and confirming the words another person speaks. It expresses an understanding of the meaning of those words and the feeling that meaning engenders in the person sharing

---

[2] See examples in *Appendix F: Templates for Knowledge Documents.*

them. Personalizing communicates one's understanding of the implications of what another person is experiencing for how the person sees him- or herself, what the person's goals and aspirations are, and how the person judges his or her ability to accomplish them. Initiating skills enable a person to help identify a course of action that will resolve the person's problem, set a goal for accomplishing that action, plan a way to achieve that goal, and act on it.

- Identifying members of one's local system – This skill enables a person to identify all the associates who are members of the person's local system. These people either affect or are affected by the person's work. Each performer must be conscious of the members of his or her local system and work in a mutually enabling way with them.
- Improving systems – These skills enable one to elevate the performance of a system by mapping, analyzing, and improving its performance as a whole.
- Information processing – With this skill, a person is able to identify the information he or she needs to resolve an issue; gather and validate that information; and systematically analyze, organize, and interpret its meaning. It is used to understand customer values and stakeholder perspectives and in all information-based problem-solving and decision-making activities. Proficiency in information processing skills infuses one's thinking, deciding, and acting with facts that are relevant and reliable and therefore support one's effectiveness.
- Root cause analysis – This set of skills enables a person to identify and describe the reasons why a particular performance outcome occurred. Examples of this skill include fishbone analysis, the 5 Whys method, Cause Analysis of Human Performance (Vitalo, 2020), and fault tree analysis. The outcome being analyzed may be the result produced by a system or a person. Root cause analysis is essential to solving problems because it identifies what factor(s) generated the problem and therefore must be eliminated in order for the problem to be corrected. It is one of a suit of skills that are subsumed under information-based problem solving. It is selected here for specific focus because there are a wide variety of methods for accomplishing root cause analysis. These methods vary in their complexity and application to different types of problems. Operations personnel need to be aware of these different approaches, their specialized uses, and how to implement them.

Knowledge and Information

The second critical-to-success resource is the documented knowledge and information one needs to produce Operations' expected results.

Knowledge

The documented knowledge needed to guide performance at the Operations level includes all the elements listed in the Life Enabling model's Strategic component (pages 251–254), with the addition of job descriptions.

A job description documents a role's purpose, responsibilities, authorities, resources, reporting relationship, coordination, performance expectations, and competency requirements. It provides the knowledge that all incumbents of that job use to prepare themselves to successfully perform the role. It educates them about what the role is, how it needs to be performed, what it must produce, and the competencies required for effectiveness. It contributes to stabilizing each incumbent's performance and making it consistent across the different people who implement the same role. It is also a key resource for developing recruitment, selection, and training programs that ensure the best candidate for a role is engaged and enabled to perform successfully.[3]

Information

The information needed to guide performance at the Operations level includes all the elements listed in the Life Enabling model's Strategic component (pages 255–256), with the addition of two new elements:

- information that connects current customer values to the features of the business's offering and its buying–benefiting experience that each addresses,
- information that connects current stakeholder values to the features of the business's offering and its buying–benefiting experience that each addresses, and
- team charter information (described on pages 403 and 404).

The values-related information enables the enterprise to eliminate unwanted features, add wanted features, and judge to what degree a feature currently satisfies its related values. It also enables performers to see the value-adding relevance of what his or her work produces. Chapter *Task 3 Understanding Customer Values* in *The Lean Champion Resource Guide* (Vitalo, Bujak, Vitalo, Bierley, et al., 2023) provides guidance for associating customer and stakeholder values to the features of the business's offering and its buying-benefiting experience.

[3] Job descriptions are discussed further in *Chapter 14*, beginning on page 398, under the topic of *Position Management*.

The team charter information performs a role analogous to a job description but for a single team. It documents each team's goal, its responsibilities, and how it will accomplish both. It sets the team's direction and accountability. It aids efficient team operation by resolving up front basic decisions about the team's responsibilities and methods. It serves as an effective tool for orienting new members—as well as nonmembers—about the team.

Communications Infrastructure

The third critical-to-success resource is a communications infrastructure sufficient to enable people to work together to accomplish goals, improve business operations, share learning, and leverage the products of their improvement efforts across the enterprise. This infrastructure must exhibit the same capabilities at the Operations level as required at the Strategic level (pages 256–257). In addition, it needs to seamlessly interface with three systems essential for realizing Operations' success: the Knowledge Management and Sharing System (KMSS), the Business-wide Suggestion System (BwSS), and the Functional Measurement and Feedback System (FM&FS).

Knowledge Management and Sharing System (KMSS)

The KMSS ensures that contributors can store, retrieve, update, and share the knowledge they uncover, develop, or create to improve their performance and that of the enterprise. It is also a repository for all other knowledge documents that support Life Enabling enterprise. Especially relevant to Operations, it provides for the documentation, storage, retrieval, and updating of standardized work documents for every work process. KMSS is described in greater detail in *Chapter 13*.

Businesswide Suggestion System (BwSS)

The BwSS collects and processes business improvement ideas from contributors that apply to the organization as a whole or to processes other than the ones that the idea contributor is involved in implementing. The system gathers these ideas, supports their review and discussion, tracks their modification, monitors their implementation and the results they produce, and provides feedback to their originators about each idea's disposition. BwSS is described in greater detail in *Chapter 13*.

Functional Measurement and Feedback System (FM&FS)

FM&FS supplies the information needed to assess the current status and progress of all performers and business activities and guides contributors in realizing success at every level of performance. It must satisfy the requirements specified in the model's Strategic component (pages 257–258), as amplified in *Chapter 13*.

The Framework of a Commercial Model and the Knowledge Contained Within Each of Its Components

Component	Results	Activities	Resources
Executive Functions	Specifies the results that Executive Functions must realize. These results always include (1) effectiveness, (2) sufficiency, and (3) synergy. Effectiveness means the organization consistently advances towards realizing its purpose. Sufficiency refers to the presence, engagement, and effective contribution of efforts by each person needed to realize the business's aims. Synergy means that those efforts integrate efficiently to accomplish the organization's purposes.	Guides one in the proper implementation of the management activities that accomplish the Executive Functions.	Guides one in defining what critical-to-success resources are required to implement the Executive Functions successfully and the essential features each must possess.

Section IV

The Executive Functions Component of the Life Enabling Model

Executive Functions keep the organization whole, capable, viable, and accomplishing its purpose. This section details the results that these functions must deliver, the activities that produce those results, and the resources needed to successfully implement those activities.

Every successful human endeavor requires two levels of activity. One level is technical performance. The second level is executive performance. The level of technical performance accomplishes the work that results in achieving the endeavor's goal. It applies the specific knowledge, skills, and proficiencies that complete the tasks that produce an output. A commercial endeavor requires many areas of technical performance to achieve its end. These include, among others, product development, marketing, finance, purchasing, logistics, production, and product support. The level of executive performance manages the endeavor as a whole. It is a meta-level focus that detects whether one's endeavor is making progress, identifies and removes barriers to progress, and adjusts one's approach to accommodate unexpected circumstances. It also ensures that a cooperative enterprise has the contributors it needs to accomplish its purpose and that they are working together effectively. Success in any endeavor is not achievable in a reliable way without both levels of activity. Without effective technical performance, nothing of substance *can be produced.* Without effective executive performance, nothing of substance *will be produced reliably.* This chapter reviews the functions that accomplish executive performance. It also provides the Life Enabling model's guidance for the first of these functions: Realizing Effectiveness.

Chapter 13

A Review of Executive Performance

As described in *Chapter 3*, there are three distinct executive functions: effectiveness, sufficiency, and synergy. Each is essential for maintaining an enterprise as a whole, capable, viable, and achieving endeavor.

- Effectiveness – This function ensures that the enterprise is demonstrably advancing toward fulfilling the aims it has defined. The executive activities that relate to effectiveness include defining purpose, setting goals, developing business plans, solving organizational problems, and improving organizational performance.
- Sufficiency – This function ensures the presence, engagement, and success of each person needed to accomplish an enterprise's purpose. The executive activities that relate to sufficiency assess the organization's people needs and acquire/develop, deploy, enable, involve, and ensure the success of each of its contributors. In an individual endeavor, they maintain the performer's focus, energy, competence, and achievement.
- Synergy – This function ensures the integration of efforts among all contributors to a cooperative endeavor. Within a Life Enabling enterprise, this means all contributors working together as a team, causing their collective efforts to produce an effect greater than the sum of their individual effects. The executive activities of communication and coordination as well as other actions that support teamwork are critical for realizing synergy.

An organization remains whole, capable, viable, and achieving when it has the people it needs to accomplish its purpose engaged fully, performing effectively, and working together in a manner that synergistically advances its success. Absent any of these elements, an organization dissipates, and its prospects of success evaporate.[1]

Realizing Effectiveness

The model's guidance for implementing the Executive Function of Effectiveness defines its purpose (above) and specifies who performs the function. It also describes what results the function must produce, the activities that accomplish those results, and the resources critical for realizing Effectiveness (Exhibit 1, beginning on the next page).

Who Performs the Executive Function of Effectiveness?

In a Capitalist enterprise, the task of realizing Effectiveness is assigned to specially designated "management" roles. Each executive/manager/supervisor is

[1] See pages 70–79 for a complete description of Executive Functions.

Exhibit 1. Summary of Guidance for the Executive Function of Effectiveness

Purpose	Ensure that the enterprise is demonstrably advancing toward fulfilling the aims it has defined.
Who Performs the Function	Every contributor to a Life Enabling enterprise is responsible for performing the function of Effectiveness. This responsibility is detailed in the role each contributor must perform, specifically in Tasks 1 through 4 (page 274). Some specialized Effectiveness tasks (e.g., the yearly Policy Planning and Deployment process) are the primary responsibility of specific teams. Nonetheless, every member of the organization actively participates in each of these activities and retains responsibility for ensuring that each team completes its work in conformance with the dictates of the Life Enabling model.
Expected Results	A Life Enabling enterprise is deemed "effective" when it realizes all the Strategic and Operations outcomes the model specifies. Short of this end, consistent progress toward realizing these outcomes indicates that the organization is advancing on success. Such progress may be monitored using the following metrics: ▪ percentage of Strategic results metrics that meet or exceed their targets, ▪ percentage of Operations results metrics that meet or exceed their targets, ▪ positive slope of the line of best fit for the degree of success in Strategic goals across the last five years (assumes maximum result not reached), and ▪ positive slope of the line of best fit for the degree of success in Operations goals across the last five years (assumes maximum result not reached).
Activities	1. Define the enterprise's business intent. 2. Build the infrastructure components essential for achieving Effectiveness. 3. Define the enterprise's yearly business plan and its continuous improvement plan. 4. Monitor the implementation of the organization's business and continuous improvement plans. 5. Detect and remove barriers hindering progress in accomplishing the enterprise's yearly plans. *Continued ...*

Exhibit 1. Summary of Guidance for the Executive Function of Effectiveness (continued)

Activities (continued)	6. Detect and realize opportunities for accelerating progress in accomplishing the enterprise's yearly plans. 7. Conduct the organization's yearly Renewal exercise.
Critical-to-Success Resources	All resources previously identified in the Strategic and Operations components, plus a Businesswide Suggestion System and a Knowledge Management and Sharing System.

responsible for the effectiveness of that portion of the enterprise over which he or she has authority. In a Life Enabling enterprise, every contributor is responsible for performing the function of Effectiveness. This responsibility is detailed in the common role each contributor must perform, specifically in Tasks 1 through 4 (page 274).

At every level of the enterprise, from the organization as a whole through each business function to each individual's workstation, every individual performs each of the activities that achieve the Executive Function of Effectiveness. As a manager of his or her own performance, each contributor ensures the effective execution of his or her specific role. Also, as an owner/member of the enterprise, each contributor assumes responsibility for ensuring the success of the enterprise as a whole.

Some specialized activities that are implemented in realizing Effectiveness are the designated responsibility of specific teams. The business leadership team, for example, is responsible for overseeing the completion of organization-wide tasks like the yearly Policy Planning and Deployment process. That team alone has representatives from every function within the enterprise and therefore is in the best position to initiate the process and integrate its final products. Nonetheless, every member of the organization actively participates in that activity and remains responsible for ensuring that it is carried out in a manner consistent with the dictates of the Life Enabling model.

The Results Effectiveness Must Produce

A Life Enabling enterprise is deemed "effective" when it realizes all the Strategic and Operations outcomes the model specifies. Short of this end, consistent progress toward realizing these outcomes indicates that the organization is advancing toward success.[2] Exhibit 2 suggests metrics one might use to judge Effectiveness.

[2] See Exhibit 1, pages 193–194, for the model's expected Strategic outcomes and Exhibit 1, page 287,

They gauge an enterprise's status on Effectiveness both in an absolute sense and in terms of progress toward absolute success.

When realized, Effectiveness energizes the collective performance of all contributors, as it either satisfies completely each contributor's personal and commercial purposes or gives evidence that satisfaction will occur. Increasing success, net of contextual factors, also confirms that people are learning from their performance and continuously improving their individual and collective efforts. Such learning elevates each contributor's pride of workmanship and confirms his or her personal growth.

Exhibit 2. Success Criteria for Gauging the Results Produced by the Executive Function of Effectiveness

Anchor	Measure	Target
Effectiveness		
Enterprise accomplishes its Strategic and Operations outcomes or demonstrates progress toward realizing them	▪ Percentage of Strategic results metrics that meet or exceed their targets	▪ 100%
	▪ Percentage of Operations results metrics that meet or exceed their targets	▪ 100%
	▪ Positive slope of the line of best fit for the degree of success in Strategic goals across the last five years (assumes maximum result not reached)	▪ True
	▪ Positive slope of the line of best fit for the degree of success in Operations goals across the last five years (assumes maximum result not reached)	▪ True

The Activities That Accomplish Effectiveness

Seven tasks accomplish the Executive Function of Effectiveness. The first two tasks are first performed at the startup of the enterprise and then maintained regularly. Tasks 3 through 7 are recycled on a yearly basis.

1. Define the enterprise's business intent.
2. Build the infrastructure components essential for achieving Effectiveness.
3. Define the enterprise's yearly business plan and its continuous improvement plan.
4. Monitor the implementation of the organization's business and continuous improvement plans.

---

for its expected Operations outcomes.

5. Detect and remove barriers hindering progress in accomplishing the enterprise's yearly plans.
6. Detect and realize opportunities for accelerating progress in accomplishing the enterprise's yearly plans.
7. Conduct the organization's yearly Renewal exercise.

These seven tasks steer the enterprise as a whole. By implementing these tasks, contributors define and continuously refine the enterprise's business intent. They establish and maintain the infrastructure needed to support its achievement. They set goals that guide technical changes at the Strategic, Operations, and Executive Functions levels and define the enterprise's continuous improvement objectives. They prioritize these goals and cascade discussion and achievement of them interactively with contributors throughout the organization. Every business function at every level of its performance personalizes these goals and creates its specific action plan to achieve them.

Together, contributors monitor the implementation of the enterprise's business and continuous improvement plans, detect and remove systemic barriers to progress, and detect and realize systemic opportunities to accelerate their implementation and elevate their successful achievement.

Each year, contributors implement an end-of-year enterprise-wide Renewal process. This process analyzes the business's effectiveness for the year ended, understands the sources of its success and the factors that hindered even greater success, extracts learning, and defines how that learning should be applied to improve next year's performance. It serves as one of the two major inputs to creating the enterprise's going-forward business and continuous improvement plans (Task 3).

Activity 1. Define the Enterprise's Business Intent

The business intent defines the end toward which the Executive Function of Effectiveness steers the enterprise. It records the enterprise's purpose, its vision, its core values, how it defines profit, the stakeholders the enterprise recognizes, and its relationship with each. The enterprise's purpose states what the business will produce for exchange, with whom, where, and why. The company's business intent also specifies the outcomes the business must produce at the Strategic level.

Activity 2. Build the Infrastructure Components Essential for Achieving Effectiveness

The infrastructure essential for realizing Effectiveness includes the following list of components:

- A standardized work document to guide each of the following activities:
  - building, improving, and disseminating standardized work;
  - performing problem solving and decision making using either information- or knowledge-based methods;
  - implementing the yearly Renewal System; and
  - implementing the yearly Policy Planning and Deployment process (Hoshin Kanri)
- An organizational structure as defined by the Life Enabling model.
- A communications infrastructure that includes
  - a Businesswide Suggestion System,
  - a Functional Measurement and Feedback System that supplies the performance information needed at every level to guide personal and organizational improvement efforts, and
  - a Knowledge Management and Sharing System that provides a central institutional repository for the enterprise's knowledge capital.

Standardized Work Documents

You must create standardized work documents to guide contributors in building, improving, and disseminating standardized work documents for processes; solving problems and making decisions; and implementing the yearly Renewal and Policy Planning and Deployment Systems.

Standardized Work for Processes

As discussed previously, standardized work documents record the current best practice for performing a technical or executive task. Together, standards support consistent performance of common tasks across the enterprise. They serve as a resource for instructing contributors in the performance of their work. They provide the baseline against which new ideas for improving a process are measured. They are therefore a critical resource in realizing Effectiveness.

The first work standard that the business must establish, therefore, is the one that guides building, improving, and disseminating standardized work documents themselves.[3] It is an essential cornerstone in the continuous improvement of the enterprise.

---

[3] While we refer to the work standards both for Building, Improving, and Disseminating Standardized Work and for Problem Solving and Decision Making as single documents, each may be an integrated set of guidance that addresses each of the different component activities that make up these tasks. This statement also applies to the work standard for the organization-wide Policy Planning and Deployment process and its Renewal System, discussed later in this chapter.

Problem Solving and Decision Making

A second organization-wide standard that the business must create guides how problem solving and decision making are performed throughout the enterprise. Contributors use this standard in their efforts to stabilize work processes, eliminate waste, add value to products and processes, and improve their personal and collective performance. Both problem solving and decision making require the use of information- or knowledge-based methods.[4] Both sets of methods are systematic and explicit. They permit participation by team members and enable collaborative action to resolve issues teams must address. They also guide individual action in the execution of one's technical and executive roles. They produce replicable outcomes and are teachable to others. The information-based methods analyze and interpret facts acquired from people, documents, direct observation, or experimentation to make decisions and solve problems. Knowledge-based methods apply a set of knowledge to logically deduce from relevant facts which choice to elect or how to correct a problem. Both methods qualify as instruments of rational processing.

Renewal System

The Renewal system guides contributors in conducting a summative evaluation of their prior year's performance. The system coordinates the performance of this once-yearly Renewal activity across the enterprise. The organization-wide improvement ideas that it generates provide input to the enterprise's yearly Policy Planning and Deployment process (see below). Contributors at each workstation and within each work team at the work process, value stream component, business function, and business leadership levels complete a Renewal activity for their prior year's personal and team performance. Each level of analysis and learning produces improvement ideas. The System guides the integration and use of these improvement ideas. Contributors pass forward those ideas that have enterprise-wide application to the business leadership team. These improvement suggestions become input to the next year's businesswide continuous improvement plan.

The Renewal Activity

Like all other efforts that mine learning from a prior performance, the Renewal activity uses the tool *Status, Reason, Learning, and Direction* (SRLD) (see below). A guide for using this tool is provided in chapter *Task 10 Learn and Share* in *The Lean Champion Resource Guide* (Vitalo, Bujak, Vitalo, Bierley, et al., 2023). An article describing how to use this tool and providing an

[4] *Appendix D* clarifies the distinction between information and knowledge. *Appendix E* provides a brief introduction to information- and knowledge-based methods.

example of its use is also available on the Internet (Vitalo and Vitalo, 2020).[5] Using the SRLD tool, contributors evaluate a past performance and understand what enabled the success that was realized and what hindered realizing even greater success. They extract learning and decide ways to use that learning to achieve a better next performance. Contributors assume responsibility for implementing those improvement ideas that are within their scope of responsibility. They pass forward to the appropriate person or team those ideas that require a broader scope of action.

Renewal is the core activity that supports every individual and team in their striving for perfection in all personal and professional endeavors. Contributors perform Renewal activities periodically throughout the year (weekly, quarterly, semi-annually) as determined by the cycle of measurement defined in the metric(s) associated with a particular performance.

At the completion of each local Renewal activity, contributors sort learning and improvement action items into those that can be locally implemented and those that require a broader scope of action. Those that require a broader scope of action are passed forward to the appropriate party.

Each team that generates and/or receives improvement ideas processes them in the same manner. First, they eliminate redundancies by integrating similar ideas they themselves generated or that were passed to them by other teams. They register with the improvement action the number of teams that pass forward a similar idea so that the breadth of relevance of each improvement suggestion is noted. This retains information important to understanding the size of benefit an improvement could generate. Contributors then organize improvement ideas by focus, type, and magnitude of benefit. Focus addresses who or what the improvement idea affects. Type refers to whether the improvement corrects a deficiency or adds new value. In general, the more directly an improvement affects a customer's receipt of benefit, the higher its priority for action is. Also, improvements that eliminate a deficiency have priority over those that add new value. Finally, contributors prioritize improvements that have a greater impact over those with lesser impact.

Once improvement ideas are prioritized, contributors responsible for implementing an improvement define a goal for that improvement and a metric for gauging its achievement and results. They develop a schedule for executing the improvements and assign responsibilities for implementing each. Together, each team monitors its execution of improvements, extracts new learning, and applies it to increase their success.

[5] See *Mining Learning From Performance*, available at http://www.vitalentusa.com/links/pdfs/mining_learning_from_performance.pdf

Once an improvement has been implemented, contributors enter the learning they generated and the results of its implementation into the businesswide Knowledge Management and Sharing System.

As stated previously, the Renewal system coordinates the performance of Renewal actions at every level of the organization with a specific focus on evaluating summative performance for the prior year (Exhibit 3). The businesswide improvement actions it generates become input to the enterprise's next year continuous improvement plan. The process may generate other insights that suggest changes in the business's approach. Those ideas become input to the enterprise's next year business plan.

Exhhibit 3. The Renewal System

Focus

- Summative Performance (Year End)
  - What we expected to achieve
  - What we achieved
  - Why we were able to achieve it
  - Why we were not able to achieve more
  - What we can learn from our analysis
  - How we can use our learning to improve

Actions

- Use the SRLD tool to learn from performance
- Sort learning and improvement action items
- Pass forward non-local improvement actions
- Organize, prioritize, coordinate, and implement local actions
- Share results of improvement actions
- Incorporate businesswide improvement ideas as inputs to the enterprise's next year continuous improvement plan
- Incorporate ideas for changes in the business's approach as input to next year's business plan

Policy Planning and Deployment (Hoshin Kanri)

The final cornerstone work standard the business creates guides its yearly Policy Planning and Deployment process (Hoshin Kanri).[6] The Hoshin Kanri method (Akao, 1991) aligns all members of a business with an integrated set of business priorities. The business-level leadership team oversees this process. The process leverages the organization's functional decomposition of work (260–264) and its interlocking team approach, described earlier (Exhibit 7, page 277). The interlocking team approach creates a personal connection from the *gemba*[7] to the broadest system level of performance and establishes a vehicle for accomplishing Hoshin Kanri.

[6] Hoshin Kanri is the Japanese term used to label this process in Lean Enterprise. "Policy planning and deployment" is the English translation of that Japanese term.

[7] A Japanese word meaning "the place where the real work is done"—that is, where people actually create the value-delivering interim and final outputs of each business function. Smalley (2016) pointed out that the correct spelling should be "genba"; however, the English spelling in common use is *gemba*.

In a Life Enabling enterprise, Hoshin Kanri produces two outputs: a deployed yearly business plan and a deployed continuous improvement plan (Exhibit 4).

Exhibit 4. Policy Planning and Deployment (Hoshin Kanri)

Focus

- Policy Planning and Deployment
  - Business Plan
  - Continuous Improvment Plan

Inputs

- For Business Planning
  - Customer information (purpose, values, success criteria, capabilities, performance context)
  - Stakeholder information (interests, expectations, concerns, preferences)
  - Commercial environment (political, social, economic, industrial, technological)
  - Current enterprise capabilities (people, structure, systems, etc.)
  - Results of Business Leadership Renewal processing
- For Continuous Improvement Planning
  - Results of Business Leadership Renewal processing
  - Passed-forward businesswide improvement ideas
  - Businesswide Suggestion System improvement ideas
  - Customer feedback on current offerings and buying–benefiting experience
  - Stakeholder feedback on their satisfaction with the business

Actions

- Business Planning
  - Gather information
  - Analyze its meaning
  - Determine impact on realizing commercial success
  - Identify changes in structure and approach that advance success
  - Set goals to realize changes
  - Establish metrics to monitor and verify goal achievement
  - Plan goal achievement
  - Work plan through the organization
  - Finalize plan
- Continuous Improvement Planning
  - Gather improvement ideas
  - Organize ideas by focus and type
  - Evaluate impact of improvement ideas
  - Prioritize improvement ideas
  - Set improvement goals
  - Establish metrics
  - Work priorities through organization
  - Finalize plan

Business Plan

The business plan may revise the enterprise's business intent or how the business will realize that intent. It specifies going-forward changes in the organization's purpose, structure, people, systems, and processes that alter its technical performance. These changes redirect the business's efforts so that they accommodate the changing world in which it will be operating.

The business-level leadership team begins the business planning process by analyzing foreseeable changes in the business's commercial environment. This analysis assesses the future status of customers, stakeholders, the commercial environment, and the enterprise's current capabilities.

The assessment of the enterprise's target customers evaluates potential changes in their customers' needs and the factors that affect their success. It uncovers any changes that are likely to emerge with regard to the purpose customers seek to accomplish, their capabilities in accomplishing it, their success criteria, and the context in which they pursue their purpose. It also detects potential changes in the values and preferences prospective customers hold with regard to the current offering designed to support their success and its attendant buying–benefiting experience.

The assessment of stakeholders seeks to uncover any future changes in their interests, expectations, concerns, and preferences.

The business-level leadership team's assessment then moves beyond prospective customers and stakeholders to evaluate potential changes to the commercial context in which the business will operate. This includes identifying anticipated social, political, economic, industry-specific, and technological factors that might affect its commerce.

The team next determines what business changes, if any, it needs to recommend so that the enterprise can advance on its purpose given future circumstances. This involves evaluating its current capabilities and approach against the new requirements for success that expected changes will demand.

Using the results of its assessments, the team devises ways to adjust the business's makeup and approach so the enterprise is maximally capable of realizing its commercial purpose. It may modify elements of its business intent, specifically what the business will produce for exchange, with whom, and where. It may modify its organizational structure or identify required changes to its approach to accomplishing its Strategic, Operations, and Executive Functions objectives. It may detect the need for contributors with a different profile of technical expertise. Where the plan defines the need for new functions or contributor roles, it also specifies its judgment as to whether these needs should be met internally or by outsourcing. In every case, the changes it identifies close every gap that exists between its current capability to succeed in the future and its required capability. No change, however, may violate the model's principles or alter the purpose commerce serves.

The team next defines goals for accomplishing the changes it identifies and creates metrics for tracking their implementation and achievement. It develops an action plan to accomplish the plan's goals. The results of the team's deliberations are documented in its draft business plan, which the team processes with contributors throughout the organization (see below).

Continuous Improvement Plan

The continuous improvement plan uses the results of the Renewal process and other inputs (e.g., the Businesswide Suggestion System) to identify ways to improve continuing activities. This plan identifies businesswide improvement goals and sets priorities for their implementation. These goals may better ensure that customers receive what they need when they need it or elevate customer value satisfaction from the business's current offerings or their related buying–benefiting experiences. The goals may target improving the coordination between business functions and suppliers or business functions and other stakeholders. Or they may focus on increasing the business's ecosystem-friendly operation or elevate the benefits communities receive from the enterprise. Goals may also target matters that relate to improving synergy across contributors, resolving performance issues in the systems and processes that crosscut functions, or elevate the capabilities of members that have organization-wide relevance.

The enterprise's continuous improvement goals result from an analysis of the business improvement ideas that flow through to the business leadership team. This wealth of thinking is organized by the focus and type of improvement. Each idea is evaluated for its potential impact on realizing the business's commercial purpose. Ideas are then prioritized within each focus category and then by type. Highest priority is given to improvements that directly affect customers, remedy deficiencies, and have a large impact. The team defines high-level goals for improvement (e.g., lower the life-cycle cost to customers of Offering Y) and establishes metrics to track both progress and accomplishment in achieving each high-level goal. The team documents the results of its deliberations in a draft continuous improvement plan. It then processes this draft plan with contributors throughout the organization (see below).

Finalizing and Deploying the Business and Continuous Improvement Plans

The business leadership team finalizes its business and continuous improvement plans using a Delphi technique approach to consensus building.[8] The business plan is finalized first. All leadership teams at each organizational level down to the work unit level meet simultaneously to receive, clarify, confirm, and identify problems and suggest improvements to the plan. The process uses a cycle of three sessions, with each session being time-limited. Each session begins with a presentation of the draft plan (or its revision), followed by members asking clarifying questions and making confirming statements of understanding. Then, each team separately discusses the plan. Members offer constructive criticisms and recommend improvements. When done, each

[8] In a large or dispersed enterprise, the process might be accomplished using virtual meetings enabled by intranet webinars.

team passes forward its endorsements, criticisms, and recommended improvements to a central organizing group that integrates the recommendations from the various peer groups. That organizing group revises the draft plan based on the feedback it receives. A revised draft is then worked through the same process. After two cycles, a proposed final plan is offered for adoption. Adoption is by consensus of all teams. Consensus means that no participants have a concern that would block their acceptance of the plan and that all participants find sufficient merit in the final plan that they can commit to making it succeed.

Once the business plan is finalized, the business leadership team develops an implementation plan. This is distributed to the organization members who will be responsible for accomplishing each business plan goal. Monitoring of progress will occur locally as well as at the business leadership level.

The same process is used to finalize the continuous improvement plan. After consensus is realized concerning the improvement plan's high-level goals, priorities, and metrics, the business leadership team conducts a second cycle of processing. Here, the team uses the same process to elicit from each organizational unit its thinking about how it will make local improvements that accomplish the high-level goals specified in the plan. A local team may simply review the slate of improvements it already has identified during its Renewal activity, associate each with the direction defined in the improvement plan, and re-prioritize its execution to conform to the plan. It may also generate new ideas should none that are relevant to the plan's high-level goals already exist. In either case, the process creates a slate of local action items extending throughout the organization that will transform the continuous improvement plan's high-level goals into realized improvements at the local level.

Since contributors apply a systems perspective at every level, their action plans incorporate cross-functional concerns. At each business level, goals and plans are owned communally. The deployment of goals and plans is complete, consistent, and integrated both vertically and horizontally at all levels. Awareness of the business's overall direction for the new year and each work area's responsibilities extends from the businesswide leadership team to the *gemba*.

Structure the Organization

The structural organization of a Life Enabling enterprise is described in *Chapter 9*, pages 258–264. Establishing this structure is the task of the Executive Function of Effectiveness. This task includes both the structure's initial definition and its reconfiguration as the nature of the business changes in response to new information and learning and the introduction of new approaches to commerce. In this way, contributors ensure that the organization's structure continuously supports the ends that structure must enable, as defined by the model (page 259).

Establish the Required Communications Infrastructure Components

Three components of the communications infrastructure already identified in the model's Strategic and Operations components specifically support the Executive Function of Effectiveness. These are a Businesswide Suggestion System (BwSS), a Functional Measurement and Feedback System (FM&FS), and a Knowledge Management and Sharing System (KMSS).

Businesswide Suggestion System (BwSS)

The BwSS collects and processes ideas for improvements from contributors that apply to the organization as a whole or to processes other than the ones that the contributor is involved in implementing. The system gathers these ideas, supports their review and discussion, tracks their modification, monitors their implementation and results, and provides feedback to their originators about the disposition of each idea submitted. This information system is part of the communications infrastructure.

The system has two components. One is the Suggestion Management subsystem. It receives, organizes, stores, retrieves, updates, reports the current status of an idea, and archives submitted suggestions. The other component is the Suggestion Disposition subsystem. It supports the processing of suggestions. These subsystems need to interconnect seamlessly with each other and with other components of the communications infrastructure.

Suggestion Management Subsystem

To be useful, this system must have the following features:

- It should capture ideas using a standard format for recording each idea. That format must record the information needed to understand what is proposed and how to evaluate its potential utility. The format should elicit who is submitting the idea and when it was inputted and updated. It should capture what improvement action is being proposed, what problem or opportunity it addresses, where this problem or opportunity exists, why its exists, what benefits the proposed idea is thought to provide, and how one might test the suggestion's usefulness.
- It should provide either online or off-line resources that a contributor may access to assist him or her in submitting the idea.
- It should acknowledge to the contributor the receipt of his or her idea, track its dispositioning status, update the contributor about that status, and permit the contributor to amend the submitted idea if needed.

Suggestion Disposition Subsystem

This subsystem supports the screening, assessment, revision, and final disposition of suggestions. The workflow for processing each submitted idea includes registering the status of each suggestion, categorizing it, assigning it for evaluation, recording the results of its evaluation, and documenting its final disposition.

Each suggestion is categorized by its focus, type, and magnitude of benefit. The stages of dispositioning are (1) received, (2) under review, (3) accepted for action, (4) executed, and (5) rejected with explanation. The only ideas accepted for action include empirical evidence as to the existence of the problem or opportunity, its root cause, the effectiveness of the suggestion in resolving the problem or realizing the opportunity, and the improvement's potential impact on business success. Any suggestion that is rejected must be discussed with its contributor *before being rejected.* Issues that concern the reviewers must be shared, and the contributor must have the opportunity to respond. Reviewers should assist the contributor in any way possible to make his or her case for the suggestion, including supporting the person in conducting an experiment or pilot to develop information about the ideas's effectiveness. The final decision should be mutually agreed upon.

Suggestions that are acted on should be tracked by the system until accomplished. At that point, the results the improvement produced should be documented in the system, and the suggestion's status should be designated as "executed."

The BwSS must rapidly process submitted ideas and ensure that adopted ideas are leveraged across the company by using them everywhere they can provide benefit. To this end, improvement actions that prove effective should be formalized into knowledge documents and entered into the Knowledge Management and Sharing System.

Finally, the businesswide Functional Measurement and Feedback System should monitor the operation of the BwSS to ensure its effectiveness. It should measure performance on such features as participation rate, number of suggestions received, time to final dispositioning, adoption rate, benefits generated, and contributor satisfaction with the system.

Functional Measurement and Feedback System (FM&FS)

The FM&FS supplies the information needed to guide decision making in realizing personal and organizational effectiveness. As stated earlier, a measurement system is deemed functional when it is complete, contains sound measures, has integrity, and is fully documented. Here, we will describe each of these features in greater detail.

A *complete* measurement system includes measures that report the status of the business's results, activities, and resources with regard to Strategic, Operations, and Executive Functions. The measures must also report the status of performance for each level of granularity in decision making and action. Thus, its metrics must gauge performance at the business level, the business function level, the value stream component level, the work process level, the work unit level, and the performer level. Here, "performer" refers to both human contributors and each self-managing, work-accomplishing machine. The measurement system must gauge the status of every feature of every element of the enterprise deemed important by its commercial model.

A measurement system has *sound* metrics when the information the metrics report is reliable, valid, and interpretable. Reliability means that each measure consistently reports the same value for a given state every time it is correctly used. If a metric is unreliable, you cannot trust what it reports. An unreliable measure, therefore, can never be valid. Validity means that a metric does, in fact, report the status of the feature it claims to report about. Interpretability means that what a metric reports can be understood in a way that guides decision making and action. This requires that the definition of a metric includes contextual information that enables its user to interpret its meaning. At a minimum, this context is supplied by the contents of the metric's success criterion. Each success criterion has an anchor, a measure, and a target. The anchor names the feature of a performer, an output, an activity, or a setting whose status needs to be known in order for contributors to steer performance toward its desired outcome. The measure describes the method for calibrating the status of the anchor. Status may be calibrated in terms of the presence or absence of a feature (Yes/No; True/False) or its quantity, quality, timeliness, or efficiency (time, cost, or cost per increment of quality). It also may be calibrated in terms of a change in any of these characteristics over instances of occurrence (e.g., time, place, performer). The measure also explains the steps one completes to calibrate its anchor's status, who should perform them, and when, and it identifies any instruments and materials to be used in making measurements. The target in a success criterion states the value that a measure must report for someone to claim that the status, as measured, matches or exceeds expectations. Simply, each success criterion tells what to check, how to measure its status, and what value, if found, justifies labeling the observed performance "successful."[9]

---

[9] Detailed guidance for building a functional measurement system is provided in chapter *Task 9 Measure Results* in *The Lean Champion Resource Guide* (Vitalo, Bujak, Vitalo, Bierley, et al., 2023).

A measurement system has *integrity* when both what it measures and how it executes its measurements align with the dictates of the business's commercial model. Thus, its results-focused measures make clear how well the business is realizing its model's expected outcomes. Its activities-focused metrics clarify whether its manner of performance in realizing the model's desired ends is consistent with the model's dictates. Its resource-focused metrics clarify whether the business has and is maintaining or developing the resources critical to the successful implementation of its business model. Additionally, the system *must not* gauge performance on any result, activity, or resource that is irrelevant or antagonistic to the commercial model the business is implementing.

Integrity also requires that the method for measuring status *does not* report a result that is achieved in a way that violates the model's principles. There are many measures of factors important to a commercial model on which you can appear to "succeed" yet produce model-defined negative consequences. For example, consider the goal of maximizing the availability of cash for use by a business. This goal is an expectation that a Life Enabling enterprise seeks to realize so that it can maximally apply its monetary resources to value-adding activities. A typical metric used to gauge the status on that anchor is called the "cash-to-cash cycle time." It reports how long cash is unavailable to a business. The shorter your business's cash-to-cash cycle, the fewer days its cash is unavailable for use. Your business's cash is out of reach when fees are uncollected from customers and when its cash is soaked up by inventory that sits on the shop floor or in storage facilities.

Uncollected customer fees are termed "receivables." How quickly a receivable is registered and how long it sits uncollected are determined by your business's Order-to-Receipt value stream and your agreement with your customers. Inventory is a function of how well your Supply Chain and Production value streams are functioning. When the systems that process inputs flow, are pulled by the customer, and are free of all waste, inventory is zero.

Typical Cash-to-Cash Cycle Measure

Number of days that inventory sits	+	Number of days that receivables are uncollected	-	Number of days payables to suppliers are unpaid

The typical cash-to-cash cycle computation adds the number of days cash is locked up in inventory to the number of days that your uncollected earnings sit as receivables and *subtracts* the days cash remains *available* to your business because it has not been spent to pay debts owed to suppliers (Ward, 2004). The last element refers to cash owed others but not yet paid. This last element creates an opportunity for reporting success on this metric while violating a tenet of the Life Enabling model. If your suppliers expect payment within 45 days and you hold their payments for 60 days, you would end up with a better cash-to-cash cycle. Delaying payments to suppliers creates a *reverse benefit* that improves your cash-to-cash cycle when you use the traditional method of computation. This reverse benefit results from action that harms suppliers. Life Enabling enterprises seek to benefit *all parties inclusively.* Solutions that optimize the availability of cash for your business cannot harm any other party (suppliers, in this case). Consequently, the method you use to compute your cash-to-cash cycle cannot credit you for *late* payment of debts to your suppliers. A cash-to-cash metric with integrity for a Life Enabling enterprise would need to adjust how the measurement is made so that it does not report progress at the expense of your suppliers.[10] The presence of any measure that can report success while violating a tenet of the model undermines the integrity of its measurement system.

A functional measurement system must also be fully *documented.* Only a documented system is publicly knowable and therefore can be assessed and improved by any contributor to the enterprise. Documentation is also essential to training people in implementing and processing measurements and to ensuring that they perform these tasks in a manner that is consistently correct. Without documentation and training, no metric within the business measurement system will be reliable, and without reliability, it cannot be valid.

In addition to satisfying the requirements for being complete and having sound measures that possess integrity and are documented, a functional system also requires that its contents be accessible to every contributor. This accessibility must enable each contributor to create an individualized management dashboard that depicts the metrics specific to his or her personal role and to the contributor's team responsibilities.

Knowledge Management and Sharing System (KMSS)

The KMSS ensures that contributors can share the knowledge they uncover, develop, or create to improve their performance, the performance of their teammates, and the enterprise as a whole. It is also a repository for all other knowledge documents. KMSS is a component within the communications infrastructure.

The system receives, organizes, stores, updates, and distributes knowledge from various sources. Its contents include the following items:

---

[10] For additional discussion of this issue and ways to resolve it, see Bierley (2006).

- Domain-specific knowledge. This includes the content knowledge that each instructional product teaches (e.g., about customer and stakeholder values, job-specific tasks) and domain-specifc knowledge documents related to the Life Enabling model and to the fields of science and technology that relate to the work of the enterprise.
- Instrumental tools.[11] These are guides, manuals, job aids, and other performance support resources that assist contributors in understanding these tools and using them effectively.
- Learning uncovered, developed, or created by contributors from the analysis of their own performance (individual and team renewal activities), continuous improvement events, literature research, experimentation, and pilots the business conducts.
- Physical tools, equipment, and materials specifications and manuals that support the use, storage, maintenance, repair, and disposal of these resources.
- Standardized work documents that communicate the current best practice for implementing each work process.
- Proven improvement ideas that have been processed through the BwSS.

So-called knowledge management systems that currently exist suffer from several maladies. First, they are built by people who do not understand the difference between knowledge and information. Thus, they contain a hodgepodge of contents. Second, they do not require the complete documentation of either procedural or decision knowledge in a standard format. Thus, their contents can be incomplete and difficult to understand. Third, their contents are not linked to their points of use. By this, we mean they are not tagged in a way that makes them readily available to people performing the work to which the knowledge relates. Fourth, they do not require each procedural or decision knowledge document to include evidence of the utility of the knowledge it documents. Hence, a user has no way of judging whether the knowledge being reported will produce results better than his or her current practice.

To avoid these failings, the KMSS must satisfy the following requirements:

- It must document *knowledge* only—either procedural or decision knowledge. Procedural knowledge guides one in accomplishing an instrumental task. Decision knowledge guides one in inferring from information what

[11] Instrumental tools include, for example, Kaizen, Quick Changeover, Total Productive Maintenance, and other behaviorally based methods that accomplish specific types of purposes.

action to take. *Appendix G* provides a template for documenting each type of knowledge.

- Each learning-generated knowledge document must be linked to a business function, a value stream component, a work process, and a task or to the performance of an activity that crosscuts the enterprise—e.g., working together as a team. If the knowledge relates to an improvement in machine or tool use, the identify of the machine or tool must be documented.
- Each knowledge entry must include evidence of its use and the results it produced. These results must always include its objectively measured effects on the performance to which it relates.
- The system must incorporate a user query and feedback component so that end users may ask clarifying questions, raise concerns, make suggestions about entries, and receive replies.
- The system must be accessible to all contributors and fully integrated with the other components of the communications infrastructure.

The Remaining Activities That Accomplish Effectiveness

Activities 3 through 7 (pages 369–370) for accomplishing Effectiveness use the infrastructure that Activity 2 builds to steer the enterprise toward its desired ends. The business leadership team initiates the Hoshin Kanri process as scheduled and produces the enterprise's going-forward business plan and its continuous improvement plan (Task 3). Contributors monitor their collective progress toward realizing the goals of these plans (Task 4). The business leadership team monitors overall progress in accomplishing the high-level goals defined in each plan. At each other level of performance, the responsible contributors monitor their progress in realizing their portion of the business and continuous improvement goals and plans.

This monitoring has built-in reflection points at which individuals and teams review progress to date and use the SRLD tool to extract learning and conceive ways to accelerate success. These regular performance review sessions are held weekly, monthly, or quarterly depending on the items being monitored and the cycle time for their status assessment. In these sessions, contributors detect and remove barriers hindering progress. They also detect and realize opportunities for accelerating progress in accomplishing the business's plans (Tasks 5 and 6).

At year's end, the summative Renewal system is activated (Task 7). That process triggers the initiation of the enterprise's yearly Policy Planning and

Deployment process (Task 3). The activities that realize the goals of Effectiveness are thus recycled as the enterprise strives for perfection in realizing Effectiveness.

Effectiveness's Critical-to-Success Resources

All the critical-to-success resources identified in the Strategic and Operations components are required for the successful performance of the Executive Function of Effectiveness. Especially important to Effectiveness are contributors' knowledge of the Life Enabling commercial model. They must also know the enterprise's end-to-end extended value stream for its production/service fulfillment business function. In addition, they must know the extended value stream for each of the business functions in which a contributor works. Also, contributors implementing some aspects of the needed infrastructure may require technical expertise in one or another specialty area—e.g., computing or economic forecasting.

Finally, the business's communication infrastructure must contain and support the Businesswide Suggestion System, Functional Measurement and Feedback System, and Knowledge Management and Sharing System.

There is no successful commercial organization without people who are capable and motivated to establish it, implement its activities, maintain its operation, and realize its purpose. Sufficiency in a Life Enabling enterprise ensures that those needed people are present, engaged in their efforts to accomplish their commercial purpose, and successful both as individuals and as contributors working to realize their enterprise's aim.

Chapter 14

The Mindset That Guides Sufficiency in a Life Enabling Enterprise

There are several unique characteristics of a Life Enabling enterprise that must inform the mindset that guides the implementation of Sufficiency.

First, the owners of a Life Enabling enterprise are its members. The members come together based on their sharing of a common purpose and approach to commerce. Their cooperative enterprise is the expression of this fact. What enables the individual's success therefore enables the enterprise's success. What enables the enterprise's success enables the individual's success.

Second, each member has two roles: frontline worker and owner. As a frontline worker, each member applies his or her expertise in a particular specialty to accomplish a value-adding task. This contribution is documented in each member's position description. As an owner, each member performs the Executive Functions that ensure that the enterprise sustains itself as a whole, capable, viable, and successful endeavor. This contribution is documented in the common role every contributor must perform (pages 273–274).

Third, the work of a Life Enabling enterprise is accomplished by two distinct types of actors: individual members and teams. Both kinds of actors assume responsibilities, make decisions, and take actions that affect the success of the commerce they cooperatively pursue. Each requires the wherewithal necessary to achieve success. Each must be fully engaged in accomplishing its purposes. Sufficiency ensures that the requirements of both individual contributors and teams are satisfied. Also, the Sufficiency function proactively ensures that no obstacles emerge to hinder the engagement and success of either type of actor.

Distinguishing Sufficiency From Human Resource Management

As you view the list of services that Sufficiency implements (Exhibit 2, page 390), you will recognize them as activities traditionally identified with the field of Human Resource Management (HRM).[1] You must not confuse the Sufficiency function with HRM as traditionally practiced. HRM activities as commonly practiced occur within a producer-focused, profit-maximizing commercial organization. We are describing these activities as implemented in a Life Enabling enterprise. The differing perspectives of HRM and Sufficiency result from this fact. Exhibit 1, next page, summarizes the salient aspects of these differing perspectives.

[1] Human Resource Management is also referred to as Human Capital Management and sometimes as Talent Management.

A producer-focused, profit-maximizing enterprise implements Capitalism. That model serves people (owners) who seek to maximize personal wealth or gain. They employ others (employees) to serve this end. Their dealings with others are based on the assumption that every person acts egoistically. Therefore, their interactions with others are always fundamentally competitive, even when they may appear to be cooperating. In every transaction, their end is always to achieve the maximum personal gain. This understanding is the foundation of Capitalism.

Exhibit 1. Comparison of Perspectives

HRM in a Capitalist Enterprise	Sufficiency in a Life Enabling Enterprise
The enterprise is made up of owners and employees.	The enterprise is made up of owners only.
Owners seek to maximize their personal profit, defined monetarily. Employees are expected to serve this end. Since employees are a cost and reduce profit, there is an inherent antagonism between the needs and wants of the owner and the employee.	Owners and members are one and the same. Their purpose is to enable their customers' success in ways that better the lives of everyone and benefit all stakeholders inclusively. Unlike monetary profit, the satisfaction that comes from enriching another's life is amplified by sharing, not reduced by it.
HRM accepts that the interests of the owners of the organization and their employees fundamentally diverge. It recognizes the owner's interests as primary.	Sufficiency is based on the understanding that the success of the individual strengthens organizational success and the success of the organization strengthens individual success.
The fundamental unit of performance in the organization is the individual employee.	The organization has dual units of performance—individual contributors and teams.
HRM sees the residents of the organization's C-suite as its customers. It seeks to advance senior management's ends by maximizing the monetary value delivered by employees while minimizing the cost of extracting that value.	Sufficiency sees its customer as the enterprise's customer. It serves customers by ensuring the presence of the people needed to maximize the value customers receive. It ensures that outcome by supporting the engagement and success of every contributor and team and advancing each contributor's emergence as an individual.

The Life Enabling model serves people who are *both* social *and* personal in their orientation. Their social orientation is reflected in their desire to be connected with others in mutually benefiting relationships. It expresses itself in their altruism toward others, even strangers, and in their preference for working cooperatively. Their personal orientation is expressed in their striving for individuation—the development of their unique personalities and full realization of their personal talents and capabilities. In this regard, they continuously learn about themselves and the world in which they live, elevate their productive capabilities, and refine their understanding of what pursuits best express who they are and advance the fulfillment of their personal potential.

These two orientations, the social and the personal, manifest themselves in their commerce with others. As an expression of their social orientation, they seek to benefit others by enabling their success in ways that better the lives of everyone. As an expression of their personal orientation, their commercial focus expresses their personal interests, applies their talents, and advances their individuation. It functions as a vehicle for their learning, growth, and emergence.

These dual orientations operate interdependently. Each is necessary for the other to thrive. With each advancement in their personal emergence, people add greater value to their benefiting of others. And, as others grow in capability, they enrich the opportunities for learning and growth for each individual with whom they interact.

The divergence in perspectives between traditionally implemented HRM and the Executive Function of Sufficiency in a Life Enabling enterprise flows from the differences in the makeup of the people who create the enterprises in which each model operates and the commercial model each employs.

Exhibit 2. Sufficiency in a Life Enabling Enterprise

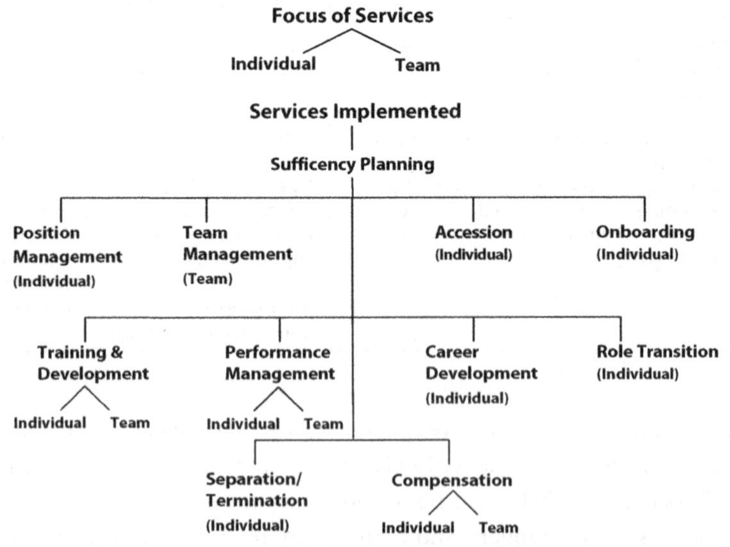

The Services Sufficiency Provides

Sufficiency uses 11 cores services to accomplish its purpose:

1. Sufficiency planning
2. Position management
3. Team management
4. Accession
5. Onboarding
6. Training and development
7. Performance management
8. Career development
9. Role transition
10. Separation/ termination
11. Compensation

Some of these services focus on individuals exclusively. One focuses on teams only. Others focus on both. Exhibit 2, prior page, depicts the focus of each service. Exhibit 3, next page, clarifies what each service provides. All services follow documented policies and procedures that member-owners approve and abide by.

The Results Sufficiency Must Produce

As with all Life Enabling business functions, Sufficiency's goal is to enable the enterprise to advance the success of its customers in ways that better the lives of everyone and benefit all stakeholders inclusively. It accomplishes its goal by realizing the following objectives: First, it must ensure the presence of people capable of fulfilling the enterprise's purpose when and where needed. Second, it must ensure that both individuals and teams are engaged and realizing success in their roles. Third, it must ensure that each contributor emerges as an individual pursuing the path that ultimately personifies the contributor's identity as a person and fully realizes his or her personal potential. Exhibit 4, page 393, provides possible outcome measures for evaluating the Executive Function of Sufficiency.

If the suite of services that produce Sufficiency is implemented as a separate business-enabling function within the enterprise—e.g., as a Sufficiency department—that function's assessment must also include the results expected from all business functions and the results expected from every enabling value stream. These results are listed in Exhibit 1, page 287. Illustrative examples of success criteria related to these outcomes appear in Exhibit 6, pages 293–294.

The Activities That Accomplish Sufficiency

The following plan of action guides the overall performance of the Executive Function of Sufficiency:

1. Establish the services needed to achieve Sufficiency.
2. Create a standardized work document for each Sufficiency service and its subprocesses.

Exhibit 3. The Services That Realize Sufficiency

Service	Explanation
Sufficiency Planning	Identifies the actions needed to sustain and improve the sufficiency of the enterprise. It profiles future contributor needs, decides sourcing (internal/external), and plans the timely fulfillment of those needs. It specifies how gaps that exist in the engagement and success of individuals and teams and the personal development of contributors will be eliminated.
Position Management	Profiles and documents every position in the company, evaluates the degree of challenge and the scope and effect of each role, and maintains position information in a current and complete state.
Team Management	Documents the charter and membership of every team in the company, evaluates the degree of challenge and the scope and effect of each team's goal, and maintains team information in a current and complete state.
Accession	Recruits, screens, and selects candidates with the competencies and qualities of character needed to implement a Life Enabling enterprise. It supports candidates in making evidence-based decisions about whether joining the enterprise aligns with their personal goals and values.
Onboarding	Educates new contributors about the company's approach to commerce, its business intent, the expectations and requirements of all contributors, and the expectations and requirements of the specific technical role the new member will perform and the work setting in which he or she will perform it.
Training and Development	Elevates the success of every contributor and team by providing them the knowledge, skills, and proficiency levels required for them to succeed in their current roles. It also ensures that they can apply that expertise effectively within their work settings.
Performance Management	Supports individuals and teams in discovering ways to improve their performance in their current roles and maximize their personal or team success.
Career Development	Supports contributors in their efforts to advance their individuation by defining a career path that best reflects their values and advances their personal growth and success.
Role Transition	Supports the movement of people to other roles on either a temporary or a permanent basis. Executes the promotion function. All movements must be based on the candidate's readiness to succeed in the new role and conform to the career path the contributor has defined.
Separation/ Termination	Facilitates a person's transition out of the enterprise. It supports the person in finding opportunities that better fit his or her goals and readiness to realize them.
Compensation	Provides for the fair and equitable sharing of the material benefits people's contributions to the enterprise generate.

Exhibit 4. Success Criteria for Gauging Sufficiency at the Enterprise Level[1]

Anchor	Measure	Target
Sufficiency		
The people the business needs to succeed are present, engaged, effective in their roles, and developing personally	▪ Percentage of accession instances wherein the people needed to implement the enterprise were present when needed and had the competencies and proficiency levels required to perform their roles (assessed quarterly)	▪ 100%
	▪ Percentage of instances wherein new hires demonstrated their readiness to successfully assume their roles post-onboarding	▪ 100%
	▪ Percentage of contributors engaged in their work as measured by a contributor engagement survey (assessed semiannually)	▪ 100%
	▪ Percentage of contributors scoring at or above expected levels on role performance metrics (assessed quarterly)	▪ 100%
	▪ Percentage of teams achieving at or above their expected levels of results on metrics measuring each team's performance (assessed quarterly)	▪ 100%
	▪ Percentage of teams scoring at or above their expected levels on a scale measuring effective teamwork (e.g., the Meeting Power Scale, Appendix G) (assessed quarterly)	▪ 100%
	▪ Percentage of all teams engaged in their work as measured by a team engagement survey (assessed semiannually)	▪ 100%
	▪ Percentage of contributors reporting full satisfaction with their personal development in the context of their commercial efforts (assessed semiannually)	▪ 100%

[1] The examples in this exhibit are abridged statements of success criteria. They are not complete. For example, the measures do not include a full description of the method by which status on each anchor is gauged.

3. Produce a yearly Sufficiency Plan.
4. Acquire or develop the intellectual products needed to implement Sufficiency services in conformance with the current Sufficiency plan.
5. Acquire the people needed to implement the enterprise through external hiring or internal development.
6. Ensure the organizational and personal success of every contributor and the success of every team.
7. Ensure the retention of every contributor when it is in the best interest of both parties.

8. Monitor the progress and success of the Sufficiency function.
9. Act to uncover and realize opportunities to improve Sufficiency and detect and eliminate barriers for realizing Sufficiency.
10. Continuously improve the performance of the Sufficiency function.

The Needed Sufficiency Services

The following guidance provides a more detailed understanding of each service and how it should operate. The policy governing each service must be adopted by members of the enterprise and incorporated in their governing agreement.

Sufficiency Planning

Sufficiency Planning[2] defines what is needed to meet the future Sufficiency needs of the business and how those needs will be met. It also corrects any detected problems in the current provision of Sufficiency services. The yearly Sufficiency Plan guides goal setting and planning for each Sufficiency service. It ensures that

1. the contributors needed to implement new roles are present, capable, and ready to contribute;
2. the people occupying discontinuing roles are redeployed or otherwise assisted;
3. the people occupying modified roles are prepared to perform those roles successfully; and
4. identified gaps in achieving the goals of Sufficiency with current contributors are remedied.

The plan describes how the enterprise, including its structure and the positions that implement it, will change.[3] It identifies what new roles and how many of each will be added to the business, what existing roles will be discontinued, and what continuing roles will be redesigned. It specifies the timeline for filling new roles, retiring discontinuing roles, and bringing online redesigned roles. Along with the timeline, the plan defines metrics for gauging progress in satisfying the business's new workforce needs.

Each workforce change triggers action by one or more Sufficiency services. For example, Position Management will need to profile new roles and redesign the roles that are changing. Training and Development will need to develop instructional resources and schedule training to prepare people to perform their

[2] The traditional designation for this activity is Human Resource Planning or Workforce Planning.
[3] This description is drawn from the company's next year business plan.

redesigned roles. Accession will need to develop screening instruments for qualifying applicants for new roles and selection tools for selecting the best candidates.

The Sufficiency Plan also identifies gaps in the effectiveness of the Sufficiency services provided to current members. It specifies goals and timelines for closing these gaps and directs actions each Sufficiency service must implement to achieve these goals. It also defines metrics that will gauge progress and achievement in remedying Sufficiency's deficits.

Preparing the Sufficiency Plan

A team of contributors completes the Sufficiency Planning process. Team members are drawn from each business function. Selection is made based on the depth and breadth of expertise of a potential team member on how his or her function produces value and the roles that accomplish that purpose. The team is aided in its work by having access to people with expertise in each of Sufficiency's 11 special services.

The Sufficiency Planning team uses three main inputs: the enterprise's yearly business plan, information describing the current state of the business's membership, and the results of the Sufficiency function's Renewal process. The information profiling current members focuses on their past and current roles, relevant demographics, and their profiles of competencies and proficiencies. The descriptions of members' current competencies is constructed from their performance on job selection criteria, their histories of training and education, the record of roles they have performed, and their level of success in performing each role.

Understanding How the Enterprise Will Change

The planning team begins by analyzing the enterprise's yearly business plan to understand how the business will change. The team registers any changes the plan makes to the enterprise's offering, buying–benefiting experience, organizational structure, extended value steams, work processes, and employed technologies. It also notes any changes in the business's throughput demands and the markets the enterprise will serve.

Determining the Future-State Workforce Needs

The team evaluates the changes described in the business plan to determine what the future roles and membership requirements of the enterprise will be. It concludes what roles, if any, will be obsolete; what roles will continue as they are; what roles will require a redesign; and what new roles will be added.

The team briefly describes the content of each new role and its major competency requirements. It completes the same task for current roles that will be modified. Position Management will later complete a formal analysis of both types of roles. The team calculates the number of contributors needed to conduct commerce in each new, modified, and continuing role. The team's analysis produces a description of the future workforce needed by the enterprise.

Identifying the Gaps Between the Future and Current Workforces

The team then compares the business's future-state requirements against its current-state member workforce. This comparison takes into account both the organization's new and continuing needs and the effects of attrition due to retirement, turnover, or other foreseeable events. It identifies all the gaps between future- and current-state membership that Sufficiency services must bridge (e.g., number of members needed, new and modified roles to analyze and fill, new competencies to be developed in continuing members).

Deciding How to Close the Gaps in Meeting Future Needs

Next, the team decides how to close the gaps it identifies. The team has three issues to resolve: how to fill new roles, how to assist members in discontinuing roles, and how to prepare members to succeed in roles that must be redesigned. The guiding rules are the following:

- Ensure that the enterprise has the workforce it needs to implement its planned direction when it needs it.
- Ensure that members who wish to continue with the enterprise have an opportunity to do so.
- Ensure that members can succeed in performing any new or redesigned role they assume.
- Ensure that every redeployment, transfer, assumption of a redesigned role, or other member-affecting action serves the business's and the member's interests inclusively.

With regard to new roles, the team's first choice is to source new roles from within, preferably by redeploying members whose roles will be discontinuing. Its second choice is to transfer current members into new roles where the new role offers a better fit for the member's career plan and he or she has the qualifications to assume that role. If time permits, either redeployment or a role transfer may be bridged by retraining members so they qualify for the new roles. The team's third choice is to engage new members to fill any remaining new roles.

With regard to discontinuing roles, the team's first choice is to find roles within the business in which the member can both succeed and advance his or her career interests. These may be new roles or roles being vacated through normal attrition. Alternatively, the roles may be temporary ones within the Sufficiency function created to facilitate the smooth transition of the workforce from its current state to its required future state. If no opportunity within the business is present, then the member must be supported in discovering opportunities outside the business that will advance his or her career path and personal development.[4]

Deciding How to Close Any Effectiveness Gaps in Sufficiency

Next, the team addresses how to remedy any gaps in the success of Sufficiency services that were uncovered during the function's Renewal activity. That activity analyzed the results of the yearly assessment of the adequacy of current services as regards ensuring the presence, engagement, and successful performance of each member in accomplishing the business's aim and in advancing their personal emergence. This assessment resulted in identifying improvements that must be made to Sufficiency services to ensure their improved performance. The Sufficiency Plan sets goals for accomplishing these improvements. It establishes a timeline for performance and metrics to monitor progress and achievement. These improvement goals are incorporated in the Sufficiency Plan and accomplished by the specific service responsible for the activity identified for remediation or improvement.

Finalizing the Sufficiency Plan

The drafted Sufficiency Plan is submitted for review and feedback to the business leadership team, the leadership team of each affected business function, and all staff implementing roles within the 11 Sufficiency services. Once finalized, the approved plan is disseminated to all members of the enterprise, and the 11 Sufficiency services begin their work to accomplish the goals the plan specifies.

Both new and changed roles require action by the Position Management and Compensation functions. The recruitment, selection, and hiring of new contributors require action by the Accession and Onboarding functions. The movement of people to new roles is the responsibility of the Role Transition service. The Training and Development and the Performance Management services pursue the plan's goals for boosting the competencies of current contributors, retraining incumbents of discontinuing or modified roles, and correcting the work setting and performance support activities or resources that require remediation. The counseling of incumbents of discontinuing roles requires action by the Career Development and possibly by the Separation/Termination service.

---

[4] See Womack (2017) for a description of how the Toyota Motor Company implemented the type of approach indicated here for supporting members when it was forced to shutdown one of its plants.

Position Management

Position Management is responsible for profiling and documenting every position in the company and maintaining its products in a complete and current state. It uses job analysis to develop position information. It uses the methods of classification to identify each position's occupational category and the methods of job evaluation to establish the significance of each position's contribution to the enterprise.

Position Information

Position information documents the purpose, responsibilities, requirements, and performance expectations of a role. Position Management uses this job information to build position descriptions, but this same information is also the critical information resource for *all* other Sufficiency services. Accession uses it to produce position announcements and develop the screening and selection instruments that support selecting new members. Onboarding uses it to prepare new members to assume their roles. Performance Management uses the information to build performance plans. Training and Development uses job information to assess training needs, prepare training plans, and develop instructional materials. The same job information is also a primary resource for constructing career ladders and career development guides.

Essentially, position information is a *sine qua non* for realizing Sufficiency. Hence, job information must be complete, valid, and current. It must be developed using legally and professionally accepted methods. And *the same information set must serve all* the Sufficiency processes; otherwise, the products these different services generate to support incumbents will be inconsistent and problematic.

Position Descriptions

A position description documents the content, requirements, and performance expectations of a specific role (Exhibit 5, next page). Position incumbents use them to understand their roles and guide their performance. The information each position description contains is also an essential input for job classification and evaluation and, usually, compensation. Sufficiency planners need position descriptions both to describe the organization's current workforce and to detect changes in the current roles members perform.

In a Life Enabling enterprise, position descriptions focus on the technical work for which the position's incumbent is responsible.[5] Each description records

---

[5] Appended to every description of a technical position is a description for the common role all contributors must accomplish.

the formal title of the position and the standard occupational classification it falls under. The position's content records its purpose, responsibilities, and outputs. With regard to outputs, it documents what must be produced, for whom, and to serve what purpose. The position's competency requirements define the knowledge, skills, abilities, and other personal characteristics needed and the proficiency level required for each to qualify as a candidate for the job.

Exhibit 5. The Topics Addressed in a Position Description

Topic	Description
Identifying Information	Records the position's job title and occupational classification.
Purpose	Describes the reason the role exists. It tells what the role—taken as a whole—should contribute to the organization.
Responsibilities	Describes the major duties and associated tasks that an incumbent performs in order to fulfill the role's purpose.
Outputs	Describes what an incumbent of the position must produce, for whom, and to serve what purpose.
Authorities	Describes the decisions, actions, and resources over which the position's incumbent has control.
Resources	Describes the assistance—human, intellectual, and material—that the incumbent may call on or use in order to support the performance of the role's duties.
Coordination	Describes with whom the incumbent must collaborate in the performance of the role, when, and what that collaboration should be.
Performance Expectations	Lists the accountabilities of the role and tells how successful performance in relation to each accountability will be measured and judged (success criteria).
Competency Requirements	Documents the knowledge, skills, abilities, and other personal characteristics and the proficiency level required for each to qualify as a candidate for the position.

The position description's authorities, resources, and coordination explain the conditions under which an incumbent must perform.

A position's performance expectations record its incumbent's accountabilities and specify the success criterion that determines his or her successful satisfaction of each. Performance expectations address both the manner of performance an incumbent must demonstrate and the results he or she must produce.

The enterprise's Functional Measurement and Feedback System tracks these role-specific success criteria.[6] Finally, every position description must contain any additional information needed for job evaluation (see below).

All position descriptions are stored in a centralized Position Management System (discussed below).

Job Classification

Job classification identifies the occupational group and the specialization within it to which each technical position belongs. Occupational classification should use the Standard Occupational Classification Manual (U.S. Office of Management and Budget, 2018). This classification system identifies all occupations in which work is performed in commercial enterprises. Classification by occupation and specialization allows position managers to group positions within occupational categories and organize them by their increasing level of significance. The result is a job progression schema within each occupation that incumbents practice. Each successive role in these schemas requires progressively higher levels of qualifications and has greater significance for a business. This progression of roles within occupations and specialty areas is the major input to building career ladders (discussed below).

Job Evaluation

Job evaluation assesses the significance to the organization of each position in a business. This evaluation uses a systematic method and a set of criteria to assign each position's value.

Job evaluation specialists use one of five methods to assign significance to a role. All of these methods require a proper job analysis and position description for the role being evaluated. The job evaluation methods are ranking, classification, factor comparison, the point-factor method, and market pricing.

A Life Enabling enterprise uses the point-factor method for job evaluation. The point-factor method requires an organization to define what characteristics of a position determine its value. Each characteristic represents a factor for evaluation. One or more scales are constructed to gauge the degree to which a position possesses each factor. When multiple scales are used, each scale evaluates a facet of the factor. Each level of a scale records an observable, measurable criterion to register its presence. The evaluation system assigns points to each level. These scales are constructed using the same process that is applied to building critical-to-quality metrics and success criteria. The evaluation system may also assign each factor a weight that specifies its relative significance with respect to

[6] The same system also tracks each member's performance with respect to the common role all members perform.

all other factors. Alternatively, it can treat all factors as equal. The result of this work is a structure of constructs and metrics that expresses a position's value from the organization's perspective.

A job evaluator judges each position's value by determining its score on each factor using the job's position description. Each factor's score is computed from the position's score on each scale used to measure the factor multiplied by the weight assigned to the factor. The Compensation system uses the points assigned to a position in its determination of the compensation the position will command.

The Life Enabling model's structure for assigning a position's value has two factors. One relates to the degree of challenge successful performance in a position presents to its incumbent. We label this factor a position's demand for *incumbent processing power.* The other factor represents the level of contribution a position makes to business success. This second factor represents the *business impact* of a position.

Demand for Incumbent Processing Power

Processing power is a person's ability to transform "givens" into "desireds." Two elements affect a position's demand for processing power. The first element is what is provided to the position's incumbent (Element 1 "Givens"). The second is the difficulty of producing the results he or she must produce (Element 2 "Desireds"). The fewer "givens" provided and the more difficult the "desireds" are to produce, the greater the position's call on its incumbent's processing power (Vitalo, 1998).

In evaluating Element 1, a job evaluator assesses two features of the position. The first is the amount of management assistance the position incorporates. The less management assistance provided, the greater the degree to which the position's incumbent must self-manage his or her performance (decide what to do, when, how, etc.). The second feature addresses the quantity and quality of the resources provided to support an incumbent's performance (adequacy of inputs and work process documentation, extent of job aids and other performance support resources provided, etc.). The higher a position's demand for self-management and the lower the level of quantity and quality of resourcing its incumbent receives to support his or her performance, the more the position's incumbent bears the burden for achieving success (Element 1).

A job evaluator assesses three features of the position's work to determine its status on Element 2 "Desireds." These are (1) the magnitude and complexity of the tasks the incumbent must perform, (2) the novelty of the output to be produced, and (3) the tolerance for error in the execution of the position. The more challenging the tasks are (magnitude and complexity), the more novel the output to be produced is, and the narrower the tolerances for error are, the more difficult are the results an incumbent must produce (Element 2).

At the highest level of demand for processing power, a position is essentially self-managed and self-resourced. An incumbent receives little more than a generalized mandate. The incumbent must deduce exactly what must be produced and how it must be produced. He or she must determine what resources are needed to fulfill the position's mandate and develop or acquire those resources as needed. Also, the output to be produced requires the execution of tasks that are large and complex in nature. The output itself is novel and has little tolerance for error.

At the lowest level of demand for processing power, the position is fully supervised and supported. An incumbent receives a detailed definition of what he or she must produce, how, and when. The position provides the resources needed to do the work it specifies and incorporates coaching and other support to ensure that the incumbent performs the role successfully. The work itself is simple in nature. The output to be produced has a proven method for production and unchallenging tolerances for error.

Positions that demand high processing power require minimal investment by the enterprise to realize the benefits they produce. This allows the enterprise to apply its saved investment to adding greater value to the benefits it provides its customers.[7]

Business Impact of a Position—Scope and Effect

The business impact of a position calibrates its effects on bettering the lives of customers in ways that benefit all stakeholders inclusively. Job evaluators estimate business impact by evaluating two elements: (1) the scope of the work performed (Element 1 "Scope") and (2) its effect on realizing the business's goal (Element 2 "Effect"). A position has significant scope when its outputs affect the work of a large number of other business activities. A position has significant effect when its activities and outputs have high consequences for delivering value to customers.

Job evaluation assesses two features to determine a position's Scope: (1) the number of business activities affected by the performance of the position and (2) the number of work-consequential people contacts a position sustains in the performance of its work. The more business activities a position's outputs

[7] This statement assumes that the compensation system for positions operative in an organization follows traditional approaches, not the one described by the Life Enabling model.

affect and the more work-consequential interactions with other contributors it sustains, the greater is the position's scope.

Job evaluation assesses three features to determine a position's Effect: (1) how much impact the role's activities and outputs have on the success of the business activities that each affects, (2) the immediacy of the position's effect on the delivery of value to customers, and (3) how consequential the role's personal contacts are for the successful performance of the people with whom it interacts. Essentially, the greater the impact a position's outputs and activities have on the business activities they affect and the more consequential its personal contacts are for the successful performance of the people with whom its incumbent interacts, the greater the effect of the role. Also, the more immediate its effects are on the delivery of value to customers, the greater the position's effect on business success.

Team Management

Team management performs a role analogous to Position Management but for teams. Every team in a Life Enabling enterprise has a mandate to produce a specified contribution to the corporate effort. This mandate is formalized in a *team charter* (Exhibit 6, next page). A team management specialist supports each team on an "as needed" basis in developing or modifying its team charter. The specialist ensures that the charter for each team is complete, current, and recorded. The Team Management service maintains all charters in a centralized Team Management System along with a record of team membership. Team specialists audit the contents of the system to ensure that they are up to date.

Team Management is also responsible for evaluating the relative significance of each team's contribution for realizing the business's purpose. For this purpose, the team management specialist uses the same two-factor model (Demand for Processing Power and Business Impact) for determining a team's significance that Position Management uses to evaluate job roles. Here, the content of the team's charter, with its attached description of the work the team will perform, substitutes for the job's position description as the source material for evaluation. As with job evaluation, the output of this assessment activity is used in assessing the team's contribution to each contributor's compensation (see *Compensation*, below).

Accession

Accession brings new contributors into the organization. It recruits, screens, and selects candidates with the competencies and qualities of character needed to implement a Life Enabling enterprise and the specific technical position being filled. It supports each candidate's evidence-based decision making about whether joining the enterprise aligns with the his or her personal goals and values. Thus, Accession is implemented in a way that benefits both the candidate and enterprise. This is the only approach consistent with the Life Enabling model.

Exhibit 6. Contents of a Team Charter

Team Goal		States the result the team will produce, for whom, the benefits it must deliver, how it will deliver them, the conditions under which it operates, and the success criteria it will apply to judge its accomplishments. It follows the same format as every functional goal statement (Vitalo, 2019). See template on page 61.
Team Responsibilities		Identifies the major duties team members must perform. These always include ▪ Implementing the process that realizes the team's goal (attach description of process). ▪ Identifying and removing barriers that hinder goal achievement. ▪ Identifying and realizing opportunities that advance goal achievement. ▪ Monitoring progress and results and extracting and leveraging learning to improve achievement. ▪ Monitoring performance as a team and elevating that performance continuously.
Connections		Identifies the individuals or other teams or groups with which the team must coordinate its efforts and describes the nature of that coordination.
Team Procedures		
	Meeting	Answers the questions: How frequently will the team meet? Where (as a default site)? For how long? Who chairs each meeting?
	Agenda	Identifies the standard issues that will appear on every meeting agenda—for example, review team goal, review meeting goal, confirm agenda, resolve action items (list), summarize meeting results, and evaluate meeting success.
	Methods	Identifies the default methods for generating ideas (e.g., brainstorming), making decisions (consensus), and taking action.
	"Red-Faced Test"	States when and how the team will check on its progress and results.
Team Success Criteria		A table detailing the success criteria for judging the team's progress and results. Each criterion is anchored in one of the elements of the team's goal (result, benefits, conditions).

Recruitment of job applicants must reach into every neighborhood. Given that most community members will lack the basic competencies needed to qualify for a role in a Life Enabling enterprise, recruitment must use innovative methods to attract capable applicants and fill needed roles.[8] These methods enable people who are interested in joining the enterprise to qualify for open positions. One example is offering open-to-all instruction through community organizations in the basic knowledge and skills required of all Life Enabling enterprise contributors (pages 252–253). Given the broad applicability of these skills for performing effectively in every living, learning, working, and social endeavor, such training will prepare community participants to better succeed in their lives, whether or not they end up applying for membership in the enterprise. Thus, this approach elevates the effectiveness of the community itself and directly contributes to fulfilling one of the enterprise's expected outcomes.

Screening candidates and selecting new members must be functionally based. This means candidates must be evaluated on their demonstrated capability to perform their roles and contribute to the enterprise. Ordinarily, character-based criteria are judged using a verified history of the candidate's prior decisions and actions. They also can be evaluated in simulations that call for the quality of conduct being evaluated. Knowledge and skills should use an assessment method that tests the candidate's role-related competencies in an application scenario. Applicants that meet or exceed the minimally required proficiency are ranked based on their scores. If this approach is problematic due to the lack of proficiency in the candidate pool, an alternative approach can be applied. In the past, when faced with this problem, we have used a candidate's ability to learn the needed skills and apply them successfully. This approach incorporates training as part of the screening process. We constructed screening events that trained applicants in the skills needed for successful performance of a role. After training, we had candidates apply their newly learned skills in a simulated work context. We observed and rated their performance. We ranked highest those candidates that demonstrated the greatest learning and the best application of the skills taught. This approach, however, does require that onboarding include the additional training needed to complete the candidate's qualifications for the role before he or she assumes it.

The just described screening and selection approaches are examples of a *functional screening and selection* system. Such systems use performance measurements of candidates in actual or simulated work scenarios. Paper and pencil

[8] Research indicates that few people make evidence-based decisions (Keen, 1981; Mintzberg, 1990; Pfeffer and Sutton, 2006; Rabin, 1998), have adequate proficiency in understanding and responding to another person's experience (Carkhuff, 1983a), or possess proficiency in the other basic performance skills required of Life Enabling enterprise contributors (pages 247–251). While these skills are readily teachable and learnable, relatively few people have had the opportunity to learn them.

assessments of constructs, such as general intelligence, are not an acceptable substitute for demonstrations of a candidate's actual capability in a real or simulated work situation.

Screening and selection always end with providing each applicant or candidate a debriefing in either an individual or group format. This meeting explores the candidate's experience of the process, shares the enterprise's perspective, and resolves discrepancies in perspective. It also extracts learning that the candidate can use to advance his or her future career planning and job seeking and the enterprise can use to improve its selection process. This closeout experience reflects the model's edict that, whatever interactions you have with others, the process should benefit both parties inclusively.

Onboarding

Onboarding educates new hires about the company's approach to commerce. It supports the new member in developing an in-depth understanding of the enterprise and the member's role. It educates new members about the Life Enabling commercial model and tests their understanding through the use of decision scenarios that require them to apply the model's concepts and principles. It instructs new members in the company's business intent, its organizational structure, the expectations and requirements of all contributors, and the expectations and requirements of the specific technical role the new member will perform. Finally, it introduces the new member to his or her teammates and the work setting within which the person will work. In summary, Onboarding provides each contributor with the information and expertise they need to be a functioning member of the enterprise and operate effectively within it.

From a Life Enabling perspective, the best onboarding strategy uses a discovery approach. In this approach, each new member studies a set of resource materials, participates in specified training experiences, explores the workplace, and interviews members of the enterprise. The new member's goal is to produce an overview of the enterprise, its approach to commerce, the candidate's work setting, and his or her role. This permits the contributor to educate him- or herself through self-directed study. It connects the new member to the enterprise in a personal way and fully supports the assumption of personal responsibility and initiative. Onboarding staff act as advisors to new members, provide them feedback on their discoveries, and otherwise support their success.

Whether onboarding uses a structured instructional approach or a self-directed approach, the new member must demonstrate his or her understanding of the enterprise, the Life Enabling model, the role the new member will assume, and the work setting in which he or she will perform. Also, the new member must demonstrate his or her mastery of all the skills instructed during the onboarding process.

Training and Development

Training and Development transfers to individual contributors and teams the competencies and required proficiency levels they need to succeed in their current roles. It focuses on teaching what are termed "training competencies." These are knowledge and skills that are not required to qualify for a role but are required to achieve full mastery of the role.[9] They are identified through job analysis of the position's duties and are documented in materials supplemental to each position description.

All training within a Life Enabling enterprise is performance-based. Its goal is to enable recipients to demonstrate proficiency in accomplishing some observable, measurable task. It transfers the knowledge and skills and establishes the proficiency levels required to achieve this end. It ensures that trainees can apply their acquired expertise in their work setting and produce better outcomes. Even when facts, concepts, and principles have been instructed, a trainee's mastery of this intellectual content is demonstrated by his or her success in using it to guide performance.

Training content is organized into curricula. Each curriculum is a set of courses that teaches a facet of the expertise needed to master an area of performance. Commercial organizations train four types of curricula: Cultural, Technical, Regulatory, and Safety.

- Cultural curriculum courses equip members of an organization to successfully implement the set of responsibilities that *every member* of a commercial organization must satisfy irrespective of their technical specialties or job level (executive, manager, supervisor, or frontline worker).[10] Common examples of such courses are ethics training and multicultural sensitivity training. The common role for contributors in a Life Enabling enterprise is described on pages 273–274. The requirements for this role are documented on pages 247–251.
- Technical curriculum courses prepare people to execute roles requiring knowledge, skills, or proficiencies that only a subset of jobs within an

[9] Competencies required to qualify for a role are used in Accession and are termed "selecting competencies." Selection competencies enable a person to perform his or her role at acceptable but not necessarily optimal levels of achievement. Mastery of training competencies and the expertise acquired through experience raise each member's level of achievement to the optimal level.

[10] The construct of "job level" is common in all commercial organizations using the dominant commercial model but is not used in a Life Enabling enterprise. As stated previously, all contributors are both executives and "frontline" contributors.

enterprise require. It is this fact alone that differentiates technical training from other training. It is not that technical training necessarily instructs people in some scientific, mathematical, or engineering task, nor that it teaches well-defined, systematic methods. All performance-based training instructs people in doing a task and provides them a well-defined, systematic process for accomplishing that task. Thus, for example, training in writing job vacancy announcements is no less "technical" in nature than training in operating a lathe.[11]

- Regulatory curriculum courses instruct people in behaviors required by a governmental body as a result of law or regulation. Training accountants in new Internal Revenue Service reporting requirements for income and expenses represents one example.
- Safety curriculum courses instruct people in the competencies required to operate in a workplace without harm and in accordance with the business's safety policies and prescribed practices. The scope and prominence of the Safety curriculum varies based on the nature of one's business. The curriculum is most pronounced in businesses dealing with hazardous materials and potentially harmful equipment or processes.[12]

The current best practice curriculum development process is referred to by its acronym, "ADDIE." The acronym stands for Analyze, Design, Develop, Implement, and Evaluate. The model was originally labeled the Systems Approach to Training (SAT). It was developed as a "best practice model" in 1975 by Florida State University for the U.S. Army Training and Doctrine Command (TRADOC) based on lessons learned from failures and successes in training (Branson, Rayner, Cox, Furman, et al., 1975; Richmond, Wrench, and Gorham, 2009). The model satisfies the requirements of U.S. Government regulations and civil case law that govern the proper way to build training content. It is the current "professional" standard for defining and building effective training curricula.[13]

The ADDIE process analyzes the tasks individuals and teams perform in their roles or the regulatory behaviors each must execute.[14] The analysis uncovers the

[11] The term "technical" is derived from the Greek word, "techne," which means practical knowledge. An interpersonal skill, such as "crediting" (i.e., expressing recognition of the worth of another person's idea or action), is as fully guided by practical knowledge as the skill of adjusting the timing on a car's engine.

[12] The Safety curriculum will incorporate those courses from the Regulatory curriculum that specifically address safety issues.

[13] There are instructional designers who see the ADDIE model as obsolete, favoring instead a form of rapid prototyping. This view fails to appreciate the breadth of purposes served by ADDIE and especially fails to understand the requirements of the regulations and case law that govern what is a legally defensible approach to defining training content.

[14] This step assumes that a current analysis of job competency requirements does not already exist.

knowledge, skills, and proficiency levels required to perform each task. It organizes the content into coherent groups of interrelated knowledge that are sized based on the estimated time required for transferring knowledge to learners. Each grouping constitutes a course or unit of instruction. Next, the process sequences these units of instruction for learning so that people successfully pass through a curriculum in the most efficient and effective manner.

Each course in a curriculum has measurable learning goals, documented instructional content, and a procedure for evaluating its outcome. It uses an active learning strategy that includes tell, show, do, repeat, and apply methods for transferring knowledge and skills and elevating proficiencies. The "do" activity provides participants an opportunity to try the skill being taught and the instructor an opportunity to observe the learner's initial grasp of it. The "repeat" activity provides practice activities for mastering the content being taught. The "apply" activities provide exercises that support each trainee's ability to use the learning acquired from the course in their job context. Together, "repeat" and "apply" verify that trainees have mastered the content being taught and can successfully use it in a job situation. Training delivery systems range from trainer-led classroom instruction through computer-implemented instructional programs to print-based self-instruction.

Training and Development targets its services to individuals and teams who need a set of knowledge or a new skill and cannot acquire that competence on their own in a timely manner. This circumstance is more likely to occur the more different the new competency is from the other competencies people already possess, the more complex the new competency is, the scarcer people demonstrating its use are, and the less proficient people are as learners. Formal training also becomes essential when errors in self-guided learning are potentially harmful or destructive.

A yearly Training Plan guides the implementation of training. It adopts the training-related priorities and goals defined in the yearly Sufficiency Plan. It identifies target populations for training, sets training goals, and defines a plan of action to accomplish those goals. It specifies metrics for monitoring progress, assessing results, and improving its success in satisfying the needs of individual contributors and the enterprise.

Performance Management

Performance Management supports members and teams in assessing their completed performance and planning their improved future performance. It results in the production of an Individual Development Plan (IDP) or Team Development Plan (TDP). The assessment uses the same Status, Reason, Learning,

Direction (SRLD) (Vitalo and Vitalo, 2020) method for learning from performance that is used in completing the enterprise's Renewal activity.

Each contributor periodically executes a summary assessment of his or her behavior and results. The metrics the contributor monitors are documented in the contributor's position description. Each metric is a success criterion for either a responsibility specified in every contributor's common role or a responsibility in the individual's technical role. Each metric has a cycle for gauging its status and that status is tracked by the organization's Functional Measurement and Feedback System. Some metrics gauge results (e.g., customer-valued features of outputs). Others measure the manner of performance (e.g., supporting the success of other contributors).

In the performance review process, each contributor assesses what factors aided and hindered his or her personal achievement (see *Factors Affecting the Outcome of Human Performance: A More Detailed Look*, pages 128–130). The learning produced from analyzing one's personal affect on performance is used by members to build their Individual Development Plans (IDPs). Each IDP identifies areas for personal development and documents the means one will use to accomplish that development. Learning from the application of SRLD to one's job performance may also provide input to the member's Career Development Plan (CDP) (see below). Other learning may provide suggestions for improving the technical processes one uses to accomplish his or her work or features of the work setting in which one performs. These "Work Process" and "Work Setting" improvement ideas may be processed within one's local work unit or forwarded on through the organization's suggestion system if they have broader ownership.

With regard to team performance, each team assesses its achievements using the success criteria documented in its team charter. These too are tracked by the organization's Functional Measurement and Feedback System. The team as a whole applies the SRLD process to generate its learning. The team assesses both its progress and results in accomplishing its mandate and the degree to which its behavior matches the standard for teamwork. In this latter assessment, an inventory such as the Meeting Power Scale (Appendix G) is used to audit team performance.[15] Also used in this assessment is a cumulative analysis of the "end of meeting evaluations" produced following each team meeting that has been held since the last performance assessment.

---

[15] The method teams use to conduct meetings and manage team performance is documented in the standardized work document for teamwork. The assessment instrument used to assess team behavior should be identified in that document as well.

The team assessment process mirrors that used by each individual. As a team, members assess what factors aided and hindered the team's achievement with regard to both its specific mandate and its teamwork. Those performance-enabling and -hindering factors that relate to team member behavior are used to build the team's Team Development Plan (TDP). Learning that points to improvements outside the team's purview (e.g., work setting) are directed to the appropriate parties.

The Performance Management specialist assists individuals and teams in executing their performance improvement planning and follow-through action on an as-needed basis.

Career Development

A career is a person's path through life. That path is each person's means for self-discovery, growth, and the full realization of his or her talents and capabilities. Said differently, a career is the endeavor through which each person's individuation and emergence unfold. Individuation is advanced by the progressive refinement of one's identity. As it proceeds, each person's unique personality develops. Emergence is the flowering of one's capabilities to live, learn, work, relate, achieve, and contribute to others.

Career development in a Life Enabling enterprise supports members in refining their understanding of the path that best serves their individuation and emergence. This support occurs even when it leads a contributor to imagine pursuits that would better fulfill their purposes but require them to leave the enterprise.

On a yearly basis, at a minimum, each member refines the definition of the career goal that best serves his or her individuation and emergence. This process involves consolidating one's learning about oneself by analyzing the personal outcomes produced by one's decisions, actions, and experiences. The career planning process extracts this learning and derives its implications for one's likes and dislikes, values, interests, expectations, talents, concerns, competencies, goals, and sense of self. It translates that understanding into potential career goals that best serve one's continued development. It supports the person in narrowing these alternatives to that choice which best advances the person's growth. It defines objectives and plans for how the member can realize his or her career goal. It concludes the process by defining a timeline for performance and metrics for gauging progress. The resulting output is the member's career development plan.

A Life Enabling enterprise provides a set of resources that enables this career-planning process. It also provides coaching assistance as required. The planning resources include a resource center (physical or virtual) that provides access to career development materials (e.g., Occupational Outlook Handbook; career planning inventories, job aids, and templates for learning about oneself; job aids for defining a career goal and building a career development plan). It also provides access to information about roles within the enterprise. This includes career ladders that document progression in technical roles.

Another enabling resource the enterprise provides is the opportunity to experience other technical roles through internship, temporary assignments, or shadowing assignments. A shadowing assignment involves observing the work of another contributor who currently performs a different technical role that is of interest to the person completing his or her career plan. The assignment exposes the contributor to the work of the target role he or she is considering and the context within which it is done. It provides a learning opportunity that can validate one's interest or demonstrate it to be misguided. It also provides a member insight into how he or she must prepare to take on that targeted role should it be a proper choice.

Career planning is always done from the point of view of the member. The goal and plan that emerge may take the person in a direction away from the enterprise. This is understood up front. The enterprise is committed to supporting every person's emergence. If it can be accommodated within the enterprise, then it is. If it cannot be accommodated within the enterprise, then the enterprise supports its members in transitioning to a situation in which they can realize their goal.

Role Transition

Role transitions include temporary details, lateral transfers, promotions, and demotions. Temporary details assign a person to a new role for a defined period of time. Lateral transfers move a person from one position to another of equal significance. Details are time limited; transfers are not. Both serve either a career development purpose or fulfill a need in a different work unit.

The Role Transitions service is an administrative service. It arranges the move, documents it in the contributor's personnel file, and updates any other affected record keeping (e.g., work unit). Both promotion and demotion, however, require more significant involvement from the Role Transition service. Both are termed "employment decisions," as they affect compensation. As such, they are governed by law, regulation, and court case findings. Knowledge of these legal requirements is essential for the correct execution of each action.

Promotion moves a person to a role that makes greater demands on his or her capabilities and is of greater significance for the enterprise. That move raises the position-based component of an incumbent's compensation. Promotion, however, is not a reward. It is the enterprise's response to a person's growth in capability and his or her desire to undertake a more challenging role. Promotion is also a means by which the enterprise meets its workforce needs or replaces an incumbent of a continuing role who moves on.

Promotion is considered a selection decision. It must be treated in the same way as filling a new role. The open position must be advertised. Candidates must qualify for the position. The selection of the best candidate must be functionally based. That selection becomes a promotion when the person selected is already a contributor and he or she is currently in a less demanding role than the one being filled.

Demotion moves a person from his or her current role to one that is less demanding, as determined by job evaluation. A demotion is termed an adverse personnel action.[16] As the term suggests, demotion is commonly viewed as a negative judgment against the person affected. In traditional businesses, it is an action taken *against* an employee. In a Life Enabling enterprise, demotion is a joint decision between the enterprise and the contributor that moves a person to a position that better matches his or her capabilities to succeed. The decision is evidence-based, using the actual performance of the contributor in his or her current role. The goal of decision making is to enable the success of the enterprise and the incumbent inclusively.

Separation/Termination

Separation actions end employment with or membership in a business. They include both voluntary (e.g., retirement or resignation) and involuntary actions (e.g., separation for cause).

The Separation/Termination service has both an administrative and an enabling facet. Administratively, it addresses the record keeping and reporting functions associated with a separation and arranges the startup of any post-separation actions (e.g., initiating retirement payments). On the enabling front, it facilitates a person's transition out of the enterprise. It engages members in a consolidation of learning from their experience as contributors to the enterprise and supports them in formulating and executing their path-forward plans. It also gathers from the exiting contributor his or her ideas about how to improve the membership experience for continuing members.

---

[16] An adverse action is a suspension without pay, demotion, or termination from employment for cause. Such actions are governed by federal and state laws, regulations, and court case findings. Knowledge of these governing requirements is necessary for the correct execution of adverse actions.

If the termination is for cause, the Separation/Termination specialist clarifies with the person the basis for the action, responds to their perspective about the action, and educates the person about his or her rights to contest the action. From the enterprise's perspective, it must learn what went wrong, why, and how it can prevent such outcomes in the future. For the terminating member, it seeks to support the person in answering these very same questions from his or her perspective should the person be open to that effort. Separation for cause is an adverse action.

Compensation

In traditionally formed businesses, there are owners and employees. The business compensates employees using base or guaranteed pay, variable pay (incentives, bonuses, monetary awards), and benefits. Owners receive equity-based compensation (e.g., dividends). In member-owned businesses, such as some Limited Liability Companies (LLCs), Partnerships, and Worker Cooperatives, members are not considered employees. Members are owners. They do not receive "salaries," and they do not own stock, which is the basis for equity distributions in C-corporations, for example.

Member-owned businesses share the material benefits they generate in three ways: they distribute ownership rights to members, they allocate profits and losses to members, and they may provide members guaranteed payments. Guaranteed payments provide an ongoing income to members between profit/loss allocations so that members can address their life needs and be free to contribute to the enterprise.

Members of the business decide how each of these methods is executed. They document the solutions they decide in the business's operating agreement. That operating agreement structures the financial and working relationships that govern the conduct of members of the company.

In a Life Enabling enterprise, the methods of compensation members elect must comply with the model's principles. The solutions we suggest in this section have a Limited Liability Company (LLC) form of business in mind but can also apply to Partnerships and Worker Cooperatives. You need to check both State and Federal statutes that address these different forms of businesses and make any adjustments that those statutes require. However, if any require an adjustment that violates a principle of the Life Enabling model, then you need to use another form of business that will comply with the model's principles.

Distribution, Allocation, and Guaranteed Payments

Distribution of ownership assigns a portion of the business's net equity to each member. Life Enabling enterprises are team endeavors. Teams are composed of members who work together to accomplish a common purpose. Each team member has equal ownership of the enterprise the team undertakes. Given that fact, the model's perspective on equity ownership is that its distribution should provide an equal share to each member. However, where a member has made a material investment in the business, that contribution should be excluded from the equity ownership distribution and assigned specifically to the ownership account of the contributor who made it. This approach requires reducing the net equity computed on the company's balance sheet by the total of such contributions and distributing the remainder equally.

Allocation of profit and loss[17] assigns to each member a portion of the net profit or loss generated by the business at the end of each fiscal year. That distribution should correspond to the personal contribution of each member to the results produced by the business. This contribution is made through the member's performance of his or her technical role and as a member of the team or teams in which he or she participates. From the model's perspective, the greater the contribution a member makes to the success of the enterprise through his or her position, the greater his or her allocation of net profit should be. Correspondingly, the lesser the allocation should be of any net loss. Similarly, the greater the contribution each member's team makes, the greater the allocation should be to the members of those teams, and the lesser the allocation should be of any net loss. This principle ensures that members and teams receive concrete feedback from their performance in the form of their net profit or loss allocations. Experiential feedback is essential to learning. It allows us to directly register the consequences of our behavior as individuals and as team members as we pursue a result we value.

Guaranteed payments are a means by which a member-owned business can provide its members an ongoing income between year-end net profit or loss allocations. A guaranteed payment differs from a salary in that its payment does not require an LLC to withhold taxes or make Federal Insurance Contributions Act (FICA) payments. "Instead, a guaranteed payment is a tax-deductible expense by the LLC that reduces the business's net profit and is reported on U.S. Return of Partnership Income (Form 1065). For the member, guaranteed payments are treated as income subject to estimated income taxes and self-employment taxes. Guaranteed payments are made whether the LLC is turning

[17] In this section on compensation, the terms "profit" and "loss" have their traditional financial meaning, which is distinct from the Life enabling model's definition of profit.

a profit or not" (Sember, 2019). From the perspective of the model, the same approach used to decide the allocation of profits and losses should be used to peg guaranteed payments.

Caveat to Contribution-Based Allocation of Net Profit or Loss and Guaranteed Payments

There is a caveat to applying the principle of equitable distribution of financial gains and losses based on the challenge met and contribution made individually and through team membership. It establishes a bottom limit in sharing profits and a top limit on sharing losses. And it establishes a bottom limit in setting guaranteed payments. In order for members to continue to contribute their cooperative efforts to the enterprise, they must be able to meet their personal material needs and those of their families. Thus, for every continuing member, the enterprise must provide a level of material support that enables him or her to satisfy those needs without resorting to government-sponsored or community-based welfare assistance programs. Remember that a Life Enabling enterprise is committed to enhancing the communities within which it operates, not draining their resources.

When a business faces the challenge of meeting its members' basic material needs with limited resources, its members must apply their problem-solving skills to discover a way to remain viable as a business. However, if the enterprise cannot resolve that issue in a manner that satisfies the material needs of its members, it cannot be in business.

Deciding Guaranteed Payments[18]

Guaranteed payments are calculated yearly. The money that is distributed is that portion of revenue generated by human performance as opposed to capital performance (i.e., revenue generated from equipment, structures, machines, inventories, land, etc.). The principle applied to assigning guaranteed payments is that each member should receive a portion of earned revenue that corresponds to that person's contribution to generating it. The process for assigning guaranteed payments begins with determining the amount of revenue to be distributed to members. It then requires developing a guaranteed payments scale and

[18] This solution for assigning variable guaranteed payments requires that the business implement all the remaining Sufficiency guidance described in this chapter. Every position and team charter, for example, must include a set of performance expectations that establish observable and measurable success criteria for evaluating successful performance. A Functional Measurement and Feedback System also must exist and objectively measure the performance of incumbents and teams against these success criteria. The appraisal system must use these evidence-based measures of performance to judge each incumbent's and team's success. Subjective assessments by supervisors are an inadequate source of evaluation, as they demonstrate little relationship with objective measures of role success (Heneman, 1986).

defining the method for pegging each member's total payment. The business uses different methods to calculate payments for new members than for continuing members.

Determining the Amount of Revenue to Be Distributed

Begin your calculation of the amount of member-distributable revenue for next year's guaranteed payments by computing the sum of last year's net profit or loss and the total dollars expended on guaranteed payments.[19] This amount provides an estimate of the net revenue your business will generate next year. Adjust this amount for any significant changes expected to occur in revenues or liabilities due either to anticipated actions by the company or to changing market conditions. This adjusted sum is the total *possible* amount of money available for use in guaranteed payments.

Next, determine the portion of that total that was generated by human performance. This represents *member-distributable revenue.* Do this by computing the percentage of the total *possible* amount of money available for use in guaranteed payments that labor produced. Use the Bureau of Labor Statistics (BLS) approach. This approach presumes that the percentage of dollar-valued output generated by a factor of production corresponds to that factor's percentage of total cost. Therefore, compute labor's portion of the total costs incurred by the business last year. Total costs include labor, capital, materials, and energy. Capital costs include the cost of equipment, structures, inventories, and land. Divide the cost of labor by the total cost to determine the percentage of revenue generated by labor. Then, multiply the total possible amount of money usable in guaranteed payments by that percentage. The resultant amount represents *member-distributable revenue.*

Creating the Guaranteed Payments Scale

Begin this work by computing the total points assigned to *all new and continuing jobs* by Job Evaluation and to *all new and continuing teams* by Team Management. Include only jobs that are occupied and those new jobs that will be occupied during the next year. Similarly, include only new or continuing teams that will be populated and active during the next year of performance.[20] This total represents the sum of the productive contributions that will be made by positions and teams to creating member-distributable revenue.

Next, divide the amount of member-distributable revenue by the total points assigned to all new and continuing jobs and to all new and continuing teams.

---

[19] Whenever possible, substitute a rolling average for this single-year data point.

[20] If either a position or team will be engaged in productive work for only a portion of the next year, adjust its assigned points to reflect this partial contribution to overall revenue generation.

This produces the dollar value of member-distributable revenue per point of evaluated productive worth of each member's position and each team.

Construct a payment scale that ranges from the lowest level of total points for a position plus its team participation to the highest level of total points.[21] Assign each level of total points its appropriate guaranteed payment by multiplying its total point score by the dollar value of each point.[22]

Assigning Guaranteed Payments to New Members

New member status applies for the first year of membership only. The model views a new member's guaranteed payments as an advance on the member's expected contribution to the enterprise. That advance requires *no repayment.* The reason is that the enterprise selects the people who join it. It makes that selection based on its judgment that the person can contribute to its success. Thus, the business owns responsibility for the initial performance of the new members it chooses. Nonperformance is a function of the business's error. Extending the new member an advance requiring no repayment is an expression of its accountability.

Assign guaranteed payments to a new member by adding together the member's position-assigned point value and a fraction of the point value assigned to each team to which the member will contribute. That fraction is the total team point value divided by the number of team members. Adjust each assignment of points to reflect how long the position will be occupied during the next year. Locate this combined position and allocated team point value on the payment scale. The amount corresponding to the member's total point value is the member's guaranteed payment for his or her first year of membership. Divide that total value by the number of payments to be issued to calculate the guaranteed payment per pay period (e.g., divide by 52 if payments are made weekly).

Guaranteed Payments for Continuing Members

Continuing members receive a variable guaranteed payment that adjusts the member's guaranteed payment by each member's prior year-end performance.

---

[21] For each team in which a position participates, the position earns $1/n$ times the points assigned to that team by Team Management. *N* refers to the number of participants in the team.

[22] The levels in a payment scale are typically organized as bands of point values, not single values. One might reasonably create such bands using the standard error of estimating point values for positions and teams. Begin with the lowest combined point value computed for a position and its associated team participation. Create the first band by adding the standard error of the estimate for assigning point values. Pay would be pegged using the central point value in the band. The next band begins with the point value that is one more than the highest value in the previous band. The process is repeated until all point values are exhausted.

First, compute the position-based guaranteed payment for a continuing member. Begin with the evaluated total points of the position the member occupies. Compute the position's guaranteed payment value by multiplying that point total by the dollar value of revenue generated per point of evaluated worth. Modify this payment to reflect the actual performance of the contributor in implementing his or her role. To make this adjustment, use the results of the member's yearly performance evaluation. Each position has a defined set of success criteria against which the member's level of achievement is registered. If performance matches the targeted value for the position, no modification of the position component of the member's guaranteed payment occurs. If performance exceeds its targeted value, the base value of the position is incremented by an amount reflective of the degree to which performance exceeded expectations. If performance falls short of its targeted value, the base value of the position is decreased by an amount reflective of the degree to which performance fell below expectations. The amount of increase or decrease should be defined and documented in the business's guaranteed payments policy.

The team component of guaranteed payment is determined in a similar manner. It begins with the evaluated total points of the team's mandate, as assigned by the Team Management service. This is translated into the team's basic guaranteed payment. That value is divided by the number of team members, and that result is the incumbent's potential team-based guaranteed payment. This amount is adjusted to reflect the team's success in accomplishing its mandate using the same method as that described above for adjusting position-based earning.

Allocating Profits and Losses

Profits and losses are allocated based on each member's contribution to business success. Again, the calculation is based on the worth to the enterprise of each member's position and the team(s) to which the member contributes. The translation of these point assignments into an allocation percentage follows a slightly different method from that used to calculate guaranteed payments. Compute the total points assigned to all jobs by Job Evaluation and to all teams by Team Management in the same way as you did for deciding guaranteed payments. Here, however, you divide the net profit or loss posted at the end of the fiscal year by that total. This gives you a *net profit or loss value per point.*

If the net profit or loss is positive (a profit), each member is allocated an amount that equals the performance-adjusted value of his or her position and team participation. First, multiply the member's position point value by the net profit or loss value per point. Adjust that total for the performance of the member in his or her position. Next, multiply the member's portion of his or her team's point value by the net profit or loss value per point. Adjust that total for the performance of the team. The member's allocation of profit is the addition of these two computations.

If the net profit or loss value is negative (a loss), the performance adjustment made is inverted. The better the performance, the less of the loss allocated to the member. For performance above expectations, reduce the member's total allocation points by the percentage by which the member exceeded expected performance. For performance that was below expectations, increase the member's total allocation points by the percentage by which the member fell short of expected performance.

The Delivery of Sufficiency Services

Every member of a Life Enabling enterprise is responsible for implementing the Executive Function of Sufficiency. The breadth of each contributor's impact on sufficiency parallels the scope of his or her role responsibilities and interactions with others. At the level of personal interactions, that scope is limited to the member's personal network of direct relationships. But each contributor also has a substantive role in implementing Sufficiency services organization-wide. At every level of the enterprise, members contribute by identifying the organization's people needs, recruiting and selecting candidates, onboarding new hires, and completing training responsibilities. They manage their own performance, plan their careers, resolve issues that detract from their personal engagement, and work with other team members to ensure the success of their teams and the efficiency with which they work together. Finally, they collectively approve the principles and practices that guide all Sufficiency services.

How the Enterprise Supports Members in Implementing Sufficiency

Any solution to supporting members in their implementation of the Sufficiency function must provide two types of assistance. First, it must provide members access to the special expertise required to properly implement each Sufficiency service. Second, it should centrally produce those products and accomplish those Sufficiency tasks that have organization-wide application.

The correct execution of many of the Sufficiency services requires special expertise. Members need access to these specialty areas of knowledge and skills. This expertise guides activities such as testing and measurement, job analysis, job evaluation, instructional systems design, role transitioning, and compensation, among others. All these tasks also require knowledge of the laws, regulations, and case law (court decisions) that govern personnel actions (e.g., the Fair Labor Standards Act (FLSA), the Employee Retirement Income Security Act of 1974 (ERISA), the Uniform Guidelines for Employee Selection, and *Burlington Northern and Santa Fe Railway Co. v. White*, 548 U.S. 53, 68, 2006).[23]

Certain Sufficiency service products and resources have businesswide use. These include, for example, onboarding materials; career development resources; and cultural, safety, and regulatory curricula. Also included are any technical curricula for positions that occur across the enterprise. It makes sense that these resources be developed centrally with participation by members from different business functions.

The structural solution for providing member support for implementing Sufficiency services depends on the size and geographical dispersion of your enterprise. The Life Enabling model views a single-activity business as its unit of implementation.[24] For a single-activity enterprise with multiple business functions, the business should use a mix of a centralized Sufficiency function and a distributed network of Sufficiency enablers.

The centralized component is a separate business function. It accomplishes tasks that affect the organization as a whole (e.g., Sufficiency Planning) and acts as a knowledge center for the expertise specific to each Sufficiency service. It also develops knowledge resources (e.g., performance support materials, training curricula, courses, career information) that apply across business functions and maintains a centralized Member Management System along with a Position and Team Management system. On a rotating basis, a current chair of the Sufficiency function's leadership team serves as a member of the business leadership team. In all regards, however, the organization-wide activities of the Sufficiency function are accomplished with the full participation of all enterprise members.

Each other business function within the enterprise should have a dedicated Sufficiency specialist who participates in its leadership team. A virtual team of Sufficiency facilitators supports this Sufficiency specialist. These facilitators are

[23] Having said this, it should also be noted that all of the expertise required to perform Sufficiency tasks can be taught to non-academically credentialed professionals. Most importantly, all people performing such tasks must first satisfy the requirements that apply to every Life Enabling enterprise contributor *and then* possess the specific technical requirements for the Sufficiency activities in which they specialize.

[24] A single-activity business focuses on satisfying the needs of a specific target market. It possesses all the components that conceive, develop, resource, produce, market, sell, distribute, and support a product or service offering targeted to satisfy the needs of a specific group of customers (e.g., produces television sets, develop instructional products). It has a single production or service fulfillment value steam. A multiactivity business is composed of more than one business (e.g., produces multiple electronic products—TVs, smart phones, computers).

members performing non-Sufficiency-related technical roles who also serve as enablers of local Sufficiency actions on an "as needed" basis. Each is trained in the expertise needed to support local action with regard to the multiple services that ensure Sufficiency. These people, for example, support the formation and success of teams; conduct local training events; support individual contributors in their efforts to learn from performance; aid members in their career planning activities; assist local teams in profiling new positions; help with recruiting, screening, and selecting new members; and support members in identifying and removing barriers to engagement.

Critical-to-Success Resources Needed to Realize Sufficiency

Realizing Sufficiency requires three essential resources in addition to all those critical-to-success resources already specified. These are the correct selection of the enterprise's form of business, people with specialty expertise in each Sufficiency-implementing service, and ready access to knowledge and information about positions, teams, members, and finances. This last requirement is essential for sharing and using the wealth of critical information and knowledge generated by each Sufficiency service (position information and job descriptions, member information, team information, performance management information, training and development records, career development plans, etc.). All of these resources are essential to the proper performance of the Sufficiency function and the realization of its expected results.

Choosing the Right Form of Business

Every enterprise must declare its form of business. The form of business an enterprise elects defines its legal status. Each form of business affects who is recognized as the enterprise's owner(s), who controls its direction, and who allocates the surplus resources it generates. Legislated laws, regulations, and case law related to each form of business can constrain or enable the actions of people who contribute their cooperative efforts to an organization adopting one or another form of business. In the case of a C-Corporation, for example, case law defines profit monetarily, and it identifies maximizing profitability for shareholders as the primary responsibility of its directors.[25]

The people who implement a Life Enabling enterprise come together to contribute their cooperative efforts based on their commonly held purpose and approach to commerce. They work together to accomplish their common commer-

[25] "A business corporation [C-corporation] is organized and carried on primarily for the profit of the stockholders. The powers of the directors are to be employed for that end. The discretion of directors is to be exercised in the choice of means to attain that end, and does not extend to a change in the end itself, to the reduction of profits, or to the nondistribution of profits among stockholders in order to devote them to other purposes" (*Dodge v. Ford Motor Co.* 170 N.W. 668 (Mich. 1919)).

cial purpose. That purpose is to maximize the delivery of value to customers in ways that benefit all stakeholders and better the lives of everyone. Profit is not defined monetarily. Each person assumes responsibility for contributing his or her technical expertise to doing the work needed to realize that common purpose. Each assumes responsibility for maintaining the enterprise as a whole, capable, viable, and achieving entity. Each is an entrepreneur. None are employees. Every decision and action to ensure Sufficiency must be founded in a proper understanding of the people who create a Life Enabling enterprise as described in *Chapter 5.*

For a Life Enabling enterprise to exist legally and, specifically, for its Sufficiency function to be realized, the form of business its members choose must allow them to act based on their commercial model's purpose, values, and implementing principles. The model has a helping purpose. It defines profit as any gain that immediately enables the business's improved achievement of its purpose. It views the development of its contributors, their growth in competence and value-producing capability, as one instance of "profit." It does not view monetary gain as "profit." Monetary gain may be used to enable the generation of profit, but money itself does not advance the achievement of the enterprise's commercial purpose.

At present, the only forms of business that can accommodate the understanding embedded in the Life Enabling model are Self-Proprietorships, Partnerships, Limited Liability Companies (LLCs), and Worker Cooperatives. Self-Proprietorships are limited to one-person ownership enterprises. Partnerships are limited in their number of members by the Companies Act 1956 (Section 11). LLCs and Worker Cooperatives are unlimited in their number of members. All four forms of businesses are subject to state regulation. That regulation may disallow their use as a form of business for a Life Enabling enterprise.[26] Also, each multimember form of business has latitude in the definition of its structure and governing rules. Hence, each enterprise must research the form of business within the jurisdictions that it will operate and identify those that will allow the Life Enabling approach to commerce. For the selected form of business its members adopt, they also must tailor its structure and governing rules to comply with the model's dictates.

The tailoring of a form of business appropriate for use as a Life Enabling enterprise is done through a governing agreement that its members create. Prior to the business's startup, the projected members of the business must construct this agreement, the basic form of which is a team charter (Exhibit 6, page 404). That charter should explicitly adopt the business's strategic intent (*Chapter 7*) as its

[26] For example, some U.S. states require that businesses that provide state-licensed professional services (e.g., legal, medical) may not form an LLC but may form a similar entity called a Professional Limited Liability Company (PLLC) (Limited liability company, 2021).

purpose and the Life Enabling model as its approach to commerce. It should address other key issues, such as distribution of ownership, how decisions are made, and how profits and losses are allocated and guaranteed payments computed. It should require the formal adoption of Sufficiency policies and the application of these policies to all members. As to decision making, it should endorse decision making by consensus, *not* majority vote. Consensus requires that all parties endorse a chosen path. This includes people who avidly embrace the solution and others who find sufficient merit in it that they can accept and uphold it as theirs. Consensus requires dialogue. Dialogue provides the opportunity for the exchange of ideas and integration of different perspectives into creative solutions that generate greater value for accomplishing the business's purpose. It ensures that any action going forward is endorsed by the whole, not imposed by a majority on the whole.

Members With Specialty Expertise

Members fulfilling Sufficiency roles must reinterpret their specialty knowledge and skills to make it applicable within a Life Enabling enterprise. As discussed previously, much of the traditional training and mindset of human resource management specialists is embedded with the thinking of Capitalism. It is inappropriate for a Life Enabling enterprise. It focuses on satisfying leadership, whom it defines as its customer. Many of its practices have no place in a Life Enabling enterprise. Two examples are incentive systems and "forced ranking" performance management systems. Thus, members with specialized Sufficiency expertise must revisit their learning and sort out what is appropriate to a Capitalist enterprise and what is applicable in a Life Enabling enterprise. They must re-imagine how to apply traditional expertise from the mindset of the Life Enabling model. As with all members of a Life Enabling enterprise, they must de-mystify their expertise, make it available to others for their use, and work with them to elevate its utility.

Communications Infrastructure

Sufficiency services require several additional centralized knowledge and information systems. These additional resources are a Position Management system, a Team Management system, a Member Management system,[27] and a Financial Accounting system. These systems are components within the enterprise's communications infrastructure and must seamlessly integrate with each other and all other components, especially the enterprise's Functional Measurement and Feedback System and its Knowledge Management and Sharing System.

[27] Traditionally referred to as a personnel management system.

The Position Management System documents each position in the enterprise, including its contents, requirements, evaluated degree of challenge, scope, and effect. It supports the tasks of job analysis, position description development and maintenance, job classification, and job evaluation. Its contents must support the implementation of all other Sufficiency services, including Sufficiency Planning, Accession, Onboarding, Training and Development, Performance Management, Career Development, Role Transition, Separation/Termination, and Compensation. Each encumbered position identifies the person who holds it and links to that person's record in the Member Management System.

The Team Management System records each team's charter, including its success criteria. It maintains information about each team's evaluated degree of challenge and its scope and effect. It also maintains a record of the team's membership and, for each member, links to that person's record in the Member Management System. The system's contents must support the implementation of other Sufficiency services, including Sufficiency Planning, Training and Development, Performance Management, and Compensation.

The Member Management System maintains demographic information about each member, as well as his or her membership information (ownership share, profit and loss allocation percentage, current guaranteed payments, etc.), current position and history of positions held, current team membership(s) and history of prior teams participated in, training and development history, and any other information relevant to satisfying the company's legal reporting requirements, executing its membership responsibilities, and supporting the implementation of Sufficiency services (e.g., Career Planning, Training and Development, Role Transitions). This system must link to the business's Financial Accounting, Position Management, Team Management, and Functional Measurement and Feedback Systems.

The Financial Accounting System monitors and maintains the flow of financial resources into the business, within the business itself, and between the business and other entities. The system manages the capital accounts of members. It provides the information that the Compensation service requires to determine the distribution of equity, the allocation of the net profit or loss, and the assignment of guaranteed payments to members. Its reports support members in their deliberations about the material status of the business and its decision making relative to that status. It also satisfies all other financial management and reporting responsibilities that are required by law or regulation.

Synergy refers to the integration of efforts among all contributors to a business. Within a Life Enabling enterprise, this means all contributors working together as a team, causing their collective efforts to produce an effect greater than the sum of their individual effects. This is the expected state of every Life Enabling enterprise.

Chapter 15

Synergy: The Canary in a Coal Mine

The Executive Function of Synergy is the least demanding of the three executive functions. The reason is that by implementing the model's Strategic and Operations components and its guidance for ensuring Effectiveness and Sufficiency, you have put in place all the requirements necessary for synergy to emerge.

The members of your enterprise are inherently social and personal in their orientation. They seek to connect with others as they pursue their emergence as individuals. They seek mutually benefiting, productive relationships and act to realize them. They recognize that their desire for productive connectedness with others and their striving for self-actualization operate interdependently. Each is necessary for the other to thrive. And, therefore, they invest in both.

They join the enterprise based on the substantive alignment between the organization's purpose, values, conduct, and needs and the individual's personal goals, values, interests, and capabilities. From their initiation as members, they are aligned, energized, and capable of performing their roles and working cooperatively with their fellow members. The infrastructure the enterprise establishes fully supports their teaming.

Members are fully engaged in their enterprise and work together both locally and across the organization. They get and give information freely. They work to accomplish their tasks in ways that enable one another's success and the success of the enterprise as a whole. They uncover problems and solve them together. They uncover opportunities to improve success, and they work together to realize them. They share ideas, appreciate the value in one another's perspective, and generate together integrative courses of action that have greater value than the individual ideas that sparked their creation.

With all contributors working together effectively as a team—stimulating one another's learning and achieving—the synergistic efforts of members produce an effect greater than the sum of their individual contributions. Synergy, therefore, is simply the natural expression of the makeup of the people who power a Life Enabling enterprise. It emerges spontaneously. Its continuance is fully enabled by the character and capabilities of its members, the design of the enterprise, and the communications infrastructure members build.

With this understanding, synergy in a Life Enabling enterprise is the equivalent of a canary in a coal mine. When a canary falters, it signals the presence of a dangerous situation. In a coal mine, that is the presence of a dangerous gas. If synergy is not alive and thriving in your Life Enabling enterprise, then it signals that your enterprise is not implementing its commercial model correctly.

The Activities That Ensure Synergy

Given that communication, coordination, and effective interdependent processing is the basic mode of operating within a Life Enabling enterprise, what actions are required to implement the Executive Function of Synergy? There are five:

1. Establish the organizational design and communications infrastructure needed to support synergy.
2. Monitor the presence of synergy.
3. Intervene to correct shortfalls in synergy.
4. Act to uncover and realize opportunities to facilitate synergy.
5. Strive for perfection in implementing the Executive Function of Synergy.

By establishing the organizational design specified for a Life Enabling enterprise, the enterprise enables people to work together smoothly to accomplish commerce. By creating the communications infrastructure specified by the model, the enterprise puts in place the underlying facilities, services, and other resources needed to share knowledge and information and allow people to connect, communicate, and collaborate with one another as a team across distances.

To ensure that synergy sustains, members must remain vigilant about its status across the enterprise. The Functional Measurement and Feedback System must track metrics that reflect the status of synergy, and this information must be monitored, assessed, and acted upon by members at least quarterly. This monitoring process must trigger problem-solving actions to correct any shortfalls in synergy at every level of its expression. Similarly, the monitoring should trigger problem-solving actions to realize any opportunities that emerge to render synergy more easily realized. These opportunities may be passed forward by members through the Businesswide Suggestion System or generated by members as they analyze previous performance, or suggested by academic research. They may also be discovered by uncovering differences in the levels of synergy realized across the enterprise and leveraging the learning from this variation to elevate synergy everywhere (Byron and Vitalo, 1991, 2004).

The enterprise strives for perfection in executing the Executive Function of Synergy by deepening its understanding of synergy and the factors that elevate it. It also continuously improves the design of its organization and its implementation of the communications infrastructure that supports all its contributors in working together as a team. It improves its monitoring of the status of synergy with regard to its speed and accuracy. It also improves the methods used to remove barriers to working together and preventing their future occurrence. Finally, it elevates the effectiveness of its means and methods for realizing opportunities to enhance teaming.

Monitoring the Status of Synergy

The status of people working together as a team must be assessed at every organizational level and at the level of the individual performer. At the enterprise level, synergy is assessed across the company's cooperative system. Within the organization, it is assessed across all business functions. Within each business function, it is assessed between work units in the same value stream component, across all components of every business function, and across all members of each business function's extended value stream. At the individual performer level, each contributor assesses the effectiveness of his or her peer-to-peer relationships with each member of the contributor's local system and each person with whom the contributor interacts in every other system with which the contributor connects.

Exhibit 1, next page, suggests anchors and partially defined measures for success criteria that might be used to monitor the status of the Executive Function of Synergy. It lists as targets the ultimate level of success an enterprise should realize if perfectly constructed and implemented.

Critical-to-Success Resources

Synergy requires all the critical-to-success resources already specified.

Exhibit 1. Success Criteria for Gauging Synergy

Anchor	Measure[1]	Target
Synergy		
People working together as a team across the enterprise's cooperative system	▪ Degree to which members of the enterprise's cooperative system apply the Life Enabling model's thinking to improving their performance in defining and pursuing their goals	▪ 100%
	▪ Presence of improvement in the degree to which members of the enterprise's cooperative system apply the Life Enabling model's thinking to improving their performance in defining and pursuing their goals[2]	▪ Yes
People working together as a team within their work units, across their functions and their extended value streams, and across all business functions	▪ Level of effectiveness of teamwork within each work unit, averaged across the enterprise, as measured by each unit's score on a scale measuring effective teamwork (e.g., the Meeting Power Scale, Appendix G)	▪ 100%
	▪ Presence of improvement in the level of effectiveness of teamwork within work units, averaged across the enterprise[2]	▪ Yes
	▪ Level of effectiveness of teamwork within each business function, averaged across the enterprise	▪ 100%
	▪ Presence of improvement in the level of effectiveness of teamwork within each business function, averaged across the enterprise[2]	▪ Yes
	▪ Level of effectiveness of teamwork between business functions, averaged across the enterprise	▪ 100%
	▪ Presence of improvement in the level of effectiveness of teamwork between business functions, averaged across the enterprise[2]	▪ Yes
	▪ Level of effectiveness of teamwork between each business function and its extended value stream members, averaged across the enterprise	▪ 100%
	▪ Presence of improvement in the average level of effectiveness of teamwork between each business function and its extended value stream members, averaged across the enterprise[2]	▪ Yes
People working together in their peer-to-peer relations	▪ Level of cooperative assistance experienced in peer-to-peer relationships, as measured using a peer-to-peer assessment inventory (example in Appendix H)	▪ 100%
	▪ Presence of improvement in the level of cooperative assistance experienced in peer-to-peer relationships[2]	▪ Yes

[1] All non-peer-to-peer measures are taken quarterly. Peer-to-peer measures are completed annually on a staggered schedule (1/12th of all employees make the assessment each month).
[2] Use this "improvement" metric if the expected performance is not 100%.

Section V

Closing

In this chapter, we summarize the contents presented in this book.

Chapter 16

Overview

This book has provided commercial guidance for that portion of humanity who either have retained or reestablished the native dispositions that describe evolved humankind (*Chapters 5 and 6*). Such people are *both* social *and* personal in their orientation. Their social orientation is reflected in their desire to be connected with others in mutually benefiting relationships. It expresses itself in their altruism toward others, even strangers, and in their preference for working cooperatively with others. Their personal orientation is expressed in their striving for individuation—the development of their unique personalities and the full realization of their talents and capabilities.

Both their social and their personal orientations manifest themselves in their commerce with others. As an expression of their social orientation, they seek to benefit others by enabling their success in ways that better the lives of everyone. As an expression of their personal orientation, their commercial focus expresses their personal interests, applies their talents, and advances their individuation. It functions as a vehicle for their learning, growth, and emergence. In this regard, they continuously learn about themselves and the world in which they live, elevate their productive capabilities, refine their understanding of what pursuits best express who they are, and advance the fulfillment of their personal potential.

Life Enabling commerce is the path through which these people fulfill their dual drives of sociality and personal emergence. Consistent with these peoples' makeup, the model's contents ensure that all commercial transactions protect, nurture, and enrich human and natural life.

Commerce

Commerce is an exchange between people, each giving the other something. It labels a comprehensive and pervasive set of behaviors that extend across every human life and all arenas of human activity. It is commerce between a man and a woman that creates human life. It is through the commerce between a child and its family that each child is protected, reared, and supported in its development and its family experiences the pride, joy, and excitement of witnessing a human life unfold. It is through our exchanges with others and our physical world that we expand our information and knowledge, develop our skills, hone our proficiencies, and progressively discover who we are as unique individuals. The traditional economic use of the term "commerce" that views it as the buying and selling of goods is myopic at best. A true understanding of human commerce must address facts descriptive of the full range of its occurrence, not just a narrow subset.

Economic Systems

An economic system or commercial model attempts to describe, predict, explain, and enable the control of commercial activity in an effort to ensure its success. People apply its thinking to guide their commercial efforts. Nations use it to guide their decision making about how they should facilitate commerce and maximize the benefits it must provide to those who control its governance.

As a human activity, each instance of commerce expresses people's motivations, goals, values, and social orientation. As *Chapter 4* explains, the foundation of every economic system is its set of assumptions about human nature and the context within which people exchange resources. It is people's makeup that determines the purpose their commerce will serve, the behaviors they will engage in to accomplish that purpose, and how they will define success. The contexts within which people exchange resources either facilitate or hinder the expression of their nature.

A model builder derives the knowledge that describes and explains commercial activity from the model's foundational assumptions. He or she extrapolates the effects human commerce will have on society as a whole by projecting the cumulative results that the commercial acts between individuals will produce.

Capitalism

Capitalism, the dominant commercial model, serves a society it posits as composed of people who act solely to satisfy their own self-interest without regard for others. Each individual's sole purpose as a producer is to maximize his or her accumulation of material wealth. This pursuit of the accumulation of wealth is never satiated. Hence, people continue to engage in commerce and continuously apply their presumed rational and informed decision making to seek out new opportunities to expand their wealth.

Capitalism also assumes that every context within which commerce occurs is free of all asymmetries between people with regard to concluding commercial transactions. This assumption is critical given the natural propensity of singularly self-serving people to just "take" what they want from others.[1] If no asymmetries of information, wealth, or power exist, then no individual can exploit another because no one has more power than the person whose resource he or she seeks. Hence, all commerce is resolved through negotiated settlements that, by definition, provide sufficient advantage to each party to warrant agreement. All such transactions are therefore deemed "free and fair."

---

[1] As documented in *Chapter 6*, empirical research supports this logical deduction.

Given Capitalism's suite of assumptions about people and the commercial context, its mechanics necessitate both the validity of its assumptions and the free action of people. Under these conditions, people wisely choose from the available offerings exactly what they need and make exchanges with others that provide them sufficient advantage to warrant agreement. It is this natural "wisdom of the market" that guides the evolution of commerce within a society along paths that continually meet society's material needs. It is this inherent rationality that external agents like governments must not disrupt.

Capitalism's Problems

As *Chapter 2* documents, Capitalism as an economic theory has no practical utility. Its failings are structural, consequential, and scientific.

Accepting for the moment its premises about people and the commercial context, the *theory* is structurally flawed. It includes constructs that do not behave in the real world as the model dictates (e.g., equilibrium), and it omits dynamic factors that have major consequences for economic activity (e.g., the effects of lending-based money creation on aggregate demand and the effects of leverage on market equilibrium).

Also, its empirically established consequences are not what it promises. It does not "raise all ships" and equitably satisfy the material needs of society as a whole. Rather, it funnels wealth to the economic elite. As Piketty's (2014) research demonstrated, Capitalism inherently advantages wealth accumulation by the already wealthy. There is no mechanism within Capitalism itself to alter this effect. Further, as empirical evidence indicates, this concentration of wealth in an elite few stifles economic growth, reduces upward mobility, and does not equitably provide for the material needs of society. It also causes social harm by reducing the access of the "non-elites" to opportunities for education, health, justice, and longevity (*Chapter 2*).

Each increment of capitalist success in wealth accumulation widens inequality within society and results in greater social and economic harm—not benefit. The continuance of this harm is sustained by the indoctrination of the exploited with the fiction that "merit" through natural giftedness and hard work is the explanation for the inequity they experience. It is also sustained by holding out to them the prospect that they too could one day become the economic elite. Yet, research shows that merit does not explain inequality (*Chapter 2* and *Appendix A*). And upward mobility is undermined by inequality, not advanced by it. Progressively, as its justifying fictions wear thin, the conditions created by Capitalism rend the fabric of social unity as it becomes manifest that there can be no true union among people who seek solely their own benefit.

The notion that Capitalism thrives on competition is also a fiction. Capitalists always seek to control markets by reducing competition. Adam Smith warned about this at the beginning of formalized Capitalism. He stated that capitalists always prefer "to narrow the competition" because it enables them to raise "their profits above what they naturally would be, to levy, for their own benefit, an absurd tax upon the rest of their fellow-citizens" (Smith, A. 1776, pp. 213–214). This quest of capitalists for control of commercial activity is a natural extension of their egoistic pursuit of maximum wealth in a context where the wealthy hold superior power in a society.

In the service of their quest for control, capitalists have always sought the instrumentality of political power. As documented in *Chapter 2* and *Appendix C*, this pursuit has succeeded. The political power they have realized has served its purpose especially in enabling the economic elite to accumulate enormous wealth by creating and exploiting opportunities for moral hazard.

The structural and consequential failures of the theory of Capitalism become understandable when one recognizes the theory's most egregious fault. Capitalism lacks any legitimacy as a practical scientific theory. As *Chapter 4* makes clear, every element of content in a deductive economic model such as Capitalism is derived from its assumptions about the nature of humankind and the commercial context. All its explanatory power rests on the validity of these assumptions. The theorems Capitalism uses to explain how commerce unfolds and what action, if any, should be taken to ensure economic success hold value only as long as its assumptions map to the reality they claim to explain. Unfortunately, Capitalism's assumptions do not map to reality. They are false. *Chapter 6* reviews in detail the empirical basis for this judgment. These empirical findings come from diverse sciences, including biology, anthropology, psychology, neuroscience, and sociology, among others. Therefore, the promotion of Capitalism by professionals and academicians as a practical economic system lacks all intellectual integrity.

As to Capitalism's failed premises, humankind is not composed *only* of people who are singularly self-regarding. It is also made up of people who are other-regarding. They desire to cooperate with others in mutually benefiting relationships. They value fairness and will sacrifice their well-being to benefit others they perceive to be in need. Additionally, people do not make "rational" decisions as a rule. Their decision making is most often affected by factors unrelated to the value-relevant features of offerings. They do not always choose exactly what they need. In fact, people frequently choose options that they later view as lacking value. Money does not drive all economic decision making. It has repeatedly been empirically demonstrated that people will elect options that do not maximize their monetary gain. In essence, one set of the assumptions (the nature of people) that underpin Capitalism's "wisdom of the market" is populated by fictions.

Also, asymmetries (e.g., information, wealth, control of the marketplace) between people do, in fact, abound. From before the emergence of formalized Capitalism, the very few in society have overwhelmingly controlled the wealth of society and the decision making of its political apparatus. In such a context, the model's laissez-faire imperative—derived from Capitalism's false assumptions—simply empowers the already wealthy and politically powerful egoists to exploit the remainder of humankind. As *Chapter 6* records, behavioral economists have repeatedly demonstrated in controlled experiments the readiness of egoistic self-maximizers to exploit others who are cooperative in nature. Thus, the second set of the assumptions (the commercial context) that underpin Capitalism's "wisdom of the market" is also populated by fictions.

Given the real-world context into which formalized Capitalism has been promulgated, its only conceivable utility is as a method of social control by the economically elite egoistic self-maximizers over the remainder of society. This is achieved by using its dictums to justify not redressing economic and political asymmetries and by rationalizing the idea that the capitalists and their pursuit of wealth accumulation is necessary for society to meet the material needs of its members.

Focus of This Book

The focus of this book, however, is *not* on the sham theory of Capitalism.[2] Its focus is on providing a commercial model that is based on three judgments, each supported empirically by the research reported in *Chapter 6*.

First, a proper science of commerce must derive its knowledge from the study of the full array of exchanges between people. To arbitrarily restrict this wide array of human behavior to a segment of its occurrence that involves exchanges in which money is involved undermines the legitimacy of its findings. It is akin to seeking to understand the animal kingdom solely by studying the marbled crab—an animal species that reproduces asexually. A true science of human commerce must incorporate facts descriptive of the full range of its expression.

Second, people's natural inclinations toward others are heterogeneous, at least as expressed in adults. A portion of adult humankind consistently function

[2] As a theoretical model of an imaginary world, Capitalism is not a "sham." Only when it is promoted as a practical model applicable in the real world is it a sham.

egoistically and act exclusively in the service of their personal gain. This conduct is observable across all their exchanges with others—not just those economists label as "commerce." However, an approximately equivalent segment of people are inclined to act in other-regarding ways. They prefer to cooperate with others and engage in mutually benefiting exchanges. If they perceive a greater need in another, they will sacrifice their own resources in an effort to remedy that need, even to the point of putting themselves in harm's way. This conduct is also observable across their interactions with others.

Our investigation of empirical studies led us to refine this initial description of egoists and other-regarding people. It uncovered that, within both groups, human behavior is nuanced. Some of those other-regarding individuals are reciprocators, and some are unconditional altruists. Reciprocators are initially cooperative but cease their cooperation when they experience others exploiting them. They also will sacrifice for others they deem worthy of such a commitment but not otherwise. Unconditional altruists do not apply these constraints to their expression of cooperation and giving. With regard to egoists, some exploit others without reserve in order to maximize their personal gains. They are resolute in their efforts to amass greater and greater gains in material wealth and power. They will take from others, even those others who act fairly toward them. Some egoists, however, are less forward leaning. One might label them "conditional egoists." While they remain egoists, they are restrained in the extent to which they will take from others. Their pursuit of personal gain appears to be limited to creating an advantaged lifestyle (comfort, security, material wealth, social status). Their egoistic roots become clear when their advantaged lifestyle is threatened. As reported in *Chapter 6*, there is considerable multidisciplinary research that supports this nuanced view of people's heterogeneous inclinations toward others.

The third judgment underpinning that no economic system designed to serve egoists can also serve other-regarding people. The reason is that the ends they pursue are diametrically opposed, as are the means they are willing to employ. One excludes concern for others, and the other includes that concern. As to means, egoists use manipulation, and the latter group uses empowerment. Capitalism serves the former group; no economic model serves the latter. And it is this latter group of humans that evolutionary theorists credit with enhancing the survivability and evolvability of our species.

The Life Enabling commercial model serves this group of other-regarding humanity. It includes in its formulation the reality that egoists exist. It also includes the fact that the contexts within which commerce occurs are rife with strong asymmetries in information and power.

The Life Enabling Model's Foundational Assumptions

The Life Enabling model makes assumptions about the nature of people but not about the state of the commercial context. It provides a detailed description of the people whose inclinations and capabilities are the foundation for its principles of commerce. While it makes no assumptions about the state of the commercial context, it does define a set of requirements that the commercial context must satisfy for the model to operate as described.

Assumptions About People's Makeup

The Life Enabling model's assumptions about humankind address issues of people's diversity, drives, inclinations with regard to others, and malleability. Each of these features of humankind has special significance for commerce.

Sameness/Differentness

The Life Enabling model assumes that people share universal qualities (sameness). These qualities are expressed in progressively distinctive ways (differentness) as individuals discover and act on their personal preferences, strengths, and interests and adapt to their specific circumstances. This process of individuation does not alter one's basic nature; it simply makes its expression increasingly unique in each person. Thus, diversity emerges as each person develops his or her own personality with its nuanced mix of values, interests, expectations, concerns, competencies, goals, and sense of self. Each individual interacting with another must personalize their application of the knowledge that applies to all people based on the makeup of the specific person with whom they are relating. This understanding applies to all exchanges between people.

Inclinations and Drives

The model further assumes that, at the beginning of life, people are inherently both social and personal in their orientation. This premise presumes that no preemptive biological deficiencies are present. People seek both connection with others in mutually benefiting relationships and their personal emergence as unique individuals. Their social orientation is reflected in their affinity for others, their desire to be connected with them, and—within the limits of their maturational development—their readiness to take into consideration the well-being of others as they decide what they will or will not do (other-regarding nature).

People's personal orientation is expressed in their striving for individuation. Individuation represents the emergence of one's singular personality and the actualization of one's full potential as a human being. This striving is enabled by people's inherent quest to learn and achieve goals. With each success, they build self-esteem and an accurate and positive sense of self-efficacy. Both fuel their continued pursuit of emergence.

In contrast to individualism, *individuation* neither implies nor avows the precedence of the individual over the interests of the social group. Rather, the dual desires for connectedness with others and individuation operate interdependently. Each is necessary for the other to thrive. Without the social component, the individual cannot realize fully his or her capabilities, as the social dimension is the source of their nurturance. It provides the stimulation that promotes the individual's physical, emotional, and intellectual development. It equips the individual with skills essential for survival and achievement. It supplies the connection to others that enriches personal experiences, elevates well-being, and provides a sense of completion. On the other hand, without the emerging individual, a social unit cannot grow either in membership or in the discovery of new ways to benefit its members and live within the world in a manner that fully develops the human species. The actualized individual, whether working alone or with others, is the fundamental source of social innovation.

Commerce, in all its variations, must enable and support both the fulfillment of people's inherent social and personal orientations; otherwise, it will undermine the survival and growth of humankind.

Cooperation, Caring, Conditionality

The model further posits that, while people's default behavior is to cooperate, share resources, and, with maturation, demonstrate a willingness to sacrifice their well-being to benefit others they perceive to be in need, for most other-regarding people, their continued cooperation with another is conditional. Its continuance depends on how they perceive the behavior of others toward them. Thus, people will work with others to achieve a commonly valued end and share their resources with them. They will act at a cost to themselves to improve the welfare of others, even strangers (altruism). But if they are treated unfairly, most of them will cease cooperation, suspend sharing,[3] and act correctively toward them. These individuals reciprocate negatively even at a cost to themselves when they experience a person being selfish, manipulative, or disrespectful. In essence, for the segment of humankind the model targets, both altruism and reciprocity are fundamental features of their relating. Altruism is displayed in the absence of past or the expectation of future interactions. Reciprocity comes into play when there is a history of a past interaction, either with or without an expectation of future interactions.

---

[3] There is empirical research that finds that a small segment of people will act cooperatively and even altruistically *unconditionally*. This research is discussed in *Chapter 6*.

One implication of conditionality for human cooperativeness, including commerce, is that people who relate positively with us intensify and sustain our cooperative inclinations toward them. Others do not. Essentially, expressions of respect, empathy, honesty, and fairness by another are necessary conditions for sustained, positive human relationships. Manipulative, competitive, or deceptive action by another undermines cooperation. Here, competitiveness refers to an individual who selfishly seeks to maximize his or her personal gain without regard for its impact on others.

Malleability of People's Fundamental Nature

While the Life Enabling model posits a set of features that define human nature at the beginning of life, it incorporates the understanding that life experiences and personal choices may enable, thwart, or alter the development and expression of that nature. Indeed, both our interactions with others in our home, school, work, social, civic, and economic settings and the choices we make may even crush the presence of our native inclinations. Hence, the model *does not* assert that human nature is fixed throughout life, nor that all people retain the inclinations native to their evolved nature.

Especially vulnerable are our affinity for others, our intrinsic striving to learn, our freedom of choice, and our success in accomplishing goals. As Deming observed, one's "[f]amily environment may shatter at an early age dignity [and] self-esteem, and thereby shatter also intrinsic motivation" (Deming, 2000, p. 108). It may also fail to nurture or aggressively destroy one's natural affinity for others. Children's intrinsic motivation to learn and achieve may be co-opted by others and funneled into activities and pursuits that represent *their* purposes and not the child's interests or needs. As adults, our work settings may frustrate our desire to produce valued outcomes by prescribing tasks but not providing the means or support needed to ensure that they can be accomplished successfully. The civic arena also has powerful enabling or destructive effects on the expression of people's native qualities. Consider a society where governing officials are manipulative and duplicitous and take actions that are contrary to the people's will and harmful to their well-being. When the people caught in such a society have no power to correct the insults and abuses imposed by their governing representatives, the civic arena becomes an agent of personal destruction. It provides a steady regimen of frustration and conditioned impotence, as all its institutions are controlled by a small segment of people whose actions are self-serving. How people react to such a circumstance varies. Many withdraw to block further undermining. Some react violently. Some displace their frustration to targets they feel they can act against, even when such action will not eliminate the real source of their misery. In their different ways, many of which end up being self-destructive, people strive to survive while the spirit of life within them is under incessant attack.

Similarly, when other-regarding and inherently cooperative people must operate within the Capitalist economic system, which is falsely applied within a context that grossly deviates from its assumptions, they are exploited or deformed. Their natural inclination to trust and be fair is manipulated by the "puffery"[4] generated by egoistic self-maximizers. These are the assertions whose only purpose is to generate their "buy behavior." They promise honesty and a commitment to provide their prospective customers "superior value" but deliver neither. Within a society dominated by Capitalism, there is no recourse for such deceit. In defense of their deceit, Capitalist companies claim that it is the buyer's responsibility to ferret out truth from falsehood and that everyone should recognize that such promises are not necessarily true. In such a society, people inclined to trust and cooperate with others must either restrain their natural cooperativeness or subject themselves to continued exploitation by egoistic self-maximizers. Either choice forces them to distort their native inclinations and undermines society as a whole. The former produces wariness in cooperating with others and hesitation even in extending help to those expressing real need. Both undermine social cohesion by introducing doubt about the intentions of others. Repeated experiences of commercial deceit and exploitation ultimately destroy trust, an element essential to commerce between people (Beugelsdijk, de Groot, and Schaik, 2004; Cardenas and Carpenter, 2008; Dincer and Uslaner, 2010; Zak and Knack, 2001).

All the destructive forces we encounter in our home, school, work, social, civic, and economic settings challenge the sustaining of our social and personal orientations. That challenge may be minimal or great depending on one's life circumstances. The greater and earlier those challenges emerge, the less likely we are to overcome them and avoid the deformity of our evolved nature. For some of us, that deformation may be reversed through our persistent struggle to live fully and the support we receive from actualized others. However, for others, that deformation becomes their embraced way of life. The Life Enabling model is targeted to guide conduct by people who have either retained their native inclinations or recovered them.

[4] "Puffery" is the term used by U.S. District Court Judge Sidney S. Stein to characterize the promises made by Capitalist enterprises to prospective customers (Neumann, 2013). On this basis, the court concluded that a consumer could not sue a commercial company for fraud based on the promises it made to win customers, since they were never intended to guide the company's conduct.

Assumptions About People's Capabilities

The Life Enabling model's assumptions also address the issues of people's freedom of choice, their ability to make effective choices, and the conditions that determine personal effectiveness. Each of these aspects of humankind has special significance for commerce.

Free and Effective Choice Making

All models that incorporate market behavior as a driver of the efficient application of resources of production and the effective satisfaction of human needs require that people make free and effective choices. Being free to choose means that people can respond to the factual circumstances that affect them. They can choose those resources they evaluate as capable of satisfying their needs. Also, they can apply their productive capabilities where they think they will yield the greatest benefit for themselves and/or others. Making effective choices means that the options people choose actually represent the best alternative for advancing their purpose in any given situation. Thus, their choice making conveys true information about their purpose and what they require to accomplish the end they seek to realize. While all free-market economic models require free and effective choice making, they do not agree on what constitutes the presence of each.

Freedom of Choice

Within Capitalism, freedom of choice is accepted as present simply based on the fact that a person makes a choice. Whether choice-shaping forces were applied by others (e.g., persuasion, even coercive persuasion, deception, or the intention limiting of a choice maker's options) is irrelevant, no matter how significant those forces may be. The logic of this judgment, as explained by Barnard (1968), is that no one *other than the person* who chooses can *effect* the act of choosing. Also, everyone can always "not choose." Hence, whatever option a person elects is elected by the person alone and must represent what he or she desired in the moment. Thus, if a person were offered the option of being a slave versus being dead, he or she could choose death. If the person elects enslavement, he or she has made a freely elected choice, since the person alone controls his or her actions (see Barnard, 1968, pp. 149–150).

The Life Enabling model's premise is that people have the potential for free choice. The model deems the development of one's potential for free choice as contingent upon one's life experiences and personal actions.

Free choice is present whenever a person selects an object, defines a goal, or chooses a course of action that expresses the person's preferences *unaffected by artificial impediments.* Such impediments to free choice may be internal or external. The model designates as "artificial" any impediment that is not defined by one's inherent capabilities. Examples of "artificial impediments" include encumbrances that are merely a function of lack of opportunity, the imposition of preferences or restriction of options engineered by others, or the result of a passively acquired conditioned inhibition. Thus, if the absence of opportunity were reversed, the limitation would disappear, and the person's choice would change. Similarly, the person's choice would change if the coercive actions of others whose intent is to control the individual's choosing were nullified or the person's passively acquired conditioned inhibitions were removed.

Freedom of choice can also be compromised by physical, emotional, intellectual, and experiential deprivations. These deprivations may be the direct consequences of the determined actions of others or byproducts of happenstance. Their methods of effect are through the depletion of energy, the engendering of confusion about oneself, the undermining of one's positive self-efficacy, and the limiting of opportunities to explore one's world and learn new skills. It can also be undermined by withheld information or misinformation, inculcation of beliefs that erode self-worth or rule out avenues for exploration and discovery that otherwise would be pursued, and passively acquired conditioned inhibitions. Conditioned inhibitions automatically close off options for thought or behavior. Essentially, any action or event that restricts what a person might entertain doing or limits the means he or she might use to do it reduces an individual's freedom of choice. The loss of freedom may be compounded by a person's progressive submission to the debilitating effects of deprivation until he or she has functionally surrendered to the dictates of internal and external circumstances.

Freedom of choice expands as a result of physical maturation and the exercise of curiosity, striving to learn, and the progressive mastery of new skills. These skills expand a child's ability to accomplish a wider variety of tasks. This progressive development adds degrees of freedom by widening the possible ends and actions the child can entertain. This development of the child's freedom must be nurtured by the adults responsible for the child until the process becomes self-sustaining. The personal process of expanding freedom is continuous as long as the native features of human nature persist and thrive within an individual and no exogenous forces impede their expression.

Freedom of Choice and Individuation

Within the Life Enabling model, the significance of free choice is greater than its implications for efficient commerce. The model identifies freedom of choice as necessary for the human process of individuation to succeed.

Individuation requires that people be able to explore their world based on their personal interests and curiosity. These interactions provide us the feedback needed to learn about ourselves—our likes and dislikes and our strengths and deficiencies. This feedback enables us to distinguish real from apparent interests and separate values and goals that are vital to us from those that are not. With each venture forward, we expand our knowledge and master new instrumental skills or strengthen existing skills. New potential goals enter our awareness. We conceive more options for action. More of these options become possible for us to accomplish. With each expansion, a broader array of opportunities unfolds that invites the person to engage in further discovery, learning, and achievement. We become less restricted in what we can conceive, undertake, and succeed at. In this way, the process of individuation expands one's freedom of choice. Each enables the advancement of the other.

Effective Choice Making

Effective decision making elects options that best advance one's purpose and values. Capitalism simply assumes that all people make effective decisions (referred to as "rational choices") based on the value-relevant features of the options under consideration. Such decisions maximize each person's realization of value. The empirical evidence reviewed in *Chapter 6* invalidates Capitalism's assumption.

The Life Enabling model defines effective decision making by the process the person uses to make a decision and by the outcome that decision produces. As to the process, effective decision making uses either information- or knowledge-based methods that are goal driven and evidence based (*Appendix E*). Information-based methods maximize the options a person considers and operationalize the values a "best choice" must satisfy. They use fact-based evidence to evaluate each option with respect to its likely success in achieving the person's goal and satisfying the decision maker's values. Knowledge-based methods apply a set of knowledge to logically deduce from relevant facts which choice to elect or how to solve a problem. Both information- and knowledge-based methods permit documentation of how the decision was made, allow participation and review by others, and support the use of outcome information to extract learning that can improve the person's future decision making. Given the probabilistic nature of all assessments, using these methods does not guarantee success. It just maximizes the likelihood that a person will realize success and supports a person's continual improvement in making choices.

As to the outcome, effective decisions should elect that alternative that best enables a person's goal achievement in ways that satisfy the person's values. Each decision of significance must be objectively assessed as to its outcome by comparing what result it produced versus what result was desired. The learning derived from this assessment is a necessary input to improving one's decision-making proficiency.

The Life Enabling model does not assume that people make effective decisions. Both internal and external factors can undermine the effectiveness of a person's decision making.

The fundamental internal factors that constrain effective choice making are (a) the accuracy with which the person understands his or her purpose, (b) the person's competence and proficiency in using information- and knowledge-based decision-making methods, and (c) the person's discipline in applying the correct process to decision making. The effectiveness of one's decision making is compromised to the degree that these elements are lacking.

As to the person's competence and proficiency in completing decision-making methods, these methods involve multiple steps. A person must master the performance of each step. Also, personal proficiency in making effective decisions must be progressively honed through application, evaluation, and the extraction of learning that advances one's effectiveness in choice making. This requires proficiency in learning from prior performance—in this case, one's previous efforts at choice making. This learning eliminates prior errors, elevates proficiency, and improves future decision making.

The fundamental external factors are the freedom to inquire, the availability of and access to all information and knowledge relevant to making one's choice, the ability to assess the validity of information, and the material resources needed to process that information and knowledge or develop it if it is absent.

Factors Determining Successful Performance

Successful commerce involves performing a wide array of commercial tasks effectively. Only successful commerce satisfies the needs of individuals and society. Thus, people must perform the tasks of commerce effectively if any economic system is to function correctly and deliver its promised benefits.

A person must understand what factors determine successful task completion in order to manage his or her own performance of commerce. In cooperative endeavors, people need this knowledge to support the success of their fellow performers. Moreover, this understanding is essential to a society when it considers what actions it should take to support its economic development. Clearly, actions that advance its members' ability to conduct effective commerce must be a primary part of any such societal program.

Capitalism's apparent perspective on this question is that differences in success between people are a function of giftedness and effort. Commercial success is the definitive evidence of these personal qualities. Consequently, society should endow those people who are already successful in commerce with added resources that will advance their expanded success.

The Life Enabling model's perspective is formed from the findings of psychological and educational research. Following Gilbert (1978), the model defines human performance as including both what the performer does (*behavior*) and the *results* he or she produces. Using the results of observation, practice, and research, the model organizes the factors that determine the outcome of human performance into three groups: the person doing a task, the work process implemented, and the work setting within which work is done.

The first group of factors, the *Person*, relates to the makeup of the performer, who may be either an individual or a team. Factors within this group include the performer's competency, capacity, and motivation. Two other performer-related factors are the accuracy and valence of the performer's judgment about his or her abilities (self-efficacy) and the performer's freedom from distraction due to physical, psychological, or social problems.

The second group of factors, the *Work Process*, relates to characteristics of the method used by the performer to produce an outcome. This group of factors includes whether the process is effective and how well it is documented. As to effectiveness, the issue is whether the process is capable of producing its target outcome if it is done exactly as designed. As to documentation, the issues are its completeness, correctness, understandability by the average performer, availability to the performer, and inclusion of both "do" and "think steps" and metrics for gauging progress and results. "Do steps" state what action to take. "Think steps" are rules that guide you in doing an action correctly.

The third group of factors, *Work Setting*, relates to the context within which a performer completes his or her work. Four types of work setting factors affect the outcome of human performance. These are (1) resources, (2) coordination, (3) expectations/feedback, and (4) incentives. Resource factors are the wherewithal needed to accomplish a task as prescribed. This includes physical resources, such as workspace, machines, tools, and materials. It also includes performance support resources, such as supervision and other performance support aids. Coordination factors address the support a performer receives from others whose work affects his or her own. These factors include the adequacy of execution of interrelated tasks by others (timeliness, correctness, consistency) and the consistency of the perspectives of people who direct task performance. Expectations factors refer to the accuracy and timeliness of information provided to the performer about what he or she is expected to do. Feedback factors include the accuracy and timeliness of the information obtained by the performer about how he or she is doing with regard to satisfying task expectations. Incentive factors relate to the presence, consistency of application, and relevance of rewards to performers for good performance.

Essentially, the likelihood that a human performance will succeed is maximized when the elements in each of these three groups of factors are optimized to support success.

Assumptions About the Commercial Context

The Life Enabling model makes no assumptions about the current state of the commercial context. Its status is purely an empirical question that every Life Enabling entrepreneur must assess. The model does have requirements that the commercial context must satisfy for its dynamics to operate as specified. These requirements flow from the model's view that the function of commerce is to serve people's growth and emergence, both individually and collectively.

Requirements

For commerce to realize its function, people must be free to choose whether or not to engage in it. They need to be able to own the resources they acquire or create. Ownership allows people to use, shape, and otherwise process their resources as best they can so that they express the intent and capabilities of the producer. Thus, people can decide what resource(s) they will work with, who they will serve, what they will offer, and all the myriad other decisions commerce entails. People can select for themselves those avenues of activity that seem to best advance their personal emergence while providing benefit to others. With the feedback they receive from the people they serve, they can hone their capabilities and sharpen their definition of what they seek to produce and provide. With the feedback they obtain from their decisions and actions, they can advance their emergence as unique individuals.

Similarly, buyers' freedom of choice requires that every market be served by multiple producers, each attempting to address the buyers' needs. To make valid selections, buyers must understand their real needs. They must use information- or knowledge-based methods to select the best offering available to them based on their value-relevant features. This requires that they have access to all the information relevant to their decision making. It also requires that they be free from pressures and other hindrances that compromise their effective decision making.

Once they have made an acquisition, buyers must assess the value delivered by their choices and use the learning from that assessment to elevate their decision-making proficiency. They also must seek redress for any harm they experience from producers, as that is valuable feedback that producers need to improve their performance. For this to occur, third-party adjudication of claims for redress of harm must be evidence based, unbiased, use information- or knowledge-based methods, and be easily accessible.

For markets to support Life Enabling commerce, they must satisfy certain additional requirements. Specifically, they must be free of artificial barriers to competition. This includes the absence of (a) coordination among producers, (b) any elements that preferentially benefit one or a subset of producers, (c) any artificial hindrances to market entry by new producers, and (d) any elements that hinder a customer's transfer from one producer to another. Finally, in each market, buyers must have the unrestricted right to seek redress for harm resulting from the actions of producers.

To What Degree Must These Conditions Be Met?

Initially, a marketplace's compliance with the model's commercial context requirements must be sufficient to allow a Life Enabling entrepreneur to establish his or her enterprise's presence in that marketplace. If an enterprise can sustain its operation, it can work progressively to expand the marketplace's satisfaction of the model's full requirements. However, as a Life Enabling entrepreneur, you can only expand a market's freedom from within if you can initially compete through excellence with sufficient success to sustain your commerce. Ultimately, the marketplace must fully comply with the model's commercial context requirements for your enterprise to thrive and fully deliver its benefits.

How the Requirements of the Marketplace Are Satisfied

As stated above, the Life Enabling model does not assume that the current state of any commercial context satisfies its requirements. Indeed, the same empirical evidence that invalidates the assumptions of Capitalism and reveals its structural and consequential problems also makes clear that few, if any, commercial contexts conform to the requirements for Life Enabling commerce.

In response to this fact, the model assigns responsibility to producers who adopt its approach to commerce to progressively transform commercial contexts from their given state to the state required for fully successful Life Enabling commerce. Thus, it is up to Life Enabling enterprises to advance people's capabilities of acting freely and making effective choices. It also is their responsibility to ensure that the marketplaces within which they do commerce satisfy all the model's remaining requirements. This assignment of responsibility to the producer is based on the fact that each producer freely chooses to implement Life Enabling commerce and selects the market in which he or she will conduct it. The producer can only succeed if all parties to commerce and the marketplace the producer enters satisfy the model's requirements.

This special producer responsibility *does not* negate any other party's responsibility for ensuring the same outcomes. Thus, while a producer must work to raise every prospective customer's free and effective choice making, it remains the responsibility of every prospective customer to raise his or her own capability to make free and effective choices.

The Realisticness of the Life Enabling Model's Assumptions

Goodwin (1991) introduced the requirement that the "realisticness" of an economic model's assumptions be established. The term "realisticness" refers to whether the assumptions made by a given theory map to the empirically established facts of the state they describe. If they do not, that failure would falsify the model's assumptions and the theorems it derives from them (*Chapter 4*).

The empirical evidence reviewed in *Chapter 6* makes clear that the assumptions underpinning Capitalism do not map to reality. In contrast, and contrary to received wisdom, the findings of empirical science do support the realisticness of the Life Enabling model's assumptions. Yes, when first read, the assumptions made by the Life Enabling model about humankind appear farfetched, especially when viewed through the image of people promulgated by the mainstream media (news, film, etc.) and our accepted notions about commerce. However, in contrast to Capitalism, the findings of empirical science uphold the judgment that a substantial portion of humanity does conform to the depiction of humankind the model presents and that its assumptions better represent humankind's evolved nature than does Capitalism's assumptions.

Evidence Concerning Sameness and Differentness

The first assumption of the model—sameness and differentness—is axiomatic. It is the fundamental assumption of science that generalizations can be made about the objects it investigates, including human beings. All the generalizations science makes about a class of objects (e.g., humankind) apply universally to class members (e.g., requirements for oxygen, nutrition, excretion of waste products, etc.). Hence, all science implicitly accepts the assumption of "sameness." It also supports the notion of differentness. No generalization about a physical object is without variation in its expression across all instances of that object. Every feature of a human being, for example, displays variation in its expression when its structure and function are measured across humans. For most features, that distribution is normal (bell-shaped curve). It has both a central tendency that represents our commonality and variation across a range of values that represents our differentness one from another.

Evidence Concerning Whether Humans Are Social Beings

Common observations of humankind support the judgment that humans are social beings. They procreate sexually, not asexually. They evidence pair bonding. Even as adults, they almost always live in groups. Their communities encompass mostly unrelated others with whom they associate in informal and formal organizations. Their offspring are born immature and helpless. Their survival is secured only through the caring of others. As parents, adult humans divert their energies from ensuring their personal survival to investing in protecting, nurturing, instructing, and guiding their child's development. Also, humans cooperate across generations in caring for their young. Finally, human relationships are not solely task-based. They have an *affective* component which, when positive, creates a strong sense of connection and, at the highest level, intimacy. This connectedness is amply demonstrated when a relationship is interrupted by a death. That loss results in the survivor's expressions of pain, grief, and mourning. All of the above observations demonstrate the essential social nature of the human species.

In addition to these naturalistic observations, the phenomenon of human sociality is fully accepted within evolutionary biology. The human species is classified as exhibiting the highest level of sociality—"eusociality"—by sociobiologists and is therefore said to be a "social animal." From the perspective of evolutionary theory, traits like sociality emerge and sustain *only when they provide a fitness advantage*. Sociality specifically has rendered the species fitter in a Darwinian sense and elevated its long-term survival capabilities (*Chapter 6*).

The fitness benefits of sociality have fostered the emergence and propagation of other phenotypic features that enhance sociality's sustainment. One of these is the superior development in humans of the neocortex of the brain. This area of the brain enables people to manipulate information, form conclusions, tailor communication with others, and coordinate complex activities. All these qualities support advanced sociality. They enable the development of complex language systems, further enabling sociality. They also enable the interpretation metaphor and other higher-order cognitive behaviors. The superior growth of the neocortex in humans has elevated each individual's ability to cognitively solve problems and accelerated the transfer of survival-enhancing tools and solutions between members of the same generation and from generation to generation (*Chapter 6*).

Research also reveals that human physiology has evolved elements that specifically enable social connectedness. Two such features are mirror neurons and the hormone oxytocin. Mirror neurons enable one individual to internally experience the behavior of another as though the observer were performing it. Research has found that the same neural circuits are activated in an observer as are activated in the observed person experiencing happiness. Similar empathic findings have been found for witnessing pain. Mirror neurons provide a physiological basis for empathy between people. Oxytocin is a hormone that serves to regulate physiology and behavior. It has been found to trigger social bonding and empathy. Its presence indicates a physiological basis for people's inborn proclivity to connect and relate with one another in caring ways. In support of another Life Enabling model assumption, it has been found that oxytocin's positive effect on human relating is conditional. Specifically, in a relationship where one party trusts another, the administration of exogenous oxytocin to either party increases the expression of prosociality by the injected party. But if the relational context is one of distrust, the injection of oxytocin triggers the opposite effect (unresponsiveness, mistrust, or hostility) (*Chapter 6*).

Further, evidence related to physical well-being supports the essential nature of human sociality. It indicates that human well-being declines in the absence of connectedness with others. Research has repeatedly demonstrated that social isolation predicts increased mortality and the rate of incidence of disease in both the general population and individuals with established illnesses. Indeed, studies have uncovered a possible biological mechanism by which psychological states like loneliness impact physiological well-being (*Chapter 6*).

Based on the breadth of available science reviewed in *Chapter 6*, the social nature of humankind appears indisputable. At a minimum, available science clearly affirms the reasonableness of the Life Enabling model's assumption as to this feature of human nature. Indeed, given the available science, if a mechanism existed that could effect the denial of human sociality or its diminution, that mechanism would threaten the fitness benefits sociality has delivered to both individuals and our species. Indeed, available science suggests that the promotion of radical individualism and human action based solely on self-interest advances a manner of living that contradicts the nature and survival requirements of evolved humankind.

Is Sociality Just Masked Self-Interest?

With apparent ignorance of all the above findings, Capitalist economists an d some biologists have continued to maintain that humankind is basically individualistic and that each human only acts egoistically to maximize material gain from every human transaction. Their definition of "rational choice" in game-theory type experiments underscores their thinking. In support of this effort, they attempt to reinterpret other-regarding behavior in whichever species it occurs as misidentified self-serving conduct.

One example of this tactic relates to the warning calls issued by a member of a species that alert others to danger and appear to benefit the warned party while endangering the caller, since the caller's vocalizations signal its location to the approaching predator. Biologists committed to the self-interest model have suggested that this act favors the caller. They propose that the caller benefits from the confusion caused by its call, thus increasing its chances of escape from harm. Another explanation ascribes a self-serving advantage to the caller by causing the predator to fail. This explanation proposes that the predator's failure lowers the frequency at which the predator returns, thereby reducing the caller's future risk of predation. However, an actual field study that tested these egoistic interpretations of an apparent other-regarding behavior failed to confirm them. None of the expected self-serving outcomes were observed. What was observed is that the caller actually raised its odds of being killed.

Analogous studies of other-regarding versus self-regarding human behavior performed by behavioral economists and reviewed extensively in *Chapter 6* also confirm that it is not possible to reinterpret other-regarding human behavior as cloaked egoism. Some people consistently do sacrifice their well-being to benefit others even when there is no possible way for them to benefit from such acts.

Evidence Concerning People's Cooperativeness and Sharing

The evidence concerning people's inclination to cooperate and share is broad, deep, and consistent in its findings. Many people will cooperate with another individual—including strangers—even when non-cooperation offers greater monetary reward. They will self-initiate reductions in benefits to themselves to provide benefit to another. Such people will shape the benefit they provide another even more favorably toward the other if the giver is aware of the other's greater need. Even when people are given the opportunity to take from others with impunity, some portion of them choose generosity over self-aggrandizement. In fact, even when people are *punished* for not participating in an activity where they can take from others, some portion of them—about 30%—will never yield their choice.

As to people's conditionality with regard to cooperation, the research supports the Life Enabling model's assumption. Some people will enforce fairness and equity in their relationships with others even at a cost to themselves if they have the opportunity to do so. They will respond to being exploited by punishing the exploiter. And they will act to protect themselves from exploitation by suspending their cooperation in situations where they lack the opportunity to correct another's exploitive or harmful behavior toward them.

Evidence Concerning People's Striving for Individuation

The striving for individuation is an uncontested construct in psychology, marketing, and the popular media—at least within Western cultures. Indeed, it seems a commonly accepted observation that, in every arena of life, people personalize their appearance, settings, associations, and pursuits. Developmental psychology recognizes striving for independence and self-identity as a stage in early human development. Marketers incorporate the concept of "tailoring" as a marketing strategy for addressing people's individualized preferences. It is claimed that producers derive market advantages when they vary their products and marketing messages to respond to the unique preferences and values of different segments of their target customers. This thinking is incorporated in the design of media products that target a specific segment of people. Media executives shape each product's content, presentation, format, and appearance specifically to appeal to the preferences of their chosen target audience.

Individuation *does imply* some internal features of humans that, from a scientific perspective, require empirical evidence to support. For example, it presumes that people perceive themselves as distinct from others. It also implies that people have both an awareness of mental states and, especially, a recognition that their mental states may vary from the mental states of others. Some clever experimentation into these issues does provide empirical support for the validity of the subtleties underlying the construct of individuation. Ironically, one component of that research has been implemented by behavioral economists. Their research into decision making indicates that people make decisions in relation to others based on their inferences about people's motivation and intent. This implies that people have a sense both of their identity as distinct from others and that the internal states of others are not necessarily the same as their own. Also, theory of mind (ToM) research by psychologists independently confirms the early development in humans of the distinction between what is in one's own mind and what is in another's. Its findings indicate that one's sense of self as distinct from others begins early in life (before age 4) and becomes more manifest with maturation.

Thus, in addition to the manifest acceptance of the concept of individuation by psychology and marketing, there is experimental evidence from behavioral economics and psychological research that supports the presence of the underlying mental mechanisms necessary for a person's pursuit of individuation—awareness of self and differentiation of self from others.

Evidence Concerning the State of Human Decision Making

The wealth of research into human decision making confirms the Life Enabling model's assumptions about people's decision-making proficiency. People do not commonly make choices based on an analysis of factual evidence concerning the value-relevant features of options. This is true independent of whether you define effective decision making using the constructs of Capitalism or the definition incorporated in the Life Enabling model. It also confirms that people frequently misjudge the value that a choice will deliver when that choice's value is measured by the satisfaction it actually provides. Even when value is defined monetarily, people wrongly differentiate between two equally valued options simply because they are described using different language that actually has the *exact same meaning*. People also make decisions based on characteristics of the offerer or other issues unrelated to the value-related features of the options they are evaluating. Additionally, people's judgments of options vary based on their prior experience even when that experience does not alter the value-relevant features of the options being considered (reference-based decision making).

Summative Judgment

As described above and documented in *Chapter 6*, the empirical evidence supports the realisticness of the Life Enabling model's foundational assumptions. Its premises about people's motives, inclinations, and capabilities are evidenced by far more than a small subset of people. Thus, they can serve as the basis for deriving how commerce unfolds when undertaken by such people. Those principles can then be used to describe, predict, explain, and enable the control of Life Enabling commerce.

The Contents of the Life Enabling Model

The Life Enabling model's approach to commerce ensures that all commercial transactions protect, nurture, and enrich human and natural life. Its contents intellectually represent the concepts, principles, methods, and outcomes of commerce that is conducted in a manner consistent with the makeup of the people described in its assumptions. The model details the results, activities, and resources needed to undertake such commerce. This includes (1) describing the people who can implement it and how they must be prepared, (2) the purpose they should pursue and the outcomes they should produce, (3) the organizational design and strategy they should adopt, (4) the form of business they should assume, (5) the competitive strategy they should employ, (6) the critical information and knowledge resources they require, (7) the measurement and feedback system their enterprises must install, and (8) the communications infrastructure necessary to support their organization members in working together to realize their common purpose.

The contents of the Life Enabling model are organized into three components: Strategic, Operations, and Executive Functions. Sections II, III, and IV detail this content.

The Strategic component provides the knowledge one needs to define a commercial enterprise's long-term goal (business intent), the results it must produce, the marketplace activities it will use to achieve those results (commercial strategy), and the organizational strategy essential to its success.

The Operations component provides the knowledge one needs to steer the day-to-day activities of every business function that contributes to its commercial success. These functions conceive, design, develop, resource, produce, market, sell, distribute, and support an enterprise's product or service offering. They also construct and implement the buying–benefiting experience associated with each offering. By applying this knowledge, entrepreneurs ensure that the daily activities of each business function produce the results that will, in aggregate, achieve the long-term outcomes that the commercial model specifies in its Strategic component.

The Executive Functions component of the model provides the knowledge one needs to maintain the commercial organization as a whole, capable, and viable enterprise that is moving forward towards its goals. It addresses each of the three distinct functions: Effectiveness, Sufficiency, and Synergy. Effectiveness ensures that the enterprise is demonstrably advancing toward fulfilling the aims it has defined. Sufficiency ensures the presence, engagement, and success of each person needed to accomplish the enterprise's aim. Synergy ensures the synergistic integration of efforts among all contributors to the business.

The model's guidance, as recorded in this book, is written in language aimed at producers. The reason is that its primary function is to explain the Life Enabling commercial model to producers and enable them to use it. The guidance the commercial model provides, however, is applicable to all parties to commerce.

Also, the model as written here guides commerce at the individual commercial agent or microeconomic level. Nonetheless, by analyzing the cumulative effects of the conduct of individuals who follow the model's guidance or by using some other suitable method, one can derive its effects for society as a whole (macroeconomic level). Also, the model's explanation of how commerce, as it defines it, unfolds and what is required for its success can support government decision makers in designing programs that can enable its flourishing (political economy level).

This chapter discusses the implications of the research findings reported in this book and extrapolates the application of the Life Enabling model from an economic system to a model for nationhood.

Chapter 17

The Nature of Commerce

Chapter 6 described human commerce's various expressions from conception through death and the critical role of other-regarding commerce in enabling human survival, well-being, fulfillment, and evolvability. As *Chapters 2* and *5* made clear, not all commerce between people results in a benefit given or received. From these observations and the research findings described in this book, we can form a general picture of commerce as a class of human behavior.

First, commerce always involves an exchange between people. Second, its expression as a human behavior extends temporally from conception through death. Third, what is exchanged can be physical, emotional, or intellectual in form. Fourth, the act of initiating an exchange between people is most often free and self-generated, but it can also be conditional (*quid pro quo*) or reciprocal ("because you did this, I will do that"). Fifth, the range of human needs commerce must satisfy extends well beyond material goods and services. These "necessities" include positive affective contact with others, comradeship, and even intimacy. They include the receipt of learning from others, which enables us to survive and emerge as self-sufficient, contributing members of society. Without the satisfaction of these necessities, people do not fully realize their physical, emotional, and intellectual potential or sustain their well-being (*Chapter* 6). Nor do the societies they create maintain their integrity and vibrancy. Sixth, while the exchange always provides each party a stimulus, that stimulus does not always result in benefit to its recipient. It can harm people's survival individually and collectively or advance both. It can thwart personal emergence and undermine social well-being, or it can enable both. It enables both when the method of production of what is exchanged, the manner of the exchange, and the effects of what is exchanged are life enabling. These are life enabling when each elevates human sociality, fosters personal emergence, and nourishes the ecosystem that supports all life. When any element detracts from one or more of these ends, the commerce they produce is life disabling.

No legitimate study of human commerce can proceed without acknowledging these fundamental qualities of commerce, framing that study within the context of this understanding, and relating its findings to this framework.

The Human Needs That Commerce Must Satisfy

The research reviewed in *Chapter 6* reveals that the necessities of life that commerce between people must satisfy to ensure the welfare of individuals and a social unit are much more than material goods and services. These necessities include positive affective contacts with others, comradeship, and even intimacy. They include the receipt of learning from others, which enables us to survive and emerge as self-sufficient, contributing members within society. Without the satisfaction of these necessities, people do not fully realize their physical, emotional, and intellectual potential or sustain their well-being. Nor do the societies they create maintain their integrity and vibrancy. Note also that all these commerce-mediated necessities require that trust, fairness, respect, and empathy prevail between people and that their other-regarding nature be nourished and sustained.

Any economic system that aims to ensure commerce's delivery of a subset of human necessities (e.g., material goods) must be evaluated against its impact on the delivery of the full range of necessities humans require commerce to provide. If either the conduct or ends an economic system advances detracts from the provision of the full range of human needs, it should be understood as harmful to humanity.

Economic Systems as Human Instrumentalities

Economic systems express the makeup and commercial purposes of the people they are designed to serve. Those people are described in the system's assumptions about human nature. As we learned in *Chapter 4*, it is these assumptions that determine each system's understanding of commerce and its guidance for conducting commerce. Given that people only adopt systems that advance their purposes, the system a person adopts must embed within it the goals, values, and images of others that are identical to its adopters.

An economic system has no potency in itself. The people each system is designed to serve apply its thinking to guide their conduct of commerce and render their work more efficient and effective. The societies they constitute or control use the economic system to guide their collective decision making about how they should advance commerce so that their intended purpose is maximally realized. It is as an instrument of these people's purposes that an economic system affects the lives of people within a society.

Two conclusions should be clear based on the above:

1. The human condition of a society is not determined by its economic system but by the nature of the people who employ that system to advance their goals and values.
2. A valid economic system may or may not be life enabling.

As regards the first judgment, an economic system or commercial model simply formalizes how the people it is designed to serve can best succeed in realizing their purposes. Its application in a society is determined by the makeup of the people who control that society. *The human condition prevalent in a society, therefore, is not determined by its dominant economic system but by the nature of the people who employ that system to advance their goals and values.* A well-formed system of thought simply renders their behavior more effective and efficient in accomplishing the ends they seek. Thus, those who rail against Capitalism for the inequality and human harm it produces are wrong headed. The cause for the harm they witness is *not* Capitalism *as a system* but the people who use it to realize their egoistic purposes (capitalists). If Capitalism were abolished and the people it represents retained the power they currently have, they would simply create a new, "improved" system to function as their instrumentality. Rebranding is useful not only for discredited businesses but for any endeavor that has been discredited and whose proponents seek to continue its work.[1]

As regards the second judgment, research documents that a subset of humans are materialistically focused egoistic self-maximizers who seek solely to benefit themselves and act exploitively toward others. A valid economic system that enables the success of such people must by necessity exploit the remainder of society by these individuals. Its guidance will enable that subset of people to more efficiently plunder the resources of all others. It also will direct their self-serving exploitation of nature's resources, as it is from these resources that they realize their greatest material gains. In so doing, they will destroy the ecosystem that supports all life.

Similarly, by privileging the wants of a solely self-serving subset of people, it will create conditions that systematically undermine the evolutionary features of humankind that have built up our species' survival fitness and our capacity for evolvability. As documented in *Chapter 2*, these features are anchored in human sociality and in all the derivative fitness advantages that sociality has provoked. The promotion of an egoistically based system denies sociality—a foundation of humankind's strength. It destroys human society by undermining the very mutuality a society needs to exist. It renders commerce unable to fulfill all the remaining necessities that humankind requires from it. By definition, a valid system that enables the success of commerce as pursued by materialistically focused egoistic self-maximizers undermines the welfare of all people. Simply stated, it is a destructive system that can only end in the undoing of evolved humankind.

---

[1] The *Great Reset*, sponsored by the world's global economic elites, has the sound of rebranding to some analysts (Lewis, 2020; Talgo, 2020). In contrast, Schwab (2020)—founder and director of the World Economic Forum, the organization sponsoring the Great Reset—sees it as the "best chance" to establish "stakeholder capitalism," a version of Capitalism incorporating other-regarding concerns. Based on a correct understanding of Capitalism, that notion is oxymoronic. Its use lends credence to the "rebranding" notion.

A Valid Version of Capitalism

Capitalism's only legitimacy as an economic system is as a theoretical model of an imaginary world (*Chapter 2*). When it is promoted as a practical model applicable in the real world, it is a sham. It fails structurally, consequentially, and, most egregiously, scientifically. It is built on an empirically false understanding of humankind. Its assumptions also falsely depict the context within which commerce occurs as devoid of asymmetries when it is, in fact, rife with them. Additionally, it fails to acknowledge and address the variety of non-materialistic necessities commerce must provide to ensure human welfare (*Chapter 6*). Currently, it serves as a social control mechanism wielded by the economically powerful, materialistically focused egoistic self-maximizers. The theory's utility is in shrouding the exploitation of the many for the personal gain of the few by providing their conduct with apparent scientific legitimacy.

Although Capitalism as a practical economic system is illegitimate, a legitimate economic model in the service of people who are materialistically focused egoistic self-maximizers (capitalists) is possible. It would acknowledge that it serves a specific subset of humankind—not all humankind—and incorporate the fact that its use would occur in a commercial context rife with asymmetries that favor already wealthy capitalists. It would also acknowledge that part of its approach to commerce would be to maintain and enhance those asymmetries so that the people whose purpose it served could continue to maximize their personal gains.

Such a system would have practical legitimacy because its assumptions would map to the real world. It would of course jettison its soothing but false constructs of equilibrium, since the commercial context does not now and, under its guidance, would never support balancing of any type. It also would surrender its promises to "raise all ships" and provide for the material well-being of all humankind.

The commercial conduct such a legitimate system would explicitly promote would map well to the exploitive practices that Capitalist enterprises currently employ—like maximizing the internalization of positive externalities and the externalization of negative ones, exploiting buyer weaknesses in knowledge and decision making, hindering a buyer's opportunity for redress from harm, and weakening the power of labor to bargain for its fair share of the material wealth it generates. These and other related practices have been documented throughout this book.

Such a properly constructed system would have the virtue of being open about who it served and what it would produce. It would possess integrity of thought—

that is, it would be structurally sound and forthrightly accurate about the outcomes it promoted. If allowed to operate within a society, it would produce the very outcomes we now observe but label as "Capitalism's consequential problems." But given this new and legitimate system, those outcomes would not be discrepant from its declared intent and, therefore, wholly appropriate.

This new, legitimate version of Capitalism would, of course, destroy society. It would be a life-disabling, not a life-enabling system. In the end, it would also destroy its implementers. This is an evolutionarily sound judgment of such a system's ultimate outcome, since the superior evolutionary fitness of humankind is grounded in its sociality and the development of the survival features that sociality has provoked. Nevertheless, this eventual destruction might well be a distant "end point," and, meanwhile, its users would realize the purpose they desire *within their lifetimes*. Indeed, very many generations of materialistically focused egoistic self-maximizers already have enjoyed the material fruits of their labors and might well continue to do so.

Can a World Dominated by Capitalists Undo Biologically Based Evolution?

The real battle that exists within the human species is not between ethnicities, "races," religions, people of different sexual orientations, or other commonly referenced identifying factors. It is not between liberals and conservatives or progressives and reactionaries. It is not even between theories of economics and economic development—e.g., Capitalism versus Socialism or globalism versus nationalism. Rather, it is between two divergent sets of humankind—those who seek to control others in the service of their own ends and those who pursue their personal growth and enable others to do likewise. We refer to the former group as egoistic self-maximizers and the latter group as other-regarding humans who strive for their personal emergence in the context of expressing their sociality (cooperative self-actualizers).

From an economic perspective, members of the former group who populate the economic elite selfishly pursue the continual accumulation of wealth and use it to gain the political power by which they can continue to extract monetary gain from their fellow citizens. From a social perspective, they are all people, independent of class or role, who resolve the satisfaction of their wants by manipulating the behavior and controlling the choices of others. They seek to control the way others think about issues that affect the satisfaction of their wants in order to ensure those people serve their ends. In contrast, cooperative self-actualizers seek to empower others so that each person individually and all members of a society collectively thrive and realize their full potential as living beings.

Although the general public is unaware of this fact, science concludes that, on the scale of evolutionary time, the battle between these subsets of humankind has been won by cooperative, other-regarding humans (*Chapter* 6). Their emergence, as viewed by evolutionary scientists, has elevated humankind's survivability and evolvability. However, on the scale of human history and with a focus on Western civilization, the battle has been won by the materialistically focused egoistic self-maximizers— that is, capitalists as defined in this book. They control every so-called developed nation and have found it beneficial to their interests to install or prop up oppressive governments in developing nations whose resources they seek to expropriate and whose political apparatus they need to control (AbuKhalil, 2019; Agee, 1975; Greenwald, 2017; Kohn and Reddy, 2017; Longley, 2019; McCoy, 2018; Schmidt, 1987; Snider, 2021). Their end is always material wealth and absolute power. Their foreign policy is always *political realism* (Korab-Karpowicz, 2018; Mosely, 2021).[2] Their preferred method is coercion, applied either militarily or economically. In modern times, this coercion is obscured through stealth, misdirection, and rationalization. As to rationalizations, they cloak their actions by claiming that they are necessitated by the nature of the world (realpolitik), as a requirement for the advancement of civilization or the defense of personal liberty, or as a necessary response to humanitarian concern for the hardships experienced by others. This last rationalization is the most insidious, since, factually, their conduct denies liberty, undermines well-being, and operates solely in the service of self-aggrandizement.

But can the dominance of materialistically focused egoistic self-maximizers in historical time undo the fitness-driven emergence of human qualities that have elevated humankind's survival as a species? Can they create a world incapable of providing the necessities required for human growth and development and the enrichment of human existence? Can the pervasive, persistent, and coherent

[2] Neorealism (Neorealism (International Relations), 2021) is the modern, depersonalized version of political realism. It provides similar behavioral guidance without reference to human nature but as a result of the rational assessment of structural conditions of the world. Kenneth Waltz, the theory's founder, identified the key structural condition as the "anarchy" that prevails between states. This condition is a function of the absence of "a sovereign body that governs the interactions between autonomous nation-states" (Kenneth Waltz, 2021). Unrecognized in this formulation is the implication that human entities—whether individuals or their social units—are naturally disinclined to cooperativeness. Hence, anarchy prevails. Unfortunately, the science reviewed in *Chapter 6*, suggests that a substantial portion of humankind is cooperative by nature and would work together with others to produce a coherent societies. This suggests that Neorealism's judgment that anarchy between nations is the natural state of international relationships is based on a distorted sample of observations or an incomplete understanding of what their observations are revealing.

advancement of behaviors and conditions antagonistic to humankind's evolved nature undo biological evolution? Consider the following reasoning.

If a culture systematically rewards one set of qualities and actions and punishes another antagonistic set *and* the people who control that culture also control the resources that support physical life, then a vehicle is established for selective breeding. This vehicle for reversing humankind's biological evolution integrates the *non-genetic* effects of cultural evolution with the evolutionary mechanism of natural selection.

The cultural mechanism propagates human qualities and actions in historical time through indoctrination and behavioral shaping. Each dominant culture passes forward its esteemed goals, values, manners of behaving, and default solutions for problems in living. These "memes" are learned, reinforced by practice, and transferred forward to subsequent generations. Cultural evolution is not itself a biological process and *has no direct effect on genetic inheritance*. But, as previously described, people are malleable.[3] We adapt ourselves to better perform the behaviors we adopt. Our adopted behavior reverberates backwards to change who we are physically, emotionally, and intellectually. Thus, complying with culturally prescribed beliefs and conduct may end up distorting aspects of our evolved nature in ways that mirror the cultural memes we adopt.

We described a concrete example of this phenomenon in *Chapter 4* wherein we discussed the change in values and behavior induced by the study of mainstream economics. The research of behavioral economists has repeatedly found that, after training in mainstream economics (Capitalism), students become more aggressive, less cooperative, and more pessimistic about the prospects of cooperation (Bauman and Rose, 2011; Etzioni, 2015; Frank, Gilovich, and Regan, 1993, 1996; Goodwin, 2014; Khadjavi and Lange, 2013; Lazear, Malmendier, and Weber , 2012; Marwell and Ames, 1981). They also are more prone to cheating than students who have had no instruction in economics. At least a portion of these effects appear to be a function of instruction in mainstream economics (Etzioni, 2015). Also, note that the characteristics that develop as a result of taking these economics courses persist (Goodwin, 2014).

> About 40% of college students in the United States take at least one economics course. Students who, two years later, have forgotten the diagrams and equations, are likely to still retain an impression that only selfishness is rational, that limitless greed is a universal human characteristic, and that economic success—of a nation, or an individual—can be assessed strictly in terms of the dollar value of consumption. Beliefs like

[3] See page 106 for a list of research studies that explore the effectiveness of various methods by which our behavior can be reshaped by the systematic actions of others and the settings within which we act.

> this are the background for a culture that will accept as perfectly normal Ponzi schemes and cooked accounts, tax fraud and tax havens, the exploitation of children, women and immigrants, and corporate expenditures to get the most favorable political environment. Institutions—from governments and legal or banking systems, to the institutions of the family or formal education—are shaped by socio-cultural norms whose roots can be traced, in some significant part, to the standard teachings of economics —especially what it says about human psychology. (Goodwin, 2014, p. 101)

Thus, in *historical time*, people and their collective perspectives can be reshaped to conform to beliefs and regimens of conduct that differ from their native inclinations.

Given the empirical research reviewed in *Chapter 2* and its appendices, we understand that the people who control the culture of Capitalist countries also control the resources that support physical life. Given this fact, a transfer of effect from the cultural to the biological realm could occur in two ways: first, through preferential breeding and second, through the Baldwin effect.

With regard to the first mechanism, those who conform to the dictates of the dominant culture prosper materially. Those who do not are progressively denied the material resources essential for life. They either adapt in historical time, die out, or—if their existence becomes too burdensome—are eliminated. If the qualities that advance the success of the rulers in historical time are reflective of a non-currently dominant genetic makeup of people, then their preferential breeding should increase the prevalence of those currently non-dominant qualities over time and, ultimately, render them dominant.[4] This presumes, however, that such people find work-arounds for the fitness benefits sociality has provided humankind by using other means (e.g., artificial intelligence, robotics, genetic engineering, cloning, or synthetic biology).

With regard to the second mechanism, another pathway to a biological impact exists through the Baldwin effect discussed in *Chapter 6*. It describes a way by which memes that are culturally passed forward can end up having genetic effects. The principle states that once an advantageous behavior appears in a population, assuming its utility sustains, it will *indirectly* reshape the genes of the species that has adopted it by generating a selective pressure for retaining mutant traits that facilitate its learning and use (Baldwin effect, 2018). In *Chapter 6*, we provided an example of how the Baldwin effect works. We imagined the development of a tool

---

[4] While it is true that fertility rates decline as income levels increase, the rich have access to alternative means to generate heirs through surrogate parenting and whatever other means sciences like synthetic biology may create.

that was critical to survival, incorporated within a culture, and passed down from generation to generation with sustaining survival value. We further imagined that the tool worked best for people who had added thumb–index finger dexterity. Accordingly, the persistence of the survival-enhancing value of that tool's use becomes a selective pressure for advantaging those species members who, by mutation, emerged with better-articulated thumbs and index fingers. Thus, culture itself can become another, albeit indirect, avenue for human evolution.

With regard to the question posed by this section, the systematically imposed culture of Capitalism would selectively advantage humans who displayed asociality on the scale of historical time, even though such a feature would—based on the evidence of evolution—diminish the fitness of humankind on an evolutionary time scale. Whether that culturally driven version of humankind could survive long enough for the Baldwin effect to operate is unknown. When the answer does emerge, it will be final. The ultimate "kill switch" for non-viable transformations in historical time is self-destruction. In evolutionary time, it is extinction.[5]

A Nation as a Life Enabling Enterprise

Barnard (1968) viewed the conceptualizations that govern the creation and management of a commercial organization as applicable to all formal organizations. He identified the state as a formal organization, albeit with a different purpose from a commercial one. As a formal organization, it is governed by the same logic that governs a commercial enterprise. Both entities are cooperative efforts seeking to accomplish a specific end. Each is organized by its purpose. That purpose is defined by its founders' and is shaped by their goals, values, beliefs, interests, and concerns. It seems, therefore, a sensible endeavor to consider what a nation organized as a Life Enabling enterprise might look like. Consider it a thought experiment.

To begin with, a Life Enabling nation can only be formed by people whose native inclinations for sociality and personal emergence are intact (*Chapter 5).* These people must also have developed qualities of character and acquired the knowledge, skills, and proficiency levels defined in the model as required for creating and sustaining a Life Enabling organization. Absent these qualities of character and competence, their efforts to establish a Life Enabling nation would fail.

Does this requirement render a Life Enabling nation a pipe dream? No. First, the research reported in *Chapter 6* makes clear that such persons do exist and not

[5] Dual inheritance theory (DIT) (Henrich and McElreath, 2007) is a formal theory that explains how human traits can be both a product of genetic evolution and cultural evolution. While the just described argument was developed independent of this theory, DIT offers a reader interested in this issue a more extensive and sophisticated exposition of how genes and culture can interact.

in small numbers. Second, the skills needed to establish and maintain a Life Enabling nation are readily trainable and easily learned by anyone interested in them. What is needed is for these people to recognize themselves and each other and acquire the capabilities they need to create such a nation.

As to forming a nation, such people would naturally join together as an expression of their sociality and common desire to enrich their opportunities for positive human associations and the mutual satisfaction of the other necessities that enable their physical and social well-being and emergence as unique, fully realized individuals. As a nation, they would act solely to protect, nurture, and enrich human and natural life and the ecosystem that supports it. It is this common purpose that would bind them together, not the territory they occupy or the ethnicity they might share. Such features (local, ethnicity) might differentiate one such Life Enabling nation from one another—but, fundamentally, they would all be aligned and could even exist as one entity. If the nature of national and international regimes deny the possibility of a physical nation, it is possible for such people to create a virtual nation independent of geography through internet mediated networking. Indeed, that may be the only way in today's world that a Life Enabling nation could emerge.

The sovereignty of a Life Enabling state would reside in its citizens. The nation's citizenry would serve as its governors. Their collective, consensus-based decision making would determine their nation's purpose and policies and direct its conduct in relation to other states. Citizens, on a rotating basis, would perform the functions of the state. Thus, as with every Life Enabling organization, every citizen would uphold two roles—one being personal and the other civic.

In their personal role, citizens would live out their lives. Each citizen would freely act on his or her inherent, other-regarding nature and pursue his or her personal emergence. In this regard, people would connect with others they choose to associate with in mutually benefiting relationships and strive to emerge as unique, productive, and contributing individuals, each fully realizing his or her human potential.

Commerce, in all its forms, would serve as the vehicle by which people fulfilled their sociality and pursued their personal lives. Every exchange between people would seek to be mutually benefiting and life enabling. As to entrepreneurial undertakings, the offerings of such undertakings would, on the one hand, be shaped by the specific interests of each citizen-producer as he or she pursued personal emergence. On the other hand, they would be shaped by the needs of the people that citizen-producer elected to serve. By undertaking such enterprise, people would fully develop their capabilities and elevate the personal emergence of their fellow humans. Each act of commerce would enrich all parties to it and the Life Enabling nation as a whole.

Moreover, each instance of an individual or cooperative enterprise would be a freestanding Life Enabling commercial organization. The manner and results of such commerce would provide all the necessities required for the nation's citizens to survive and thrive as humans and for the continuing health of their life-sustaining ecosystem. If the commercial efforts of citizens included the exchange of resources with others outside their state, their conduct would be no different. Every exchange would abide by the values of the Life Enabling model and seek to maximize the life-enabling benefits realized by every party inclusively.

In their civic role, citizens would undertake the performance of the Executive Functions of a Life Enabling organization as described in Section IV of this book. It is in this role that every citizen would undertake the work of governance and ensure that the nation is sustained as a whole, capable, and viable entity moving forward towards its goals. Through their collective action, they would establish the nation's organizational structure and build the infrastructure[6] necessary for pursuing the nation's purpose. They would implement this role of governance as a team with the participation of all citizens, making decisions by consensus, not by majority vote. Their governance work would ensure that an environment capable of nurturing and supporting the social and personal capabilities of every citizen existed, functioned, and continuously improved in satisfying its purpose.

The nation's governmental organization would follow the design of a Life Enabling enterprise. It would be a tiered system of interlocking civic teams extending from each neighborhood outward to encompass the nation as a whole. The citizens making up each local team would rotate in their participation in more distant teams and work together vertically and horizontally to ensure the harmoniously implemented, continuous improvement of their nation in achieving its purpose. Each team would manage from a systems perspective and ensure that no local changes it undertook resulted in the diminution of their nation's overall ability to realize its purpose.

Governance would focus singularly on creating an infrastructure that enables the physical and social well-being and personal emergence of every citizen, as well as the sustained viability of their ecosystem. Its responsibilities and accountabilities would be defined by the Executive Functions component of the Life Enabling model (Effectiveness, Sufficiency, and Synergy). It would address all civic issues in

---

[6] By infrastructure we mean the physical, social, intellectual, and environmental facilities and services that are needed to sustain the nation, the emergence of its citizens, and the ecosystem that supports all life.

the same manner as the Life Enabling model described for commercial organizations using information- or knowledge-based decision making and problem solving.

Work teams implementing specific governance tasks would come into existence as needed and would be dissolved once their tasks were accomplished. The sustained continuance of a centralized governance team would be based on a documented need for action that was best implemented on a non-local basis. Its self-elimination would be its factual, not aspirational, goal.

Citizens would implement all governance services in a manner consistent with the model's Operations guidance (Section III). Thus, they would begin by understanding the needs and preferences of the people to be served by the purpose each service undertook to accomplish. They would proceed by comprehending the perspectives of all stakeholders to that purpose. They would manage their service activities from a systems perspective and design outputs and implement processes that maximize the benefit delivered to their constituents and all stakeholders inclusively. They would also establish waste-free, optimized processes to accomplish their purposes and strive for perfection—the ultimate achievement of which would be the elimination of the need for their service to exist. Their civic work would serve as another vehicle for the fulfillment of sociality and their striving for personal emergence.

The activities for accomplishing the Executive Function of Effectiveness would be, with adaptations, the yearly backbone activities of governance. These are to: (1) define/refine the nation's purpose and intent, (2) build the infrastructure components essential for achieving Effectiveness, (3) define the nation's yearly domestic infrastructure development plan and its continuous improvement of governance plan, (4) monitor implementation of the nation's plans, (5) detect and remove barriers hindering progress in accomplishing the nation's yearly plans, (6) detect and realize opportunities for accelerating progress in accomplishing the nation's yearly plans, and (7) conduct the nation's yearly Renewal exercise. The focus of governmental action at the national level would be resolving issues that affect the nation as a whole or are beyond the capabilities of local citizen action and require action with the broadest involvement of citizenry.

Governance's performance of its Sufficiency and Synergy functions would likewise comply with the dictates of the Life Enabling model. Sufficiency would ensure the presence of citizens who were capable and motivated to establish, implement, maintain, and realize the nation's life-enabling purpose and fulfill their dual roles as citizens. Citizenship would be open to all people who demonstrate the qualities of character and necessary competencies to participate in and contribute to a Life Enabling nation. The nation would provide development opportunities for people who do not qualify for citizenship but desire to. Sufficiency would also support every citizen's engagement in his or her nation's efforts to accomplish its purpose and succeed both as individuals and as citizens in realizing their personal and national aims.

The function of Synergy would implement the same activities as described in the Life Enabling model (*Chapter 15*). It would begin with establishing the organizational and communications infrastructure needed for citizens to work together in realizing their national intent. This same infrastructure would also serve to support people's interactions with one another as they pursue their personal lives and their cooperative commercial activities. The function of Synergy would proceed by monitoring the presence of synergy across the nation, intervening to correct shortfalls in synergy, acting to uncover and realize opportunities to facilitate synergy, and striving for perfection in the interdependent and synergistic cooperation of all citizens toward realizing their nation's purpose.

The above description of citizenship and governance is far removed from our real-world experience of both. As citizens, we are largely passive entities. We may be able to speak our minds, but we have little to no agency in governmental decision making. Our experience of governance is one dominated by the existence of a formal bureaucracy composed mostly of people unknown to us and led by people who fashion an image of themselves that is intended to persuade us of their importance. They are the people who make governance decisions and take actions that shape the nation we live in. Despite the language suggesting that power lies in the hands of the people, in the final analysis it does not. Politically speaking, as documented in *Chapter 2* and *Appendix C*,[7] there are the ruled (the many) and the rulers (the few). Our experience of governance is as something *apart from us* whose actions are directed *at us*.

In your effort to grasp the description of the governance activities of a Life Enabling nation, remember that the people of such a nation *are factually its governors*. They implement the governance roles. There are no politicians or bureaucrats. By every citizen's makeup and competent striving, he or she ensures that governance focuses on creating a nation that enables every citizen to live out their lives as they choose in social and physical contexts that enrich everyone's success. Governance takes no action that is contrary to the nation's expressed purpose as defined by its citizens because it is citizen action that implements governance. All citizens rotate through the roles of governance. All citizens participate directly in managing governance activities. They decide *by consensus* what governance will do using the

[7] See *Chapter 2, Political Power,* pages 32–49, and *Appendix C: The Economic Fruits of Political Power.*

same mechanisms described in the Life Enabling model for ensuring full participation by members in a commercial enterprise's decision making and action. Citizens monitor, measure, evaluate, and improve governance. They regularly assess the nation's performance against the model's defined metrics to determine whether it is accomplishing its objectives and acting in the manner they prescribe.

As to foreign policy, a Life Enabling nation would perceive all other nations as actual or potential members of its cooperative system (*Chapter 8*). It would work with them as the model describes. It would seek to engage them in constructive, mutually benefiting relationships. Its conduct in international affairs would absolutely comply with the core values of the model that shapes it as a nation. A Life Enabling nation would have no "three-letter agencies" (NSA, CIA, DIA, etc.) operating in secret to self-servingly manipulate the actions of other nations and its own citizens. It would conduct no secret wars nor sponsor death squads or "targeted assassinations" nor use economic coercion to enforce its will over other nations. It would work to resolve issues with others by working with them to understand their concerns and find solutions that integrate the realization of each party's interests. It would never initiate aggression, but would respond if forced to by the actions of others. It would never employ the fiction of pre-emptive attacks, as these are cloaks for making one's own aggression seem defensive in nature. It would never celebrate war, only regret its occurrence and learn from it, as every war is a marker of human failure. The only action worthy of celebration is moving forward together in harmony to fully realize humankind's sociality, advance every individual's striving for emergence, and ensure the viability of the ecosystem that sustains all life. War is always destructive of these ends.

The above sketch of how a Life Enabling nation would appear and behave is offered solely as a suggestive beginning for a thinking through of the question. Even so, take note of the differences between such a nation and the Capitalist nations that dominate the developed world. Domestically, Capitalist nations are controlled by their economic elites. They focus on the protection and advancement of monetary wealth and, in that process, advantage the already wealthy and advance systemic inequality that undermines social cohesion and disables the survival and emergence of the majority of their citizens. In these "liberal democracies," economic elites leverage their wealth to sustain and enhance their political control. Their claimed "free-market economies" stagnate competition as they resolve themselves into concentrated commercial sectors populated by fewer and fewer large enterprises. Their foreign policy follows the dictates of *political realism* (Korab-Karpowicz, 2018; Mosely, 2021). That doctrine shares as its root the very same view of humankind as Capitalism. It asserts that "[h]uman beings [are] inherently egoistic" and act solely with regard to self-interest "to the extent that self-interest overcomes moral principles" (Korab-Karpowicz, 2018, chap. 1, para. 76). Indeed, one virtue of the theory of political realism is its honesty. That honesty makes it a perfect compliment to a *valid version* of Capitalism (pages 464–466). Its sole focus in foreign affairs is on amassing power and using that power to control the conduct of other nations. Its reasoning is that any nation that fails to act egoistically in the service of its self-interest will end up being subject to the self-interests of other nations. Ideally, the state a nation following its doctrine ultimately strives to create, is world hegemony.

This brief chapter addresses the actual state of marketplace commerce and its personal implications for creating and sustaining a Life Enabling enterprise. It provides a warning to every Life Enabling entrepreneur. If you do not heed this warning and address it in your business planning, you will doom your commercial efforts.

Chapter 18

Warning to Life Enabling Entrepreneurs

The Life Enabling model is for use by people who retain or reestablish the native qualities of humankind described in *Chapter 5*. If you are such a person, you must also develop the character and competencies defined in the model itself. You cannot assume that you possess these capabilities without objective verification. You certainly are not likely to have the competencies specified in the model unless you have been fortunate enough to have crossed paths with others who could demonstrate and teach them to you.

You will also require a quality of character we have not yet discussed. This is courage. It is not the uncertainty of marketplace success that will require your courage. No. If you are capable of implementing this model, there is little doubt that you will realize marketplace success. While we have not addressed the empirical data on this question, there is a great deal of research evidence supporting the superior performance of enterprises that incorporate even a few of the features of a Life Enabling enterprise (e.g., Combs, Liu, Hall, and Ketchin, 2006; Grasso, 2015; Hendricks and Singhal, 1997; Jones and Kato, 2005; Kenexa Corporation, 2012; Stockamp, 2005; Womack, Jones, and Roos, 1991).[1]

No, the challenge that will test your mettle will be from the producer-focused, profit-maximizing firms that populate the commercial markets you enter and the industry groups they control. As the previously cited quote from Adam Smith observed, firms owned and managed by capitalists seek to limit competition. Control of the marketplace is the most efficient path to maximizing profits. Thus, once they recognize your existence, they will view your Life Enabling enterprise as a threat to their hegemony.

There are two aspects of the threat your enterprise poses. The first is your emerging commercial success. The second is your rewriting of the rules that govern the existing commercial context. As your enterprise succeeds and grows, the perception of these threats will increase.

At first, your success will detract from their firms' profits. Soon, however, it will become clear that your continued success presents an even greater danger. Your mode of operation presents prospective customers an alternative to their exploitive approach to doing commerce. It jeopardizes their fiat-based path to wealth accumulation. Your enterprise empowers people by offering them options that truly add value to their purposes and by providing them with the tools they need to make free and effective choices. Even worse, your enterprise continuously

[1] Given the dominance of producer-focused, profit-maximizing enterprises, most but not all of the metrics used in these studies relate to success as defined by such organizations.

raises the bar that any competitor must hurdle to match your performance because you continuously improve all your operations and your offerings. Every aspect of your enterprise undermines the marketplace control that Capitalist enterprises seek. Control provides a sure thing. Absence of control introduces uncertainly. One has to chance innovating new solutions or incrementally improving existing ones through learning. Success in accomplishing these outcomes is not assured. Also, those actions reduce profit by redirecting revenue into uncertain research and development investments.

Even if a Capitalist enterprise were willing to assume some level of risk, it would soon discover that it was unable to match your enterprise's performance. The operating principles of a Capitalist enterprise do not permit the type of performance attainable by a Life Enabling enterprise. A Capitalist enterprise cannot allow the type of distributed, learning-driven, teamed performance achievable by a Life Enabling enterprise. That approach requires a person to relinquish self-interest as his or her driving motive. It requires *power sharing* and the equitable distribution of material gains based on verifiable contribution, not position or privilege. It annuls a capitalist's singular purpose—namely, to maximize his or her personal gains.

The resilient relationship your enterprise builds with each member of its cooperative system further deepens its threat to Capitalist enterprises. These bonds develop because your approach incorporates improving their success, not exploiting your power in relation to them as, for example, many large companies do with regard to their suppliers. Everything you do elevates others. Everything a Capitalist enterprise does seeks to constrain others and capture them in one-sided relationships that enrich the enterprise alone.

Given the alternative, who would choose to do business with someone who takes their welfare into consideration and whose words were genuine commitments? You offer substantive promises, not "puffery." You provide "customer care" that actually shows care for your customers. You forsake gimmicks and deceptive devices that give less while charging more. You push for changes that advantage your customers, not yourself alone. You create an experience of fairness that people naturally respond to in a positive way. And once that experience is present in a marketplace, customers gradually begin to expect and then demand that other producers match it. They express this demand through their buying behavior.

The threats your enterprise pose are absolutely intolerable for a Capitalist enterprise. Your success—no matter how beneficial it is to the population as a whole—is an existential threat to all the existing producer-focused, profit-maximizing enterprises that populate each producer-controlled market you enter. They will not yield control easily. They and their industry groups will use all their economic and political power to thwart your efforts to do commerce. The level of attack you will experience will be the measure of the level of threat to their hegemony and wealth accumulation that you present. The methods used against you will be unconstrained. They will be selected based on expediency alone. When you challenge these people, understand that you are entering a life-and-death struggle, for that is how they will perceive it.

Human Service/Public Sector Organizations

Most people readily accept the notion that "businesses" operate differently from non-profit organizations performing human service or public sector work. They do not. Not making a profit for one's organization does not mean you are not making a profit for yourself as an executive or professional worker in such an organization. Nor does it mean that you are not running the organization in a way that serves your preferences as its decision maker, not the preferences or needs of the people the organization exists to serve.

Capitalists, as we define them in this book, exist in every walk of life—from street cleaners to the presidents of nations (see Footnote 17, page 30). Executive positions, even in public service organizations, pay salaries in the upper 15% income bracket and offer other rewards (e.g., status, security, special privileges and benefits, social standing). And when an egoistic self-maximizer leads a non-profit organization, he or she operates according to the same principles as the executive of any producer-focused, profit-maximizing enterprise.[2]

Consider examples from your own experience. How often have you encountered a primary healthcare provider who sets an appointment time, then makes you wait for your appointment and never offers an apology? If you imagine that delays have to occur because of their limited funding or the nature of the work your care provider delivers, you are wrong. The senior author has managed multiple community mental health programs where people were seen when they were scheduled and not one person in need was ever turned away. At one of these institutions, people initially waited some 17 days before they could be received into care. Within six months, in two waves of changes, that was reduced to zero days with no one turned away, no increase in staffing, and no overtime. The first wave reduced the wait time to 3.4 days despite a 27% increase in demand. The second wave provided immediate intake to service. Service flowed and was available on

[2] These public sector capitalists may, however, belong to that subset of egoists who are less forward leaning (see page 7). While they remain egoists, their preferred end is creating an advantaged lifestyle for themselves rather than the maximum accumulation of wealth. Their egoistic roots become clear when their advantaged lifestyle is threatened.

demand. The methods for ensuring this result are documented in the chapters on Operations in this book (Section III). They are not new. They do not require genius to implement. They only require that public service executives operate based on their commitment to serve the public. They require that care providers actually place first the people who seek their care and invest effort in ensuring that obstacles to the delivery of service are removed.[3]

When traditionally run, not-for-profit human service community organizations are confronted with another organization that applies the principles and practices of Life Enabling commerce, they too react with alarm. They are the established entities. Their funding flows based on their reputation. Their deferential position within the panoply of public service enterprises assures their continued funding. When the poor performance of such agencies is challenged (delayed service, failure to serve the severely impaired, skewed services to only majority community members, refusal to work with one or another group of people in need), their funding sources and regulators defer to their explanations for why this or that "apparent" failing is not a failing at all. After all, they are the "professionals," and their institutions are the respected ones in their sphere of public service. *And without anyone else offering a service that does not have such failings, their statements remain unchallengeable.*

But when an agency without such failings emerges, the established incumbents' controlled space of operation and the legitimacy of their excuses for why more or better service cannot be provided are threatened. Now, their egoistic mode of operation must change, or the source of the challenge that threatens their control and continued egoistic operation must be eliminated. No other alternative is possible without compromising their modus operandi and the desired personal comfort and privilege it provides.

Not-for-profit enterprises may have much fewer financial resources than for-profit enterprises, but when run by egoistic self-maximizers, they behave no differently. They will attack you and your service enterprise with all the resources they can muster. They will leverage every political connection they have to denigrate your work, harass your funding sources, and even attack your professionalism. Ultimately, they will act as ruthlessly as any producer-focused, profit-maximizing firm.

---

[3] Other applications of improvement methods at the same mental health center increased the time therapists worked face-to-face with their clients from 49% of their workweek to 62%, raised clients' reports of benefits from care from 70% to 92% after 3 years, and reduced broken treatment rates from 84% to 35%. Similar service improvement gains are reported for another community mental health program using the same approach to commerce (Carkhuff, 1983, pp. 102–115). For a description of a client-focused approach to mental health care delivery, see Vitalo (1975).

APPENDICES

Not everyone agrees that inequality in wealth and income is problematic. Some proponents of Capitalism maintain that it is essential to sustaining a vibrant economic system. Mankiw (2013) argued that inequality is a positive economic factor. It shows that rewards are available for those who are skilled, hard-working, and innovative. This motivates others in a society to emulate these meritocratic qualities. Mankiw proffered J. K. Rowling, Stephen Spielberg, and Steve Jobs as evidence. Freeland (2013) offered support for this thinking, stating that "many of the ultra-high-net-worth individuals flourishing in today's global economy are admirable entrepreneurs, and we would all be poorer without them." Gordon (2013) characterized Mankiw's defense of the top 1% as arguing, "High earners are high earners because they have made 'significant economic contributions.'"

In response to Mankiw's exemplars, Baker (2013) pointed out that his choice of Jobs and Rowling as capitalist success stories is ironic,

> since the wealth of both individuals is so obviously dependent on the intervention of the government in the form of patent and copyright monopolies. These monopolies are a prize awarded by the government as a way to provide incentives for creative work. These are quintessential forms of government intervention, they are 180 degrees at odds with the free market. (Baker, 2013)

More pointedly, however, Piketty's (2014) exhaustive analysis of rising inequality concluded *that merit is not its cause*. He stated that assertions of merit-based inequality of wealth are typically made in opposition to any laws that might restrain the actions of capitalists—for example, "labor laws or social legislation" (Piketty, 2014, p. 85). Rather, the upward spiral in accumulated wealth and the resulting spiraling upward of inequality is a function of the initial state of wealth inequality at the introduction of Capitalism augmented by three factors. These are the preferential rate of return on capital relative to labor income growth, the law of cumulative returns, and the power of inheritance. His data reveals that escalating inequality is independent of talent or merit. It is driven by the mechanisms of Capitalism. As Adam Smith (1776) observed, "Money, says the proverb, makes money. When you have got a little, it is often easy to get more. The great difficulty is to get that little" (p. 81).

Other empirical evidence also undermines Mankiw's argument that it is the financial elite's unusual skill set and entrepreneurial creativity that account for their unequal generation of wealth. Bakija, Cole, and Heim (2012) investigated who the *actual* high earners in the United States are. They found that just 6.1% of these financial elites come from the arts, media, sports, computer, math, engineering, and other creative or technical fields. In contrast, "executives, managers, supervisors, and financial professionals account for about 60 percent of the top 0.1 percent of income earners in recent years, and can account for 70 percent of the increase in the share of national income going to the top 0.1 percent of the income distribution between 1979 and 2005" (2012, p. 2).

As to these elites' unusual skill set, Hogan and Kaizer (2005) reported that empirical studies indicate that "[e]stimates of the base rate for managerial incompetence in corporate life range from 30% to 75%" (p. 175). DeVries and Kaiser (2003) reported that only 50% of executive appointments are considered successful. The reasons for failure they identified included poor relationships, inability to create teamwork, and inability to think strategically. Kaiser (2011) updated the findings on executive success. He reported the results of eight studies that found executive failure rates between 40% and 67%.

Perhaps the data that questions the competence of the managerial class can be read a different way. Perhaps the data really suggest that those who *do* succeed produce prodigious results for their companies and are worth the median pay of $17 million received by Fortune 500 chief executive officers (CEOs) in 2014 (Mullaney, 2015). Well, not really. Evidence also suggests the elite levels of compensation do not mean elite levels of firm performance.

In response to the question, "How tightly is CEO pay tied to performance," Mullaney (2015) responded, "Not very tightly at all." He reported the findings of a study investigating the relationship between executive pay and firm performance published in the *Journal of Management*. "It found that variations in company performance account for only about 5 percent of the variation between how much companies pay their top executives."

In dissent to this judgment about the lack of relationship between CEO compensation and firm performance, Sigler (2011) completed a study to demonstrate that, indeed, CEO pay *does* relate to company performance. While the study *statistically* confirmed the author's expectation, Sigler overlooked the *extreme smallness* of the relationship he uncovered. Based on his reported regression coefficients (Sigler, 2011, Table 2, p. 7), successful firm performance appeared to account for less than 1% of total compensation. Sigler emphasized that the relationship was statistically significant despite how little effect the relationship had on determining CEO pay.

A study by Cooper, Gulen, and Rau (2016) further reinforces the smallness of the relationship between CEO pay and a firm's financial performance. They found that the firm's performance accounted for only 7.2% of the total variance in CEO compensation (2016, see Table 1, p. 36).

From the above studies, one implication is clear. Some 93% to 99% percent of the reason CEOs are paid so highly *is not due to their positive effect on company performance.* In the language of Capitalism, *it is not due to merit.*

Perhaps elite compensation is related to *anticipated* performance? "We pay high to get the best." Cooper, Gulen, and Rau (2016) investigated the relationship between CEO pay and a company's performance *going forward.* They found that CEOs' compensation above normative levels is *negatively* related to the future financial returns of the firms they lead. The authors observed that managers in the top decile of compensation made investment decisions, concluded mergers, and used more debt to pursue their ends—all with negative economic consequences for their firms.

As perhaps the coup de grâce to the linkage of compensation to merit, Morgenson (2006) reported that "[s]ome [CEO] employment agreements actually stipulate that they will provide bonuses even if company performance declines." She described one such agreement in which the CEO of a major media corporation would receive a $4.25 million (2006 dollars) bonus if earnings fell 6.25 percent, "and an earnings decline of 14 percent translates to a $3.52 million bonus."

Even when there is no clause to ensure a bonus for non-performance, Steven Clifford (2017) reported that 40% of the companies that comprise the Dow Jones Industrial Index "adjusted their earnings upward when calculating their CEO's bonus in 2015." Clifford was directly involved in crafting CEO compensation packages for over 20 years. He continued, "Consider what Nationwide Mutual Insurance did in 2011. That year, the company decided that claims from an unexpected succession of tornadoes shouldn't count against its CEO's performance measures, which doubled his bonus. (And here I thought weighing the risks of unusual occurrences was what insurance was all about.)"

What Drives Escalating CEO Pay?

If neither a firm's growth in its inherent value nor its prior or future financial performance drives high levels of CEO compensation, what does? Researchers have identified at least two factors. One is how CEO compensation is set. The second is the linking of CEO incentives to positive changes in stock price value. Together, these factors suggest that the bottom line reason for escalating CEO compensation is that CEOs effectively control their own level of compensation.

How CEO Compensation Is Set

CEO compensation is most frequently decided using a peer benchmarking process (Bizjak, Lemon, and Nguyen, 2009). Directors commission a survey of current CEO compensation for a set of selected companies. They do this both when they set the compensation level for an open position and when they revise the compensation being paid to a current CEO. These compensation findings are ranked, and directors typically peg the compensation of their CEO positions at the median or higher level (e.g., the 75th percentile).

The issues with peer benchmarking are several. For one, the selection of companies used to benchmark CEO pay can skew a compensation package upward. If a firm benchmarks against companies with greater revenues than its own, it will automatically find higher CEO compensation packages than if it benchmarks against companies with like revenues. The larger the firm, the larger the CEO compensation. Cheng (2011) studied peer selection practices using 15,000 corporate filings over a four-year period. He found that "[c]ompanies tend to select peers that are between 0.5 to two times their revenue size." Bizjak, Lemon, and Nguyen (2009) found that selected "peer firms are systematically larger, have better performance, and have more highly paid executives" (p. 4). This systematic choice of larger companies as benchmarks drives compensation upward.[1]

Reinforcing this upward compensation bias, Cheng also found that "Highly paid CEOs are the most prevalent peers for benchmarking." Cheng's finding about using highly paid CEOs as benchmarks was reinforced by Fauklender and Yang (2007). They reported,

> [W]e find that firms appear to select highly paid peers to justify their CEO compensation and this effect is stronger in firms where the compensation peer group is smaller, where the CEO is the chairman of the board of directors, where the CEO has longer tenure, and where directors are busier serving on multiple boards. (Fauklender and Yang, 2007)

Perhaps the most obvious problem with peer benchmarking is that the process *automatically ratchets CEO compensation upward* with each cycle. When companies set their CEOs' compensation by choosing a higher than median-level reference point, the median level of all CEO compensation packages is automatically increased. Even if they choose just the median level, simply by definition they will be raising that median level half the time. By definition, half of all CEOs are paid

---

[1] It should be noted that these authors found the source of bias differed between firms that were in the S&P 500 index and those that were not. They still concluded, however, that "[f]irms in the S&P 500 appear to choose peers in a manner that justifies their high pay" (Bizak, Lemon, and Nguyen, 2009, p. 5).

below the median. When one of that group is then paid at the median level, the entire distribution moves upward. If a company also benchmarks against the highest-paid CEOs or companies with greater revenues than their own (as research indicates they do), that adds even greater velocity to the upward movement of CEO compensation for all CEOs. It automatically raises the pay of all peer-benchmarked CEOs at their next cycle of compensation setting.

As Whoriskey (2011) noted, the practice of peer benchmarking "has long been controversial because, as critics have pointed out, if every company tries to keep up with or exceed the median pay for executives, executive compensation will spiral upward, regardless of performance."

If you are imagining that stockholders can balance these upward compensation forces, they cannot. "Under the 2010 Dodd-Frank law, public companies must hold an advisory shareholder vote on executive compensation every three years. But the vote is nonbinding unless a company decides otherwise" (Mullaney, 2015).

Also hindering the correction of this upward accelerating compensation dynamic is that both the CEO and his or her board have a vested interest in not altering it. Obviously, the upward cycle directly benefits the CEO, but board membership itself brings benefits to board members. For example, membership brings reimbursement through stock options or direct compensation. Sherman (2018) reported, "The median director pay at the largest U.S. companies was above $250,000 in 2015. This means that half of the directors of the boards of major corporations earned more" than this amount.[2] He also noted that "[c]orporations continue boosting director pay, year after year, faster than they do for their regular employees." In fact, the average "pay for directors has skyrocketed in the 21st century compared to pay for regular workers. According to Fortune magazine, compensation rates [for directors] at the largest U.S. public companies increased nearly 20 percent since 2012." Sherman added that the average board member puts in just "a few hours a week on the job." Board membership brings other benefits as well. These include social status, business connections advantaging one's career, and insider information. All these benefits enhance one's wealth accumulation.

As Zingales (2017) observed, "The primary way for board members to lose their jobs is to criticize the incumbent chief executive officer." Since the CEO is also the chairman of the board in just over 50% of the companies comprising the S&P 500 index (Larcker and Tayan, 2016), an action against the CEO would be seen as an attack on the board's chairperson. Lawler (2012) reported that

[2] In a recent conversation with the Chief Financial Officer (CFO) of a multibillion dollar corporation, the CFO informed me that the remuneration for directors in 2021 is typically $500,000 or more.

> [b]oard members typically want to be looked upon positively by the CEO and other senior executives in order to get on and remain on corporate boards. A board member who argues for paying individuals below the market is not likely to be a respected or valued board member, at least in the eyes of the executive team of the company. (Lawler, 2012)

He also noted that

> Some members of corporate boards have an even greater self-interest in making sure that the compensation of the CEO continues to go up, up, and up. *They are the CEOs of other companies.* You don't have to be a compensation expert to realize that if you vote for one of your peers to have a higher salary, you are effectively voting for your own salary to go up. (Lawler, 2012)

When any CEO's pay increases above the existing median, it raises the reference salary for all CEOs.

Thus, not only are the upward-spiraling incomes of the majority of the financial elite *not* a function of their exceptional creative skills or other forms of merit, but—at least for CEOs—it is to a large extent under their own control. As Piketty (2014) stated, "It is only reasonable to assume that people in a position to set their own salaries have a natural incentive to treat themselves generously, or at the very least to be rather optimistic in gauging their own marginal productivity" (p. 332). Actually, such behavior is only expected from people who are egoistic self-maximizers. Empirical research (e.g., Andreoni, 1995; Korenok, Millner, and Razzolini, 2014; Yamagishi, Li, Takagishi, et al., 2014) says that this group of people is only a portion of humankind. But perhaps Piketty should be forgiven since, under the regimen of Capitalism, all people are assumed to strive solely to maximize their own gains. And it is reasonable to suspect that, in a Capitalist enterprise, it would be such people who would rise to the top.

Linking CEO Incentives to Stock Price Change

A second source of accelerating CEO compensation is the tying of incentive pay to positive changes in a company's earnings per share and stock price value. The concept originally expressed a firm's intent to reward CEOs for increasing shareholder value—the monetary return a shareholder receives for investing in the company. The thinking was that a CEO who improved the inherent productive value of the company would increase its revenues and profits. This would enable the company to pay higher dividends to shareholders, improving shareholders' return on their investment. It would also make each unit of stock in the company more valuable, thereby increasing the market value of the company. Shareholders would reap that added market value either through leveraging their stock's value to make additional investments or through sale of their stock.

Unfortunately, incentive systems that are not carefully thought out are subject to "gaming." Gaming refers to behavior that triggers an incentive payout without actually improving the intended target outcomes. Here, the gaming was enabled by a Securities and Exchange Commission regulatory change with regard to firms buying back their own stock. Stock buybacks were illegal until the Securities and Exchange Commission legalized them in 1982. They were considered a form of stock manipulation. A buyback reduces the number of shares in circulation. By reducing the number of shares outstanding, the same level of earned income results in a *higher earnings per share* (EPS) result. It also elevates the company's share price, as fewer shares of stock are available for purchase. What it does not do is increase the inherent productive value of the company. Nonetheless, the apparent improvement in EPS and in the price of a firm's stock triggers the payment of CEO bonuses aimed toward rewarding CEOs for increasing shareholder value. Hence, CEOs can reward themselves handsomely by simply buying back the firm's stock without improving the intrinsic value of the firm they oversee.

This "gaming" of the incentive system has been further enabled by both reduction in taxes on corporations and the Federal Reserve's policy to maintain an artificially low federal funds interest rate. That rate determines the interest charged on corporate loans.[3] Thus, CEOs have been able to use both savings produced by lower taxation and borrowing enabled by the lower cost of debt service to buy back their firms' stock. As Alsin (2017) reported "American companies have been spending wildly lately, but that cash isn't being used for R&D or innovation. Rather, it's being spent to buy up gobs of company stock." As a result, bonus payments triggered by improvements in EPS and stock price have escalated. In 2017, these bonus payments accounted for 32% to 47.5% of total CEO compensation in S&P 500 companies.

Keep in mind that these buybacks *do not improve the intrinsic value of the company*. Indeed, they harm its future performance. For example, an empirical study of the effects of EPS-motivated stock buybacks found a positive relation between buybacks and the incidence of subsequent "reductions in employment and investment, and a decrease in cash holdings" (Almeida, Fos, and Krunkund, 2016). The authors concluded: "Our evidence suggests that managers are willing to trade off

[3] That rate also determines the interest paid on the savings account balances of average citizens. As an aside, the same Federal Reserve policy that artificially makes corporate loans cheap and boosts the growth of asset markets dominated by the economic elite has cost average savings account holders an estimated four trillion dollars since its inception in 2008 (Pollock, 2021). In essence, the Federal Reserve's policy has represented a silent transfer of wealth from the average citizen to the already rich.

investments and employment for stock repurchases that allow them to meet analyst EPS forecasts" and garner the bonuses associated with them. Other evidence for the negative effects of stock buybacks on the intrinsic value of a company has been provided by Ayres and Olenick (2017); Brettell, Gaffen, and Rohde (2015a, 2015b); and Lazonick (2014).

As perhaps a final blow to economic fairness, these bonuses are a tax deduction for the firms giving them. That means the average taxpayer is subsidizing the escalating CEO payouts (Americans for Tax Fairness, 2014) and its additive contribution to the upward-spiraling inequality that harms them.

The Powell Memorandum (Powell, L.F., 1971) presents an example of a long-term, comprehensive indoctrination program targeting the public and political decision makers. Its purpose was to instill the conviction that Capitalism is the only effective and democratically consistent economic system known. Lewis F. Powell conceived the program in response to a request from Eugene B. Snyder, Jr. At the time, Snyder was the chair of the United States Chamber of Commerce. Powell wrote the memorandum just before his nomination to the U.S. Supreme Court, where he remained an esteemed justice for the remainder of his career.

Powell opened his memorandum with this statement: "No thoughtful person can question that the American economic system is under broad attack. This varies in scope, intensity, in the techniques employed, and in the level of visibility." Powell's footnote clarifies that by the "American economic system," he meant "Capitalism or the profit-system."

Alarmingly for Powell, the voices of criticism came "from perfectly respectable elements of society: from the college campus, the pulpit, the media, the intellectual and literary journals, the arts and sciences, and from politicians." He noted bewilderingly that the capitalists themselves were allowing this chorus of criticism to grow despite the levers of power they possessed to control its emergence. Specifically, he refereed to their monetary contributions to higher education institutions and their roles as trustees on university boards. To this he added the power they possessed to influence mass media outlets through their advertising expenditures, noting further that these outlets were themselves Capitalist enterprises.

Powell named a number of examples of those who threatened Capitalism, but he singled out Ralph Nader, the consumer advocate who fought for car safety as "perhaps the single most effective antagonist." He characterized the arguments against tax breaks and other economic benefits for business as examples of "rifle shots [against Capitalism] which undermine confidence and confuse the public." Clearly, the memorandum was a "call to arms" in the service of Capitalism. Powell shamed current business leaders who had failed to mobilize in their own interests by labeling their behavior as "appeasement" and "ineptitude."

Powell outlined a long-term plan to guide collective action to re-establish Capitalism's supremacy. He stated,

> Strength lies in organization, in careful long-range planning and implementation, in consistency of action over an indefinite period of years, in the scale of financing available only through joint effort, and in the political power available only through united action and national organizations. (Powell, L.F., 1971, p. 11)

The plan targeted universities "to address the campus origin of this hostility" to Capitalism. It recommended forming a cadre of social scientists to advocate for Capitalism, a speakers bureau to promote the dissemination of a pro-Capitalism stance, and systematic evaluation of textbooks by "eminent scholars who believe in the American system" to challenge anti-Capitalism content. The speakers bureau should include "attractive, articulate and well-informed speakers," and its leaders should "exert whatever degree of pressure—publicly or privately—[that] may be necessary to ensure opportunities to speak." Given the one-sided nature of this effort and the stated intent of his entire program as a whole, Powell's added statement that "[t]he objective always must be to inform and enlighten, and not merely to propagandize" (1971, p. 19) seems more than a little disingenuous, even more so given the remainder of his proposal.

The education thrust, he stated, should also address the hiring of faculty supportive of Capitalism and extend down from graduate-level education to secondary education. While Powell advised, "Reaching the campus and the secondary schools is vital for the long-term," he added, "Reaching the public generally may be more important for the shorter term." To reach the public, Powell proposed that a second cadre of people be assembled. It should be composed "of eminent scholars, writers and speakers, who will do the thinking, the analysis, the writing and the speaking." They must be thoroughly familiar with the media and possess the qualities needed to be persuasive. Media targets included television, radio, scholarly journals, and publishing (books, articles, and pamphlets). The program should also use paid advertisements to promote its messages.

Two additional theaters of battle are politics and the courts. In Powell's words, "In final analysis, the payoff ... is what government does" (1971, p. 24). Incredibly, Powell lamented how little influence in government American business had. Recall that his memorandum was issued just 10 years after President Eisenhower warned the nation of the growing power of the "military-congressional-industrial complex" in his farewell address from the White House on January 17, 1961. Even in 1971, the mantra "As GM goes, so goes the country" still had resonance. Nonetheless, Powell was seemingly shocked and angered by the weakness in influence businesses possessed. He commented that "current examples of the impotency of business, and of the near-contempt with which businessmen's views are held, are the stampedes by politicians to support almost any legislation related to 'consumerism' or to the 'environment'" (1971, p. 25).

His answer to business's political weakness was a two-pronged attack. First, the previously discussed methods of persuasion to be implemented with educational institutions, mass media, and the public would provide indirect means to shape political decision making. The second prong of his proposed attack was direct. He based it on "the lesson that political power is necessary; that such power must be assiduously cultivated; and that when necessary, it must be used aggressively and with determination without embarrassment and without ... reluctance." He advised that "There should be not the slightest hesitation to press vigorously in all political arenas for support of the enterprise system. Nor should there be reluctance to *penalize politically* [italics added] those who oppose it" (1971, p. 30). In other words, punish those who disagree.

As to the courts, Powell again recommended assembling a cadre of highly competent lawyers able "to appear as council amicus in the Supreme Court" and advocate the positions favoring Capitalism.

The last venue for action Powell recommended was to find ways to mobilize the power of corporate stockholders to influence public opinion and government decision making.

In a final call to action, Powell urged, "It is time for American business—which has demonstrated the greatest capacity in all history to produce and to influence consumer decisions—to apply its great talents vigorously to the preservation of the system itself" (1971, p. 30).

As an argument against any notion that his just described program of propaganda and indoctrination was a threat to freedom, Powell aligned its purpose with that of ensuring the continuance of individual freedom. He did this by reasserting that Capitalism alone is consistent with individual freedom and democracy. Throughout his memorandum, Powell was oblivious to the fact that shaping people's thinking and actions *to conform to what someone else thinks they should be* through programs of propaganda, indoctrination, and punishment *inherently undermines individual freedom*—whether it is implemented by capitalists, communists, liberals, conservatives, or whomever.

As to the memorandum's impact, Cray (2011) reported that soon after the memo was made public in 1973 by Jack Anderson, a news reporter,

> the [U.S. Chamber of Commerce's] board of directors formed a task force of 40 business executives (from U.S. Steel, GE, ABC, GM, CBS, 3M, Phillips Petroleum, Amway and numerous other companies) to review Powell's memo and draft a list of specific proposals to "improve understanding of business and the private enterprise system," which the board adopted on November 8, 1973.
>
> Powell's Memo is widely credited for having helped catalyze a new business activist movement, with numerous conservative family and corporate foundations (e.g. Coors, Olin, Bradley, Scaife, Koch and others)

thereafter creating and sustaining powerful new voices to help push the corporate agenda, including the Business Roundtable (1972), the American Legislative Exchange Council (ALEC - 1973), Heritage Foundation (1973), the Cato Institute (1977), the Manhattan Institute (1978), Citizens for a Sound Economy (1984 - now Americans for Prosperity), Accuracy in Academe (1985), and others.

Because it signaled the beginning of a major shift in American business culture, political power and law, the Powell memo essentially marks the beginning of the business community's multi-decade collective takeover of the most important institutions of public opinion and democratic decision-making. At the very least, it is the first place where this broad agenda was compiled in one document. (Cray, 2011)

Do financial elites realize economic advantages from their pursuit of political power? What, if any, results does the application of political power produce, and are these outcomes beneficial to the financial elite alone or to the larger society as well?

Money, Political Power, and Its Outcomes

"Most political scientists continue to insist that we lack clear evidence that the inequality of political resources translates systematically into markedly unequal influence over American government" (Pierson, 2015). Prior research has supported the idea that the median voter "decides" policy outcomes. "Elections are really about giving the people what they want. Money, they claim, has negligible impact on elections" (Parramore, 2016).

Several authors have challenged this accepted judgment (Jacobs and Page, 2005; Gilens and Page, 2012; Zingales, 2017). These challenges address the incompleteness of prior studies and their use of bivariate analyses.

As to incompleteness, Zingales (2017) pointed out that prior studies focused narrowly on the effect of contributions alone or the correlation between the views of the median voter and policy outcomes. The focus on contributions alone is too narrow given the broad array of methods of influence available to wealthy individuals and corporations.[1] Also, using reported contributions fails to account for dark money contributions (Jacobs and Page, 2005; Pilkington and Siddiqui, 2019). Dark money contributions are political contributions funneled through non-profit organizations set up for this purpose. These organizations are not required to disclose their donors. They can receive unlimited donations from individuals or corporations and use them to support their favored political candidate or policy position. Finally, researchers' focus on the correlation between median voter opinions and policy outcomes fails to account for the indirect effects of promotional campaigns to shape public opinion so that it aligns with the positions of the economically elite.[1]

As to the use of bivariate analyses in prior studies, such studies fail to account for sources of influence other than the single one they target. As a result, these studies are unable to partial out the unique effect of each voice (citizen, financial elite, business corporations) given the presence of other voices. When research designs simultaneously evaluate all major voices of influence on policy in one study, "the prior findings appear to be largely or wholly spurious" (Gilens and Page, 2014, p. 573). Using multivariate designs, both Jacobs and Paige (2005) and Gilens and Page (2014) showed that the average citizen has no independent effect on

[1] See examples in *Appendix B: A Detailed Look at the Powell Memorandum.*

policy decision making. Essentially, "ordinary citizens get what they want from government *only when they happen to agree with elites or interest groups that are really calling the shots* [italics added]" (Gilens and Page, 2014, p. 573). It is the economic elites and business interest groups who are the most powerful influencers of government decision making.

The preferential political influence of financial elites and business groups produces outcomes that affect society as a whole. If these results benefit wealthy individuals and Capitalist corporations but harm society in general, then the economic system that enables this outcome is dangerous to society. Evidence consistently supports the conclusion that the results produced by the two groups of wealth powerhouses can be categorized as benefiting them *alone*. These benefits enable financial elites and corporations to accelerate their wealth accumulation, enhance their ability to exert political influence, and protect themselves from any negative consequences resulting from their conduct. Of special concern are the opportunities for the exercise of moral hazard their influence creates.

A Sample of the Results Realized

This sample of results produced by the economically elite's exercise of political power is minuscule compared to the universe of actual results that have been documented. It is offered for illustrative purposes only. The examples include the huge transfer of wealth from the public to the banks, reduced enforcement of laws, concentration of market power, giveaways of the people's assets for private wealth accumulation, preferential taxation, and opportunities to exercise moral hazard.

Federal Government Borrowing From Banks Rather Than Self-Funding

Perhaps the largest monetary gain by Capitalist corporations from the general public results from the little-known fact that the U.S. government does not need to borrow from private banks to fund its deficit spending. That borrowing cost the U.S. taxpayers a half-trillion dollars in *2018 alone*. All that money was transferred from the public to private, for-profit banks.

"The irony is that the United States does not need to carry a debt to bondholders [private lenders] at all. It has been financially sovereign ever since President Franklin D. Roosevelt took the dollar off the gold standard domestically in 1933" (Brown, 2019). The U.S. government can draw "on credit from its own central bank [the Federal Reserve]; and since there was no longer a need for gold to cover the loan, the central bank would not have to borrow. It could just create the money on its books." This is essentially what it is doing in its multi-trillion-dollar bailout of the banks since 2008 and the more recent multi-trillion-dollar bailout of asset markets due to the U.S. government's response to the COVID-19 pandemic.

So, how did the banks achieve their unneeded but highly profitable role as U.S. debt holders? Brown (2019) reported that, "[a]fter the dollar went off the gold standard in 1933, Congress could have had the Fed just print money and lend it to the government, cutting the banks out. But Wall Street lobbied for an amendment to the Federal Reserve Act, forbidding the Fed to buy bonds directly from the Treasury as it had done in the past." That prohibition "was written into the Banking Act of 1935 at the behest of those bond dealers that have an exclusive right to purchase directly from the Fed."

A historical review of that action on the website of the New York Federal Reserve quotes Marriner Eccles, chairman of the Federal Reserve from 1934 to 1948, as stating, "I think the real reasons for writing the prohibition into the [Banking Act] ... can be traced to certain Government bond dealers [private lenders] who quite naturally had their eyes on business that might be lost to them if direct purchasing were permitted" (Brown, 2019). From 2000 through 2018 alone, this unneeded transfer of wealth to Capitalist banks cost taxpayers *just over $7.6 trillion* in interest expense on outstanding government debt (U.S. Department of the Treasury, 2019).

And the same process of passing money through banks when it is unnecessary to do so continues today. Just recently, the Paycheck Protection Program enacted by the U.S. Congress authorized approximately $350 billion in loans to small businesses to help them survive during the forced COVID-19 lockdown (Abrams, 2020). While the Small Business Administration (SBA) has been a major lender to such enterprises, "the Senate wanted these funds to go through banks instead of the Treasury Department or the SBA" (Abrams, 2020). The rationale was to speed the lending process. Instead, it "created mass confusion and frustration," as banks were not geared up to handle the process, and each bank had different loan application procedures. Loan applicants had to jump through different hoops depending upon which bank they approached. Worse still, every loan incurred an unnecessary cost that was collected by the banks. Banks took "in 1% to 5% in fees" (Sullivan, 2020). That cost reduced the amount of money available to small businesses. As Sullivan (2020) reported, "Banks handling the government's $349 billion loan program for small businesses made more than $10 billion in fees—even as tens of thousands of small businesses were shut out of the program."

Reduced Law Enforcement

For the 30 years from 1970 through 1999, the U.S. Federal Trade Commission (FTC) brought an average of 15.7 cases per year under the Sherman Antitrust Act.[2] Between 2000 and 2014, enforcement dropped dramatically to 2.8 cases per year, even as mergers and acquisitions resulting in market concentration increased (Zingales, 2017, p. 121).

As a specific example of reduced enforcement, consider the FTC's dropping of the antitrust case against Google while European regulators continued the case:

> A leaked FTC staff report ... concluded that Google had unlawfully maintained its monopoly over general search and search advertising by 'scraping content from rival vertical web sites,' 'by entering into exclusive and highly restrictive agreements with web publishers that prevent publishers from displaying competing search results or search advertisements,' and 'by maintaining contractual restrictions that inhibit the cross-platform management of advertising campaigns.' Nonetheless, the FTC unanimously decided to drop the case. (Zingales, 2017, p. 123)

Zingales asked what role, if any, the frequent visits paid by Google employees to the White House played. "[B]etween Obama's first inauguration and the end of October 2015, employees of Google and associated entities visited the White House 427 times, including 21 small, intimate meetings with President Obama" (2017, p. 123).

Of course, the most notorious example of reduced law enforcement is the doctrine of "too big to jail." This doctrine is identified with former President Obama's U.S. Attorney General Eric Holder. He proclaimed that the size of some banks precluded bringing criminal charges against them for wrongdoing because "if you do bring a criminal charge—it will have a negative impact on the national economy, perhaps even the world economy" (Delamaide, 2013). "'Stunning' is how Sen. Charles E. Grassley (R-Iowa) described Holder's remarks before the Senate Judiciary Committee on Wednesday. 'After hearing today's testimony, big bankers know that if they commit financial crimes, they can expect a passive response from the Justice Department'" (Douglas, 2013).

Concentration of Market Power

One of the effects of reduced antitrust regulation is market concentration. Grullon, Larkin, and Michaely (2018) reported that, "[i]n the last two decades, over 75% of U.S. industries have experienced an increase in concentration levels." They also found that this concentration has led to higher profit margins and

---

[2] Section 2 of the Sherman Act makes it unlawful to "monopolize, or attempt to monopolize, or combine or conspire with any other person or persons, to monopolize any part of the trade or commerce."

more profitable M&A (merger and acquisition) deals without any evidence of improved operational efficiency. In other words, the surviving firms' increased profitability was not a function of producing greater value or the same value more efficiently but as a result of possessing greater "pricing power" through market concentration. As an added negative consequence, Zingales (2017) noted that the increased corporate wealth that market concentration yields provides these companies still greater political power.

Giveaways of the People's Assets for Private Wealth Accumulation

The Center for Public Integrity (2000) reported that, "[i]n 1997, broadcasters lobbied and received portions of the digital broadcast spectrum—worth, according to some estimates, upwards of $70 billion—for free" (p. 4). The action received little coverage by national news programs. One story that did air appeared on CNN/FN. It reported that "Congress agreed to *loan the broadcasters* [italics added] the valuable digital spectrum .... The 'loan' was interest-free; in fact, the principal never had to be paid back" (The Center for Public Integrity, 2000, p. 4).

Preferential Taxation

In terms of personal income taxes, the financial elite have done well. "A study of the top 400 taxpaying households showed that just the reduction of effective individual income tax rates between 1995 and 2007 ... was worth a mean of $46 million per year for each of these fortunate 400" (Hacker and Loewentheil, 2013). Other tax benefits to financial elites have been even greater. Approximately 60% of their earnings come from capital gains, and capital gains income receives a preferential tax rate over ordinary income. The tax rate on income of $434,551 from selling stock held longer than a year is 15%. But if that same income came from labor, it would be taxed at 35% (Tarver, 2021).[3]

Hedge fund managers do not qualify for the capital gains reduced tax rate. Their income does not derive from money at risk in investments. Rather, their income is labor based. Adams-Mott (2018) reported that a Forbes 2017 compensation survey "determined the top earning hedge fund manager of 2017 made $2 billion, with each of the top four earners making over the $1 billion mark. The lowest earner in the top 25 earned $200 million in the same year." To save these managers from having their earnings taxed as other labor income is, Congress created the "carried interest" provision. This provision allows hedge fund managers, whose income is generally defined as a percentage of their fund's earnings, to benefit from a capital-gains-like tax rate. "While the tax legislation passed on Jan. 1 [2013] increased the top individual-income [labor-

[3] Note that the richest 10% of Americans owned 84% of all stocks in 2017 (Wile, 2017).

based] tax rate to 39.6 percent from 35 percent for couples making more than $450,000 and individuals making more than $400,000, it left carried-interest income taxed at just 20 percent" (de Rothschild, 2013), producing an enormous windfall for hedge fund managers.

Even in the midst of the economic crisis produced by the government's response to the COVID-19 pandemic, the financial elite are able to realize extraordinary benefit. MacLeod (2020) reported

> Hidden away in the Coronavirus Aid, Relief, and Economic Security (CARES) Act is a series of Republican tax cuts that will save the ultra-wealthy $90 billion in 2020 alone. According to a report from the Joint Committee on Taxation (JCT), a nonpartisan congressional body, almost 82 percent of the benefits of the tax breaks will go to just 43,000 Americans who make over $1 million annually. In contrast, less than three percent will go to the great majority who earn less than $100,000 per year [approximately 91% of taxpayers as of 2016].

Have the preferential tax benefits for the economic elite generated economic growth benefits for the remainder of society? Apparently, they have not. Krueger (2012) found that "Across all businesses, job growth was much weaker" *after the tax reductions* implemented from 2001 through 2007 than in the 1990s. Linden (2011) reported that, since the 1950s, the top margin tax rate has dropped from 92% to just 28%. He found that "in years when the top marginal rate was lower than 39.6 percent ... annual real growth averaged 2.1 percent." However, "when the [tax] rate was 39.6 percent or higher, real growth averaged 3.8 percent."

Opportunities for Moral Hazard

The reduced law enforcement discussed earlier is one major factor in increasing opportunities for moral hazard, as self-serving illegal behavior goes unpunished. Another enabler is government actions that allow the capitalist investors to escape the consequences of faulty business decisions.

This benefit allows firms and investors to privatize the gains from their risky investments while their losses are borne by the general public. It insulates them from the consequences of poor business decisions and the risk inherent in enterprise. It treats "losses as a responsibility that society as a whole must shoulder ... through taxpayer-funded subsidies or bailouts" (Privatizing profits, socializing losses, 2019). In essence, it allows egoistic self-maximizers to exploit moral hazard for their private gain.

Nankin, Umansky, Schmidt, and Klein (2008) reported 14 major taxpayer bailouts of Capitalist companies between 1970 and 2009. Not included in their list was the bailout of American banks between 1982 and 1985 due to loans they extended to foreign governments (Mexico and other Latin American governments) that were unable to repay them (Treadway, 2010). Vasquez (2002) reported that the "largest U.S. banks had made sovereign loans in excess of their [banks'] capital." If those borrowers defaulted, the banks would be insolvent. The government pulled money "out of a variety of hats including the Federal Reserve, the US Treasury, the US Strategic Petroleum Reserve, the Department of Agriculture, the Bank for International Settlements and of course the IMF, [and] bailed out Mexico. Bailouts of the other defaulting Latin countries soon followed, with the IMF taking a leading role" (ibid.). These government bailouts acted to prevent the banks' threatened losses. They allowed the defaulting nations to repay their loans, and the American banks suffered no losses. Instead, the citizens of the United States did. Treadway cited other examples not included in Nankin, Umansky, Schmidt, and Klein's list. These bailouts are the Second Mexican Crisis (1994–1995), the Emerging Market Crises (1997–2002), the Long-Term Capital Management bailout (1998), and the post-NASDAQ bubble bailout (2002). Other bailouts not included were the auto industry bailouts from 2008–2014 (Amadeo, 2019). Those bailouts cost U.S. citizens $10.2 billion.

The most-cited recent example of privatizing gains and socializing losses is the post-2008 financial crisis bailout of banks and insurers. The Troubled Asset Relief Program (TARP) of 2008 authorized the Treasury to spend $700 billion of taxpayer money (though only $426.4 billion was actually used) to rescue these firms, many of which had contributed to the crisis through reckless—but enormously profitable—investments in risky mortgage-backed derivatives.

Some of the failing firms' employees were awarded multimillion-dollar bonuses despite accepting money from TARP and the Federal Reserve. By contrast, the homes of 2,330,483 ordinary citizens were foreclosed on in 2008.

As of 2018, the Congressional Budget Office estimated that "the government's total subsidy costs—including those already realized and those stemming from outstanding and anticipated transactions—will be $32 billion" (Congressional Budget Office, 2018, p. 1).

But the TARP portion of the bailout is minuscule compared to the total costs of the bailout of the banks by the U.S. taxpayer. Collins (2015) reported that "[t]he Special Inspector General for TARP summary of the bailout says that the total commitment of government is $16.8 trillion with the $4.6 trillion already paid out. Yes, it was trillions not billions and the banks are now larger and still too big to fail."

Collins went on to chronicle some of the crimes for which these institutions were being bailed out. Two examples are falsely rating toxic mortgaged-backed securities as AAA-quality investments and banks betting against their own customers that the securities they sold them as good investments would fail (JP Morgan and Goldman Sachs).

Purpose

This guide teaches you to distinguish knowledge from information.

Importance

Both knowledge and information are necessary for rational decision making and problem solving. Each, however, has different uses. Unless you can distinguish one from the other, you will not know whether you are using the right resource for your task, and you will undermine your success.

Description

Knowledge

Knowledge is mental content that labels or describes a class or category of objects and their characteristics, operation, and relationships. This type of knowledge is called declarative knowledge. The label "house" and the description of its characteristics such as "it is a physical structure" and "it serves as a residence for people" are examples.

Knowledge may also detail a set of activities that accomplish a task. This type of knowledge is called procedural knowledge. The set of instructions that provide step-by-step guidance for assembling a child's toy is an example of procedural knowledge.

A special feature of knowledge is that it applies whenever it is used to guide the performance it addresses no matter where or by whom it is used. For example, "house" is the label for a category of structures that serve as dwellings for one or more persons. It can be used anywhere at any time to determine whether a structure is a house. The step-by-step instructions for assembling a toy also can be used to assemble any instance of that toy at any time.

Finally, the term "knowledge" applies only to ideas that have been made explicit by being documented. This documentation may be in words, mathematical symbols (e.g., $E = mc^2$), or images (e.g., a flow diagram).[1]

Information

Information is mental content that tells about a specific person, place, thing, or activity at a given time. It is the equivalent of news. For example, Matthew M. lived at 1816 Sutphin Boulevard, Jamaica, New York, during 1990. This fact informs us where Matthew M. lived during the specified period. It applies to no other person and no other time.

---

[1] Some people label expertise or knowledge embedded in people "tacit knowledge," following Polyani (1959). This confuses "knowledge" with "know how." Knowledge is mental content that has been made explicit by documenting it. As "documented know how," it can be critiqued, verified, transferred, and improved by the shared efforts of people through the practice of science. "Know how" or "tacit knowledge" lacks all the just mentioned features of knowledge. Our use of the term "knowledge" corresponds to what Polyani called "explicit knowledge."

Uses of Knowledge

Knowledge allows us to label, organize, relate, explain, predict, and control the contents of our world. It also enables us to accomplish tasks in a consistently correct manner. To appreciate its utility, consider the declarative knowledge associated with the label "apple." One element of that knowledge relates to the apple's structure. Our knowledge of the structure of an apple allows us to predict that, when we slice an apple in half, we will find at its center a hard core with seeds. When a piece of equipment breaks down, we can use the knowledge contained in its maintenance manual (e.g., a "fault tree") to discover why it has broken down. That knowledge guides us in observing the equipment's status with regard to specific features, interpreting what that status means, and understanding the cause of the equipment's problem.

That same manual might also guide us in fixing the problem. Here, its instructions, if complete, will support us in managing our performance of the repair. Its instructions will tell us what tools and materials we will need, educate us as to the sequence of steps we will execute, and provide tips to ensure each step is done correctly. When we finish, the instructions will guide us in checking whether we did the task correctly. In this way, knowledge allows us to control our own performance and ensure its success.

Documented instructions also allow multiple people to coordinate their efforts by clarifying what each person will do and how their activities must flow together. When people do the same work in different places, written instructions support them in being consistent in their parallel execution of that work. When that knowledge is taught to new hires, it enables novice performers to rapidly master the work they must accomplish and accelerate their career advancement. Exhibit D1, next page, summarizes the uses knowledge may serve.

Uses of Information

Information describes what we or others have experienced or imagine that we will experience. It reports the status of persons, places, things, or activities at a point in time (e.g., John was shaking his fist; Mike was sweating). When it describes past experiences, it records history. When it presents what we imagine will happen, it tells our premonitions about the future.

Information can contrast different observations or experiences, as in reporting the results of an experiment. "In our experiment, Method A produced the course materials in 23 hours. Method B produced the materials in 61 hours." It can also describe the *apparent* connections between two or more persons, places, things, or activities (e.g., "When Mac studied more than 15 hours a week, his grades were B or higher").

Exhibit D1. Some Uses That Knowledge and Information Support

Type	Use It To ...

Knowledge	▪ Define, describe, and detect the presence of a type of physical object.
	▪ Define a logical object (e.g., the concept of truth or freedom) and detect whether its use in a given situation is correct.
	▪ Label and organize things and experiences.
	▪ Describe the features that an object has and their relationships with each other.
	▪ Predict how an object will behave.
	▪ Predict the effects an object will have on other objects.
	▪ Interpret what collected information means.
	▪ Guide task performance:
	  ▪ Guide you in deciding whether a task is appropriate to do.
	  ▪ Guide you in preparing to do a task.
	  ▪ Guide you in sequencing your actions.
	  ▪ Guide you in executing an action correctly.
	  ▪ Guide you in verifying that you did a task correctly.
	▪ Enable coordination between multiple people doing a task together.
	▪ Enable consistency of performance between people doing the same task in parallel.
	▪ Provide the content needed to teach others a skill and speed their progress toward competence.
	▪ Keep expertise for future use and improvement.

Information	▪ Describe the status of a particular person, place, thing, or activity (e.g., "The car's engine temperature was 175°F."). ▪ Contrast two or more persons, places, things, or activities (e.g., "Sarah's living room was 244 square feet in area. Her kitchen was just 100 square feet."). ▪ Describe the *apparent* connection between two or more persons, places, things, or activities (e.g., "When Mac studied more than 15 hours a week, his grades were B or higher."). ▪ Record history. ▪ Report the findings of pilots or experiments. ▪ Select what knowledge is appropriate to apply.

Information, however, cannot *guide* our decisions or actions. The reason is that it only describes what was observed *in the past* and *in a particular time and place.* It does not explain what that observation means, why it occurred, or whether the same observation would occur at another time or place or even whether another observer of the original event would report it the same way.

While information cannot guide decision making or action, it can help us identify what knowledge is appropriate to apply in making a decision or taking an action. For example, each piece of equipment has a model number associated with it. We can use that model number (information) to locate the repair guide that can help us repair that piece of equipment. The repair instructions also will direct us to obtain information about the status of one or another gauge or part of the equipment. We apply the guide's knowledge to that information to diagnose the problem and indicate what action to take. Thus, knowledge and information work together to enable us to achieve our goals.

Distinguishing Between Knowledge and Information

Exhibit D2, next page, provides a learning aid that distinguishes knowledge from information. The type of knowledge depicted in this example is "procedural knowledge." Study the guide and then complete the practice exercise on page 510.

Exhibit D2. Guide for Distinguishing Between Knowledge and Information

	Knowledge	Information
Definition	Names or describes a class of objects and their characteristics, operation, and relationships or a set of activities that accomplish a task.	Tells about a person, place, thing, or activity at a given time.
Applicability	Applies across instances of time and place.	Applies to a specific time (point or period), place, and setting.

Example of Knowledge

Task: Determine whether a tax return properly identifies the taxpayer

Input  Stack of Tax Returns

Process

1. Verify that a name appears in the name box.
2. Verify that a complete address appears in the address boxes.
3. Verify that a social security number appears in the SSN box.
4. Verify that the name and SSN match.
5. Stamp the return.
   If all verifications succeed, then stamp the return "Good to Go"; else stamp it "Return to Sender."
6. Send letter.
   If the return is stamped "Return to Sender," then send letter to taxpayer; else send no letter.

Output

▶ Tax return stamped "Good to Go"

- OR -

▶ Tax Return stamped "Return to Sender"
Letter notifying taxpayer of the problem
Letter with return sent to the taxpayer

Example of Information

Letter to Jack Whatsus Informing him that his tax return was rejected

U.S. Internal Revenue Service

Dear Jack Whatsus,

Your 2022 tax return is being sent back to you because you failed to provide all the identifying information we require.

Your Uncle Sam
June 21, 2023

Practice Exercise: Which Is Knowledge and Which Is Information and Why?

Use the following practice exercise to test your skill in distinguishing knowledge from information. Which example is knowledge? Which is information?

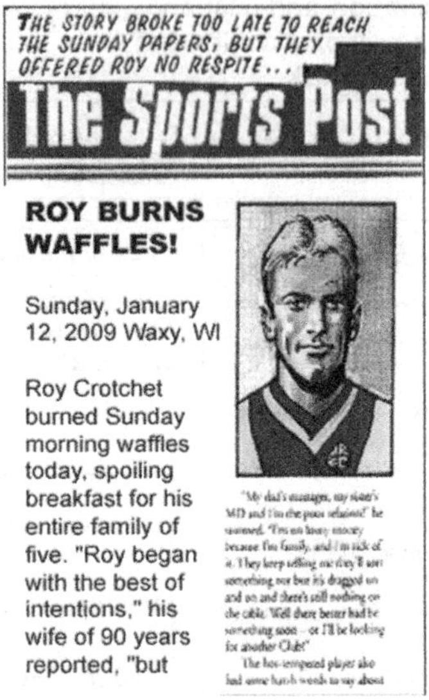

THE STORY BROKE TOO LATE TO REACH THE SUNDAY PAPERS, BUT THEY OFFERED ROY NO RESPITE...

The Sports Post

ROY BURNS WAFFLES!

Sunday, January 12, 2009 Waxy, WI

Roy Crotchet burned Sunday morning waffles today, spoiling breakfast for his entire family of five. "Roy began with the best of intentions," his wife of 90 years reported, "but

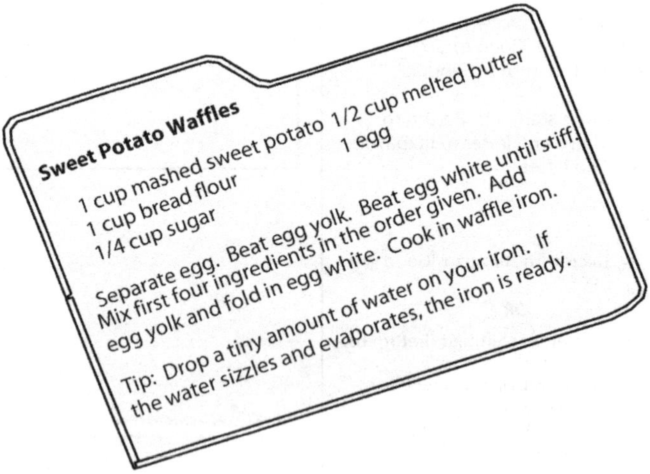

Sweet Potato Waffles

1 cup mashed sweet potato 1/2 cup melted butter
1 cup bread flour 1 egg
1/4 cup sugar

Separate egg. Beat egg yolk. Beat egg white until stiff. Mix first four ingredients in the order given. Add egg yolk and fold in egg white. Cook in waffle iron.

Tip: Drop a tiny amount of water on your iron. If the water sizzles and evaporates, the iron is ready.

Answer:

The top item is information. It reports something that happen to a specific person at a specific time. The bottom item is knowledge. It guides a person in making waffles. Its utility is not restricted to a specific time and place.

Decision making chooses an option. Problem solving eliminates a barrier to accomplishing a purpose or realizes an opportunity for improved success. There are different ways to accomplish these actions. Some require no knowledge at all. They are inborn. Others require specialized knowledge and, occasionally, the mastery of scientific theories (e.g., general relativity) or complex statistical tools (e.g., general linear modeling, structural equation modeling).

Three Groups of Methods

We organize the methods for making decisions and solving problems into three groups: biological, information based, and knowledge based (Vitalo, 2023). These groups differ in whether they require the manipulation of mental content (facts and ideas) and what their primary input is (sensory data alone, information alone, or knowledge and information). *Biological processing* methods make a choice or act to solve a problem automatically in response to a specific stimulus. These methods include instinct, reflexive behavior, autonomic responding (Silvert, Delplanque, Bouwalerh, Verpoort, and Sequeira, 2004), and habit. None require "thinking." Their primary input is sensory data, either from generated from within oneself or from outside. Solutions produced by instinct, reflex, and autonomic responding are unlearned. For example, withdrawing your hand from a flame is an unlearned, reflexive problem solution. A habit is the automatic expression of a previously learned behavior. Habits are generated by trial and error learning, unconscious imitation, or conditioning methods. Learning to ride a bike is an example of trial and error biological processing. Saying "please" or "thank you" are most often conditioned behaviors. *Information-based* methods analyze and interpret facts acquired from people, documents, or by direct observation or experimentation to make decisions and solve problems. Using an opinion poll to decide whether to run for office is a case of information-based processing. *Knowledge-based* methods apply a set of knowledge to guide one in making a decision or completing a task. Following a recipe that directs you in baking a cake is a simplistic but real example of knowledge-based processing. Both information- and knowledge-based methods qualify as rational processing. While each group of methods adds to one's personal capability to act effectively, only information- and knowledge-based methods are useful in *cooperative* endeavors. Only these methods can be taught, learned, and performed with the participation of others.

Why Group Processing Methods?

We group methods primarily to facilitate understanding them and their proper uses. Methods within the same category share important characteristics (e.g., how solutions are developed, how fast or slow they execute, what their advantages and disadvantages are). Thus, what one learns about the features of a group of methods instantly informs them about each method within that group.

Exhibit E1. Profile of the Three Groups of Problem-Solving and Decision-Making Methods

Feature	Group		
	Biological	**Information**	**Knowledge**
Input(s)	Data—the raw input from sensory organs.	Information—symbols (words, numbers, graphics, or images) that report about a person, place, thing, or operation at a point in time.	▪ Knowledge—mental content that guides performance. ▪ Information needed to do the performance.
Output	Decision or action.	Decision or action and how it was arrived at.	Decision or action and how it was arrived at.
Methods	▪ Instinct, reflex, autonomic responding. ▪ Learned habit (via imitation, trial and error, conditioned responding).	▪ Case-based methods. ▪ Sense of the people methods. ▪ Information-based problem-solving/decision-making methods.	▪ Knowledge-Inference-Action (K-I-A) with variations in knowledge representation and inferencing rules.
Examples	▪ Learning to walk, unconscious activation response to threatening stimuli, riding a bicycle, learning the alphabet, etc.	▪ Adopt someone else's approach or choice (Case based). ▪ Use what most people you ask suggest (Sense of the people). ▪ DMAIC, Toyota's A3 method, and Ford's Global 8D Method (Information-based problem solving). ▪ Criterion-based decision making (Information-based decision making).	▪ Decision tables, decision trees, flow diagrams, fault tree analysis, knowledge-based expert systems.
Advantages	▪ Methods and their mechanisms are inborn. ▪ Methods require fewest input resources. ▪ Fastest response times for inborn behaviors and for habits acquired by biological learning methods. ▪ Solutions are resilient to extinction.	▪ Leverages facts specific to problem or decision. ▪ Allows for participation by others. ▪ Can be fast when information sources are readily available. ▪ Solutions can be explained. ▪ Safer approach when dealing with situations that may have harmful consequences.	▪ Allows for participation by others. ▪ Generates solutions having proven validity and uses facts that are specific to the task at hand. ▪ Processing speed can be very fast when knowledge and needed information are readily available. ▪ Least-risky approach to solving problems for which wrong answers have harmful results. ▪ Solutions can be explained.
Dis-advantages	▪ Slow in learning a solution (except inborn responses). ▪ Highest-risk approach when solving problems in which wrong answers have harmful consequences. ▪ Limited social utility—methods use singleton performance and generate solutions that may be demonstrated but not explained.	▪ Method must be learned and sometimes requires complex skills. ▪ Transferring solutions to new situations requires confirming that the new situation matches the original situation in all important features. ▪ Solutions are specific to the situation in which each is developed. Consequently, in dealing with fast changing circumstances, prior solution have limited utility.	▪ Acquiring knowledge may require the investment of more time and resources than other approaches. ▪ Methods must be learned. ▪ Some methods require complex skills.

Exhibit F1. A Template for Documenting Procedural Knowledge

Knowledge Item	Clarifying Question
Task	What is the proper name of the task this knowledge guides?
Point of Use	Where is the task done? Business function/component/work unit.
Source	Identify the source(s) that supplied this knowledge.
Purpose	What does this task accomplish?
Benefit	Why is accomplishing this purpose important? What business benefits does its correct performance generate?
Start	When is the task performed? What triggers its startup?
Performer	Who should perform this task? (Name the job role and any special qualifications the person needs.)
Input	What resources must be provided to do this task? (Include access to people, information, facilities, equipment, materials, tools, funds, etc.)
Output	What will the task have produced when it is done? (List all tangible product or service outputs the task yields, including interim and final outputs. Note which are interim and which are final.)
Method	How is the task performed? What steps do you do to get ready?[1] ***Tip:*** For each step, what behaviors accomplish the step, why is each important, and how is each done? What tips, if followed, would ensure successful performance of the step? What steps do you do to make it execute the task? ***Tip:*** For each step, what behaviors accomplish the step, why is each important, and how is each done? What tips, if followed, would ensure successful performance of the step? What steps do you do to follow up after you finish? ***Tip:*** For each step, what behaviors accomplish the step, why is each important, and how is each done? What tips, if followed, would ensure successful performance of the step?
Check Steps	Record the steps you take to ensure that you have done the task correctly.
Definitions	List special terms relevant to the task, and state what each means.
Case Example	Describe an example of the task being done.
Results Produced	Describe, in observable and measurable terms, what benefits using this procedural knowledge has generated.
References	List all source documents that support the validity of this knowledge.

[1] Record the steps in the order each should be performed.

Exhibit F2. A Template for Documenting Decision Knowledge

Knowledge Item	Clarifying Question
Decision	What is the proper name of this decision?
Point of Use	Where is the decision taken? Business function/component/work unit.
Source	Identify the source(s) that supplied this knowledge.
Purpose	What question or issue is this decision resolving?
Benefit	Why is this decision important? What business benefits does a correct decision generate?
Start	When is the decision made? What causes it to be addressed?
Performer	Who should make this decision? (Name the job role and any special qualifications the person needs.)
Decision Outcomes	What are the final judgments one might conclude when decision making is done?
Decision Factors	▪ What factors do you need to consider in making this decision? ▪ For each factor, what are you looking to detect? ***Tip:*** For example, one factor to consider in deciding whether to drive through an intersection is the color of the traffic light. To evaluate this factor, you would need to detect whether the color is red, yellow, or green.
Decision Flow	Build a decision tree. 1. Write the first factor the decision maker should consider at the top. 2. Draw a decision tree (^) under the factor with a branch for each possible outcome. ***Tip:*** For example, if the factor was "color of the traffic light," the tree would have three branches—Red, Yellow, and Green. 3. For each branch, ask what factor is considered next. 4. Repeat Steps 2 and 3 until all factors have been addressed and all possible outcomes have been concluded.
Tips	List the guidelines a decision maker should keep in mind in deciding the status of each factor?
Definitions	List special terms relevant to this decision making and state what each means.
Case Example	Describe an example of this decision being made.
Results Produced	Describe, in observable and measurable terms, what benefits using this decision knowledge has generated.
References	List all source documents that support the validity of this knowledge.

The Meeting Power Scale provides feedback on the focus, efficiency, results, and participation achieved in a team meeting. It supports team members in sharing their understanding of how well they worked together to fulfill the mandate documented in their team charter.

Instructions

Evaluate the effectiveness of your meeting by rating the extent to which you agree or disagree with each statement listed in this inventory. Also, at the end of the survey, list your major observations about how the meeting took place and record any ideas you have about what the team should keep doing, stop doing, and start doing to make its meetings better.

Use the following scale to respond to each survey statement. Circle the number that reflects your level of agreement or disagreement with each statement.

Statement	Strongly Disagree	Disagree	Agree & Disagree	Agree	Strongly Agree
1. Read the statement, then respond with your level of agreement or disagreement by circling a number to the right.	1	2	3	(4)	5

After you have responded to each statement and recorded your ideas at the end of this survey, compute your average rating for each meeting factor: Meeting Focus, Meeting Efficiency, Meeting Results, and Group Participation.

Any factor whose average rating fell below "4" needs improvement. Look to the particular items in that factor to identify where to focus your improvement efforts. Also, look at the observations and suggestions you recorded at the end of the survey for ideas about how to improve the team's meetings.

Statement	Strongly Disagree	Disagree	Agree & Disagree	Agree	Strongly Agree
Meeting Focus					
1. An agenda was prepared prior to the meeting.	1	2	3	4	5
2. Participants had an opportunity to contribute to the agenda.	1	2	3	4	5
3. At a minimum, the agenda stated the time and place of the meeting and the meeting's goal, and it recorded the meeting's topics, the person leading each topic, and the action required for each topic.	1	2	3	4	5
4. The agenda supported achieving the mandate of your team.	1	2	3	4	5
5. The objectives of the meeting were stated clearly.	1	2	3	4	5
Meeting Efficiency					
6. The meeting began on time and where the agenda specified.	1	2	3	4	5
7. Ground rules were established at the beginning of the meeting.	1	2	3	4	5
8. The agenda was followed throughout the meeting.	1	2	3	4	5
9. As each topic was completed, the action required by the team was taken (e.g., discussion, decision).	1	2	3	4	5
10. As each topic was completed, the meeting leader summarized the issue, discussion, and resulting action.	1	2	3	4	5
11. Only one topic was covered at a time.	1	2	3	4	5
12. Only one person spoke at a time.	1	2	3	4	5
13. The group stayed on task and kept superfluous information to a minimum.	1	2	3	4	5
14. At the end of the meeting, the team concluded what next steps it would take to follow through on the results of the current meeting.	1	2	3	4	5
15. The meeting ended on time.	1	2	3	4	5

Statement	Strongly Disagree	Disagree	Agree & Disagree	Agree	Strongly Agree
Meeting Results					
16. The meeting goal was accomplished.	1	2	3	4	5
17. Participants were satisfied with the team's process and decisions.	1	2	3	4	5
18. When decisions were made to take an action, the action was planned (i.e., a person was designated as responsible, a "drop-dead date" for the action was set, and a plan was devised or requested).	1	2	3	4	5
19. All questions were resolved before the meeting ended or were tabled to be continued at the next meeting.	1	2	3	4	5
20. Before the meeting ended, there was a review of the agenda, a summary of accomplishments, and a review of agreed-upon next steps.	1	2	3	4	5
21. The meeting closed with a process check of what worked well, what did not work well, and what lessons the team should take forward to improve its success.	1	2	3	4	5
Group Participation					
22. Everyone had equal opportunity to express their points of view.	1	2	3	4	5
23. Differences in opinion among participants were elicited and explored.	1	2	3	4	5
24. Participants listened attentively to one another.	1	2	3	4	5
25. Participants clarified what other people were saying and why by asking clarifying questions.	1	2	3	4	5
26. Participants confirmed that they understood what other team members said before offering their own point of view.	1	2	3	4	5
27. When expressing a difference in opinion, participants offered a constructive criticism. They pointed out the value of the other member's idea, specified their concern about it, and offered or invited suggestions for resolving their concern.	1	2	3	4	5

Statement	Strongly Disagree	Disagree	Agree & Disagree	Agree	Strongly Agree
28. Participants hitchhiked on each other's ideas in a constructive way. They acknowledged a connection between the other person's idea and their own, added value to the original idea, and checked back to elicit the other person's thoughts about what they said.	1	2	3	4	5

List Your Major Observations of How the Meeting Took Place

Suggestions

Please review your observations about the meeting. Based on those observations, suggest what the team should "Keep Doing," "Stop Doing," and "Start Doing" to make its meetings better.

Keep Doing

Stop Doing

Start Doing

Associate to Whom You Are Providing Feedback:

Name: ______________________________

Function: ____________________________

Role: ________________

Please rate how frequently I have demonstrated the following behaviors in my working with you.	Not at All	Infrequently	About Half the Time	Frequently	All the Time
1. I show interest in your perspective on issues that relate to both of us.	1	2	3	4	5
2. I identify your needs and concerns about issues that relate to both of us.	1	2	3	4	5
3. I incorporate your thinking in my decisions and plans for issues that relate to both of us.	1	2	3	4	5
4. I respond to queries from you.	1	2	3	4	5
5. I resolve issues that relate to both of us cooperatively, using mutually agreed upon information- or knowledge-based methods.	1	2	3	4	5
6. I provide support to you when you need it in a manner that is helpful.	1	2	3	4	5
7. I provide you the information you need in a timely and complete manner.	1	2	3	4	5
8. I resolve issues related to coordinating our use of the same resources in a way that benefits both our success.	1	2	3	4	5
9. I work with you to improve our ability to support each other's success while advancing the success of the business as a whole.	1	2	3	4	5

Over ...

Additional Feedback

Please record below your suggestions for what I can do to enable us to work together successfully.

1. What should I keep doing?

2. What should I stop doing?

3 . What should I start doing?

BIBLIOGRAPHY

Abdela, A. & Steinbaum, M. (2018). The Unitied States has market concentration problems. Retrieved August 7, 2021, from https://www.ftc.gov/system/files/documents/public_comments/2018/09/ftc-2018-0074-d-0042-155544.pdf

AboutLawsuits. (2009). Bad drug test results routinely hidden by pharmaceutical companies: Study. *Aboutlawsuits.com*. Retrieved August 4, 2019, from https://www.aboutlawsuits.com/bad-drug-test-results-routinely-hidden-by-pharmaceutical-companies-study-6160/

Abrahamson, E., & Park, C. (1994). Concealment of negative organizational outcomes: An agency theory perspective. *Academy of Management Journal, 37*(5), 1302–1334. Retrieved June 1, 2011, from https://web.archive.org/web/20120206140512/http://journals.aomonline.org/amj/images/awards/1994.pdf

Abrams, R. (2020). PPP loan plan a mess so far for small businesses riding out coronavirus crisis. *USA Today*. Retrieved May 18, 2020, from https://www.usatoday.com/story/money/usaandmain/2020/04/07/ppp-loan-plan-rollout-disaster-small-businesses/2963901001/

AbuKhalil, A. (2019). The angry Arab: U.S. role in Lebanon's crisis goes unrecognized. *The Consortium News*. Retrieved November 24, 2020, from https://consortiumnews.com/2019/12/04/the-angry-arab-u-s-role-in-lebanons-crisis-goes-unrecognized/

Ackerman, F. (1999). Still dead after all these years: Interpreting the failure of general equilibrium theory. Global Development and Environment Institute, Tufts University. Retrieved 3/24/2022, from https://sites.tufts.edu/gdae/files/2019/10/00-01Ackerman_StillDead.pdf

Adams-Mott, A. (2018). How much do hedge fund managers make? *Chron*. Retrieved May 6, 2019, from https://work.chron.com/much-hedge-fund-managers-make-23556.html

Agee, P. (1975). *Inside the company: CIA diary*. New York: NY, Stonehill Publishing Company.

Akao, Y. (1991). *Hoshin Kanri: Policy deployment for successful TQM*. Portland, OR: Productivity Press Inc.

Alexander, C. S., Miesing, P., & Parsons, A. L. (2004). *How important are stakeholder relationships?* Retrieved September 28, 2019, from https://www.albany.edu/~pm157/research/stakeholders.pdf

Almeida, H., Fos, V., & Kronlund, M. (2016). The real effects of share repurchases. *Journal of Financial Economics, 119*(1), 168–185.

Alonzo, W. J. (1998). The role of kin selection theory on the explanation of biological altruism: A critical review. *Journal of Comparative Biology, 3*(1), 1–14.

Alsin, A. (2017). The ugly truth behind stock buybacks. *Forbes Magazine*. Retrieved May 7, 2019, from https://www.forbes.com/sites/aalsin/2017/02/28/shareholders-should-be-required-to-vote-on-stock-buybacks/#53b0b8116b1Moysiche

Amadeo, K. (2019). Auto industry bailout: Was the big 3 bailout worth it? *The Balance*. Retrieved May 7, 2019, from https://www.thebalance.com/auto-industry-bailout-gm-ford-chrysler-3305670

Amadeo, K. (2019a). Savings and loan crisis explained. *The Balance*. Retrieved May 21, 2019, from https://www.thebalance.com/savings-and-loans-crisis-causes-cost-3306035

American Heritage Dictionary (3rd ed.). (1992). Boston, MA: Houghton Mifflin.

Americans for Tax Fairness. (2014). *Tax subsidies for CEO pay*. Retrieved February 28, 2019, from https://americansfortaxfairness.org/files/10-ATF-Tax-Subsidies-for-CEO-Pay-fact-sheet.pdf

Ames, M. (2014). The Techtopus: How Silicon Valley's most celebrated CEOs conspired to drive down 100,000 tech engineers' wages. Retrieved November 23, 2021, from https://web.archive.org/web/20140214070152/http://pando.com/2014/01/23/the-techtopus-how-silicon-valleys-most-celebrated-ceos-conspired-to-drive-down-100000-tech-engineers-wages/

Amihud, Y., & Lev, B. (1981). Risk reduction as a managerial motive for conglomerate mergers. *Bell Journal of Economics, 12*, 605–616.

Andreoni, J. (1990). Impure altruism and donations to public goods: A theory of warm-glow giving. *The Economic Journal, 100*, 464–477. Retrieved February 28, 2018, from https://econ.ucsb.edu/~tedb/Courses/UCSBpf/warmglow.pdf

Andreoni, J. (1995). Cooperation in public-goods experiments: Kindness or confusion? *The American Economic Review, 85*(4), 891–904. Retrieved February 20, 2018, from https://www.cs.sfu.ca/~lshia/personal/econ/papers/AndreoniAER95.pdf

Andreoni, J., & Miller, J. H. (1996). *Giving according to GARP: An experimental study of rationality and altruism.* Working Paper No. 9601. Social Systems Research Institute, University of Wisconsin at Madison.

Andreoni, J., & Miller, J. H. (2002). Giving according to GARP: An experimental test of the consistency of preferences for altruism. *Econometrica, 70*(2), 737–753.

Andrews, E. (2007, December 18). Fed shrugged as subprime crisis spread. *The New York Times.* Retrieved August 8, 2016, from http://www.nytimes.com/2007/12/18/business/18subprime.html

Asch, S. (1955). Opinions and social pressure. *Scientific American, 193*(5), 31–35. Retrieved May 21, 2015, from www.columbia.edu/cu/psychology/terrace/w1001/readings/asch.pdf

Ayres, R., & Olenick, M. (2017). *Secular stagnation (or corporate suicide?).* Instead Working Paper. Retrieved February 27, 2019, from https://ruayres.wordpress.com/2017/07/11/secular-stagnation-or-corporate-suicide/#more-772

Badger, E. (2014). Pollution is segregated, too. *The Washington Post.* Retrieved March 5, 2019, from https://www.washingtonpost.com/news/wonk/wp/2014/04/15/pollution-is-substantially-worse-in-minority-neighborhoods-across-the-u-s/

Baker, D. (2013). The bigger problem with Mankiw's plan to give everything to the one percent. *Center for Economic and Policy Research.* Retrieved February 17, 2019, from http://cepr.net/blogs/beat-the-press/the-bigger-problem-with-mankiws-plan-to-give-everything-to-the-one-percent

Baker, T. (2005). *The medical malpractice myth.* Chicago: IL, University of Chicago Press.

Bakija, J., Cole, A., & Heim, B. T. (2012). *Jobs and income growth of top earners and the causes of changing income inequality: Evidence from U.S. tax return data.* Retrieved May 29, 2019, from https://web.williams.edu/Economics/wp/BakijaColeHeimJobsIncomeGrowthTopEarners.pdf

Baldwin effect. (2018, January 7). In *Wikipedia.* Retrieved January 18, 2018, from https://en.wikipedia.org/w/index.php?title=Baldwin_effect&oldid=819170138

Bandura, A. (1977). *Social learning theory.* Englewood Cliffs, N.J: Prentice Hall.

Bandura, A. (1982). Self-efficacy mechanism in human agency. *American Psychologist, 37*(2), 122–147. Retrieved March 10, 2020, from https://pdfs.semanticscholar.org/8bee/c556fe7a650120544a99e9e063eb8fcd987b.pdf

Bandura, A. (1994). Self-efficacy. In V. S. Ramachandran (Ed.), *Encyclopedia of human behavior* (Vol. 4, pp. 71–81). New York, NY: Academic Press. Retrieved February 21, 2012, from http://www.des.emory.edu/mfp/BanEncy.html

Bandura, A. (1997). Self-efficacy: The exercise of control. New York: W.H. Freeman and Company.

Banerjee, N., & Song, L. (2015, October 8). Exxon's business ambition collided with climate change under a distant sea. *Inside Climate News.* Retrieved October 27, 2015, from http://insideclimatenews.org/news/08102015/Exxons-Business-Ambition-Collided-with-Climate-Change-Under-a-Distant-Sea

Banerjee, N., Song, L., & Hasemyer, D. (2015, October 16). Exxon's own research confirmed fossil fuels' role in global warming decades ago. *Inside Climate News.* Retrieved October 27, 2015, from http://insideclimatenews.org/news/15092015/Exxons-own-research-confirmed-fossil-fuels-role-in-global-warming

Banerjee, N., Song, L., & Hasemyer, D. (2015a, October 17). Exxon believed deep dive into climate research would protect its business. *Inside Climate News.* Retrieved October 27, 2015, from http://insideclimatenews.org/news/16092015/exxon-believed-deep-dive-into-climate-research-would-protect-its-business

Bardsley, N. (2008). Dictator game giving: Altruism or artefact? *Experimental Economics, 11,* 122–133. Retrieved March 27, 2018, from http://faculty.cbpp.uaa.alaska.edu/jalevy/protected/BardsleyDictatorExpeEcon2008.pdf

Barnard, C. I. (1968). *The functions of the executive.* Cambridge, MA: Harvard University Press.

Baron-Cohen, S., Leslie, A. M., & Frith, U. (1985). Does the autistic child have a "theory of mind"? *Cognition, 21*(37), 37–46.

Bartik, T. J., & Hershbein, B. J. (2018). *Degrees of poverty: The relationship between family income background and the returns to education.* Upjohn Institute Working Paper 18-284. Kalamazoo, MI: W.E. Upjohn Institute for Employment Research. Retrieved May 12, 2020, from https://research.upjohn.org/cgi/viewcontent.cgi?article=1302&context=up_workingpapers

Bauman, Y., & Rose, E. (2011). Selection or indoctrination: Why do economics students donate less than the rest? *Journal of Economic Behavior & Organization, 79*(3), 318–327.

Beaty, W. (1996). Virginia power takes its own energy saving advice. *Electric Light and Power, 74*(3), 22.

Becker, J., Stolberg, S. G., & Labaton, S. (2008, December 21). White House philosophy stoked mortgage bonfire. *The New York Times.* Retrieved April 8, 2016, from http://www.nytimes.com/2008/12/21/business/21admin.html

Becker, S. W., & Eagly, A. H. (2004). The heroism of women and men. *American Psychologist, 59*(3), 163–178.

Beckert, S. (2014, December 12). Slavery and capitalism. *Chronicle of Higher Education.* Retrieved October 25, 2018, from https://www.chronicle.com/article/SlaveryCapitalism/150787

Benson, G., & Lawler, E. (2015). *Revised employee involvement: Research foundations.* Center for Effective Organizations. CEO Publication G15-03 (650). Retrieved October 26, 2018, from https://ceo.usc.edu/revised-employee-involvement-research-foundations/

Benson, G. S., Kimmel, M., & Lawler, E. E., III. (2013). Adoption of employee involvement practices: Organizational change issues and insights. *Research in Organizational Change and Development, 21,* 233–257.

Berman, J. (2013). Eric Holder's 1999 memo helped set the stage for "too big to jail." Retrieved July 18, 2018, from https://www.huffingtonpost.com/2013/06/04/eric-holder-1999-memo_n_3384980.html

Bernays, E. (1928). *Propaganda.* New York, NY:: Horace Liveright.

Berns, G. S., Chappelow, J., Zink, C. F., Pagnoni, G., Martin-Skurski, M. E., & Richards, J. (2005). Neurobiological correlates of social conformity and independence during mental rotation. *Biological Psychiatry, 58*(3), 245–253. https://doi.org/10.1016/j.biopsych.2005.04.012

Bernstein, J. (2013). *The impact of inequality on growth.* Center for American Progress. Retrieved May 11, 2020, from https://www.americanprogress.org/wp-content/uploads/2013/12/BerensteinInequality.pdf

Berkshire Hathaway Inc. (2002). *2002 annual report*. Retrieved May 25, 2019, from http://www.berkshirehathaway.com/2002ar/2002ar.pdf

Bethell, T. (2001). A map to nowhere: The genome isn't a code and we can't read it. *The American Spectator*. Retrieved July 19, 2016, from http://www.colin.org/SmallStuff/MapNowhere.html

Betts, S. (2018, March 8). Hope man kills rabid raccoon after it tussles with dog. *The Camden Herald*, *150*(10), A1 and 10A.

Beugelsdijk, S., de Groot, H. L. F., & van Schaik, A.B.T.M. (2004). Trust and economic growth: A robustness analysis. *Oxford Economic Papers*, *56*, 118–134.

Bialik, C. (2007). How much are frivolous lawsuits really costing you? *The Wall Street Journal*. Retrieved March 31, 2011, from http://blogs.wsj.com/numbersguy/how-much-are-frivolous-lawsuits-really-costing-you-95/

Bierley, J. J., Jr. (2006). *Cash-to-cash cycle*. Retrieved January 14, 2008, from http://www.vitalentusa.com/learn/cash_to_cash.php

Bikhchandani, S., Hirshleifer, D., Welch, I., (1992). A theory of fads, fashion, custom, and cultural change as informational cascades. *The Journal of Political Economy*, *100*(5), 992–1026.

Bizjak, J. M., Lemmon, M., & Nguyen, T. (2009). Are all CEOs above average? An empirical analysis of compensation peer groups and pay design. *Journal of Financial Economics*, *100*, 538–555. Retrieved May 29, 2019, from https://papers.ssrn.com/sol3/papers.cfm?abstract_id=1364775&download=yes

BlessingWhite, Inc. (2008). *The state of employee engagement 2008*. Princeton, NJ: BlessingWhite, Inc. Retrieved January 24, 2009, from http://www.blessingwhite.com/%5Ccontent%5Creports%5C2008EmployeeEngagementNAOverview.pdf

Blount, S. (1995). When social outcomes aren't fair: The effect of causal attributions on preferences. *Organization Behavior and Human Decision Processes*, *63*, 131–144.

Blumenthal, E. (2018, November 2). HBO and Cinemax go off the air for Dish and Sling TV over programming dispute with AT&T. *USA Today*. Retrieved November 8, 2018, from https://www.usatoday.com/story/money/2018/11/02/att-hbo-cinemax-dish-sling-tv-dispute-over-programming/1860427002/

Bolton, G. E., & Katok, E. (1998). An experimental test of the crowding out hypothesis: The nature of beneficent behavior. *Journal of Economic Behavior & Organization*, *37*, 315–331.

Bouchard, M. (2008). Why markets go bad. Retrieved December 4, 2020, from https://www.tmcnet.com/usubmit/-why-markets-go-bad-/2008/07/18/3555312.htm

Bourguignon, F. & Morrisson, C. (2002). Inequality among world citizens: 1820-1992. *The American Economic Review*, 92(4), pp. 727-744. Retrieved August 5, 2021, from http://www.salasweb.info/cursos/desigualdad/BourguignonMorrison2002.pdf

Boyd, R., & Richerson, P. J. (1988). The evolution of reciprocity in sizable groups. *Journal of Theoretical Biology*, *132*(3), 337–356.

Branson, R. K., Rayner, G. T., Cox, J. L., Furman, J. P., King, F. J., Hannum, W. H. (1975). *Interservice procedures for instructional systems development* (TRADOC Pam 350-30 NAVEDTRA 106A). Ft. Monroe, VA: U.S. Army Training and Doctrine Command, August 1975. (NTIS No. ADA 019 486 through ADA 019 490).

Brettell, K., Gaffen, D., & Rohde, D. (2015). The cannibalized company: Part 1. *Reuters*. Retrieved February 27, 2019, from https://www.reuters.com/investigates/special-report/usa-buybacks-pay/

Brettell, K., Gaffen, D., & Rohde, D. (2015a). The cannibalized company: Part 2. *Reuters*. Retrieved February 27, 2019, from https://www.reuters.com/investigates/special-report/usa-buybacks-cannibalized/

Brill, S. (2018). How baby boomers broke America. *Time Magazine*. Retrieved May 1, 2019, from http://time.com/5280446/baby-boomer-generation-america-steve-brill/

Brown, E. (2019). The banking model that's bankrupting Americans. *Truthdig*. Retrieved June 25, 2019, from https://www.truthdig.com/articles/the-banking-model-thats-bankrupting-americans/

Bubble. (2018). In *Investopedia*. Retrieved October 10, 2018, from https://www.investopedia.com/terms/b/bubble.asp

Buchanan, M. (2008, July 19). Why economic theory is out of whack. *The New Scientist, 2665*, 32–35. Retrieved September 5, 2018, from http://www.archimedesfinancial.com.au/files/omic_theory_is_out_of_whack___Buchan__Jul08__0.pdf

Bujak, C. J., & Vitalo, R. L. (2014). The possibility of misinterpreting improvements in the value added ratio (VAR). Retrieved October 28, 2014, from http://www.vitalentusa.com/learn/possibility_misinterpreting_improvements_in_var.php

Bukhari, J. (2017). Famed investor predicts historic market drop. *Fortune*. Retrieved October 10, 2018, from http://fortune.com/2017/03/09/stock-market-sell-bubble

Burger, J. M. (2009). Replicating Milgram: Would people still obey today? *American Psychologist, 64*(1), 1–11. https://doi.org/10.1037/a0010932

Burns, A.D. (2008). Six Sigma lessons from Deming, Part 2. *Quality Digest*. Retrieved February 22, 2012, from http://www.qualitydigest.com/inside/six-sigma-article/six-sigma-lessons-deming-part-2

Bushman, B. J., & Anderson, C. A. (2001). Media violence and the American public. *American Psychologist, 56*(6/7), 477–489.

Byron, J. S., & Bierley, P. V. (2003). *Working with others training program*. O'Fallon, MO: Lowrey Press.

Byron, J. S., & Vitalo. R. L. (1991). Quality improvement through exemplar-based productivity analysis. *American Productivity and Quality Center*, Brief 82. Retrieved September 11, 2020, from https://www.researchgate.net/publication/334576869_Quality_Improvement_Through_Exemplar-Based_Productivity_Analysis#fullTextFileContent

Byron, J. S., & Vitalo, R. L. (2004). *Using working with others training sessions to drive employee involvement*. Retrieved January 15, 2008, from http://www.vitalentusa.com/learn/drive_ei.php

Camerer, C. F. (2003). *Behavioral game theory: Experiments in strategic interaction*. Princeton, NJ: Princeton University Press.

Cameron, L. A. (1999). Raising the stakes in the Ultimatum Game: Experimental evidence from Indonesia. *Economic Inquiry, 37*, 47–59.

Campbell, D. (1969). Reforms as experiments. *American Psychologist, 24*, 409–429.

Caporael, L. R., Dawes, R. M., Orbell, J. M., & Van de Kragt, A. J. (1989). Selfishness examined: Cooperation in the absence of egoistic incentives. *Behavioral and Brain Sciences, 12*(4), 683–739.

Cappelen, A. W., Nielsen, U., Sorensen, E., Tungodden, B., & Tyran, J. (2012). *Give and take in Dictator Games*. NHH Dept. of Economics Discussion Paper No. 14/2012. Retrieved April 16, 2018, from https://ssrn.com/abstract=2135511

Cardenas, J. C., & Carpenter, J. (2008). Behavioural development economics: Lessons from field labs in the developing world. *Journal of Development Studies, 44*(3), 337–364.

Carkhuff, R. R. (1969). *Helping and human relations*. New York, NY: Holt, Rinehart, and Winston, Inc.

Carkhuff, R. R. (1971). *The development of human resources*. Amherst, MA: Human Resource Development Press, Inc.

Carkhuff, R. R. (1975). The gold star schedule. In R. R. Carkhuff, *Belly to Belly Back to Back* (pp. 17–19). Amherst, MA: Human Resource Development Press, Inc.

Carkhuff, R. R. (1977). *The art of helping III.* Amherst, MA: Human Resource Development Press, Inc.

Carkhuff, R. R. (1983). *Sources of human productivity.* Amherst, MA: Human Resource Development Press, Inc.

Carkhuff, R. R. (1983a). *Interpersonal skills and human productivity.* Amherst, MA: Human Resource Development Press, Inc.

Carkhuff, R. R. (1986). *Human processing and human productivity.* Amherst, MA: Human Resource Development Press, Inc.

Carkhuff, R. R. (1988). *The age of new capitalism.* Amherst, MA: Human Resource Development Press, Inc.

Carkhuff, R. R., & Anthony, W. A. (1979). *The skills of helping.* Amherst, MA: Human Resource Development Press, Inc.

Carkhuff, R. R., & Berenson, B. G. (1967). *Beyond counseling and psychotherapy.* New York, NY:: Holt, Rinehart, and Winston, Inc.

Carnegie Hero Fund Commission. (2018). 20 Carnegie Heroes named for extraordinary heroism. Retrieved March 22, 2018, from http://www.carnegiehero.org/awardees/

Caux Round Table. (2017). Principles for business. Retrieved February 14, 2017, from http://www.cauxroundtable.org/index.cfm?menuid=8

CBS News (2021). Only half of U.S. households donated to charity, worst rate in decades. Retrieved August 17, 2021, from https://www.cbsnews.com/news/charity-donations-us-households-decline/

Cerasoli, C. P., Nicklin, J. M., & Ford, M. T. (2014). Intrinsic motivation and extrinsic incentives jointly predict performance: A 40-year meta-analysis. *Psychological Bulletin, 140*(4), 980–1008.

Chappell, B. (2019). U.S. income inequality worsens, widening to a new gap. Retrieved May 8, 2020, from https://www.npr.org/2019/09/26/764654623/u-s-income-inequality-worsens-widening-to-a-new-gap

Chappello, J. (2020). Gini index. *Investopedia.* Retrieved May 8, 2020, from https://www.investopedia.com/terms/g/gini-index.asp

Chen, J. (2016, August 14). Man saves woman and her dog from drowning in sinking convertible in Louisiana. *US Magazine.* Retrieved March 25, 2018, from https://www.usmagazine.com/celebrity-news/news/man-saves-woman-her-dog-from-drowning-in-sinking-convertible-w434387

Cheng, D. (2011). *Executive pay through a peer benchmarking lens.* ISS Corporate Services. Retrieved May 29, 2019, from http://www.shareholderforum.com/sop/Library/20110721_ISS.pdf

Chetty, R., Friedman, J. N., Saez, E., Turner, N., & Yagan, D. (2017). Mobility report cards: The role of colleges in intergenerational mobility. Retrieved March 17, 2019, from http://www.equality-of-opportunity.org/papers/coll_mrc_paper.pdf

Chetty, R., Grusky, D., Hell, M., Hendren, N., Manduca, R., & Narang, J. (2017). The fading American dream: Trends in absolute income mobility since 1940. *Science, 356*(6336), 398–406. Retrieved May 11, 2020, from https://science.sciencemag.org/content/356/6336/398.full

Chetty, R., Stepner, M., Abraham, S., Lin, S., Scuderi, B., Turner, N., Bergeron, A., & Cutler, D. (2016). The association between income and life expectancy in the United States, 2001–2014. *Journal of the American Medical Association, 315*(16), 1750–1766.

Chimerine, L., & Eisenbrey, R. (2005). *The frivolous case for tort reform.* Economic Policy Institute Briefing Paper #157. Retrieved June 19, 2011, from http://www.epi.org/page/-/old/briefingpapers/157/bp157.pdf

Choma, R. (2014). Millionaires' club: For first time, most lawmakers are worth $1 million-plus. Retrieved April 23, 2019, from https://www.opensecrets.org/news/2014/01/millionaires-club-for-first-time-most-lawmakers-are-worth-1-million-plus/

Cingano, F. (2014). *Trends in income inequality and its impact on economic growth*. OECD Social, Employment and Migration Working Papers, No. 163, OECD Publishing, Paris, https://doi.org/10.1787/5jxrjncwxv6j-en

Clark, J. (2011). What is the revolving door? Retrieved April 25, 2019, from https://people.howstuffworks.com/what-is-the-revolving-door.htm

Clark, M. S., Boothby, E. J., Clark-Polner, E., & Reis, H. T. (2015). Chapter 16: Understanding prosocial behavior requires understanding relational context. In D. A. Schroeder & W. G. Graziano (Eds.), *The Oxford handbook of prosocial behavior* (pp. 329–345). New York, NY: Oxford University Press.

Clarke, R. (2004). Open source software and open content as models for eBusiness. Retrieved October 22, 2013, from http://www.rogerclarke.com/EC/Bled04.html#BM

Clifford, S. (2017). How companies actually decide what to pay CEOs. *The Atlantic*. Retrieved May 30, 2019, from https://www.theatlantic.com/business/archive/2017/06/how-companies-decide-ceo-pay/530127/

Coffey, C., Revollo, P. E., Harvey, R., Lawson, M., Butt, A. P., Piaget, K., Sarosi, D., & Thekkudan, J. (2020). *Time to care*. Oxfam International. Retrieved May 8, 2020, from https://oxfamilibrary.openrepository.com/bitstream/handle/10546/620928/bp-time-to-care-inequality-200120-en.pdf

Cohan, W. D. (2015). How Wall Street's bankers stayed out of jail. *The Atlantic*. Retrieved May 25, 2019, from https://www.theatlantic.com/magazine/archive/2015/09/how-wall-streets-bankers-stayed-out-of-jail/399368/

Cohan, W. D. (2017). Jamie Dimon's $13 billion secret—revealed. *Vanity Fair*. Retrieved December 8, 2020, from https://www.vanityfair.com/news/2017/09/jamie-dimon-billion-dollar-secret-jp-morgan/amp

Cole, S. W., Hawkley, L. C., Arevalo, J. M., & Cacioppo, J. T. (2011). Transcript origin analysis identifies antigen-presenting cells as primary targets of socially regulated gene expression in leukocytes. *Proceedings of the National Academy of Sciences, 108*(7), 3080–3085.

Collins, C., & Hoxlie, J. (2017). *Billionaire bonanza: The Forbes 400 and the rest of us*. Institute for Policy Studies. Retrieved May 8, 2020, from https://inequality.org/wp-content/uploads/2017/11/BILLIONAIRE-BONANZA-2017-Embargoed.pdf

Collins, M. (2015). The big bank bailout. *Forbes Magazine*. Retrieved May 20, 2019, from https://www.forbes.com/sites/mikecollins/2015/07/14/the-big-bank-bailout/#66aca2262d83

Combs, J., Liu, Y., Hall, A., & Ketchen, D. (2006). How much do high-performance work practices matter? A meta-analysis of their effects on organizational performance. *Personnel Psychology, 59*, 501–528. Retrieved October 14, 2020, from https://www.greenleaf.org/wp-content/uploads/2013/11/PersonnelPsych.pdf

Congressional Budget Office. (2018). *Report on the Troubled Asset Relief Program—March 2018*. Retrieved June 26, 2019, from https://www.cbo.gov/system/files/115th-congress-2017-2018/reports/53617-tarp-march2018.pdf

Cooper, C. (2014). Drugs companies "routinely withhold results of medical trial" from doctors, researchers and patients. *The Independent*. Retrieved August 4, 2019, from https://www.independent.co.uk/life-style/health-and-families/health-news/drugs-firms-routinely-withhold-results-of-medical-trials-from-doctors-researchers-and-patients-9035740.html

Cooper, G. (1998). *Research into cognitive load theory and instruction design at NSWU.* School of Education Studies, University of New South Wales, Sydney, NSW 2052, Australia. Retrieved August 24, 2013, from http://dwb4.unl.edu/Diss/Cooper/UNSW.htm

Cooper, M. J., Gulen, H., & Rau, R. (2016). *Performance for pay? The relation between CEO incentive compensation and future stock price performance.* Retrieved March 11, 2019, from https://online.wsj.com/public/resources/documents/CEOperformance122509.pdf

Corak, M. (2013). *Income inequality, equality of opportunity, and intergenerational mobility.* IZA DP No. 7520. Retrieved February 17, 2019, from http://ftp.iza.org/dp7520.pdf. Also, a briefer version at: *Journal of Economic Perspectives*, 27(3), 79–102. Retrieved February 17, 2019, from https://pubs.aeaweb.org/doi/pdfplus/10.1257/jep.27.3.79

Côté, S., House, J., & Willer, R. (2015). High economic inequality leads higher-income individuals to be less generous. *Proceedings of the National Academy of Sciences, 112*, 201511536. Retrieved April 23, 2018, from http://www.pnas.org/content/pnas/early/2015/11/18/1511536112.full.pdf

Cottini, E., Kato, T., & Nielsen, N. W. (2009). *Adverse workplace conditions, high-involvement work practices and labor turnover: Evidence from Danish linked employer-employee data.* Discussion Paper No. 4587, November 2009. Retrieved May 30, 2011, from http://ftp.iza.org/dp4587.pdf

Council on Foreign Relations. (2019). Robert E. Rubin: Chairman Emeritus; Former Secretary of the U.S. Treasury. Retrieved April 25, 2019, from https://www.cfr.org/expert/robert-e-rubin

Cox, J. C., Sadiraj, K., & Sadiraj, V. (2002). *Trust, fear, reciprocity, and altruism* (Working Paper). University of Arizona. Retrieved April 12, 2018, from http://excen.gsu.edu/jccox/working_papers/trustfear.pdf

Cox, J. C., Sadiraj, K., & Sadiraj, V. (2006). *Implications of trust, fear, and reciprocity for modeling economic behavior.* Andrew Young School of Policy Studies Research Paper Series No. 07-15. Retrieved April 12, 2018, from https://ssrn.com/abstract=976036

Coyle-Shapiro, J., & Kessler, I. (2002). Exploring reciprocity through the lens of the psychological contract: Employee and employer perspectives. *European Journal of Work and Organizational Psychology, 11*(1), 69–86.

Cray, C. (2011). The Lewis Powell Memo - corporate blueprint to dominate democracy. *Common Dreams.* Retrieved August 23, 2021, from https://www.commondreams.org/views/2011/08/25/lewis-powell-memo-corporate-blueprint-dominate-democracy

Crony capitalism. (2019). In *Wikipedia.* Retrieved April 2, 2019, from https://en.wikipedia.org/w/index.php?title=Crony_capitalism&oldid=883351215

Cushman, J. H., Jr. (2015, October 8). Highlighting the allure of synfuels, Exxon played down the climate risks. *Inside Climate News.* Retrieved October 27, 2015, from http://insideclimatenews.org/news/08102015/highlighting-allure-synfuels-exxon-played-down-climate-risks

Cutler, D. M., Poterba, J. M., & Summers, L. H. (1988). *What moves stock prices?* Working Paper No. 2538, National Bureau of Economic Research, Cambridge, MA. Retrieved May 7, 2020, from http://www.nber.org/papers/w2538

Dabla-Norris, E., Kochhar, K., Ricka, F., Suphaphiphat, N., & Tsounta, E. (2015). *Causes and consequences of income inequality: A global perspective.* International Monetary Fund. Retrieved May 11, 2020, from https://www.imf.org/external/pubs/ft/sdn/2015/sdn1513.pdf

Dahl, R. A., & Lindblom, C. E. (2000). *Politics, economics, and welfare.* New Brunswick, NJ: Transaction Publishers.

Dale, S., & Krueger, A. B. (2011). *Estimating the return to college selectivity over the career using administrative earnings data.* NBER Working Paper No. 17159. Retrieved March 17, 2019, from https://www.nber.org/papers/w17159.pdf

Dawes, R. M., Orbell, J. M., Simmons, R. T., & van de Kragt, A. J. C. (1986). Organizing groups for collective action. *American Political Science Review, 80,* 1171–1185.

Dawes, R. M., & Thaler, R. H. (1988). Anomalies: Cooperation. *Journal of Economic Perspectives, 2*(3), 187–197. Retrieved February 20, 2018, from http://econ.ucsb.edu/~oprea/176/Cooperation.pdf

de Navarro, J. M. (1925). Prehistoric routes between Northern Europe and Italy defined by the amber trade. *The Geographical Journal, 66*(6), 481–503.

de Rothschild, L. F. (2013). A costly and unjust perk for financiers. *The New York Times.* Retrieved May 31, 2019, from https://www.nytimes.com/2013/02/25/opinion/carried-interest-an-unjust-privilege-for-financiers.html

Deci, E. L., Koestner, R., & Ryan, R. M. (1999). A meta-analytic review of experiments examining the effects of extrinsic rewards on intrinsic motivation. *Psychological Bulletin, 125*(6), 627–668.

Delamaide, D. (2013). Holder admits megabanks are "too big to jail." *MarketWatch.* Retrieved May 31, 2019, from https://www.marketwatch.com/story/holder-admits-mega-banks-are-too-big-to-jail-2013-03-07

Deming, W. E. (1950). *Elementary principles of the statistical control of quality: A series of lectures.* Tokyo, Japan: Nippon Kagaku Gijutsu Renmei.

Deming, W. E. (1967). What happened in Japan. *Industrial Quality Control, 24*(2), 89–93.

Deming, W. E. (1975). On probability as a basis for action. *The American Statistician, 29*(4), 146–152.

Deming, W. E. (1982). *Quality, productivity and competitive position.* Cambridge, MA: Massachusetts Institute of Technology Center for Advanced Engineering Study.

Deming, W. E. (1982a). *Out of crisis.* Cambridge, MA: Massachusetts Institute of Technology Center for Advanced Engineering Study.

Deming, W. E. (1988). Quality and the required style of management—the need for change. *Journal for Quality and Participation, 17*(7), 1–2.

Deming, W. E. (2000). *The new economics: For industry, government, education* (2nd ed.). Cambridge, MA: Massachusetts Institute of Technology Center for Advanced Engineering Study.

Deming, W. E. (2013). Lectures and meetings: Deming's 1950 lecture to Japanese management. Translated from Japanese transcript. Retrieved August 27, 2013, from http://hclectures.blogspot.com/1970/08/demings-1950-lecture-to-japanese.html

Democracy Now! (2011, January 25). Do you know the full story behind the infamous McDonald's coffee case and how corporations used it to promote tort reform? http://www.democracynow.org/2011/1/25/do_you_know_the_full_story

Devanny, J. (2020). Who owns America today? Retrieved December 7, 2020, from https://www.abbevilleinstitute.org/blog/who-owns-america-today/

Devereux, M. P., Lockwood, B., & Redoano, M. (2004). *Do countries compete over corporate tax rates?* University of Warwick, Coventry, England. Retrieved August 20, 2018, from https://warwick.ac.uk/fac/soc/economics/staff/blockwood/dlrrev.pdf

DeVries, D. L., & Kaiser, R. B. (2003). *Going sour in the suite: What you can do about executive derailment.* Paper presented at the Maximizing Executive Effectiveness workshop, Miami, FL.

Dewey, J. (1910). *How people think.* Retrieved December 11, 2007, from http://www.brocku.ca/MeadProject/Dewey/Dewey_1910a/Dewey_1910_a.html

Diekmann, A. (2004). The power of reciprocity. *Journal of Conflict Resolution, 48*(4), 487–505. Retrieved March 17, 2015, from www.communicationcache.com/uploads/1/0/8/8/10887248/the_power_of_reciprocity.pdf

Dijksterhuis, A., & Knippenberg, A. (1998). The relation between perception and behavior, or how to win a game of trivial pursuit. *Journal of Personality and Social Psychology, 74*(4), 865–877. Retrieved August 6, 2017, from https://www.researchgate.net/publication/13710149_The_Relation_Between_Perception_and_Behavior_or_How_to_Win_a_Game_of_Trivial_Pursuit

Dilger, D. E. (2007). Microsoft's outrageous Office profits. Retrieved July 2, 2020, from https://web.archive.org/web/20170809215009/http://www.roughlydrafted.com/2007/09/09/microsoft%e2%80%99s-outrageous-office-profits/

Dincer, O. C., & Uslaner, E. M. (2010). Trust and growth. *Public Choice, 142*, 59–67.

Dodge v. Ford Motor Co. 170 N.W. 668 (Mich. 1919). Retrieved January 29, 2020, from https://h2o.law.harvard.edu/cases/3965

Douglas, D. (2013). Holder concerned that megabanks too big to jail. *The Washington Post.* Retrieved from https://www.washingtonpost.com/business/economy/holder-concerned-megabanks-too-big-to-jail/2013/03/06/6fa2b07a-869e-11e2-999e-5f8e0410cb9d_story.html

Draper, S. W. (2016, May 11). The Hawthorne, Pygmalion, placebo and other effects of expectation: Some notes. Retrieved May 25, 2018, from http://www.psy.gla.ac.uk/~steve/hawth.html

Dunbar, R. I. M. (1998). The social brain hypothesis. *Evolutionary Anthropology, 6*(5), 178–190.

Dunbar, R. I. M., & Schultz, S. (2017). Why are there so many explanations for the primary brain evolution? *Philosophical Transactions of the Royal Society: Biological Sciences, 372*, 20160244.

Durden, T. (2019). John Bolton openly admits he wants Maduro out, American oil companies in. *Zerohedge.com.* Retrieved January 29, 2019, from https://www.zerohedge.com/news/2019-01-28/venezuela-regime-change-good-american-oil-companies-says-john-bolton

Economic Mobility Project. (2009). Opinion poll on economic mobility and the American Dream. Washington, D.C.: Pew Charitable Trusts. Retrieved from http://www.pewstates.org/research/analysis/opinion-poll-on-economic-mobility-and-the-american-dream-85899378651.

Economic Policy Institute. (2018). The productivity–pay gap. Retrieved February 26, 2019, from https://www.epi.org/productivity-pay-gap/

Egan, A. (2018). Alan Greenspan: "We have a stock market bubble." *CNN Business.* Retrieved October 10, 2018, from https://money.cnn.com/2018/01/31/investing/alan-greenspan-bubble-stocks-bonds/index.html

Eisenhardt, K. (1989). Agency theory: An assessment and review. *Academy of Management Review, 14*(1), 57–74. Retrieved from https://pdfs.semanticscholar.org/8488/a9a8c56dd19be9f4e9e7793ed0ded2cd7782.pdf

Elliott, L. (2019). World's 26 richest people own as much as poorest 50%, says Oxfam. *The Guardian.* Retrieved May 3, 2019, from https://www.theguardian.com/business/2019/jan/21/world-26-richest-people-own-as-much-as-poorest-50-per-cent-oxfam-report

Engel, C. (2011). Dictator games: A meta analysis. *Experimental Economics, 14*, 583–610.

Enomoto, T. (1995). The individual in the group. In P. Graham (Ed.), *Mary Parker Follett profit of management* (pp. 240–245). Washington, D.C.: Beard Books.

Erikson, E. H. (1988). *Identity and the life cycle.* New York, NY: W. W. Norton & Company.

Etzioni, A. (2015). The moral effects of economic teaching. *Sociological Forum, 30*(1), 228–33. Retrieved August 20, 2021, from https://www.uv.es/sasece/docum2015/Etzioni-2015-Sociological_Forum.pdf

Falk, A., & Fischbacher, U. (2000). *A theory of reciprocity.* University of Zurich, Working Paper Series, Working Paper No. 6, ISSN 1424-0459. Retrieved October 24, 2011, from http://www.econ.uzh.ch/static/wp_iew/iewwp006.pdf

Falk, A., & Fischbacher, U. (2001). *A theory of reciprocity.* Institute for Empirical Research in Economics Working Paper No. 6. CESifo Working Paper Series No.457. Retrieved July 18, 2018, from https://ssrn.com/abstract=203115 [27 pp.]

Fang, L., & Lerner, S. (2020). Coronavirus treatment developed by Gilead Sciences granted "Rare Disease" status, potentially limiting affordability. *The Intercept.* Retrieved January 8, 2021, from https://theintercept.com/2020/03/23/gilead-sciences-coronavirus-treatment-orphan-drug-status/

Faulkender, M. W., & Yang, J. (2007). *Inside the black box: The role and composition of compensation peer groups.* AFA 2008 New Orleans Meetings Paper. Retrieved February 19, 2019, from https://ssrn.com/abstract=972197

Federal Reserve History. (2019). Garn-St Germain Depository Institutions Act of 1982. Retrieved May 20, 2019, from https://www.federalreservehistory.org/essays/garn_st_germain_act

Fehr, E. (2005). *The nature of human altruism.* Carl Snyder Memorial Public Lecture—UCSB, March 7, 2005. Retrieved July 20, 2018, from https://www.coursehero.com/file/7622769/altruismppt/

Fehr, E., Fischbacher, U., & Gächter, S. (2002). Strong reciprocity, human cooperation and the enforcement of social norms. *Human Nature, 13,* 1–25. Retrieved March 2, 2018, from http://www.vwl.tuwien.ac.at/lva/expoek.ps/artikel/altruismus_und_reziprozitaet/strong_reciprocity_human_cooperation_and_enforcement_of_social_norms.pdf

Fehr, E., & Gächter, S. (2000). Cooperation and punishment in public goods experiments. *The American Economic Group, 90*(4), 980–995.

Fehr, G., Kamm, A., & Jäger, M. (2014). *The behavioral change matrix: A tool for evidence-based policy making.* FehrAdvice & Partners AG. Retrieved December 22, 2020, from https://www.fehradvice.com/wp-content/uploads/2014/08/behavioral-change-matrix-fehr-advice.pdf

Ferguson, T. (1995). *Golden rule: The investment theory of party competition and the logic of money-driven political systems.* Chicago, IL: University of Chicago Press.

Ferguson, T., Jorgensen, P., & Chen, J. (2016). *How money drives US Congressional elections.* Working Paper No. 48. Institute for New Economic Thinking. Retrieved July 17, 2018, from https://www.ineteconomics.org/uploads/papers/WP_48_Ferguson_et_al.pdf

Financial Samurai. (2014). The median net worth of U.S. households over time has gone nowhere. Retrieved April 23, 2019, from https://www.financialsamurai.com/the-median-net-worth-of-us-households-over-time-has-gone-nowhere/

Fletcher, M. A. (2013). Research ties economic inequality to gap in life expectancy. *The Washington Post.* Retrieved February 28, 2019, from http://www.washingtonpost.com/business/economy/research-ties-economic-inequality-to-gap-in-life-expectancy/2013/03/10/c7a323c4-7094-11e2-8b8d-e0b59a1b8e2a_story.html

Floyd, J. (2018). White collar crime increases, prosecutions decrease. Retrieved March 2, 2019, from https://www.johntfloyd.com/white-collar-crime-increases-prosecutions-decrease

Follett, M. P. (1995a). Power. In P. Graham (Ed.), *Mary Parker Follett profit of management* (pp. 97–119). Washington, D.C.: Beard Books.

Follett, M. P. (1995b). Constructive conflict. In P. Graham (Ed.), *Mary Parker Follett profit of management* (pp. 67–87). Washington, D.C.: Beard Books.

Ford, H. (1922). Quotation from *Ford News*, January 15, 1922, issue. Retrieved August 2, 2019, from https://www.thehenryford.org/collections-and-research/digital-resources/popular-topics/henry-ford-quotes/

Ford, H. (1988). Today and tomorrow. Portland, OR: Productivity Press.

Forrester, J.W. (1991). System dynamics and the lessons of 35 years. Retrieved November 23, 2021, from http://matema.ujaen.es/jnavas/web_master/archivos/articulos%20forrester/forrester1.pdf

Forrester, J.W. (2010). System dynamics: The foundation under systems thinking. Massachusetts Institute of Technology Cambridge. Retrieved November 23, 2021, fromhttp://static.clexchange.org/ftp/documents/system-dynamics/SD2011-01SDFoundationunderST.pdf

Forsythe, R., Horowitz, J. L., Savin, N. E., & Sefton, M. (1994). Fairness in simple bargaining experiments. *Games and Economic Behavior*, *6*(3), 347–369.

Frank, R. H., Gilovich, T., & Regan, D. T. (1993). Does studying economics inhibit cooperation? *Journal of Economic Perspectives*, *7*(2), 159–171. Retrieved December 3, 2020, from https://www.aeaweb.org/atypon.php?return_to=/doi/pdfplus/10.1257/jep.7.2.159

Frank, R. H., Gilovich, T., & Regan, D. T. (1996). Do economists make bad citizens. *Journal of Economic Perspectives*, *10*(1), 187–192. Retrieved December 3, 2020, from https://pubs.aeaweb.org/doi/pdfplus/10.1257/jep.10.1.187

Freeland, C. (2013). The problem with too many millionaires. *The New York Times*. Retrieved May 29, 2019, from https://www.nytimes.com/2013/06/21/us/21iht-letter21.html

Friedman, M. (1953). *Essays in positive economics Part I—The methodology of positive economics*. Retrieved August 10, 2015, from www.econ.umn.edu/~schwe227/teaching.s11/files/articles/friedman-1953.pdf

Friedman, M. (1970, September 13). The social responsibility of business is to increase its profits. *The New York Times Magazine*. Retrieved from http://www.umich.edu/~thecore/doc/Friedman.pdf

Frye, A., & Campbell, D. (2011, February 18). Buffett says pricing power beats good management. *Bloomberg News*. Retrieved April 21, 2011, from http://www.bloomberg.com/news/2011-02-18/buffett-says-pricing-power-more-important-than-good-management.html

Gallagher, R. (2018). Google plans to launch censored search engine in China, leaked documents reveal. *The Intercept*. Retrieved January 29, 2019, from https://theintercept.com/2018/08/01/google-china-search-engine-censorship/

Gallup, Inc.(2017). *State of the American workplace*. Gallup, Inc. Retrieved March 12, 2017, from https://www.gallup.com/file/workplace/257549/State_American_Workplace_Report.pdf

Gallup, Inc.(2020). Satisfaction with the United States. Retrieved December 8, 2020, from https://news.gallup.com/poll/1669/general-mood-country.aspx

Gallup Management Journal. (2002, October). Gallup study finds that many employees doubt the ethics of corporate leaders. *Gallup Management Journal*. Retrieved January 24, 2009, from http://gmj.gallup.com/content/829/Gallup-Study-Finds-Many-Employees-Doubt-Ethics-Corporate-Leaders.aspx

Gelhaus, A. (2008, September 12). When it comes to food, package size matters. Retrieved May 15, 2020, from https://www.aol.com/2008/09/12/iwhen-it-comes-to-food-package-size-matters/

Giancola, J., & Kahlenberg, R. (2016). True merit: Ensuring our brightest students have access to our best colleges and universities. *Jack Kent Cooke Foundation*. Retrieved March 2, 2019, from https://www.jkcf.org/research/true-merit-ensuring-our-brightest-students-have-access-to-our-best-colleges-and-universities/

Gibbs, M. E. (1980). *The effects of extrinsic rewards on work performance, job satisfaction and intrinsic motivation* (Doctoral dissertation, Texas Tech University). Retrieved February 21, 2014, from http://repositories.tdl.org/ttu-ir/bitstream/handle/2346/12332/31295000046499.pdf?sequence=1

Gilbert, T. F. (1996). *Human competence. Engineering worthy performance.* Washington, D.C.: The International Society for Performance Improvement.

Gilens, M., & Page, B. I. (2014). Testing theories of American politics: Elites, interest groups, and average citizens. *Perspective on Politics, 12*, 564–581. Retrieved July 17, 2018, from https://scholar.princeton.edu/sites/default/files/mgilens/files/gilens_and_page_2014_-testing_theories_of_american_politics.doc.pdf

Gilson, D., & Rios, E. (2016). 11 charts that show income inequality isn't getting better anytime soon. *Mother Jones Magazine*. Retrieved December 3, 2018, from https://www.motherjones.com/politics/2016/12/america-income-inequality-wealth-net-worth-charts/

Golden, D. (2003). Many colleges bend rules to admit rich applicants. *The Wall Street Journal*. Retrieved March 2, 2019, from https://online.wsj.com/public/resources/documents/Polk_Rich_Applicants.htm

Goodnight, C. J., & Stevens, L. (1997). Experimental studies of group selection: What do they tell us about group selection in nature? *The American Naturalist, 150*, S59–S79.

Goodwin, N. (1991). Chapter 11: Stories that blow up: How to anticipate when the realisticness of assumptions will matter. In *Social economics: An alternative theory: Building anew on Marshall's principles* (pp. 227–256). New York, NY: St. Martin's Press. Retrieved August 9, 2015, from http://www.ase.tufts.edu/gdae/pubs/te/Chapter11.pdf

Goodwin, N. (2014). The human element in the new economics: A 60-year refresh for economic thinking and teaching. *Real-World Economics Review, 68*, 98—118. Retrieved August 20, 2021, from http://www.paecon.net/PAEReview/issue68/Goodwin68.pdf

Goodwin, N., Harris, J., Nelson, J. A., Roach, B., & Torras, M. (2017). *Microeconomics in context* (3rd ed.). New York, NY: Routledge.

Goranson, R. E., & Berkowitz, L. (1966). Reciprocity and responsibility reactions to prior help. *Journal of Personality and Social Psychology, 3*(2), 227–232.

Gordon, C. (2013). Defending the top 1 percent—and failing at it. Retrieved January 13, 2021, from https://iowapolicypoints.org/2013/07/03/defending-the-top-1-percent-and-failing-at-it/

Goulder, A. (1960). The norm of reciprocity. *American Sociological Review, 25*, 161–178. Retrieved November 18, 2013, from http://media.pfeiffer.edu/lridener/courses/normrecp.html

Govan, T. P. (1950). The rich, the well-born, and Alexander Hamilton. *The Mississippi Valley Historical Review, 36*(4), 675–680. Retrieved July 5, 2016, from http://www.jstor.org/stable/1895524

Grandia, K. (2011). Bonner & Associates: The long and undemocratic history of astroturfing. *The Huffington Post*. Retrieved July 23, 2020, from https://www.huffpost.com/entry/bonner-associates-the-lon_b_269976

Grasso, L. P. (2015). Performance measurement in a Lean organization: The case of the Wiremold company. Retrieved October 14, 2020, from http://www.bobemiliani.com/goodies/wm_cases/04wiremold_pm_case.pdf

Greenwald, G. (2017). Trump's support and praise of despots is central to the U.S. tradition, not a deviation from it. *The Intercept*. Retrieved November 20, 2020, from https://theintercept.com/2017/05/02/trumps-support-and-praise-of-despots-is-central-to-the-u-s-tradition-not-a-deviation-from-it/

Greenwald, G. (2021). The journalistic censorship industry suffers well-deserved blows. *Scheerpost*. Retrieved February 26, 2021, from https://scheerpost.com/2021/02/09/the-journalistic-censorship-industry-suffers-well-deserved-blows/

Greenwald, G. (2021a). Congress escalates pressure on tech giants to censor more, threatening the first amendment. Retrieved February 26, 2021, from https://greenwald.substack.com/p/congress-escalates-pressure-on-tech

Greenwald, G. (2021b). House Democrats, targeting right-wing cable outlets, are assaulting core press freedoms. Retrieved February 26, 2021, from https://greenwald.substack.com/p/house-democrats-targeting-right-wing

Greenwood, V. (2018). Theory suggests that all genes affect every complex trait. *Quanta Magazine*. Retrieved July 20, 2018, from https://www.quantamagazine.org/omnigenic-model-suggests-that-all-genes-affect-every-complex-trait-20180620/

Gross, D. (2019). How elite US schools give preference to wealthy and white "legacy" applicants. *The Guardian*. Retrieved March 2, 2019, from https://www.theguardian.com/us-news/2019/jan/23/elite-schools-ivy-league-legacy-admissions-harvard-wealthier-whiter

Grullon, G., Larkin, Y., and Michaely, R. (2018). Are U.S. industries becoming more concentrated? *Review of Finance*, 23(*4*), pp. 697–743. Retrieved August 9, 2021, from https://academic.oup.com/rof/article-pdf/23/4/697/28935115/rfz007.pdf

Guerrero, S., & Barraud-Didier, V. (2004). High-involvement practices and performance of French firms. *International Journal of Human Resource Management*, *15*(8), 1408–1423. Retrieved May 30, 2011, from https://poliformat.upv.es/access/content/group/DOC_27028_2007/Referencias/Guerrero_Barraud2004%20High-involvement%20practices%20and%20performance%20of%20French%20firmsB.pdf

Gyles, C. (2015). Skeptical of medical science reports? *Canadian Veterinarian Journal*, *56*(10), 1011–1012. Retrieved from https://www.ncbi.nlm.nih.gov/pmc/articles/PMC4572812/#b1-cvj_10_1011

Hacker, J. S., & Loewentheil, N. (2013). How big money corrupts the economy. *Democracy Journal*, *27*(Winter 2013). Retrieved March 29, 2019, from https://democracyjournal.org/magazine/27/how-big-money-corrupts-the-economy

Hamilton, W. D. (1964). The genetical theory of social behaviour I. *Journal of Theoretical Biology*, *7*, 1–16.

Hamilton, W. D. (1964a). The genetical theory of social behaviour II. *Journal of Theoretical Biology*, *7*, 17–52.

Handfield, R. (2011). *What is supply chain management?* Retrieved March 27, 2014, from http://scm.ncsu.edu/scm-articles/article/what-is-supply-chain-management

Haney, C., Banks, W. C., & Zimbardo, P. G. (1973). Interpersonal dynamics in a simulated prison. *International Journal of Criminology and Penology*, *1*, 69–97.

Harada, T. (2010, November 12). *Summary of notes from Art Smalley interview with Mr. Harada.* Retrieved March 18, 2014, from http://artoflean.com/documents/pdfs/Harada_interview_on_Jidoka.pdf

Häring, N., & Douglas, N. (2012). *Economists and the powerful.* New York, NY: Anthem Press.

Harness, J. (2009). Companies renamed to hide from bad reputations. Retrieved July 22, 2019, from https://www.neatorama.com/2009/09/10/companies-renamed-to-hide-from-bad-reputations/

Harras, G., & Sornette, D. (2008). Endogenous versus exogenous origins of financial rallies and crashes in an agent-based model with Bayesian learning and imitation. *Swiss Finance Institute Research Paper Series.* Retrieved October 16, 2018, from http://ssrn.com/abstract=1156348

Harter, J. K., Schmidt, F. L., & Killham, E. A. (2003). *Employee engagement, satisfaction, and business-unit-level outcomes: A meta-analysis.* The Gallup Corporation, Princeton, NJ. Retrieved April 14, 2016, from http://www.nova.edu/ie/ice/forms/meta_analysis_july_2003.pdf

Harter, J. K., Schmidt, F. L., Agrawal, S., & Plowman, S. K. (2013). *The relationship between engagement at work and organizational outcomes: 2012 Q12 meta-analysis.* Retrieved April 14, 2016, from https://www.employeeengagement.com/wp-content/uploads/2013/04/2012-Q12-Meta-Analysis-Research-Paper.pdf

Hasemyer, D., & Cushman, J. H., Jr. (2015, October 22). Exxon sowed doubt about climate science for decades by stressing uncertainty. *Inside Climate News.* Retrieved October 27, 2015, from http://insideclimatenews.org/news/22102015/Exxon-Sowed-Doubt-about-Climate-Science-for-Decades-by-Stressing-Uncertainty

Hayes, A. (2019). Perfect competition. *Investopedia.* Retrieved June 3, 2020, from https://www.investopedia.com/terms/p/perfectcompetition.asp

Hendricks, K. B., & Singhal, V. R. (1997). Does implementing an effective TQM program actually improve operating performance? Empirical evidence from firms that have won quality awards. *Management Science, 43*(9), 1258–1274.

Heneman, R. L. (1986). The relationship between supervisory ratings and results-oriented measures of performance: A meta-analysis. *Personnel Psychology, 39*(4), 811–826.

Henrich, J., Boyd, R., Bowles, S., Camerer, C., Fehr, E., Gintis, H., & McElreath, R. (2001). *In search of homo economicus: Behavioral experiments in 15 small-scale societies.* AEA Papers and Proceedings, May 2001. Retrieved September 4, 2017, from http://www.umass.edu/preferen/gintis/Anthro%20AER%202001.pdf

Henrich, J., Boyd, R., Bowles, S., Camerer, C., Fehr, E., Gintis, H., . . . Barr, A. (2005). "Economic man" in cross-cultural perspective: Behavioral experiments in 15 small-scale societies. *Behavioral and Brain Sciences, 28*(6), 795–815.

Henrich, J., & McElreath, R. (2007). Dual-inheritance theory: The evolution of human cultural capacities and cultural evolution. In L. Barrett & R. Dunbar (Eds.), *Oxford handbook of evolutionary psychology* (pp. 555–570). New York, NY: Oxford University Press.

Henry, J. (2012). The price of offshore revisited. *Tax Justice Network.* Retrieved February 15, 2019, from http://taxjustice.nonprofitsoapbox.com/storage/documents/The_Price_of_Offshore_Revisited_-_22-07-2012.pdf

Herman, E. S., & Chomsky, N. (2002). *Manufacturing consent: The political economy of the mass media.* New York, NY: Pantheon.

Herzberg, F. (1987). One more time: How do you motivate people? *Harvard Business Review,* September–October, Reprint 87507 (entire). Retrieved August 8, 2012, from http://www.facilitif.eu/user_files/file/herzburg_article.pdf

Hill, A., Wang, J., Levi, J., Heath, K., & Fortunak, J. (2020). Minimum costs to manufacture new treatments for COVID-19. *Journal of Virus Eradication*, *6*(2), 61–69. Retrieved January 8, 2021, from https://www.sciencedirect.com/science/article/pii/S2055664020300182

Hirano, H. (1990). 5 Pillars of the Visual Workplace. Portland, OR: Productivity Press.

Hirschman, A. O. (1977). *The passions and the interests: Political arguments for capitalism before its triumph*. Princeton, NJ: Princeton University Press.

Hirschman, A. O. (1982). Rival interpretations of market society: Civilizing, destructive, and feeble? *Journal of Economic Literature*, *20*, 1463–1484.

Hoffower, H. (2018). From hiding their mansions on Google Maps to building $500,000 panic rooms, rich people are sparing no expense to keep their lives private and secure. *Business Insider*. Retrieved March 5, 2019, from https://www.businessinsider.com/rich-people-spending-more-privacy-security-2018-11

Hofling, C. K., Brotzman, E., Dalrymple, S., Graves, N., & Pierce, C. M. (1966). An experimental study in nurse–physician relationships. *The Journal of Nervous and Mental Disease*, *143*(2), 171–180.

Hogan, R., & Kaizer, R. B. (2005). What we know about leadership. *Review of General Psychology*, *9*(2), 169–180.

Holder, E. (1999). *Bringing criminal charges against corporations*. Retrieved July 18, 2018, from https://www.justice.gov/sites/default/files/criminal-fraud/legacy/2010/04/11/charging-corps.PDF

Holland, J. (2013). Hundreds of Wall Street execs went to prison during the last fraud-fueled bank crisis. Retrieved May 26, 2019, from https://billmoyers.com/2013/09/17/hundreds-of-wall-street-execs-went-to-prison-during-the-last-fraud-fueled-bank-crisis/

Hossein-Zadeh, I. (2014). Class interests as economic theory. *Counterpunch*. Retrieve September 9, 2015, from http://www.counterpunch.org/2014/11/14/class-interests-as-economic-theory

Hosseini, H. (2003). The arrival of behavioral economics: From Michigan, or the Carnegie School in the 1950s and the early 1960s? *Journal of Socio-Economics*, *32*, 391–409.

Hosseini, H. (2010). Unfettered capitalism: Why it is neither efficient nor just. *Humanomics*, *26*(2), 99–111.

House, J. S. (2001). Social isolation kills, but how and why? *Psychosomatic Medicine*, *63*, 273–274.

Hunter, E. (1983). Coercive persuasion: The myth of free will? *Air University Review*, January–February 1983.

Iacoboni, M. (2009). Imitation, empathy, and mirror neurons. *Annual Review of Psychology*, *60*, 653–670.

Individualism. (2017a). In *Encyclopædia Britannica*. Retrieved June 16, 2017, from https://www.britannica.com/topic/individualism

Individualism. (2017b). In *Merriam-Webster.com*. Retrieved June 16, 2017, from https://www.merriam-webster.com/dictionary/individualism

International Consortium of Investigative Journalists. (2013, April 2). Secret files expose offshore's global impact. Retrieved February 15, 2019, from https://www.icij.org/investigations/offshore/secret-files-expose-offshores-global-impact/

Irons, J. (2009). *Economic scarring: The long-term impacts of the recession*. Economic Policy Institute Briefing Paper #243. Retrieved September 11, 2018, from https://www.epi.org/publication/bp243/

Isaacs, K. P., & Choudhury, S. (2017). *The growing gap in life expectancy by income: Recent evidence and implications for the Social Security retirement age*. The Congressional Research Service. Retrieved February 20, 2020, from https://fas.org/sgp/crs/misc/R44846.pdf

Jacobs, L. R., & Paige, B. I. (2005). Who influences U.S. foreign policy? *American Political Science Review, 99*(1), 107–123.

Jefferson, T. (1813). Thomas Jefferson's letter to John Adams (October 28, 1813). Retrieved October 28, 2018, from http://www.bigeye.com/aristocracy.htm

Jensen, M. (1994). Self-interest, altruism, incentives, and Agency Theory. *Journal of Applied Corporate Finance, 7*(2), 40–45. Retrieved September 28, 2015, from http://papers.ssrn.com/sol3/papers.cfm?abstract_id=5566

Jensen, M., & Meckling, W. (1976). Theory of the firm: Managerial behavior, agency costs, and ownership structure. *Journal of Financial Economics, 3*, 305–360.

Jensen, M., & Meckling, W. (1994). The nature of man. *Journal of Applied Corporate Finance, 7*(2), 4–19.

Jerrim, J. (2013). *Family background and access to "high status" universities*. The Sutton Trust. Retrieved December 8, 2020, from https://johnjerrim.files.wordpress.com/2013/07/john-jerrim-report-final.pdf

Johnson, H. T., & Kaplan, R. S. (1991). *Relevance lost: The rise and fall of management accounting*. Boston, MA: Harvard Business School Press.

Jones, J. M. (2016). American trust in political leaders, public at new lows. *Gallup*. Retrieved March 6, 2019, from https://news.gallup.com/poll/195716/americans-trust-political-leaders-public-new-lows.aspx

Jones, D. C., & Kato, T. (2005). *The effects of employee involvement on firm performance: Evidence from an econometric case study*. William Davidson Institute Working Paper No. 612, Revised May 2005. Retrieved May 30, 2011, from http://www.iza.org/conference_files/TAM2005/kato_t2130.pdf

Jones, D. T., & Womack, J. P. (2009). *Seeing the whole: Mapping the extended value stream*. Cambridge, MA: Lean Enterprise Institute.

Joulin, A., Lefevre, A., Grunberg, D., & Bouchaud, J-P. (2008, December 2). Stock price jumps: News and volume play a minor role. Retrieved October 5, 2018, from http://arxiv.org/abs/0803.1769v1

Kagel, J. H., Kim, C., & Moser, D. (1996). Fairness in ultimatum games with asymmetric information and asymmetric payoffs. *Games and Economic Behavior, 13*, 100–110.

Kahneman, D. (1997). New challenges to the rationality assumption. *Legal Theory, 3*(2), 105–124.

Kahneman, D., Knetsch, J. L., & Thaler, R. H. (1986). Fairness and the assumptions of economics. *Journal of Business, 59*(4), S285–S300.

Kahneman, D., Knetsch, J. L., & Thaler, R. H. (1986a). Fairness as a constraint on profit seeking: Entitlements in the market. *The American Economic Review, 76*(4), 728–741.

Kahneman, D., & Tversky, A. (1979). Prospect theory: An analysis of decision under risk. *Econometrica, 47*(2), 263–292.

Kaiser, R. B. (2011). *Going sour in the suite. The root causes of leadership failure*. Paper presented at AB London, May 25, 2011.

Kanigel, R. (1997). *The one best way: Frederick Taylor and the enigma of efficiency*. Cambridge, MA: MIT Press.

Karelina, K., Norman, G. J., Zhang, N., Morris, J. S., Peng, H., & DeVries, A. C. (2009). Social isolation alters neuroinflammatory response to stroke. *Proceedings of the National Academy of Sciences, 106*(14), 5895–5900. Retrieved April 27, 2021, from https://www.pnas.org/content/pnas/106/14/5895.full.pdf

Katz, C. (2012). People in poor neighborhoods breathe more hazardous particles. *Scientific American*. Retrieved March 5, 2019, from https://www.scientificamerican.com/article/people-poor-neighborhoods-breate-more-hazardous-particles/

Keating five. (2019). In *Wikipedia*. Retrieved May 23, 2019, from https://en.wikipedia.org/w/index.php?title=Keating_Five&oldid=895122712

Keen, P. W. (1981). Information systems and organizational change. *Communications of the ACM, 24*(1), 24–33. Retrieved December 4, 2022, from https://dl.acm.org/doi/pdf/10.1145/358527.358543

Keen, S. (2012). *Instability in financial markets: Sources and remedies.* INET Conference, Berlin. April 12–14, 2012. Retrieved September 12, 2018, from https://keenomics.s3.amazonaws.com/debtdeflation_media/2012/04/KeenINET2012InstabilityFinancialMarkets02.pdf

Keen, S. (2016, August 13). The need for pluralism in economics. Retrieved January 28, 2018, from http://www.debtdeflation.com/blogs/2016/08/13/the-need-for-pluralism-in-economics/

Keen, S. (2017). *Can we avoid another financial crisis?* Cambridge, UK: Polity Press.

Kendrick, M. (2020). I've lost all trust in medical research—the financial muscle of Big Pharma has been busy distorting science during the pandemic. *RT News*. Retrieved July 14, 2020, from https://www.rt.com/op-ed/493732-big-pharma-pandemic-covid/

Kenexa Corporation. (2012). High performance organizations and macroeconomic performance. Retrieved October 14, 2020, from https://www.slideshare.net/jonathanescobarmarin/high-performance-organizations-and-macroeconomic-performance

Keynes, J. M. (1937). The general theory of employment. *Quarterly Journal of Economics, 51*(2), 209–223.

Keyte, B., & Locher, D. (2004). *The complete lean enterprise: Value stream mapping for administrative and office processes.* New York, NY: Productivity Press.

Khadjavi, M., & Lange, A. (2013). Prisoners and their dilemma. *Journal of Economic Behavior & Organization, 92*, 163–175.

Khan, A. (2007, September 14). Employee engagement a winning formular for success. *American Chronicle*. Retrieved January 17, 2010, from http://www.americanchronicle.com/articles/view/37656

Klien, E. (2006, July 11). The medical malpractice myth: Forget tort reform. The Democrats have a better diagnosis. *Slate Magazine*. Retrieved March 31, 2011, from http://www.slate.com/id/2145400/

Kohn, M., & Reddy, K. (2017). Colonialism. In E. N. Zalta (Ed.), *Stanford encyclopedia of philosophy.* Retrieved November 24, 2020, from https://plato.stanford.edu/archives/fall2017/entries/colonialism/

Korab-Karpowicz, W. J. (2018). Political realism in international relations. In E. N. Zalta (Ed.), *Stanford encyclopedia of philosophy* (Summer 2018 ed.). Retrieved November 15, 2020, from https://plato.stanford.edu/archives/sum2018/entries/realism-intl-relations/

Korenok, O., Millner, E. L., & Razzolini, L. (2014). *Taking, giving, and taking aversion in dictator games.* Retrieved April 17, 2018, from http://excen.gsu.edu/center/media/Razzolini.pdf

Kreibig, S. K., Whooley, M. A., & Gross, J. J. (2014). Social integration and mortality in patients with coronary heart disease: Findings from the Heart and Soul Study. *Psychosomatic Medicine, 76*, 659–668.

Krueger, A. B. (2012). The rise and consequences of inequality in the United States. *Center for American Progress*. Retrieved May 26, 2019, from https://cdn.americanprogress.org/wp-content/uploads/events/2012/01/pdf/krueger.pdf

Krugman, P. (2012, March 27). Banking mysticism. *The New York Times*. Retrieved November 29, 2018, from https://krugman.blogs.nytimes.com/2012/03/27/banking-mysticism/

Kuyea, O. L., & Sulaimonb, A. A. (2011). Employee involvement in decision making and firms performance in the manufacturing sector in Nigeria. *Serbian Journal of Management*, *6*(1), 1–15. Retrieved May 30, 2011, from http://www.sjm06.com/6_1_2011_full%20text/6%281%292011_1.pdf

Kuznets, S. (1955). Economic growth and income inequality. *The American Economic Review*, *45*(1), 1–28. Retrieved February 12, 2019, from https://www.aeaweb.org/aer/top20/45.1.1-28.pdf

Lakner, C. & Milanovic, B. (2015). Global income distribution: From the fall of the Berlin Wall to the Great Recession. The World Bank Economic Review Advance Access published August 12, 2015. Retrieved August 5, 2021, from https://www.gc.cuny.edu/CUNY_GC/media/LISCenter/brankoData/wber_final.pdf

Lamare, A. (2016). How rich are the Supreme Court justices? Retrieved April 23, 2019, from https://www.celebritynetworth.com/articles/celebrity/rich-supreme-court-justices/

Lambert, S. (2010). *Business models*. Retrieved October 22, 2013, from http://www.audiencedialogue.net/documents/Businessmodels_Lambert_000.pdf

Lane, J. (2006). The myth of the frivolous lawsuit. *Tort Deform*. Retrieved March 31, 2011, from http://www.tortdeform.com/archives/2006/09/the_myth_of_the_frivolous_laws.html

Larcker, D. F., & Tayan, B. (2016). *Chairman and CEO: The controversy over board leadership structure*. Rock Center for Corporate Governance at Stanford University Closer Look Series: Topics, Issues and Controversies in Corporate Governance No. CGRP-58; Stanford University Graduate School of Business Research Paper No. 16-32. Retrieved June 7, 2021, from https://ssrn.com/abstract=2800244

Lawler E. E., III. (1999). Employee involvement makes a difference. *Journal for Quality and Participation*, *22*(5), 18–20.

Lawler, E. E. (2012). Outrageous executive compensation: Corporate boards, not the market, are to blame. *The Huffington Post*. Retrieved February 19, 2019, from http://www.huffingtonpost.com/ed-lawler/outrageous-executive-comp_b_1973923.html

Lawler, E. E., III, Mohrman, S. A., & Benson, G. (2001). *Organizing for high performance*. New York, NY: John Wiley & Sons, Inc.

Lawler, E. E., III, Mohrman, S. A., & Ledford, G. E., Jr. (1995). *Creating high performance organizations*. San Francisco: Jossey-Bass.

Lazear, E. P., Malmendier, U., & Weber, R. A. (2012). Sorting in experiments with application to social preferences. *American Economic Journal: Applied Economics*, *4*(1), 136–163.

Lazonick, W. (2014). Profits without prosperity. *Harvard Business Review*. September 2014. Retrieved February 27, 2019, from https://hbr.org/2014/09/profits-without-prosperity

Lerner, J. D., & Arias, M. G. (2017). Nudging in developing nations. In A. Samson (Ed.), *The behavioral economics guide 2017* (pp. 66–73). Retrieved December 22, 2020, from https://www.behavioraleconomics.com/

LeVine, S. (2018). U.S. startups are in a surprising 13-year slump. *Axios*. Retrieved June 24, 2019, from https://www.axios.com/startups-slump-13-years-artificial-intelligence-us-ef914164-78f7-4783-b912-2ea50a06968d.html

Lewis, N. (2020). An elite-led "Great Reset" post-Covid? Retrieved November 19, 2020, from https://www.rt.com/op-ed/507108-great-reset-wef-globalist/

Lewis, N., & Bruenig, M. (2017). The wealthiest 1% inherited an average of $4.8 million. Retrieved May 11, 2020, from https://www.peoplespolicyproject.org/2017/10/10/the-wealthiest-1-inherited-an-average-of-4-8-million/

Liebeck v. McDonald's Restaurants. (2011). In *Wikipedia*. Retrieved June 7, 2021, from https://en.wikipedia.org/w/index.php?title=Liebeck_v._McDonald%27s_Restaurants&oldid=1026836672

Limited liability company. (2021, January 14). In *Wikipedia*. Retrieved January 29, 2021, from https://en.wikipedia.org/w/index.php?title=Limited_liability_company&oldid=1000235023

Linden, M. (2011). The myth of the lower marginal tax rates. *Center for American Progress*. Retrieved, from https://www.americanprogress.org/issues/economy/news/2011/06/20/9841/the-myth-of-the-lower-marginal-tax-rates/

Lindert, J. G., & Williamson, J. G. (2012). *American incomes 1774–1860*. National Bureau of Economic Research Working Paper 18396. Retrieved December 8, 2020, from https://www.nber.org/system/files/working_papers/w18396/w18396.pdf

Lipton, E. (2014, October 30). Hard-nosed advice from veteran lobbyist: "Win ugly or lose pretty." *The New York Times*. Retrieved December 16, 2014, from http://www.nytimes.com/2014/10/31/us/politics/pr-executives-western-energy-alliance-speech-taped.html

List, J. (2007). On the interpretation of giving in dictator games. *Journal of Political Economy*, *115*(3), 482–493. Retrieved March 22, 2018, from https://web.archive.org/web/20180308164441/http://home.uchicago.edu/jlist/papers/dictator_game.pdf

List of recessions in the United States. (2018, September 9). In *Wikipedia*. Retrieved September 11, 2018, from https://en.wikipedia.org/w/index.php?title=List_of_recessions_in_the_United_States&oldid=858834124

Liu, H., & Wang, Z. (2005). Effects of social isolation stress on immune response and survival time of mouse with liver cancer. *World Journal of Gastroenterology*, *11*(37), 5902–5904.

Longley, R. (2019). Gunboat diplomacy: Teddy Roosevelt's "big stick" policy. Retrieved November 24, 2020, from https://www.thoughtco.com/gunboat-diplomacy-4774988

Lucido, G. (2015). Chicago's safest and most dangerous neighborhoods for the money. Retrieved March 5, 2019, from http://www.chicagonow.com/getting-real/2015/07/chicagos-safest-and-most-dangerous-neighborhoods-for-the-money/

Luhby, T. (2019). The top 26 billionaires own $1.4 trillion—as much as 3.8 billion other people. *CNN*. Retrieved February 13, 2019, from https://edition.cnn.com/2019/01/20/business/oxfam-billionaires-davos/index.html

MacLeod, A. (2020). GOP tax cuts in Coronavirus relief bill give 82% of benefits to millionaires and billionaires. *MintPress*. Retrieved June 19, 2020, from https://www.mintpressnews.com/82-percent-benefits-coronavirus-relief-fund-go-to-millionaires-billionaires/266674/

Macleod, A. (2020a). Public outcry follows Gilead decision to charge $3000 for COVID drug that costs pennies to produce. *MintPress*. Retrieved July 6, 2020, from https://www.mintpressnews.com/public-outcry-gilead-charges-3000-covid-19-drug-cost-pennies/269110/

Mainstream economics. (2015). In *Wikipedia*. Retrieved September 28, 2015, from https://en.wikipedia.org/w/index.php?title=Mainstream_economics&oldid=668899751

Mäki, U. (1986). Rhetoric at the expenses of coherence: A reinterpretation of Milton Friedman's methodology. *History of Economic Thought and Methodology, 4*, 127–143. Retrieved August 10, 2015, from http://repub.eur.nl/pub/6214/18383.pdf

Malkiel, B. G. (1977). The valuation of closed-end investment company shares. *Journal of Finance, 32*, 847–859.

Mankiw, N. G. (2013). Defending the one percent. *Journal of Economic Perspectives, 27*(3), 21–34. Retrieved May 29, 2019, from https://scholar.harvard.edu/files/mankiw/files/defending_the_one_percent_1.pdf

Market. (2018). In *Investopedia*. Retrieved January 30, 2019, from https://www.investopedia.com/terms/m/market.asp

Marshall, A. (1982). *Principles of economics* (8th ed.) Philadelphia, PA: Porcupine Press.

Marwell, G., & Ames, R. (1981). Economists free ride, does anyone else? *Journal of Public Economics, 15*, 295–310. Retrieved August 20, 2021, from http://econ.ucsd.edu/~jandreon/Econ264/papers/Marwell%20Ames%20JPubE%201981.pdf

Materialism. (2018). In *Merriam-Webster.com*. Retrieved August 15, 2018, from https://www.merriam-webster.com/dictionary/materialism

McCambridge, J., Witton, J., & Elbourne, D. R. (2014). Systematic review of the Hawthorne effect: New concepts are needed to study research participation effects. *Journal of Clinical Epidemiology, 67*, 267–277. Retrieved January 6, 2021, from https://researchonline.lshtm.ac.uk/id/eprint/1380017/1/1-s2.0-S0895435613003545-main.pdf

McCoy, A. W. (2018). A new age of gunboat diplomacy—and a new area of conflict. *Salon*. Retrieved November 24, 2020, from https://www.salon.com/2018/04/16/gunboat-diplomacy-and-the-ghost-of-captain-mahan_partner

Meckstroth, D. J. (1991). *Does employee involvement improve the performance of U.S. industry?* Manufacturers Alliance for Productivity and Innovation, 1200 18th Street NW, Washington, D.C.

Meehan, B., Rosenberg, S., & Duke, C. (2018). How to double savings rates: A case study of nudging for good. In A. Samson (Ed.), *The behavioral economics guide 2018* (pp. 80–85). Retrieved December 22, 2020, from https://www.behavioraleconomics.com/

Melis, A. P., & Semmann, D. (2010). How is human cooperation different? *Philosophical Transactions of the Royal Society B, 365*, 2663–2674.

Mertonian norms. (2020, November 3). In *Wikipedia*. Retrieved January 6, 2021, from https://en.wikipedia.org/w/index.php?title=Mertonian_norms&oldid=986862945

Meyers-Levy, J., Zhu, R. J., & Jiang, L. (2010). Context effects from bodily sensations: Examining bodily sensations induced by flooring and the moderating role of product viewing distance. *Journal of Consumer Research, 37*, 1–14.

Milgram, S. (1963). Behavioral study of obedience. *The Journal of Abnormal and Social Psychology, 67*(4), 371–378.

Milius, S. (1998, September 12). The science of eeeeek: What a squeak can tell researchers about life, society, and all that. *Science News*. Retrieved January 10, 2018, from https://www.thefreelibrary.com/The+science+of+eeeeek%3a+what+a+squeak+can+tell+researchers+about+life%2c...-a021156998

Mill, J. S. (1844). *Essays on some unsettled questions of political economy*. London: John W. Parke.

Miller, N. E., & Dollard, J. (1941). *Social learning and imitation*. New Haven, CT: Yale University Press.

Milman, O. (2019). Microsoft joins group seeking to kill off historic climate change lawsuits. *The Guardian*. Retrieved May 25, 2019, from https://www.theguardian.com/technology/2019/may/01/microsoft-joins-group-seeking-to-avoid-climate-change-lawsuit

Minsky, H. P. (1992). *The financial instability hypothesis*. The Jerome Levy Economics Institute Working Paper No. 74. Retrieved June 7, 2021, from https://ssrn.com/abstract=161024

Mintzberg, H. (1990). The manager's job: Folklore and fact. *Harvard Business Review*, March/April 1990, pp. 163–176. Retrieved June 7, 2021, from http://rafael.glendale.edu/ppal/Busad%20101/mintzbergmar1990.pdf

Mirochnik, M. (2010). Credit default swaps and the financial crisis. *Columbia University Academic Commons*. Retrieved February 21, 2021, from https://academiccommons.columbia.edu/doi/10.7916/D84T6SC8

Mirror neuron. (2018, February 3). In *Wikipedia*. Retrieved February 7, 2018, from https://en.wikipedia.org/w/index.php?title=Mirror_neuron&oldid=823752231

Moffatt, M. (2017). What is volatility clustering? Retrieved October 15, 2018, from https://www.thoughtco.com/volatility-clustering-in-economics-1147328

Molenberghs, P., Cunnington, R., & Mattingley, J. B. (2009). Is the mirror neuron system involved in imitation? A short review and meta-analysis. *Neuroscience and Biobehavioral Reviews, 33*, 975–980.

Molina, J. A., Giménez-Nadal, J. I., Cuesta, J. A., Gracia-Lazaro, C., Moreno, Y., & Sanchez, A. (2013). Gender differences in cooperation: Experimental evidence on high school students. *PLOS ONE, 8*(12), e83700.

Moody, J., McFarland, D., & Bender-de Moll, S. (2005). Dynamic network visualization. *AJS, 110*(4), 1206–1241. Retrieved October 19, 2017, from http://www.soc.duke.edu/~jmoody77/ajs_online.pdf

Morgenson, G. (2006). Big bonuses still flow, even if bosses miss goals. *The New York Times*. Retrieved May 30, 2019, from https://www.nytimes.com/2006/06/01/business/01bonus.html

Moseley, A. (2021). Political realism. *Internet Encyclopedia of Philosophy*. Retrieved April 8, 2021, from https://iep.utm.edu/polreal/

Moysich, A. (1997). The savings and loan crisis and its relationship to banking. In *History of the eighties: Lessons for the future. Vol. 1, An examination of the banking crises of the 1980s and early 1990s* (pp. 167–188). Federal Deposit Insurance Corporation (FDIC). Retrieved from https://www.fdic.gov/bank/historical/history/167_188.pdf

Mullaney, T. (2015). Why corporate CEO pay is so high, and going higher. *CNBC*. Retrieved May 9, 2019, from https://www.cnbc.com/2015/05/18/why-corporate-ceo-pay-is-so-high-and-going-higher.html

Murray, C. (2016). Did you grow up in a bubble? These ZIP codes suggest you did. Retrieved May 12, 2020, from https://www.pbs.org/newshour/economy/did-you-grow-up-in-a-bubble-these-zip-codes-suggest-you-did

Nankin, J., Umansky, E., Schmidt, K. K., & Klein, S. (2008). History of U.S. gov't bailouts. *ProPublica*. Retrieved May 19, 2020, from https://www.propublica.org/article/government-bailouts

Nelson, R. R. (2003). The market economy, and the scientific commons. *Research Policy, 33*, 455–471.

Nemoto, M. (2009). Total quality control and the Toyota Production System. In K. Shimokawa & T. Fujimoto (Eds.), *The birth of lean* (pp. 171–215). Cambridge, MA: Lean Enterprise Institute.

Neorealism (international relations). (2021). In *Wikipedia*. Retrieved April 8, 2021, from https://en.wikipedia.org/w/index.php?title=Neorealism_(international_relations)&oldid=1014682917

Neumann, J. (2013). S&P has unusual defense. *The Wall Street Journal*. Retrieved July 2, 2020, from http://online.wsj.com/article/SB10001424127887324235304578439010216689372.html

New York Times Editorial. (1990). The biggest scandal ever. *The New York Times*. Retrieved May 23, 2019, from https://www.nytimes.com/1990/05/29/opinion/the-biggest-scandal-ever.html

Nowak, M. A., Tarnita1, C. E., & Wilson, E. O. (2010). The evolution of eusociality. *Nature, 466*(7310), 1057–1062. Retrieved January 10, 2018, from https://www.ncbi.nlm.nih.gov/pmc/articles/PMC3279739/pdf/nihms329641.pdf

Oaks, A. (2015, June 28). 4 reasons you should tailor your marketing strategy to your industry. Retrieved February 10, 2018, from https://rabidofficemonkey.com/4-reasons-tailor-marketing-strategy-industry/

Ohno, T. (1988). *Toyota production system*. New York, NY: Productivity Press.

Okasha, S. (2013). Biological altruism. In E. N. Zalta (Ed.), *Stanford encyclopedia of philosophy* (Fall 2013 ed.). Retrieved February 16, 2018, from https://plato.stanford.edu/archives/fall2013/entries/altruism-biological

OpenSecrets.org. (2020). Personal finances. Retrieved June 17, 2020, from https://www.opensecrets.org/personal-finances/top-net-worth

Parramore, L. (2016). Stark new evidence on how money shapes America's elections. *Institute for New Economic Thinking*. Retrieved July 17, 2018, from https://www.ineteconomics.org/perspectives/blog/stark-new-evidence-on-how-money-shapes-americas-elections

Peck, E. (2016). The 62 richest people on earth now hold as much wealth as the poorest 3.5 billion. *The Huffington Post*. Retrieved May 2, 2019, from http://www.huffingtonpost.com/entry/global-wealth-inequality_us_56991defe4b0ce4964242e09

Peek, G. A. (2003). *The political writings of John Adams*. Indianapolis, IN: Hackett Publishing Company, Inc.

Perelman, M. (1984). *Classical political economy*. Totawa, NJ: Rowman & Allanheld, Publishers.

Pew Research Center. (2020). In views of U.S. democracy, widening partisan divides over freedom to peacefully protest. Retrieved September 8, 2020, from https://www.pewresearch.org/politics/2020/09/02/in-views-of-u-s-democracy-widening-partisan-divides-over-freedom-to-peacefully-protest/

Pfeffer, J., & Sutton, R. I. (2006). *Hard facts, dangerous half-truths, and total nonsense*. Boston, MA: Harvard Business School Press.

Philippon, T. (2019). Monopolies cost Americans $300 a month. *The Guardian*. Retrieved December 7, 2020, from https://www.theguardian.com/commentisfree/2019/nov/13/america-was-once-the-land-of-free-markets-now-theyre-becoming-a-myth

Phillips, K. (2002). *Wealth and democracy*. New York, NY: Broadway Books.

Phillips, K. (2009). *Bad money*. New York, NY: Penguin Books.

Pierson, P. (2015). *Goodbye to pluralism? Studying power in contemporary American politics*. Paper presented at the Wildavsky Forum for Public Policy, Goldman School of Public Policy, Berkeley, CA, April 9, 2015.

Piketty, T. (2014). *Capital in the twenty-first century* (A. Goldhammer, Trans.). Cambridge, MA: Harvard University Press.

Piketty, T. (2020). *Capital and ideology* (A. Goldhammer, Trans.). Cambridge, MA: Harvard University Press.

Pilkington, E., & Siddiqui, S. (2019). Democrats go after political "dark money" with anti-corruption measure. *The Guardian*. Retrieved May 30, 2019, from https://www.theguardian.com/us-news/2019/feb/13/political-funding-dark-money-anti-corruption-trump

Pirenne, H. (1960). *Economic and social history of medieval Europe.* New York, NY: Harvest Book HB-14, Harcourt Brace & Company.

Pluralism in economics. (2015). In *Wikipedia.* Retrieved September 9, 2015, from https://en.wikipedia.org/w/index.php?title=Pluralism_in_economics&oldid=653764560

Pollin, R. (2002). *Wage bargaining and the U.S. Phillips Curve: Was Greenspan right about "traumatized workers" in the 1990s?* Department of Economics and Political Economy Research Institute (PERI) University of Massachusetts-Amherst Amherst, MA. Retrieved February 24, 2017, from http://courses.umass.edu/econ797a-rpollin/Pollin--Was%20Greenspan%20Right%20about%20Traumatized%20Workers.pdf

Pollock, A.J. (2021). Since 2008, monetary policy has cost american savers about $4 trillion. Retrieved November 18, 2021, from https://wolfstreet.com/2021/11/17/since-2008-monetary-policy-has-cost-american-savers-about-4-trillion/

Polyani, M. (1959). *The study of man.* Chicago, IL: The University of Chicago Press.

Powell, A. (2016). The costs of inequality: More money equals better health care and longer life. *U.S. News.* Retrieved March 5, 2019, from https://www.usnews.com/news/articles/2016-02-23/the-costs-of-inequality-more-money-equals-better-health-care-and-longer-life

Powell, L. F. (1971). Confidential memorandum: Attack of the free enterprise system. Retrieved January 9, 2019, from https://scholarlycommons.law.wlu.edu/powellmemo/1/

Pressman, S. D., Cohen, S., Miller, G. E., Barkin, A., Rabin, B. S., & Treanor, J. J. (2005). Loneliness, social network size, and immune response to influenza vaccination in college freshmen. *Health Psychology, 24*(3), 297–306.

Prisoner's dilemma. (2018, February 19). In *Wikipedia.* Retrieved February 21, 2018, from https://en.wikipedia.org/w/index.php?title=Prisoner%27s_dilemma&oldid=826467510

Pritchard, J. (2018). Moral hazard: Definition and examples. Retrieved October 18, 2018, from https://www.thebalance.com/moral-hazard-what-it-is-and-how-it-works-315515

Privatizing profits, socializing losses. (2019). In *Investopedia.* Retrieved May 7, 2019, from https://www.investopedia.com/terms/p/privatizing-profits-and-socializing-losses.asp

Profit. (2016). In *Oxford Living Dictionaries.* Retrieved December 10, 2020, from https://www.lexico.com/definition/profit

Prupis, N. (2016). 'This is what consumers want': General Mills to start labeling GMOs. *Common Dreams.* Retrieved May 21, 2016, from http://www.commondreams.org/news/2016/03/18/what-consumers-want-general-mills-start-labeling-gmos

Rabin, M. (1998). Psychology and economics. *Journal of Economic Literature, 36*(1), 11–46.

Rakoff, J. S. (2014, January 9). The financial crisis: Why have no high-level executives been prosecuted? *The New York Review of Books.* Retrieved July 17, 2018, from http://www.nybooks.com/articles/2014/01/09/financial-crisis-why-no-executive-prosecutions/

Rappa, M. (2000). Business models on the web. Retrieved October 22, 2013, from http://digitalenterprise.org/models/models.html

Regulatory capture. (2016). In *Investopedia.* Retrieved June 26, 2016, from http://www.investopedia.com/terms/r/regulatory-capture.asp

Richmond, V. P., Wrench, J. S., and Gorham, J. (2009). Communication, affect, & learning in the classroom. Retrieved February 22, 2013, from http://www.cios.org/readbook/cal/cal.pdf

Rickards, J. (2012). Repeal of Glass-Steagall caused the financial crisis. *U.S. News*. Retrieved February 21, 2021, from https://www.usnews.com/opinion/blogs/economic-intelligence/2012/08/27/repeal-of-glass-steagall-caused-the-financial-crisiss

Rizzuto, R., & Schoenberg, S. (2013). Sen. Elizabeth Warren rips Treasury officials' response to HSBC's confession to drug money laundering charges. Retrieved March 2, 2019, from https://www.masslive.com/politics/index.ssf/2013/03/sen_elizabeth_warren_rips_offi.html

Robinson, H. (1997). *Using poka-yoke techniques for early defect detection*. Paper presented at the Sixth International Conference on Software Testing Analysis and Review (STAR'97). Retrieved February 19, 2016, from https://faculty.washington.edu/apurva/502/Readings/Lean/pokasoft.pdf

Roll, D. (2005). *An introduction to 6S*. Retrieved January 15, 2008, from http://www.vitalentusa.com/learn/6s_article.php

Rosenthal, R. (1994). Interpersonal expectancy effects: A 30-year perspective. *Current Directions in Psychological Science, 3*(6), 176–179. Retrieved March 14, 2016, from http://www.lscp.net/persons/dupoux/teaching/JOURNEE_AUTOMNE_CogMaster_2011-12/readings_deontology/Rosenthal_1994_interpersonal_expectancy_effects_a_review.pdf

Rosenthal, R., & Rubin, D. B. (1978). Interpersonal expectancy effects: The first 345 studies. *Behavioral and Brain Sciences, 1*, 377–386.

Roth, A. E., Prasnikar, V., Okuno-Fujiwara, M., & Zamir, S. (1991). Bargaining and market behavior in Jerusalem, Ljubljana, Pittsburgh, and Tokyo: An experimental study. *Bargaining and Market Behavior, 81*(5), 1068–1095. Retrieved July 22, 2018, from https://pdfs.semanticscholar.org/25a3/58ebd149b09a14f64e487efb8aa4871ee986.pdf

Rother, M., & Shook, J. (2003). *Learning to see*. Cambridge, MA: The Lean Enterprise Institute.

Rutherford, S. T., & Bassler, B. L. (2012). Bacterial quorum sensing: Its role in virulence and possibilities for its control. *Cold Spring Harbor Perspectives in Medicine, 2*(11), 1–25.

Saad, L. (2016). Americans' confidence in government takes positive turn. *Gallup*. Retrieved March 6, 2019, from https://news.gallup.com/poll/195635/americans-confidence-government-takes-positive-turn.aspx

Saez, E. (2020). *Striking it richer: The evolution of top incomes in the United States*. Retrieved May 8, 2020, from https://eml.berkeley.edu/~saez/saez-UStopincomes-2018.pdf

Sahlins, M. (2008). *The Western illusion of human nature*. Chicago, IL: Prickly Paradigm Press, LLC.

Samuelson, W., & Zeckhauser, R. (1988). Status quo bias in decision making. *Journal of Risk and Uncertainty, 1*(1), 7–59.

Sauter, M. B., & Suneson, G. (2019). The net worth of the American presidents: Washington to Trump. *24/7 Wall Street*. Retrieved April 24, 2019, from https://247wallst.com/special-report/2019/02/26/the-net-worth-of-the-american-presidents-washington-to-trump-2/2/

Say's law of markets. (2018). In *Investopedia*. Retrieved August 27, 2018, from https://www.investopedia.com/terms/s/says-law.asp

Schmidt, H. (1987). *Maverick Marine*. Lexington, KY: The University Press of Kentucky.

Schwab, C. (2020). Now is the time for a "great reset." Retrieved November 19, 2020, from https://www.weforum.org/agenda/2020/06/now-is-the-time-for-a-great-reset/

Schweyer, A. (2009). *The economics of engagement*. Human Capital Institute. Retrieved October 31, 2011, from http://www.incentivecentral.org/pdf/Final_Economics_of_Engagement.pdf

Sember, B. (2019). The basics of LLC guaranteed payments. Retrieved April 13, 2020, from https://www.legalzoom.com/articles/the-basics-of-llc-guaranteed-payments

Senge, P. (1990). *The fifth discipline: The art and practice of the learning organization.* New York, NY: Doubleday.

Sherman, F. (2018). What does a director on a corporate board get paid? Retrieved February 20, 2019, from https://work.chron.com/director-corporate-board-paid-19587.html

Shewhart. W. (1980). *Economic control of quality of manufactured products.* Milwaukee, WI: ASQ Quality Press.

Shibayama, S. (2014). Academic commercialization and changing nature of academic cooperation. *Journal of Evolutionary Economics, 25*, 513–532.

Shimokawa, K., & Fujimoto, T. (Eds.). (2009). *The birth of lean.* Cambridge, MA: Lean Enterprise Institute.

Sigler, K. J. (2011). CEO compensation and company performance. *Business and Economics Journal, 2011*, 1–8.

Silvert, L.; Delplanque, S.; Bouwalerh, H.; Verpoort, C.; & Sequeira, H. (2004). Autonomic responding to aversive words without conscious valence discrimination. *International Journal of Psychophysiology*, 53, 135-45.

Simcoe, M., Valdes, A., Liu, F., Furlotte, N. A., Evans, D. M., Hemani, G., ... Pirro, G. (2021). Genome-wide association study in almost 195,000 individuals identifies 50 previously unidentified genetic loci for eye color. *Science Advances, 7*(11), (eabd1239), 1–11.

Singh, L. K. (2010). Whither efficient markets? Efficient market theory and behavioral finance. Retrieved October 23, 2018, from http://post.nyssa.org/nyssa-news/2010/05/whither-efficient-markets-efficient-market-theory-and-behavioral-finance.html

Sippel, R. (1997). An experiment on the pure theory of consumer's behaviour. *The Economic Journal, 107*(444), 1431–1444.

Sirotta, D. (2014). Too big to punish. Retrieved July 18, 2018, from https://www.creators.com/read/david-sirota/09/14/too-big-to-punish

Smalley, A. (2016). Is it genba or gemba? Retrieved October 31, 2020, from http://artoflean.com/index.php/2016/03/25/is-it-genba-or-gemba/

Smith, A. (1776). *An inquiry into the nature and causes of the wealth of nations.* An Electronic Classics Series Publication. Retrieved March 25, 2019, from https://eet.pixel-online.org/files/etranslation/original/The%20Wealth%20of%20Nations.pdf

Smith, C. H. (2017). Do the roots of rising inequality go all the way back to the 1980s? Retrieved December 8, 2020, from https://web.archive.org/web/20190501142627/https://washingtonsblog.com/2017/03/roots-rising-inequality-go-way-back-1980s.html

Smith, D. (2011, August 1). Tailor marketing strategies to customer preferences. Retrieved February 10, 2018, from http://www.dmnews.com/digital-marketing/tailor-marketing-strategies-to-customer-preferences/article/208054/

Smith, V. L. (1998). The two faces of Adam Smith. *Southern Economic Journal, 65*(1), 1–19. Retrieved March 9, 2018, from https://www.researchgate.net/profile/Vernon_Smith4/publication/227577210_The_Two_Faces_of_Adam_Smith/links/55eee6fa08aef559dc449fb0/The-Two-Faces-of-Adam-Smith.pdf

Snider, A. (1994). Citizen's revolt. *Mother Jones*. Retrieved May 14, 2020, from https://www.motherjones.com/politics/1994/09/citizens-revolt/

Snider, T. (2021). The dark side of Eisenhower's foreign policy. *Responsible Statescraft*. Retrieved October 7, 2021, from https://responsiblestatecraft.org/2021/08/12/the-dark-side-of-eisenhowers-foreign-policy/

Sociality. (2020, November 29). In *Wikipedia*. Retrieved December 30, 2020, from https://en.wikipedia.org/w/index.php?title=Sociality&oldid=991245033

Spreitzer, G. M. (1995). Psychological empowerment in the workplace: Dimensions, measurement, and validation. *Academy of Management Journal, 38*(5), 1442–1465. Retrieved May 31, 2011, from http://webuser.bus.umich.edu/spreitze/PsychEmpowerment.pdf

Spreitzer, G. M. (2007). *Taking stock: A review of more than twenty years of research on empowerment at work*. Center for Effective Organizations, Marshall School of Business, University of Southern California-Los Angeles. Retrieved May 31, 2011, from http://ceo.usc.edu/pdf/T071511.pdf

Sreevatsan, A. (2018). British Raj siphoned out $45 trillion from India: Utsa Patnaik. Retrieved December 31, 2022, from https://www.livemint.com/Companies/HNZA71LNVNNVXQ1eaIKu6M/British-Raj-siphoned-out-45-trillion-from-India-Utsa-Patna.html

Staff. (2016). 90 percent of public lacks trust in US political system. *The Associated Press–NORC Center for Public Affairs Research*. Retrieved March 6, 2019, from https://popularresistance.org/90-percent-of-public-lacks-trust-in-us-political-system/

Steverman, B. (2020). Americans to inherit $764 billion this year, mostly tax-free. Retrieved May 8, 2020, from https://www.yahoo.com/news/americans-inherit-764-billion-mostly-050100545.html

Stewart, M. (2018). The 9.9 percent is the new American aristocracy. *The Atlantic*. Retrieved November 22, 2018, from https://www.theatlantic.com/magazine/archive/2018/06/the-birth-of-a-new-american-aristocracy/559130

Stockamp, D. R. (2005). The strategic benefits of revenue cycle improvement. *Healthcare Finance Management, 59*(9), 74–76, 78, 80.

Street, P. (2017). Impeach the U.S. Constitution. *Truthdig*. Retrieved February 9, 2021, from https://www.paulstreet.org/impeach-the-u-s-constitution/

Sullivan, L. (2020). Small business rescue earned banks $10 billion in fees. *NPR News*. Retrieved May 18, 2020, from https://www.npr.org/2020/04/22/840678984/small-business-rescue-earned-banks-10-billion-in-fees

Sussman, R. W., Garber, P. A., & Cheverud, J. M. (2005). Importance of cooperation and affiliation in the evolution of primate sociality. *American Journal of Physical Anthropology, 128*(1), 84–97.

Sutter, R. (2006). *2006 update on tort cost trends*. Towers Perrins. Retrieved March 31, 2011, from http://www.towersperrin.com/tp/getwebcachedoc?webc=TILL/USA/2006/200611/Tort_2006_FINAL.pdf

Swanson, E. (2013). GMO poll finds huge majority say foods should be labeled. *The Huffington Post*. Retrieved May 21, 2016, from http://www.huffingtonpost.com/2013/03/04/gmo-poll_n_2807595.html

Swift, A. (2016). Americans' trust in mass media sinks to new low. *Gallup*. Retrieved March 6, 2019, from https://news.gallup.com/poll/195542/americans-trust-mass-media-sinks-new-low.aspx

Taibbi, M. (2011, February 16). Why isn't Wall Street in jail? *Rolling Stone*. Retrieved March 4, 2011, from http://www.rollingstone.com/politics/news/why-isnt-wall-street-in-jail-20110216

Taibbi, M. (2013). The last mystery of the financial crisis. Retrieved May 25, 2021, from https://www.rollingstone.com/politics/politics-news/the-last-mystery-of-the-financial-crisis-200751

Taibbi, M. (2014). *The divide: American injustice in the age of the wealth gap*. New York, NY: Spiegel & Grau.

Talgo, C. (2020). What is the Great Reset? Retrieved November 19, 2020, from https://townhall.com/columnists/christalgo/2020/06/19/what-is-the-great-reset-n2570919

Tarver, E. (2021). Income tax vs capital gains tax. (2019). In *Investopedia*. Retrieved May 6, 2019, from https://www.investopedia.com/ask/answers/052015/what-difference-between-income-tax-and-capital-gains-tax.asp

Taylor, F.W. (1911). The principles of scientific management. Retreived February 18, 2010, from http://socserv2.socsci.mcmaster.ca/~econ/ugcm/3ll3/taylor/sciman

Thaler, R. H. (1988). Anomalies: The ultimatum game. *The Journal of Economic Perspectives*, *2*(4), 195–206.

The Center for Public Integrity. (2000). Off the record: What media corporations don't want you to tell you about their legislative agendas. Retrieved June 7, 2021, from https://web.archive.org/web/20011216192924/http://www.publicintegrity.org/downloads/otr.pdf

Theory of mind. (2018, January 26). In *Wikipedia*. Retrieved February 12, 2018, from https://en.wikipedia.org/w/index.php?title=Theory_of_mind&oldid=822383235

The Spaced-Out Scientist (2017). Single parents worldwide: Statistics and trends. Retrived October 12, 2021, from https://spacedoutscientist.com/2017/07/18/single-parents-worldwide-statistics-and-trends/

Thompson, D. (2010). Google's CEO: "The laws are written by lobbyists." *The Atlantic*. Retrieved April 25, 2019, from https://www.theatlantic.com/technology/archive/2010/10/googles-ceo-the-laws-are-written-by-lobbyists/63908/

Thucydides. (1951). *The complete writings of Thucydides: The Peloponnesian wars*. New York, NY: Random House.

Thurner, S., Farmer, J. D., & Geanakoplos, J. (2012). Leverage causes fat tails and clustered volatility. *Quantitative Finance*, *12*(5), 695–707.

Tobin, J. (1963). *Commercial banks as creators of money*. Cowles Foundation for Research in Economics at Yale University. Retrieved December 5, 2020, from http://cowles.yale.edu/sites/default/files/files/pub/d01/d0159.pdf

Towers Perrin. (2008). *Closing the engagement gap: A road map for driving superior business performance*. Retrieved May 5, 2010, from http://www.biworldwide.com/info/pdf/Towers_Perrin_Global_Workforce_Study.pdf

Toyoda, A. (2010, February 9). Toyota's plan to repair its public image. *The Washington Post*. Retrieved March 18, 2014, from http://www.washingtonpost.com/wp-dyn/content/article/2010/02/08/AR2010020803078.html

Toyota Traditions. (2007). No more than one cup's worth of water can fit into a single cup. To hold more water, you need more cups. Retrieved January 8, 2021, from http://www.toyota-myanmar.com/about-toyota/toyota-traditions/philosophy/no-more-than-one-cups-worth-of-water-can-fit-into-a-single-cup-to-hold-more-water-you-need-more-cups

Treadway, P. T. (2010). Privatize the gains, socialize the losses. *The Big Picture*. Retrieved May 7, 2019, from https://ritholtz.com/2010/02/privatize-the-gains-socialize-the-losses/

Trivers, R. L. (1971). The evolution of reciprocal altruism. *The Quarterly Review of Biology*, *46*(1), 35–57.

Truax, C. B., & Carkhuff, R. R. (1967). *Toward effective counseling and psychotherapy.* Chicago, IL: Aldine Publishing Company.

Tuchscherer, M., Kanitza, E., Puppea, B., Tuchschererb, A., & Stabenow, B. (2004). Effects of postnatal social isolation on hormonal and immune responses of pigs to an acute endotoxin challenge. *Physiology & Behavior, 82*(2–3), 503–511.

Tulip mania. (2018). In *Wikipedia*. Retrieved October 10, 2018, from https://en.wikipedia.org/w/index.php?title=Tulip_mania&oldid=857818544

U.S. Department of Justice. (1994, July 16). Microsoft agrees to end unfair monopolistic practices. Retrieved June 1, 2019, from https://www.justice.gov/sites/default/files/atr/legacy/2006/04/11/msjudge.pdf

U.S. Department of the Treasury. (2019). Interest expense on the debt outstanding. Retrieved June 25, 2019, from https://www.treasurydirect.gov/govt/reports/ir/ir_expense.htm

U.S. Office of Management and Budget. (2018). Standard occupational classification manual. Retrieved January 28, 2021, from https://www.bls.gov/soc/2018/soc_2018_manual.pdf

van Schaik, C. P. (2006). Why are some animals so smart? *Scientific American, 294*(64), 7130–7137. Retrieved January 12, 2018, from http://faculty.bennington.edu/~sherman/how%20do%20animals%20work%3F/orang%20intelligence.pdf (pagination in this reprint reads 30–37).

van Schaik, C. P., & Burkart, J. M. (2011). Social learning and evolution: The cultural intelligence hypothesis. *Philosophical Transactions of the Royal Society B, 366*, 1008–1016.

van Vugt, M., Roberts, G., & Hardy, C. (2009). Competitive altruism: Development of reputation-based cooperation in groups. In R. Dunbar & L. Barrett (Eds.), *Oxford handbook of evolutionary psychology* (1st ed.) (pp. 521–540). New York, NY: Oxford University Press.

Vasquez, I. (2002). A retrospective on the Mexican Bailout. *Cato Journal, 21*(3), 545–551.

Vazirani, N. (2007). *Employee engagement.* SIES College of Management Studies Working Paper Series. Retrieved May 23, 2014, from http://www.siescoms.edu/images/pdf/research/working_papers/employee_engagement.pdf

Vickrey, W. S. (1964). *Microstatics.* New York, NY: Harcourt, Brace, and World.

Vitalo, R. L. (1975). Guidelines for the functioning of a helping agency. *Community Mental Health Journal, 111*, 170–179.

Vitalo, R. L. (1998). Personal capital. Vital Enterprises, Austin, TX.

Vitalo, R. L. (2014). Lean insanity. Retrieved January 19, 2015, from http://www.vitalentusa.com/learn/lean_insanity.php

Vitalo, R. L. (2017). Deming revisited: The real quality model for commerce. Vital Enterprises. Retrieved November 29, 2017, from http://www.vitalentusa.com/links/pdfs/deming_revisited-Vitalo.pdf

Vitalo, R. L. (2019). Building a useful goal statement. Retrieved August 6, 2019, from http://www.vitalentusa.com/learn/building_a_useful_goal_statement.php

Vitalo, R. L. (2020). Chester I. Barnard: A summary and analysis of his thinking. Austin, TX: Vital Enterprises.

Vitalo, R. L. (2022). Completing a cause analysis for a failed task. Retrieved December 29, 2022, from https://www.vitalentusa.com/learn/cause_analysis_failure.php

Vitalo, R.L. (2023). Three types of methods for guiding personal action. Vital Enterprises. Retrieved August 8, 2023, from https://www.vitalentusa.com/learn/3_methods.php

Vitalo, R. L., & Bujak, C. J. (2019). Why Lean management's rubrics cannot tell us what Lean's view of people is. Retrieved May 4, 2020, from http://www.vitalentusa.com/learn/why_lm_rubrics_not_enough.php

Vitalo, R. L., & Bujak, C. J. (2021). Why Toyota is not Lean Thinking's 'Rosetta Stone.' Retrieved October 31, 2021, from http://www.vitalentusa.com/learn/toyota_not_lean_rosetta_stone.php

Vitalo, R. L., & Bujak, C. J. (2022). The missing pieces in the Lean Enterprise Model. Retrieved June 12, 2019, from http://www.vitalentusa.com/learn/missing_pieces_in_the_lean_enterprise_model.php

Vitalo, R. L.; Bujak, C. J.; Vitalo, J. P.; Bierley, P. V.; & Ruffino, B. J. (2023). The lean champion's resource guide. Austin, TX: Lowrey Press.

Vitalo, R. L., Butz, F., & Vitalo, J. P. (2003). *Kaizen desk reference standard.* O'Fallon, MO: Lowrey Press.

Vitalo, R. L., Byron, J., Bierley, P. V., & Holmberg, C. (2008). The high-performing learning organization. Retrieved October 23, 2008, from http://www.vitalentusa.com/learn/hplo_model.php

Vitalo, R. L., & Vitalo, J. P. (2020). *Mining learning from performance.* Retrieved April 6, 2014, from http://www.vitalentusa.com/links/pdfs/mining_learning_from_performance.pdf

Wade, M. J. (1977). An experimental study of group selection. *Evolution, 31*(1), 134–153.

Walden, D. (Ed.). (1993). Kano's methods for understanding customer-defined quality. *Center for Quality of Management Journal, 2*(4), entire issue. Retrieved December 19, 2007, from http://cqmextra.cqm.org/cqmjournal.nsf/issues/vol2no4

Ward, P. (2004). Cash-to-cash is what counts. *Journal of Commerce, 5*(7), 54–55. Retrieved January 15, 2008, from http://www.hitachiconsulting.com/downloadPdf.cfm?ID=57

Washington, G. (2011). Settling prosecutions for pennies on the dollar is a type of bailout. Retrieved March 2, 2019, from https://georgewashington2.blogspot.com/2011/01/settling-prosecutions-for-pennies-on.html

Washington, G. (2016). Every single bloody market is manipulated . . . see for yourself. *Zerohedge.com.* Retrieved August 7, 2021, from https://web.archive.org/web/20160418065951/https://www.zerohedge.com/news/2016-04-14/markets-are-manipulated

Wellins, R. S., Bernthal, P. B., & Phelps, M. (2005). *Employee engagement: The key to realizing competitive advantage.* Developmental Dimensions International (DDI). Retrieved June 2, 2011, from http://www.ddiworld.com/DDIWorld/media/monographs/employeeengagement_mg_ddi.pdf

Wenner, D., & Zollman, K. (2017, November 2). How to end international tax competition. *New York Times.* Retrieved August 20, 2018, from https://www.nytimes.com/2017/11/02/opinion/ending-international-tax-competition.html

Whaples, R. (1995). Where is there consensus among American economic historians? The results of a survey on forty propositions. *The Journal of Economic History, 55*(1), 139–154.

Whitney, M. (2017). Yellen's effed up attack on working people, sad. *Counterpunch*, March 17. Retrieved March 17, 2017, from http://www.counterpunch.org/2017/03/17/yellens-effed-up-attack-on-working-people-sad/

Whoriskey, P. (2011). Cozy relationships and "peer benchmarking" send CEOs' pay soaring. *The Washington Post.* Retrieved February 19, 2019, from https://www.washingtonpost.com/business/economy/cozy-relationships-and-peer-benchmarking-send-ceos-pay-soaring/2011/09/22/gIQAgq8NJL_story.html

Wile, R. (2017). The richest 10% of Americans now own 84% of all stocks. *Money.* Retrieved May 19, 2020, from https://money.com/stock-ownership-10-percent-richest

Willingham, E. (2019). Wealth care or concierge medicine? Two-tiered medical care is a growing trend. *Association of Healthcare Journalists*. Retrieved March 6, 2019, from https://healthjournalism.org/blog/2019/02/wealth-care-or-concierge-medicine-two-tiered-medical-care-is-a-growing-trend/

Wilson, E. O., & Hölldobler, B. (2005). Eusociality: Origin and consequences. *Proceedings of the National Academy of Sciences, 102*(38), 13,367–13,371.

Wilson, G. (2006). The effects of external rewards on intrinsic motivation. Retrieved November 18, 2013, from http://www.abcbodybuilding.com/rewards.pdf

Wilson, M. R. (2017). Lobbying's top 50: Who's spending big. *The Hill*. Retrieved April 24, 2019, from https://thehill.com/business-a-lobbying/business-a-lobbying/318177-lobbyings-top-50-whos-spending-big

Wimmer, H., & Perner, J. (1983). Beliefs about beliefs: Representation and constraining function of wrong beliefs in young children's understanding of deception. *Cognition, 13*(1), 103–128.

Womack, J. P. (2010). Back to work. Message posted to Jim Womack's E-letters, archived at https://web.archive.org/web/20100302065114/http://www.lean.org/common/display/?o=1366

Womack, J. P. (2016). You can't make countries great without great jobs. Retrieved May 4, 2020, from https://planet-lean.com/womack-great-jobs-smes/

Womack, J. P. (2017). Jim Womack on the lean shut-down of Toyota Australia. *Planet Lean*. Retrieved on October 3, 2021, from https://planet-lean.com/jim-womack-toyota-australia-lean/

Womack, J. P., & Jones, D. T. (2003). *Lean thinking* (Rev. ed.) New York, NY: Free Press.

Womack, J. P., Jones, D. T., & Roos, D. (1991). *The machine that changed the world*. New York, NY: HarperCollins Publishers.

Woolf, S. H., Aron, L., Dubay, L., Simon, S. M., Zimmerman, E., & Luk, K. X. (2015). How are income and wealth linked to health and longevity. *Center for Society and Health*. Retrieved March 6, 2019, from https://www.urban.org/sites/default/files/publication/49116/2000178-How-are-Income-and-Wealth-Linked-to-Health-and-Longevity.pdf

Wu, T. (2018, November 11). How AT&T fooled the Federal Judiciary. *New York Times*. Retrieved November 8, 2018, from https://www.nytimes.com/2018/11/07/opinion/att-hbo-antitrust.html

Wudneh, E., Acharya, A., Ashraf, A., Krishnan, R., & Tohid, H. (2016). The mystery of the mirror neuron system. *ARC Journal of Radiology and Medical Imaging, 1*(2), 1–4.

Yaari, M. E., & Bar-Hilell, M. (1984). On dividing justly. *Social Choice Welfare, 1*, 1–24. Retrieved February 22, 2018, from https://www.researchgate.net/publication/225221212_On_Dividing_Justly

Yamagishi, T., Li, Y., Takagishi, H., Matsumoto, Y., & Kiyonari, T. (2014). In search of homo economicus. *Psychological Science, 25*(9), 1699–1711.

Yang, A. (2018). *The war on normal people: The truth about America's disappearing jobs and why universal basic income is our future*. New York, NY: Hachette Books.

Zak, P. J. (2017). The neuroscience of trust. *Harvard Business Review*, January–February. Retrieved January 8, 2021, from https://hbr.org/2017/01/the-neuroscience-of-trust

Zaitchik, A. (2018). How big pharma was captured by the one percent. *The New Republic*. Retrieved April 19, 2021, from https://newrepublic.com/article/149438/big-pharma-captured-one-percent

Zaitchik, A. (2022). Owning the sun: a peoples history of monopoly medicine from aspirin to covid-19 vaccines. Berkeley: CA: Counterpoint Press.

Zak, P., & Knack, S. (2001). Trust and growth. *Economic Journal, 111*, 295–321.

Zingales, L. (2017). Towards a political theory of the firm. *Journal of Economic Perspectives, 31*(3), 113–130.

Zucman, G. (2016). *The hidden wealth of nations*. Chicago, IL: University of Chicago Press.

Zucman, G. (2019). Global wealth inequality. *Annual Review of Economics, 11*, 109–138. Retrieved May 10, 2020, from https://www.annualreviews.org/doi/pdf/10.1146/annurev-economics-080218-025852

GLOSSARY

5 Whys	A method for uncovering the causes of a problem by successively asking the question "why?", prompting knowledgeable people to share their ideas about the reasons the problem exists. It is useful in circumstances where people knowledgeable about the problem are available.
5S	A method for organizing workplaces and guiding workers, popularized by Hiroyuki Hirano (1990). The five Ss refer to five Japanese words—seiri, seiton, seiso, seiketsu, and shitsuke. Seiri means to separate needed and unneeded materials and to remove the latter. Seiton means to neatly arrange and identify needed materials for ease of use. Seiso means to conduct a cleanup campaign. Seiketsu means to do seiri, seiton, and seiso at frequent intervals and to standardize your 5S procedures. Shitsuke means to form the habit of always following the first four Ss. The origin of 5S is rooted in the works of two American pioneers who were scrupulously studied by Japanese managers. These were Frederick W. Taylor's *Scientific Management* (1911) and Henry Ford's *Today and Tomorrow* (1988). Indeed, Ford's CANDO program (Cleaning up, Arranging, Neatness, Discipline, Ongoing improvement), which builds on Taylor's work, appears as the obvious origin for 5S.
6S	A method that uncovers and implements changes to a workplace that enable it to most efficiently and safely support the work processes implemented within it. It builds on 5S by adding a sixth S that stands for "Safety." It adds a focus on safety within workplace improvement events to ensure that every change enhances workplace utility and job safety. See also *5S*.
A3 problem solving	A version of information-based problem solving that identifies the problem, describes the context within which it occurs, measures its impact, specifies a goal for improvement, uncovers root causes using the 5 Whys method, generates and implements solutions, measures the improvements made, reports outs the results of the effort, and follows up to ensure that the improvements are sustained. First used by the Toyota Motor Company.
Acquiring–benefiting experience	Refers to all the activities an enterprise or one of its functions must engage in to access, acquire, prepare to use, and use a supplied resource; maintain it in a useful state between uses; produce value for the enterprise's customers with it; and dispose of it or its byproducts.
Anchor	A component of a success criterion. It identifies a feature of an object, activity, or setting whose status needs to be known in order to just the success of a performance. See also *Measure*, *Target*, and *Success criteria*.
Andon cord	A signaling device located along a work process. When activated, it signals that a process has gone awry and stops the process.

Annual renewal activity	See *Renewal activity*.
Autonomation	Usually defined as "automation with a human touch." The human touch added to the automation is vigilance and judgment. Essentially, the automated component of a machine or process detects instances of out-of-bounds, signals their occurrence, and stops operations so that the problem can be fixed.
Batch output	A unit of output composed of more than one instance of a product or service. For example, a batch output might be a pallet of cylinders, a carton of eggs, or a bundled suite of related customer services.
Batch processing	Producing an offering in units that are composed of more than one instance of a product or service output.
Burning bridge strategy	A tactic that uses an external threat to motivate action or eliminates the option for no action. For example, "Unless we cut costs by 25%, we will be out of business in six months."
Business	A human enterprise encompassing serving the specific needs of a defined set of people that implements the Strategic, Operations, and Executive Functions components of a commercial model.
Business function	An internalized business activity that relies on a unique set of expertise to produce an output that advances the success of the enterprise within which it operates. Each business function has a unique workflow that accomplishes its purpose by progressively transforming the inputs it receives into the outputs it contributes to the business. This workflow is called a *value stream*. Examples are Purchasing, Engineering, Production, or Information Technology. Some business functions deliver value directly to customers (e.g., Production) and others deliver value indirectly (e.g., Purchasing) . The latter enable the success of functions that deliver value directly. See *Value stream*, *Enabling value stream*, and *Extended value stream*.
Business intent	States the enterprise's purpose, its vision, its core values, how it defines the meaning of profit, the stakeholders the enterprise recognizes, and its relationship with each. It also specifies the outcomes the business must produce at the Strategic level for it to claim success. The purpose component of the statement expresses what the business will produce for exchange, with whom, where, and why.
Business model	A set of ideas that describe how a business intends to generate revenue and realize profit. If focuses on answering questions like "Who will pay for your offering?" "What will you provide?" "To whom?" and "Why will they pay for it?" An example of a business model is "bait and hook." Contrast with *commercial model*.

Buying–Benefiting experience	Includes all the activities the customer must engage in to access, acquire, prepare to use, and use an offering to accomplish the customer's purpose; maintain it in a useful state between uses; and dispose of it and its byproducts.
Capability indices (Cp and Cpk)	Measure the ability of a process to consistently produce an output that meets the customer's expectations. One index, Cp or Pp, assesses whether the width of variation, within a specified range around its normative output, matches the width between the customer's upper and lower limits of acceptance (customer tolerance). A second index, Cpk, verifies that a process's band of variation always includes an acceptable output value, as defined by a customer. A process may possess an acceptable band of variation, but if the typical output it produces is not centered within that band, then some of its outputs will fail to satisfy customer expectations.
Capitalist	In this book, the lower-case term "capitalist" refers to a person who uses his or her means for the production of goods and services to egoistically pursue the maximization of personal wealth. Since every functional human being inherently possesses the means of production, the discriminating factor for being a capitalist is one's status as an egoistic self-maximizer. The "wealth" element that is typically associated with the concept of capitalist serves only to amplify the scale of one's capabilities to achieve one's ends. It is the end the person pursues in his or her exchanges with others that defines the person as a capitalist. When we capitalize the "c," we are referring to the economic theory.
Cash-to-cash cycle	Calculates the time operating capital (cash) is out of reach for use by your business. Cash is out of reach when it is uncollected from customers and when it is soaked up by inventory that sits on the shop floor, in office storage areas, or on computer disks. The speedier your cash-to-cash cycle, the fewer days your cash is unavailable for use in producing value.
Clarifying	Asking questions to uncover the elements of what someone is thinking so you have the complete picture of another person's viewpoint.
Commerce	An exchange between people, each giving the other something. Its expression as a human behavior extends temporally from conception through death. What is exchanged may be physical, emotional, or intellectual in form. The exchange between people is most often free and self-generated, but it can also be conditional (*quid pro quo*) or reciprocal ("because you did this, I will do that"). While the exchange always provides each party a stimulus, that stimulus is not always satisfying or beneficial.

Commercial model	A theory that attempts to describe, predict, explain, and enable the control of commerce in an effort to ensure its success. Such theories guide the conduct of entrepreneurs in focusing their commercial efforts and the design, development, and management of their business enterprises. They also advise how a society can provide for the generation and distribution of the necessities for human life. Commercial models may be empirically developed or deduced from a set of assumptions about the nature of people and the context within which they exchange resources (Vickrey, 1964). Both Capitalism and the Life Enabling model are examples of deductive commercial models. We view a commercial model and an economic system as being the same.
Common cause variation	Variation in the performance of a system that appears even when the system is implemented exactly as specified in its design. It can be removed only when the system's design is modified.
Commercial strategy	Specifies what a commercial enterprise will offer to whom to generate revenue; where it will enter into commerce; how it will attract, win, and retain customers; and how it will realize profit as defined by the enterprise's commercial model.
Competency	A knowledge, skill, ability, or other personal characteristic (KSAO) that enables a person to successfully perform a task. "Other personal characteristics" are sometimes referred to as traits. One example is "cooperativeness," especially if the task requires multiple people coordinating their efforts.
Competitive strategy	See *Commercial strategy*.
Conditioned inhibition	The trained absence of a response that otherwise would occur. It automatically closes off an option for thought or behavior.
Conditions of performance	Specifies the authority and resourcing a performer of a task can use in accomplishing a task and any constraints he or she must abide by while accomplishing the task (e.g., time to completion, "must do" and "must not do" actions).
Confirming	Saying in fresh terms what you understand the person has said to you so you can verify your understanding of what someone thinks, feels, and has expressed.
Constructive criticism	Recognizing the value in a shared idea while expressing a concern and inviting or offering a suggestion for resolving the concern.
Coordination among producers	Refers to an action by a group of firms that is intended to improve their profits by coordinating their reactions to each other's business decisions. One example might be producers in an industry agreeing to uniformly raise prices, not based on each firm's own capabilities or circumstances but in response to a price

	rise announced by one producer. Coordination among producers may include tacit or expressed collusion, which may or may not be lawful. It always disadvantages the buyer by limiting competition among sellers and raising prices.
Cooperative system	The larger system of entities that is centered on the business enterprise itself and composed of all those external groups essential to its commercial success (e.g., supplying industries, communities, governmental bodies, etc.).
Core values	The principles of conduct an organization must abide by if it is to realize the purpose its commerce serves. Core values derive from the dictates of the commercial model the organization adopts.
Cp or Pp	See *Capability indices*.
Cpk or Ppk	See *Capability indices*.
Crediting	Recognizing another person's good idea or action by identifying the behavior, saying specifically what you like about it, what that says about the person, and how it contributes to the team's efforts.
Critical path	The series of steps in a process that must be completed in sequence for the process to be completed. All other tasks can be done in parallel to this sequence. The time consumed by all the tasks on the critical path determines the minimum time needed to carry out an operation.
Critical-to-quality (CTQ) metric	An observable and measurable standard used to gauge the presence of a customer value. Each metric translates a need or value of the user into a measurable characteristic of your offering.
Culture	The totality of behavior patterns, artifacts, beliefs, institutions, and all other products of human work and thought that emanate from a social unit aligned around a common goal and upholding a common set of values. These memes define how people work together and the nature of their relationships with each other and others outside their group.
Customer	The person who uses your offering to accomplish a purpose.
Customer segment	A group of people who share common traits that affect the definition of value as applied to an enterprise's product or service offering and the buying–benefiting experience it provides. Each segment's experience of value differs and requires a somewhat different response to satisfy.
Cycle time	The rate at which a unit of product exits a work process. A unit is one completed output but not always one item. For example, a unit of output might be a pallet of cylinders or a carton of eggs. See Vitalo (2014) for other ways cycle time is defined.
Decision factors	Issues the decision maker must consider in making a decision.

Decision flow	Depicts the sequence in which a person considers decision factors and what he or she concludes based on the status of each factor. It is the equivalent to the "process" section or work flow map of a work standard.
Decision outcomes	A list of the final judgments one concludes when decision making is done. It is the equivalent to the "output" section of a process document.
Decision tree	A tool used to guide decision making. It consists of a series of individual judgments. Each judgment is put in the form of a question. Below the question two lines in the form of an inverted "V." Each branch is labeled with a possible answer. Trees usually have two branches but may have as many branches as there are possible answers to the question. The tree begins at the top with a "root node," the first question asked, and ends at the bottom with multiple "leaf" nodes, each of which states a conclusion.
Deductive model	A system of ideas deduced from a set of assumptions that attempt to describe, explain, and predict the behavior of a phenomenon. Its contents are not induced from empirical research. Its theorems do not have the scientific foundations of a natural science such as physics or biology (Vickrey, 1964). The real-world utility of such a model depends on its internal consistency and whether its premises map to scientifically established facts.
"Delighter" value	Identifies a feature of an offering or the customer's buying–benefiting experience that, when absent, goes unnoticed but, when present positively excites the customer. One of Noriaki Kano's three value types.
Delivery chain	Refers to the group of organizations external to the business that deliver its outputs to its customers and support customers in extracting benefit from them.
Demand Flow Technology (DFT)	A systematic methodology for making a process flow in response to customer demand.
Departmentation	Divides a business into work units and associates these work units vertically and horizontally so that the business operates most effectively and efficiently. Its output is represented by the various "boxes" that appear on a company's organizational chart (or charts). Each box identifies a distinct work group.
Design failure mode and effects analysis (DFMEA)	A process for identifying potential failure modes in a product or system and their causes and effects.
Design for Excellence (DFX)	A set of rules, guidelines, and methodologies used to analyze the way a product has been designed. It ensures a design's manufacturability, ease of assembly, testability, and lowest cost,

	among other features important to satisfying consumer values.
Development need	A specific deficiency in a person's capacity, motivation, competence, or other personal characteristic that must be eliminated for the person to successfully perform his or her role.
DMAIC	The acronym for "define, measure, analyze, implement, and control." These are the terms used to describe the steps of problem solving by practitioners of Six Sigma™.
Dos and don'ts	A list of steps, resources, or coordination that a performer or team either must or may use in doing its work (do's) and actions the performer or team cannot do (don'ts).
Economic system	See *Commercial model.*
Ecological system	The dynamically interacting systems of organisms, the communities they make up, and the non-living components of their environment (Ecology, 2019).
Effective decision making	Describes decision making whenever it uses information- or knowledge-based methods that employ all relevant information and yield outcomes that advance one's purpose.
Effectiveness	Refers to the executive function that ensures the enterprise is demonstrably advancing toward fulfilling the aims it has defined. The executive activities that relate to effectiveness include setting goals, developing plans, solving organizational problems, and improving performance.
Employee engagement	Means that contributors are aligned with the organization's purpose, energized, focused, and striving to accomplish their work, including investing discretionary effort to this end. What constitutes alignment with the organization's purpose varies in meaning based on the commercial model being applied. Discretionary effort expresses itself in the form of extra time, brain power, and energy invested (Vazirani, 2007).
Employee involvement	Refers to the degree to which management involves employees in accomplishing the business's purposes. At the lower end of involvement, managers have employees focus on doing their assigned work to expectations. Management communication is specific to the tasks employees must complete and to feedback on their levels of achievement. All decision-making, goal-setting, planning, and problem-solving activities are the direct responsibility of the manager. At the higher end, employees operate in autonomous teams. In such teams, employees within a single work unit or process are cross-trained to execute all jobs associated with the process and have delegated authority to both set and achieve goals. As a team, they make decisions, establish plans, and manage their implementation. As they implement these plans, they uncover and realize opportunities to improve success and identify and solve problems that hinder that success. Management assumes the role of resource provider and

	coach and in this ways supports their performance.
Enabling business function	A business function that produces product or service outcomes that indirectly deliver value to customers by enabling the performance of those business functions that deliver value directly to the customer (e.g., the production or service fulfillment value stream).
Engagement	See *Employee engagement*.
Evolvability	The ability of a species to generate solutions that enhance its capability to survive and thrive in an environment.
Evolved humankind	A term that refers to the collection of fitness-enhancing features that the current state of the human species expresses. Their presence is a product of evolution.
Extended value stream	Represents the flow of input resources from suppliers into and through a business function's value stream and its output from that value stream to and through its successful use by its recipient. Each of the organizations that contribute to that flow is represented in it. Every business function has an extended value stream. See *Value stream.*
Extrinsic motivation	Effort exerted in the performance of a task that flows from some reason other than one's natively valuing the work itself and what it is intended to produce. Extrinsic motivators may be positive (e.g., awards, corner office, pay, prestigious title) or negative (threat of unemployment). See also *Induced motivation*.
Externality	A cost or benefit experienced by a party who did not participate in the commercial transaction causing the cost or benefit. A benefit is called a positive externality, and a cost is called a negative externality. Air pollution experienced in eastern states in the United States caused by coal-burning power-generating companies operating in the western states is an example of a negative externality. The pollination of apple trees in an apple orchard by a nearby bee keeper's bees during their normal course of activity is an example of a positive externality.
Final output	The output generated by a value stream that passes outside it to an end user. See *Value stream*.
Flow	Describes a process in which work moves through it without interruptions or delays at a pace that matches customer demand (takt). Establishing flow in every operation is one task in optimizing work processes. See also *Takt*.
Free choice	Describes choice making whenever a person selects an object, defines a goal, or chooses a course of action that expresses the person's preferences, unaffected by artificial impediments.
Foundational knowledge	Refers to the set of concepts, principles, and relations used to explain the "why" underlying observed facts (inductive knowledge

	systems). In a deductive knowledge system, it is the set of assumptions from which the system's judgments and directives are deduced.
Gemba	A Japanese word meaning "the place where the real work is done"—that is, where people actually create the interim and final outputs of each business function. Smalley (2016) points out that the correct spelling should be "*genba*"; however, the common English spelling is *gemba*.
Ground rules	Define a common set of expectations for appropriate behavior while working with others that all parties endorse and obey.
Group	A collection of two or more items. As an approach to accomplishing work, each member of a group has a separate responsibility that defines his or her accountability. These assignments are designed so that, when all are done, some larger purpose is accomplished. In a group, an individual can succeed even if the collective purpose of the group fails. Contrast with *Team*.
Hitchhiking	Adding your thinking to another's idea while recognizing his or her contribution.
Hoshin Kanri	See *Policy Planning and Deployment*.
Income	Monetary value acquired through either labor (i.e., the expenditure of one's personal time, effort, and expertise) or rents (i.e., money earned from one's existing base of wealth). The former includes wages, salaries, bonuses, and "other remuneration statutorily defined as labor related" (Piketty, 2014, p. 18). The latter includes dividends, interest, profits, capital gains, and other rents.
Individualism	Our use of the term refers to an understanding of humankind that places the interests of the individual above the interests of the social group. This meaning reflects the primary dictionary definition (Individualism, 2017a).
Individuation	The process by which people become differentiated from one another; the development of one's unique personality. Individuation progressively refines the definition of one's interests, values, goals, and other personality features so they each more exactly represents one's unique perspective. The striving for individuation is the desire to develop one's singular personality and to acquire the capabilities needed to realize its promise.
Induced motivation	Effort exerted in the performance of a task that flows from some reason other than one's natively valuing the work itself and what it is intended to produce. Barnard identifies two ways to induce motivation: the method of incentives (e.g., pay, privilege, status) and the method of persuasion. Persuasion changes people's minds through coercion, rationalization, or indoctrination (Barnard, 1968, p. 149). See also *Extrinsic motivation*.

Inequality	The unequal distribution among different groups in a society of financial wealth and income and opportunities for personal growth and development.
Inferencing	Drawing a conclusion from observed facts (information processing) or making a logical judgment by applying knowledge to a given issue (knowledge processing).
Informal organization	Barnard defined the informal organization as "the aggregate of personal contacts and interactions and the associated groupings of people" (Barnard, 1968, p. 115) that "occur and continue without any specific conscious joint purpose" (Barnard, 1968, p. 114). These informal organizations transfer information among their participants, affect their attitudes, and influence their behavior.
Information	Mental content that tells about a person, place, thing, or activity at a point in time. It is the equivalent of "news."
Information-based decision making	A systematic process that analyzes and interprets facts to conclude a decision. The process defines a decision's goal, identifies the key values that depict the best solution, establishes weights to differentiate the importance of values, generates alternative choices one might conclude, evaluates how well each alternative satisfies the decision values, and selects the best alternative based on the results of that evaluation. The criterion-based decision-making method is an example of information-based decision making.
Information-based problem solving	A systematic process that analyzes and interprets facts to solve a problem. The process describes the problem, uncovers its root causes, develops solutions, and takes action to eliminate the problem's causes. It typically uses some degree of statistical analysis to evaluate the information gathered and draw conclusions about its meaning. Examples of information-based problem-solving methods are PDCA, A3, and DMAIC, among many others. They all represent the same backbone process using somewhat different language.
Interdependent processing	People thinking together to solve a problem in a way that advances a common goal.
Interim output	An output generated during the execution of work process that is used to produce a final output.
Interlocking teams	A cascading set of teams that ties together all levels of workers from the shop or office floor to corporate governance in a common effort to accomplish the business's purpose. In this mechanism, each higher-level team is populated by the current chair of each lower-level team. On every team, there are people who can personally represent lower-level perspectives as the team accomplishes its work. This interlocking team approach creates a personal connection from the gemba to the highest level of leadership and establishes a framework for accomplishing

	Hoshin Kanri.
Intrinsic motivation	Effort exerted in the performance of a task that flows from one's natively valuing the work itself and what it is intended to produce.
Jidoka	A system for rapidly detecting defects and preventing their multiplication.
Kaizen	Pronounced *ki-zen*. It is a Japanese word constructed from two ideographs, the first of which represents change and the second goodness or virtue. Kaizen is used in two ways. Its first use expresses a value or principle that guides one' approach to all he or she does. Its second use refers to a process-improvement method. As a value or principle, kaizen is synonymous with continuous improvement or striving for perfection through learning. It flows from W. Edwards Deming's teaching that every worker in a business should "[i]mprove constantly and forever the system of production and service" (Deming, 1982a, p. 49). As a process improvement method, Kaizen uses an information-based problem-solving strategy to uncover and remove waste and thereby increase a process's value-added ratio. In this book, the lower-case version of "kaizen" refers to the principle of continuous improvement. The upper-case version of "Kaizen" refers to the process improvement method.
Kanban	A signal (a card, light, or sound) that triggers activity upstream from where it occurs. A kanban system enables pull by triggering activity in upstream operations (operations that occur before the point where the kanban is triggered) only when a downstream activity is accomplished (production kanban system). It is also used to signal replenishment of materials and supplies as they are needed (replenishment kanban system).
Knowledge	Mental content that names or describes a class of objects or their characteristics, relationships, or operation. Knowledge, unlike information, applies across instances of time, place, and person. For example, the knowledge that all cars have a vehicle identification number (VIN) applies to all cars manufactured anywhere. In contrast, the VIN for my car (information) applies only to my car at this point in time.
Knowledge-based problem solving	Applies knowledge to solve problems through the use of inferencing. The knowledge you use directs you to the information that is important for you to consider. It tells you what to conclude given the information you find. A common example is the use of fault tree analysis to detect the likely cause of an instance of equipment failure.
Lead time	The time it takes for an output to move all the way from request to completion. It may or may not match cycle time. For example, if an output requires 100 hours to build but the builder only has 10 hours per week to apply to it, the cycle time is 100 hours, and

	the lead time is 10 weeks. See Vitalo (2014) for other ways lead time is defined in Lean manufacturing literature.
Lean enterprise (Lean manufacturing)	A business improvement metrology derived from the findings of the study of the Toyota Production System (TPS) and other Japanese companies' approaches to producing products and services. These original findings have been refined and elaborated into "Lean thinking." It formalizes Toyota's strategic perspective and the operating methods known as the Toyota Production System into its depiction of a "Lean enterprise."
Leverage	With regard to measuring a person's productive capability, leverage refers to one's ability to raise or lower the productivity of others. Leverage positively raises one's productive capability whenever the individual elevates the success of a colleague and lowers their productive capability whenever the person detracts from the success of another.
Market	A market is a physical or virtual setting that allows buyers and sellers of a specific good or service to interact in order to facilitate an exchange (Market, 2018).
Market strategy	See *Commercial strategy*.
Materialism	With regard to human motivation, refers to a dominant desire for wealth and material possessions with little interest in ethical or spiritual matters. With regard to philosophy, the theory that physical matter is the only reality and that everything can be explained in terms of matter and physical phenomena (Materialism, 2018).
Mean	The arithmetic average of all numbers in a set of numbers.
Measure	Tells the metric you will use to gauge status on the anchor of a success criterion and how you will make that measurement. A metric may note the presence or absence of a feature or its quantity, quality, timeliness, or efficiency (time or money), or it may gauge a change in any of these characteristics. The method of measurement explains the steps one completes to calibrate status, who should perform them and when, and identifies any instruments and materials to be used. See also *Anchor*, *Success criteria*, and *Target*.
Median	The value that is at the mid-point in a set of values that are ordered from highest to lowest and in which there is an odd number of values. If the number of values in the set is even, then the median is the average of the two values in the middle—e.g., for the set 1, 34, 56, 77, 81, and 89, the median is the average of 56 and 77, or 66.5.
Mode	The number that occurs most often in a set of numbers. For example, in the set 21, 33, 43, 23, 12, 11, 33, and 65, the mode is 33. A set of numbers may have more than one mode, as when several values appear with equal frequency. Also, a set of numbers

	may have no mode, as when every number appears just once.
Muda	The Japanese word for waste. As defined within Lean Enterprise literature, it refers to any activity that, when first implemented, does not materially change a product or service output in a way for which a well-informed and reasonable customer is willing to pay. Our definition of waste differs from this definition of *muda*. See *Waste*.
Multiactivity company	A company composed of more than one business. See also *Business*.
Mura	A Japanese term for unevenness, irregularity, or inconsistency. An example would be work processes that have wait states or interruptions or workloads that vary greatly across time.
Muri	A Japanese term for overburden, unreasonableness, or absurdity. It refers to any form of excess, as in inventory, excessive demands on workers, or the overburdening of equipment.
"Must be" value	Identifies a feature of an offering or the customer's buying–benefiting experience that, when absent, leads to rejection of the offering. Its presence, however, does not produce satisfaction. One of Noriaki Kano's three value types.
Offering	A final product or a service output a business provides to a customer. See also *Product offering* and *Service offering*.
Organizational strategy	Guides the formation of the business. It identifies what its critical-to-success resources are for long-term success and the essential features each must possess and how the enterprise should organize itself structurally and socially to succeed.
Other-regarding behavior	Refers to the tendency of some people to take into consideration the well-being of others as they decide what they will or will not do. It is an expression of human sociality. See *Sociality*.
Outcome	Defines a result. Includes an output and a state it should satisfy when produced. Examples are cost reduction plan [output] that generates a 12% reduction in unit cost [desired status] or software design [output] that satisfies all client requirements [desired status].
Output	The object a work process generates. It may be a physical (e.g., a car or an electric mixer) or intellectual object (e.g., a report, study, design, plan, contract, or an instructional product).
Paper Kaizen	A team process improvement activity that does not require a process to physically exist or be observed in operation. The team maps a proposed or documented work process. Using this map, it conducts a virtual walkthrough of the process to detect instances of waste. It then revises the work process to eliminate that waste and documents the improved work process.

Performance	Doing a behavior and producing a result. Both elements together define performance.
Performance gap	The difference between an expected and observed manner of performance (behavior) or the results it has produced.
Poka-yoke	A Japanese term usually interpreted as "mistake proofing." It refers to a physical or mental aid that ensures that a task is done correctly. A jig is an example of a physical poka-yoke device, and a conceptual template or framework that guides a person in describing a commercial model is an example of a mental poka-yoke device.
Policy Planning and Deployment	A yearly planning process that involves all members of a business in building the subsequent year's business and improvement plans. The process aligns all contributors in accomplishing the plans. The process ensures consistent and coherent performance toward a common goal. The most common English translation for this Japanese term is policy (hoshin) deployment (kanri) or policy management.
Political economy	The study of the role of public policy in influencing the economic and social welfare of a political unit. Its purpose is to devise ways by which governmental action or non-action can enable the economic growth and success of a society.
Processing power	One of the two components that measure a person's productive capability. It refers to a person's ability to transform 'givens' into 'desireds.' The less 'givens' (resources) provided to a person for accomplishing a task and the more difficult the 'desireds' are that the person must produce—the greater is the demand on a person's processing power and, if success is realized, the greater is the person's productive capability. See also *Leverage*.
Product offering	The final output (e.g., a finished car) or service output (e.g., a prescription for corrective lens) produced by a production system or value stream. See also *Output* and *Value stream*.
Production Preparation Process (3P)	Refers to a teamed method that creates and/or validates potential product and process designs to ensure that they are least complex, require the fewest resources, are easy to manufacture, and fully satisfy customer values.
Profit	The advantage or benefit that is gained from doing something.
Pull	Describes a process in which customer demand triggers the flow of activity that transforms resource inputs into a finished product. Pull systems operate in reverse. A customer purchase (or shipped product) cascades a signal backwards through the system that triggers startup of the operation signaled.
Quality function deployment (QFD)	A method for improving existing offerings and designing new offerings so that they provide greater value to customers. It involves building a matrix that interacts customer values with

	features of an existing or proposed offering. It uncovers missing, inadequate, or unneeded features and otherwise assists in detecting opportunities to deliver added value to customers. It also can be applied to improving work processes.
Quick changeover	A process for reducing the time elapsed from the production of the last good part to the production of the first good part after a new setup. Also referred to as "Single Minute Exchange of Die" (SMED).
Realisticness	A term coined by Goodwin (1991) that refers to whether the assumptions made by a given theory map to the empirically established facts of the state they describe. If they do not, that failure would falsify the model's assumptions and the theory derived from them.
Regulatory capture	The process by which regulatory agencies become dominated by the very industries they are charged with regulating. Regulatory capture results in a regulatory agency formed to act in the public's interest instead acting in ways that benefit the industry it is supposed to be regulating (Regulatory capture, 2016).
Reliability	Refers to a measurement tool's consistency in reporting the same value for a given state every time it is correctly used. See also *Repeatability* and *Reproducibility*.
Renewal activity	A personal or team activity that uses the SRLD tool to evaluate a past performance, understand what enabled the success that was realized and what hindered realizing even greater success, extract learning, and decide ways to use that learning to achieve a better next performance.
Renewal system	An organization-wide team activity that conducts a summative evaluation of the enterprise's performance at every level of its activity in order to extract learning that will advance greater future success.
Repeatability	Refers to a measurement tool's ability to produce the same reading for a given state of what it is measuring independent of the person doing the measurement, the age of the tool, and where the sample registers on the range of possible values the tool reports. It is said to represent the inherent precision of the measurement tool.
Replenishment	Refers to the restocking of a work station with the materials used to complete the generation of its contribution to a value stream's output.
Reproducibility	Refers to a measurement tool's ability to produce the same reading every time an operator measures the same sample that has a constant state. Reproducibility is essentially equivalent to the construct of reliability. See also *Reliability* and *Repeatability*.
"Satisfier" value	Identifies a feature of an offering or the customer's

	buying–benefiting experience that creates greater satisfaction the more it is present and less satisfaction the more it is missing. One of Noriaki Kano's three value types.
Secondary gain	A benefit derived indirectly from some action, condition, or event. It is typically not obvious to the casual observer.
Selective pressure	A factor that challenges an organism's survival—e.g., reduced food supply, climate change, population density, emergence of a new predator, or the emergence of life-challenging problems that require a cooperative approach to resolve.
Self-efficacy	A person's belief in his or her ability to complete tasks and reach goals. It may be accurate or inaccurate and positive or negative. It is accurate when this belief is based on one's actual success in real-world situations. When accurate and positive, it enhances future success. When inaccurate, it undermines future success. When it is negative, it retards future learning and success because it renders one hesitant to undertake new activities.
Sensitivity (of a measure)	Refers to a measure's ability to detect small changes in the status of a feature.
Service offering	The result of an activity performed for a customer on some object provided by the customer. Service outputs are identified by what they alter (people, things, settings, or activities) and how they alter it (e.g., toasters repaired, custom-designed homes built, flower gardens established, work processes improved, workers trained to analyze the root causes of operating problems).
Single Minute Exchange of Die (SMED)	A methodology for reducing the time spent in setting up a machine to produce a new output. It provides a rapid and efficient way of converting a manufacturing process from running the current product to running the next product. Sometimes referred to as "Quick changeover."
Sociality	Refers to the degree to which members of an animal species tend to associate in groups and form cooperative societies. See also *Other-regarding behavior*.
Special cause variation	Variation in performance due to some event or action that represents a deviation from the implementation of a system as it was designed. Its cause is detectable and correctable through the application of problem-solving methods.
SRLD	See *Status, Reason, Learning, and Direction (SRLD)*.
Stakeholder	A person, group, or other entity that either affects or is affected by the actions of an enterprise. While each stakeholder has a "stake" in the direction, conduct, and outcomes of a commercial organization's actions, a company only attends to the stakeholders recognized by the commercial model it is applying. Each commercial model offers its own guidance for which

	stakeholders to recognize and how they should be "attended to."
Standardized work	Refers to the development, maintenance, and use of a written description of each work process's goal and output; how the process should be set up, implemented, and checked; and what its expected performance is. The document records the current "best practice" version of the process.
Status, Reason, Learning, and Direction (SRLD)	A tool that supports people in analyzing a past performance and understanding what factors enabled the success they realized and what factors hindered even greater success. It turns these insights into items of learning and then generates an action item that leverages each learning into improved future performance. Each action item directs an improvement in contributors, work processes, or work settings.
Sufficiency	The executive function that ensures the presence, engagement, and success of each person needed to accomplish the enterprise's aim. The activities that implement Sufficiency include assessing the organization's people needs and acquiring/developing, deploying, enabling, involving, and ensuring the success of each of its contributors, both as individuals and as contributors for realizing their enterprise's aim.
Supply chain	The organizations external to a business that produce and deliver the business's inputs. Every business is part of someone's supply chain.
Success criteria	Benchmarks that focus and guide the measurement of performance and its interpretation. Each success criterion is composed of three elements—an anchor, a measure, and a target. Each anchor defines a focus for evaluation. It identifies who or what you will measure the status of. The measure tells the metric you will use to gauge status on the anchor and how you will make that measurement. The target specifies the result the measurement must yield to satisfy expectation. See also *Anchor*, *Measure*, and *Target*.
Synergy	It refers to the integration of people's efforts in a way that efficiently accomplishes their organization's purpose. Within a Life Enabling enterprise, synergy means all contributors working together as a team, causing their collective efforts to produce an effect greater than the sum of their individual effects. Ensuring the presence of synergy is one of the three executive functions described in the model.
Takt	The rate at which a unit of product must exit a work process to satisfy customer demand. Takt time is computed by dividing the number of product or service units of output customers demand over a given period of time (e.g., a day or week) by the total available production time for the period. For example, if customers demand 240 widgets per day and the factory operates eight

	hours per day (480 minutes), takt time is 30 widgets per hour, or one widget every two minutes. If customers want two new products designed per month and the company operates 160 hours per month, the takt time for a new design is one every 80 hours.
Target	A component of a success criterion. It identifies the result on a measure that one must achieve for performance to be judged "successful." See also *Anchor, Measure, and Success criteria.*
Team	Two or more people who commit to accomplishing a common goal together. Each member of the team assumes full responsibility for making the team as a whole succeed. Even when responsibilities are divided among members, each member stands ready to pick up another's activity if he or she cannot complete it. This is because teams operate as a single performer. In a team, no individual succeeds unless the collective purpose of the team is achieved. Contrast with *Group.*
Team charter	Performs a role analogous to a job description but for teams. It records each team's goal, its responsibilities, and how it will accomplish both. It sets the team's direction and accountability. It aids efficient team operation by resolving basic decisions about the team's role and methods up front. It serves as an effective tool for orienting new members—as well as nonmembers—about the team.
Total Productive Maintenance (TPM)	A system of activities that maximize equipment effectiveness. It is a company-wide equipment maintenance program that covers each machine's life cycle and requires participation by every employee. It incorporates three activities: autonomous maintenance, predictive maintenance, and equipment improvement. TPM programs also include the implementation of 5S.
Training	A systematic process using instructional methods (e.g., introductory experiences; tell, show, do, repeat, and apply activities; modeling; performance feedback; remediation) that results in a person being able to perform a task successfully or with greater proficiency if successful performance is already realized.
Unspoken value	Characteristics of an offering or an element of the buying–benefiting experience that a customer desires but is either not recognized by the customer until it is pointed out or is recognized but goes unmentioned.
Utility	When used in mainstream economics, it refers to the satisfaction received from consuming a good or service. Except in this specific use, its meaning in this book is its common dictionary definition—namely, the quality or condition of being useful in accomplishing a purpose.
Validity	Evaluates whether a measurement tool actually describes the status of the feature that it claims to report about.
Value	Some feature of an object, activity, or setting that enables its

	recipient to achieve the purpose he or she seeks to accomplish in a way that satisfies all his or her preferences and provides a better life for everyone. Within Life Enabling commerce, value received must be real, life-enhancing, and its judgment must be evidenced based. Objective assessment uses measurements of the effects of the benefit provided on the recipient's achievement of his or her desired goal and well-being. Subjective assessment measures the benefit received as experienced by each recipient.
Value-added ratio (VAR)	The proportion of an operation's total cycle time that is consumed by activities that materially change a product or service output in a way that satisfies a customer value. It is common to find this proportion to be between 5% and 15% in most business work processes. See Bujak and Vitalo (2014) for a detailed discussion of VAR and its correct computation.
Value engineering	A systematic approach to ensuring that the necessary functions in an offering are provided at the least cost. Value is the ratio of the worth of a function to its cost. Value can therefore be manipulated by either improving the function's utility or reducing the cost of its inclusion. It is a primary tenet of value engineering that basic functions be preserved and not be reduced as a consequence of pursuing value improvements.
Value stream	The end-to-end flow of work and control information that transforms a business function's inputs into its final product or service output. Its name derives from the expectation that each step in the process adds value to the work in progress as it advances toward becoming the value stream's final output.
Values framework	A breakout of the components and features of an offering or its related buying–benefiting experience. Customer values information (value, type, importance, satisfaction) is associated with the elements represented in these frameworks. These frameworks guide you in collecting and analyzing customer values information and provide a structure for storing those findings for easy use. They also assist you in evaluating and improving your current offerings and their associated buying–benefiting experiences.
Variation	The observed differences in the measured value of some feature of a process or its output across instances of its occurrence. No two observations of the same process or behavior yield exactly the same results when measured with sufficient sensitivity. See also *Common cause variation* and *Special cause variation*.
Waste	Any activity or other expenditure of resources that does not materially change a product or service offering or a customer's buying–benefiting experience in a way that satisfies a customer value.
Wealth	The total of one's assets—i.e., anything tangible or intangible

	that can be owned and controlled to produce monetary value through sale, rent, or productive use. Examples include non-financial assets, such as land, dwellings, commercial inventory, machinery, and patents, and financial assets, such as bank accounts, mutual funds, stocks, insurance policies, and pension funds, among others (Piketty, 2014).
Work process	A sequence of activities that accomplish a task and produce an output.
Working with others skills	A set of four skills defined by Byron and Bierley (2003). Two of the skills enable getting information and ideas from others correctly (clarifying and confirming). The remaining two skills (constructive criticism and hitchhiking) enable giving one's own information and ideas in ways that keep people working together. Clarifying and confirming skills ensure that a person accurately gets the information and ideas others offer. Constructive criticism and hitchhiking enable people to work cooperatively to improve each other's ideas and generate the best solutions to problems together. These skills eliminate the misunderstanding and friction that waste time and energy, destroy collaboration, and preempt best solutions.

INDEX

AUTHORS

Raphael L. Vitalo, Ph.D.

Raphael L. Vitalo received his doctorate in clinical psychology from the University of Massachusetts at Amherst. He has authored 50 professional articles, technical reports, and chapters in the areas of psychology, education, business management and commerce, information systems, and artificial intelligence. He has designed, managed, and implemented more than 400 projects serving public and private sector organizations in the areas of strategic planning, organizational effectiveness, performance management, workforce productivity, business process reengineering, risk management, knowledge engineering, information systems design and development, and expert systems design and development.

Christopher J. Bujak, B.S.M.E.

Christopher J. Bujak is a managing partner of Continual Impact, a consulting group providing consulting and training in continuous improvement. Chris is a mechanical engineer with extensive postgraduate training and experience in the application of Lean Manufacturing and Six Sigma methodologies and tools. As global director of continuous improvement (CI) for Air Products and Chemicals, Inc., Chris was one of the principle developers of an integrated CI model that included Lean Enterprise, Six Sigma™, and other critical enabling elements. This global initiative yielded $13 million (2021 current U.S. dollars) in savings during its first year of implementation, $21.1 million in its second year, and over $68 million in its third year. His work with Continual Impact has reached some 200 organizations, with more than 4,000 people trained and engaged in continuous improvements efforts. His recent focus has been on public health organizations across the U.S.

Made in the USA
Monee, IL
05 November 2026

67809041R00334